CORRECTION SYMBOLS

ab	Incorrect abbreviation (33c-d)	*no ,*	Comma unnecessary (26q)
act	Use active voice (9d)	*no* ¶	New paragraph unnecessary (4)
ad	Misused adjective or adverb (22)	*n*	Incorrect use of numbers (33a-b)
agr	Error in subject-verb agreement (1...)	*p*	Punctuation error (25-30)
aud	Audience not cl...	⊙	Period (25a)
awk	Awkward sente...		...n mark (25b)
bib	Bibliographic fo... (37c-d)		...tion point (25c)
ca	Incorrect use of...		...(26)
cap	Use a capital lette... (32)		...n (27)
cit	Citation missing or incorrect (37)		...phe (28)
co	Coordination (7a)		...n marks (29)
corr	Make corrections indicated (3e)	— ⊙ ( ) / [/] /	Dash, colon, parentheses, brackets, slash, (30a-e)
cs	Comma splice (17)	· · ·	Ellipsis mark (30f)
d	Faulty diction (11)	-	Hyphen (30g)
dang	Dangling modifier (23a)	*par,* ¶	New paragraph needed (4)
det	Use concrete details (2b, 4c)	¶ *coh*	Paragraph not coherent (4b)
dev	Develop essay more fully (2b-d, 3a)	¶ *dev*	Paragraph not developed (4c-d)
div	Word not divided correctly (30g)	¶ *rev*	Paragraph needs revision (4e)
draft	See sections on preparing drafts (3, 38c-e, 40i)	¶ *un*	Paragraph not unified (4a)
emph	Inappropriate emphasis (9)	*pass*	Inappropriate passive voice (9d)
fig	Inappropriate figurative language (12)	*plan*	Revise essay plan (1, 2a)
frag	Sentence fragment (18)	*pl*	Error in plural use (31c)
gd	Good word or sentence	*pro*	Error in pronoun use (21)
gl/gr	Refer to glossary of	*prf*	Proofread (3c, 38d)
gl/us	grammatical terms (Appendix E) or to glossary of usage (Appendix D)	*purp*	Purpose unclear (lc)
		red	Redundant (14a)
gr	Error in grammar (17-24)	*ref*	Faulty pronoun reference (21a-c)
id	Incorrect idiom (11e)	*rep*	Needless repetition (14a)
ital	Underline to indicate italics (34)	*rev*	Revise (3b, 4e, 14a, 38c)
		ro	Run-on sentence (17)
k	Awkward construction	*shift*	Confusing shift (24)
lc	Use a lower case letter (32e)	*sp*	Spelling error (31)
lmt	Topic not sufficiently limited (1b, 35a, 40c-e)	*sub*	Subordination (7b)
		sxl	Sexist language (15)
log	Faulty logic (6, 39)	*t*	Error in verb tense (20)
misp (or mm)	Misplaced modifier (23b-e)	*thesis*	Thesis unstated or unclear (2c)
		trans	Transition required (4b-5&6)
ms	Incorrect manuscript form (3d)	*uc*	Use a capital letter (32)
no cap	Capital letter not needed (32e)	*var*	Vary sentence structure (10, Appendix C)
		vb	Error in verb form (20)
		wdy	Wordy (14)
		ww	Wrong word (11, 16b-c)
		∧	Something missing (13)
		//	Faulty parallelism (8)
		?	Unclear
		⌒	Close up space
		#	Insert space

The McGraw-Hill
COLLEGE
HANDBOOK

The McGraw-Hill
COLLEGE
HANDBOOK
Second Edition

Richard Marius
Harvard University

Harvey S. Wiener
The City University of New York

McGRAW-HILL BOOK COMPANY
New York   St. Louis   San Francisco   Auckland   Bogotá   Caracas
Colorado Springs   Hamburg   Lisbon   London   Madrid   Mexico
Milan   Montreal   New Delhi   Oklahoma City   Panama   Paris
San Juan   São Paulo   Singapore   Sydney   Tokyo   Toronto

This book was set in Caledonia by Progressive Typographers, Inc.
The editors were Michael R. Elia, Emily Barrosse, and David Dunham.
The cover was designed by Joan Greenfield.
The designer was Merrill Haber; the production supervisor was
Joe Campanella.
Arcata Graphics/Kingsport was printer and binder.

1234567890   KGPKGP   89321098

ISBN 0-07-040398-8

          Library of Congress Cataloging-in-Publication Data
Marius, Richard.
   The McGraw-Hill college handbook/Richard Marius, Harvey S.
Wiener.— 2nd ed.
      p.   cm.
   Includes index.
   ISBN 0-07-040398-8
   1. English language — Grammar — (date) 2. English language — Rhetoric.
I. Wiener, Harvey S. II. McGraw-Hill Book Company. III. Title.
PE1112.M33 1988
808'.042 — dc19
                    87-25057
                      CIP

About the Authors

Richard Marius has been the Director of Expository Writing at Harvard since 1978, in charge of a required freshman course that all Harvard students must take as well as a program that includes a large writing center, an upper-division writing course, and interdisciplinary work in writing across the undergraduate curriculum.

He was born on a farm in Tennessee and worked on a small county newspaper for five years while he was finishing high school and taking a degree in journalism from the University of Tennessee, Knoxville. Later he took the M.A. and the Ph.D. at Yale and served as an editor for the Yale Edition of the Complete Works of St. Thomas More. He is the author of two biographies, *Luther* published in 1974 and *Thomas More* published in 1984. *Thomas More* was a finalist in the nonfiction category for the American Book Award. He has published two novels, *The Coming of Rain* in 1969 and *Bound for the Promised Land* in 1976. He is finishing a third novel. He writes a regular book review column for *Harvard Magazine*, and his articles have appeared in publications as diverse as *Esquire* and the medieval journal *Traditio.*

He has published many articles about the teaching of writing, and he has written or coauthored three writing textbooks, including the *McGraw-Hill College Handbook.* He is also at work on the McGraw-Hill *College Rhetoric.*

Before he assumed his present position, he taught European history for two years at Gettysburg College and fourteen years at the University of Tennessee.

Harvey S. Wiener, University Associate Dean for Academic Affairs of the City University of New York, codirects the National Testing Network in Writing (NTNW) and College Assessment Program Evaluation (CAPE). He was founding president of the Council of Writing Program Administrators. Dr. Wiener is the author of many books on reading and writing for college students and their teachers, including *The Writing Room* (Oxford, 1981). Dr. Wiener is a member of the Standing Committee on Assessment for the National Council of Teachers of English and he is chair of the Teaching of Writing Division of the Modern Language Association (1987). He has taught writing at every level of education from elementary school to graduate school. A Phi Beta Kappa graduate of Brooklyn College, he holds a Ph.D in Renaissance literature from Fordham University. Dr. Wiener has won grants from the National Endowment for the Humanities, the Fund for the Improvement of Postsecondary Education, and the Exxon Education Foundation.

Contents

BOOK ONE
The Writing Process

I. Writing Essays and Paragraphs   3

1. Planning a Paper   5
  a Using prewriting techniques   7
  b Limiting the subject   19
  c Picking an approach to suit the topic   21

2. Developing a Paper   24
  a Considering the audience   24
  b Choosing the evidence   28
  c Defining the main idea and writing a thesis statement   31
  d Expanding ideas and organizing a rough outline   33

3. Writing and Revising a Paper   40
  a Preparing the first draft   40
  b Revising the draft   49
  c Proofreading   60
  d Preparing the final draft   60
  e Making necessary changes and corrections   64

4. Writing Strong Paragraphs   74
  a Building unified paragraphs   75
  b Building coherent paragraphs   87
  c Supporting the controlling idea with details   105
  d Constructing opening and closing paragraphs   117
  e Revising paragraphs   122

II. Writing Clear and Effective Sentences 125

5. **Basic Sentence Elements 127**
   a Basic sentence structure 131
   b The eight parts of speech 140
   c Recognizing the structure of familiar sentence patterns 163
   d Learning the difference between phrases and clauses 164

6. **Sentence Logic 178**
   a Eliminating irrelevant details 180
   b Organizing sentence elements for emphasis 183
   c Establishing cause and effect 184
   d Limiting generalizations 188
   e Avoiding mixed images 190
   f Using concrete words for writing definitions 191

7. **Coordination and Subordination 194**
   a Using coordination to give equal ideas equal value 195
   b Giving emphasis by subordinating minor ideas 199

8. **Parallelism 208**
   a Using parallelism to compare and contrast 209
   b Using correlatives for parallel forms 210
   c Using parallelism in lists and outlines 211
   d Using repetition to emphasize parallelism 211
   e Maintaining parallelism with relative pronouns 213

9. **Emphasis 215**
   a Periodic sentences 216
   b Placement of parenthetical expressions 217
   c Cumulative sentences 218
   d The active voice 220
   e Repetition of key words or phrases 221
   f The very short sentence 222

10. **Variety 224**
    a Sentence patterns and lengths 224
    b Rhetorical questions 226
    c Exclamations 227
    d Inverted subject and verb 228
    e Free modifiers and absolutes 229

III. Using Words Effectively 233

11. **Appropriate Diction 235**
    a Use of slang 238

　　b　Dialect in writing　　240
　　c　Jargon　　240
　　d　Obsolete words, foreign words, and technical
　　　terms　　241
　　e　Idioms　　245
　　f　Connotations　　247

12.　Imagery and Figurative Language　　249
　　a　Nouns that convey concrete images or report
　　　action　　249
　　b　Metaphors and similes　　251
　　c　Clichés　　255

13.　Including Needed Words　　258
　　a　The necessary parts of verbs　　258
　　b　Use of *that*　　259
　　c　Articles, prepositions, and pronouns　　260

14.　Avoiding Wordiness　　264
　　a　Editing to eliminate unnecessary words　　264
　　b　Eliminating common phrases　　269
　　c　Combining sentences　　271
　　d　Eliminating jargon and overblown language　　273

15.　Avoiding Sexist Language　　275
　　a　Avoiding sexist labels and clichés concerning
　　　women　　275
　　b　Avoiding the use of *he, him, his,* and *himself* as
　　　indefinite personal pronouns　　276
　　c　Avoiding cumbersome constructions　　277
　　d　Avoiding artificial coinages　　277

16.　Using a Dictionary and Thesaurus　　279
　　a　Dictionaries for the college writer　　279
　　b　Entries in a standard desk dictionary　　283
　　c　Using a thesaurus　　288

BOOK TWO
Rules and Options

IV.　Writing Correct Sentences　　293

17.　Correcting Run-ons and Comma Splices　　295
　　a　Using end marks to set off independent clauses　　295
　　b　Using a comma and a coordinating conjunction　　297
　　c　Using a semicolon between independent
　　　clauses　　297

    d   Using subordination to correct comma splices or run-on sentences   300

    e   Looking for words, phrases, and punctuation that may cause run-on errors or comma splices   301

    f   Examining drafts for run-on errors and comma splices   304

18. Correcting Sentence Fragments   307

    a   Changing fragments into complete sentences   309

    b   Recognizing words and phrases that may begin fragments   314

    c   Examining drafts for fragments   317

    d   Recognizing acceptable uses of sentence fragments   319

19. Agreement of Subject and Verb   322

    a   Singular verbs with singular subjects ending in *-s*   323

    b   Plural verbs with plural subjects not ending in *-s*   324

    c   Singular verbs and singular pronoun subjects   324

    d   The pronouns *I* and *you*   324

    e   Plural verbs with plural pronoun subjects   325

    f   Plural verbs with subjects joined by *and*   326

    g   Agreement with the verb *to be*   327

    h   Intervening phrases between subjects and verbs   328

    i   Agreement with *or, either . . . or,* and *neither . . . nor*   329

    j   Indefinite pronouns   330

    k   Agreement in inverted sentences   332

    l   *There* or *here* at the beginning of a sentence   332

    m   Relative pronouns as subjects   332

    n   Agreement with subjects and linking verbs   333

    o   Collective nouns   333

    p   Noun subjects plural in form but singular in meaning   334

20. Verb Forms   337

    a   Principal parts of verbs and their uses in showing tenses   337

    b   Uses of the simple present tense   346

    c   Correct sequence of tenses   347

    d   Using mood accurately   349

    e   Active and passive voice of verbs   352

    f   Use of the infinitive form   355

    g   Common errors in the use of verbs   358

21. Pronouns 362
a Referring clearly to antecedents 363
b Agreeing in number with antecedents 365
c Avoiding broad references with *this, that, they, it, which,* and *such* 367
d The expletive *it* and the pronoun *it* 368
e Using *one* and *you* 369
f Using *I, my, me,* and *mine* 370
g Avoiding placement of a pronoun after a noun 371
h Cases of pronouns 373

22. Adjective and Adverb Modifiers 379
a Adjectives to modify nouns or pronouns 380
b Adverbs to modify verbs, adjectives, and adverbs 383
c Adverbs modifying whole sentences 385
d Improper use of adjectives as adverbs 386
e Use of adverbs and adjectives with verbs of sense 387
f Adjectives and adverbs spelled alike 387
g The positive, comparative, and superlative degrees 389

23. Dangling Modifiers and Misplaced Parts 396
a Dangling or misplaced participles 397
b Misplaced prepositional phrases 401
c Misplaced clauses 403
d Confusing placement of adverbs or adverbial phrases 404
e Placement of one-word modifiers defining degree, extent, or limitation 405

24. Confusing Shifts 407
a Consistency in verb tenses 407
b Consistency in verb moods 410
c Consistency in voice 413
d Consistency in person and number of nouns and pronouns and in manner of addressing reader 414
e Shifts in point of view 415
f Excessive emotion in writing 417

V. Understanding Punctuation 421

25. End Marks 423
a Uses of the period 423
b The question mark 424
c Exclamation marks 425

26. Commas 427

a   Independent clauses joined by coordinating conjunctions   427

b   Introductory phrases and clauses   428

c   Absolutes   430

d   Participial modifiers   431

e   Commas used to prevent confusion   431

f   Nonrestrictive clauses and phrases   432

g   Items in series separated by commas   434

h   Commas separating two or more adjectives   435

i   Parenthetical words and phrases   436

j   Direct quotations   436

k   Direct address   437

l   Commas replacing words in sentences   437

m   Commas used for emphasis   438

n   Commas used in addresses and place names   438

o   Commas used in dates   439

p   Commas with coordinating conjunctions in series   439

q   Faulty or needless commas   440

27. Semicolons 444

a   Joining independent clauses   444

b   Joining main clauses separated by a conjunctive adverb   445

c   Separating elements in a series   446

d   Separating elements in elliptical constructions   446

e   Separating elements in reference notes   447

28. Apostrophes 449

a   Showing possession of nouns and indefinite pronouns   449

b   Indicating omission of letters or numbers   454

c   Plural of words stressed as words   455

d   Possessive forms of personal and relative pronouns and of the pronoun *it*   455

29. Quotation Marks 457

a   Direct quotations   459

b   Use of other punctuation with quotation marks   461

c   Titles of essays, chapters, and sections in books or periodicals   462

d   Indicating special use of a word or phrase   462

e   Avoiding apologetic quotation marks   463

30. Other Marks of Punctuation 465

a   The dash   465

b The colon 466
c Parentheses 468
d Brackets 469
e The slash 471
f Ellipses 472
g The hyphen 474

VI. Understanding Mechanics   477

31. Spelling   479
a Careful reading and pronunciation as a spelling aid   480
b Principles of spelling   482
c Regular and irregular forms of the plural   487
d Spelling lists   490
e Hyphens forming compound words and adding clarity   496

32. Capitalization   498
a Capitalizing the first word of a sentence   498
b Capitalizing proper nouns and their abbreviations   500
c Titles of written works and works of art or architecture   503
d Dialogue within quotation marks   504
e Consistent capitalization and unnecessary capitals   504

33. Numbers and Abbreviations   510
a Words versus figures for numbers   510
b Figures for statistical information, dates, times of day, and addresses   511
c Full spelling rather than abbreviation in essays   512
d Abbreviations for familiar titles   515
e Common acronyms   516
f Words typically used with times, dates, and figures   516
g Latin abbreviations   517

34. Italics   518
a Titles of books, magazines, other types of literary works, works of art, and musical works   519
b Foreign words and phrases   520
c Words stressed as words   521
d Names of ships, trains, and air or space vehicles   522
e Underlining for emphasis   522

BOOK THREE
Special Writing Tasks

VII. Writing a Research Paper   527

35. Starting a Research Project   529
   a   Choosing a subject and developing a limited topic   530
   b   Learning about libraries   534
   c   Making a preliminary bibliography   535

36. Planning to Write from Sources   548
   a   Exploring sources and developing a thesis and rough plan   548
   b   Taking notes from sources   550
   c   Organizing notes to help focus ideas   554

37. Citing and Documenting Sources   558
   a   Integrating material from sources with your writing   559
   b   Different formats for documenting sources   565
   c   MLA documentation format   566
   d   APA documentation format   586
   e   Other systems of parenthetical references   591
   f   Footnotes and endnotes   592
   g   Avoiding plagiarism   602

38. Developing, Writing, and Revising the Research Paper   605
   a   Revising the thesis   605
   b   Writing a formal outline   607
   c   Writing the first draft   610
   d   Editing the first draft   611
   e   Preparing the final version   611
   f   Sample research papers   612

VIII. Other Writing Tasks   661

39. Writing Logical Arguments   663
   a   Using arguments to draw conclusions   663
   b   Using logic in arguments   665
   c   Inductive reasoning   666
   d   Deductive arguments   675
   e   Argument from authority and from experience   681
   f   Checklist for making good arguments   684

40. Writing about Literature   698
   a   Examining the assignment carefully   698

b Reading with care and attention   699
c Prewriting and developing a thesis   700
d Considering the paper's audience and purpose   701
e Various approaches to literary analysis   702
f Choosing an essay topic   704
g Studying poetry to write about it   707
h Literary devices and terms   710
i Writing first and subsequent drafts   717

41. Writing an Essay Exam   726
a Reviewing notes   726
b Writing out questions in advance   727
c Reading questions and outlining responses   727
d Justifying opinion with concrete details   728
e Reading and improving your answer   729

42. Business Writing   730
a Accepted business standards for letters   730
b Addressing envelopes clearly and completely   742
c Memos   742
d Job application letters and resumes   744

Appendixes

A   Study Techniques   751
B   Writing with a Word Processor   756
C   A Sampler of Prose for Imitation   766
D   Glossary of Usage   773
E   Glossary of Grammatical Terms   789
Acknowledgments   810
Index   815

Preface

To the Teacher

The McGraw-Hill College Handbook assumes that students must practice writing regularly if they are to become good writers. We counsel continual revision and show students how to do it. We believe in the truth behind the remark of a French writer that he never finished a piece of writing; when faced with a deadline, he abandoned his work to the printer, but he could always revise it some more if he had the time.

We have had time during the past three years to revise this book carefully, helped by the wise advice of many teachers who have successfully used the first edition in their classrooms all over America.

Throughout our efforts on the revision, we maintained precisely the same simple goal that motivated us from the start several years ago: that a handbook should be an easy-to-use tool for good writing. We have tried to make this one sharp and efficient. We aimed for clear writing, accurate explanations that are easy to understand, and informative and engaging exercises.

The McGraw-Hill College Handbook focuses as much on process as it does on product. Too often in the past handbooks have spent too much time showing students a correct writing product without telling them how to get there. In our chapters on process we have given a realistic account of how writers write.

We expect this book to be used in freshman composition classes and in other classes in writing, language, or literature offered in English departments. We value literature, long the staple of freshman writing courses, and so we draw many examples from it. But we also believe that students should learn how to write for courses in all departments.

Therefore we have assumed throughout the work on both the first and second editions that our handbook will be used across the curriculum wherever students write. Our book uses examples from history, psychology, economics, physics, biology, business, engineering, sports (to name a few areas) to illustrate our conviction that good writing has been done in many fields.

Indeed our society requires clear presentations of accurate information if people are to make sensible decisions. And no matter what form it takes — journal articles, books, speeches, newspaper reports, television scripts — most information comes to us, either directly or indirectly, through the medium of writing.

We worked hard in the first edition to teach students a good writing process, and we have reworked those sections in the second edition. Hardly any writer writes without studying the subject carefully beforehand and then writing several drafts on the way to publication. We have provided three drafts of a typical freshman student's paper, showing peer commentary in the early draft as well as commentary by the instructor in a later draft. And, of course, we show the changes made by the writer at each step along the way to final draft. Students who follow our trail through process will arrive much more confidently at a piece of work that will make them proud of their efforts and their accomplishments.

We have also looked for a middle ground between the extreme positions about rules for writing. We have tried to be neither too rigid nor too flexible in our presentation and interpretation of the rules. We do not believe that writers are inspired to write by learning the rules first; people want to write because they have something to say. As they continue to write, most people want to know how to communicate more clearly and effectively. Therefore we have shown how good writers communicate with different audiences. We also observe that good writers sometimes break some of the "rules" of writing, but we make a distinction between those rules that can be broken now and then and those that cannot. We do not teach that the rules of writing are carved in granite; neither do we teach that they are written in sand. Our philosophy is that writing is guided by principles rather than rules, and we have tried to state those principles clearly and to illustrate them by the work of good contemporary authors.

We have added several important features to the second edition. A chapter on argument will help students use some of the traditional methods of argumentation in their papers. We have been careful to give students the wisdom of traditional rhetoric without burdening them with a multitude of difficult terms, and we hope that in reading our chapter on argument students will write better arguments on their own and will recognize the arguments that other writers make in their work.

We have added a chapter on writing about literature, taking into account the knowledge that many freshman writing courses where this book will be used require students to write papers about fiction, drama, and poetry. We have expanded our chapter on business writing, including instructions on how to write effective office memos—probably the most common form of written communication being used in America today.

We have expanded the section on research papers dramatically, thereby providing an even fuller view of the issues in library work than we had in the last edition. To emphasize the need for good writing in all fields, we have included a student research paper on black holes, a scientific topic, in addition to a paper about Willa Cather's short stories. Because a handbook should incorporate current standards, the scientific research paper uses the APA style of referencing and the literary paper illustrates the 1984 MLA style.

Other additions and changes include thoroughly revised grammar sections and an expanded Appendix, "Writing with Word Processors." We have updated many examples and exercises, striving to keep our work lively and relevant to students' needs.

Reviewers and users of the first edition of *The McGraw-Hill College Handbook* commented warmly on its stylistic excellence. But following our own counsel about revision, we have rewritten much of the book to make it even more clear and timely. We think we have produced a handbook that can be read with pleasure and used by both those students who are already excellent writers and by those who have some of the basic difficulties that all hard-working English teachers recognize. We have worked especially hard to write genuinely helpful exercises.

Our book is marked by humor that is never condescending. In its examples it also gives a large place to women and to minorities. We think that it is a book for the modern age and yet a book that also embodies the strengths of tradition.

Supplements

We have provided a package of aids that teachers will find helpful throughout the course, and supplements that students will find useful in enhancing their work.

For teachers, the aids consist of:
- Annotated Teacher's Edition of the handbook
- Instructor's Manual
- Diagnostic Tests
- Additional Exercises

For students, the supplements include:
- *The McGraw-Hill College Workbook*, which includes exercises that may be assigned by the teacher.
- *The McGraw-Hill Self-Study College Workbook*, which is designed, as its title implies, primarily for self study.

Acknowledgments

We are grateful to the many people who helped us with this book in both its first and second editions. Teaching English composition is probably the most difficult job in any university. Perhaps it is the very difficulty of our profession that makes its members feel so strongly the sense of mutual obligation and respect that binds us all together. We have been the beneficiaries of those helpful sentiments from the many teachers in the field who have reviewed the manuscript of this book at its various stages, and we could not have done our work without their searching commentaries and their generous encouragement.

Because so much of the structure and personality of the first edition persists throughout this revision, we would like once again to thank and acknowledge all those who helped with their reviews of the many drafts of the previous edition.

Jay Balderson — Western Illinois University
John C. Bean — Montana State University
Kathleen L. Bell — University of Miami, Coral Gables
Richard H. Bullock — Northeastern University
Joseph J. Comprone — University of Louisville
Harry H. Crosby — Boston University
Robert M. Esch — University of Texas at El Paso
James A. Freeman — University of Massachusetts at Amherst
Dennis R. Gabriel — Cuyahoga Community College
Frank Hubbard — California State University, Sacramento
Lee A. Jacobus — University of Connecticut, Storrs
Russ Larson — Eastern Michigan University
Peter D. Lindblom — Miami-Dade Community College
Joe Lostracco — Austin Community College
Sheila J. McDonald — C.W. Post Center, LIU
Donald A. McQuade — Queens College, CUNY
Sharon Niederman — Metropolitan State, Denver
Jack B. Oruch — University of Kansas, Lawrence
Karen Reid — Midwestern State University
Kathleen W. Ritch — Santa Fe Community College, Gainesville
Annette T. Rottenberg — University of Massachusetts at Amherst
Donald C. Stewart — Kansas State University, Manhattan
John Stratton — University of Kansas, Little Rock
Margaret A. Strom — Eastern Maine Technical Institute
Sebastian J. Vasta — Camden Community College

And to those users of the first-edition handbook and the reviewers of the second-edition drafts, who helped us to make the improvements we have made in this edition, also thanks.

John C. Bean — Seattle University
Kathleen Bell — Old Dominion University
Mark Coleman — Potsdam College
Larry Corse — Clayton State College
Joe Glaser — Western Kentucky University
Rosalie Hewitt — Northern Illinois University
Pat C. Hoy II — United States Military Academy —West Point
Beverly Huttinger — Broward Community College
Larry P. Kent — William Rainey Harper College

Patricia Maida	University of DC
David A. Martin	University of Wisconsin—Milwaukee
Joseph McLaren	Mercy College
Albert H. Nicolai, Jr.	Middlesex County College
Della H. Paul	Valencia Community College
Donnetta Heitschmidt Suchon	Daytona Beach Community College
Carroll L. Wilson	Somerset County College

We have had lots of fun working on the handbook from the beginning. We have had the pleasure of thinking through our own long experience as deeply engaged classroom teachers of writing and the difficult delight of thinking through our glorious English language in its lively American version. We have worked far into the night again and again on the writing of both the first and the second editions. We have put our heads together to come up with genuinely new approaches both to the writing process and to understanding our language. We have had the satisfaction of reading through some of the best English prose, both old and new, to illustrate our instructions. And we have laughed often.

We owe many debts. Phillip Butcher, editor-in-chief at McGraw-Hill, and Emily Barrosse, senior editor in English, have supported us from the beginning with generosity, interest, and good humor. Mike Elia, the developmental editor in charge of this book, has talked to both of us almost daily on the telephone.

David Dunham with his usual intelligence and efficiency moved the manuscript through the production process, somehow keeping the book on schedule while incorporating our last-minute efforts to correct and to improve it. Merrill Haber's design has proved to be both practical and handsome.

We are grateful to Seiji Yamada for allowing us to use elements from one of his term papers in our section on research.

Both our families have put up with our long evening silences as we clacked away at our computers in remote rooms of our homes. Our wives perhaps deserve special commendation for their patience when we sometimes appeared from our sanctuaries to read parts of our work aloud to them in that perpetual enthusiasm of writers who think that after they have done hard work they have got it right and want the confirmation of praise from those dear to them. They did praise, and we return to them now our loving thanks.

Perhaps most remarkable , we have worked closely with each other now for almost a decade with a mutual respect and affection that endure.

Richard Marius
Harvey S. Wiener

To the Student

To the Student

The best way to use this book is to keep it handy as a reference. From time to time, pick it up and browse through it at random. When your teacher refers you to a section of the handbook, study the section and do the exercises to fit the principles in your mind. By all means read Chapters 1 through 4 before you begin to write your first paper.

The Index and the plan of the text outlined on the inside back cover will help you locate information that deals with your special problems and interests. The correction symbols and the directory of special features on the inside front cover will help you find special sections quickly.

The ability to write well can give you both pleasure and power. You owe it to yourself to discover the joy of writing, the excitement of expressing your ideas, your feelings, your thoughts, your discoveries, your arguments about everything from the daily events in your life to the demands of a perilous yet promising future. As you learn to write well, you will also discover that people are more likely to respect and accept your opinions, because you can express yourself in writing that engages and persuades your readers.

No handbook can make writing easy; good writing always takes hard work. But we hope that *The McGraw-Hill College Handbook* can make writing less difficult for you and can give you both guidance and pleasure along the way.

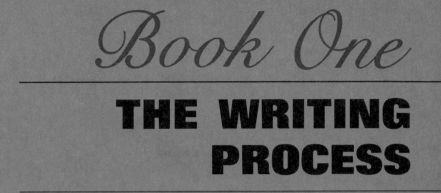

Book One

THE WRITING PROCESS

PART ONE
Writing Essays and Paragraphs

PART TWO
Writing Clear and Effective Sentences

PART THREE
Using Words Effectively

PART ONE

WRITING ESSAYS AND PARAGRAPHS

	Chapte
Planning a Paper	1
Developing a Paper	2
Writing and Revising a Paper	3
Writing Strong Paragraphs	4

CHAPTER ONE

Planning a Paper

Most writing teachers require a paper within the first class session or two. It is often a personal experience paper, something about yourself or your observations. Or maybe you will write about your first reactions to college life, the chaos of registration, or the challenge of choosing a program of study. Some teachers will ask you to write about something you have been thinking about lately, perhaps something you have been studying in another class.

You may have to write outside of class on a topic such as a description of a room you know well, a scene you have observed, a person you have met recently, or your experience on a part-time job. Your instructor may simply tell you, "Write about anything you want to write about, but give me five pages."

To help you do that early assignment, the first part of this handbook describes the writing process. The writing process includes all the steps we take from the moment we decide we must write something until the time we finish our final draft. Writing process involves deciding on a topic, a decision we call *invention*. It involves gathering notes, making outlines, deciding on an introduction and a conclusion, and all the drafts that writers produce on their way to a final version. It may involve writing trial sentences or paragraphs that you may want to insert later on in your paper. The writing process involves all the thinking you do about a paper whether you are actually writing it at the moment or not.

Writing is not one act; it is many. It is not a series of steps that can be neatly set up one after another. Many parts of the writing process may go on at the same time. Writers work through successive drafts: rethinking what they are trying to say; looking for the right organization, the right words, the right arguments, the right evidence to cause their readers to take them seriously. They may begin with one idea that they want to explore; but as they write, they may discover that they really want to explore a topic that they originally thought was a side issue. As they put words on paper, their minds are continually active, rethinking their purposes and their expressions. Almost no professional writer sits down at a desk and writes a piece through exactly as it will eventually appear in print.

Experienced writers usually begin with a fairly broad topic — a historical period or a person, a problem such as water pollution or child care for working parents, a personal memory of an influential experience. A writer must decide which part of the topic is interesting enough and limited enough to be treated in an essay.

Students may be told, "Write about an experience or a person who has had great influence on your life." A student who has come to a large, urban university from a farm may ponder the differences between rural life and city life: "I want to write about farm life." But what exactly will she write? "Farm life" as a topic is far too broad. She must find some thesis, some unifying subject, that she can use to weave various memories and reflections together in an essay.

Professional writers go through much the same process. Someone — an editor, an agent, a friend — suggests a general topic: "Why don't you write a piece about farming?"

"How many pages do I have?"

"Oh, do five or six double-spaced pages."

In five or six double-spaced pages, you cannot write a complete autobiography. You cannot tell every detail about farm life. You must limit your topic to something you can cover in the assigned space. You might write about the architecture of old barns or different jobs different people do on a working farm or the different qualities of various breeds of cattle or the special concerns of the dairy farmer or the problems small farmers are having now with debt. To write well, you must have a specific subject within the broad, general topic of farming.

Professional writers have the same difficulties as inexperienced writers. Now and then they begin with a clearly defined topic. "The writer Orson Orwell is in town. I'll interview him about his latest book, *Famous Bird Dogs.*" But most of the time they start with a more general idea: "I think I'll do something on dogs," "I'd like to write about clocks," "It would be fun to write about various forms of chairs," "I had an interesting life as a young person; I'd like to write about that." Once they have that broad idea, they have to cut it down, to limit it, to give it focus.

One way of giving the idea focus is to learn more about it. Writers read up on topics. They use libraries. They consult their journals or their old letters. They talk to experts, to friends, perhaps to members of their families. In whatever way, they find information on the topic or they ponder the information they already have. They take notes. Gradually, the limitations of the paper come to them: "I want to write about farm life in Tennessee," "I want to write about my own experience growing up on a farm in Tennessee before I came to college," "I want to write about my father."

As the topic grows in their minds, writers may jot down lists in a preliminary effort to organize their thoughts. They try out sentences. They may change their minds about their topics. They keep striving to find something that will fit the design of their essays. Sometimes they make outlines. They write drafts. They polish and revise. Finally they stop because they have a deadline to meet. A French writer early in this century said writers never really finish a piece of work; they only get to the place where they must abandon it.

From the time you *consider* writing something until you actually *produce* a final manuscript, you do certain things. Sometimes you can skip one thing or another; more often you must do them all. Most readers can tell when you have rushed through an assignment without spending enough time putting a paper together carefully. A brick mason must fit every brick exactly in place; otherwise the wall will look slapped together and will be so fragile that it might fall down with a push. Writing a paper is similar. Do it carelessly, and people can tell.

1a
Use prewriting techniques to explore your subject before you write your first draft.

No one set of steps can make you a writer. Each of us develops his or her own process. But every process involves a step we usually call *prewriting*. **Prewriting** covers all the steps that writers take before they write a draft. Prewriting lets you limber up. You brainstorm to make ideas come, perhaps making lists of things you want to cover. You try out some sentences. You play with words and phrases, following them where they take you without worrying about order or completeness. You see where your own impulses, thoughts, and interests lead before you investigate your topic rigorously. You may write a rough outline; you may make a list of various subjects you want to cover; you may ask yourself questions.

The following suggestions for prewriting come in no absolute sequence. You can use them in any convenient order. All of them will help you develop and record ideas. They will also help you give some shape to your essay.

1 Think about your subject.

Good writing begins with clear thinking. Although this point may seem obvious, many students start writing an essay before they have thought about it. Most of us need time to let our ideas on a topic develop and ripen. As you consider a subject — either one that your instructor requires or one that you choose for yourself — take your feelings and impulses seriously. You like some things about a subject; you dislike others. Why? Once you start thinking hard about why you have the feelings you do, you may have an idea for a paper.

Some thinking is direct. You pursue an idea and try to develop it. Other thinking is random. You may be doing something unrelated to writing — jogging or riding a bike or rushing to class — and an idea will pop into your mind. If you make yourself think about your subject before you start writing, you may nurture **inspiration** — the sudden, imaginative flash that may define, shape, or clarify a topic.

You should think about your audience. Who will read your paper? What do your readers know already about your topic? What can you tell your readers that they don't know? What thoughts do you have about a subject that your readers may not have had themselves? What do you want your readers to think about you as a writer and a person?

Honesty is essential. Readers hate dishonesty, and you should want your readers to think you are an honest person. They should not imagine that you are writing something out of a desire to brag about yourself or to get at your enemies. They should not think you are trying to be cute or otherwise false. They should not think that you are showing off. Writing is a social act; your readers want to believe that you take them seriously, that you respect them, that you do not want to waste their time, that you are writing within a community of communication where both you and they belong.

Think hard about your subject, and try to keep those thoughts as honest as you can. Honesty in judgment is the first step to having a good and an original paper once you have decided on the general definition of your topic.

2 Learn about your topic.

Good writing flows out of abundance. You must know a lot about your topic to write about it well. Good writing comes from bringing many parts of your experience to the writing task.

Good writers study their subjects. They spend time in libraries. They read popular magazines as well as serious books. They talk to experts.

They try out ideas on friends. They think about their subject when they watch television or films; often they will see something that will make them understand their subject in a different way. They recall past experiences. They make comparisons. A person writing an autobiographical account about an important experience will read other autobiographical accounts to see how other writers have handled similar topics. A student writing about her failure at basketball may gather valuable insights from a roommate who has starred on the ice hockey team. The two sports are not the same, but perhaps the experiences the two women have in sports are worth comparing. Comparisons are excellent devices for learning. Someone writing about one of Charles Dickens's novels may see Dickens more clearly by thinking of the differences between Dickens and Joan Didion.

A person from a farm in Tennessee will not be the only rural person at the university. It might be helpful for that student to go talk with others from similar backgrounds, to compare experiences. Someone from a farm in Iowa may say, "I remember how good a cold glass of water tasted when we had worked an hour in the cornfields," and the person from Tennessee will think about drinking water in the cool shade of a cedar while getting in hay in August.

No matter how familiar you may be with a subject, you can see it better if you talk to another person also acquainted with it or with a subject akin to the one you are writing about.

It is always a good idea to talk to someone about any paper you intend to write, even if that person is not an expert on the subject. A good listener may ask you important questions or point out where you seem confused or confusing. If you can talk to an expert or to someone who has had similar experiences, that person may have information that you do not have. Your acquaintance may recommend experts you might not otherwise know. Friends who know nothing about your topic may become so interested in what you are saying that you feel encouraged to pursue it, or they may know books you have not read or recall conversations or thoughts that will help you formulate your own ideas.

Not least among the benefits of talking to someone else is the clarity you may get in your own mind from hearing yourself discuss the subject. Talking a subject out is a good way to know what you are thinking, to discover those areas where you don't have enough information, where you must study some more. Talking is a good way to lubricate your mind. Ideas flow when you talk about them. Talking about your topic is also an excellent way to narrow it down to something manageable, something you can do in the space you have. Your teacher may divide your writing class into small groups so that you can talk to others in the group about what you are doing and listen to them tell you what they are doing.

3   Jot down ideas in an informal list.

As soon as you can, start jotting down things you may want to write about in your paper. Moving a hand across a page seems to move the brain. The more you write, the more inspiration you get. Carry your list around with you, perhaps in a small notebook. Let it grow over several days as your thoughts develop and become more specific — one or two sentences or phrases scribbled in the morning, another few dashed off as you return from class, perhaps something jotted down in class itself.

Try not to tighten up or be self-conscious. Your list is your private property. No one else will see it. Be bold. Be absurd. Free-associate. By writing freely, you may unblock ideas in your mind. Although at first chaotic, these ideas may come together later on. They are the rough ore a miner digs out of the ground; they may look like rock and dirt at first, but if you work hard with them, you will discover that they contain gold.

COUNTRY LIFE

living on a farm and hearing the silence at night

My father had a job as teacher in the high school in the consolidated school.

He loved farming.

He had been brought up on a farm and determined to farm, even if it did not make him any money.

We raised our food. Most of it at least.

beauty of nature

But nature is hard, too.

snakes and birds

killing pigs

the country church

Why did the preacher's wife leave him?

the time I broke the egg in my pocket when I was four or five

the cat I shot in the foot

City people are different.

How trite can you get! Of course city people are different. But how are they different?

They live faster.

They have more organization to their lives.

the first time I ever saw a subway

baseball games between community teams: Dixie Lee Junction vs. Turkey Creek

the difference between that sort of baseball and the Mets or the Red Sox

the harshness of nature

My father's two personalities: school principal and farmer

his names for everything

He taught us the names of birds, of trees, of plants, and of animals.

how proud he was when Peggy learned to be a good mechanic

working together

his death; the drunk driver

We moved away.

This list records many fragmentary ideas about country life by a student brought up on a farm and trying to work out a subject for the first paper he will do in his writing class. He has been told to write something about his personal experience. But he might follow the same process in any assignment he was given.

As he thought about his subject, he realized that what he was thinking about most was the influence of his father on him while he was growing up.

Now he made another list.

SUBJECT: MY FATHER'S LEGACY

My father left me no money.

He left me a lot of pleasures.

his own pleasure about farming

You can have so much pleasure by enjoying the things you do every day.

He was not a daring man.

He tried the farm out, and he liked it, and that's where he stayed.

I can't even say he tried the farm out; that was all he ever knew.

his fascination with small things

Tell the story of how he stopped me and kept me from disturbing the woodcock. The mother woodcock on her nest. I didn't see her. He suddenly put his hand on my arm. We were walking through that little sliver of woods that separates the pasture from the hay field, and he saw her before I did and put his hand on my arm and made me stop talking.

Tell something about the community?

the Baptist church on the hill?

the socials we had?

My father used to be the master of the games at church socials.

He had such a good time with the young people.

But he was tough in school.

He said he didn't want people to go away from school and remember him as just a good old man. He wanted to be tough enough on them so they wouldn't be surprised when they went to college.

He didn't tell everybody to go to college.

"Carpenters make a good living," he said. "And there's nothing wrong with being a good carpenter."

But he did tell a lot of people to go to college.

He always said people from our school were just as smart as anybody; they shouldn't stay home from college just because they thought it might be hard.

the names of things

poison sumac; poison ivy; red maples; red oaks; white oaks; white pines; loblolly pines. Larks, thrashers, all those birds. King snakes. Copperheads. Corn snakes.

What was it he called the pileated woodpecker?

Why did he go to school in Virginia?

"Don't kill anything unless it's dangerous to you or you're going to eat it."

He died in the accident, hit head-on by a drunk driver.

The driver was a senior in the high school.

He'd been to a party where people were drinking hard liquor.

He cried and cried when he found out what he had done.

This list is still not organized. But the writer has begun to define a limited topic and to see ways of limiting and defining the topic even more. Although this is to be an autobiographical paper, the writer must still sort out what he knows and what he does not know about his father. He must also sort out what is interesting, what reveals character, what seems most significant in his father's life and influence. Notice that the list contains some questions. The writer will try to answer some of those questions; others will turn out to be insignificant. Successive revisions of the list will eliminate some points, expand others, and add some that are not now on it. Writing the list prepares you for the writing of the paper itself.

Your first paper in a college writing class will often be a personal-experience paper. Since you know a lot about the subject already, you can often jot down a large number of thoughts like those above.

You can use the same process in composing a paper from texts. As you read a short story, a poem, a drama, or some other text that you must analyze in a paper, you can jot down ideas about it. When you are going to write about any text, it's always a good idea to read it through quickly before you take any notes. But when you go back through and read it again, you can start writing down some thoughts about it. Jotting down such thoughts will stimulate your mind to think other thoughts.

In many college writing classes, you will read James Joyce's short story "The Dead." Here is an example of the sort of thoughts you might jot down as you read the story.

Who are "The Dead" in this story?

Kate and Julia Morkan hold an annual dance.

They've been having it for years.

Now they are old. Are they "the dead"?

Gabriel is the center of the story. The narrator takes his point of view. It is a third-person story; Gabriel doesn't tell it himself. But the narrator knows what Gabriel is thinking. The narrator is looking over his shoulder.

It's a snowy night. The snow is mentioned early in the story, and it is the last thing mentioned in the story. What is the significance of the snow? Is the snow like time, burying people silently? Is this a story about time?

Gabriel Conroy. What is the significance of the name Gabriel? Does it refer to the Gabriel who will blow his horn when the world ends? Gabriel an angel. The Gabriel of the Bible brings people to judgment. Does this Gabriel bring people to judgment? He judges people all the way through the story. He's unhappy. A very unhappy man at a party where people want him to be happy.

Why is Gabriel unhappy?

He's married.

Is he unhappy about his marriage?

Is he unhappy because he lives in Ireland?

4   Ask yourself questions about your subject.

To stimulate ideas, writers frequently ask themselves questions about a subject. We have seen some questions in the two preliminary outlines sketched above. How do you know what questions to ask? One good way of organizing questions is to think of the five *w*'s of journalism. Reporters are taught to ask *who, what, when, where,* and *why*. For almost any subject that you approach, you can ask several versions of each of these questions. They help you explore your subject.

To use the journalistic questions, you may write your subject at the top of the page. Then, with ample space for your answers, write down as questions *who, what, where, when,* and *why*. You may want to add the question *how*.

You might proceed in the following way:

Who was my father?

Who am I because of him?

Who is my mother?

Who are the people who meant most to me?

Who are the people most different from me because of the farm?

Who is my brother?

Who is my sister?

Who was the person who killed my father in the wreck?

Who were some of the most important people in my father's life?

What did my father like about the farm?

What made him become a schoolteacher?

What did we do to win the conflict against nature?

What is nature?

What did we do on the farm?

What did he teach us?

What did he dislike about the farm?

What did my mother dislike about the farm?

When did my father and mother buy the farm?

When did I first start thinking about being different?

When did I realize that my father loved the farm more than he loved his teaching?

Why did my father go to school in Virginia?

Why did my mother fall in love with him?

Why did she consent to live on the farm?

Where was our farm?

Where did my father grow up?

Where did my father teach?

Where did he learn everything he knew about nature?

You can ask many of these questions. They operate like a searching program on a computer, running through your memories and making some of them stand out for the purposes that you are gradually selecting in your paper. As you ask as many versions of these questions as possible, you start uncovering material that will fit well with your paper. You cannot answer all the questions you raise; you will not want to answer them all because the answers to some of them will not contribute to your paper. But raising a great many questions will help you scan your subject, seeing things in it that may make your writing interesting.

5   Write nonstop for a stated time period.

Filling up a page with your writing may help overcome some of the nervousness that often grips people when they sit down to write. Make yourself sit at a table or a keyboard and spin sentences out ten minutes at a time. Do not get up in that time. Do not stop writing. Do not try to preserve any order. You can leap around all over the place in a writing exercise like this. The ideas will flow. You can gather them up later into coherent forms.

It may be painful to keep your pen or your keys on the computer or the typewriter moving. But do not stop. Do not look back to see what you have written. Do not erase or cross anything out. Do not stop to check spelling or grammar. Do not stop for *anything* until the time you have set for the exercise is up. Write whatever comes to mind without censoring or correcting. Writing nonstop forces you to *produce.* You can *edit* later on. If you worry too much about being correct, you may block your thoughts. Remember, you alone will see this prose. You should not trouble yourself about how it looks. Try to write complete sentences. And when you look back over the sentences done in this fashion, you will find some ideas there worthy of further exploration.

The student writing about his memories of his father wrote the following thoughts in a half hour without getting up from his desk and without pausing to consider whether he was organizing things well, spelling all the words correctly, or getting all the grammar right

I was scared to death when I got to the college and saw all these people who knew things I didn't know and who talked about things I had only seen on television and who looked at me like I was a refugee from a zoo when I said, yes, I really did grow up on a farm, although my father was a high school teacher. But he had grown up on a farm, and he never got it out of his system, I guess, and he taught school because he or we couldn't make a living out of the farm by itself, but he loved to farm. Nobody can make a living farming on fifty acres. When you consider what schoolteachers make, I guess you'd have to say that my father was an odd one — using school teaching to make money enough to let him stay on the farm. He loved tractors, and he loved putting hay in the barn and fixing things and turning up the soil, and I loved it, too. Well, I loved most of it. I really didn't like being up in the hot barn with the sun beating down on the galvanized iron roof and making the loft as hot as an oven and the hay down my back in my shirt and the sweat rolling off my body and making all the hay and the dust stick to me. Well, this isn't a paper about my miseries in the barn loft. I had to milk morning and night. Three cows, and to tell the truth, I never did like cows much, and especially in the wintertime I didn't like to go down to the barn in the dark at six in the morning, and we couldn't go places because we had to milk every day, and my father didn't trust other people to take care of the cows. No, I hated the cows and milking and the tedium of having to be there morning and night at the same time, and cows are dangerous, too. There were lots of things wrong with growing up like that, but I didn't think about them at the time. Well, maybe they weren't "wrong," but I guess you would have to say they were hardships, conflicts. It's always work. We never could go anywhere because we had to milk the cows, and we couldn't or my father wouldn't trust anybody to milk the cows for him, although my mother said she thought he was just making an excuse not to have to go anywhere. He didn't like to leave the farm when he didn't have to. I wondered if he might be afraid to go somewhere else. But we did work hard; we all worked hard. We worked together, too, and I loved that. He was always cheerful. When we did some dumb thing, he didn't get mad at us. Like the time I forgot to set the disk harrow right and ran the tractor over the whole upper field where we were going to plant a new stand of hay, and he came out and said, "What are you doing?" And I said, "I've harrowed the field," and he said, "You haven't harrowed the field; you've just run the tractor and the harrow over the field. If you're going to break the clods, you have to set the harrow at an angle. Let me show you." So he showed me, and he slapped me on the leg in a friendly way, and he said, "OK, Champ. Now you're ready to disk-harrow the field; so I had to do it all over again. I think my father loved the farm because it gave him something to do all the time; it occupied his mind. He could see things happen because of his work. It wasn't like working in a corporation where you decide something and pass it on up the way, and somebody else decides on your decision, and by the time something gets done, it's so far away from you that you don't seem responsible for it. We were responsible for everything that happened on the farm. And it kept all of us together. He had been in a close family. We were all a close family. We worked side by side in the fields, and we were a team. We knew what to expect of each other; we knew what we could do and what we couldn't do, and I think my father liked that predictability. It was a hard life. But it was an orderly life, and we all counted for something. There was work that had to be done, and if we didn't do the work, it wouldn't get done, and we'd all suffer. We all had to work together to make it, and there was a lot of satisfaction in that, a lot of pleasure. He took so much pleasure in teaching us things. The names of birds, the names of plants, the names of animals, the names of snakes. "Never kill anything unless it's dangerous or you plan to eat it," he said. A good motto for living in nature. He wouldn't let us kill the king snakes in the corncrib because they ate the rats that ate the corn. I'd rather have the rats myself. But we let the king snakes alone. They kept the copperheads away, too.

After rereading these sentences, the writer might see some of the things he wants to emphasize in his main essay. He might see other things that he decided were not so important. These sentences are a long way from a finished essay. But the ideas are beginning to flow. The writer is beginning to get his thoughts in order.

6 Draw a subject tree.

You can draw a subject tree by taking a sheet of paper and making a rough drawing of a tree and then writing in possible subjects along the various branches of your tree. You don't have to be a good artist to draw the tree. It's just a device to tie together various related ideas.

The subject tree allows you to jot down ideas in a rough organization, seeing where the various ideas lead. As you can see, the accompanying subject tree produces a number of ideas that can be developed into a paper. Making up a subject tree will often give you confidence because it will show you that you have more to write about in relation to a general subject than you thought when you started. The subject tree breaks knowledge down into manageable chunks, and you can then put those chunks together in a paper.

Subject Tree

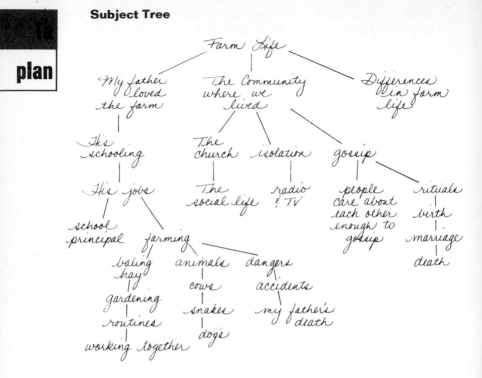

7 Browse in the library, or do research on your subject.

For many topics, reference books, other texts, and magazine articles will suggest ideas you have not thought of yourself. Several hours of browsing in the library and taking notes give many writers just the materials they need to develop a specific topic with confidence. You may also wish to interview people who know about your topic. Many interesting papers do not depend on libraries. Writing a personal-experience paper, for example, may not require you to work in the library. But other topics will always be much better if you do some general reading about them. Researching a subject always broadens your understanding and provides important details you can draw on later.

Using these prewriting techniques individually or in combination, you can record the mixed impressions you have about a subject. Once you put some ideas on paper, you can start to narrow your topic into something you can manage in an essay.

Exercise 1.1 Use some of the prewriting techniques explained on the previous pages to explore one or more of these general subjects:

1. exploration in space
2. drugs and athletes
3. alcohol abuse
4. pollution
5. violence in the movies
6. novels with happy endings
7. gun control
8. advertising of tobacco and alcohol
9. exercise
10. computers
11. religion and morals
12. getting angry
13. gender roles for children
14. feminism and parenthood
15. teaching in high school

1b

Limit your subject.

When you must choose your own subject, you may immediately decide what you want to write about. A friend of yours may have been injured in an automobile accident caused by a drunk driver. You may decide to write about how beer and wine are advertised on television and to try to analyze the appeals that ad writers are making to young people. Occasionally topics pop into your head, and you find that you can write well about them.

But most writers arrive at their topics by a slow, uneven process. You may want to write about religion and morals. But thousands of books have been written on that subject. You must bring it down to an essay you can manage in five or six pages. You want your essay to be interesting, to grab attention but not to be vulgar. And if you write in general about religion and morals, you will probably not interest anyone. But suppose you write about the differences among Christians, Moslems, and Jews when it comes to the drinking of alcohol? Suppose you write about the problems of separation between church and state in this country, taking an issue such as prayer in the public schools or federal aid to church-supported schools or the teaching of religion in the public schools? Suppose you write about the various constitutional issues involved in the choice of textbooks for public schools? Find out what various religious groups have said on these subjects and you may have the basis for a fine paper.

You may want to write about physical exercise. But you can look at any large newsstand and see perhaps a dozen or more magazines covering various forms of exercise—bicycling, walking, jogging, weight lifting, wrestling, and so on. How do you limit your topic so you can write about some aspect of exercise that will interest your readers? If you refuse to limit your topic and stay with making general ramblings about a general subject, your work will be tedious. Don't be satisfied with being tedious.

Sharpening your subject to make it more interesting may take much thought. You may find it easier to develop a specific topic if you take a series of steps to limit it progressively:

Too broad	Still too broad	Less broad	Still less broad
exercise	good exercises	jogging	the effects of jogging on the heart and blood pressure
	bad exercises	manic jogging	the damage excessive jogging does to the knees and feet
farm life	my sixteen years on a farm	my father's place in my memories of farm life	the major ways my life on the farm makes me different from city friends
	nature	farmers and nature	nature as beauty and destructive force in farm life
pollution	pollution of the air	pollution of the air in the home	pollution caused by wood stoves
	pollution of the water	acid rain	the controversy between the U.S. and Canada over acid rain
computers	computers in education	computers in writing courses	how the computer changed my writing process
	computers in the home	what computers can and cannot do in the home	a comparison between the extravagant claims made for computers in magazines published in 1982 and the realities of today

Even topics in the column "Still less broad" may be narrowed further. Only you can decide how much to limit your own topics for papers. That decision depends on the physical demands of the task—minimum or maximum length, for example—and how much time you have to write. Once you do limit a topic, your ideas about it will expand. Record those ideas as they come to you, and add them to your prewriting materials.

Exercise 1.2   Using the columns above as a model, limit, in a series of steps, any five topics from Exercise 1.1.

1c
Pick the approach that suits your topic best.

Long ago, teachers established four general "modes" of writing and speaking—description, narration, exposition, and argumentation. Most writing involves a combination of these modes. You rarely find a description that does not involve narration, a narration that does not have some description in it, or an exposition or argument that does not include the other two. Many papers may include all four modes. But it helps to know the different modes so you can think about what you are doing as you write and so you can decide which mode ought to predominate in your paper.

Description provides some sort of visual image of a scene, an object, or a person:

Our house stood on a hillside in a grove of maples and oaks.

Narration tells a story, usually in chronological sequence:

I heard the shriek of brakes, the crash, and then the scream. Nick had tried to straighten his tie in the rearview mirror, lost control of his car, and crashed through the window of the bank. He was on his way to the bank to make his last car payment. He stepped out of the wreck unharmed and said to the loan officer, against whose desk the car had come to rest, "Do we have insurance for this?"

Exposition explains.

The Second Amendment of the Constitution of the United States guaranteeing the right of citizens to keep and bear arms does not mean that just anybody can walk around town with a loaded machine gun.

Argument usually maintains a point of view against other, opposite points of view.

Although some of them are very funny, beer commercials should be outlawed from television.

Much college writing is predominantly expository because college papers usually explain texts, statistics, observations, or whatever. The line between an expository paper and an argumentative paper may be thin. You may explain your interpretation of a short story, for example, to prove that someone else's interpretation is incorrect. Then your exposition drifts over into argument.

Think about the four modes as you plan your writing, for they can help you clarify the purpose of your paper. The chart below shows how a writer might develop the same general subject along four distinct lines once a specific purpose is established.

━━ **GENERAL SUBJECT: GROWING UP ON A TENNESSEE FARM** ━━

Mode	Purpose
Description	To present a picture of our house and our community in the foothills of the Great Smoky Mountains
Narration	To describe how my family happened to live there and to tell some of the stories that illustrate what sort of man my father was and how he influenced my life
Exposition	To explain some of the attitudes my father had and what effect they had on his life
Argument	To persuade readers that living on the farm with my family was valuable, even in a world where farming is a declining way of life

These topics will help the writer of the paper better understand why he is writing the paper and what ought to go into it. You can use them in this way for almost any paper you write once you have narrowed the topic down to something you can handle in an interesting way.

You can see how easy it is to move from one mode to another. You can also see that the final purpose of your paper will lead you to emphasize one of these modes above all the others. If your purpose is to present a convincing argument, you may want to keep description and narration to a minimum. If you want to write a straight news story about an accident, you may not want to make any arguments at all: you will tell what happened; you will write a narrative. If you are explaining the various steps doctors take in treating an accident victim, you may find that telling the story of an actual accident is a distraction.

Always keep your major purpose clearly in mind. Once your purpose is clear, it will be easy to choose the rhetorical mode that best suits your aims in writing the paper and emphasize that mode in your writing. The writer of the paper who wants to recall his father and farm life decided, in looking at the different modes, that he did not want to make a strong argument about his father or farm life. There was little to argue about. No one was likely to dispute his account of farm life or his memories of his late father. The topic lent itself much more to narration, to telling illustrative stories about his family's experiences on a small Tennessee farm. Readers could then take their own lessons from his story — as we do from most narratives.

Exercise 1.3   Choose one of the topics you have thought of for a paper and jot down some thoughts about the modes you would use to develop it. Answer these questions, perhaps by devoting a short paragraph to each: What would you describe in this paper? What would you narrate? What would you explain? What would you argue?

CHAPTER TWO

2

Developing a Paper

As you get further into developing a paper, you will do several things to shape it and to give it a clear focus. There is no special order to this process, but here are parts of it that you must consider. You are still using prewriting techniques at this stage of your work.

2a
Consider your intended audience.

Who will read your writing? Avoid thinking of your audience only as the teacher who will evaluate your paper. Write to appeal to others—your friends, the other members of the class, or other people you know. Try to write to engage the attention of people you respect. Always remember that your readers could be doing other things. Try to interest them. Try to be so clear that they have no trouble understanding you. Try to make them willing to stop doing something else so they can have the pleasure of reading what you write.

In many respects, you create your audience as you write. If you write sensibly, interestingly, clearly, and with occasional flashes of wit, you will draw the sort of audience that does most of the reading in America. If you write with passionate emotion and uncompromising anger towards everyone who disagrees with you, your audience will be a small group of fanatical true believers whose emotions rule their way of looking at the world. These people read only material they either love or hate. They do not read to be persuaded of a point of view because they have made up their minds already. If you write in a dull, plodding effort to fill pages and not to take any risks, you will get a dull, plodding audience of a few people who will read your prose because they have nothing better to do at the moment. Or you will get an audience of one: your teacher, who is paid to read your writing no matter how dull it is. You will probably never find a more patient audience than the teacher. Always remember that in life beyond school, you have to write for people who do not have to read your work and who will put it down quickly when it bores them.

1   You should always think of writing within a community of discourse.

A **community of discourse** is a group with certain interests, knowledge, and expectations and with certain conventional ways of communicating with each other. We usually belong to several communities of discourse. Baseball fans make up a community of discourse; they talk and write about the game in familiar ways, and they understand each other even though people outside the community may not know what they are talking about. Every baseball fan would understand this sentence:

> Mickey Mantle switch-hit for the Yankees for eighteen seasons, compiling a .298 lifetime batting average and an astonishing slugging average of .557.

For someone outside the baseball fan's community of discourse, such a statement is gibberish. But consider this statement from the community of discourse that includes biologists:

> Endocytosis of liposomes occurs in a limited class of cells: those that are phagocytic, or able to ingest foreign particles. When phagocytic cells take up liposomes, the cells move the spheres into subcellular organelles known as lysosomes, where the liposomal membranes are thought to be degraded.
> —MARC J. OSTRO

To a biologist, these sentences convey clear thoughts; to people outside the community of discourse made up of biologists, they are gibberish — just like the baseball fan's language to the nonfan. Historians, specialists in literature, economists, philosophers, astronomers, model-railroad enthusiasts, pilots, engineers, salespeople, stockbrokers, dentists, surgeons, and thousands of other groups have their own communities of discourse within which certain expectations control the way members communicate with each other. Writers within these disciplines must know what will interest others, what is new, what is old, how members of the community think, and what language they use to appeal to one another.

You don't have to define *switch-hitter* to a baseball fan. You don't have to define *liposomes* to a biologist. But you would have to define both these terms to readers outside these two communities of discourse.

You determine your audience in part by how much you think you have to explain. Are you writing for people who already know a lot about your subject? Or are you writing for those who might be interested only if you can relate your subject to something in their own experience, which does not happen to include much knowledge about your subject? As we have seen, certain words require no explanation within a given community of discourse because everyone understands them. Once a writer broadens his or her purpose to include people outside a relatively narrow community of discourse, more explanation becomes necessary.

In a college writing class, you will usually assume that your audience includes the other members of the class. What do they know about your subject? What do you have to tell them if they are to make sense of what you are saying? If everybody in the class has read *King Lear*, you don't have to summarize the plot; if nobody has read it, a short summary will be in order.

Part of the expectations of any community of discourse involve style or tone. For any community, you should write as though you respect the reader and respect the subject that presumably interests you both. A professional historian does not write, "Gee whiz, Bismarck was one smart dude, but the bottom line was that he was bad news for Europe." Serious historians don't write that way. Other historians, reading such a sentence, would immediately decide not to take the writer seriously. Unfair? Perhaps. But that is the way communities of discourse work. Readers familiar with conventional ways of approaching knowledge rebel at reading a style radically different from the conventional style of that community of discourse. Yes, language does change, and communities of discourse change their expectations. But the process is slow, and you cannot speed it up by writing in an overheated style, full of slang and street-wise language.

A serious historian will write, "Bismarck's greatness as a German statesman is undisputed, but it was not a moral greatness, and his policies eventually helped bring on the slaughter of World War I." The tone indicates a serious interest in a serious historical question. It also represents respect for the expectations of historians when they read about history. They will take this historian seriously because they see a serious style.

2 Keep the same tone in writing to both experts and others.

Over years of experience, writers come to feel most comfortable with one tone. Whether you address scholars or high school students, do not use slang words that seem to condescend or jargon that seems to say much more than it really does. Scholars will not have to be told that the action in *King Lear* supposedly takes place before Britain became Christian; high school students will probably have to be given that information. They may not know that people lived in Britain before Christianity arrived. But to neither would you write, "When you get right down to it, everybody in the play was hyper, and old Lear was the most hyper guy in the whole bunch. Cordelia was a real sweetie, but she didn't have too many smarts if you ask me."

To neither audience would you write, "The highly idiopathic and narcissistic ego-gratification impulse in Lear, while problematic, transpires in an empirical evolution manifestly evident to the discriminating audience as sanguinary self-destruction."

In writing the personal-experience papers you may be assigned at the beginning of a composition course, you have a little more freedom. Autobiography is often more relaxed than history, philosophy, science, and other academic disciplines.

But often in autobiography, you must explain more than you might explain in a history essay. You have to tell your readers enough about your personal experience to let them understand it. You have to give them enough details to enable them to understand why you feel as you do about various matters. They have to know enough to understand why some things in the experience happened as they did. They have to know why you care enough to tell the story.

3 Ask yourself what you expect the audience to know.

Whoever your readers may be, give them enough knowledge to read your work comfortably. Do not try to alter your style so that you use big, complicated words with one group and breezy or slangy words with another. As you work through your writing life, writing as much as you can, you will develop the style that suits you. Stick with it.

In much of the writing you will do after college, you will be trying to appeal to many different audiences. At work, your audience may include your boss, those you supervise, the owners of the business, potential consumers, and the government agency that regulates what you do. For different groups of readers, the same subject demands different approaches. You must explain things to some groups that you do not have to explain to others. You may, with intimate associates, say some things and use some words that you would not use with readers you know less well. But in whatever you write, your best approach is always to use a flexible style that conveys seriousness without rigidity, fairness without groveling, and friendliness without embarrassing informality that could be considered condescension.

4 In thinking about your audience, keep the journalistic questions in mind.

Whenever you introduce a new character or a new piece of information, ask yourself if your readers know who the character is, what is happening, why it is happening, where it is happening, and when it is happening. Journalists try to answer these questions in the first couple of sentences of a story.

> A fire in a rooming house at 221 Broadway left fourteen people homeless early this morning. The blaze, apparently starting in a Christmas tree, engulfed the frame building in a matter of moments. No one was killed, but several tenants were hospitalized for injuries caused when they jumped to safety from their windows.

Such a story tells what happened, where it happened, who was involved, why it happened, and when it happened. It makes a good beginning for a news story, although you will not usually use such a beginning in college papers.

Still, the questions need to be answered whenever you introduce new information in a paper. When you bring in a new character, always give the full name and accompany it with some sort of identifying tag. "Burriss Young, the dean in charge of the fellowship competition, organized the interviews." When you say that something happened, tell where and when it happened; and if you can tell why it happened, so much the better.

Exercise 2.1   For the topic that you have chosen to write about, ask the journalistic questions. Make up as many of these questions as possible. You should end with a list of questions and answers. Who are you going to write about? Who would be interested in your essay? Who would know about the subject? What happened that you are going to write about? Why did it happen? Why were these people involved? When did it happen? Where? What is the most important question that you want to answer for the paper you are going to write?

2b
Choose the evidence and details you need to make your points.

When you make assertions, provide some evidence to back them up. You may have strong opinions, but few readers accept opinions merely because a writer believes them passionately. You must present evidence that others can accept. If your teacher writes "Be specific" in the margin of a paper, she is probably asking you for some details that support some assertion you have made.

If you say, "Faulkner sometimes seems to get lost in his prose and to lose readers, too," quote a text from Faulkner as evidence for your assertion. You may say, "Dickens lamented the plight of the poor in nineteenth-century England, but he seemed to have no solution except the hope that some good rich people would be generous." If you make such an assertion, give some examples from Dickens's novels to support it. If you say, "James Baldwin puzzled over the Swiss villagers who had never seen a black as much as they puzzled over him," back your statement up with something from Baldwin's essay "A Stranger in the Village."

2b

dev

1   Consider different kinds of evidence and details.

A paper filled with assertions and lacking details that constitute evidence is nearly always a bad paper. Evidence varies. You may use one kind of evidence for one paper, another kind for a different essay.

Source of evidence	Kind of evidence
Personal experience and observation	Concrete sensory details. Describe specific actions, colors, sights, sounds, smells, and tastes to re-create an experience for a reader.
	Dialogues and indirect quotations. Reproduce the words people say so you can enliven a scene.
	Tell stories of events you have witnessed that make you believe something.
Authorities: books, periodicals, TV, radio, films, interviews	Quotations, paraphrases, summaries. Support your points by quoting the words of authorities or by restating their ideas in your own words.
Statistics and cases	Use data (often from charts, graphs, and tables) to lend force to your assertions.
Inferences	Draw conclusions that seem to come from the evidence, though they may not be explicit in the evidence itself.

If you write about a trial you have observed in your local courthouse, you may want to capture the drama by using the details arising from language of the senses, recording the appearance of the courtroom, the actions of the various participants, the smells of the surroundings, and the various sounds that will evoke the scene for your readers. You might write about the bored expressions of the jurors, the no-smoking signs hanging over the bench where the judge sits smoking a cigarette, the professional courtesy of the opposing lawyers, the appearance of the defendant, the nervousness of witnesses, your own difficulties in deciding who is telling the truth, your conversations with other spectators.

You might choose to take a historical approach, reading the transcript of a famous trial and studying books and articles written about it afterwards. You might quote from the evidence given at the trial and quote from the books and articles written afterwards to prove that the evidence was true or false, good or bad.

For yet another kind of paper, you might study the statistics for convictions and sentencing for various kinds of crimes among different age, gender, and ethnic groups. Who is most likely to be sentenced to death in this country? What groups experience the greatest rates of crime? The questions are endless, and the evidence is readily available in various government documents your reference librarian can help you find.

2   Use inferences carefully and wisely.

In both your observations and your use of data, you will have the chance to infer things. When we **infer**, we try to make sense of our observations by reasoning about them on the basis of experience or what we often call *common sense.* We awake in the morning and see snow on the ground; when we went to bed last night, the sky was clear and there was no snow anywhere in sight. So on seeing the snow, we infer that it fell during the night even though we did not see it happen. **Inference** is the way the mind operates to tell us what happened even when we did not see it happening.

The defendant was found with a Colt revolver in his pocket. Two of the bullets had been fired. Ballistics tests show that the bullets that killed the victim exactly match bullets fired from this revolver. The victim had quarreled violently with the defendant. But the defendant says that he found the gun in the gutter, already fired, outside the victim's house and was planning to take it to the police when he was arrested. What do you infer? Such questions are the stuff of thrillers in the movies, but they are also a part of real life, where we infer things every day.

3   Fit different kinds of evidence and details together.

These various kinds of details to form evidence do not exclude one another. A paper rooted in statistical or quoted evidence also benefits from the concrete sensory details that engage readers. A newspaper story recently told us that government debt in the United States was approaching a trillion dollars. It illustrated a trillion dollars by saying that that was enough money to give every ant in the United States a dollar bill. Or that if you put a trillion dollar bills end to end, they would reach the star Alpha Centauri, which is over four light years from earth. By converting numbers into something we can visualize, at least to a degree, we make the numbers more vivid.

It is impossible to say exactly when in the writing process your attention should turn to evidence and details. Some writers begin to consider it only after they write a thesis statement (see 2c) or as they write a rough draft (see 3a). Others think about details earlier, as they formulate and refine the evidence they need to support their topic.

2c

dev

When you consider your chosen topic and the audience you have in mind, think about the kinds of evidence that will best suit your purpose. Ask yourself how you will gather the details to create the evidence you need. For most papers, you will find questions like these helpful:

1. What experiences in my own life will help me make this topic interesting?

2. What have I read recently in books, newspapers, or magazines — or what can I read before I write — that will help me support my topic?

3. What have I heard on the radio or observed on television or in the movies that will help me support my topic?

4. What have I learned in recent conversations with friends, parents, relatives, teachers, and associates that will help me support my topic?

5. What do people in my audience know about my topic? What will interest them? What will bore them? What may even surprise them?

Exercise 2.2   Return to the topics you limited in Exercise 1.2 (or limit some new topics of your own choosing). For each topic, state your reason for writing about it, describe your intended audience, and suggest some probable sources of the kinds of evidence and details that you could use to develop the topic.

2c

Think through the main idea of your composition, and write a thesis statement.

Define your main idea, or **thesis** — the essential thing you want to say about your subject — before you plan and write your paper. As you write and revise, you may change your mind about your thesis. Writers often start a paper and discover that their original thesis is not exactly what they want to say. Then they formulate a new thesis. That is all part of the writing process, and you should accept the proddings of your own mind to change your thesis when those proddings become insistent.

But you will save yourself much time, and you will write much more to the point, if you formulate a main idea before you begin your first draft. You may change it slightly or transform it into something altogether different later on. But you may very well keep the same main idea from first to last draft. Having a thesis focuses the mind and helps you control the sentences and paragraphs that make up your composition. It is usually helpful to formulate your thesis as an argument: What is the most important thing I want my readers to think about my subject? Do I want them to do something? If so, what do I want them to do?

Once you have narrowed the focus of your topic, construct a thesis statement. **A thesis statement** may be one sentence. Or it may be a couple of sentences or even a short paragraph that tells your readers what they are going to be reading, what tone you are going to use in your piece. It also tells readers why they should read what you have written. It lets them know what to expect and lets them decide whether they want to go on with your work. It usually describes your position on the subject as well. What do you think about the subject? If you are writing about organic gardening, for example, your readers should know right away whether you believe in organic gardening or whether you will argue that it is a waste of time and money. Your thesis statement may also include the two or three major arguments you intend to use to support your proposition. The following limited topics at the left led writers to produce the thesis statements at the right.

Limited topic	Possible thesis statement
surprise endings in fiction	The good surprise ending, as in William Faulkner's short story "A Rose for Emily," makes us feel that we should have expected it, for in subtle ways the writer prepares us for it throughout the story.
the effects of jogging on the body	Despite its many advantages, jogging can cause serious injuries to the feet, the knees, and the back.

In the first example, the thesis states the topic — surprise endings. Her thesis claims that a surprise ending is good if it makes us think we should have expected it all along. We expect the paper to prove that thesis with evidence drawn from Faulkner's short story "A Rose for Emily." In the second example, we have a list of bodily parts that jogging can injure. We expect the paper to discuss the effects of jogging on the feet, the knees, and the back, bringing in medical evidence that the writer has found in various publications.

Limited topic	Possible thesis statement
passenger trains in the United States	Passenger trains can do great service in American transportation if Americans will only realize that transportation is too important to be supported only by the people who travel.

32 Writing Essays and Paragraphs

local court-room drama	The murder trial I witnessed this summer made me reflect on how extraordinary and painful events are quickly brought under control in our society by being wrapped up in routine procedures (like those in a courtroom) that make the extraordinary ordinary.
school architecture at home in my high school	The architects of our high school at home thought they would save on fuel by having many classrooms without windows, but the result was disaster.
photographs in the library collection	The old photographs in our library not only show the clothing styles of past times but also how families thought of themselves as units grouped around the oldest male.
advertising in two popular journals	The advertising in *Rolling Stone* and *The New York Times* helps show us many things about the differences in the audiences for the two publications.
a comparison between Hemingway and Faulkner	Hemingway and Faulkner both wrote about men proving themselves in conflicts with large and dangerous animals — Hemingway's characters with bulls and Faulkner's with bears. But at heart both Hemingway's and Faulkner's characters were after self-knowledge.
my growing up on a fairly isolated farm	I spent the first sixteen years of my life on a farm in Tennessee, and my father gave me some of my most vivid memories.
my battle to control my heavy drinking	The morning when I woke up in the seat of my car in a barnyard, not knowing how I got there, my head pounding with the worst hangover in my life, was the moment I realized I had to stop drinking so much alcohol.

Exercise 2.3 Write a broad phrase that covers the subject of the paper you will write. Then write a thesis statement to focus the paper.

2d

To develop your paper, expand your informal written ideas, group them by subject, and organize them in a rough outline.

As you write your thesis statement, you will probably think of more ideas related to your topic and ways to expand ideas you have already recorded. Do not hesitate to add these new ideas to your prewriting papers. It is important to include as many points as you can to help you write. You may start with one thesis statement and, as you begin to write a draft, discover that your thesis—what you really want to write about—is changing.

Next, examine all your prewriting materials and put together related thoughts. You can do this in many ways: cutting and pasting, drawing lines and arrows from one point to a related one, or identifying ideas that belong together with a letter or a symbol in the margin. Some writers look at their lists or jottings produced in prewriting and recopy them into groups of connected thoughts.

As you read your materials, look for some principle to guide you in clustering ideas. For instance, which points on one page depend on points you have made on other pages? If you tie together related ideas before you write, you can improve your chances for producing a clear and logical paper.

1 Choose a method for arranging your information.

As you group your ideas, think about ways of organizing them. Of course there are many possible ways of arranging the thoughts you have grouped together. However, at this stage, most writers find it helpful to consider the following common methods for arranging information in an essay:

Chronological

A **chronological arrangement** relates events as they happen in time. Narratives are usually chronological. The writer of the paper about local courtroom drama (page 29), for example, will probably begin with the opening of the trial and continue, event by event, to the end.

Spatial

You can choose a logical starting point and then move through space systematically. If you are told to describe a painting in a local art gallery or in an art book, for example, you might look at the central focus of the painting and then move outward to the edges of the canvas. If you were asked to describe a landscape, you might write about its most dominant impression and then move, a step at a time, to the less noticeable features that contribute to the whole.

General to Specific, or Specific to General

You may see a relation between a general point and some specific points that would support it. To group these related points together, you can move from a general statement to specific details, or you can arrange your points the other way around. The writer about surprise endings in fiction could begin with the general statement that surprise endings involve careful preparation. She would then support that general statement with specific information from Faulkner's "A Rose for Emily."

The essay about the high school with the windowless rooms could begin with a series of specific statements about incidents in those rooms — children sweating from being overheated in the wintertime, feeling gloomy at being cut off from the sun, the grade curve being lower in those rooms than in rooms with windows, teachers assigned to those rooms quitting their jobs at a much higher rate than others. Then there could come the general statement that the reason all these incidents took place was the gloominess of windowless rooms designed by an architect for heating efficiency rather than for learning. We often see popular magazine articles begin with anecdotes. Having presented the anecdote to whet our interest, the writer tells us why the anecdote means something in a larger context. This sort of introduction moves us from the specific to the general.

By Importance

Some points will seem less important than others in supporting an idea. You may make an argument in the opening paragraph of your paper, then support it by points that climb from the less important to the more important. If your last points have great emotional appeal, you might say that your argument builds in a **crescendo,** a gradual increase of intensity that reaches a peak of such force that readers must pay attention to it and take it seriously. The student writing about the need for passenger trains could build to a crescendo by arguing first that passenger trains are a graceful and convenient way to travel, then that American train service is worse than that of any other major country in the world, then that all major countries subsidize their railroads, then that railroads offer a way to keep from choking cities with automobile fumes, and finally that a good passenger railroad system provides a sense of community for people who cannot afford air transport and yet want to travel comfortably and with dignity.

The writer has to decide which ideas are more or less important than others, and different writers may make different choices — just as different writers make different arguments.

These principles of organization should be especially useful to you during this early planning stage, though you may alter or abandon the sequence you have planned once you start to write.

2   Create a rough outline.

When you put your ideas in sequence, you create a rough outline to expand and develop. **Rough outlines** are informal, private conveniences for the writer, and they follow no prescribed format. From prewriting material, one writer prepared this rough outline for a composition.

dev

Tentative thesis statement: My father's love for his family farm in Tennessee made him a special kind of person and created the legacy that he gave to his children.

Introduction: Tell what home was in my childhood—a farm in Tennessee and my father's place on the farm and our family life together until he was killed in a car accident.

1. First steps
   Earliest memories: Who was in our family; who my father was; who my mother was; why they married; what we did; what sort of life we had; where we lived; where we did things; why we lived there; when these things happened.

2. What characterized farm life: The routines of farm life; the things my father used to love to do. His love of nature, of planting things, of looking at things on the farm, of knowing the names of things, of seeing it all as a great experience. Why did he like the farm so much? It was familiar. It was a relief from his job as a school principal. Did he like being a school principal? I never knew.

3. What we did in the community—church, parties, funerals, telling stories, knowing each other. The community where everybody knew everybody else. Different from the city where you don't know your neighbor next door. Our life in the church. Church every Sunday. Long, boring sermons. But it was a great thing to talk after church, especially in warm weather, when people took their time exchanging news—gossip, I guess—before they went home to Sunday dinner.

4. The advantages of farm life over city life—healthier, safer, more secure.

5. The disadvantages—isolation, not knowing many things that city children know, no travel, no real vacations.

6. Why everything changed. My father was killed in a car wreck. We had to leave the farm.

7. Conclusion: How things are now with the farm and with me.

You can also write up a fully developed formal outline if you want. (See 38-b.) But a rough outline will usually suffice. As you develop the first draft of your paper, you may change your rough outline to include some new ideas. But even if you do not follow your original outline exactly, it can provide a first check on unity and coherence. A paper has **unity** if all the ideas support the thesis. A paper has **coherence** when each thought in the paper flows logically into the next, allowing readers to follow the connections from one point to the next.

Sometimes unity and coherence flow quickly into your writing without much effort. An idea comes to mind in a flash and you write it down clearly, it leads logically to another idea, and somehow every sentence seems to flow easily into the next. But most of the time we all have to work hard to achieve unity and coherence in our writing. Unity and coherence usually develop as you write successive drafts of your paper. Writing a rough outline can help save time by helping you see the points you want to make, evaluate them, rearrange them, perhaps eliminate some of them, and perhaps add some more before you start to work.

3   Check your rough outline.

Checking his rough outline, for example, this writer saw that he should tell his story within a broad chronological framework. He planned now to begin with his earliest childhood on the farm and then come forward to the time when he left the farm and moved to the city. But he realizes that within that broad framework, he does not have to be strictly chronological. His father is dead; he wants to remember him and to tell other people what kind of man he was and to imply, at least, some of the influence that his father had on him. To perform this task he can tell several stories about his father without having to say, "This happened when I was six, and this happened when I was ten, and this happened when I was fourteen, and this happened when I was sixteen." He can be selective in the order that he tells various stories while still following a general chronological sequence. So the dominant modes in his paper will be narration and description, and the general design of the paper will be of several shorter stories put together to make a larger story. Good narratives often have such a design so that the shorter incidents or stories become like the separate beads strung on a thread that make up a necklace; only instead of a necklace, the separate stories make a broader narrative.

This writer sees some difficulties in his outline. When he wrote it, he was still toying with the idea of defending farm life and of arguing that it is better than city life. Then he could argue that despite appearances, his father had given him the best possible life. That's when he put in part 4. But now as he looks at the outline, he begins to wonder if that argument is necessary. He added part 5 to show that farm life also has many disadvantages, and he decides that his paper may lose coherence if he tries to argue that one is better than the other. Maybe it is sufficient to tell his story without any argument at all. He will think about this issue as he writes.

With all the prewriting that he has done, he now has a lot of material for his paper. But he must now ask himself if he can reasonably expect to get all this information into one essay. That is a serious question for a writer to ponder. Perhaps the only way to answer it is to produce a rough draft. The mind generally works better when you are writing a draft than when you are writing a rough outline.

Even so, you should always jot down a rough outline before you start writing a draft. It will help you see the shape and direction of your paper and will help you decide what you have to say and how you will go about saying it. It will raise helpful questions about limitations. Can you say everything you want to say in the space you have available? If not, how do you say those things most interesting to you and most likely to be interesting to your readers?

If you develop a rough outline, you may save yourself a lot of time later on. Sometimes you may do several drafts of such an outline — just as you will do several drafts of a paper. Each draft allows you to think more about your subject before you commit yourself to writing. This preliminary organization may not do everything you hope it will do. You will almost certainly change some things once you start writing. But a strong organizational effort at the beginning will save you much time in the writing process and give you confidence that you do have something worthwhile to say.

This student must also consider his audience. Why would anyone want to read about his father? Why would anyone want to read about farm life in Tennessee? Why would anyone care what happened to the family after his father died?

The writer recognizes, perhaps unconsciously, some advantages he enjoys with his paper. We love stories. When we hear stories about people, we identify with them and want to know how the story comes out because in some sense we are living through it with the characters. The main characters in an autobiographical piece should usually be someone readers would like to know. Sometimes we do get interested in characters who are so bad that we view them with horrified fascination. But most of the time we want to like the main characters in an autobiographical piece.

We also want some tension in the stories we read, whether they are fact or fiction, personal experience or novel. Something must happen. There must be some movement to the story. There should be some conflict, either between characters or between a character and some trial or challenge presented early in the narrative. When we read novels or short stories, or when we see plays or movies, we like to see something happening, a problem set at the beginning, characters moving through incidents related to solving the problem, finally solving it or being overwhelmed by it. When you write a personal-experience piece, you should find an incident that has some conflict, some tension, some problem in it; and you should let your audience know of that tension right away. Then the essay should move toward some resolution, some sense of conclusion or finality in which the problem or the conflict is resolved.

Exercise 2.4   Make a rough outline of a subject you are thinking of writing about in a paper. Write a tentative thesis statement. Then write a series of statements that support that thesis. Exchange outlines with another student in your class. Ask that student to read your outline just as you read the outline that he or she has prepared for a paper. Discuss with each other the following questions:

1. Is the thesis clear enough and limited enough to provide for a good paper?
2. Does every heading in your outline support the thesis statement?
3. Can you write interestingly about the subject of the paper in the time you have before the assignment is due?
4. Does your outline provide for a satisfying conclusion?

CHAPTER THREE

Writing and Revising a Paper

This chapter will take you through a sample writing process that will involve producing drafts of a paper. Follow it carefully to see how the writer can help you understand what you are doing in drafting your own composition.

3a
Prepare the first draft of your composition

With the results of your prewriting and your rough (or formal) outline close at hand, you can start writing. Don't try to make it perfect. This is a first draft and therefore a *rough* draft! The ideas that pop into your head during your prewriting and while you build an outline will only begin to take shape as you develop statements and fill in details on your first draft.

Don't worry too much about errors of fact, questionable spellings, or awkward constructions. Write your first draft as fast as you can. At this stage, you should concentrate on producing a flow of ideas. When you have a draft in front of you, you can change it, correct the misspellings, smooth out the rough places, and shape the whole into a pleasing design.

Mark the places where you think you may have problems. Later you can go back and work on them. Leave wide margins. You need room for additions and corrections. Some writers triple-space after each typewritten line or skip a line or two after each handwritten one so they can insert a later improvement easily.

40

Don't worry about a title now. If you can think of one, fine. If not, develop your title later. Here is the first draft of the essay by a student named Tim about his early life on a farm in Tennessee. For this assignment early in the term, the instructor asked students to write on this topic: "What experience more than any other has shaped you as a person?" The comments were made by peer reviewers in the class.

My Father's Farm

Our farm was about thirty miles from Knoxville in a county called Bourbon that is very beautiful. Or at least it was beautiful when I was growing up there in the 1960s, although now it has changed a lot, and it is not so beautiful any more. Anyway, I was born there and grew up there until I was a sophmore in high school and my father got killed in a car wreck, and we had to move.

Do you need to tell us all this in your first paragraph?

spelling?

I want to write about my father, I want you to know him as I knew him. He was born on the farm, and he never did want to leave it, although he went to college and majored in education and became a school teacher. My father's Uncle Edward hated the farm and went off to school and never returned. "Bob was crazy about the place," Uncle Edward said. "I never could see it myself." I wondered if my father just didn't have enough confidence to leave the farm. Uncle Edward became a lawyer.

Is this a run-on sentence?

Maybe you really want to write about your father in this piece.

Writing and Revising a Paper **41**

Very successful. My father never was successful. Maybe he wouldn't take a risk.

But he was good to us. He didn't want much out of life. And yet he wanted everything out of life--satisfaction, love, some object for his work.

You can't make a living by farming alone, and my father wanted to do something to keep the cash flow going, as they say, but to let him live where he wanted to live. And that was the farm. He got a job teaching, but pretty soon he got to be the principal of the high school. Anyway, he went off to college in Virginia. Because that's where his father wanted him to go, since his father had a big thing about Virginia, thinking all the people there were aristocrats or something, but he never was happy any place else but the farm, and he majored in education because he had his heart set on coming back and he didn't know what he could do except teach.

My mother didn't feel so hot about living on the farm, I don't think she ever got used to it. She was from Richmond, and they met in college, and I guess they loved each other

You sound too inform through he I think yo can compre

Don't you think th is too informal

because they got married and she came back to
live on the farm with him after college.

   I was the oldest, and I had a brother and a
sister younger than me. We all learned to do
all the farm work. My sister learned to drive *I like this part.*
the tractor when she was six years old, and by
the time she was eight, she could drive while
we put up hay. We had two tractors. With the
big one my father would pull the baler through
the field, dropping off the bound up bales. <u>Me</u> *Subject? My brother and I?*
<u>and my brother picked</u> the hay bales up after my
father <u>run</u> the baler through the field, and we *Did you leave out a helping verb?*
put them on the wagon that was pulled behind
the tractor, and my sister drove, and people
thought it was wonderful to see an eight-year-
old girl driving that tractor like she'd been
doing it all her life. Well, she had been doing
it a big part of her life.

   Our community was very close, everybody knew *These are interesting details, but do they go with the paper? Are you writing about the farm or the community?*
everybody else. People were helpful, and when
you were in trouble, you could depend on a lot
of help. When I was very small, too young to
drive the tractor, my father got sick. I don't
know what kind of sickness it was, but he was

in bed for a long time. But some of the
nieghbors came and did our plowing for us, and
they didn't charge anything. It was just the   *Spelling?*
way you did in my nieghborhood.

   My father always wore a suit to his job at
the high school. When he put on his suit in the
morning. He became like a different person. I
think he hated his suit. He always said wool
scrached his skin. He wore cotton on the place. *Check spe*
                                                 here.
Blue jeans. Long cotton underwear in winter   *Aren't the*
time. But he wore a suit to school. He stood up *sentence*
                                                 fragments
straight and got quiet when he put on his suit   *Do you w*
                                                 to use i
and seemed to think about everything he was   *for empha*
going to say before he said anything. We rode
to school with him. I mean my brother, my
sister and me. He didn't have much to say to us
then. You know how it is; he had to think about
everything he had to do during the day, all the
teachers he had to supervise and all those
students, and he didn't want to talk. He was
always so talkative, but you know how it is
when you've got a big job a head of you, you've
got to think about it, and I don't think my
father ever much liked being a school principal.
People liked him, but he didn't like bossing

people. He never said, but that's just my opinion. We called his school work ''suit work.'' We thought it was funny.

We came home on the school bus because he always worked late. There were always papers to fill out and letters to write and reports. School principals make a lot of reports, but who reads them? My father wrote reports and got everything in on time, and then at five o'clock or so he came home. As soon as he came home, he changed his clothes, he put on blue jeans or <u>kakis</u> and an old <u>flanell</u> shirt, and he was out *Spelling?* to the garden or to the barn or somewhere. And he got to work.

And everthing about him changed then he was like another person. He was relaxed and calm *I really like this. But could you pull it together?* and happy, and he'd talk to us about the different kinds of trees on the place and the different kinds of birds and different kinds of cows and chickens and all that. They're even different kinds of grass. That's something you don't suspect about a farm. It seems so simple. But really it's very complicated. You have to know a lot of names, my father knew them all. *This is a comma splice.* He knew the loblolly pine and the Virginia pine and the white pine. He knew the red maple and the silver maple and the mountain maple. He knew poison ivy and poison oak and taught us how to know them and avoid them and how to tell the difference between the poison sumac that grew in a marshy place along the creek in the lower field and the smooth sumac that grew in the woods.

I like names o things

He loved wild flowers. Things that looked like weeds to me to him were beautiful, and he could hold a dandilion in his hand and marvel over it like it was a star that had fallen down to earth. Sometimes we walked back up in the mountains, and he'd carry a little notebook in his shirt pocket, and he'd write down the names of all the flowers he saw. It was like a contest with him. To see how many flowers he could see in a day. When the honeysuckle was blooming, he'd pull off some of the little blossoms and show us how to suck the necter out of them.

And the birds. He loved to look at birds. Once we were walking through a field, and he stopped me all of a sudden by just lying a hand on my

Don't (this.

arm, and he pointed, and I couldn't see anything, but then real slow I saw a bird the color of leaves sitting on a nest. "It's a woodcock," he said real quite. And he made me walk around so we wouldn't disturb her.

It was fun working with him. He loved to be out in the open and to have us with him, and when we got through doing something--getting in *Maybe you could compress this.* the hay, for example--he'd talk about how much fun it was to work together. It was fun. Hard work but fun. He loved to plant things and to watch them grow up. And he loved to harvest things. He said we were his finest crop, and he couldn't wait to see what we'd turn out to be.

We didn't think we were specially happy or unhappy. We just lived from day to day, and some days we were happy, and some days we were so tired that we thought we were unhappy. But I guess in the end you'd have to say we were definitely happy.

But then in my <u>sophmore</u> year in high school *Spelling* my father was killed in a car wreck. A drunk driver hit him one night when he was coming home after a school board meeting. My father had a bag of corn seed on the back seat of the *This is good.*

car when he was killed. I guess his last

thoughts were about planting something.

My mother thought that we should move back

to Richmond. She had family there, she had *Comma splice.*

lived on the farm only because my father wanted

to live there. We sold the place for a pretty

penny. Knoxville was spreading out. Lots of

people were commuting. A lot of people were

selling off land for divisions. And so we did,

too. My mother got a good job in Richmond. So

everything turned out all right.

This last summer I went back. My father has

a brother in Knoxville who works for TVA, and I

went to spend a couple of weeks with him, and

he drove me back down to the old homeplace.

Everything was changed. Our house had been

bulldozed away. Streets had been laid out. There

were alot of houses built and others going up.

We had a driveway running down from the house *I like th details. B*

to the highway, and at the bottom next to the *I wish ending tc*

highway we had a couple of big maple trees. *this st*

They are gone, and in their place is a couple *papir we a little*

of brick pillars with a sign on them. It says *stronger.*

"Happy Valley Subdivision." I was really

unhappy when I looked at that. I realized how

happy we had all been on the farm and how it

was all gone, and it never will come back again.

Notice that Tim concentrated on recording his thoughts and did not worry about correctness. Obviously many errors appear in these pages. Tim has marked some words and sentences that he wants to check during revision. Many ideas in this draft are unclear and far from their final shape. There are problems with language and with form. Here and there the tone is too informal. Some sentences are confused. Some thoughts are repeated unnecessarily.

Exercise 3.1   Without looking ahead in this book, rewrite Tim's paper. Pretend you are Tim. Write in the first person as if these events happened to you. Try to put yourself in his place and live these events in your mind. You may reorganize the draft in any way you want. Try to cut out the unnecessary details. Make the language a little more formal without making it stiff. Then compare your draft with Tim's second draft on pages 52–59.

3b
Revise your first draft.

After you complete the first draft of a paper, take a long break. Put some time and distance between you and your paper to clear your mind.

When you return to your draft, be prepared to reread it carefully several times and to make changes in content, word choice, and sentence structure. As you revise, you will cut some things out and add others. You will change some words, substituting more precise language for generalities. You may want to shift sentences from one place to another or shorten or combine them. Often you may find yourself reorganizing parts of your paper completely.

Think of a title for your paper. If you have a title already, look at it carefully and revise it, if necessary. It should suit your thesis and should engage the reader's attention without being too general, too long, or too cute.

Revised drafts can get messy. Whenever yours gets too messy to read easily, rewrite it as a new draft. If you are using a computer, you can mark up your printed copy, make all the changes on the computer, and run off a new and clean printed copy. Writing habits and skills vary, but most writers need to do at least two drafts. Professional writers and good student writers nearly always do more. With computers, counting drafts may be difficult because you may do so much editing from the screen. But it's always good to print out drafts along the way and to study them as a text off the computer screen.

When you have produced a readable draft, show it to someone whose opinion you trust. Don't ask that person, "What do you think of my paper?" The person will almost always say, "I like it." Ask, rather, "What do you think I am trying to say?" As your friend tells you back what he or she thinks you are trying to say, you may discover that you have not made your purposes clear. Once you and your friendly reader have agreed that the most important issue is what you are trying to say in the paper, you can then discuss some better ways to achieve your purpose. You might want to go in a new direction altogether. Or you might want to straighten out a few confusing places in the paper as you have written it.

Make things as clear as you can. Many sentences will require radical changes to make your ideas easier to understand. Start by fixing the problems you marked in your first draft. Then answer any questions readers may have raised as they talked with you about your paper. Thereafter, you should check every draft slowly and thoughtfully for errors. Mark your sentence boundaries clearly with periods or other end marks. Look for troublesome verbs, vague pronoun references, and misspelled words.

The following checklist focuses on key elements to consider when you revise.

POINTS TO CONSIDER WHEN REVISING

A. Revising ideas
   1. Is the thesis clear? (See 2c.)
   2. Does the paper speak consistently to the same audience? (See 2a.)
   3. Are there enough details to support your major points? (See 2b.)
   4. Does the paper show unity? Do all the ideas relate clearly to each other? (See 2d.)
   5. Is the paper coherent? Do ideas flow logically and smoothly from one to the other? (See 2d.)
   6. Are ideas stated in precise language? (See 4c-1, 12c, 16.) Should any words be replaced by more accurate or appropriate ones?
   7. Does each sentence state its information clearly? Is there sentence variety to hold the readers' interest? When read aloud, do the sentences sound right to the ear? (See Chapters 9–10.)
   8. Are there any unnecessary words that can be eliminated? (See 14a.)

B. Revising for essay structure
1. Does the introduction capture and hold the reader's interest?
2. Does the conclusion complete the ideas established and supported in the paper? (See 4d-2.)
3. Does the title engage the reader's attention?

C. Revising for correctness
1. Sentence completeness
   a. Are periods and other end marks used to set off complete statements? (See 17a.)
   b. Are there any run-on sentences that should be separated by end marks or combined with connecting words and suitable punctuation? (See 17e.)
   c. Are there any sentence fragments that can be corrected by joining them to other sentences, by adding subjects or verbs, or both? (See 18a-1 through 3.)
2. Sentence logic
   a. Are parallel ideas expressed in parallel forms? (See Chapter 8.)
   b. Have you corrected all the needless shifts in tone or point of view? (See Chapter 24.)
   c. Do modifiers stand near enough to the words they describe to avoid ambiguity?
   d. Are the references to pronouns clear? (See Chapter 23.)
   e. Do subordinate sections relate correctly to main clauses? (See 7b-1.)
3. Verbs
   a. Do subjects and verbs agree? (See Chapter 19.)
   b. Are verb tenses correctly formed and consistent? (See 20a-c.)
   c. Have you corrected all unnecessary shifts in tense, mood, voice, number, or emphasis? (See Chapter 24.)
4. Punctuation and mechanics
   a. Are punctuation marks clearly and firmly written? Do end marks, commas, colons, and semicolons serve the meaning of sentences? Are apostrophes placed to show possession or contraction? (See Chapters 25–30.)
   b. Are quotation marks used in pairs to set off someone's exact words? (See 29a.)
   c. Do italics, numbers, and symbols follow conventional uses? (See Chapters 33 and 34.)
   d. Do capital letters follow the conventions of American English? (See Chapter 3.) Is the title of the theme correctly capitalized and punctuated?
   e. Have troublesome words been checked in a dictionary for accurate spelling? (See 22c.)

The writer of the preceding draft reconsidered his work carefully. He found some errors in grammar and spelling and some confusion in diction. But he realized that correcting these errors was not the major task he faced. He had to shape the thoughts in this piece of free writing into a coherent essay. That took some careful revising.

He also had to think about his audience. Who would read this paper? How could he make the paper appeal to people who did not know his father and who had no sense of farm life? How could he sustain interest to the end? What was the main problem or issue that he wanted to introduce early in the essay so he could get people to read on to see how it all ended?

He went back to his rough outline and studied it and compared it with his piece of free writing. This process gave him a little better sense of what he wanted to say and how he wanted to shape his essay. He put the draft down beside his keyboard after making some marginal notes to himself, and then he wrote the following draft.

His teacher had asked the class to turn in a rough draft so she could comment on it and make suggestions before the students did the final draft. So Tim turned in the following draft to her, and her comments appear at the bottom.

My Father's Legacy

I grew up on a small farm in Tennessee about *This is*
nice begin
thirty miles southwest of Knoxville. I left the *But see*
comments
farm when I was a soph*o*more in high school *the end*
because my father was killed in a car wreck,
and I spent the rest of <u>adoliscence</u> in Richmond, *spellin*
Virginia. But the memories of farm life and my
This run
father's love of the farm stay with me more *error ma*
than anything else the experience of growing up *your ide*
unclear.
on a farm shaped me as a person.

We lived on the farm because my father had
lived there before us. He never wanted to
leave, although he did recognize that you can't
make a good living by farming alone nowadays,

and he went to college in Virginia and majored in education and became a school teacher. That way he could teach in the nearby county seat town of Bourbonville and bring in some cash to supplement what we drew out of the farm. But <u>in any case</u> we stayed on the farm, and he taught school to make ends meet.

You can compress this

He was good at his job, and when I was little, <u>he got to</u> be principal of the high school. But his real passion was not teaching but the farm. He never was happy any place but the farm. He loved it.

informal?

My mother <u>didn't feel so hot about living</u> on the farm. (I guess I've already shown that) She was from Richmond, and her folks were well off. They didn't think much of my dad. For one thing he took their only daughter off to Tennessee, and for another he didn't ever make any money. She and my father met in college and fell in love, and he persuaded her to come down to Tennessee despite the fact that her folks didn't want her to marry him and then didn't want her to leave Virginia.

too informal

You don't need this.

There were three children in the family. I was the oldest. My brother Edward was two years younger than <u>me</u>, and my sister Peggy was two years younger than Edward. Peggy learned to

pro

drive the tractor when she was six years old, and by the time she was eight, she could drive while we put up hay. We had a couple of tractors. With the big one my father would pull the baler through the field, dropping off the bound up bales. Me and my brother picked the ~pro ssh~ hay bales up after my father had run the baler through the field, and we put them on the wagon that was pulled behind the tractor, and my sister drove, and people thought it was wonderful to see an eight-year-old girl driving that tractor like she'd been doing it all her life. Well, she had been doing it a big part of ~You don~ ~need th~ her life.

My father loved the farm. He loved to drive a tractor, to work on engines, to plow, to plant things, to put up hay. He gardened, sometimes working late by the light of the moon when it was full. Sometimes in the summer time he would make a pot of coffee when he got up around sunrise, and he would walk out to his garden with a coffee cup and look at the growing things like he was a king admiring his kingdom.

My father always wore a suit to his job at the high school. When he put on his suit in the morning. He became like a different person. He stood up straight and got quiet and seemed to think about everything he was going to say

~See 18. N~ ~reason fo~ ~fragment~

before he said anything. The three of us rode
to school with him in his old Ford. He never
had much to say to us then. You know how it is.
You have to think about what you're going to do
during the day, and if you have a lot of
teachers and a whole high school full of
students depending on you, you have to think
about it. We called this part of his work
"suit work" because he wore a suit to do it.
<u>We thought that was funny</u>.

*You don't
need this.*

We came home on the school bus because he
always worked late. There were always papers to
fill out and letters and reports to write.
"Nobody reads these reports," he said. "But I
still have to write them." Around five o'clock
he came home, changed into blue jeans or khakis
and an old flannel shirt, and he went out to
the garden or to the barn or to the fields to
work.

And everything about him changed then. He
was like another person. He was relaxed and
calm and happy. Now he taught us about all the
incredible things in nature all around us. And
he'd talk to us about the different kinds of
trees on the place and the different kinds of
birds and different kinds of cows and chickens
and even the different kinds of grass.

*I like this
transition*

My father seemed to know the names of

everything. He knew the loblolly pine and the Virginia pine and the white pine, the difference between red oak and white oak, and the red maple and the silver maple and the mountain maple. He knew poison ivy and poison oak and taught us how to know them and avoid them and how to tell the difference between the poison sumac that grew in a marshy place along the creek in the lower field and the smooth sumac that grew in the woods and didn't raise an itching rash on your skin.

He loved wild flowers, things that looked like weeds to me were beautiful to him. He could hold a dandelion and marvel over it like it was a star that had fallen down to earth. *Good simi*
Sometimes we walked in the mountains a few miles from our house, he always carried a little notebook in his shirt pocket, and he wrote down *Two com* the names of all the flowers he saw. It was a *splices* contest with himself to see how many flowers he *check* *this* could see in a day. Honeysuckle especially *See 17.* pleased him. He'd pull off some of the little blossoms and show us how to suck the nectar out of them.

He loved wild birds. He knew all their names *Shorten* and their habits. Once we were walking along *sentence.* the edge of a field, and he suddenly laid a *Make it* hand on my arm and made me stop and put his *into sev* *sentences* other hand up in a gesture of silence, and he pointed towards the ground, and I couldn't see anything, but then real slow I saw a bird the color of leaves sitting on a nest. She was just about the color of the leaves around her, and she was sitting there still as could be and looking at us. "It's a woodcock," he said real quiet. And he made me walk around so we wouldn't disturb her. It really makes me feel good on looking back to think about how he respected nature and didn't want to disturb anything in nature he didn't have to; I really loved that about him.

I don't think you need this. We can see the man here. You don't have to tell us your feelings.

It was fun working with him. He laughed and made us all laugh. He loved to be out in the open and to have us with him, and when we got through doing something--getting in the hay, for example--he'd talk about how much fun it was to work together. Most of it was fun. Hard work but fun.

You can compress this.

He loved to plant things and to watch them grow up. He planted peas on Valentine's Day, and when the first green shoots came up out of the soil of his garden, he said, "I don't care what the calendar says; it's spring. It's really spring." And he was happy. He always said we were his finest crop, and he couldn't wait to see what fruit we'd bear.

As it turned out, he didn't get to see what we turned out to be, he was killed in a wreck during my sophomore year in high school. A drunk driver hit him one night when he was coming home after a school board meeting. My father had a bag of corn seed in the back seat of the car when he was killed. I guess his last thoughts were about planting something.

My mother decided to move us back to Richmond. We didn't want to go. The farm was home, and we couldn't think about living anywhere else. But Mom had family in Richmond, and she didn't like the farm much anyway.

This last summer I went back to see my father's brother who lives in Knoxville, my uncle Edward. He drove me back to the old homeplace. Nothing was the same. The house was vanished--bulldozed away, Uncle Edward said. Streets had been laid out through our fields. Houses had been built along the streets. It was all very depressing. I realized how happy we had all been on the farm and how it was all gone, and it never will come back again.

But I also realized that some things will stay in me as long as I live. I'll always remember how the farm brought our family together. I'll always remember my father and the things he taught me. I'll remember the names of the trees and the names of the birds and how he marveled at the woodcock sitting on her nest. My Mom's father, my grandfather, has always said that if my Dad had spent as much time on business as he spent on birds, he would have left me a legacy. But he did leave me a legacy even if he didn't leave me any money. He took time to notice things that other people never saw. I hope I can always do the same.

Tell me more about the conflict here. Put it in the first paragraph.

This is a good draft, and it can be a better one. You have a fine topic—your father's legacy to you. Be sure that everything in the paper tells us about that legacy.

You tell us too many times that your father loved the farm. We can tell that from what you tell us about him. Perhaps you used the verb "loved" too much in the essay. It's a good word. But you don't want to repeat any word again and again.

Your conclusion has a good idea. But I'd like to see you think about it a little and develop it more. One of the most interesting remarks is what your grandfather said about your father and the birds. I know that may be painful for you, but you might work that up into a theme for the paper.

Note the places where I have marked some errors in the margins of your paper. These errors are easily fixed.

Now and then I've suggested that you rewrite a sentence, especially when you get a little too informal. I won't rewrite the sentence for you. But take a look at the places I have marked to see if you can make them clearer, better. Watch for comma splices.

Shorten the piece. It's too long as it stands. I'm looking forward to the final draft of this paper. You're telling a good story well.

Exercise 3.2 Study this draft. Compare it with your own earlier attempt to revise the free writing that provided the first draft of the paper. See if you can tell why the writer made the changes he made in his first draft. Discuss with other members of your class how you would revise the paper, the questions you wish the writer would answer, the things you think he could delete without injury to the whole.

The final version of Tim's paper appears in 3e. You will see how different it is from the version you just read.

3c
Proofread your paper for errors.

Both before and after you prepare your final draft, comb your paper for mechanical mistakes and correct them. This step is called **proofreading.** Proofreading requires careful examination of each line on the page. Proofread your last rough draft before you turn it into your final draft, and proofread again as you prepare your final draft for submission. Hold a ruler or a blank sheet of paper beneath the line you are studying. Examine each sentence carefully for missing words and punctuation. Check each word carefully for missing or incorrect letters. Proofreading a paper by reading backwards from the last sentence to the first is another good technique. It helps you to focus on isolated units and to catch errors easily overlooked in the context of surrounding sentences. Some writers touch the point of a pencil to each syllable to help them read more slowly. It is always a good idea to read your paper slowly aloud to yourself.

Tim has an advantage in that his teacher read a rough draft of his essay and made some suggestions about changes. Many teachers do not have time to read rough drafts, and so you may be on your own when you prepare your final draft. That is all the more reason for you to pay careful attention to what you do.

3d
Prepare the final draft.

Follow your instructor's guidelines for correct manuscript preparation in each course. The papers you submit for your instructor's evaluation must be clean and relatively free of handwritten corrections. But it is *always* better to write in a correction than to turn in clean pages with misspellings or other obvious errors.

Remember that your instructor must grade many papers, remaining alert and careful through them all. Messy papers make life hard for the busy teacher. But sometimes you will find a mistake in a paper just as you are ready to hand it in. Always correct the mistake, but do so as neatly as you can.

GENERAL MANUSCRIPT REQUIREMENTS

Margins

1. Leave margins of 1 ¼ or 1 ½ inches at the top, sides, and bottom of each page. Do not fold margins. You can mark off the four marginal areas with light pencil lines to keep your words from straying into them.
2. Indent all paragraphs.

Title

1. Center the title on the first page, 1 ½ inches below the top margin, or on the first line for handwritten copies.
2. Leave one line of space below the title.
3. Capitalize the first letter of all *major* words in the title, including the first and last words, no matter what part of speech they are.

    Jumping for Fitness and Popularity

4. Capitalize the first letter of prepositions of four or more letters.

    Once Upon Life's Highway

5. Do *not* use a period at the end of the title; do not underline the title or enclose it in quotation marks. (The title of a book, an article, or a poem that appears within your title does need correct punctuation. See 29c and 34a.)
6. A title on the cover page requires all-capital letters. If you use a cover page, use the title again at the top of the first page of your manuscript.

Cover page

The cover page usually includes your name, your class number, the submission date, and the professor's name. However, your instructor may have different requirements.

Format

1. Write on one side of each page only.
2. Number all pages consecutively, starting with page two of your composition. The first page is not numbered but is considered page one nonetheless. (Do not count the cover page or, if you submit one, the outline page.)

3. Use arabic numbers in the upper right hand corner or centered at the top of each page. Be consistent in whatever form of pagination you use.

Typed and word-processed papers

1. Use 8 ½ × 11 unlined white bond paper, not onionskin, and not the paper treated to allow corrections with pencil erasers. (Eraseable paper smudges easily and often becomes unreadable.)
2. Use *only* black ribbon; if the type looks faded, change the ribbon. Nothing is so hard for a teacher as to be forced to make out an almost illegible paper typed with an exhausted ribbon.
3. Double-space between lines; indent paragraphs five spaces.
4. After periods, question marks, exclamation points, and colons, use two spaces; after commas and semicolons, use one space.
5. Do not use a space before or after a hyphen. To type a dash, use two consecutive hyphens (--) without any spacing between the dash and the words on each side.

   ```
   Dashes--as in this example--set off thoughts
   for emphasis.
   ```

6. Make corrections with a typewriter eraser, a correcting tape on the typewriter, or with correction fluid. Do not strike over incorrect letters. For minor errors discovered after you have removed your pages from the typewriter, use a pen with blue or black ink.
7. If you use a computer, be sure you have not left in words you intended to delete or deleted words you intended to leave in.
8. Type should be clean enough to make clear, sharp letters.
9. Dot matrix printers used with word processors should have true descenders. That is, the tails on the letters *g, j, p, q,* and *y* should come down below the baseline for the rest of the type. (See Appendix B.)
10. Remember to use adequate margins. (A left margin set at 10 and a right margin set at 70 are acceptable.)
11. In general, a manuscript prepared on a word processor is more readable if the right margin is *not* justified. Printers with proportional spacing may justify the right margin.
12. If you use a computer printer with tractor-fed continuous-form paper, be sure you tear off the perforated strip on each side of the paper, and be sure to separate each page.

Handwritten papers

1. Use 8 ½ × 11 paper with lines spaced about ⅜ inch apart. (For a clear layout, you can skip every other line.)
2. Use blue or black ink; write on one side only.
3. Indent the first line of every paragraph about an inch.
4. Make occasional corrections with an ink eraser or correction fluid, or draw a neat line through words you want to delete. Write in the new words above the deletions, using skipped lines and marginal space for additions.

5. Make your handwriting readable. Use firm, clear periods at the end of sentences, and leave space before the next sentence. Dot *i*'s and *j*'s directly above the letter. Avoid loops and curlicues, especially when you make capital letters. Make sure readers can distinguish between the *r* and the *n*, the *v* and the *u*, the *o* and the *a*, the *l* and the *t*, and the *e* and the *i*. Be careful to round off the letter *h* so it does not look like the letters *l* and *i*. Be sure to make the letters *m* and *n* so they do not look like the letter *u* combined with another letter or standing alone.

Here is the first page of the final typed paper on farm life.

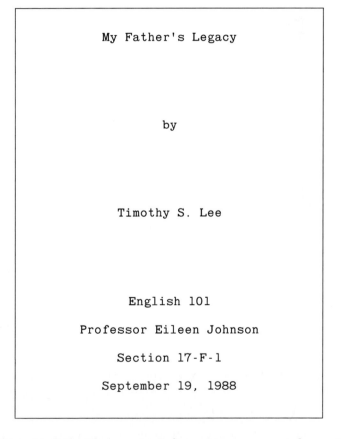

```
                My Father's Legacy



                        by



                Timothy S. Lee




                  English 101

            Professor Eileen Johnson

                Section 17-F-1

             September 19, 1988
```

Exercise 3.3   Choose a topic from your own personal experience and prepare a composition based on it. Try to write about an experience that shaped you as a person or that marked a turning point in your life. Follow guidelines 1a through 3d. As you write, be sure to save the following materials that you can put in a large envelope to present to your teacher.

1. Notes made during your prewriting
2. A limited topic
3. A statement of purpose for your paper, a description of the kind of people you would like to read the paper, and a description of the nature and sources of your supporting details
4. A thesis statement
5. An outline (See 38b-1, for different sorts of outlines.)
6. A first draft
7. A second draft and any subsequent drafts that may be necessary
8. A final draft

3e
Make the necessary changes and corrections after your instructor has commented on your paper.

When your instructor returns your graded paper, read it over carefully. Study the summary remarks that describe the strengths and weaknesses of your work. Examine the marginal notations, and be prepared to make revisions based on the commentary you find there.

You can learn to prevent errors next time around by correcting your mistakes and by responding to suggestions about style, form, and content.

Your instructor may evaluate your paper with a combination of comments, questions, and marking symbols. An alphabetical list of common correction symbols keyed to this handbook appears on the inside front cover of your book. If you see / / in the margin of your paper, for example, the list on the inside cover tells you that / / is a shorthand notation for faulty parallelism and that Chapter 8 explains the problem and how to correct it.

If your instructor writes chapter and section numbers only, check the inside back covers of this handbook for a quick guide to the plan of the text. If your instructor writes ≠ *coh* in the margin of your paper, for example, the plan on the inside back cover tells you that ≠ *coh* refers to paragraph coherence. After you read that section, you should understand the problem and some strategies for correcting it.

As you reread your paper, correct all the errors and make required revisions. Pay special attention to places where your instructor may have asked for more information. If, for example, you mention a name, your instructor may ask for some identification. You may have written this: "According to John Simon, the English language is in decline." Your instructor may write, "Who is John Simon?" You should revise by saying, "According to John Simon, literary critic and author of *Paradigms Lost*, the English language is in decline." If you don't understand a comment or a symbol, make an appointment to discuss the paper with your instructor.

GUIDELINES FOR MAKING CORRECTIONS
━━━━━━━ ON EVALUATED PAPERS ━━━━━━━

1. Follow your instructor's guidelines for revisions. Some instructors read drafts and make comments *before* the paper goes into final form. Others encourage full rewriting based on comments written on final drafts. Be sure to correct errors before you do complete revisions of graded papers.

2. Learn the symbol and comment system your instructor uses.

3. Make all corrections called for by marking symbols and comments. Use a pencil or a different color of ink to make corrections so that your instructor can readily see what you have done.

4. As you make corrections, draw a line through the marginal symbol to help yourself keep track of what you have finished.

5. Write short corrections clearly, directly above the error noted by your instructor.

6. Rewrite any weak sentences in the margin (if there is room) or on the reverse side of the page. If you rewrite on the reverse side of the page, put an arrow in the margin to let your instructor know to turn the page over to see your revision.

7. Keep a record of your mistakes from theme to theme. Any writer tends to fall into patterns of error. If you keep a record of your errors, you can discover your own patterns and so be on the lookout for the errors you are most likely to make.

━━━━━━━━━━━━━━━━━━━━━━━━━━━━━━━

Here is the final draft of the paper "My Father's Legacy," accompanied by commentary from the instructor, who used questions, marking symbols, and suggestions for revision.

```
"If your father had been as interested in

business as he was in birds, he might have left

you a legacy." That was the growling comment

of my grandfather, my mother's father, last
```

year when I went back to see the farm where I
grew up in Tennessee. My grandfather had not
wanted his daughter to marry my father; and
once they were married he did not want her to
go off to live on a farm.

We lived on the farm because my father never
wanted to leave the place where he had grown
up. His father barely made a living off the
farm, and my father knew he would have to have
outside income to make ends meet if he stayed
on the place. So he got a scholarship to a
college in Virginia, supplemented the
scholarship with a part-time job as a janitor
in a college building, majored in education and
became a school teacher.

He and my mother met in an English class.
They were required read each other's papers
before handing them in to the teacher. He wrote
a paper about birds, she was surprised that a
man would be interested in such things. And
that was how it started.

Her parents--especially her father--objected
to the marriage from the first. Her father told
her that my father would never make any money.
They did not want her to live on a farm far
from home. They never came to visit as long as
we lived there.

Mother loved the city with its broad streets,

its people, and its things to do. She studied to be an architect, and she wanted to live in a city where architects could find work. I don't think she was happy on the farm. Perhaps she was not happy with my father. Once when she was angry at him, my mom said, ''You don't have any ambition.'' She apologized again and again for saying that, but it may have been true. Still, she never complained much except when she had to fight off the cockroaches that came in from the woods or when she ran into snakes in her flower garden or when the roof leaked because the house was so old and my father was to busy to fix it.

My father eventually became principal of the high school in nearby Bourbonville. But his real passion was the farm and the natural world that thrived there.

He sang when he drove a tractor, and at a distance we could hear his tenor voice rising above and carrying beyond the puttering sound of the gasoline engine. He gardened, sometimes working late by the light of the moon when it was full. Sometimes he made a pot of coffee when he got up around sunrise, and he walked out to his garden with a coffee cup and looked at the growing things like a king admiring his kingdom.

I was the oldest child. My brother Edward was two years younger than I, and my sister Peggy was two years younger than Edward. My father taught Peggy how to drive a tractor when she was 6 years old. By the time she was 8, she *~n (see 33l* could drive while we put up hay. We had two tractors. With the big one my father would pull the baler through the field, droping off the *sp* bales. Edward and I lifted the bales onto the flat-bed wagon pulled behind the tractor that my sister drove.

We always had something to talk about with each other--the new calf, the work we would do that day or the work we had done, the angus cow who had butted down a fence post yet again and run off into the neighborhood, the king snake my mother found in the robins mud-plastered *√ 28* nest in the yard and the crys all the other *pl 31c* birds made around the snake as he made his meal on the robin's blue eggs.

We learned what we were good at and what we were bad at. ''Nobody can be good at everything'' my father said. I got to be good *ß 26* at working on engines, but Edward loved to read. ''Just like his namesake, my brother,'' my father said. He was proud of the good grades Edward made in school. But he was also proud because Peggy loved engines, and by the time she was eleven, he had taught her to be a fine mechanic.

My father always wore a suit to his job at the high school. When he put on his suit in the morning he became a different person. He stood up straight and got quiet and seemed to think about everything he was going to say before he said anything. He drove us to school in his old Ford. He never had much to say to us on those mornings. He seemed absorbed in the work he was going to have to do that day--"suit work," we called it, the work of being a school principal. And when my father put on his suit, we took it as a signal that we should be quiet.

We came home on the school bus because he always worked late. He always had papers to fill out and letters and reports to write. Around five o'clock he came home, changed into blue jeans or khakis and an old flannel shirt, and he went out to the garden or to the barn or to the fields to work.

Everything about him changed <u>then</u>. He was relaxed and calm and happy. He wasn't the school principal <u>then</u>; he was our teacher, and the farm was our book. He taught us about the different kinds of trees on the place and the different kinds of birds and different kinds of cows and chickens and even the different kinds of grass.

You repeat these thens very close to each other. Another word?

He seemed to know the names of everything. *pl*
He knew the loblolly pine and the Virginia pine
and the white pine. He knew the red maple and
the silver maple and the mountain maple. He
knew poison ivy and poison oak and taught us
how to know them and avoid them and how to tell
the difference between the poison sumac that
grew in a marshy place along the creek in the
lower field and the harmless, smooth sumac that
grew in the woods.

Plants that were weeds to me were wild
flowers to him. He could hold a dandelion and
admire it as if it were a star fallen to earth.
Sometimes we drove over to the mountains a few
miles from our house and took hikes on Sunday
afternoons, especially in the Spring when it   *Cap 32*
was first getting warm. He always carried a
little notebook in his shirt pocket, and he
wrote down the names of all the flowers he saw.
It was a contest with himself to see how many
flowers he could see in a day. When the
honeysuckle was blooming. He'd pull off some of   *frag 18*
the little blossoms and show us how to suck the
nectar out of them. "It's natural candy," he
said. "And it doesn't rot your teeth."

He saw things we sometimes might have missed.
Once we were walking along the edge of a field,
and he suddenly laid a hand on my arm and made

me stop and put his other hand up in a gesture of silence, and he pointed towards the ground. I couldn't see anything at first except the dried grass, but then I saw a bird the color of leaves sitting on a nest. "It's a woodcock," he said real quiet. And he made me walk around *adj and* so we wouldn't disturb her.

He loved to plant things and to watch them grow up. He planted peas on Valentine's Day, and when the first shoots came up out of the soil of his garden, he said, "I don't care what the calendar says; its spring. Its *us* really spring." And he was happy. He always said we were his finest crop, and he couldn't wait to see what fruit we'd bear.

My father was killed in a wreck during my sophomore year in high school. A drunk driver hit him one night when he was coming home after a school board meeting. My father had a bag of corn seed in the back seat of the car when he was killed. His last thoughts must have been about planting something.

A developer bought our farm. My mother moved us back to Richmond, to her family, and she went back to being an architect. And we have lived well.

This last summer for the first time in almost three years, I went back to visit my father's brother, my Uncle Edward, in Knoxville. He drove me back to the old homeplace. Nothing was the same. The house had vanished--bulldozed away, Uncle Edward said. Streets had been laid out through our fields. Houses were built or being built along the streets.

My grandfather was wrong. True, my father did not leave me any money. But he left me the memory of his pleasure at hard work and growing things, his good humor, his love, his silent wonder at the sight of the woodcock nesting in the grass against a background of leaves. I remember how much he hoped for all of us. And I remember all the times he said, "Good job. Good job." He made me believe I can do a good job and be happy with what I have, and that is a legacy beyond anything my grandfather can imagine.

*Much l
ending-
matche
your
introd*

This is a very nice piece that evokes both sadness and pleasure. You have a clear thesis now, and you stay with it all the way through. I like the way you begin with the word legacy and end with it. I enjoyed the many good stories you tell. But you never do tell us any of your father's faults. Surely he had some. You might talk about them just enough to make more believable all the good memories you have of him. He sounds like a great person, and he will still be great if you admit some shortcomings.

Now and then your language is a little too informal. And I think some parts of the essay don't fit together as well as they should. I've marked some places where you might weave things together a little better. Try to work on those comma splices.

But this is a good paper, and I enjoyed reading it.

Exercise 3.4   Divide your class into small groups, and compare this final draft of Tim Lee's paper with the previous two drafts. Where has he revised sentences? Where has he changed paragraphs around? Where has he added new information? Where has he deleted material? Why do you think he has made each of the changes he has made? Do you approve of all the changes, or do you think he has deleted some things that he should have kept from previous drafts? Now discuss all these changes in the class as a whole.

Exercise 3.5   Following the instructor's comments on the theme on pages 72–73, make corrections and any necessary revisions.

Exercise 3.6   When your instructor returns the composition you prepared for Exercise 3.3, follow the instructor's guidelines and make all necessary corrections and revisions.

CHAPTER FOUR

Writing Strong Paragraphs

Paragraphs divide a text up into manageable units that organize writing and make reading easier. The first sentence of a paragraph is indented several spaces from the left margin of the page. The indentation serves as a signal; it lets us know when a paragraph begins; it tells us that the paragraph before the indentation has ended.

Without paragraphs, any printed text would appear as a long, monotonous column of type. We are so familiar with the appearance of paragraphs that we often take them for granted. But they became common only in the nineteenth century as a device to break up the sameness of appearance on the printed page. The paragraph then proved to be valuable as a means of breaking up a long discourse into smaller units of meaning—a sort of processing of thought into bite-sized intellectual chunks for the mind of both writer and reader alike.

The history of the paragraph as a printer's device should help you recall an essential fact about them: paragraphs do not stand alone; they are not essays in themselves. Once in a while you may write a single paragraph for some special purpose—as a caption to a picture, for example, or as a brief memo in an office. But much more commonly, paragraphs are not written for their own sake but as part of the flow of a larger text. In a college writing course, paragraphs form steps along the way to making the point that a writer wants an essay to make. Paragraphs have meaning as they are joined together to reach the goal of the essay.

Paragraphs usually comprise several sentences. Those sentences usually support a main point, some train of thought that binds the sentences together in a common purpose. Another way of thinking of a paragraph is to visualize it as a team of horses pulling a wagon; the horses are sentences; the wagon is the general idea that those sentences carry along in the essay. The sentences have to be connected and carefully arranged if they are to pull their load. Otherwise the lines will get tangled up, and the thought will become hopelessly confused.

4a

Build unified paragraphs.

We expect paragraphs to have some common purpose, some point that all the sentences of the paragraph work together to make. Paragraphs achieve unity if they support a controlling idea.

1 Give each paragraph a controlling idea.

Every paragraph should have a **controlling idea,** a main thought that all of its sentences support and clarify. Often a lead sentence will express that controlling idea as a generalization:

> Everyone knows that sports teams must have nicknames, but selecting an appropriate one is fraught with peril. Alabama, for instance, may be proud of the Crimson Tide, but it sounds like a bloodbath or a serious algae problem. Notre Dame's famous jocks are ossified as the Fighting Irish, though Hibernian-American athletes are about as rare in South Bend as they are on the Boston Celtics. Nothing exposed the nickname crisis more than the 1982 NCAA basketball championship game played between the Georgetown Hoyas and the North Carolina Tar Heels. Even if you know what a hoya or a tarheel is, the only sensible strategy is to forget it. (For those overwhelmed by a need to know, hoya is short for *Hoya saxa!* a garbled Greek and Latin cheer meaning "What rocks!," and tarheel originated during the Civil War as a disparaging term for folks from the Carolina pine forests.) Few knew what the Fort Wayne Zollner Pistons were when a pro basketball team played under that name. (They were players owned by Fred Zollner, who also happened to own a piston factory in Fort Wayne.) The early vogue of naming a team for a person seems to have come to an end with Paul Brown, the original coach of the Cleveland Browns. Fans who found the cult of personality distasteful at least were grateful that he wasn't named Stumblebrenner.
>
> — JOHN LEO

This paragraph begins with a general statement made, tongue in cheek, about the oddities of the nicknames for athletic teams. Having made that broad statement, John Leo fills his paragraph with supporting information.

How do you define a controlling idea? The traditional method has been to put it into a **topic sentence,** a general statement usually coming at the beginning of the paragraph and supported by all the following sentences. A topic sentence may limit and define the topic by presenting a strong opinion or an attitude about it. That is what writer John Leo does in the humorous paragraph quoted above. Or the topic sentence may make a simple statement of fact that will be supported by later sentences in the paragraph.

Wars have been waged over water. In recent decades, India and Pakistan fought over rivers they shared; also Israel and Syria, and Iraq and Syria. In 1964, notes resources expert Richard J. Barnet, in *The Lean Years,* a water dispute between two states of the United States led to a legal battle and "language reminiscent of the sort that France and Germany used to employ just before they went to war." ("The aggressive policies of the State of Iowa," read one Supreme Court brief, "have caused great consternation to the State of Nebraska and its citizens, and have threatened to result in armed conflict on the part of landowners and the State of Iowa and its representatives.")

— Jonathan Weiner

The topic sentence, "Wars have been waged over water," introduces a paragraph whose controlling idea is neatly stated. The other sentences support the controlling idea expressed in the topic sentence.

You can often add to the clarity of your writing by shaping the first sentence in a paragraph to express, in exact language, the controlling idea you want to convey. Compare the following topic sentences:

1. My father spent the first years of his childhood in Chicago.
2. My father spent the first years of a difficult childhood in Chicago.

Both these sentences make a general statement about a topic — the father's childhood in Chicago. But no controlling assertion gives direction to the topic in sentence 1. Many things happen in childhood.

In a good paragraph, the writer selects details that develop a central idea. And in some paragraphs that central idea is expressed by a topic sentence that is a sort of general summary of what the rest of the paragraph is about. In the paragraph below, the first sentence makes a broad and general statement; the second sentence develops the general statement more specifically. The paragraph that comes after it will report difficulties in the father's childhood that will show how hard it was. See how the limited topic sentence works in the following paragraph.

My father spent the first years of a difficult childhood in Chicago. His father deserted the family, leaving a wife and five small children. At age eight, my father was the oldest. His mother had to take in washing and had to clean house for rich people on Michigan Avenue just to keep her family together. My father cleaned up yards for ten cents an hour when he was eleven. He got a paper route when he was twelve and had to crawl out of bed at five in the morning, seven days a week, winter and summer, to deliver the papers before breakfast. He gave all the money he made to his mother for family expenses. Because they could not afford doctors, my father was left partly deaf by a childhood disease. *Every sentence in the paragraph supports the general statement made in the topic sentence. Every detail illustrates the idea of a difficult childhood to back up the general assertion made at the beginning.*

In the following paragraphs, each topic sentence makes a generalization that limits and controls the topic.

Although smoking has been a popular habit for centuries, it has always had its enemies. Some American Indians advised young braves not to smoke too much because tobacco would cut their wind in a hunt or in battle. King James I of England called smoking "a branch of the sin of drunkenness, which is the root of all sins." Ben Jonson, the playwright, said smoking was "good for nothing but to choke a man and fill him full of smoke and embers." Popular slang called cigarettes "coffin nails" long before the medical evidence on the harm from smoking was complete. Now every package of cigarettes and every advertisement for cigarettes must carry a warning from the Surgeon General that smoking is injurious to health.

—Dick Curry

The first sentence announces the topic, asserting that smoking has always had its enemies. Note how this topic sentence helps the writer limit and control the paragraph. Every sentence that follows supports this main idea.

Teenagers are almost endemic to the mall—some of them are so fiercely loyal that they call themselves "Mall Rats." Such self-confessed examples include Michelle and her friends, teenagers of both sexes between the ages of 12 and 15, who hang out at Hillsdale Shopping Center near San Francisco. "A Mall Rat is someone who is here every day," Michelle says. The primary reason is social; it's where kids strut their stuff. "We put on our cool faces and walk around and try to meet girls, and scare all the other guys," says Dan, who frequents Detroit malls. The loyalty of Mall Rats is sometimes extreme. When his family moved, one boy in the Washington, D.C., area insisted on bicycling five miles every day to his old mall so he could be with his friends.

— WILLIAM SEVERINI KOWINSKI

The topic sentence comes first; it provides an organizing framework for the sentences that follow. The topic sentence tells the reader why the writer has chosen these details to present and gives direction to the paragraph.

But many paragraphs do not begin with a summary topic sentence. Paragraphs that tell stories, paragraphs that describe, even some paragraphs that explain do not have a general statement that unites everything else in the paragraph. The absence of a topic sentence in many paragraphs is a legacy of paragraph history. As we said above, paragraphs do not stand by themselves; they take their place within a flow of discourse, and so the meaning of some paragraphs depends on what comes before them in other paragraphs.

Always the most important sentence in setting the stage for the paragraph is the first sentence, even if it does not tell you much about the topic. The first sentence announces the subject, and the rest of the paragraph develops its controlling idea by building on some thought expressed in the first sentence. The controlling idea may not be specifically expressed in a sentence of its own, but when you read a good paragraph you can always express its controlling idea in a sentence if you set yourself to doing so.

Sometimes the first sentence simply introduces the topic for the paragraph without summarizing what will be said about the topic. The second sentence may then be a summary of what is to come.

The steam locomotive evokes nostalgia among many people. *The nostalgia is better than the experience of the steam locomotive ever was.* The steam locomotive was a dirty, dangerous, and generally disagreeable companion to American life for well over a century. It spread filthy black smoke over large areas of every city it served, and it usually left a thick film of oily grime on the face of every passenger in the cars behind it. It started fires along the sides of the tracks in woods and fields. It was so heavy that it pounded rails until they broke, and when it crashed and turned over — as it frequently did — it poured deadly fire and steam on the fireman and the engineer in the cab. It had so many moving parts under high stress that it often broke down, stranding passengers for hours. And it was absurdly inefficient and costly to operate.

The second sentence is a summary topic sentence in this paragraph. It tells you that the paragraph will describe the disadvantages of steam locomotives. But the first sentence leads into the topic, even though it does not tell you what the paragraph will say about steam locomo-

tives. Everything else in the paragraph takes the lead from the topic introduced in the first sentence.

Sometimes the first sentence in the first paragraph of a longer work will begin the description of a scene. Several similar sentences will follow. The final sentence in this type of first paragraph may sum up the scene and explain why it is important to the meaning that the paragraph expresses. Or a following paragraph may explain the scene depicted in the first. Such scene-setting first paragraphs are often used to begin articles in popular magazines because they make readers want to know what is going to happen next. Although the first sentence in such a paragraph is not, strictly speaking, a topic sentence, it sets the direction for what comes next and introduces the controlling idea of the paragraph.

The bands are marching, the tailgates swinging open for the ritual of picnics and parties. The beverages are heady, the boosterism infectious, the old school colors vivid and bright. *This is college football, as the television slogan goes, a great way to spend an autumn afternoon.*

—*Newsweek*

A summary topic sentence comes last, uniting all the concrete details in the earlier sentences and explaining why the writer has put them in. But the first sentence introduces the topic, even though it does not make a general statement about it.

Often an introductory paragraph in an essay or an article simply tells a story. The first sentence begins with a striking detail, and the following sentences build on it. A later paragraph introduces the topic that the story illustrates. The role of the first sentence in such a paragraph is to catch the interest of readers and to make them keep on reading.

Georges Randrianasolo, Madagascar's leading naturalist, grabbed the doorframe of our descending helicopter and stared uneasily at the limestone pinnacles below us. From horizon to horizon, erosion had sculptured rock into spires a hundred feet tall, some whetted so thin at their peaks that the setting sun gleamed as if sinking behind an entire skyline of Empire State Buildings. Malagasy —the people of Madagascar— call these rocks *tsingy*, or spikes, and say that in the tsingy there is hardly enough flat land to plant your whole foot.

—ALISON JOLLY

The first sentence in this opening paragraph from a National Geographic *article about Madagascar sets a dramatic scene by telling a story about landing by helicopter in a dangerous region of Madagascar, an island nation off the southeastern coast of Africa. The rest of the article describes Madagascar and relates many of its problems and opportunities.*

When a paragraph begins by stating the controlling idea in general terms, the second sentence often limits the idea. The rest of the paragraph builds then on that second sentence. In the following paragraph, the first sentence makes a general statement about how the police of Birmingham, Alabama, handled the arrest of civil rights demonstrators in the 1960s. The second sentence makes a limiting statement about the general subject introduced by the first. The rest of the paragraph flows from that more limiting statement to the topic sentence that is the next to the last sentence in the paragraph.

It is true that they have been rather disciplined in their public handling of the demonstrators. In this sense they have been rather publicly "nonviolent." But for what purpose? To preserve the evil system of segregation. Over the last few years I have consistently preached that nonviolence demands that the means we use must be as pure as the ends we seek. So I have tried to make it clear that it is wrong to use immoral means to attain moral ends. But now I must affirm that it is just as wrong, or even more so, to use moral means to preserve immoral ends. *Maybe Mr. Connor and his policemen have been rather publicly nonviolent as Chief Prichett was in Albany, Georgia, but they have used the moral means of nonviolence to maintain the immoral end of flagrant racial injustice.* T. S. Eliot has said that there is no greater treason than to do the right deed for the wrong reason.
— MARTIN LUTHER KING, JR.

The first sentence introduces a topic King now addresses after having told many of the details of police conduct during the demonstrations for civil rights in Birmingham. The police did not beat demonstrators as they had often done in the past; but they did arrest them and put them in jail. Having introduced this topic, King thinks about its meaning, and he condemns the motivation of those making the arrests. Once he wrote that first sentence, he committed himself to exploring what he meant by it. A first sentence in a paragraph always commits a writer to exploring some meaning contained in that sentence.

Some paragraphs introduce the topic with a direct quotation that focuses attention on the information to come. But again, the general subject of the paragraph is signaled by the first sentence. Here is a paragraph from David Donald's biography of the writer Thomas Wolfe introducing the chapter on how Wolfe broke into print. Note how he uses a quotation from a letter to Wolfe's sister Mabel to introduce a paragraph that develops the thesis of this chapter.

"My greatest deficiency is a total lack of salesmanship," Wolfe wrote Mabel while he was still working on his novel. He recalled that in trying to place his plays he had sent the scripts to only two or three

producers and, when they did not respond promptly, had peremptorily demanded that they be returned. "I have never known where to go, where to turn, or what to do," he explained, but he predicted: "This time, certain friends will probably attend to that part of it for me."

— DAVID HERBERT DONALD

The first sentence announces that the rest of the paragraph will concern Wolfe's difficulties and hopes involved in getting his first novel published. The sentence does not summarize the rest of the paragraph as we might expect a standard topic sentence to do. But it does introduce a subject that will be treated in the other sentences.

Some paragraphs introduce the topic by posing a question at the beginning. The rest of the paragraph offers some kind of response to the question. The response may be a firm answer, or it may suggest an answer or report an answer that someone has given. In the following paragraph, the biographer of the poet William Carlos Williams reports on Williams's response to the question in the first sentence. (Ed is the poet's brother.)

But wasn't truth, after all, an act of intuitive faith, something that left poor logic far behind? Truth, he told Ed that same month, was not something reasoned out but something intuitively grasped, something believed in. "Don't reason from feelings or rather don't reason at all," he told his brother. For he saw now that truth was not something arrived at by syllogisms and proofs, but something grasped by a quantum leap of faith. Truth was, after all, an intuitive insight into the essence of a thing, something radiantly perceived in a moment.

— PAUL MARIANI

The same paragraphs you have examined demonstrate the range of possibilities writers have developed for making their topics clear. The main idea in a paragraph may appear in a topic sentence that expresses a dominant impression about the topic. The topic sentence may be a general summary statement. It may also be a limited statement that the rest of the paragraph develops. This summary of the paragraph may appear in the first sentence or in the middle or at the end — or such a summary statement may not appear at all. Whether or not the topic of the paragraph is directly stated and summarized, it must be clear. Both writer and reader should be able to say in a sentence what the paragraph is about. The first sentence always leads into the topic in some way, usually by mentioning a word that the rest of the paragraph will develop.

The standard topic sentence is most valuable when you are writing paragraphs about ideas, when you are explaining something, or when you are making an argument. Such paragraphs usually help an essay develop its thesis step by step. The topic sentences define those steps clearly and help both writer and reader know where they are going. In narratives and

¶ un

in descriptions you may often write paragraphs that do not have a topic sentence. But in all paragraphs, the first sentence should have a word or words that are developed in the following sentences. When you write that first sentence, pause a moment and think of what words in it introduce the main ideas you want to express in the paragraph. Then explore those ideas.

Exercise 4.1 Write a couple of pages very swiftly on something that happened to you recently — a parking problem, a talk with a friend about some important event, some victory that you had, something good or something bad that happened to you. Don't pause much over your composition. Get it on paper quickly. Now study your composition and see how the first sentence in each of your paragraphs introduced the subject you explored in the rest of the paragraph. You will usually discover that when you write quickly about something that happened to you recently, your paragraphs develop naturally.

Now write a couple of pages about something you have been thinking about lately — the ideas expressed in a difficult course, something you have been reading about in the newspapers, some thoughts that have been on your mind. See if the paragraphs you construct develop naturally from the first sentence. How many of your paragraphs have a standard topic sentence in them?

If the whole class does this exercise together, exchange papers, read them aloud, and discuss the paragraph structure.

Exercise 4.2 For a paragraph on each of any five topics below, construct a topic sentence that states the topic and offers an opinion about it, an attitude toward it, or a reaction to it.

1. reactions against terrorism
2. looking for a summer job during college
3. advertisements for cigarettes
4. studying efficiently
5. the pleasures of reading
6. the value of learning to write well
7. the most popular music group now recording
8. the way rock stars rise and fall
9. volunteer work for public service during college
10. the value of your favorite form of exercise

Exercise 4.3 Take each of the following statements as the topic sentence for a paragraph, and write a paragraph developing the subject.

1. My neighborhood was a good (or bad) place to live when I was growing up.
2. The parking problem at this school has been handled badly by the administration.
3. I choose my friends because they have some special qualities.
4. I most fear _____.

Exercise 4.4   State the topic of each of the following paragraphs in your own words. Then tell whether or not the writer states that topic in a topic sentence. Also, explain what words in the first sentence of each paragraph are developed as the subject for the paragraph itself.

Hutton hiked to the margins of glaciers in the heights of the Alps — great seas of ice, in some places thousands of feet thick. Glaciers can last almost as long as the lofty mountain peaks on which they lie; the ice melts a little each summer but is replenished by fresh snows each winter. Hutton noticed boulders embedded in the ice of some glaciers, and more boulders lying on the slopes just below them, rock and rubble that the ice had apparently picked up from the ground as it grew, and then dropped again when it shrank. Hutton put two and two together. Some of these Swiss glaciers, he decided, must once have flowed down from their eminences and filled more than a few Swiss valleys. The glaciers must have plucked up thousands of boulders as they traveled forward and then dropped their loads when they receded, the way a tide strews pebbles on a beach — hence the misfit boulders lying in the valleys, far from any modern glacier.

This insight, like many of Hutton's finest, was unpopular in his lifetime. Misfit boulders, or *erratic blocks,* had long been considered to be irrefutable evidence of Noah's Flood. They were supposed to have been tumbled up hills and down dales by the churning biblical waters. In those days, many people felt as if a dark crack were slowly widening between the world as explained by science and the world as revealed in Holy Writ. Any hypothesis that threatened to widen the crack was frightening. A theory that both geologists and theologians could respect was accepted with gratitude and relief. So the Flood theory prevailed, and Hutton's was ignored.

— JONATHAN WEINER

There is a coarse and boisterous money-making fellow in the outskirts of our town, who is going to build a bank-wall under the hill along the edge of his meadow. The powers have put this into his head to keep him out of mischief, and he wishes me to spend three weeks digging there with him. The result will be that he will perhaps get some more money to hoard, and leave for his heirs to spend foolishly. If I do this, most will commend me as an industrious and hard-working man; but if I choose to devote myself to certain labors which yield more real profit, though but little money, they may be inclined to look on me as an idler. Nevertheless, as I do not need the police of meaningless labor to regulate me, and do not see anything absolutely praiseworthy in this fellow's undertaking, any more than in many an enterprise of our own or foreign governments, however amusing it may be to him or them, I prefer to finish my education at a different school.

— Henry David Thoreau

More than Northerners, civilians of the South found that the war affected every facet of their daily lives. Almost from the beginning Confederates began to feel the pinch of the shortages. Theirs was an agricultural society, primarily devoted to raising cotton and tobacco. When the war closed Northern markets and the Union blockade cut off those in Europe, bales and hogsheads piled up. Confederate authorities urged farmers to grow grain instead. Having the utmost confidence in Jefferson Davis, "our worthy President (at once soldier and statesman)," the Jones family willingly responded to this appeal. Cotton planting at 2,000-acre Arcadia, largest of their plantations, was limited in the 1862 season to one acre for every field hand. Wrote Charles C. Jones, Jr., approvingly: "Every bushel of corn and blade of grass will be greatly needed for the support of our armies."

— *We Americans*

2   Make all sentences in a paragraph support the main idea.

Every paragraph needs a logical structure based on the main point of the paragraph. The succession of sentences and the flow of ideas help bring that structure about. Any sentence that distracts readers from the main idea violates the architecture of the paragraph. In the following paragraph, several sentences wander away from the main idea.

After vigorous exercise, the body enters a dangerous period that cooling off can help prevent. When you are swimming or running, a large blood supply from the heart brings your arms and legs the oxygen required for muscle activity. **The human heart works like a pump. When the right upper chamber of the heart (the *auricle*) fills with blood, blood rushes down into the right lower chamber (the *ventricle*). When this chamber fills, the strong muscles in its wall pump tired blood into an artery that speeds the blood to the lungs.** As you exercise, the muscles squeeze, and blood going back to the heart gets an added push as long as you move your limbs. But if you stop suddenly, all this extra blood stays there: your arm and leg muscles are no longer helping your heart pump the blood around. Blood that remains in the arms and legs is blood kept away from vital organs like the brain. But if you *cool off*, that is, slow down your activity gradually, you'll help bring your pulse rate and your body temperature down slowly, you'll help your muscles rid themselves of metabolic waste, and, most important, you'll keep the blood flowing normally through your body.

The controlling idea of this paragraph may be stated like this: Stopping vigorous exercise suddenly can cause a strain on the heart and other body organs, but a gradual cooling off after activity can prevent serious problems. Now look at the sentences in boldface. These details of how the heart operates are interesting. But they distract the reader from the controlling idea of the paragraph. These sentences have no place here, though they may work well in another part of the paper. The paragraph is clearer and reads more smoothly with the distracting sentences removed.

Check the sentences in your paragraphs carefully against your main idea, and remove any sentences that do not support that main idea.

Exercise 4.5   The following paragraphs contain sentences that distract from the controlling idea that should direct the paragraph. Locate those sentences, and rewrite the paragraph without them. Although the paragraphs deal with similar information, they have different controlling ideas. Discuss the differences, and show how they help you decide which sentences do not belong.

When I was in college, I worked at the circulation desk of the library at night. Many of those nights were cold and bitter, and I could sometimes stand in the nearly empty silence of the library and hear the wind howling around the tower above the desk and the snow pecking against the high stained-glass window over the main entrance. My job was fairly complicated compared to similar jobs now. Students brought their books to me to be checked out, and I stamped a sticker in the back of the book with a date when the book would be due back in the library. Students had to sign a card which I also stamped with the due date. Then I had to file it in the proper place. When books were returned, I had to find the card, replace it in the book, mark through the borrower's name, and place the book on a cart to be taken to the stacks and replaced on the shelves. It took me a minute or so to check a book out, longer to check a book in again — sometimes much longer because someone had misfiled the card, and I had to hunt for it. Now students have identification cards that have bar codes on them. The books have bar codes, too, and someone working at a circulation desk with a light pencil and a computer can check a book out or in with a couple of strokes taking only seconds.

When I was in college I worked at the circulation desk of the library at night. Many of those nights were cold and bitter, and I could sometimes stand in the nearly empty silence of the library and hear the wind howling around the tower above the desk and the snow pecking against the high stained-glass window over the main entrance. Students seldom came to the library on snowy nights. Those were my favorite evenings to work, for I had leisure to read and to think. Checking out the books was a fairly complicated business that took a lot of time. It was nothing like today's library where every book has a bar code in the back, and every student has a bar code on his or her student identification card enabling books to be checked in and out in seconds by means of a light sensor attached to a computer. The library was warm, and the snow piling up outside added to the silence that libraries normally have so that during snowstorms, everything was peaceful. Perhaps it was that peacefulness that made me willing to explore books and ideas I might not otherwise have thought about. For it was on one of those quiet snowy nights that I happened to pick up, for the first time, Faulkner's *Absalom, Absalom,* the first novel of his that I had read. And my life was never the same afterward.

Exercise 4.6   Write out the controlling idea for each of the following paragraphs. Explain how each sentence in each paragraph supports that controlling idea.

Psychophysicists who study food tastes have found four basic tastes: sweet, sour, salty, and bitter. There are wider variations in what people call sweet or bitter than in what they call sour or salty — variations we are only now beginning to understand. We have found, too, that there is not one but a number of receptor mechanisms in the mouth for bitterness, which may explain why people are sensitive to some bitter foods and not others. We have also discovered that certain substances can suppress one or more of the four tastes.

—LINDA BARTOSHUK

Some children dedicate themselves to being ridiculous, their behavior conjuring up memories of old Mack Sennett comedies and floppy-footed clowns. We have encountered a considerable number of these children in our counselling work over the last two decades. They are usually brought in for evaluation and treatment as "behavior problems"; they may be doing badly in school, be in conflict with everyone in the family, or have threatened to run away from home. Whatever the immediate difficulty, we have been impressed in each case with a theatrical clumsiness, a clownish awkwardness.

—SEYMOUR AND RHODA LEE FISHER

To begin with, there was the nature of the country. The front line, ours and the Fascists', lay in positions of immense natural strength, which as a rule could only be approached from one side. Provided a few trenches have been dug, such places cannot be taken by infantry, except in overwhelming numbers. In our own position or most of those round us a dozen men with two machine-guns could have held off a battalion. Perched on the hill-tops as we were, we should have made lovely marks for artillery; but there was no artillery. Sometimes I used to gaze round the landscape and long—oh how passionately!—for a couple of batteries of guns. One could have destroyed the enemy positions one after another as easily as smashing nuts with a hammer. But on our side the guns simply did not exist. The Fascists did occasionally manage to bring a gun or two from Zaragoza and fire a very few shells, so few that they never even found the range and the shells plunged harmlessly into the empty ravines. Against machine-guns and without artillery there are only three things you can do: dig yourself in at a safe distance—four hundred yards, say—advance across the open and be massacred, or make small-scale night-attacks that will not alter the general situation. Practically, the alternatives are stagnation or suicide.

—George Orwell

4b
Use a variety of methods to build coherent paragraphs.

In coherent paragraphs, thoughts and pieces of information follow one after the other, connected in ways that are easy for readers to see and understand. Writers use various methods to make these connections and to make ideas flow smoothly so that readers do not feel that something has been left out, that questions have been unanswered, or that new information has been suddenly introduced without reason. As you use these methods, you must think carefully about the sequence of ideas you follow in each paragraph.

You can achieve coherence by carefully arranging the information in a paragraph. That arrangement requires you to look carefully at the first sentence in the paragraph to see what ideas in it you want to develop in the following sentence. To make the paragraph coherent, the ideas in the second sentence must be closely related to the ideas in the first.

Pronouns help coherence by referring to nouns that have already been introduced and identified. You can also help coherence by repeating important words or phrases, by using parallel structures, and by using transitional words and expressions. You should combine these techniques as necessary to write paragraphs that hold together around a central theme or topic.

In the following paragraphs, boldface print indicates some of the devices that lend coherence to the paragraph. Study them carefully to see those ideas that are developed, those words that tie previous information to new information being introduced, and how various thoughts are explained.

Experience gained on the Santa Fe Trail was compara- 1
tively unimportant, and might be misleading. Conditions there 2
were very different. The distance was only half as far, and the 3
country was nearly all open and level. **Even more important,** as 4
the expression "Santa Fe trade" indicates, that trail was used 5
by traders, and not by **emigrants.** When the Oregon and Cali- 6
fornia **emigrants** imitated the Santa Fe traders, **they** nearly 7
always came to grief — as **in using big wagons, forming large** 8
companies, and **organizing in military fashion.** 9

On the other hand, the **emigrants** made use of a general 10
backlog of experience with teams and wagons. Every **farmer** 11
knew a good deal about that sort of thing, and **he** had probably 12
made journeys of several hundred miles. What had to be faced, 13
to get to California, were the new conditions — **the tenfold-** 14
long pull, the untamed Indians, the lack of supply points, the 15
difficult country of deserts and mountains. But in the handling 16
of the wagon itself most of the men were already **proficient,** 17
and this **proficiency** was essential to the success of the covered- 18
wagon migration. 19

— GEORGE R. STEWART

In both paragraphs, a logical plan controls the arrangement of information. Each of the two paragraphs starts with a generalization. Supporting elements appear in ascending order of importance, the most dramatic statement in each paragraph appearing last. The pronouns they *and* he *in lines 7 and 12 connect with nouns stated earlier,* emigrants *and* farmer. *Repetition of the word* emigrants *in lines 6, 7, and 10 and the use of* proficient *and* proficiency *in lines 17 and 18 advance the flow of ideas by repeating important thoughts. Repetition is usually good in a paragraph when it expands on a thought previously mentioned; repetition is usually bad when it repeats a previous thought without adding anything new to it. In lines 7 to 9, the writer uses a series of gerund phrases as objects of prepositions. (A gerund is a participial form of a verb used as a noun.* Forming large companies *is a gerund phrase. See 5d-1.) In lines 14 to 16, he uses a series of appositives to expand the thought expressed in the phrase* the new conditions. *(An appositive is a noun that follows another noun, adding information about that previous noun. See 5b-2.) In both cases, the repeated grammatical structure adds coherence to the paragraphs. Finally, the use of the expressions* even more important *(line 4) and* on the other hand *(line 10) and the dramatic use of* but *to open a sentence (line 16) act as transitions, carrying thought smoothly from one idea to another.*

Coherence is a difficult matter. Sometimes you can obey all the formal rules and still have trouble developing a paragraph so that a reader can follow it easily without being bogged down in useless repetition or feeling that something has been left out. The main rule for coherence in paragraphs is to keep developing ideas by expanding on words or thoughts expressed in the first sentence and the succeeding sentences. Then be sure that all the sentences in the paragraph develop an idea that can be expressed in a summary sentence, whether you write that summary sentence into the paragraph or not.

Here is a paragraph that demonstrates some simple truths about coherence: the introduction to an article about the first pilots to fly around the world nonstop, a flight that ended successfully on Christmas eve, 1986.

What a grand Christmas gift it was — the "last first" in aviation, a nonstop flight around the world on the gossamer wings of one of the strangest looking craft ever built. *Voyager,* made of paper, graphite and resin, was a cross between a glider and a graphite fishing rod, and it looked like the result of the mating of a seagull and a pterodactyl. The pilots were Dick Rutan, 48, a Vietnam War flying ace, and Jeana Yeager, 34, a gentle but steely Texan who never talks when she can be doing. Flying *Voyager,* said Yeager, was like riding on the back of an eagle.

— SAM MOSES

The paragraph begins with an exclamation and a long phrase. The next sentence picks up the thought expressed in both the words "flight around the world" and "strangest looking craft ever built." The word Voyager *gives the name of this strange craft; the sentence tells why it was strange. In the next sentence, the word* pilots *looks back to* Voyager *and to* craft. *Planes have pilots, and when we see the word* pilots, *we make the connection between it and the aircraft just described. The following sentence repeats both the name* Voyager *and the name of one of the pilots mentioned in the previous sentence,* Yeager, *and it tells something she said. All these sentences are tied together by the interconnections of these words. We could summarize the paragraph in a sentence like this: "A bizarre aircraft called* Voyager, *piloted by a man and a woman, successfully made the first nonstop flight around the world." The development of one idea after the other is controlled by a central thought that binds all the other thoughts in the paragraph together.*

Here are some devices that will help you achieve coherence in different kinds of paragraphs that you may write.

1 Arrange paragraph ideas according to a logical plan (see also 4a-2).

How you organize information in a paragraph is related to your main point and what you want to say about it.

You can arrange information **spatially** by locating the reader somewhere in a scene and then moving through physical space — from back to front, from top to bottom, from left to right, or in some other logical way. In describing landscapes, paintings, buildings, streets, and various other things, you may choose to move your readers carefully across space.

You may learn to write paragraphs such as the one below by standing in front of the scene you want to describe and mentally blocking it off in sections. If you carry a notebook, you can jot down some things you see in each section.

Spatial Arrangement

I walked out on the bridge and looked down at the lock. The canal flowed into the lock through a sprung wooden gate just under the bridge. It ran between two narrowly confining walls for about a hundred feet. Then, with a sudden boil and bubble, it broke against another gate, spilled through, and resumed its sluggish course. The walls of the lock were faced with big blocks of rust-red sandstone. Some of the stones were so huge that they could have been hoisted into place only with a block and tackle. It was beautiful stone, and it had been beautifully finished and fitted. Time had merely softened it. Here and there along the courses I could even make out the remains of a mason's mark. One device was quite distinct — a double-headed arrow. Another appeared to be two overlapping equilateral triangles. I went on across the bridge to the house. The windows were shuttered and boarded up, and the door was locked. No matter. It was enough just to stand and look at it. It was a lovely house, as beautifully made as the lock, and as firmly designed for function. It gave me a pang to think that there had once been a time when even a lock tender could have so handsome a house. A phoebe called from a sweet-gum tree in the dooryard. Far away, somewhere down by the river, a mourning dove gave an answering sigh. I looked at my watch. It was ten minutes after ten. I started up the towpath.

— BERTON ROUECHÉ

We look down from the bridge into the canal at the bottom of the lock. Then we examine the walls of the lock. Looking at the house, we then move to a tree in the dooryard and after that to a place far away down by the river. The scene unfolds through logical movement in space.

Another way to present information in a paragraph is chronologically. In a **chronological arrangement,** events are organized as they happen, one after another. Earlier incidents come before later ones. We tell stories in the narrative mode.

Chronological Arrangement

The sun rose slowly out of the hazy sea as we hiked through the great olive grove at the foot of Mount Iouktos on Crete. By seven o'clock, we had started our slow climb up the mountain, following a trail that twisted back and forth as it snaked its way toward the summit. We left the olive trees behind quickly and entered a rocky world where a few poplars cast an occasional weak shade. By ten o'clock, the sun had burned the haze off the sea, and its heat bore down on us. We quickly became thirsty, but we had brought no water. By eleven, we were drenched with sweat, and the heat made everything shimmer so that the tumbled rocks seemed to dance crazily in the harsh sunlight. By now we could see for miles down the island of Crete, and to the west the huge bulk of Mount Ida rose into the hot blue sky. By noon, nearly crazy with heat, thirst, and fatigue, we got to the top. There we found a little church, and just beside it was a cistern with a bucket attached to a long rope. We dropped the bucket down into the darkness of the cistern and heard a great, reassuring splash. Quickly we pulled the bucket to the top and drank greedily. Then we sat in the shade of the church and looked out over one of the most beautiful landscapes I had ever seen.

—DICK CURRY

The writer's intent here is to capture the experience as it happened, describing one event at a time. The description begins at the bottom of the mountain early in the day and ends at the top of the mountain around noon. The ascent of the climbers proceeds as the sun climbs in the sky and the heat increases hour by hour, and the story ends with the climb over.

Spatial and chronological arrangements often work together. In both of the sample paragraphs above, chronological and spatial order contribute to the coherence of the paragraph.

You can arrange paragraph elements according to **importance,** starting with the least significant or least dramatic information and building to a climax with the most significant or most dramatic.

Order of Importance

Shakespeare came to London at a fortunate time. If he had been born twenty years earlier, he would have arrived in London when

4b

¶ coh

underpaid hacks were turning out childish dramas about brown-paper dragons. If he had been born twenty years later, he would have arrived when the drama had begun to lose its hold on ordinary people and was succumbing to a kind of self-conscious cleverness. But his arrival in London coincided with a great wave of excitement and achievement in the theatre, and he rode with it to its crest. William Shakespeare brought great gifts to London, but the city was waiting with gifts of its own to offer him. The root of his genius was Shakespeare's own, but it was London that supplied him with the favoring weather.

— MARCHETTE CHUTE

The fact that London, at the time he arrives, gave Shakespeare just the right environment for his talents is the most important fact in this paragraph, and it comes last.

Paragraphs may be arranged inductively or deductively. An **inductive scheme** builds through successive instances to support a generalization that comes at the end of a paragraph. In other words, the writer presents details one after the other and finally draws a conclusion from them. In a **deductive arrangement,** the generalization comes first, and the particular details succeed it in the paragraph. (See Chapter 39.)

Inductive Arrangement

We huddled together in the cool spring night, whispering in hoarse voices, thrumming with the excitement that vibrated through the crowd gathering in the parking lot outside the Ames train station. All the way home from Des Moines we had hugged each other, laughed, cried, and hugged each other again. When we passed through the small farming towns between Des Moines and Ames, we rolled down the windows of the Harbingers' station wagon and shouted down the quiet streets, "We beat Marshalltown in seven overtimes! We beat Marshalltown in seven overtimes!" It had a rhythmic beat, a chant we repeated to each other in unbelieving ecstasy. We beat Marshalltown in seven overtimes! For the first time in ten years, Ames High School had won the state basketball championship. Most of us sophomores felt nothing so important could ever happen to us again.

— SUSAN ALLEN TOTH

The last sentence states the generalization that the paragraph details support.

Deductive Arrangement

Other scientific investigations also exerted considerable influence on present-day painters and sculptors. Inventions like the microscope and telescope, with their capacity to enlarge, isolate and probe, offer the artist provocative new worlds to explore. These instruments, which break up structures only to examine them more fully, demonstrate how details can be magnified and separated from the whole and operate as new experiences. Repeatedly, artists in recent years have exploited this idea, allowing one isolated symbol to represent an entire complex organism. Miró often needs merely part of a woman's body to describe all women, or Léger, one magnified letter of the alphabet to conjure up the numberless printed words that daily bombard us.

—KATHERINE KUH

Supporting details about scientific inventions and their effect on artists follow the generalization stated in the first sentence.

Information in the paragraph about childhood in Chicago (4a-1) is also arranged deductively.

Exercise 4.7   Explain the method of arrangement used in each paragraph below.

Then a strange blight crept over the area, and everything began to change. Some evil spell had settled on the community; mysterious maladies swept the flocks of chickens; the cattle and sheep sickened and died. Everywhere was a shadow of death. The farmers spoke of much illness among their families. In the town the doctors had become more and more puzzled by new kinds of sickness appearing among their patients. There had been several sudden and unexplained deaths not only among adults but even among children, who would be stricken suddenly while at play and die within a few hours.

—RACHEL CARSON

The preacher preached a wonderful rhythmical sermon, all moans and shouts and lonely cries and dire pictures of hell, and then he sang a song about the ninety and nine safe in the fold, but one little lamb was left out in the cold. Then he said: "Won't you come? Won't you come to Jesus? Young lambs, won't you come?" And he held out his arms to all us young sinners there on the mourners' bench. And the little girls cried. And some of them jumped up and went to Jesus right away. But most of us just sat there.

—LANGSTON HUGHES

Once in a long while, four times so far for me, my mother brings out the metal tube that holds her medical diploma. On the tube are gold circles crossed with seven red lines each—"joy" ideographs in abstract. There are also little flowers that look like gears for a gold machine. According to the scraps of labels with Chinese and American addresses, stamps, and postmarks, the family airmailed the can from Hong Kong in 1950. It got crushed in the middle, and whoever tried to peel the labels off stopped because the red and gold paint came off too, leaving silver scratches that rust. Somebody tried to pry the end off before discovering that the tube pulls apart. When I open it, the smell of China flies out, a thousand-year-old bat flying heavy-headed out of the Chinese caverns where bats are as white as dust, a smell that comes from long ago, far back in the brain. Crates from Canton, Hong Kong, Singapore, and Taiwan have that smell too, only stronger because they are more recently come from the Chinese.

— MAXINE HONG KINGSTON

2   Use pronouns to link ideas.

By replacing nouns, pronouns help achieve coherence, joining one part of a paragraph to another. Pronouns with antecedents refer the reader to a previously identified noun and help the writer to connect the ideas in a paragraph without having to mention the nouns again and again.

When you use pronouns, pay special attention to the antecedents. Readers must always find it easy to determine which words pronouns are referring to. When they are used well, pronouns fix attention on the ideas that help hold a paragraph together and make it coherent.

When a mother is afraid that **her** child will die when **it** has only a pimple or a slight cold we speak of anxiety, but if **she** is afraid when the child has a serious illness we call **her** reaction fear. If someone is afraid whenever **he** stands on a height or when **he** has to discuss a topic **he** knows well, we call **his** reaction anxiety; if someone is afraid when **he** loses **his** way high up in the mountains during a heavy thunderstorm we would speak of fear. Thus far we should have a simple and neat distinction; fear is a reaction that is proportionate to the danger one has to face, whereas anxiety is a disproportionate reaction to danger, or even a reaction to imaginary danger.

— KAREN HORNEY

Each of the pronouns in boldface refers clearly to a noun or indefinite pronoun that comes before it. The pronouns give unity to the paragraph by focusing the sentences on the persons having the reactions described by the writer as anxiety *and* fear.

3 Repeat important words or phrases to connect ideas.

Repetition helps bind sentences together in a paragraph. By repeating key words you can help readers follow your line of thought. As we have said before, you want to make sure that every repetition includes some new information along with what is repeated. That information should develop some thought important to your essay.

> We do not **choose** to be born. We do not **choose** our parents. We do not **choose** our historical epoch, or the country of our birth, or the immediate circumstances of our upbringing. We do not, most of us, **choose** to die; nor do we **choose** the time or conditions of our death. But within all this realm of choicelessness, we do **choose** how we shall live; courageously or in cowardice, honorably or dishonorably, with purpose or in drift. We **decide** what is important and what is trivial in life. We **decide** that what makes us significant is either what we do or what we refuse to do. But no matter how indifferent the universe may be to our choices and decisions, these choices and decisions are ours to make. We **decide**. We **choose**. And as we **decide** and **choose,** so are our lives formed. In the end, forming our own destiny is what ambition is about.
>
> — JOSEPH EPSTEIN

The boldface words choose *and* decide *provide dramatic linkage of ideas, connecting thoughts smoothly while emphasizing the issue of choice and decision as the writer sees it. The new informaton provided in each repetition concerns what is open to choice and decision. The sense of choice is repeated again and again; what is chosen is different each time.*

4 Use parallel structure to link ideas.

You can tie thought units together in your paragraphs by repeating the forms of clauses, phrases, or sentences. In the paragraph below, parallelism dramatically links Macaulay's statements about Britain's King Charles I (1600–1649), the only English king to be judged a criminal by his people and executed by beheading. Macaulay wrote two centuries after the event, at a time when some English romantic historians were defending King Charles. Macaulay wanted to set the record straight. He thought Charles was a rotten king, and here he gives his reasons, at the same time attacking Charles's defenders.

> We charge him with having broken his coronation oath; and we are told that he kept his marriage vow! We accuse him of having given up his people to the merciless inflictions of the most hot-headed and hard-hearted of prelates; and the defense is, that he took

his little son on his knee and kissed him! We censure him for having violated the articles of the Petition of Right, after having, for good and valuable consideration, promised to observe them; and we are informed that he was accustomed to hear prayers at six o'clock in the morning! It is to such considerations as these, together with his Van Dyck dress, his handsome face, and his peaked beard, that he owes, we verily believe, most of his popularity with the present generation.

— Thomas Babington Macaulay

The subject-verb-object structure opens each of the first three sentences: "We charge him," "We accuse him," "We censure him." Also, a semicolon follows each attack on Charles and precedes each apology made by historians favorable to him. The grammar and syntax of the sentences heighten the contrast between Macaulay's assertions and those of his opponents.

As Macaulay's example points out, the use of extended parallelism in a paragraph works especially well in argument. Here is a more modern example, a paragraph from the famous "Letter from Birmingham Jail" by the Reverend Martin Luther King, Jr., during the civil rights struggle of the 1960s. (This essay was also quoted on page 80.)

We have waited for more than 340 years for our constitutional and God-given rights. The nations of Asia and Africa are moving with jetlike speed toward gaining political independence, but we still creep at horse-and-buggy pace toward gaining a cup of coffee at a lunch counter. Perhaps it is easy for those who have never felt the stinging darts of segregation to say, "Wait." But when you have seen vicious mobs lynch your mothers and fathers at will and drown your sisters and brothers at whim; when you have seen hate-filled policemen curse, kick and even kill your black brothers and sisters; when you see the vast majority of your twenty million Negro brothers smothering in an airtight cage of poverty in the midst of an affluent society; when you suddenly find your tongue twisted and your speech stammering as you seek to explain to your six-year-old daughter why she can't go to the public amusement park that has just been advertised on television, and see tears welling up in her eyes when she is told that Funtown is closed to colored children, and see ominous clouds of inferiority beginning to form in her little mental sky, and see her beginning to distort her personality by developing an unconscious bitterness toward white people; when you have to concoct an answer for a five-year-old son who is asking: "Daddy, why do white people treat colored people so mean?"; when you take a cross-country drive and find it necessary to sleep night after night in the uncomfortable corners of your automobile because no motel will accept you; when you are humiliated day in and day out by nagging signs reading "white" and "colored"; when your first name becomes "nigger," your middle name becomes "boy" (however old you are) and your last name becomes "John," and your wife and mother are never given the respected title "Mrs."; when you are harried by day and haunted by night by the fact that you are a Negro, living constantly on tiptoe stance, never quite knowing what to expect next, and are plagued with inner fears and outer resentments; when you are forever fighting a degenerating sense of "nobodiness"—then you will understand why we find it difficult to wait. There comes a time when the cup of endurance runs over, and men are no longer willing to be plunged into the abyss of despair. I hope, sirs, you can understand our legitimate and unavoidable impatience.

—THE REVEREND MARTIN LUTHER KING JR.

The parallelism here lies in the repetition of the word when, *followed by a clause depicting the humiliations of segregation as seen from the eyes of American blacks. The repetition of the word acts as a sort of hammer, beating home the judgment that segregation is evil. Note especially the parallel form represented in this opening clause: "But when you have seen vicious mobs lynch your mothers and fathers at will and drown your sisters and brothers at whim. . . ."*

5 Use appropriate transitional expressions to make your thoughts flow smoothly from sentence to sentence.

Transitional expressions are words or phrases that tell a reader something like this: "I am now leading you carefully from the point that I have just made to the point that I am about to make. Don't let me lose you." The most obvious transitional expressions are words such as *moreover, furthermore, and, but, or, nevertheless, then, still,* and *likewise.* These expressions look back to the thought just expressed and announce that readers will now move to a related but slightly different point.

Many couples who want to adopt a child run into frustrating difficulties. They may have a comfortable home and financial security. **And** they may be loving and generous people. **But** they may be too old for the standards set by the adoption agency. **Or** they may discover that no children are available. **Then,** when a child is available, the couple may be charged an exorbitant fee. **Nevertheless,** couples who want to adopt a child usually persevere, **and** their determination usually pays off.

In the boldface words in this paragraph, the word and *helps add a thought. The words* but *and* or *indicate contrasts. The word* then *says that something happens after something else.* Nevertheless *contrasts previous ideas with one of the final ideas in the paragraph.*

Writing Strong Paragraphs   **97**

4b

¶ coh

In the list below, transitional expressions are classified according to what they do in sentences. Choose transitional expressions to make the connections you want to make between your various ideas.

To show relations in space

above, adjacent to, against, alongside, around, at a distance from, at the, below, beside, beyond, encircling, far off, forward, from the, in front of, in the rear, inside, near the back, near the end, nearby, next to, on, over, surrounding, there, through the, to the left, to the right, up front

To show relations in time

afterward, at last, before, earlier, first, former, formerly, further, furthermore, immediately, in the first place, in the interval, in the meantime, in the next place, in the last, later on, latter, meanwhile, next, now, often, once, previously, second, simultaneously, sometime later, subsequently, suddenly, then, therefore, third, today, tomorrow, until now, when, years ago, yesterday

To show something added on to what has come before

again, also, and, and then, besides, further, furthermore, in addition, last, likewise, moreover, next, nor, too

To give examples or to intensify points

after all, as an example, certainly, for example, for instance, indeed, in fact, in truth, it is true, of course, specifically, that is

To show similarities

alike, in the same way, like, likewise, resembling, similarly

To show contrasts

after all, although, but, conversely, differ(s) from, difference, different, dissimilar, even though, granted, however, in contrast, in spite of, nevertheless, notwithstanding, on the contrary, on the other hand, otherwise, still, though, unalike, while this may be true, yet

To indicate cause and effect

accordingly, as a result, because, consequently, hence, since, then, therefore, thus

To conclude or summarize

finally, in brief, in conclusion, in other words, in short, in summary, that is, to summarize

Well constructed paragraphs may hold together without obvious transitional words and phrases. You should not use such expressions unless you feel a special need for them. You can write sentences like the following and know that readers will assume that you are speaking of cause and effect.

> I discovered that he lied to me about where he had been that night. I never trusted him again.

You do not have to say this:

> I discovered that he lied to me about where he had been that night. Accordingly, I never trusted him again.

You can assume that readers will recognize the cause-and-effect relation without your having to throw in the word *accordingly*. A good general rule to follow in writing holds that prose should be efficient. That is, you should generally delete words not necessary to the meaning you want to convey. Unless transitional words are necessary to express your meaning, you should not use them. Readers may mentally add words like *for example, thus, however*, and *nevertheless* as they read. Also, you have already seen how linking devices other than transitional expressions can work in your paragraphs. (See 4b-1 through 4.)

Even the punctuation in a sentence can serve as a connecting device. Notice how the dash and the colon in the two examples below link ideas without stating transitions directly (see also 30a and 30b).

> Some penny-arcade war machines were also busy — the familiar American sound of the thump and whine of miniature electronic holocausts.
>
> —GEORGE PLIMPTON
>
> *The dash acts as a transition here. Plimpton might have written "and thus I heard" or some other transitional phrase in place of the dash. But the dash does the job well enough without any special transitional phrase.*

> The computer has had many effects on American life: used as a word processor, it has revolutionized the way people write; used to read bar codes on products bought in supermarkets, it has speeded up the checkout line; used in banks, it has reduced the number of checks people must write; used by credit-card companies, it has vastly speeded up billing procedures — and has sometimes enraged customers by billing them for the wrong amounts.
>
> *Instead of using a colon, the writer of this paragraph could have said "for example." But the colon indicates that what will come after-*

wards illustrates the sentence before the colon or else is caused by whatever is reported in the sentence before the colon.

The rule comes down to this: don't use transitional expressions unless you *must* use them to be clear. How can you know if you should use them? You must read your writing carefully and see if it answers all the questions it needs to answer. Sometimes you must use transitional devices. But a steady repetition of *moreover, furthermore, nevertheless, but,* and so on can easily bore your readers. If you can develop your thoughts without using obvious transitional expressions, you are more likely to write in a lively and readable style.

Exercise 4.8   Rewrite the following paragraphs, putting in transitional devices where they are needed and taking them out where they are not needed. Compare your revisions with the revisions done by other members of your class. Be prepared to explain why you have removed a transitional device, why you have put one in, or why you have left one in the original paragraph.

Writing is difficult for almost everybody, even professional writers. Specifically, writing requires hours of concentrated work. Furthermore, writers must usually withdraw from others while they are doing their writing. Moreover, writing exposes many writers to a constant sense of failure because they do not think they are doing well. Consequently, many writers stop writing at the peak of their careers. For example, Thomas Hardy thought that he wrote novels badly and stopped after writing some of the greatest novels in the English language. In the same way, Virginia Woolf fell into such despair about her work that she eventually committed suicide. Accordingly, we can see that both teachers and students who think that a writing course can make writing easy are perhaps pursuing a false hope. In other words, a writing course may make one's writing better, but it may not make it easier to do.

The house stood on a shady street in the suburbs. Surrounding it, the neighborhood was filled with similar houses. It was a comfortable place, large and square, with three floors and a basement and a broad covered porch across the front. In the rear, a large backyard allowed the family to picnic in warm weather. The backyard was surrounded by a pleasant wooden fence, too high for anyone to see over. Therefore, it was a private place, and people could sit there and talk or read or merely think without being disturbed. On the other hand, the house itself was old. As a result, the furnace needed replacing. Furthermore, the windows let in drafts of cold air in winter and, likewise, hot air in summer. Often people told us how much they like our house. And in truth, we liked it, too. But it was not an ideal place. Still, I am glad to have lived there growing up, and, not withstanding its disadvantages, I miss it.

Henry VIII remains the king of England best known to Americans. Of course, they do not like him very much. They remember the fate of his wives, especially those whom he had beheaded. Henry was hard on his friends, too. He often had them put to death when they did something that displeased him. For example, he had Thomas More and Thomas Cromwell beheaded, and, in addition, he had Robert Barnes, a former religious adviser of his, burned at the stake. Nevertheless, he gave England great benefits merely by surviving as long as he did because he kept his country from the civil war that might have broken out if he had died without an heir. Hence, it may be that he deserves some praise, although certainly no one can much admire his character.

6   Link ideas together from one paragraph to the next.

In an essay, coherence *between* paragraphs is as important as coherence *within* paragraphs. Using the devices explained in previous sections, you can help your readers follow the direction of your thought as you move from one paragraph to the next in your writing.

The opening sentence of a paragraph in the body of an essay usually looks back to information in the previous paragraph and forward to information about to be disclosed. Boldface print in the excerpts below shows how that first sentence in a paragraph looks both backward and forward.

When Africans first got to New York, or New Amsterdam as the Dutch called it, they lived in the farthest downtown portions of the city, near what is now called The Bowery. Later, they shifted, and were shifted, as their numbers grew, to the section known as Greenwich Village. The Civil War Draft Riots in 1863 accounted for the next move by New York's growing Negro population.

After this violence (a few million dollars' worth of property was destroyed, and a Negro orphanage was burned to the ground) a great many Negroes moved across the river into Brooklyn. . . .

—LeRoi Jones

The phrase "after this violence" connects the ideas of the two paragraphs. The phrase refers to the violence of the Civil War Draft Riots mentioned in the last sentence of the previous paragraph. The word after *indicates something yet to come. Jones tells us then that "a great many Negroes moved across the river into Brooklyn." That helps establish the topic of the next paragraph, which will be about the experience of blacks in Brooklyn. So the phrase "after this violence" looks backward to the previous paragraph and forward to the new paragraph that the phrase introduces.*

Among those who now take a dim view of marijuana are Dr. Sidney Cohen, a drug expert at the University of California at Los Angeles, who once described marijuana as "a trivial weed," and Dr. Robert L. DuPont, former director of the National Institute on Drug Abuse, who had lobbied for marijuana's legalization.

According to these and other experts, it is no longer possible to say that marijuana is an innocuous drug with few if any health effects aside from intoxication.

— JANE E. BRODY

The words "according to these and other experts" connect the paragraphs by referring readers to the point developed in the previous paragraph. The rest of the opening sentence of the second paragraph states the major point to be developed in that paragraph, the dangers of marijuana.

This sort of connection signals a slight turn of the writer's thought to develop an idea from one of the words in a previous paragraph. Such connections show the writer moving forward, adding new thoughts to earlier information, giving readers the sense that they have some reason to keep on reading.

In the body of an essay, the first sentence of a new paragraph usually provides the link to ideas in the preceding paragraph. Occasionally, however, the last sentence in a paragraph will point forward.

Why is marking up a book indispensable to reading it? First, it keeps you awake. (And I don't mean merely conscious; I mean wide awake.) In the second place, reading, if it is active, is thinking, and thinking tends to express itself in words, spoken or written. The marked book is usually the thought-through book. Finally, writing helps you remember the thoughts you had, or the thoughts the author expressed. **Let me develop these three points.**

If reading is to accomplish anything more than passing time, it must be active. . . .

— MORTIMER J. ADLER

The sentence in boldface type at the end of the first paragraph announces Adler's intention to explain some of the things he says in this paragraph about marking up books. He will develop these thoughts in the next paragraph. This sort of formal announcement aims at carrying readers smoothly from one part of an essay to another. It is sometimes used in scholarly writing where the material is dense and difficult to understand and writers want to be sure that they are taking readers along with them.

In the following example, we have an entire paragraph used as a bridge leading from one part of a critical essay to another. Such paragraphs may serve to carry readers over material where they might otherwise be lost.

I have, I hope, cleared the ground for a dispassionate comparison of certain aspects of Shakespeare's technique in the Henry VI plays with his technique in the "romance" histories. Now, perhaps, some general remarks about the structure of the trilogy will be helpful.

— PAUL DEAN

This short paragraph joins two parts of an essay about the three plays Shakespeare wrote about the English king, Henry VI. The first sentence reminds readers of points made earlier about some of the dramatic techniques Shakespeare used in those plays. Now Dean, the author of the essay, announces a fairly major shift from that discussion to another, this one bearing on the structure of the three plays, called a trilogy.

There is an expression called "the peak experience," a moment which, emotionally, can never again be equalled in your life. I had mine, that first day in the village of Juffure, in the back country in black West Africa.

— ALEX HALEY

This two-sentence paragraph provides a dramatic link for what is clearly a turning point in the essay. The device is especially useful when you think that the two parts of an essay are very different from each other and you want to be sure that the reader sees the connection.

Exercise 4.9 Discuss in class the various devices used to build coherence within and between paragraphs in the following selection from Frances Fitzgerald's article on a retirement community called Sun City near Tampa, Florida.

Ask yourself these questions: What major theme joins all these paragraphs? What words carry the theme from one paragraph to the next? How do the last sentences in each paragraph look forward to the next paragraph? How do the first sentences in each paragraph look back to the last paragraph?

The younger generation in this country has grown up with the notion that people should reach the age of sixty-five and reach it in good health. But Americans now over sixty belong to the first generation to do that. Modern medicine has increased longevity to some degree, but, just as important, it has alleviated some of the persistent, nonfatal maladies of the body. Throughout history, of course, some people have reached their eighties in excellent health, but until this century the majority of Europeans and Americans aged as many people still do in the poorest countries of the world — suffering irreversible physical decay in their forties and fifties. Philippe Aries reminds us that until recently chronological age had very little meaning in European society; the word "old" was associated with the loss of teeth, eyesight, and so on. The very novelty of health and physical vigor in those past sixty-five is reflected in the current struggle over nomenclature. Since the passage of the Social Security Act, in 1935, demographers have used the age of sixty-five as a benchmark and labeled those at or over it as "the old" or "the elderly." The terms are meant to be objective, but because of their connotations they have proved unacceptable to those designated by them. Sensitive to their audience, gerontologists and government agencies have substituted "older people," "the aging," or "senior citizens." These terms, being relative, could apply to anyone of almost any age, but, by a kind of linguistic somersault, they have come to denote a precise chronological category.

People now over sixty-five live on a frontier also in the sense that the territory is fast filling up behind them. By the end of the century, if current demographic trends hold, one in eight Americans, or slightly more than 12 percent of the population, will be sixty-five or over. The increase will at first be relatively small, because the number of children born in the thirties was a relatively small one; but then, barring catastrophe or large-scale immigration, the numbers will start to climb. In the years between 2020 and 2030, after the baby-boom generation reaches its seniority, some fifty-five million Americans, or nearly 20 percent of the projected population, will be sixty-five or over. How the society will support these people is a problem that Americans are just beginning to think about. Politicians have been considering the implications for Social Security and federal retirement benefits, but they have not yet begun to imagine all the consequences in other realms.

The younger generation assumes that at sixty-five people leave their jobs and spend five, ten, or fifteen years of their lives in a condition called retirement. But there, too, the generation now around sixty-five has broken new ground. Historically speaking, the very notion of retirement — on a mass scale at any rate — is new, and dates only from the industrial revolution, from the time when a majority of workers (and not just a few professionals) became replaceable parts in organizations outside the family. The possibility of retirement for large numbers of people depended, of course, on the establishment of adequate social-insurance systems, and these were not created until long after the building of industry. In this country, whose industrial evolution lagged behind that of Western Europe, the possibility came only with the New Deal. The Social Security Act of 1935 created an economic floor for those who could not work. More important, it created the presumption that American workers had a right to retire — a right to live without working after the age of sixty-five. This presumption led, in turn, to the establishment of government, corporate, and union pension plans that allowed workers to retire without a disastrous loss of income. But these pension plans did not cover very many people until some time after World War II. Even in 1950, 46 percent of all American men sixty-five and over were still working or looking for work. In 1980, only 20 percent were.

— FRANCES FITZGERALD

4c

Put enough details in your paragraphs to develop and support your controlling idea.

Paragraphs are usually weak when they contain nothing but general statements.

> The parking problem here at school is terrible. It sometimes takes hours and hours to find a space. Why can't the administration do something about it? Students are late to class because they can't find a parking space, and then they miss things in the lecture, and they do poorly on their final exams. With all the money the university is spending on football, you would think that they could put a little of it into student parking. It's especially hard on commuter students.

Compare that general paragraph with this one, which is much more specific:

> On Friday of last week, I drove to school, arriving at 9:45 for a ten o'clock class. A parking sticker that cost me $250 for the year announces from the windshield of my car that I have the right to park in any student parking lot. But on Friday, I drove around parking lot A, parking lot B, and parking lot C without finding a space. Finally, in desperation, I drove up to parking lot M a mile away from my class. There I found plenty of parking, but by the time I raced to the Mahan Building, where my accounting class was in progress, it was 10:20, and Professor Lewis stopped his lecture as I came in and said, "Well, we are certainly happy that Mr. Jenkins has decided to join us this morning. I hope you

didn't disturb your sleep just to be with us, Mr. Jenkins." I felt my face turn hot, and I knew I was blushing from anger and embarrassment. I should have come earlier and parked in lot **M** at the beginning. But my own problem did lead me on a greater quest that is the subject of this paper. What is the nature of the parking problem here, and what can be done about it?

The author of the first paragraph blows off steam but does not provide any worthwhile information. The author of the second paragraph tells us a story and provides many specific details that help us imagine the scene.

1 When you can, use concrete details to support the main idea of your paragraph.

Sensory details support paragraphs well—mention of colors, actions, sounds, and sensations of taste, touch, and smell. More specific details are nearly always better than general details. Rather than make a series of generalizations about the parking problem at your school, it is much better to tell a story that illustrates the problem. Rather than say "The room was shabbily furnished," say, "Three old wooden kitchen chairs, a broken-down couch with a filthy cover, and a deeply stained folding card table were the only furniture in the room."

Sensory language appeals to that part of the imagination that helps us join our experience to the experience of the writer. We have experienced a word like *furniture* only as an abstraction. It does not call up much of anything specific in our minds. But we have seen old wooden kitchen chairs, and mention of these words helps us imagine the scene better because we can bring concrete memories to it.

Sensory language, an essential quality of fiction, also adds life, clarity, and vividness to nonfiction prose, as you can see from this excerpt from "Ida's Fields," by Susan Hand Shetterly:

> The day our fire department burned Ida's house, smoke carried from the rotted timbers and cracked linoleum and old cedar shakes. Ida was dead, and the house with its caved-in kitchen floor and ruined roof on that long stretch of empty road was considered a hazard by the town selectmen. We could smell the fire from our place and see smoke through the trees. By nightfall, bulldozers had pushed the charred rubble into the cellar hole and covered everything Ida had owned with a clean layer of dirt. Everything, that is, but her fields.
>
> While she was alive, Ida did not let anyone walk those fields. It was rumored that if she caught you on them—and she was vigilant —she'd be looking at you down the barrel of a 12-gauge. She wore a nylon wig that looked like a brush fire flaming out of control, and beneath it, her face was a sour pucker. She died at ninety-three. That

last year, she lived in one room of the house and spent her days perched like a caged bird at the window that looked out on the lovely roll of the fields.

I have walked them at least a hundred times since her death. It is one field, actually, folded into five parts. At the fold lines, streams sing out in a January thaw. In the spring, they flood. But by August, they have vanished. As the field drops south towards the road, a line of granite breaks through it, as sharp as the vertebrae on the spine of a large, old animal. Ten apple trees grow on either side.

— SUSAN HAND SHETTERLY

Think of the difference in effect if Shetterly had written this: "For safety reasons the fire department burned down the empty house of an old woman who had died, and since then I have been walking around her place." Her skill lies in noticing details and then calling them up to support her writing.

Statistics and cases are the language of facts and figures. You can often use them effectively to support a topic. **Statistics** are numerical data; **cases** are specific instances involving real people and events. When you can use statistics well, they give authority to your statements and make readers think that you know what you are talking about. Then they will take your writing seriously. Statistics can often help your interpretation of a situation. Notice in the following selection how the numbers in the first paragraph and the dramatic use of a case study in the second help the writer make his point that although many American Indian children leave the reservation to attend public schools, some tribes feel a strong need to preserve their traditional schools on their reservations.

In 1969 there were 178,476 Indian students, ages five to eighteen, enrolled in public, Federal, private and mission schools. Approximately 12,000 children of this age group were not in school. Of the total in school, 119,000 were in public schools, 36,263 in boarding schools operated by the Bureau of Indian Affairs, 16,100 in Bureau day schools, 108 in Bureau hospital schools, and 4,089 in dormitories maintained by the Bureau for children attending public schools. The Bureau operated 77 boarding schools, 144 day schools, 2 hospital schools, and 18 dormitories. The number of Indian children being educated in public schools has steadily increased, aided by the financial assistance provided local school districts under the Johnson-O'Malley Act of 1934 (which provided financial support, in cooperation with the Department of Health, Education, and Welfare, to aid federally affected areas). The closer relationship between state school systems and the Indian system has been welcomed by many Indian groups. Sixty-one tribes have established compulsory education regulations that conform with those of the states where they live.

On the other hand, some more traditional Indian groups have rebelled at efforts to close down reservation schools. The attempt of the Bureau of Indian Affairs to close down, on July 1, 1968, a small grade-school at Tama, Iowa, created an instant reaction. Forty-five Mesquakie Indian children were attending school there on the reservation purchased by their ancestors, a separate body of the Sac tribe which, with the Fox, had a hundred years earlier been pushed out of Iowa into Kansas. The Mesquakie Indians, who had not been consulted about the closing of the school, promptly sought judicial relief. They got it in September 1968, in the Federal District Court at Cedar Rapids, when United States District Court Judge Edward J. McManus ordered the school reopened in the fall. The Mesquakie were able to call upon a number of influential white friends in their attempt to retain their Indian school. The validity of integration into a white school system that is often both distant from and cold toward Indian values can be questioned, as the Mesquakie questioned it.

—WILCOMB E. WASHBURN

Using statistics like these requires a great deal of research and hard work. But if you are going to make meaningful generalizations about large groups of people, you must find the statistical information to support those generalizations, especially if the generalizations are central to the point you are making in your essay.

Always try to think of specific examples to support your generalizations. Even when you are writing about your personal experience, readers want to know why you think the way you do, why you make the general statements that you make, and why you look on the world as you do. You can help them by telling them incidents that have formed your opinions.

It was almost a third of a century since Sacco and Vanzetti had been tried, yet the ghost of their trial still seemed to haunt the courthouse. Scarcely a day passed while I was on jury duty but some reference to it came up. It shadowed us all. We served in the same paneled room with the marble-faced clock where Sacco and Vanzetti had been tried and sentenced. There was the same enclosure for the prisoners that Sacco-Vanzetti partisans referred to as a "cage"—as if the two defendants had been exhibited like animals in a zoo. Actually, it was a waist-high metal lattice, slightly higher in the back, with nothing formidable or forbidding about it. Our white-haired sheriff, Samuel Capen, in his blue-serge cutaway, its gleaming brass buttons embossed with the state seal, and his white staff of office that he wielded like a benevolent shepherd, had been sheriff at the time of the great trial. In the overlong lunch hours he would sometimes talk about it, telling of the day Sacco and Vanzetti were sentenced, how Vanzetti made his famous speech, and how Judge Thayer sat with his head bent and never looked at him. I don't suppose any doubts had ever crossed the sheriff's mind as to the guilt of the two Italians or the rectitude of Massachusetts justice.

—Francis Russell

In this paragraph, in a chapter describing his early interest in the famous murder trial of Nicola Sacco and Bartolomeo Vanzetti in 1920, Russell reports some of his experiences on jury duty in Dedham, Massachusetts, in the same courthouse where Sacco and Vanzetti had been tried and sentenced to death.

As you develop paragraphs in an essay, you will draw upon many devices to support your points. Like Francis Russell, you may give some concrete details that evoke a mood or recapture a scene. Not every point that you make in a paragraph can or should be supported by concrete details. Especially in a long essay, a paragraph may build a series of generalizations or abstractions without providing supporting data. But every good writer knows that effective writing uses details. Details remind readers of their own experiences. They allow readers to bring their own imaginations to what they are reading. Without them, readers remain vague about what the writer is trying to say, and if they do understand, they may not be convinced.

Exercise 4.10 Read the following selections and identify the details that support the controlling idea of each paragraph.

When I first saw a water shrew swimming, I was most struck by the thing which I ought to have expected but did not; at the moment of diving, the little black and white beast appears to be made of silver. Like the plumage of ducks and grebes, but quite unlike the fur of most water mammals, such as seals, otters, beaver or coypus, the fur of the water shrew remains absolutely dry under water; that is to say, it retains a thick layer of air while the animal is below the surface. In the other mammals mentioned above, it is only the short, woolly undercoat that remains dry, the superficial hair tips becoming wet, wherefore the animal looks its natural color when underwater and is superficially wet when it emerges. I was already aware of the peculiar qualities of the waterproof fur of the shrew, and, had I given it a thought, 1 should have known that it would look, under water, exactly like the air-retaining fur on the underside of a water beetle or on the abdomen of a water spider. Nevertheless the wonderful, transparent silver coat of the shrew was, to me, one of those delicious surprises that nature has in store for her admirers.

—Konrad Z. Lorenz

We can understand though how the poet got his reputation as a kind of licensed liar. The word poet itself means liar in some languages, and the words we use in literary criticism—fable, fiction, myth—have all come to mean something we can't believe. Some parents in Victorian times wouldn't let their children read novels because they weren't "true." But not many reasonable people today would deny that the poet is entitled to change whatever he likes when he uses a theme from history or real life. The reason why was explained long ago by Aristotle. The historian makes specific and particular statements, such as: "The battle of Hastings was fought in 1066." Consequently he's judged by the truth or falsehood of what he says—either there was such a battle or there wasn't, and if there was he's got the date either right or wrong. But the poet, Aristotle says, never makes any real statements at all, certainly no particular or specific ones. The poet's job is not to tell you what happened, but what happens: not what did take place, but the kind of thing that always does take place. He gives you the typical meaning, recurring, or what Aristotle calls universal event. You wouldn't go to *Macbeth* to learn about the history of Scotland—you go to it to learn what a man feels like after he's gained a kingdom and lost his soul. When you meet such a character as Micawber in Dickens, you don't feel that there must have been a man Dickens knew who was exactly like this: you feel that there's a bit of Micawber in almost everybody you know, including yourself. Our impressions of human life are picked up one by one, and remain for most of us loose and disorganized. But we constantly find things in literature that suddenly co-ordinate and bring into focus a great many such impressions, and this is part of what Aristotle means by the typical or universal human event.

— Northrop Frye

2   Choose an appropriate form to develop your paragraphs.

No book can list every possible kind of paragraph, but the following examples offer several varieties for study and imitation.

Narration

Use narrative paragraphs to tell a story in chronological order, relating the events one after the other as they happened in time.

Banyan Street was the route Lucille Miller took home from the twenty-four-hour Mayfair Market on the night of October 7, 1964, a night when the moon was dark and the wind was blowing and she was out of milk, and Banyan Street was where, at about 12:20 A.M., her

1964 Volkswagen came to a sudden stop, caught fire, and began to burn. For an hour and fifteen minutes, Lucille Miller ran up and down Banyan Street calling for help, but no cars passed and no help came. At three o'clock that morning, when the fire had been put out and the California Highway Patrol officers were completing their report, Lucille Miller was still sobbing and incoherent, for her husband had been asleep in the Volkswagen. "What will I tell the children, when there's nothing left, nothing left in the casket," she cried to the friend who called to comfort her. "How can I tell them there's nothing left?"

— Joan Didion

Covering a brief span of time, this narrative relates events in a clear sequence. Notice the use of detail that makes readers form pictures in their minds of what happened.

Process Analysis

Use process analysis in paragraphs to explain how to do something or how to make something. Here is a paragraph on how to check the inflation on your bike tires if you don't have an air pressure gauge with you:

There's a great *curb-edge test* you can do to make sure your tires are inflated just right. Rest the wheel on the edge of a curb or stair, so the bike sticks out into the street or path, perpendicular to the curb or stair edge. Get the wheel so you can push down on it at about a 45 degree angle from above the bike. Push hard on the handlebars or seat, depending on which wheel you're testing. The curb should flare the tire a bit but shouldn't push right through the tire and clunk against the rim. You want the tire to have a little give when you ride over chuckholes and rocks, in other words, but you don't want it so soft that you bottom out. If you are a hot-shot who wants tires so hard that they don't have any give, you'll have to stick to riding on clean-swept Velodrome tracks, or watch very carefully for little sharp objects on the road. Or you'll have to get used to that sudden riding-on-the-rim feeling that follows the blowout of an overblown tire.

— Tom Cuthbertson

You can follow these directions because they break down a process into simple steps that follow one after the other. In all process writing, you must break the process down into steps and list the steps one after another exactly as they follow in the process itself; by all means, do not leave any of the steps out.

Comparison

Organize paragraphs by using comparisons that may include both similarities and differences.

You may make comparisons between conditions existing at two or more different times or between people, places, or things existing at the same time. But be sure that your comparisons are sensible. You can compare any two things with each other—a freight train with a short story, for example. Both have a beginning, a middle, and an end. But such meaningless and trivial comparisons will annoy your readers. Annoyed readers usually stop reading.

The following paragraph compares a Russian tank, the T-34 of 1942, with earlier Russian tanks and also with the German tanks that the Russians encountered in World War II. Because the comparison involves weapons of two armies at war with each other, it is clearly a meaningful comparison.

The new T-34s coming into action in 1942 had better guns and engines. And they retained the broad tracks that made them more mobile and more weatherworthy than German vehicles. In mud or snow they could—quite literally—run rings around the panzers. The turret of the earlier T-34 had been difficult to operate, and its large hatch was vulnerable to grenades and satchel charges; the hatch had been replaced by a smaller opening for the commander and a second one for the gunner. The rear overhang over the turret —a favorite place for the German tank-killer squads to plant their mines—was eliminated, and handrails were welded onto the rear deck so that infantrymen could be carried to counter enemy antitank teams.

—JOHN SHAW

Notice especially the careful detail that this comparison involves.

Classification

Use classification in paragraphs to sort out things or people into groups of similar individuals. Often you will want to divide a large group into several smaller parts so that readers can see different elements in a group that, at first glance, may seem to be without variation.

Classification helps organize complicated information so that it can be managed in steps by the writer.

People who understand high finance are of two kinds: those who have vast fortunes of their own and those who have nothing at all. To an actual millionaire a million pounds is something real and comprehensible. To the applied mathematician and the lecturer in economics (assuming both to be practically starving) a million pounds is at least as real as a thousand, they having never possessed either sum. But the world is full of people who fall between these two categories, knowing nothing of millions but well accustomed to think in thousands, and it is of these that finance committees are mostly composed. The result is a phenomenon that has often been observed but never yet investigated. It might be termed the Law of Triviality. Briefly stated, it means that the time spent on any item of the agenda will be in inverse proportion to the sum involved.

— C. Northcote Parkinson

Parkinson, in a humorous way, classifies people's sense of money into two sorts. This classification allows him to describe each sense of money and to come to a conclusion that explains why finance committees spend so much time arguing over relatively minor matters in the budget.

Causal Analysis

Organize paragraphs around an explanation of cause and effect when you want to explain why something happened or when you want to explain the effects of some happening. Here are two paragraphs that give the cause and effect of the plague called the Black Death that ravaged Europe in the fourteenth century:

In October 1347, a fleet of Genoese merchant ships from the Orient arrived at the harbor of Messina in northeast Sicily. All aboard the ships were dead or dying of a ghastly disease. The harbor masters tried to quarantine the fleet, but the source of the pestilence was borne by rats, not men, and these were quick to scurry ashore. Within six months, half of the population of the region around Messina had fled their homes or succumbed to the disease. Four years later, between one-quarter and one-half of the population of Europe was dead.

The Black Death, or plague, that devastated Europe in the 14th century was caused by bacteria that live in the digestive tract of fleas, and in particular the fleas of rats. But at that time, the disease seemed arbitrary and capricious, and to strike from nowhere. One commentator wrote: "Father abandoned child, wife husband, one brother another, for the plague seemed to strike through breath and sight." The pestilence was widely held to be a scourge sent by God to chasten a sinful people.

— Chet Raymo

The writer of these paragraphs carefully spells out the cause of the Black Death and gives some of its effects in the Europe of its time.

Definition

Use paragraphs to define objects, concepts, ideas, terms, political movements, and anything else that may be important to your essay. A useful definition first identifies something as a member of a class of similar things; then it states how it differs from everything else in its class. Simple, concrete objects may often be identified in a single sentence if they require definition at all.

A typewriter is a small tabletop machine—operated by a keyboard activated by human fingers—that allows a writer to produce writing on paper more quickly and more legibly than by handwriting.

Here a typewriter is first classified as a small tabletop machine. What distinguishes it from a copier, a stapler, a table saw or whatever is that it is operated by a keyboard activated by human fingers and that its purpose is to allow a writer to produce writing on paper more quickly and more legibly than by handwriting.

Definitions of more abstract terms may require an entire paragraph or several paragraphs. Paragraphs that define usually come near the beginning of an essay so that writers may be sure their readers understand a term to be used throughout.

We have a roster of diseases which medicine calls "idiopathic," meaning that we do not know what causes them. The list is much shorter than it used to be; a century ago, common infections like typhus fever and tuberculous meningitis were classed as idiopathic illnesses. Originally, when it first came into the language of medicine, the term had a different, highly theoretical meaning. It was assumed that most human diseases were intrinsic, due to inbuilt failures of one sort or another, things gone wrong with various internal humors. The word "idiopathic" was intended to mean, literally, a disease having its own origin, a primary disease without any external cause. The list of such disorders has become progressively shorter as medical science has advanced, especially within this century, and the meaning of the term has lost its doctrinal flavor; we use "idiopathic" now to indicate simply that the cause of a particular disease is unknown. Very likely, before we are finished with medical science, and with luck, we will have found that all varieties of disease are the result of one or another sort of meddling, and there will be no more idiopathic illness.

—Lewis Thomas

A paragraph like this one defines a term much more subtly and in much greater complexity than does either a common dictionary definition or the brief definition of a typewriter *that we saw above.*

Writers frequently combine patterns. The paragraphs by Chet Raymo and Lewis Thomas, for example, use narrative to help develop cause and effect and definition. The paragraph by C. Northcote Parkinson involves causal analysis as well as classification. When you write an essay, you should not feel obligated to use only one method of development in each paragraph. But your paragraphs will be more coherent if you decide which method of development should be most important in that paragraph for your purposes.

Exercise 4.11   Discuss the various techniques used in the following paragraphs — narrative, process analysis, comparison, classification, cause and effect, or definition.

The figure that comes to me oftenest, out of the shadows of that vanished time, is that of Brown of the steamer *Pennsylvania* — the man referred to in a former chapter, whose memory was so good and tiresome. He was a middle-aged, long, slim, bony, smooth-shaven, horse-faced, ignorant, stingy, malicious, snarling, fault-hunting, mote-magnifying tyrant. I early got the habit of coming on watch with dread at my heart. No matter how good a time I might have been having with the off-watch below, and no matter how high my spirits might be when I started aloft, my soul became lead in my body the moment I approached the pilot-house.

I still remember the first time I ever entered the presence of that man. The boat had backed out from St. Louis and was "straightening down." I ascended to the pilot-house in high feather, and very proud to be semi-officially a member of the executive family of so fast and famous a boat. Brown was at the wheel. I paused in the middle of the room, all fixed to make my bow, but Brown did not look around. I thought he took a furtive glance at me out of the corner of his eye, but as not even this notice was repeated, I judged I had been mistaken. By this time he was picking his way among some dangerous "breaks" abreast the woodyards; therefore it would not be proper to interrupt him; so I stepped softly to the high bench and took a seat.

— MARK TWAIN

Exactly what happens when GNP [gross national product] falls or lags? The pace of business activity slows down. There is less demand for consumer goods and services, less demand for plant and equipment and other business items. Some businesses fire people; other businesses hire fewer new workers. Because our labor force is steadily growing as our population swells, even a small decrease in the willingness to take on new workers spells a sharp rise in unemployment for certain groups, such as young people. When a recession really deepens, as in 1980, it is not just the young who cannot find work, but experienced workers find themselves thrown out of work.

— ROBERT HEILBRONER AND LESTER THUROW

In December of 1862, Benjamin Butler was replaced in New Orleans by General Nathaniel Banks—who was immediately offered a bribe of $100,000 to approve a shady deal. A disillusioned Banks wrote his wife that "everybody connected with the government has been employed in stealing." He commented sadly: "I never despaired of my country until I came here."

Banks was by no means the only one who despaired of what he witnessed in the free-spending wartime years. The New York *Herald* coined a new epithet—"shoddy"—to describe the whole era. Originally, the word referred to a flimsy material used by profiteering contractors to make Army uniforms that were so poor they tended to disintegrate in the rain. "The world has seen its iron age, its silver age, its golden age and its brazen age," pronounced the *Herald*. "This is the age of shoddy." It was characterized by "shoddy brokers in Wall Street, or shoddy manufacturers of shoddy goods, or shoddy contractors for shoddy articles." On Sundays, concluded the *Herald*, these men became "shoddy Christians."

—DALE JACKSON AND THE EDITORS OF TIME-LIFE BOOKS

People react strongly and variously to being queued. Russians line themselves up without being told. Moscow theater audiences file out, last row first, like school children marching out of assemblies. In America, on the contrary, theatrical performances break up like the Arctic ice in springtime. Commuters and the constitutionally impatient gather themselves for a dash up the aisle, while the rest of the audience is still applauding. Fidgeters and people who can't bear having anyone ahead of them sidle across rows to emergency exits, while placid souls who seem to enjoy the presence of others drift happily up the aisle with the crowd. In Moscow, the theater is emptied faster. In New York, you can get out fast if you're willing to work at it.

—CAROLINE BIRD

Exercise 4.12 Discuss what paragraph form you would use to develop these topics. Choose from narration, process analysis, comparison, classification, causal analysis, and definition.

1. The meaning of intelligence
2. An embarrassing or humorous moment
3. Types of teachers
4. How to repair a flat tire
5. American democracy and ancient Greek democracy
6. Why teenagers drop out of school

Exercise 4.13 Use the topics below to practice writing paragraphs according to the method listed by each number.

1. *Narration:* *(a)* a fishing trip, *(b)* what you did last Saturday morning, *(c)* a time you were lost, *(d)* your first dance
2. *Process analysis:* *(a)* cooking a simple recipe, *(b)* operating a food processor, *(c)* how to study for an exam, *(d)* throwing a curve ball, *(e)* learning to type
3. *Comparison:* *(a)* a novel and a film based on the novel, *(b)* a pet dog and a pet cat, *(c)* two college courses, *(d)* downhill skiing and cross-country skiing, *(e)* rowing and canoeing, *(f)* German war aims in 1914 and in 1939
4. *Classification:* *(a)* jobs for college students, *(b)* clothing styles for different sorts of people, *(c)* kinds of television watchers, *(d)* planets in the solar system, *(e)* fantastic movies and police movies
5. *Causal analysis:* *(a)* some effects of nuclear war, *(b)* why some children have trouble learning to write, *(c)* why more women are smoking cigarettes, *(d)* how high unemployment rates affect teenagers
6. *Definition:* *(a)* democracy, *(b)* fascism, *(c)* religion, *(d)* women's rights, *(e)* rock music, *(f)* jazz, *(g)* country music, *(h)* spectator sports, *(i)* a fan

3 Write paragraphs of appropriate length.

There are no absolute rules for the length of a paragraph. Writers for newspapers and magazines often favor short paragraphs of a few sentences, totaling one hundred words or so. Many professional essayists prefer paragraphs that fill a half page or a full page of print. As you look back through the sample paragraphs in this chapter, you can see many different lengths.

A new paragraph signals a change of subject — slight or large — so a paragraph should be long enough to let readers absorb and remember its subject. Introductory paragraphs are generally shorter than paragraphs in the body of a paper. Within the body of your paper, it is a good idea to strike a balance between short and long paragraphs.

A good general rule is to have an indentation on each typed page. But use your judgment to decide how long your paragraphs should be.

4d
Construct opening and closing paragraphs that suit your thesis and hold your readers' attention.

Your opening paragraph should announce the general topic of your essay and be interesting enough to make people want to read on; the opening paragraph usually implies a promise you make to the reader to do something in your essay. Your concluding paragraph should end with that promise kept.

1 Write opening paragraphs that seize the attention of readers as you introduce your subject.

Your opening paragraphs must win over readers trying to decide whether to read your work. Your opening paragraphs set the tone for everything else in your essay, announcing not only your subject but also the sort of audience you want to read your work.

A few audiences may expect your opening paragraphs to outline everything you intend to do in your essay. Descriptions of scientific experiments almost always start with such an outline, called an **abstract** in scientific circles. But if you are writing about some personal topic or about something you wish to explain or report, your first paragraphs usually give only an inviting glimpse of what lies in store for the reader.

Note how the opening paragraphs that follow introduce a subject and set the tone for the piece.

It is a modern plague: the first great pandemic of the second half of the 20th century. The flat, clinical-sounding name given to the disease by epidemiologists — acquired immune deficiency syndrome — has been shortened to the chilling acronym **AIDS**. First described in 1981, **AIDS** is probably the result of a new infection of human beings that began in central Africa, perhaps as recently as the 1950's. From there it probably spread to the Caribbean and then to the U.S. and Europe. By now as many as two million people in the U.S. may be infected. In the endemic areas of Africa and the Caribbean the situation is much worse. Indeed, in some areas it may be too late to prevent a disturbingly high number of people from dying.

—ROBERT C. GALLO

This paragraph seizes a reader's attention by relating some shocking information. It sets a tone of serious concern combined with careful objectivity about the facts.

Spring is a glorious time to be in the Kansas Flint Hills, especially if the rains have been plentiful. The bluestem grasses have lost their winter gray and brown in favor of a deep rich green, a color that will soon fade with the coming of the hot summer sun. Even if spring is brief, as it is in some years, it is sufficient. The clean sweet smells carried on the gentle warm breeze blowing up from the southwest carry a freshness that the nostrils have not sensed since the Indian summer days of fall. "The hills," as the local cattlemen call the land, have none of the flaming beauty of the forested New England mountains or the majesty of the Rocky Mountains. Rather, the gentle contour of the rolling carpet of grass stretching from horizon to horizon is soft and restfully inviting. It is peaceful because the hand of man is little in evidence. Most of the Flint Hills are still virgin prairie, much as they were a century or more ago when the Indian's cattle — buffalo — grazed on the tall grasses. Today the white man's cattle have replaced the shaggy monsters of the past.

— DAVID DARY

This is the opening paragraph of a book called Cowboy Culture, *an account of how cowboys lived on the western plains in the nineteenth century. Here is a carefully written and beautiful description that leads rather slowly into the theme of cattle raising, which itself introduces the main theme of the book, the story of the men who raised the cattle and took them to market.*

I spent several days and nights in mid-September with my ailing pig, and I feel driven to account for this stretch of time, more particularly since the pig died at last, and I lived, and things might easily have gone the other way round and none left to do the accounting. Even now, so close to the event, I cannot recall the hours sharply and am not ready to say whether death came on the third night or the fourth night. This uncertainty afflicts me with a sense of personal deterioration; if I were in decent health I would know how many nights I had sat up with a pig.

— E. B. WHITE

This paragraph introduces a personal-experience narrative. It sets a tone of sadness and lets readers know that the essay will be about the death of a pig — an unusual subject but one that may interest them because it has so moved the writer.

In the following introduction, the writer tells readers just what to expect in the essay to come. Introductory paragraphs that summarize the paper to follow are especially popular among science writers. They assume a previous interest by the specialists who will read those papers. Those interested in the topic can quickly see the argument of the paper and decide if they want to keep reading.

In this paper I shall consider several educational issues growing out of A. R. Jensen's paper, "How Much Can We Boost IQ and Scholastic Achievement?" (Jensen, 1969.) The first deals with the question of how education should adjust to the incontestable fact that approximately half the children in our schools are and always will be below average in IQ. Following this, I take up some of the more moot points of the "Jensen controversy"— what does heritability tell us about teachability? What are the prospects for reducing the spread of individual differences in intelligence? And what are the educational implications of possible hereditary differences in intelligence associated with social class and race? — ending with some implications that these issues have for educational research.

— CARL BEREITER

Note that most writers cannot assume the professional interest on the part of readers that Bereiter assumes here. That is why blueprint beginnings are common in professional journals in medicine and science and in other publications where readers are seeking technical information. In most other writing, readers must be wooed into reading an essay. To win them over, writers must use more imaginative techniques than the so-called blueprint beginning that gives the plan of the essay in the first paragraph. The blueprint says "I am going to tell you about the World Series. I am going to tell you about the first game, the second game, and about all the other games until I get to the seventh game. I'm going to tell you a lot of interesting things about the players and coaches, and I'm going to describe many of the plays that happened on the field." Blueprint beginnings usually signal a boring style.

2 Write concluding paragraphs that complete your essay without summarizing it.

If you write a scientific, technical, or academic paper, you may be expected to summarize everything you have said at the end of the paper. But there are far more imaginative ways to conclude an essay. Most professional writers make it a rule never to end a story or an essay with a summary.

A good concluding paragraph will complete the paper logically and clearly, perhaps drawing a conclusion that expresses some meaning to be found in the information presented in the essay. The following paragraphs express the general meaning of the essays they conclude.

Does this terrible tale have a moral? Yes. In the past two decades one of the fondest boasts of medical science has been the conquest of infectious disease, at least in the wealthy countries of the industrialized world. The advent of retroviruses with the capacity to cause extraordinarily complex and devastating disease has exposed that claim for what it was: hubris. Nature is never truly conquered. The human retroviruses and their intricate interrelation with the human cell are but one example of that fact. Indeed, perhaps conquest is the wrong metaphor to describe our relation to nature, which not only surrounds but in the deepest sense also constitutes our being.

—ROBERT C. GALLO

This paragraph, the last in the article introduced by the paragraph beginning "It is a modern plague" in 4d-1, sums up the general lesson that may be learned from the study of AIDS, the lesson that human beings will never fully make nature do what they want it to do. Hubris, the destructive pride that makes us imagine we are more powerful than we are, may make us think that we have conquered nature. But AIDS and the retrovirus that causes it show that nature can always surprise us. Notice that the first paragraph speaks of AIDS; this last paragraph also refers to the disease.

As the sixteenth century was ending, the ranching industry was firmly established in the New World. It had spread northward on two fronts, one up the western and one up the eastern slope of the majestic Sierra Madre. It had swept more than a thousand miles from where it began southwest of Mexico City less than a century before. And the *vaquero* had become an integral part of the spreading cattle-related culture that emphasized the mounted horseman.

—DAVID DARY

This paragraph concludes the chapter begun by the introductory paragraph you read in 4d-1. Notice that just as the first paragraph speaks of cattle, so does the last, in the phrase "cattle-related culture." The last sentence speaks of the vaquero, *the Spanish word for "cowboy," and the chapter itself has discussed the development of cattle ranching on the plains by the first white settlers, who were Spanish.*

The news of the death of my pig traveled fast and far, and I received many expressions of sympathy from friends and neighbors, for no one took the event lightly, and the premature expiration of a pig is, I soon discovered, a departure which the community marks solemnly to its calendar, a sorrow in which it feels fully involved. I have written this account in penitence and in grief, as a man who failed to raise his pig, and to explain my deviation from the classic course of so many raised pigs. The grave in the woods is unmarked, but Fred can direct the mourner to it unerringly and with immense good will, and I know he and I shall often revisit it, singly and together, in seasons of reflection and despair, on flagless memorial days of our own choosing.

—E. B. WHITE

The death of the pig mentioned in the first paragraph of White's article (4d-1) is mentioned again in this last paragraph. He concludes with a mention of the grave—something we might expect when the essay has been about a death.

Exercise 4.14 Take any popular magazine that you enjoy reading and look at all the articles in it, carefully comparing the first and last paragraphs of each article. What relation do you see between the two paragraphs even before you read the article? Discuss in class or with friends interested in writing the connections between each first and last paragraph that you survey.

Exercise 4.15 Take one of your own essays and compare the first and last paragraphs. What similarities do you note between them?

Exercise 4.16 Write several first paragraphs for articles or essays that you are thinking of writing. Make them interesting and appealing. See if you can make them introduce your subject without merely summarizing what you are going to say in the essay.

4e
Revise any loose paragraphs for unity, coherence, and development.

As you revise the rough draft of your essay, make sure that your paragraphs are unified, coherent, and well developed. You may want to add elements, eliminate elements, or subordinate one element to another. Because the controlling idea of your paragraph should guide any changes you make, start by rereading your paragraph carefully to determine the controlling idea that you want to express. A paragraph like the one that follows requires revision in an essay.

LOOSE PARAGRAPH

Wood-burning stoves are helping many Americans beat the cost of fossil fuels and save money. Wood is still plentiful in the United States. Many states set off parts of their state forests where residents can cut designated trees at no charge. Some wood stoves give off emissions that may cause cancer. But the technology of wood stoves has improved so that they can be very safe as well as efficient. The federal government now has standards that wood stove manufacturers must meet. Unfortunately, wood stoves are sometimes bulky and ugly and take up too much space in small rooms. Sometimes they make rooms too hot. Many homeowners who have gone to wood stoves for heat report savings of hundreds of dollars each year over the former price of heating their houses with oil. And many of them enjoy the exercise of cutting wood.
In this paragraph, the controlling idea is clearly stated in the first sentence. Everything else in the paragraph should relate to the idea that wood stoves save money. The issues of availability and safety,

though important, do not suit the topic of this paragraph. In the same way, the sentences about the disadvantages of wood stoves have no place in a paragraph about costs. The sentence about the technology of wood stoves may belong in a paragraph about costs because technology has made wood stoves more efficient, that is, cheaper to operate. Smoother connections between sentences would make the chapter more coherent, and the paragraph would benefit from added details about the availability of wood and about the efficiency of wood stoves.

Here the paragraph has been revised with the above points in mind.

REVISED PARAGRAPH

Wood-burning stoves are helping many Americans beat the high costs of fossil fuels. In recent years, the prices of oil and gas have come down, but these are limited fuels, and the prices are bound to rise again. So the availability of cheap fuel is still worth considering—and wood is cheap in some parts of the United States. A cord of word, a stack measuring $4 \times 4 \times 8$ feet, costs just over a hundred dollars in a typical heating season. Many states like Massachusetts and Montana set off parts of their state forests where residents can cut designated trees at no charge. On a warm summer morning, one may see dozens of families sawing trees and loading vans or pickup trucks with logs for use as a winter fuel. Not only can wood be obtained cheaply, but also the technology of wood stoves has improved; the new models are far more efficient than the old ones. Now a family can heat a house with a wood stove with a minimum of waste or expense. A good airtight wood stove heats a room far more efficiently than does a conventional fireplace or a Franklin stove. Many homeowners who have turned to wood stoves for heat report savings of hundreds of dollars each year over the price of heating their houses with oil.

—DICK CURRY

All sentences now support the idea of saving money with wood-burning stoves. The writer has added details: he names two states that make forests available for wood users, and he provides a lively image to imply the popularity of such programs. An example about efficiency adds substance to the paragraph, too. Transitional expressions like in fact, but also, *and* now *connect ideas smoothly.*

Exercise 4.17   Revise the following paragraphs for unity, coherence, and development.

The blizzard began early on the morning of February 6. The snow began falling before dawn. The flakes were small and hard.

The snow itself was very thick. By nine o'clock, six inches of white covered the streets. Commuting traffic was reduced to a crawl. None of this affected me, since the schools were closed, and I stayed home, warm and cozy by the fire. I read the morning newspaper and kept refilling the coffee mug that sat beside me on a glass-topped table. By ten-thirty, the streets were impassable, and motorists were abandoning their cars. By noon, the offices in the city that had opened despite the storm were closing and sending workers home. At three o'clock, the mayor declared a state of emergency and asked schools, churches, and synagogues to give shelter to people stranded by the storm. Seeing all those people gathered together in houses of worship gave you a nice feeling about human nature, which some writers have claimed is evil. By six o'clock, the city was locked in the enchantment of a profound silence. Two feet of snow lay in the streets, and more was falling.

Just after World War II a "portable radio" was a large, rectangular box with tubes; a heavy, expensive battery; and a handle on top that allowed the radio to be lifted out of the trunk of the car and carried a short distance to the beach or a picnic table. No one would have thought of carrying a portable radio on a long hike in the mountains or for any distance at all. And if you ask me, that was a good thing! Today, portable radios, or boom boxes as they are sometimes called, can make people in subway cars or buses miserable because the adolescents who carry them turn the volume up as loud as they can. Back when portable radios first came out, people used them to listen to the news, soap operas, jazz music, sports, and singing commercials. But with the invention of the transistor, the portable radio has become the daily companion of millions, truly portable, a small object that can be tucked into a shirt pocket or hooked onto a belt and carried anywhere.

PART TWO

WRITING CLEAR AND EFFECTIVE SENTENCES

	Chapter
Basic Sentence Grammar	5
Sentence Logic	6
Coordination and Subordination	7
Parallelism	8
Emphasis	9
Variety	10

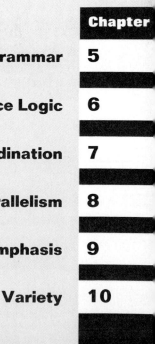

0

CHAPTER FIVE

Basic Sentence Grammar

To write well, you must know how to use the elements of the English sentence — elements traditionally called *grammar*. **Grammar** is two things:

1. A collection of patterns that make sense in sentences
2. The language we use to talk about such patterns

The first definition of *grammar* is much more important than the second. We use grammar all the time as a set of patterns that make sense. Most of us use grammar well enough to make language do what we want it to do — help us communicate with other people. We learn the patterns of the English sentence when we learn to talk, and we use them every day all our lives.

The word *patterns* is essential to understanding grammar. We react to sentences as patterns. They happen to be patterns developed over several hundred years of use by English-speaking people, and they are not always logical. But then no special logic governs many of the patterns we encounter in daily life. For example, we encounter the familiar pattern of the stop sign almost every day. If instead of using white letters on a red octagon, we had been using blue letters on a gold, diamond-shaped sign for many years, the diamond shape would be the controlling pattern for all stop signs. But somebody decided some time ago that stop signs should have the pattern we now recognize as official. We don't change the pattern just because some people believe that blue and gold are prettier colors than red and white.

The patterns of the English sentence are much the same. We are used to them. We cannot change them on whim. We learned these patterns from others, usually from our parents. We discovered early in life that they work because large numbers of people agree on their meaning.

We probably started by giving something a name that got results. "Milk!" we shouted, and somebody gave us milk. A little later we said, "Give me milk." Still later we said, "Will you please give me some milk?" or "I prefer milk, please." These are complicated sentences for children; no child can talk about them with a grammarian. But a child can make them work.

As we grow older, we learn to work all kinds of thoughts into the basic sentence patterns. If you hear somebody say "I picked up the telephone," you know what the speaker means. The pattern is familiar. But if somebody says "Picked I the telephone up," you run it through your mind again. What is this person trying to say? The pattern is not right. People don't say "Drove I the car this morning to work" or "Stood bravely he resisting the last until." If you wrestle with these sentences, you can probably make sense of them. But you wouldn't want to do much of this wrestling because it is so opposed to what we regard as normal communication. The patterns are not right, and we dislike the surprise these unfamiliar patterns give us.

The sense of pattern is so strong in us that we can frequently understand a sentence even when we don't know what every word in it means. If somebody says "Give me the phlumpis on the table," we hear the pattern, recognize it as a request or a command, and look on the table to see what the "phlumpis" is. The pattern tells us to do something with something called a "phlumpis," and we do it. The pattern is grammar in action.

There are only a few basic sentence patterns, although as you will see in 5c, you can make some changes in the basic form of any sentence. The most common pattern is the sentence that tells us that something does something to something else.

The man next door kills ants by spraying them with window cleaner.

This is a simple pattern. The man next door acts on the ants. It may seem odd to kill ants with window cleaner. But the sentence tells you that the man next door does it. You can imagine him pumping away with his bottle of window cleaner aimed at the ants.

You can substitute nonsense words in a pattern and still have an idea of what the sentence means.

The aardcam next door grinks ants by cooming them with dab.

Despite your confusion here, you know that something called an "aardcam" is the actor in this sentence. You know that "grinks" expresses the main act and that "cooming" expresses a helping act to the main act. And "dab" is some kind of tool, some instrument, something used in this action. You know that something is doing something to the ants because you recognize a basic pattern of the English sentence.

There are other patterns, including the one that tells us that something acts but that nothing receives the action.

The telephone is ringing.

The telephone is not doing anything to anybody. It's just ringing. Many sentences follow this same pattern.

The thermometer exploded.

The flowers bloom.

The child cried.

She arrives tomorrow.

The dog sat.

gr

Another pattern describes state or condition of being. The actor in the sentence simply exists in a certain way. There is no action but rather a statement that something *is* (or was or will be) something or that it exists with a certain quality.

The telephone is black.

The man was old and feeble but still witty and interesting.

My mother is an engineer.

Cousin Helga was a riverboat captain.

In the first sentence, you recognize from the pattern that the writer wants to make a statement about a telephone. The telephone isn't doing anything to anybody; it isn't doing anything at all in this sentence except existing as something black. And the man in the next sentence isn't doing anything. He is described as being a certain way—old, feeble, witty, interesting.

Another pattern tells that something is acted upon. When you read such a sentence, you expect to discover that from the viewpoint of the writer, the recipient of the action is the most important object or person in the sentence.

My brother was hit by a wheelbarrow this morning.

Obviously the most important person in this sentence is the recipient of the action—"my brother." "My brother" didn't act. He was acted upon. We recognize this pattern and understand its importance because we know that the normal pattern of expressing action in a sentence is differ-ent. Usually the actor is the most important element in the sentence and goes first. When the recipient of the action goes first, we are alerted to expect an unusual emphasis.

The basic patterns help sentences make sense. That is what the word **sentence** means — a group of words that make sense. They make sense because they communicate by using patterns that we recognize and ex-pect. We can all understand the sense of the following statements:

It rained last night.

The dust on the book made me sneeze.

Bicycle racing is becoming popular in the United States.

The Boston Red Sox lost the 1986 World Series.

She wrote three books before she was thirty.

Our knowledge of patterns tells us when we don't have a sentence. When we don't have a sentence, we don't have a familiar pattern that communicates. We are not fooled by the words pretending to be sen-tences below. Each group of words looks like a sentence at first glance, but it is not.

Shafts of light into the misty mountain valleys.

Favor capital punishment.

The most frequently abused drugs.

Each group begins with a capital letter and ends with a period — just like a sentence. But by itself, not one group makes sense. None of the groups has a pattern we recognize as a sentence. To each group, we must add words to make a pattern that communicates a sensible statement.

The rising sun threw shafts of light into the misty mountain valleys.

Polls show that most Americans favor capital punishment.

The most frequently abused drugs and therefore those most harmful to the general population are alcohol and tobacco.

To talk intelligently about these sentence patterns, you do not have to know grammatical terms such as *subject, verb, participle, direct object, indirect object*, and all the rest. But if you know the terms, your talk about language can be more precise. The rest of this chapter will introduce the most basic terms to you. But even so, you do not have to know grammati-cal language to recognize that something is wrong with an incomplete pattern, a group of words that does not communicate anything that makes sense.

Exercise 5.1 Some of the word groups below are sentences, and some are not. Mark each sentence with an *S*. Use an *X* to indicate an incomplete sentence. Discuss your decisions with other members of your class.

1. Soft steps in the hallway.
2. Riding along the edges of the reservoir and watching the birds in the water.
3. She spoke carefully.
4. After an introductory course, you.
5. Attempted to explain why the dinosaurs became extinct.
6. With a sly, cold smile.
7. Prices rose, but supplies remained plentiful.
8. When nothing else will help.
9. A terrible headache the morning after.
10. The dog barked as though asking us to remember her.

Exercise 5.2 In the preceding groups of words that are *not* sentences, add words that will make them sentences. Use your creativity to make the sentences interesting.

5a

Learn the basic structure of the English sentence.

Most sentences name something and then make some statement about the thing named. The part of the sentence that names what the sentence is about is called the *subject*. The part of the sentence that makes a statement about the subject is called the *predicate*.

Subject	Predicate
The sun	shines today.
Liberty	prevails in the world.
Our love	died last summer.
Charles	is allergic to cigarette smoke.
Sarah	repairs automobiles.
The students	forgot their rough drafts.
Penn State	went undefeated.
My car	was stolen last night.
Rex	is a huge dog.

gr

All these sentences name something and make an assertion about it. Each sentence tells you that the subject does something or that something is done to the subject or that the subject exists in a certain way. Questions, of course, do not make statements. But they do name a subject and then ask something about it.

> Is Charles allergic to cigarette smoke?
>
> Does Sarah repair automobiles?
>
> Was my car stolen last night?

gr

Sentences that give commands or make requests often imply the subject. If the subject is implied, it is always the person spoken to. You can supply the subject by adding the word *you*. The word *you*, then, is the subject of a command or request that does not specifically name some other subject.

> [You] Bring me the report.
>
> [You] Pass the spaghetti.

Here are two necessary qualities of any sentence.

1. The boundaries of the sentence are clearly marked off by a capital letter at the beginning and a period, a question mark, or an exclamation point at the end.

2. Within these boundaries, every sentence contains at least one subject and one predicate that fit together to make a statement, ask a question, or give a command.

1 All sentences have a subject and a predicate and tell one of three things.

1. The subject does [or did or will do] something.

2. Something is done to the subject.

3. The subject exists in some state or condition.

The Subject

The subject and the words that describe it are often called the *complete subject*. Within the complete subject, the word (or words) serving as the focus of the sentence may be called the *simple subject*. To get to the simple subject, you remove all the describing words that may provide added information about the simple subject. Grammarians are not always consistent in the names they use for elements of the sentence. The word *subject* can be used for either the complete subject or the simple subject. The **simple subject** may be a thing, person, place, action, idea, name, or anything else that serves as the element the predicate makes a statement about.

In the following sentences, the complete subjects are underlined once and the simple subjects are in boldface:

The quick brown **fox** jumps over the lazy dog.

Buckner lost the game with his error in the last of the ninth.

The huge black **clouds in the west** told of the coming storm.

Sometimes a subject is **compound;** that is, a conjunction such as *and* or *but* (see 5b-5) connects two or more words that serve as subjects of the sentence.

Original **thinking** and bold **design** have distinguished her architectural career.
Two subjects, thinking *and* design, *are joined by the conjunction* and. *The subject is compound.*

The Predicate

The **predicate** asserts something about the subject. The predicate, together with all the words that help it make a statement about the subject, is often called the *complete predicate.* In the complete predicate, the word (or words) that reports or states conditions, with all describing words removed, is called the *simple predicate* or the *verb.* Here, too, there is some overlap in terminology. The word *predicate* can be used for the complete predicate or for the simple predicate, and *verb* can be used instead of *simple predicate.*

In the following sentences, the complete predicates are underlined and the simple predicates (the *verbs*) are in boldface.

The quick brown fox **jumps** over the lazy dog.

Buckner **lost** the game with his error in the last of the ninth.

The huge black clouds in the west **told** of the coming storm.

Original thinking and bold design **have distinguished** her architectural career.

Like subjects, predicates may also be compound. In a compound predicate, two or more verbs are joined by a conjunction:

The huge black clouds in the west **told of the coming storm and ended** our picnic.

Two verbs, told *and* ended, *are joined by the conjunction* and. *The predicate is compound.*

Sometimes a verb combines with an auxiliary verb (also called a *helping verb*) to form a verb of more than one word. **A helping verb** aids a main verb by adding a sense of time or progression to the sense of the main verb. (See section 5b-1.) When a main verb combines with a helping verb in a sentence, we call the resulting element a *verb phrase.* The verb phrases are in boldface in the sentences below.

Original thinking and bold design **have distinguished** her architectural career and **have made** her rich.

Gold **was discovered** in California in 1848.

He **might have seen** that film before.

The oldest building on campus **would have been demolished** if not for her generous contribution to save it.

2   Learn to recognize subjects and predicates.

Being able to locate subjects and predicates in your own sentences helps you check on their logic, clarity, and correctness. One way to find the two sentence components is to look at what the sentence says and to ask two questions about its meaning:

1. Who or what is the sentence about? *(subject)*

2. What statement is the sentence making about the subject? *(predicate)*

Consider this sentence:

Some harmless snakes imitate poisonous snakes in color and behavior.

Questions	Answers
1. Who or what is the sentence about?	Some harmless snakes *(subject)*
2. What statement is the sentence making about the subject?	Imitate poisonous snakes in color and behavior *(predicate)*

Simple Predicates

Perhaps the best way to find these basic sentence components is to start by looking for the verb (the *simple predicate*).

Remember that verbs express action or state of being.

Churchill *spoke* to England.
action

The hippopotamus *was* beautiful.
state of being

You can identify verbs by finding the action words or the words that show state of being (see 5b-1).

But it is even easier to find verbs if you remember that they may change their form according to the different ways they may be used in a sentence. Because verbs change their forms to show time, or *tense* (see 5b-1), you can locate verbs easily by forcing such a change in a sentence. If you use a word like *yesterday, today,* or *tomorrow* at the start of a sentence whose verb you are trying to identify, the word that changes will be the verb. Only the verb will change in the sentence.

I eat green vegetables.

Yesterday, I *ate* green vegetables.
Eat *changed to* ate; eat, *therefore, is the verb in the original sentence.*

Mr. Smith goes to Washington.
Tomorrow, *Mr. Smith* will go *to Washington. The word* goes *changed to* will go; goes *is the verb in the original sentence.*

Another way to locate verbs is to memorize the verbs that serve as **auxiliaries,** that is, helpers, to other verbs. There are only a few of them. These auxiliaries are always verbs and never anything else. They often signal the presence of another part of the verb phrase close by in the sentence. Or they serve alone as verbs in sentences (see page 339). The most common helping verbs are *am, is, are, was, were, shall, will, could, would, have, has, had, do, does, did, be, been, might, can, may,* and *must.*

Another good way to test a word you think may be a verb is to use *I, he, she, it, you, we,* or *they* before the word. If you make sense with this combination, the word you are testing is a verb.

Word	Test	Verb?
try	I try she tries	yes
olive	I olive (?) they olive (?)	no

5a
gr

laughingly	they laughingly (?)	no
laugh	they laugh	yes
laughing	I laughing they laughing	no

See 5b-1 and Chapter 20, for further information about verbs.

=========== **FINDING AND TESTING VERBS** ===========

1. Change a sentence by using *yesterday, today,* and *tomorrow* at the beginning. The word that changes is a verb.

He played shortstop.

Tomorrow he will play shortstop.

Today he plays shortstop.
The word that changes is *play. Play* is the dictionary form — the form you find listed in alphabetical order in the dictionary — of the verb.

2. Learn the most familiar helping verbs.

3. Use *I, she, it, you, we,* or *they* before the word you think is a verb.

VERB: Swim I swim
NOT A VERB: thing I thing

Simple Subjects

Once you find the verb, you can find the subject easily. Just put the verb in a question asking who or what does the action of a verb. Say the word *who* or *what;* then say the verb. The answer to your question will be the subject of the sentence. Note how the questions work for the following sentences; verbs and verb phrases are in boldface.

We **have been working** all night.
Who has been working all night? We *is the subject of the sentence.*

Trout fishing **is** a popular sport in northern New England.
What is a popular sport in northern New England? Trout fishing.
Trout fishing is the subject of the sentence.

Lee **invaded** the north twice during the Civil War.
Who invaded the north twice during the Civil War? Lee is the subject of the sentence.

He **was looking** for his car.
Who was looking for his car? He is the subject.

Generally, subjects of verbs are **nouns or pronouns,** words that name persons, places, things, ideas, or objects (see 5b-2 and 3). But other words may sometimes be subjects.

Exercise 5.3   Write five sentences. Draw a dividing line between the complete subject and the complete predicate. Then draw a line under the simple subject and the simple predicate.

Example

My writing <u>assignments</u> in school/<u>have always caused</u> me much difficulty.

Other Predicate Parts

The verb is the most important word in the predicate because we have to have a verb to make a statement about a subject. In a very simple sentence, a verb can be a predicate all by itself. But in more complicated sentences, complete predicates may also include objects, complements, and various words called *modifiers* that help describe other elements. All these elements work like interlocking parts to make a sentence convey an understandable thought.

Direct Objects

Catholic missionaries established the school.
The word missionaries *is the subject of this sentence. The missionaries acted through the verb* established. *What did they establish? They established a school. The word* school *is the direct object of this sentence.*

The **direct object** tells who or what receives the action done by the subject and expressed by the verb. Not every sentence has a direct object, but many verbs require one to complete their meaning. Such verbs are called *transitive verbs* from the Latin *trans-* meaning "across". A **transitive verb** carries action from the subject across to the direct object.

So if there is a direct object in a sentence, a subject is doing something to it. You can begin to think about direct objects by imagining sentences that express a vigorous action. Direct objects are in italics, verbs are in boldface.

Snopes **burned** *barns* all over the county.
William Faulkner **wrote** many *books.*
The Jets **beat** the *Colts* in famous Super Bowl III.

But some direct objects receive action that is not so vigorous.

The children **crossed** the *street*.

I **have read** that *story*.

We **heard** the distant *voice*.

In every example above, the verb is transitive. It reports an action done by the subject to the direct object.

A verb that does not carry action to a direct object is an **intransitive verb**. An intransitive verb reports action done by a subject, but it is not action done to anything. In the following sentences, the verbs are intransitive:

The ship **sank** within three hours after the collision.

Our dog **died** in the summer.

She **jogs** to keep fit.

In looking for direct objects in sentences, ask *what* or *whom* after the verb. The answer to the question will be the direct object.

The children crossed the street.
Crossed what? *Crossed the* street. *The word* street *is the direct object.*

She saw him at the beach.
Saw whom? *Saw* him. *The direct object is* him.

Indirect Objects

Many times a verb will report an action on a direct object and will tell for whom or for what the action is done. Someone may say, "My partner brought me a hamburger." The direct object is *hamburger,* which receives the action of the verb *brought.* But the purpose for the action is expressed by *me.* The hamburger was brought *for* me. So *me* is the indirect object. If you ask *to whom* (or *to what*) or *for whom* (or *for what*), you can find the indirect object. Indirect objects occur fairly infrequently and are usually used with verbs such as *give, ask, tell, sing,* and *wrote.*

He sang *me* a song.
He sang a song for whom? *The answer is* me. *The indirect object is* me.

I wrote *Amelie* a letter.
I wrote a letter to whom? *The answer is* to Amelie. Amelie *is the indirect object.*

The Miss Liberty celebration gave *us* pride in America.

Ask *the teacher* your question.

Jack told *George* the whole funny story.

Direct objects and indirect objects, like subjects, are generally nouns or pronouns, or they are word groups that act like nouns or pronouns. (See 5b-2 and 3.)

Complements

Complements complete descriptions of subjects and objects.

Subject complements are located on the other side of the verb from the subject and add to the description of the subject. The verb that joins a subject and its complement is called a *linking verb*. **A linking verb** does not express an action from subject to object; it links or joins a subject to some further description of itself not included in the subject.

The most common linking verbs are the "to be" verbs—*is*, *are*, *was*, and *were*. But there are many others. Observe the subject complements after the linking verbs in the following sentences.

My father is *a welder*.
Welder *describes the subject* father. *The subject and its complement are linked by the verb* is.

America looked *good* to me after my long absence.
Good *completes the meaning of the subject*, America, *by describing it. The verb* looked *links the subject and the subject complement.*

The university was *a large and frightening place*.

The parking permit was *a hunting license*.

I became *frustrated* when I could never find a parking place.

I was often *late* to class.

My professors were *impatient* with me for my tardiness.

Object complements come immediately after direct objects and help complete the description of the direct object by the verb. Object complements are always nouns or adjectives (see 5b-2 and 4), and they are never separated from the direct object by a comma.

She called me *a bonehead*.

She said I drove her *crazy*.

My aunt dyed her hair *blue*.

I liked my eggs *scrambled*.

He got all the answers *right*.

We shut the door *tight*.

Like subject complements, object complements add to the description of the object. Complements may be nouns, pronouns, or adjectives. (See 5b-2 and 4.)

Exercise 5.4   Write five sentences with subject complements and five sentences with object complements. Discuss your sentences in class or in small groups with other students to see if they agree with your understanding of these terms.

5b

Learn the basics of English grammar by becoming familar with the eight parts of speech.

The eight parts of speech are verbs, nouns, pronouns, adjectives, adverbs, conjunctions, prepositions, and interjections.

When we say that each word in English can be classified as a part of speech, we mean that it can do some things in a sentence but not other things.

Words are like actors, able to play some roles but not others. For example, an eighty-year-old man cannot play Peter Pan or Superman and convince his audience. But he can play King Lear or the grandfather in a television soap opera. In a similar way, every word plays at least one part of speech, and some words can play several parts, just as some actors can play several roles. For example, the word *act* can be a noun or a verb. If you say "The second act begins in five minutes," *act* is a noun. If you say "We act as if we know what we are doing," *act* is a verb.

But although a word may play two or even three parts of speech, no word can play all the parts, and some can play only one. You will puzzle people if you say "Her dog was much more act than mine." In this sentence, *act* tries to play the part of an adjective, and it cannot do the job. But you can add *-ive* to *act* and get the word *active*, which is an adjective and a different part of speech from *act*. Then you can say easily, "Her dog was much more active than mine."

You can classify words according to the function they perform in sentences. *Subject, predicate,* and *direct object* are classifications based on sentence function.

Or you can classify words according to their part of speech. *Noun, verb,* and *pronoun* are examples of classifications based on parts of speech. Sometimes the parts of speech and the parts of the sentence are called by the same word. A conjunction is both a part of speech and a part of a sentence. So is a preposition. But the classification is useful. In the following sentence, compare the two systems of classification.

December brought us icy streets and heavy snow.
We can classify the words in this sentence in two different ways, by the function each word performs in the sentence and by the part of speech each word plays. If we classify by function, December *is the subject,* brought *is the simple predicate,* us *is the indirect object,* icy *is an adjective,* streets *is a direct object, and* is *a conjunction,* heavy *is an adjective, and* snow *is a direct object. If you classify the words in the sentence as parts of speech,* December *is a noun,* brought *is a verb,* us *is a pronoun,* icy *is an adjective,* streets *is a noun, and* is *a conjunction,* heavy *is an adjective, and* snow *is a noun. Notice that we have some overlap between function and part of speech. The words* icy *and* heavy *function as adjectives within the sentence and as adjectives among parts of speech.*

Exercise 5.5   Fill in the blanks in the following sentences with any words that make sense. The word in parentheses at the end of each sentence tells you the part of speech that will go in the blank. But don't worry about that. Look at the names of the parts of speech, but use your own intuition to fill in the blanks. The exercise will prove that you have a feel for the parts of speech even if you don't readily come up with the names of them. You will then build your confidence as you study the other sentences. Later in this chapter, you will learn the names of the various parts of speech.

1. The dinosaurs _____ extinct millions of years ago. (verb)
2. Emma bought _____ a hamburger for lunch. (pronoun or noun)
3. The _____ broke on the car. (noun)
4. The leaves on the maple tree in the yard _____ red. (verb)
5. The English poet Coventry Patmore _____ many poems about young love. (verb)
6. "_____," he cried. "That hurt." (interjection)
7. The English troops retreated _____ from Lexington. (adverb)
8. Collecting guidebooks was _____ hobby. (pronoun)
9. I had to buy textbooks _____ supplies on the first day of the semester. (conjunction)
10. Alcohol is one of the _____ dangerous common drugs. (adverb)
11. He wanted me to stay, _____ I had to go. (conjunction)
12. Our arrival was delayed _____ we had a flat tire. (conjunction)
13. The _____ that he found in his driveway turned out to be stolen. (noun)
14. She welded the _____ to the bicycle. (noun)
15. Come _____ my house for the party. (preposition)
16. It rained all _____ the game. (preposition)

17. France _____ California produce some of the finest wines on earth. (conjunction)
18. The buffalo _____ the wide green plains of the West. (verb)
19. The _____ problem was how to buy a car without going into debt. (adjective)
20. The _____ bicycle is much more complicated than its ancestors. (adjective)
21. His father bought him a _____ coat for his birthday. (adjective)
22. We painted the house _____. (adjective)
23. The game turned into a _____. (noun)
24. The New York Mets began playing baseball _____ 1962. (preposition)

1 Verbs

Verbs report action, condition, or state of being.

Verbs are the controlling words in predicates, but verbs themselves are controlled by subjects in that the subject determines the person and number of its verb.

Verbs have three persons. In the **first person singular,** I speak of myself.

I love music.

I am tired of sitting at this computer.

I feel good.

I enjoy writing.

In the **first person plural,** we speak or write of ourselves:

We watched the movie last night.

We sing at the slightest excuse.

We like to go out together.

We used to be friends.

In the **second person singular and plural** (the forms are the same), you are addressed.

You told me the truth about him.

You look happy today.

You are going to England next year?

You have always loved cars.

You can do it.

In the **third person singular**, someone speaks or writes about somebody or something who is not being addressed.

He promised to do his share of the work.

He exploits people by his grin and his flattery.

She was taken in by him for a while.

She learned to mistrust him.

It is raining right now.

It makes Lucy feel good.

In the **third person plural**, someone speaks or writes about more than one person or about more than one object.

They tried to calm him down.

They walked along the beach.

They ate supper together.

They used to whistle at crossings, their steamy shout echoing across the night land.

The form of the verb changes according to the person and number of the subject. (See Chapter 20.) If a subject mentions only one thing, we say that it is *singular*. If it mentions more than one thing, we say that it is *plural*. "A dog" is singular. The plural form is "the dogs." Verbs must reflect these differences in subjects by having a singular or a plural form.

Verbs also show whether the action of the sentence is taking place now, took place in the past, or will take place in the future. Study the following chart.

	Singular	**Plural**
First person:	I read.	We read.
Second person:	You read.	You read.
Third person:	She reads.	They read.
First person:	I loosen.	We loosen.
Second person:	You loosen.	You loosen.
Third person:	It loosens.	They loosen.
First person:	I build.	We build.
Second person:	You build.	You build.
Third person:	He builds.	They build.

All the verbs in this chart are in the present tense. Notice that the only change that takes place is in the third person singular; a final -s is added to the common form of the verb. Most — but not all — verbs will add this -s in the third person singular.

Verbs must agree with the person of the subject. In the present tense the rule usually requires you to add an -s to the verb in the third person singular. In other tenses the rule usually means making a change in the helping verb.

I run   he runs

I am running   he *is* running

Helping Verbs and Verb Phrases

The final word in a verb phrase, that is, a verb combined with a helping verb, we call the *main verb.* The **main verb** carries the primary meaning of the verb phrase. In the following sentences, the verb phrases are underlined; HV appears over each helping verb; and MV appears over each main verb.

        HV HV   MV   HV MV
The plane will have left before we can get to the airport.

    HV HV   MV   HV MV
He had been walking for hours before he was found.

    HV MV
He is biking to Vermont from Boston.

     HV MV
They will arrive in time for the game.

                          HV   MV
Contrary to his opinion, he does not have any imagination.

            HV   HV MV
Cy Young has always been considered one of the best pitchers in baseball history.

Notice that on occasion words not part of the verb phrase come between the helping verb and the main verb, as in the last two sentences above. Neither *not* nor *always* is a verb. They are both adverbs. (See 5b-4.) Sometimes helping verbs come in clusters. Common helping-verb clusters are "used to," "are going to," "might be able to," "could have," "have to," "ought to," and "about to."

English is rich in helping verbs, though the helpers are not so numerous that you cannot easily memorize them. See how helping verbs change the sense of the main verb *build* in the following sentences.

They are building a house right now.

I used to build houses.

I am going to build a house next month.

People should build houses with sturdy materials.

Contrary to your expressed doubts, I do build houses.

They were about to build the house when the bank refused their application for a loan.

Sometimes particles are added to verbs. **Particles** are short words that never change their form no matter how the main verb changes. They sometimes look like other parts of speech, but they always go with the verb to add a meaning that the verb does not have by itself. Look at how a change in particles changes the meaning of the verb *made* in the following sentences.

5h

gr

Harry made *up* with Gloria.

He made *off* with my pen.

She made *out* her application.

She made *good* on her promise.

They made *over* the basement into a playroom.

The crowd made *way* for the President.

We made *back* our losses.

Sometimes other words come between the verb and its particle.

I always *looked* words *up* in the dictionary if I didn't know them.

Jack *put* me *up* in the spare room when I visited.

His enemies *made* Roscoe *out* to be a liar.

Time of Verbs

Verbs have three simple times, or *tenses*. (The word *tense* means "time.")

PRESENT: She works every day.

PAST: She worked yesterday.

FUTURE: She will work tomorrow.

You can form the simple past tense of most verbs by adding a final *-ed* to the common form of the present or a simple *-d* if the common form of the present ends in *-e*.

PRESENT: I *save* a little money every month.

The dogs in our neighborhood *bark* at night.

PAST: I *saved* a thousand dollars last year.

The dog next door *barked* all night long.

But many verbs in English are irregular. That is, the simple past tense is very different from the common form of the present.

PRESENT: We *grow* tomatoes every year on our back porch.

I *run* four miles every day.

PAST: We *grew* corn back in Iowa.

Coe *ran* the mile in three minutes and forty-six seconds in August 1981.

The future tense of verbs is always formed by adding *shall* or *will* to the common form of the present.

PRESENT: I often *read* in bed.

FUTURE: I *will read* you a story before bedtime.

See Chapter 20 for a full discussion of verbs.

Exercise 5.6   Underline the verb phrases in the following sentences. Include particles as part of the verb phrase. Write *HV* over the helping verbs and *MV* over the main verbs.

1. Nomads in Arabia are now wearing sunglasses.
2. Has she rebuilt the Jeep engine?
3. Fees rise every year at universities in America.
4. She ought to be here any minute.
5. We sent out for pizza every Saturday night.
6. Our friend Tom White has spent Thanksgiving with us for years.
7. They used up all the ribbons for the printer.
8. He was running after the car.
9. People are moving to California every day.
10. They made out their route to northern Burma.
11. Composition teachers have been using handbooks for years.
12. Mr. Tang might have stayed with us more than a year.
13. Carla has never answered his letter.
14. Could you find out their plans?

2 Nouns

Nouns are the names we use for people, places, animals, things, ideas, actions, states of existence, colors, and so forth.

In sentences, nouns serve as subjects, objects, and complements.

Common nouns name ordinary things. They are not capitalized unless they begin a sentence. Common nouns include the following words and thousands more.

profession, color, man, beauty, woman, democracy, philosophy, rope, students, desks, cattle, library, justice, baseball, music, geometry, synagogue, car, glove, showcases, horses, proficiency, ability, tension, glory, defeat, smell, house

Proper nouns are the names given to persons, places, and things to set them off from others in a group. The common noun "man" does not set an individual off as much as the proper noun "John" or "Mr. Wilcox." The common noun "building" does not set off as distinctly as the proper noun "The McGraw-Hill Building." Proper nouns are capitalized any time they are used. Proper nouns include the following and thousands more:

Germany, Department of Transportation, Greek Orthodox, Helen, Ms. Howard, General Dynamics, Belmont, Tennessee, Amtrak, Donald A. Stone, Frenchman, New York, Omaha

Compound nouns consist of two or more words that function as a unit. They include common nouns like *heartache, mother-in-law, father-in-law, great-grandmother,* and *world view.* Compound nouns may be proper nouns — *International Business Machines, Federal Bureau of Investigation, Suez Canal.*

How do you recognize nouns? Sometimes nouns reveal themselves by their endings. Words that end in *-ty, -tion, -sion, -or, -ism, -ist, -ment, -ness, -ship, -ture, -ance,* and *-ence* are usually nouns. But be careful! Some words with these endings may also be verbs.

Jackson made *mention* of you in his letter. (noun)

I hope you will *mention* my request to him. (verb)

One of the best tests for a noun is to see if you can put the article *a, an,* or *the* in front of it and still make sense in your sentence. For example, you can say, "He promised he would *mention* my request to his boss." But you cannot make sense by saying, "He promised he would *the mention* my request to his boss." So you know that *mention* in this sentence is not playing the part of a noun. But you can say, "Jackson made a mention of you in his letter." In this sentence, you know that *mention* is a noun.

Nouns can be singular or plural. You usually form the plural by adding *-s* or *-es*. (See 31c-1 and 2.)

Singular	Plural
nest	nests
dog	dogs
humanist	humanists
bush	bushes
church	churches

You can form the possessive of nouns by adding -'s or a simple apostrophe (') to show ownership or special relation.

Singular	Possessive
girl	girl's
guests	guests'
insect	insect's
neighbors	neighbors'

These qualities of plurality and possession can help you identify nouns in sentences. If you can make a word plural or make it show possession, it is a noun.

THREE TESTS FOR NOUNS

1. Use *a*, *an*, or *the* before the word.

Word	Test	a Noun?
book	the book	yes
injure	an injure	no

2. Make the word plural.

Word	Test	a Noun?
egg	eggs	yes
soon	soons	no

3. Make the word show possession.

Word	Test	a Noun?
child	the child's blanket	yes
criticize	the criticize's thing	no

Nouns function typically as subjects, objects, and complements. They may also be appositives. When a noun (and any words that modify it) follows another noun to describe or add information about the first noun, we call such a noun an *appositive*. The word *appositive* comes from an old French word that means "to set beside." In grammar, **appositives** are nouns set beside one another and referring to the same person, place, or thing. One of the nouns may be separated from the other by various modifiers.

Wilson hit to the first baseman, Bill Buckner
The words first baseman *and* Bill Buckner *refer to the same man. The name "Bill Buckner" is in apposition to "first baseman" because the two terms are placed next to each other.*

She loved her old car, a LaSalle.
The words car *and* LaSalle *refer to the same automobile. They are side by side in the sentence; so they are in apposition to one another.*

Elizabeth Blevins, an experienced marathoner, chased the purse snatcher until she saw a police car and got the officers to help her catch the exhausted young man.
The noun marathoner *and its modifiers* an *and* experienced *appear after the name* Elizabeth Blevins *to add information about the subject. The word group* "an experienced marathoner" *is in apposition to the name* Elizabeth Blevins.

Exercise 5.7   Write a short paragraph about something you did yesterday. Use nouns as subjects, objects, and complements. Try your hand at writing a noun in apposition to another noun.

3   Pronouns

Like nouns, pronouns serve as subjects, objects, and complements in sentences.

There are different kinds of pronouns, and we use them for different purposes.

Most pronouns stand for nouns and help us avoid the monotony of repeating the same noun over and over again. Without pronouns, we could not express some thoughts. We say this: "Lanier Smythe bought the house, measured it, drew up a floor plan for it, and then redesigned it. She hired a carpenter, but she did much of the labor herself, and at the end she had demonstrated her architectural talents to herself and anybody who cared to look."

Without pronouns, we would have to say something like this: "Lanier Smythe bought the house, measured the house, drew up a floor plan for the house, and then redesigned the house. Lanier Smythe hired a carpenter, but Lanier Smythe did much of the labor, and at the end Lanier Smythe had demonstrated Lanier Smythe's architectural talents to Lanier Smythe and to many others."

Such sentences would be unbearably dull, clumsy, and confusing. Without the use of the pronoun *anybody,* we could not even express the idea we find in the words "anybody who cared to look" in the first version.

Most pronouns refer to nouns that have already appeared in the text. In the sentence above, the name Lanier Smythe is a proper noun, and the word *she,* used several times later, is the pronoun. "Lanier Smythe" is therefore the *antecedent* of the pronoun *she.* In the same sentence, *house* is a noun antecedent of the pronoun *it.* Always be sure your readers know what nouns your pronouns stand for. Pronouns that lack a clear antecedent cause great confusion. Failure to have a clear antecedent is a little like making your readers shop in a supermarket where someone has torn all the labels off the cans.

gr

> "I've got it," he said. It moved slowly as he held it by the neck. We looked at it, and we all agreed that we had never seen anything like it before. It was ugly and big but sluggish and seemingly did not want to bite.

When we read a text like this one, we all immediately ask, "What is the *it?* " Until we know the antecedent to *it,* we don't know what is being talked about. Other cases of the missing antecedent may be a little easier to solve. But any time the antecedent is missing when we need it, our reading suffers, and we become confused and sometimes cross.

Personal pronouns are pronouns that refer to one or more persons. Personal pronouns include *I, you, he, she, it, we,* and *they.* (Personal pronouns may be classified according to case as either subjective, objective, or possessive. See Chapter 21.)

Indefinite pronouns do not require an antecedent. Though most pronouns refer to antecedent nouns, some pronouns may stand without an antecedent. Such pronouns let us make statements about a member of a group when we are unable to name which one we mean. They do stand for something, but what they stand for usually comes in a word, phrase, or clause *after* the pronoun in the sentence.

> *Everybody* in the room heard the crash.
>
> *Anything* you do to help will be appreciated.
> Everybody *in the first sentence above receives its meaning from the following phrase* "in the room." Anything *receives its meaning from the following clause* "you do to help."

Reflexive pronouns refer to the noun or pronoun that is the subject of the sentence. Reflexive pronouns can serve as direct or indirect objects to show that a subject is doing an action to itself.

She allowed *herself* no rest.

He loved *himself* more than he loved anyone else.

Intensive pronouns have the same form as reflexive pronouns. Intensive pronouns add a special emphasis to nouns and other pronouns.

I *myself* have often made that mistake.

President Harding *himself* played poker and drank whiskey in the White House at a time when the United States Constitution prohibited the sale and use of alcoholic drinks.

Reflexive and intensive pronouns have the same form; they always end in *-self.*

Demonstrative pronouns point out nouns or other pronouns that come after them. To see if a pronoun is demonstrative, see if you can imagine using it while pointing your finger at the noun it indicates.

That is the book I want.

This is the place.

These are my friends.

Are *those* the books you bought?

Relative pronouns join word groups containing a subject and verb to nouns or pronouns that the word groups describe. (Such word groups are called *clauses.* See 5d.) Some relative pronouns change their form depending upon their use in a sentence. (See Chapter 21.)

Dravot in Kipling's story was the man *who* would be king.
The words who would be king *describe the man by telling which man is meant.* Who *is a relative pronoun.*

The tools *that* I lost in the lake cost me a fortune to replace.

The doctor *whom* you recommended has been suspended for malpractice.

Possessive pronouns show possession or special relations.

She was *my* Aunt.

Our door is always unlocked.

Their cat sets off my allergies.

gr

The fault was *ours,* and the worst mistake was *mine.*

Your amplifier is driving me crazy.

His speciality was finding flaws in the work of others.

Interrogative pronouns (*who, which,* and *what*) introduce questions.

What courses are you taking?

Who kept score?

Which of the glasses is mine?

Here are the most common pronouns. Review them briefly and think of ways you might use them in sentences:

I, me, mine, myself, yourself, yourselves, we, our, ours, ourselves, you, yours, he, she, it, they, himself, herself, itself, themselves, his, hers, its, them, their, theirs, one, ones, oneself, everybody, anybody, anyone, everyone, that, this, which, who, whom, these, those, whoever, whichever, whomever

For a fuller discussion of pronouns, see Chapter 21.

Exercise 5.8   Fill in the blanks with any pronouns that make sense. See how many different pronouns you can use in each blank.

1. _____ always wanted to put a small motor on _____ hang glider.
2. _____ house is on the street next to _____ school.
3. _____ who can square-dance is welcome to _____ party.
4. The President _____ said he would be at the party.
5. _____ is in charge of _____ goat?
6. _____ must we do to pay _____ mechanic?
7. _____ of the parts must be replaced?
8. The snake was _____ , but I kept quiet when _____ was found on the couch of the adjoining apartment.
9. "The most important principle in dancing," _____ told _____ "is to think of the music and not _____ feet."
10. When _____ drove the car through _____ kitchen window, the impact ruined _____ cake _____ happened to be in the oven at the time.
11. The movie was so bad that _____ left in the middle of it and told _____ waiting outside not to see _____ .
12. _____ magazine comes every Tuesday, and _____ immediately sits down and reads _____ .

13. He pointed to _____ broken rocks over there and said _____ were the cause of the shipwreck.
14. Divers _____ go down deep in the ocean must be careful to avoid nitrogen poisoning in their blood when _____ rise to the surface again.
15. The potato, _____ came originally from the New World, became a primary food in Ireland, _____ was a poor country.
16. We built the house _____ and saved thousands of dollars, but the effort cost _____ hundreds of hours of labor and devoured _____ time.
17. _____ in the stadium could have won the lottery.
18. _____ who plays baseball well is not necessarily a fine athlete.
19. You can take _____ you want.
20. Tell _____ that _____ should feed and water _____ unicorn every day.

5b

gr

4   Adjectives, Articles, and Adverbs

Adjectives and adverbs add qualities to other words.

They describe other words more fully or more definitely. Adjectives and adverbs **modify** other words; that is, they change, expand, limit, or otherwise help describe the words to which they relate. You can sometimes recognize adjectives and adverbs because they have **comparative** or **superlative forms,** that is, forms that indicate degree. Take the adjective *large,* for example.

>   Positive degree: She owned a *large* hat.
>
>   Comparative degree: Her hat was *larger* than mine.
>
>   Superlative degree: She owned the *largest* hat in the theatre.
> *One object is* large; *between two, one is* larger; *among three or more, one is* largest.

And here is the adverb *sadly.*

>   Positive degree: My visitors said goodbye *sadly.*
>
>   Comparative degree: They spoke *more sadly* than I did.
>
>   Superlative degree: I spoke *most sadly* when they told me they had decided not to leave.
> *When no degrees of "speaking sadly" are being compared, we use the simple adverb* sadly. *But when two degrees of speaking sadly are being compared, we have to say "more sadly." When more than two degrees or kinds of speaking sadly are being compared, we have to say "most sadly" of the greatest.*

Adjectives

Adjectives modify nouns and pronouns. That is, they help describe nouns and pronouns in a sentence, giving those words qualities that they do not have by themselves. See how different adjectives change the meanings in the following sentences:

The *pale* sun shone through the *gloomy* clouds.
The *bright* sun shone through the *white* clouds.
The *scalding* sun shone through the *thin* clouds.

Adjectives may be located immediately before or immediately after the words they modify, although they usually come before.

The *tired, thirsty,* and *impatient* horse threw its rider and went back to the barn.
The horse, *tired, thirsty,* and *impatient,* threw its rider and went back to the barn.

An adjective modifying the subject of a sentence sometimes appears on the opposite side of a linking verb from the subject.

The horse looked *tired, thirsty,* and *impatient.*
My friend was *late,* and I was *worried.*

In describing nouns, adjectives answer a number of questions: Which one? What kind? How many? What size? What color? What condition? Whose?

Which one? *That* man was the murderer.
What kind? The *dead* leaves clung to the *old* tree.
How many? The train had *six* cars.
What size? The *tall* building is Holyoke Center.
What color? The *brown* grass showed that we needed rain.
What condition? *Sick* people often have no energy.
Whose? *My* coat is the one with the rip in the sleeve.

A TEST FOR ADJECTIVES

Ask *"Which one?" "What kind?" "How many?" "What size?" "What color?" "What condition?" "Whose?"* A word that answers one of these questions is an **adjective.**

One small child lingered on the empty playground while the hard rain hammered down on the black pavement.

One	*small*	child
How many?	What size?	
lingered on the	*empty* playground while the	*hard*
	What condition?	What kind?
rain hammered down on	the	*black* pavement.
		What color?

5b

gr

The articles *a*, *an*, and *the* function as adjectives, but they lack the power of description we find in other adjectives.

The articles *a* and *an* are indefinite and singular; they call attention to one of several things without being particular about which one.

He sent me *a* card.
There are many different cards; he sent me one. The sentence does not say which of the many he sent.

Richard III cried, "*A* horse, *a* horse, my kingdom for *a* horse"
Any horse would do; the king did not have any special horse in mind.

The article *a* appears before words that begin with a consonant sound. The article *an* appears before words that begin with a vowel sound.

a dish, a rose, a year, an apple, an entreaty, an hour, an ideal, an enemy, a friend, an umbrella, a union, an understanding

Notice that many English words that begin with the vowel *u* sound as if they begin with the consonant *y*; these words are preceded by *a*:

a university, a union, a united land

The word *Europe* begins with the vowels *eu* that also has the sound *y*. So we speak of "*a* Europe at peace" or "*a* European in America." A few English words that begin with the consonant *h* have a vowel sound and are preceded by *an*.

an hour, an honest man, an honor, an honorable schoolboy

The article *the* is used with both singular and plural nouns. It always denotes a definite noun. It always means "this and not any other." Often the difference between using *a* or *an* and using *the* depends on the writer's idea of how specific the following noun is.

He came down off *the* mountain and found *the* road.
The writer has a particular mountain and a particular road in mind, and no other mountain and no other road will do.

He came down off *a* mountain and found *a* road.
The use of the indefinite a seems to show that the writer does not know or care what mountain the man descended or what road he found. Maybe the man himself didn't know. Something else about the sentence is much more important to the writer than naming the mountain or locating the road.

Adverbs

Adverbs add shades of meaning to words or sentence elements that cannot be modified by adjectives.

Since adjectives can modify only nouns and pronouns, adverbs are left to modify anything else in the sentence that can be modified. They most commonly modify verbs, adjectives, and other adverbs, but they sometimes modify prepositions, phrases, clauses, and even whole sentences (see 22b and c).

Adverbs answer several questions. Study each of the sentences below. The question the adverb answers is in parentheses at the end of the sentence. The adverbs are in boldface.

He **cheerfully** gave up the money. (How?)

Sometimes I wonder what she means. (How often?)

I **intensely** dislike having to look for a parking place. (To what degree?)

Odysseus, following the defeat of Troy, turned **homeward.** (Where?)

Yesterday I took my last exam. (When?)

--- **A TEST FOR ADVERBS** ---

Ask *"How?" "How often?" "To what degree?" "Where?" "When?"* A word that answers one of these questions to describe a verb, an adjective, or another adverb is an **adverb.**

Afterward she stood	*there*	*very*	*quietly.*
When?	Where?	To what degree?	How?

Adverbs may modify by affirmation:

He will *surely* call home before he leaves.

They may also modify by negation. *Not* is always an adverb.

They shall *not* pass.
We will *never* see anyone like her again.

Many adverbs end in *-ly,* and you can make adverbs of most adjectives simply by adding *-ly* to the adjective form.

Adjective	Adverb
large	largely
crude	crudely
beautiful	beautifully

But beware! A great many words that may function as adverbs do not end in *-ly.*

> often, sometimes, then, when, anywhere, anyplace, somewhere, somehow, somewhat, yesterday, Sunday, before, behind, ahead, seldom

And many adjectives end in *-ly.* Here are just a few examples:

> costly, stately, lowly, homely, measly, manly, womanly

In addition to their roles as modifiers, some adverbs also can serve to connect ideas logically between clauses. These are the **conjunctive adverbs,** words and phrases like *accordingly, consequently, hence, however, indeed, meanwhile, moreover, nevertheless, on the other hand,* and *therefore.* (See 17e.)

Descartes said, "I think; therefore I am."

He opposed her before she won the primary election; however, he supported her afterwards in her campaign.

Swimming is an excellent exercise for the heart and for the muscles; medical researchers have discovered, *on the other hand,* that swimming does not strengthen the bones as jogging and biking do.

Unlike *coordinating conjunctions* (see 4b-5), conjunctive adverbs cannot bind clauses together. If you use one of the conjunctive adverbs between clauses, you must also use a semicolon or a period. This rule makes it easy to tell a conjunctive adverb from a coordinating conjunction. Conjunctive adverbs may shift positions within a clause:

CLAUSES JOINED BY A COORDINATING CONJUNCTION:
Swimming is an excellent exercise for the heart and for the muscles, *but* medical researchers have discovered that swimming does not strengthen the bones as jogging and biking do.

CLAUSES JOINED BY A CONJUNCTIVE ADVERB: Swimming is an excellent exercise for the heart and for the muscles; *on the other hand,* medical researchers have discovered that swimming does not strengthen the bones as jogging and biking do.
In the first example, the coordinating conjunction but joins two independent clauses with the help only of a comma. In the second example, the conjunctive adverb "on the other hand" must have the stronger help of a semicolon to join the two independent clauses.

The best test for an adverb is to find what it modifies and then to ask yourself the adverb questions. If a modifier does not help describe a noun, a pronoun, or some other noun substitute, it has to be an adverb. If it does modify a noun, a pronoun, or some other noun substitute, it cannot be an adverb.

Exercise 5.9   In the following sentences, underline the adverbs and draw a circle around the adjectives.

1. He walked the dog happily down the moonlit street at a few minutes past midnight, unaware that hostile eyes were watching him from a darkened window in a house everyone thought was empty.
2. Solar heat offers many advantages to homeowners who want to save money in the long run; but in the short run solar heat is expensive because both the equipment and its installation have high costs.
3. The Japanese planes roared swiftly in over the battleships at Pearl Harbor early in the morning of Sunday, December 7, 1941, when most of Honolulu and most of the sailors on the ships were sound asleep.
4. Handbooks are valuable instruments for sharpening your knowledge of grammar and writing, but they cannot serve you well unless you truly want to write well and work hard to improve.
5. I learned to appreciate Hebrew by hearing our cantor sing during the Sabbath services on Friday nights, but I went for years and never understood exactly what the songs meant because I did not know the language well enough.

5 Conjunctions

Conjunctions join elements within a sentence.

These elements may be words, or they may be groups of words like clauses or phrases. (See 5d-1 and 2.)

Coordinating conjunctions (or, simply, **coordinators**) join elements of equal weight or function. The common coordinating conjunctions are *and, but, or, for,* and *nor.* Some writers now include *yet* and *so* among the coordinating conjunctions.

She was tired *and* happy.

The town was small *but* pretty.

The road was steep, rough, *and* winding.

They must be tired, *for* they have climbed all day long.

You may take the green *or* the red.

He would not leave the table, *nor* would he stop insulting his host.

Correlative conjunctions — that is, conjunctions used in pairs — also connect sentence elements of equal value. The familiar correlatives are *both . . . and, either . . . or, neither . . . nor,* and *not only . . . but also.*

Neither the doctor *nor* the police believed his story.

The year 1927 was *not only* the year Lindbergh flew solo nonstop across the Atlantic *but also* the year Babe Ruth hit sixty home runs.

Subordinating conjunctions (or **subordinators**) join dependent or subordinate sections of a sentence to independent sections or to other dependent sections. (See 5d-2.) The common subordinating conjunctions are *after, although, as, because, before, if, rather than, since, that, unless, until, when, whenever, where, wherever,* and *while.* There are several others.

The stylus will not track records *if* there is not enough weight on it.

Although the desert may look barren and dead, a vigorous life goes on there.

He always wore a hat *when* he went out in the sun.

Stories about divorce are common on television and in the movies *because* so many Americans have been divorced.

For the use of coordinators and subordinators to improve your writing, see Chapter 7.

6   Prepositions

Prepositions are short words that never change their form. When followed by a noun or pronoun, they form a prepositional phrase.

They unite a noun or pronoun into a prepositional phrase. The noun or pronoun is the object of the preposition, and the prepositional phrase gives to the noun or the pronoun the sense of an adverb or adjective.

> Suburban yards now provide homes *for wildlife* that once lived only *in* the *country.*
>
> *The preposition* for *relates the object* wildlife *to the noun* homes; *the preposition* in *relates the object* country *to the verb* lived.

The preposition, its noun, and any modifiers attached to the noun make up a **prepositional phrase.** Prepositional phrases act as adjectives and adverbs. The main function of prepositions is to allow nouns and pronouns to modify other words in the sentence. Here are the common prepositions:

about	beyond	on
above	by	over
across	despite	since
after	down	through
against	during	to
along	except	toward
amid	excluding	under
among	following	underneath
as	from	until
at	in	up
before	including	upon
behind	inside	via
below	into	with
beneath	like	within
beside	near	without
between	of	

Some prepositions consist of more than one word:

according to	except for	instead of
along with	in addition to	on account of
apart from	in case of	up to
as to	in front of	with regard to

because of	in place of	with reference to
by means of	in regard to	
by way of	in spite of	

Prepositions usually come before their objects. But sometimes, especially in questions, they do not. Grammarians debate whether or not prepositions should end a sentence. Most writers favoring an informal style will now and then use a preposition to end a sentence.

> Which lake does she live *by?*
> *Compare "By which lake does she live?" This choice is more formal.*
> His frequent complaining is hard to put up *with.*
> *The idiom "to put up with" ends in a preposition and, to most people, sounds natural here. You could rewrite the sentence: "It is hard to put up with his frequent complaining." Or "I find it hard to put up with his frequent complaining." But what you gain in formality (the preposition no longer ends the sentence), you lose in emphasis. "His frequent complaining" is the most important information in the sentence and belongs first. In this sentence, you might choose to change the wording: "His frequent complaining is hard to tolerate." Whether one chooses this option depends on the taste of the writer.*

Many words used as prepositions can be used as other parts of speech. They also often serve as adverbs or as subordinating conjunctions.

> He arrived *after* midnight.
> *The preposition* after *introduces a prepositional phrase with an adverbial sense modifying the verb* arrived.
> Jill came tumbling *after.*
> *Here,* after *is a simple adverb.*
> *After* Jack broke his crown, Jill fell down, too.
> After *is a subordinating conjunction.*

7   Interjections

Interjections are forceful expressions, usually written with an exclamation point, though mild ones may be set off with commas.

They are not used often in formal writing except in quotations of dialogue.

| Hot dog! | Wow! |
| Ouch! | Hooray! |

"Wow!" Davis said. "Are you telling me that there's a former presidential adviser who hasn't written a book? Hot dog!"

A journalist covering Davis's remarks might quote the interjections Davis used. But the journalist would not use such words in the body of his or her own text.

8   Words can play different parts of speech.

Always remember that the same word may be used for several different parts of speech in different sentences or in different parts of the same sentence. How the word is used will determine what part of speech it is.

The *light* drizzle foretold heavy rain. (adjective)
The *light* glowed at the end of the pier. (noun)
As you *light* the candle, say a prayer. (verb)

The cobra glided *outside*. (adverb)
The child played on the *outside*. (noun)
The mongoose waited *outside* the house. (preposition)
The famous *outside* linebacker was terrified at this scene. (adjective)

When will he come home? (adverb)
He will come *when* he is ready. (conjunction)
They decided the where and the *when* immediately. (noun)

Exercise 5.10   Write original sentences in which you use each word below according to the directions. Use a dictionary when you need assistance. The dictionary will always show the various ways words are used, and it will often give examples that will help you create sentences of your own.

1. Use *jump* as a noun, a verb, and an adjective.
2. Use *beyond* as an adverb, a preposition, and a noun.
3. Use *after* as an adverb, a preposition, and a conjunction.
4. Use *book* as a noun, a verb, and an adjective.
5. Use *lapse* as a noun and a verb.
6. Use *effect* as a noun and a verb.
7. Use *honor* as a noun, a verb, and an adjective.

5c

Learn to recognize the grammatical structure of familiar sentence patterns.

You have already seen how important sentence patterns are in our language. We learn to talk not by studying grammar but by hearing patterns in action and then learning to use these patterns to make "sentence sense." The chart below illustrates the most typical sentence patterns.

Pattern 1 **Subject** **+ Verb**

We	laughed.
The flowers	bloomed.
The house	was destroyed.

Pattern 2 **Subject + Verb + Direct object**

Ann	used	the jackhammer.
Dickens	wrote	*David Copperfield.*
She	told	the story.

Pattern 3 **Subject** **+ Verb** **+ Subject complement**

Our house	was	large and cold.
He	looked	good.
The crowd	became	noisy.
The contract	seemed	fair.

Pattern 4 **Subject + Verb** **+ Direct object + Object complement**

They	called	Lindbergh	a fool.
He	named	his son	John.

Pattern 5 **Subject + Verb + Indirect object + Direct object**

Lee	gave	Longstreet	the orders.
Smoke	gives	me	a headache.

The basic patterns of sentences can be rearranged in many different ways.

Subject complement + Verb   + Subject

Fair   lie   the fields of England.

Direct object   + Subject + Verb

These bones   he   removed.

5d

Learn the difference between phrases and clauses.

A **phrase** is a group of related words without a subject and a predicate. In sentences, all phrases can play the role of a part of speech—usually a verb, an adjective, an adverb, or a noun.

> They *were watching* the game. (verb phrase)
>
> The child ran *into the lake.* (prepositional phrase acting as an adverb)
>
> The yellow penalty flag *on the fifty-yard line* lay there silently while the fans cheered hysterically for the 109-yard punt return and while the halfback danced in the end zone, waving the football over his head. (prepositional phrase acting as an adjective)
>
> *Grinning happily,* she made a three-point shot. (participial phrase acting as an adjective)
>
> *To succeed in writing,* you must be willing to revise again and again. (infinitive phrase acting as an adverb)
>
> *Diving for treasure* is sometimes dangerous. (gerund phrase acting as a noun)
>
> He *might have survived* if he had sat down at once when he knew he was lost and had started a fire. (verb phrase)

A **clause** is a group of grammatically related words containing both a subject and a predicate. Clauses may be independent or dependent. An **independent clause** can usually stand by itself as a complete sentence. A **dependent,** or **subordinate, clause** often cannot stand by itself because it is introduced by a subordinating conjunction or a relative pronoun and therefore the clause alone does not make sense. But the main test for a dependent clause is to see if it serves as a noun, an adjective, or an adverb within another clause. (For a further discussion of nouns, adjectives, and adverbs, see 5b-1, 2, and 4.) An independent clause does not serve as a part of speech in another clause.

She ran in the marathon because she wanted to test herself.
The independent clause "She ran in the marathon" can stand by itself as a complete sentence. The dependent clause "because she wanted to test herself" cannot stand by itself. The independent clause does not serve as a part of speech for another clause. The dependent clause serves as an adverb modifying the verb ran *in the independent clause, answering a question adverbs can answer: "Why did she run?"*

She said she felt exhausted after fifteen miles.
The independent clause "She said" cannot stand by itself as a complete sentence. But it is an independent clause because it does not serve as a part of speech for another clause. The dependent clause "she felt exhausted after fifteen miles" can stand by itself as a complete sentence. But it is a dependent clause because it serves as a noun and a direct object for another clause. What did she say? She said she felt exhausted after fifteen miles. You can test dependent clauses like this one to see if the subordinator that *will go before the clause. (She said* that *she felt exhausted after fifteen miles.)*

They took what they could find.
The independent clause is "They took." The dependent clause, "what they could find," serves as a noun and as the direct object for the independent clause.

When we had done everything possible, *we left the wounded to the enemy.*
The independent clause is "we left the wounded to the enemy." The dependent clause is "When we had done everything possible." It serves as an adverb modifying the verb left.

1   Learn to identify various types of phrases.

The following list includes the various kinds of phrases that you may find in English sentences.

Prepositional Phrases

Prepositional phrases (see 5b-6) always begin with a preposition and always end with a noun or pronoun that serves as the object of a preposition. The noun or pronoun in the phrase can then help to describe something else in the sentence. A prepositional phrase generally serves as an adjective or an adverb in the sentence where it occurs.

The tree *in the yard* is an oak.
The prepositional phrase "in the yard" is an adjective modifying the noun tree. *Which tree?* The tree in the yard.

He arrived **before breakfast.**
The prepositional phrase is an adverb modifying the verb arrived.
When did he arrive? Before breakfast.

To identify an adjective prepositional phrase or an adverb prepositional phrase, use the same tests that you used for simple adjectives and adverbs. (See 5b-4.) If the prepositional phrase answers one of these questions, it probably serves as an adjective: Which one? What kind? How many? What size? What color? What condition? If the prepositional phrase answers one of these questions, it probably serves as an adverb: How? How often? To what degree? Where? When? Because phrases (and clauses) that function as adverbs often tell why, be sure to add *why?* to your list of questions.

Ditmars's book *about North American snakes* sold well *because of its outstanding photographs.*
Which of Ditmars's books? The one about North American snakes. *The phrase is an adjective modifying the noun subject* book. *Sold well why?* Because of its outstanding photographs. *The phrase is an adverb modifying the verb* sold.

Without prepositions and prepositional phrases, we could not express many simple thoughts. The prepositional phrases in the following sentences are in boldface.

They sat **on the grass.**

She sat **at her desk.**

In both these sentences, the prepositional phrases function as adverbs, modifying the verbs. The prepositional phrase "on the grass" in the first sentence answers the adverb question *Where?* Where did they sit? No adverb in English can answer the question so that you know they sat on the grass. You cannot say, "They sat grassly." The same is true of the adverb question *Where?* in the second sentence. You can't say, "She deskly sat." But you *can* say, "She sat at her desk."

Similarly, when prepositional phrases are used as adjectives, they may relate a noun to the rest of the sentence in a way not possible for any adjective.

The road *over the mountain* was safer than the one *by the sea.*

If you say, "The mountain road was safer than the seaside road," you may not express the meaning you want, especially if you mean the road that crosses the mountain and not the one that runs along the mountain crests. But some prepositional phrases are almost exactly interchangeable with adjectives or adverbs.

ADJECTIVE: He lived in the *corner* house.

PREPOSITIONAL PHRASE: He lived in the house *on the corner.*

ADVERB: The child read the ancient map *easily.*

PREPOSITIONAL PHRASE: The child read the ancient map *with ease.*

Verbal Phrases

Verbals are words formed from verbs. But they do not function as verbs in sentences. There are three kinds of verbals—infinitives, participials, and gerunds. Verbals can stand alone as parts of speech, or they can have words attached to them to make a verbal phrase.

Infinitives and Infinitive Phrases

The infinitive of any verb except the verb *to be* is formed by putting the infinitive marker *to* before the common form of the verb in the first person present tense.

Verb	Infinitive
go	to go
make	to make

Infinitives and infinitive phrases function as nouns, adjectives, and adverbs. Here, too, the tests for adjectives and adverbs come in handy.

To finish his novel was his greatest ambition.
The infinitive phrase functions as a noun, the subject of the sentence.
He made many efforts *to finish his novel.*
The infinitive phrase functions as an adjective modifying the noun efforts. Which efforts? The efforts to finish his novel.
He rushed *to finish his novel.*
The infinitive phrase functions as an adverb modifying the verb rushed. Why did he rush? To finish his novel.

Participles and Participial Phrases

Participles are made from verbs. **Present participles** suggest some continuing action. **Past participles** suggest completed action. The present participle of verbs is formed by adding *-ing* to the common present form of the verb. The past participle is usually made by adding *-ed* to the common present form of the verb, but past participles are frequently irregular. That is, some past participles are not formed by adding -ed but rather by changing the root of the verb.

I have *biked* five hundred miles in two weeks.
The past participle of the regular verb bike *is formed in the regular way by adding* -d *to the root form of the verb.*

I have *driven* five hundred miles in a morning.
The past participle of the irregular verb drive *is formed by adding* -n *to the root form of the verb.*

Because they do represent action, participles can be used in many different ways. They can be used as part of a verb phrase to indicate action done by a subject. But when they are used in other sorts of phrases, they take on other kinds of meaning.

Creeping through heavy traffic, the messenger on the bike yelled angrily at pedestrians.
The present participial phrase modifies messenger *and serves as an adjective. The action of creeping here could be expressed in this sentence: "The* creeping *messenger on his bike yelled angrily at pedestrians."*

Insulted by the joke, the team walked out of the banquet.
The past participial phrase modifies team *and serves as an adjective. The* insulted *team walked out of the banquet.*

Drawn down to the highway by the lights, the deer stood helplessly in the road.
The past participial phrase modifies deer *and serves as an adjective. Though it would not be good style, you could say, "The drawn-down-to-the-highway-by-the-lights deer stood helplessly in the road."*

Gerunds and Gerund Phrases

The **gerund** is simply the present participle used as a noun. The **gerund phrase** includes any words and phrases attached to the gerund so that the whole serves as a noun.

Walking is one of life's great pleasures.
The gerund is the subject of the verb is.

Walking swiftly an hour a day will keep you fit.
The gerund phrase is the subject of the verb phrase will keep.

She praised his *typing*.
The gerund typing *serves as a noun and as the direct object of the verb* praised.

He worked hard at *typing the paper*.
The gerund phrase is the object of the preposition at.

Absolute Phrases

An **absolute phrase** is made by attaching a noun or a pronoun to a participle without a helping verb. Remember: a helping verb would make the participle part of a verb phrase.

> *Her body falling nearly a hundred miles an hour,* she pulled the rip cord, and the parachute opened with a heavy jerk.
> The storm came suddenly, *the clouds boiling across the sky.*

The absolute phrase modifies the whole sentence in which it appears. That is, absolute phrases do not modify any particular words or word groups in the way that participial phrases do.

> *Falling nearly a hundred miles an hour,* she pulled the rip cord, and the parachute opened with a heavy jerk.
> *By removing the noun* body *and its modifier,* her, *we turn the absolute phrase into an adjective participial phrase modifying* she.

Exercise 5.11   Write sentences using the following phrases.

1. was leaving (verb phrase)
2. on the head (prepositional phrase)
3. the train having arrived (absolute phrase)
4. to use a computer (infinitive phrase)
5. lying in the dark (participial phrase)

Exercise 5.12   Identify the clauses in each of the following sentences. Tell whether each clause is dependent or independent.

Example

> When he was a pilot on the Mississippi River in his youth, Samuel Clemens learned the lore of the people along its banks.
> *The first clause is "When he was a pilot on the Mississippi River in his youth." It is dependent. The second clause is "Samuel Clemens learned the lore of the people along its banks." It is independent.*

1. Before she set out on the Appalachian Trail, she had to buy a good backpack.
2. Movies are often made from successful novels.

3. Although Americans feel nostalgic about trains, they don't ride them very often.
4. When knighthood was in flower, life was bloody and short.
5. Women now do many things that society prevented them from doing only a few years ago.
6. In college football, the running game is more important than it is in the pros.
7. Soccer is a coming sport in the United States because it is much cheaper and safer to play than high school football.
8. The state of Texas has decided that high school athletes must pass all their academic work if they are to play sports.
9. George Armstrong Custer and the Seventh Cavalry perished because they attacked a village where thousands of Indian braves were ready to fight.
10. Medical evidence has been building up for years to prove that cigarette smoking causes lung cancer and heart disease.

5d

gr

Exercise 5.13   Identify the phrases in boldface in the following sentences. Tell what kind of phrase each one is and how it is used in the sentence.

1. The sheriff entered the bar, **his hands hovering over his pistols.**
2. "Where is that cat?" he shouted, **his eyes darting around the room.**
3. **Whispered softly and urgently,** the question was passed along the bar.
4. **Opening the door softly,** the cat walked into the room.
5. **Over the barroom** a great hush fell as the sheriff and the cat stared at each other.
6. The sheriff wiped his eyes **to see better.**
7. "Time's up for you, cat," the sheriff shouted **in the great, expectant silence.**
8. **Licking his fur indifferently and sitting down,** the cat seemed to nod behind the sheriff.
9. **Frightened and dismayed,** the sheriff looked behind him.
10. A thousand cats were softly padding **through the open door.**

2   Learn the basic kinds of clauses and their uses.

Unlike phrases, clauses have subjects and predicates. Clauses may be independent or dependent. Sometimes we call independent clauses *main clauses* and dependent clauses *subordinate clauses.*

An **independent clause** can usually stand on its own as a complete sentence. A dependent clause cannot. A dependent clause always acts as a part of speech for another clause; an independent clause never serves as a part of speech for another clause.

> *He swam across the lake* after the sun set.
> *The independent clause* "He swam across the lake" *can stand grammatically as a complete sentence. The dependent clause* "after the sun set" *does not make complete* "sentence sense" *by itself. It must be connected to an independent clause.*

> *He claimed* that he swam across the lake after the sun set.
> "He claimed" *is an independent clause. But* claimed *is a transitive verb and must take a direct object. (See 5a-2.) So* "He claimed" *cannot stand alone as a sentence. It is an independent clause because it does not play the role of a part of speech for another clause. The dependent clause* "that he swam across the lake" *serves as a noun that acts as the direct object of the verb* claimed. *The dependent clause* "after the sun set" *serves as an adverb for the verb* swam *in the previous dependent clause.*

A practical way to recognize dependent clauses is to see if they are introduced by a subordinating word or group of words. (See 5b-5 and 7b-1.) **Dependent clauses** are subordinate to other clauses. That is, a dependent clause serves another clause as an adjective, an adverb, or a noun. The subordinator tells you that the clause to follow is to serve another clause.

> I am going to bed *because I am tired.*
> *The subordinator* because *tells us that the clause in which it appears serves another clause. In this sentence, the subordinate clause* "because I am tired" *serves as an adverb (see 5b-4) in the clause* "I am going to bed." *Why am I going to bed? Because I am tired.*

Here are some of the subordinating conjunctions that may introduce a subordinate or dependent clause:

after, although, as, because, before, if, once, since, that, though, till, unless, until, when, whenever, where, wherever, while, as if, as soon as, as though, even after, even if, even though, even when, for as much as, in order that, in that, so that, sooner than

Some subordinators are relative pronouns:

what, which, who, whom, whose, that

The subordinators *that* and *which* are sometimes left out of sentences before dependent clauses. In the following sentences, the dependent clauses are in boldface, and the subordinator has been omitted.

Many poor people in Latin America believe **they can gain dignity only by revolution.**

She said **she would enroll in evening school and work during the day.**

We thought **the Mets might win the pennant this year.**

Dependent clauses always act as nouns, adjectives, or adverbs for another clause.

Noun Clauses

Noun clauses act as subjects, objects, and complements.

That English is a flexible language is both glory and pain.
The noun clause serves as the subject of the verb is.

He told me *that English is a flexible language.*
Here the noun clause is the direct object of the verb told.

His response was *that no response was necessary.*
The noun clause is the subject complement of the linking verb was.

Adjective Clauses

Adjective clauses modify nouns or pronouns; relative pronouns are used to connect them to the words they modify.

The contestant *whom he most wanted to beat* was his father.
The adjective clause modifies the noun contestant. *Which contestant? The contestant* whom he most wanted to beat. *The relative pronoun* whom, *which stands for its antecedent* contestant, *serves as the direct object of the infinitive* to beat. *Compare: "He most wanted to beat the contestant."*

The computer *that I wanted* cost too much money.
The adjective clause modifies the noun computer. *The relative pronoun* that *serves as the direct object of* wanted. *Compare: "I wanted the computer."*

The journey of Odysseus, *which can be traced today on a map of Greece and the Aegean Sea,* made an age of giants and miracles seem close to the ancient Greeks.
The adjective clause modifies journey. *The relative pronoun* which *serves as the subject of* can be traced.

Adverbial Clauses

Adverbial clauses serve as adverbs, usually modifying the verb in another clause. Adverbial clauses are often introduced by the subordinators *after, when, before, because, although, if, though, whenever, where,* and *wherever,* as well as by many others.

After we had talked for an hour, he began to look at his watch.
The adverbial clause modifies the verb began. *Began when?* After we had talked for an hour.

If you learn to type, writing will be less of a chore.
The adverbial clause modifies the verb phrase "will be."

Although he loved to cook, he hated to clean up the kitchen afterward.
The adverbial clause modifies the verb hated.

He reacted as swiftly *as he could.*
The adverbial clause modifies the adverb swiftly.

The desert was more yellow *than he remembered.*
The adverbial clause modifies the adjective yellow.

5d

gr

Exercise 5.14   Write sentences using the following dependent clauses. Tell whether you make each an adjective, an adverb, or a noun.

1. because we were afraid
2. when he saw the elephant
3. as soon as she could
4. after she had won the state lottery
5. although he wrecked the car
6. where the dinosaur bones were found
7. wherever she drew the plans
8. before the fire started
9. though the night had long since fallen
10. if she would turn down her radio

3   Learn to identify sentences as simple, compound, complex, or compound-complex.

It will not necessarily make you a better writer to know whether a sentence is simple or compound or whatever it is. But by studying this section, you will be able to understand some things about the structure of language and the structure of your own writing that may help you think better about what you are doing. If your writing teacher says, "You are using too many simple sentences in your papers," you will have to know what a simple sentence is. Reviewing this section may also help you add some variety to your writing as you think more precisely about your own style.

The Simple Sentence

A **simple sentence** contains only one clause, and that clause is independent, able to stand alone grammatically. A simple sentence may have several phrases. It may have a compound subject or a compound verb. It can even have both a compound subject and a compound verb. But it can have only one **clause**—one subject and one verb that combine to make a clear statement. The following are simple sentences.

Large land reptiles have been unable to evolve in the presence of large land mammals.

The bloodhound is the oldest known breed of dog.

Each sentence is simple; each contains only one independent clause and no dependent clause.

He staked out a plot of high ground in the mountains, cut down the trees, and built his own house with a fine view of the valley below.

The verbs staked, cut, *and* built *make a compound predicate for the subject,* he. *But the sentence has only one independent clause and no dependent clauses.*

Historians, novelists, short-story writers, and playwrights write about characters, design plots, and usually seek the dramatic resolution of a problem.

The LaSalle, the DeSoto, and the Pierce Arrow once flourished as American automobiles but then, like dinosaurs meeting a new climate, declined and finally became extinct.

Though these sentences are both fairly complicated, they are both simple sentences because each has only one clause.

Singing, brawling, shouting, laughing, crying, and clapping every moment, the fans turned out every night hungry for a pennant.

Despite its numerous phrases, this sentence has only one clause— naturally, an independent clause. So it is grammatically a simple sentence.

The Compound Sentence

A **compound sentence** contains two or more independent clauses, usually joined by a comma and a coordinating conjunction—*and, but, nor, or, for, yet,* or *so.* A compound sentence does not contain a dependent clause. Sometimes the independent clauses are joined by a semicolon, a dash, or a colon. The following are compound sentences.

The sun blasted the earth, and the plants withered and died.

He asked directions at the end of every street—but he never listened to them.

The trees on the ridge behind our house begin to change in September: the oaks start to redden; the maples pass from green to orange; the pines become more dark.

A compound sentence may consist of a series of independent clauses joined by commas, with a conjunction before the last clause.

They searched the want ads, she visited real estate agents, he drove through neighborhoods looking for for-sale signs, and they finally located a house big enough for them and their cats.

The Complex Sentence

A **complex sentence** contains one independent clause and one or more dependent clauses. In the following sentences, the independent clause is in regular type, and the dependent clause is in boldface type.

He consulted the dictionary **because he did not know how to pronounce the word.**

She asked people **if they approved of what the speaker said.**

Although football players are reputed to be the most powerful athletes in team sports, the winners of the World Series beat the winners of the Super Bowl in a tug-of-war on network TV one year.

The Compound-Complex Sentence

A **compound-complex sentence** contains two or more independent clauses and at least one dependent clause. In the following sentences, boldface type indicates dependent clauses, and regular type indicates independent clauses.

She discovered a new world in historical fiction, but she read so much **that she had no time to write anything of her own.**

Although Carrie Nation may seem ridiculous in retrospect, her belief **that God had called her to break up saloons with her hatchet** was widely applauded in her time, and she influenced many Americans to vote for the prohibition amendment.

After Abraham Lincoln was killed, an angry and bewildered government could not determine **how many conspirators there were,** and **since John Wilkes Booth, the assassin, was himself soon shot and killed,** he could not clarify the mystery, **which remains to this day.**

Exercise 5.15 Classify the following sentences as simple (S), complex (CX), compound (CD), or compound-complex (CC).

1. The winter of 1542 was marked by the tempestuous weather throughout the British Isles: in the north, on the borders of Scotland and England, there were heavy snowfalls in December and frost so savage that by January the ships were frozen into the harbor at New-castle.

— ANTONIA FRASER

2. Prints, with woodblocks as the oldest form, began life humbly, not as works of art but as substitutes for drawings or paintings when multi-ples of a single image were needed, probably as long ago as the fifth century A.D. in China.

— JOHN CANADAY

3. The female belted kingfisher, distinguished by a rusty band across her breast, lays six to eight pure white eggs on a bed of sand or regurgitated fish bones.

— ALEXANDER WETMORE

4. Although America has some fine native cherries, some of the very best wild cherries to be found came originally from seedlings of cultivated varieties, and the birds have been the chief agents of scat-tering the seeds.

— EUELL GIBBONS

5. The notion of the painter as a sort of boon companion to the hangman is carried on by Leonardo, who was fond of attending executions, perhaps to study the muscular contortions of the hanged.

— MARY MCCARTHY

6. Once a month I would ride ten miles down the wretched mountain road to Winchester, go to confession, hear mass, and take commu-nion.

— WILLIAM ALEXANDER PERCY

7. Huey had found another issue that would help to move him along the path to the governorship.

— T. HARRY WILLIAMS

8. When he had eaten seven bananas, Mr. Biswas was sick, whereupon Soanie, silently crying, carried him to the back verandah.

— V. S. NAIPAUL

9. The people who developed the English language were more inter-ested in making distinctions between boats than they were in the differences between colors and feelings, not to speak of tastes and smells.

— WALTER KAUFMANN

10. Inside the tough-talking, hard-jogging man of 40 who is identified largely by his work, there is a boy trying not to cry, "Time is running out."

— GAIL SHEEHY

Exercise 5.16 Combine the following groups of sentences into complex, compound, or compound-complex sentences. You will often have to add conjunctions or relative pronouns. Sometimes you will want to delete some words. See how many combinations you can work out from each group.

1. A pitcher can throw a baseball faster than ninety miles an hour. Batters may be severely injured if they are hit. Every batter must wear a helmet at the plate.
2. Ultralight planes now swoop down valleys and soar over mountains. They are hardly more than hang gliders with engines. The engines are small. The ultralights may fly at thirty to forty miles an hour.
3. Orson Welles terrified America with his radio presentation of *War of the Worlds* in 1938. Hitler was pushing Europe into war. News bulletins regularly interrupted broadcasts. Welles made the program sound like a news broadcast. He made people think that Earth was being invaded from Mars.
4. The Mississippi Delta has some of the richest farmland in the world. It grows more cotton than any comparable area on earth. It was not thickly settled until after the Civil War. Mosquitoes gave people in the Delta yellow fever.
5. Almost a million accountants now work in the United States. The profession is still growing. Positions will increase by 30 percent over the next ten years. These figures have been reported by the Bureau of Labor Statistics.

CHAPTER SIX

Sentence Logic

Every sentence should make a statement that may be easily understood by readers. Short, simple sentences offer little difficulty:

> The world came to life at dawn.
>
> The Mets won the 1986 World Series.
>
> The snow fell softly all night long.

Such sentences clearly answer all or some of the five questions we ask when we read anything: Who? Where? What? When? Why? *What* came to life? The world. *What* happened? The world came to life. *When?* At dawn. *Who* won the 1986 World Series? The Mets. *What* did the Mets do? They won the 1986 World Series. *When?* 1986.

When we read any sentence, we look for answers to some of these questions. Any sentence must give us some of these answers if it is to tell us anything. Even when your sentences are long and complicated, you may simplify your thinking about them by asking which of these questions they answer. And sometimes you will see that you need to answer more of these questions than your sentence manages. What questions does the following sentence answer?

> To ride a horse into battle would have been to come to the field already prepared for flight, and such was against the Saxon battle ethic, which decreed that if a man's lord died on the field, he could not leave it alive.
>
> —JAMES BURKE

The most important question answered here is Why? Why *did Saxon warriors not fight on horseback? Because the horse offered a chance for flight, and the Saxon battle ethic made flight impossible. Who is this sentence about? The Saxon warrior who came to fight under the leadership of a lord. What are we talking about here? The custom of not riding a horse into battle.*

Few sentences will answer all five W questions. But every sentence must answer one or more of them clearly. If your sentence does not answer at least one of these questions, or if it gives a vague, weak, or confusing answer, you should rewrite it. Study the following sentence to see how many W questions it answers:

Every day meteorites plunge to Earth and add at least a quarter of a ton to our planet's mass.

—Roy A. Gallant

What are we talking about? Meteorites. *What happens?* They plunge *to earth and add at least a quarter of a ton to our planet's mass.* When? Every day.

In a clear sentence, we quickly see the interrelations of the questions the sentence answers. We feel uncomfortable when parts of a sentence do not answer related questions. What is going on here? Am I missing something? Questions like these confuse readers and then irritate them.

Born in Lincoln, Nebraska, my mother always loved potato chips.
The who *of this sentence is "my mother." The* what *is "loved potato chips." The* where *is "Lincoln, Nebraska." But what do these questions have in common? Does being born in Lincoln, Nebraska, make people love potato chips? The writer may have something in mind to connect the various pieces of information in this sentence. But as it stands, it consists of two apparently unrelated ideas. It tells* who — *"my mother." It tells* what — *"always loved potato chips." It tells* where — *"Lincoln, Nebraska." It tells* when — *"always." But it does not tell* why. *Why does being born in Lincoln, Nebraska, have anything to do with loving potato chips?*

Clarence, who learned to type when he was fifteen years old, had a ruddy complexion.
The sentence tells us who. *"Clarence." But it gives us two seemingly unrelated answers to the question* what? *Clarence learned to type when he was fifteen; he had a ruddy complexion. What do these answers have to do with each other?*

When you ask someone a direct question, you expect a coherent reply. When someone gives you several unrelated answers to the question, you are confused. You want a clear, logical, and direct answer. You want to understand as quickly as you can. Your sentences, answering questions for your readers, should give those answers as efficiently as possible.

6a

Prune away irrelevant details.

Unnecessary information may confuse your readers by blurring the central thought of your sentence. Everything in a sentence must support the central statement. In casual conversation, you might say something like this.

> Clifford Jenkins — you know, his brother runs the restaurant right next to the stadium where people regularly get food poisoning — well, Clifford took the opening kickoff and ran it back 103 yards for a touchdown.

But when you are writing, you must trim away irrelevant statements that enter your conversation.

> Substitute running back Clifford Jenkins ran the opening kickoff back 103 yards for a touchdown.

In the rapid writing of a first draft, you may throw in irrelevant details as you try to put down everything you know about a topic. When you revise, cut out these details so that everything in each of your sentences will contribute to the major statement you wish to make in it.

> **FIRST DRAFT:** *The Adventures of Huckleberry Finn,* by Mark Twain, who lectured widely in the United States and Great Britain, received only one review when it was published in 1884. *Why does Mark Twain's lecturing have anything to do with his book,* The Adventures of Huckleberry Finn?

> **REVISED:** *The Adventures of Huckleberry Finn,* by Mark Twain, received only one review when it was published in 1884.

Often you can revise a sentence so that all the details you throw into your first draft can be made to support the major purpose of the sentence:

> Although Mark Twain lectured widely in the United States and Great Britain and was well known to the public, *The Adventures of*

Huckleberry Finn received only one review when it was published in 1884.

In this version, the principal questions answered by the sentence are these: What happened? When did it happen? What happened was that Mark Twain's The Adventures of Huckleberry Finn *received only one review. That happened when it was published in 1884. Although Mark Twain was a well-known figure, his story of Huckleberry Finn received only one review. The introductory statement makes us think that we might have expected one thing but that something else happened. We know why the two statements are connected.*

But you should never cram your sentences with too many ideas. As a general rule, you should aim at stating one central idea in every sentence. When you have several important ideas to communicate, put them in separate sentences.

MIXED IDEA: World War I began on July 28, 1914, when the Austrians, whose army was huge but badly commanded and badly supplied and was also made up of many rival nationalities, attacked the city of Belgrade, in what was then called Serbia, though today it is a part of the nation of Yugoslavia.

This sentence is confused because it contains too much information. What is its main purpose? Is it to tell us when the war began? Or is it to tell us why the Austrian army was much weaker than it appeared? Or is it to tell us where Belgrade is?

REVISED: World War I began on July 28, 1914, when the Austrians attacked the city of Belgrade in what was then called Serbia. The Austrian army was huge, badly commanded, and badly supplied, but the Serbians were no match for it by themselves, and so they had to call on the Russians for help. The Austrians thereupon called upon the Germans for help against the Russians. The Germans decided to defeat the French first before turning their attention to fighting Russia. In that way, the Germans hoped to avoid war on two fronts. Suddenly all Europe was in conflict.

Each independent clause or sentence in this version makes one clear statement. Each statement fits closely to the statement that comes after it. To understand the general purpose of this text, we can ask the question "What happened?" What happened was that an attack on one city in Serbia quickly expanded into a general European war. Step by step these sentences and independent clauses within sentences lead us to an answer to the question, "What?" or "What happened?"

When in an early draft you create a sentence with mixed ideas, you can often revise by making a separate sentence for each idea. Sometimes you may be tempted to throw in unnecessary information to show readers how much you know. Then you must revise by eliminating the unnecessary information altogether.

MIXED IDEAS: Small computers, which have become a new source of trade rivalry between the United States and Japan, have at their heart a tiny silicon chip, which may contain thousands of circuits capable of millions of different combinations.

The major statement in this sentence concerns the tiny silicon chip at the heart of small computers. The information about the place of the computer in trade rivalry between the United States and Japan may belong in another sentence later on in the paper. But here it blurs the focus of the main statement in this sentence.

REVISED: Small computers most often have at their heart a tiny silicon chip, which may contain thousands of circuits capable of millions of different combinations.

Exercise 6.1   Rewrite the following sentences to clarify the main statement in each of them. You may choose to revise to make two sentences with related thoughts if you want to express two distinct main statements. You may want to leave out some of the information given in the sentences so that the statements you preserve will be clear.

1. My mother, who always hated to wash windows or clean house but preferred to work in her flower garden, worked on newspapers for twenty years in places as diverse as Beaumont, Texas, and Montgomery, Alabama.
2. Notoriously hard to spell and difficult grammatically, the English language has spread all over the world largely because of the power and influence of the United States and the British Empire and Commonwealth.
3. Scurvy, a disease once common among sailors who spent many weeks at sea, can be prevented by eating citrus fruits, which grow in warm climates and can be preserved at sea because of their thick skins.
4. Born in 1809, when the independence of the United States had been recognized by Great Britain for less than thirty years, Abraham Lincoln was the only American President forced to wage a civil war to preserve the unity of that nation.
5. If Lincoln had not sent ships to supply the federal garrison at Ft. Sumter in Charleston harbor, the British might have recognized the Confederacy as an independent nation so that they might ensure a steady supply of southern cotton to British textile mills, which by 1861 were using steam engines.

6. The greatest center for making glass in the Middle Ages was Venice in Italy, which is today endangered by flooding and is noted for its canals and its gondolas.

7. Terrorism is one of the frightening symbols of modern society because it is violent, bloody, and merciless and often completely anonymous, since the terrorists sometimes do not know and do not care who their victims are, but they know that a bomb exploding in an airport or a bullet tearing through the body of a police officer will get publicity, which they think will make them look important in the eyes of the world, and they think that if they are important, they may be able to get their way.

6b

Organize the elements of your sentences to give the greatest emphasis to the most important parts of your statements.

The most emphatic places in a sentence are at the beginning and at the end. The human mind picks up beginnings and endings better than it picks up middles. That is one reason most sentences begin with the subject. The person, place, or thing that the sentence is going to be about comes first so that readers will have it in their minds for the rest of the sentence. Think about your sentences enough to have a clear idea about those elements that you most want to emphasize.

> **WEAK AND ILLOGICAL:**   When you are looking for a good book, try *The Adventures of Huckleberry Finn,* which you will find to be a great one.

> **BETTER:**   *The Adventures of Huckleberry Finn* is one of the greatest books in American literature.

> **WEAK AND ILLOGICAL:**   He opposed Russian tyranny in Poland, Czechoslovakia, and Afghanistan very strongly. However, he did not want nuclear war, which would be a calamity, as everyone would agree.

The illogic in this sentence comes from the weakness of the language that reports such important thoughts. Serious thoughts should have an emphatic place in the sentence that reports them.

BETTER: Although he strongly opposed Russian tyranny in Poland, Czechoslovakia, and Afghanistan, he feared the calamity of nuclear war.

6c

Clearly establish cause and effect in your sentences.

6c

logic

Be logical when you attribute an effect to a cause, and avoid statements that imply causal relations that you do not intend.

English syntax often helps make statements about cause and effect. (**Syntax** is the name we give to the customary ways of putting words together to form phrases, clauses, and sentences.) The most obvious example is the use of *because* to introduce a dependent clause.

> The experiment failed *because* the lab technicians had not cleaned the instruments.

> The airship *Voyager* succeeded in making the first nonstop round-the-world flight *because* it could carry so much fuel relative to its light weight.

Words such as *for, since, therefore, thus,* and *so* also make causal connections between one part of a sentence and another or between sentences.

> *Since* his doctor ordered him to stop drinking coffee, he says he feels much better.

> He felt sad and lonely and depressed, *for* no one in the dorm seemed to like him.

> She worked hard, *so* she could graduate in three years.

> The temperature during the storm hung just below the freezing point. Therefore the snow stuck to the branches of the trees and to the electric and telephone wires, causing much damage.

Often adverbs like *when, after,* and *before* imply cause-and-effect relations.

> *When* they had biked for four hours, they were hungry.
> *The use of the clause introduced by* when *implies that the biking caused them to get hungry.*

> *After* Scarlett saw how much Ashley grieved for Melanie, she realized that he had always loved his wife.

The use of the clause introduced by after *implies that Scarlett's awareness that Ashley had always loved his wife came because she saw how much Ashley grieved for Melanie.*

Sometimes placing two ideas close together in a sentence implies a cause-and-effect relation.

6c

logic

She had a great talent for design, and she did well in architecture.
Putting the two statements together implies that one helps cause the other. You could make the causal relation more explicit: Because she had a great talent for design, she did well in architecture.
Jack bought a video cassette recorder, and he and his family started watching movies at home every night.
The cause of Jack's watching movies at home with his family was that he bought a video cassette recorder.

Confusion may arise when a writer puts two ideas together so that readers think some cause-and-effect relation exists between them when in fact the writer intends no such thing.

In 1950 the most popular song in America was "Tennessee Waltz," and the United States went to war in Korea.
Was the popularity of "Tennessee Waltz" the cause of the Korean War? A reader may think that the writer means just that. The thought needs filling out to clarify the writer's point: that two different and contradictory things were happening at the same time, not that one was the cause of the other.
In 1950, when the most popular song in America was the slow, dreamy "Tennessee Waltz," the United States went to war in Korea, and a peaceful dream ended for thousands of young men.
Now the thoughts are joined; the peacefulness of the "Tennessee Waltz" is contrasted with the end of the peaceful dream for those young men who went off to fight in Korea.

Confusion may also result from the joining of a dependent clause to an independent clause in such a way that a cause-and-effect relation seems to be implied.

When he saw the movie *Casablanca*, my friend Bert had a heart attack.
Did the movie Casablanca *cause Bert to have a heart attack? Probably not. But a rapid reader might think that it did. Again, a solution is to fill out the thought so that readers will not think you are implying cause and effect.*

While he was watching the movie *Casablanca* last week, my friend Bert had a heart attack. He looked to be in perfect health, and he was enjoying himself, but suddenly he was doubled over with a near-fatal seizure.

Some words establish negative relations. These include words like *but, although,* and *however.* Often we wish to make a statement that sets up certain expectations in the minds of readers. But we wish to tell them that these expectations will not be fulfilled. We say things like this:

Although seat belts save lives in automobile accidents, most motorists refuse to wear them.
Although tells us that an expectation will not be met. Seat belts save lives in automobile accidents; we should expect people to wear them. But they refuse to wear them. The expectation fails. Although lets us know that there will be an expectation and that it will fail.

Here are some other examples of statements that raise expectations that a word in the sentence shows us are not fulfilled.

I would love to graduate at the head of my class; *however* I hate to study.
The triathlon, a race where contestants swim, bike, and run great distances, has become one of America's rapidly growing sports. *But* many people still think triathloners are crazy.

Words like *but, however,* and *although* tell us that we might expect some relation of cause and effect but that in fact the expected relation does not exist. Use these words only when you are trying to set up an expectation that you wish to contradict.

Confusion results if you use one of these words to join two statements that are unrelated to each other.

Although I like to read, television is exciting.
The first statement, "I like to read," does not have any clear relation to the second statement, "television is exciting." What does liking to read have to do with exciting television? The writer meant to say something else.

Although I like to read, it is easier for me to watch an exciting television show in the evening when I am too tired to concentrate on the printed page.
Now the relation is clear. When I say "I like to read," you expect me to say that I read every evening. But I contradict that expectation by saying that I find it easier to watch television at night when I am too tired to concentrate on the printed page.

Be sure to establish clear relations between statements joined by *although, however, but,* and other such words. Adding some information will often show readers how you relate the statements in your own mind.

> *Although* my Aunt Anastasia was old, I loved to hear her stories about her childhood in Greece.
> *Does the writer mean that she is surprised to discover that old people are interesting?*

> *Although* my Aunt Anastasia was old and spoke slowly in a soft voice I could scarcely hear, I sat for hours by her chair, straining to hear the stories she told about her childhood in Greece.
> *Now we have enough information to understand the* although *that begins the sentence, and the sentence logic is plain.*

Be especially careful to make clauses beginning with *if* and *when* show a clear causal relation to the rest of the sentence. Sometimes writers will say this:

> *If* you see that movie, it is great.
> *The implication here is that if you do* not *see the movie, it is* not *great. The writer means to say something else.*

> *If* you see that movie, you will agree that it is great.
> *Now the clause beginning with* if *has a clear causal connection to the rest of the sentence.*

Some writers will say this:

> *When* you see the Grand Canyon for the first time, all the photographs cannot show how grand it is.

They mean to say this:

> *When* you see the Grand Canyon for the first time, you will realize that all the photographs of it you have seen cannot show how grand it is.

Exercise 6.2 Where necessary, rewrite the following sentences to eliminate faulty patterns of cause and effect. Be creative. Use your imagination to add information when it is necessary to establish sentence logic.

1. Personal computers were unknown twenty years ago, and Elvis Presley was in his prime.
2. Steroids have been shown to produce a host of illnesses including cancer while they are helping build huge, muscular bodies for weight lifters and football players, and athletes often use them.

3. Aspirin is a potent pain reliever because some doctors believe that too much aspirin may damage the kidneys.
4. If you see a Woody Allen movie, he captures the humor and suffering of middle-class urban men and women today.
5. When you go to college, many teachers love to write and talk to students about research and writing.
6. Although seat belts save lives, my friend Jack was severely injured when he was thrown out of his car when it hit a curb and the door flew open.
7. I wrote five drafts of my paper, but writing is difficult for me.
8. Athens, Greece, is the most polluted city in Europe now, and the Acropolis draws millions of tourists every year, and the fumes from cars passing in the streets are destroying the marble monuments from antiquity.
9. If you go to Monticello, the earth gets wet and fragrant after a spring rain.
10. Although the Natural History Museum has a great collection of dinosaur bones, those giant and now extinct reptiles flourished for millions of years on the earth.

6d
Limit generalizations.

Avoid sweeping statements that assert too much on too little evidence. Whenever you are tempted to say that all members of a group share some quality or when you are tempted to say that something has been the best or the worst of a class, or when you start to use words such as *always* and *never*, be sure your statement is limited enough to be true. Sweeping generalizations give the impression that the writer has not studied the material enough to be aware of the exceptions that serious observers know about. If you make sweeping generalizations, you will risk losing authority with your readers.

FAULTY GENERALIZATION: Students nowadays lack dedication and seriousness, and they never read anything worthwhile.

BETTER: Some students I have known lack dedication and seriousness, and they seldom read anything but the sports pages and the comics.

FAULTY GENERALIZATION: Football coaches think they are the symbols of real Americanism because they are emotional, hardworking, and dedicated to winning.

BETTER: Many fans believe that football coaches are symbols of real Americanism because they are emotional, hardworking, and dedicated to winning.

FAULTY GENERALIZATION: There never has been another play as good as *Macbeth.*

BETTER: *Macbeth* stirs audiences because Macbeth's flaws are so much the flaws of all of us—ambition that may overpower every tender feeling in its drive to the top.

6d

logic

FAULTY GENERALIZATION: Hemingway didn't believe in his own manhood because his mother kept him dressed up like a little girl for such a long time so that he always had to go around proving himself.

BETTER: The heroes in Hemingway's novels are continually trying to prove their manhood by being brave in dangerous situations, and in real life Hemingway tried to project a vigorous manly image that now seems almost foolish. Was he trying to prove something to himself? His mother dressed him in girl's clothes until he was ready to go to school. It may be that he was cursed throughout his life with the fear that perhaps he was not manly enough.

> **Exercise 6.3**   Rewrite the following sentences to qualify sweeping generalizations. Don't be afraid to change words if the changes help you improve the sentences.

Example:

Sweeping Generalization
> Everyone is agreed that Faulkner's story "A Rose for Emily" is not one of his better works because it is too melodramatic.

Limited Generalization
> Some critics tell us that Faulkner's story "A Rose for Emily" is not one of his better works because, they say, it is too melodramatic.

1. In Detroit the other day, the driver of one car shot another driver who dented his fender. This kind of thing happens because people in big cities carry pistols in the glove compartments of their cars.
2. My cousin Charles was furious because he could not get anybody to speak English when he asked directions in Paris no matter how much

he shouted at them. His experience proves that the French all hate the Americans except when France needs American help in time of war.

3. Members of the crime syndicates are always photographed smoking cigars, and the cigar has long been regarded as a symbol of success by everyone who thinks about such things.

4. The recent photographs of the ship *Titanic* lying on the bottom of the Atlantic Ocean since it sank in 1912 prove that travel by ship was much more dangerous than travel by airplane is today.

5. Colstrop's necktie was found at the scene of the murder along with his wristwatch, his notebook, and a pair of his trousers. So he was the killer, and the police have arrested him.

6e

Avoid mixed images.

Carelessness in using colorful, figurative language can confuse readers. (See 12b and 12c.) This confusion is especially likely to occur when we rely on familiar, overworked expressions called *clichés*. Here are some common clichés:

acid test	dead as a doornail
bottom line	launch out into the deep
cold, hard facts	nipped in the bud
cold light of day	noses to the grindstone

There are hundreds more. You can usually recognize a cliché because the beginning almost immediately makes us think of the end. When we hear somebody say, "It's like looking for a needle in a _____," we can fill in the blank with *haystack.* If we hear that someone is as neat as a _____, we can fill in the blank with *pin.*

Clichés have a sameness to them, a predictability, that makes for dead language. And sometimes they can lead to unintentional humor, when writers forget what they are saying in an effort to be colorful.

People in every walk of life can climb the ladder of success by launching out into the deep and keeping their noses to the grindstone.

If we think of these images at all, we are bound to be confused. Is there a ladder on the boat that is going to launch out into the deep? And how are we going to climb that ladder if we must haul a grindstone up with us?

He took off like a rocket in his new job and came up smelling like a rose.

Can you imagine a rocket that smells like a rose?

She was as busy as a bee, and the bottom line was that her drawings sold like hotcakes.

It is hard to imagine a bee that would make hotcakes or that would be concerned with the bottom line.

6f

logic

Exercise 6.4   Rewrite the following sentences to eliminate the mixed images. You may wish to change a cliché altogether and write a simple, declarative sentence.

Example:

Mixed Images

My opponents wish to put their heads in the sand and ride roughshod over those like me who point to the skeletons in their closets.

Revised

My opponents wish to hide from reality and attack anyone who calls attention to their previous faults.

1. She burned the midnight oil until the crack of dawn.
2. He insisted on passing the buck; so he nipped his chance for success in the bud and made his prospects as dead as a doornail.
3. We've got to get the lead out if we expect to improve the bottom line.
4. They took the primrose path, but it became painfully obvious that they were doomed to disappointment.
5. My opinions ran off him like water off a duck's back.
6. She called a spade a spade and sometimes acted like a bull in a china shop so that people avoided her like the plague.
7. They agreed to split the work and the profits fifty-fifty, but Horace wouldn't buckle down and put his shoulder to the wheel; so there was a fly in the ointment right off the bat.

6f
When you define a word, use other concrete words.

Don't define a word by repeating it or by using one of its cognates.

> **REPETITIOUS DEFINITION:**   A grammar book teaches you grammar.
> *If you don't know what grammar is, this definition will not help you; if you do know what grammar is, you do not need the definition.*

BETTER: A grammar book explains the system of rules about word endings and word order that allows a language to communicate.

REPETITIOUS: A floppy disc is a disc used in a computer.

BETTER: A floppy disc is a small, flat, circular sheet of magnetized plastic that looks a little like a 45 rpm phonograph record. It is used in personal computers to store information much as a tape is used in cassette recorders.

Words should not be defined by their cognates. **Cognates** are words that come from the same root. *Grammar* and *grammatical* are cognates. So are *describe* and *description, narrate* and *narration, compute* and *computer,* and *nostalgic* and *nostalgia.*

REPETITIOUS: A community is a group with communal interests that communicates within itself.

BETTER: A community is a group that shares similar ceremonies, goals, habits, and patterns of work as well as information about its members.

REPETITIOUS: Students of ancient history study ancient persons and events.

BETTER: Students of ancient history explore the art, artifacts, and literature of the period that began with the invention of writing about three thousand years before Christ and ended with the fall of the Roman Empire in the West.

Avoid definitions that use the words *is when.*

AWKWARD AND UNCLEAR: Fascism is when you have a dictator who wears a uniform and controls everybody with the secret police and won't allow freedom of the press or assembly.

BETTER: Fascism is a political system usually characterized by a military dictator ruling the state with the help of secret police. A Fascist state may use terror and strict censorship of the press to limit popular assemblies and suppress freedom of speech.

Exercise 6.5   Rewrite the following sentences to give proper definitions. Use the dictionary when necessary. (See 16b.)

1. An accident is when you have something happen accidentally that is unexpected and usually harmful, although accidents can be lucky, too.
2. A traffic jam is when traffic is jammed up on the streets.
3. Inflation is when you have inflated prices.
4. A quarterback is a back on a football team.
5. A poet is a man or a woman who writes poetry.
6. The English House of Commons is the representative body of the common people in Great Britain.
7. Oil lubricates because it is extremely oily.
8. Anger is when somebody gets angry at somebody else.
9. Beauty is when you think that something is beautiful.
10. A bookshelf is a shelf where books are placed.

CHAPTER SEVEN

Coordination and Subordination

Distinguish between main ideas and subordinate ideas in your sentences.

A pleasing style includes a variety of sentences. Variety includes different forms and elements to keep readers alert and expectant. (See Chapter 10.) No matter how varied you make your sentences, always keep readers on track by making a distinction between your major statements and the subordinate elements that support these statements. Your major statements are usually those you develop from sentence to sentence. Your minor statements are usually those that help add information to major statements. Your readers should be able to follow a train of ideas from sentence to sentence in your prose. Improper coordination or subordination can interrupt that flow and can make your readers struggle to understand the main points you are trying to make in your essays.

IMPROPER COORDINATION: The children played happily, and the cars were parked haphazardly along the street, and the buildings on each side were old and falling down.
The main thought in this sentence is difficult to find. Are we learning about cars or about streets or about children? But when we reorganize our thoughts, we can subordinate some ideas to the main statement we want to make.

REVISED: The children played happily in the streets between the parked cars and the dilapidated buildings.
Now we know that the main thought in this sentence is that the children played happily. In addition to their happy playing, we have the details that cars were parked along the streets and that the adjoining buildings were dilapidated.

194

Sometimes confusions caused by improper sentence coordination are more complicated.

IMPROPER COORDINATION: In the fields the cattle grazed placidly, and we heard nothing but the soft hum of insects and the singing of birds, and for the moment we were safe from pursuit.
This writer is trying to depict a vivid scene. But the triple compound sentence prepares us to believe that all these statements are closely related. Were we safe from pursuit because the cattle were grazing and because we heard nothing but the soft hum of insects and the singing of birds? The writer apparently meant something else, but this sentence makes that meaning obscure.

REVISED: In the fields the cattle grazed placidly, and we heard nothing but the soft hum of insects and the singing of birds. For the moment, we were safe from pursuit.
Separating the last independent clause from the first two eliminates the impression that the thoughts expressed in all three are closely related. The first two clauses describe the scene; the last one, now an independent sentence, describes something slightly different—our safety.

Avoid attaching clauses to each other unless there is some clear relation between them. Always be sure that the elements you join with various coordinating devices do indeed have equal status in the statements you wish to make. When elements are not equal or do not have a clear cause-and-effect relation, separate them or else subordinate them.

NOT THIS: Chunks of ice floated in the pond, and he swam across it at its greatest width.

BUT THIS: Although chunks of ice floated in the pond, he swam across it at its greatest width.

7a
Give equal ideas equal value by proper coordination.

Establish equal emphasis between parts of a sentence by using coordinating conjunctions or suitable punctuation or both.

1 Coordinate words, phrases, or clauses, giving them equal emphasis to expand sentence ideas.

The conjunction *and* always calls for equal emphasis on the elements that it joins.

> The bear ate the food in camp.
> The bear *and* her cubs ate the food in camp.
> *In the first sentence, the subject is* bear. *It acts with the verb* ate *to make a statement. In the second sentence, the coordinating conjunction* and *makes a compound subject of the noun* bear *and the noun* cubs *so that both of them act together through the verb. The conjunction* and *joins equal elements.*

In the following sentences, notice how the conjunction *and* joins equal elements.

> The bear *and* her cubs ate the food in camp *and* destroyed our tent.
> At the end of our climb, we were hot *and* tired.
> He drank only coffee, tea, *and* milk for a week.
> She ran the marathon swiftly *and* tirelessly.
> After reading her book *and* thinking about her arguments, I decided she was right.

When *and* is used to join unequal elements, confusion results. This confusion is called *faulty parallelism.* (See Chapter 8.)

> His favorite pastimes were reading, walking, *and* he liked to skate on frozen ponds in winter.
> *In this sentence, the words* reading *and* walking *prepare us to find a similar word after* and, *a word used as a gerund, such as* skating *or* singing *or* thinking. *Instead, we do not find another gerund but an independent clause, and we feel that something has been left out. We can amend the sentence in a couple of ways.*
> His favorite pastimes were reading, walking, and skating.

A comma can sometimes replace the *and* in a series:

> He zigzagged, fell, rolled, ran into my waiting hand.
> —E. B. WHITE
> *The comma after* rolled *coordinates the verbs in the sentence without the use of* and.
> Wistfully, admiringly, the old voice added, "It's snug in here, upon my word!"
> —KATHERINE MANSFIELD

Mansfield could have said, "Wistfully and admiringly," but she chose to eliminate the and and use a comma instead. Even so, wistfully and admiringly are equal adverbs in the sentence.

The conjunction *or* also joins equal sentence elements. It is not as common as *and.*

He could go by bus *or* by train.

They knew that they must work out their differences over money *or* else get a divorce.

Many convicted criminals have suffered neglect *or* abuse *or* both from their parents.

Confusion and a breakdown in parallelism can arise when *or* joins unequal elements.

They could see a movie, a play, *or* talk all night.

We feel that something is missing in such a sentence. We hesitate, go back over it to see if we have read it correctly, and then see that the breakdown in parallelism makes it seem that they could "see talk" all night. The writer must mean this instead:

They could see a movie or a play, *or* they could talk all night.

2 Coordinate thoughts you wish to stress equally by joining short, consecutive sentences.

With careful use, coordination can establish clear relations among equal elements in a sentence. Devices for coordination may make your prose more vivid.

They hesitate, and they regret, and sometimes they petition; but they do nothing in earnest and with effect.
— HENRY DAVID THOREAU

Written as short, consecutive sentences, Thoreau's statement might not stress the close relations in these thoughts. He is denouncing the caution and the lack of effectiveness in some people. The roll of clauses joined by commas builds to a strong impact.

When you use *and, but, or, for, yet, nor,* or *so* to connect independent clauses and thus coordinate related statements of equal importance, use a comma.

7a

CO

To act is to be committed, and to be committed is to be in danger.
— JAMES BALDWIN

I buried my head under the quilts, but my aunt heard me.
— LANGSTON HUGHES

In both these sentences, two related statements are joined by a coordinating conjunction that gives each statement a clear connection to the other.

7a

co

You can also use a semicolon to connect related statements that are equally important.

We walked, and he talked; the musical irresistible voice seemed to set the pace of our march.
— EMLYN WILLIAMS

Here the semicolon joins two independent clauses, giving them equal status without the help of a coordinating conjunction.

Sometimes both a semicolon and a coordinating conjunction introduce an independent clause. (See 27a.)

The hands of the man who sawed the wood left red marks on the billets; and the forehead of the woman who nursed the baby was stained with the stain of the old rag she wound around her head again.
— CHARLES DICKENS

Here both the semicolon and the coordinating conjunction and *serve to join two independent clauses.*

Exercise 7.1 Rewrite the following sentences to provide proper coordination of elements. You may want to write more than a sentence for some of the examples.

1. He loved to shave in the morning because he liked the softness of shaving cream, the clean feel of the razor on his cheek, the smell of his after-shave, and he enjoyed taking a shower, too.
2. We drove to Baltimore last month, and to Wilmington the month before that, and next month we hope to drive to Providence.
3. Police officers in old movies often seem hard, cynical, and yet they are honest.
4. Truck drivers in this country complained bitterly about the 55-mile-an-hour speed limit, the high price of diesel fuel, and many of them refused to slow down.
5. Our friends would eat out on Saturday night, go to a movie, visit with each other, or they would do something else to have a relaxing good time.

7b

Give major ideas the emphasis they should have by subordinating minor ideas.

Subordination helps focus attention on major ideas. In many sentences, some ideas depend on others. For example, one condition or event may cause another; one event may come before another; one observation may explain another. Subordination establishes the dependence of one idea on another by shifting emphasis away from supporting elements so that major statements become clear.

7b

sub

1 Subordinate the less important to the more important in your sentences so your readers can tell the difference.

In the following sentences, readers would have trouble discerning the statements that carry the major line of thought that the writer wants to pursue.

Columbus discovered the New World in 1492. He made his voyage in three ships. They were tiny and frail. He did not believe that the world was flat. No educated person in that time believed that the world was flat. Columbus was well educated. The Greeks had taught that the world was round. They had taught that two thousand years before Columbus. On a round world, a sailor might head west. In the west, he would eventually get to lands others had found by sailing east. Columbus never believed he had discovered a "new world." Columbus wanted to find a new route to China and to other lands in Asia. Others had reached those lands. They had sailed around the southern tip of Africa to get there. Columbus thought the world was much smaller than it is. He thought he could get to Asia in about a month. Suppose America had not been in the way. He would have had a voyage of three or four months. He did not find the East Indies or China or Japan. America was in the way. It is a good thing America was in the way. Columbus might have sailed his three ships into an enormous ocean. His sailors might have starved to death. The ocean would have been far larger than anything Columbus could have imagined.
Each sentence in this paragraph is clear. But together, in this version, the sentences create confusion because they do not show proper subordination.

This is a revised version:

> With three tiny ships, Christopher Columbus discovered the New World in 1492, although he never understood just what he had done. Neither he nor any other educated person in his time believed that the world was flat. From the time of the Greeks two thousand years earlier, the educated had believed that the world was round and that by sailing west, a ship might arrive in Asia without having to sail around the tip of Africa. Because Columbus thought the world was much smaller than it is, he expected to find the East Indies, China, or Japan. Instead he found America, and had this continent not been in the way, he might have sailed his crews to starvation in an enormous ocean far larger than any sea he had imagined.

Much more is involved in this revision than a simple combining of sentences, but the sentence combining does help. The writer has put down a series of short and seemingly disconnected sentences in a first draft. Then, in the second draft, he has thought about the main ideas he wants to present, and he has subordinated some lesser ideas to these main statements.

The appropriate placing of words and phrases in a sentence helps subordinate ideas clearly. Sometimes writers rely on key words to state the precise relations between major and minor ideas. These key words, often called *subordinators* (see 5b-5), help to build subordinate clauses. Commas may also set off subordinate sections from a part they modify, especially when some subordinated element opens the sentence. (See 26b.)

For subordinate sections that show	Use one of these subordinators	Example
place	where	*Where* the road forks, you will find the graveyard.
condition	as, as if, unless, provided, since, although, if	*Unless you object*, I will plug my ears at the rock concert.
cause or purpose	since, because, as long as, in order that, so that, that	*Because great horned owls are so big*, they sometimes kill and eat cats.
time	after, as, whenever, while, as soon as, when, before, until, once, since	*Until you remove the engine head*, you cannot see the pistons.

| manner | how | He taught me *how to throw a curve.* |
| concession | although, even, though, even if, even when, though | *Although she looked tiny,* she was a superb police officer. |

How you place a subordinator in relation to the clause it introduces will affect the meaning of a sentence.

She did not eat *because she was angry.*
In this sentence, her anger kept her from eating.

She was angry *because she did not eat.*
In this sentence, her anger was caused by her not eating.

When the police arrived, the burglars ran away.
In this sentence, the arrival of the police caused the burglars to flee.

When the burglars ran away, the police arrived.
In this sentence, the burglars were already gone when the police got there. The sentence may imply that the police did not do their duty.

After he completed a fifty-yard pass, we cheered him.
The sentence implies that the completed pass caused the cheers.

After we cheered him, he completed a fifty-yard pass.
The sentence implies that the cheers caused the completed pass.

Relative pronouns—*who, whom, that, which, what, whoever, whomever, whose*—also signal subordinate elements in a sentence. Notice how the use of subordinators speeds up the pace of the following sentences.

WITHOUT SUBORDINATORS: My cousin does my taxes every year. He is an accountant. He helps me with many suggestions. These suggestions allow me to take several deductions. These deductions reduce my tax bill considerably.

WITH SUBORDINATORS: Because my cousin is an accountant, he does my taxes every year, suggesting several deductions that reduce my tax bill considerably.

WITHOUT SUBORDINATORS: Many amateur pilots fly ultralight aircraft. The ultralight aircraft was developed from the hang glider. Somebody decided to attach a small engine to a hang glider. Ultralight aircraft are hardly more than a tubular frame, a simple motor, flimsy wings, and a tail. The ultralight reduces flight to the essentials.

WITH SUBORDINATORS: Many amateur pilots fly ultralight aircraft, which were developed when somebody decided to attach a small engine to a hang glider. Because they are hardly more than a tubular frame, a simple motor, flimsy wings, and a tail, ultralight aircraft reduce flight to the essentials.

Clauses, phrases, and single words can all be subordinate units in a sentence, highlighting the major assertion of the sentence while providing supporting information. The subordinate element usually enlarges on some element in the main part of the sentence. As you rethink your first drafts, keep clearly in mind the main thoughts you want to communicate. Subordinate other elements to these main thoughts.

7b

sub

2 Join a series of short sentences or a string of poorly coordinated clauses by using embedding techniques.

Short sentences are easy to understand, but several of them coming one after another may be monotonous, even if they are all clear and correct. Short sentences may be confusing because they make it hard for readers to pick out the direction of your thought. The papers you write should have a clear direction or, as we have called it before, a *thesis*. You obscure that thesis sometimes with short, choppy sentences. You can make your purposes more clear if you use both subordinators and embedding techniques. The embedded elements may be short phrases that you write into a longer sentence to replace shorter sentences.

Good writers can compress a great deal of clear information into a few words by using embedding techniques. Don't abbreviate your sentences so that they are unclear, but you can often combine thoughts into efficient, lively sentences that readers can quickly understand.

SENTENCES WITHOUT EMBEDDED ELEMENTS: She was sad. She did not look back. She mounted the seawall. She was bowed by her burden of failure, sorrow, and self-contempt.

SENTENCE WITH EMBEDDED ELEMENTS: Sadly, without looking back, she mounted the seawall, bowed by her burden of failure, sorrow, and self-contempt.

—CONSTANCE HOLME

Several of the sentences in the first version have been reduced to modifiers in the second version. We say that the ideas expressed in the several sentences in the first version have been embedded *in the second.*

SENTENCES WITHOUT EMBEDDED ELEMENTS: We can turn poetry toward biology. We can suggest a closer relationship between them. This creation of a relationship would follow a long line of similar suggestions. Other disciplines have made these suggestions.

SENTENCE WITH EMBEDDED ELEMENTS: To turn poetry toward biology and to suggest a closer relationship between them is only to follow in a long line of similar suggestions made by other disciplines.
— ELIZABETH SEWELL

Several separate sentences in the first version have been changed to embedded elements in the second version.

7b

sub

SENTENCES WITHOUT EMBEDDED ELEMENTS: That stick has an explosive charge. The coyote tugs at it. It shoots some cyanide into the mouth of the coyote.

SENTENCE WITH EMBEDDED ELEMENTS: That stick has an explosive charge that shoots some cyanide into the mouth of the coyote who tugs at it.

SENTENCES WITHOUT EMBEDDED ELEMENTS: The White Star liner *Titanic* was the largest ship the world had ever known. The *Titanic* sailed from Southampton on her maiden voyage to New York on April 10, 1912.

SENTENCE WITH EMBEDDED ELEMENTS: The White Star liner *Titanic*, largest ship the world had ever known, sailed from Southampton on her maiden voyage to New York on April 10, 1912.
— HANSON W. BALDWIN

SENTENCES WITHOUT EMBEDDED ELEMENTS: She was falling asleep. Her head was bowed over the child. She was still aware of a strange, wakeful happiness.

SENTENCE WITH EMBEDDED ELEMENTS: Even as she was falling asleep, head bowed over the child, she was still aware of a strange, wakeful happiness.
— KATHERINE ANNE PORTER

By varying techniques, you can embed several enriching thoughts within one base sentence, transforming a whole group of ideas into a statement in which unstressed elements modify main ideas precisely. By using coordination along with subordination, you can expand your options for embedding and transforming sentences.

The fissions generate heat, and in a power reactor this heat produces steam, which drives electric turbines.

— JEREMY BERNSTEIN

The comma and the conjunction and *connect two independent clauses through coordination; the comma and the relative pronoun* which *subordinate an idea by means of a relative clause. The prepositional phrase* "in a power reactor" *embeds a subordinate idea, too.*

Equality with whites will not solve the problems of either whites or Negroes if it means equality in a world society stricken by poverty and in a universe doomed to extinction by war.

— MARTIN LUTHER KING JR.

The conjunctions either . . . or *coordinate two objects of the preposition* of; *the conjunction* and *coordinates two prepositional phrases. A subordinate clause begins at the word* if. *The participial phrases —* "stricken by poverty" *and* "doomed to extinction by war" *— embed ideas. All seven prepositional phrases serve subordinating functions as well.*

Exercise 7.2   Using the techniques of subordination illustrated in 7b-1 and 2, revise the following sets of sentences. Make any necessary changes to create logical, correct sentences. You might want to see how many different combinations you can make of each example. Compare your work with that of others in your class.

Example:

Television beats us with athletic contests now. We see championship basketball. We see the league play-offs in baseball. We see the World Series. We see the National Football League play-offs. We see the Super Bowl. Perhaps the Super Bowl is the greatest spectacle of all. The Super Bowl has become an international TV event. We see so much that we cannot remember any of it. Who can recall who played in the Super Bowl in 1987? Who played in the World Series in 1986? Who won the National Basketball League Championship in 1987, and whom did that team beat in the finals?

Revision

Television beats us with athletic contests now — championship basketball, the league play-offs in baseball, the World Series, the National Football League play-offs, and, perhaps the greatest spectacle of all, the Super Bowl, which has become an international TV event. But who can remember who played in the 1987 Super Bowl or the 1986 World Series or who won the 1987 National Basketball League Championship or whom that team beat in the finals?

1. Bilingual education is expanding in many schools. It is designed for children. The native language of these children is not English. It may be Spanish. It may be Chinese. It may be Vietnamese. It may be Korean. It may be some other language.

2. This auditorium was huge. The acoustics were terrible. The tenor nearly screamed at us. But no one could hear him beyond the ninth row. The soprano looked as if she was trying. But her voice sounded like a whisper in the balcony. The singers walked off the stage. They had played only two-thirds of the first act. The baritone was in tears.

3. Henry James began his novel *The Portrait of a Lady* in the spring of 1879. He wrote parts of the preface more than twenty-five years later. The novel has been one of his most enduring works. It is still in print.

4. A uniform can symbolize a worker's status. Status means power. People see authority in some uniforms. A doorman in an apartment building shows by his uniform that he can let people in. He can also keep people out. A policeman by his uniform shows that he has authority to make people stop. Sometimes uniforms are not prescribed. But people try to wear clothing that makes them look as if they belong. Male college professors used to wear tweed jackets. Their tweed jackets were a kind of uniform.

5. I read the same want ads over and over. I was looking for a job as a word processor in Dallas. I wanted to work at night. I had moved to Dallas the day before. I did not have a job. Finally I found the right ad. It asked for someone to do word processing. The hours were from midnight until 8:00 A.M. I love to work at night when it is quiet and to sleep during the day.

6. Computers were large only a decade ago. Few people used them for word processing. The small computer changed all that. Now many homes have small computers. Almost every office uses computers. Young people learn how to use computers early. Often they learn about computers in grade school. College students write papers on computers. Often they save their money and buy computers themselves. A good computer for word processing now costs less than seven hundred dollars.

7. She wanted to study engineering. Her friends discouraged her. Her parents did not believe engineering was a good profession for a woman. She knew they were wrong. She decided to major in engineering in college. She told her parents she was majoring in home economics. They were happy with her choice. Only on graduation day did they learn the truth. Then she graduated at the head of her class in engineering. She went to work for four times what her father was making. He had been in his job twenty-five years.

3 Avoid using so many subordinate structures—clauses or phrases—that you obscure the main statement of a sentence.

Although subordinating elements of a sentence help clarify your main statement, you can do too much of a good thing. Too much subordination may distract your readers and confuse your main statement. It is always good to write sentences that make a clear statement. Subordinate elements may add important information to that statement. But if you add too much information, the main statement may get fuzzy.

LESS CLEAR: He was a stamp collector of considerable zeal who bought stamps at the post office on the day they were issued and fixed them with loving care in large books which had leather bindings, treasuring them not merely for themselves but for the enormous profit that he hoped to gain from them in the passage of years when they had increased in value.

MORE CLEAR: A stamp collector of considerable zeal, he bought stamps at the post office on the day they were issued and fixed them carefully in large, leatherbound books. He prized them not for themselves but for the enormous profit he hoped to gain from them when, after many years, they had increased in value.

LESS CLEAR: Jackson Bingle, leader of the rock group called the Howlers, who had been known for his ability to scream over the sound of drums, a primal shriek that had amazed critics and delighted audiences while dismaying parents, learned during his annual physical, administered by Dr. T. J. Summers, head physician of Whooping Crane Hospital, that he had lost seven-eighths of his hearing, so he told reporters this morning.

MORE CLEAR: Jackson Bingle told reporters this morning that he had lost seven-eighths of his hearing. Bingle, leader of the rock group called the Howlers, had been known for his ability to scream over the sound of the drums. His was a primal shriek that had amazed critics and delighted audiences. It also dismayed parents. Bingle said he learned of his hearing loss during his annual physical administered by Dr. T. J. Summers, head physician of Whooping Crane Hospital.

Exercise 7.3 Revise this passage by combining sentences through subordination and coordination.

(1) Abused children learn poorly. (2) They feel unloved. (3) They feel stupid. (4) They may listen to a question. (5) They may even be

7b

sub

able to answer it. **(6)** But they give up right away. **(7)** It is easier for them to say "I don't know" than to respond. **(8)** Such an answer suits their feelings of worthlessness. **(9)** Some abused children deliberately avoid answering questions. **(10)** They turn away from any question. **(11)** They purposely disobey instructions. **(12)** They seem to want negative results from teachers. **(13)** It is difficult to teach these children anything.

Exercise 7.4   Revise the following sentences to eliminate excessive subordination. You will have to write at least two sentences for each one in the examples. One point of this exercise is to get you in the habit of clarifying the major statements in sentences.

1. The Paul Newman movies, which nearly always end with an upbeat final scene, have beguiled Americans for years, during which time many movies have been either somber or else nonsensical, causing many adults to quit going to see movies at all.
2. The new sun creams, which contain various sun-blocking chemicals, help protect against skin cancer, long a hazard to people who spend much time in the sun, and against aging, which seems to be at least partly a consequence of the ultraviolet rays of the sun, and they have also been shown to retard the graying of hair.
3. Literacy should mean not only the ability to read and write, which is an essential skill in our culture, but also the ability, which is very much appreciated by academics, businesspeople, and professionals, to talk about many topics with intelligence — which may be another way of saying that true literacy embraces curiosity and the love of learning.
4. When books began to be printed in the fifteenth century, often considered the high point of the Renaissance, many people out of a form of snobbery refused to have printed books in their libraries, much as some people refuse today to allow paperbacks on their shelves, and in consequence printers tried to make printed books look as much like manuscripts as possible so that those books today are difficult to read even when we know the language they are written in, since often the type looks like handwriting.

CHAPTER EIGHT

Parallelism

Parallel constructions in sentences bind related thoughts together and give them more force.

In parallel constructions, the same form is repeated in a balanced way. The elements in a parallel construction are equal or nearly equal in grammatical structure and importance. Parallel constructions may help you make lists, join similar ideas, or build emphasis. The coordinating conjunctions *and, but, or, nor,* and *yet* always join parallel structures.

The simplest parallel structure is the series with two or more elements in it:

She loved to read *magazines* and *newspapers.*

She loved to read *books, magazines,* and *newspapers.*
The series of nouns joined by the conjunction and *provides a list of words telling what she liked to read.*

At Gettysburg in 1863, Abraham Lincoln said that the Civil War was being fought to make sure that government *of the people, by the people,* and *for the people* might not perish from the earth.
Here prepositional phrases are joined in a parallel construction. Each phrase is equal grammatically to the other two.

He *did the dishes, ran the vacuum, put out the garbage,* and *walked the dog.*
A compound predicate, here with four verbs, is placed in parallel form. Each element in the series includes a transitive verb and a noun that serves as a direct object.

He runs marathons, and *she runs* sprints, but *they train* together.
A series of independent clauses, each with an active verb, makes a parallel form.

Many athletes live *to hear* the roar of the crowd, *to feel* the love of their fans, and *to enjoy* the attentions of reporters.
A series of infinitive phrases forms a parallel structure.

She walked home slowly, *smelling* the aroma of wood smoke, *seeing* the decorated streets, and *feeling* at peace with the world.
A series of participial phrases at the end of the predicate modifies the subject, she.

8a

8a

Use parallelism to compare and contrast.

Parallelism helps make comparisons and contrasts more emphatic.

WEAK: She preferred *to buy* a house rather than *renting* one.
The contrasting elements to buy *and* renting *are not parallel;* to buy *is an infinitive, and* renting *is a participle.*

BETTER: She preferred *to buy* a house rather than *to rent* one.
The two infinitives are parallel.

BETTER: She preferred *buying* a house to *renting* one.
The two participles make a parallel form.

WEAK: The new library was larger than the old one, more beautiful than any other building on campus, and *it cost too much money*.
The parallel form breaks down in the final, italicized clause. The first two elements, larger *and* more beautiful, *are comparative adjectives, and readers expect another comparative adjective to follow them.*

PARALLEL: The new library was *larger* than the old one, *more beautiful* than any other building on campus, and *more expensive* to build than anyone had imagined.
The revision includes the comparative adjective "more expensive."

8b

Use parallel forms for coordinating elements like both . . . and, either . . . or, neither . . . nor, not only . . . but also, and whether . . . or.

8b

//

Pairs like these, often called *correlatives*, always indicate a choice or a balance between equal elements. Because the equality is important to the sense of the sentences where these elements appear, it should be expressed in the parallel form that makes it stand out.

WEAK: Most soldiers in the Civil War were *neither heroic nor were they cowardly*.
The adjective heroic *does not balance the clause* "nor were they cowardly."

BETTER: Most soldiers in the Civil War were *neither heroic nor cowardly*.
Now the contrasting adjectives, heroic *and* cowardly, *are equal grammatically, emphasizing the equality of form indicated by the words* neither *and* nor.

WEAK: The parking lot for commuters was *both small* and *it was crowded*.
The adjective small *does not balance the clause* "it was crowded."

BETTER: The parking lot for commuters was *both small and crowded*.
The two adjectives give equally important descriptions of the parking lot.

The magazine was not only *the first thing he read in the morning* but also *the last thing he looked at before bed*.
The parallelism is maintained by an adjective clause modifying the noun thing *in each element.*

Our economic future depends on whether we *love automobiles* or *leave them*.
The parallel forms are the verb love *with its direct object* automobiles *and the verb* leave *with its direct object* them. *They imply an equal choice.*

8c

Use parallelism in making lists and outlines.

WEAK: Americans now rely on the automobile because:

1. cities are sprawling; public transport is poor.

2. habit.

3. the cheapness of gasoline for so long.

4. parking lots provided for employees and students by businesses and schools.

5. general convenience.

6. shopping malls depend on automobiles.

In this list, the meaning could be much clearer if every numbered item completed a sentence begun by the lead thought: "Americans now rely on the automobile because." The meaning would be even clearer if every numbered item were parallel with every other item.

BETTER: Americans now rely on the automobile because

1. cities are sprawling, and public transport is poor.

2. they have formed the habit of driving cars everywhere.

3. gasoline was cheap for a long time.

4. automobiles are convenient.

5. businesses and schools provide parking lots for employees and students, encouraging them to drive.

6. shopping malls were built to depend on automobiles.

Each of these numbered items begins with a noun or nouns introducing a clause. Each item would complete the heading by making a complete sentence.

8d

You may emphasize parallelism by repeating important words introducing parallel elements.

WITHOUT A REPEATED INFINITIVE MARKER: They thought it was better *to* agree than quarrel.

WITH A REPEATED INFINITIVE MARKER: They thought it was better *to* agree than *to* quarrel.

The infinitive marker to *is repeated before* agree *and* quarrel *to emphasize the parallelism.*

WITHOUT A REPEATED PREPOSITION: They searched for the lost keys *in* the house, yard, and street.

WITH A REPEATED PREPOSITION: They searched for the lost keys *in* the house, *in* the yard, and *in* the street.
The repetition of the preposition in *emphasizes the parallel form and helps call attention to the difficulty of the search.*

WITHOUT A REPEATED ARTICLE: For the handicapped, getting an education is often *a* tribulation, necessity, and victory.

WITH A REPEATED ARTICLE: For the handicapped, getting an education is often *a* tribulation, *a* necessity, and *a* victory.
Repetition of the article a *before each noun stresses the parallel form and emphasizes the nouns that make up the series.*

WITHOUT A REPEATED CONNECTIVE: I decided to leave when I realized *that* I had offended him, he was angry, and my apology would do no good.

WITH A REPEATED CONNECTIVE: I decided to leave when I realized *that* I had offended him, *that* he was angry, and *that* my apology would do no good.
The repetition of the connective that *emphasizes the parallelism of these three dependent noun clauses and makes the clauses more emphatic.*

Note that the sentences *without* the repeated elements in these examples are correct and parallel. But repetition of an element may help you add a certain kind of emphasis to your sentences. You do not always have to make that choice, but from time to time, repetition will strengthen your style.

Exercise 8.1   Rewrite the following sentences to create parallel forms.

1. Harrison Ford was a hot-rod driver in *American Graffiti*, a rocket-ship pilot in *Star Wars*, and he played Indiana Jones, the archaeologist in *Raiders of the Lost Ark*.
2. Orson Welles starred on radio, he directed and appeared in movies, and toward the end of his life advertised wine on television.
3. We biked around the reservoir, over the hills, enjoyed the country roads, and we ended at the ice-cream store.
4. He was not a good writer, and he couldn't speak very well either.

5. Many people in America are unhappy because of jobs not leading anywhere, with their families, and they don't like where they live either.

Exercise 8.2   Revise the following sentences to repeat introductory words before parallel forms to make the parallelism more striking.

8e

//

1. The new ultralight aircraft can land on a sandbar, back lot, or small street.
2. She promised to help out in the day or night.
3. They piled their books on the sofa, tables, and beds.
4. She made three promises — that she would try the machine out, write up a report about it, and tell her friends if she liked it.
5. The railroad tracks passed through a tunnel and then over a river and highway.

8e

If you begin a clause with *and which, and that, and who*, or *and whom*, be sure that it follows a clause that begins with *which, that, who,* or *whom*.

FAULTY: The peach tree, with its sugary fruit and which was not known in the Middle Ages, seems to have developed from the almond.
The and *must join two equal grammatical elements. But here it tries to join the prepositional phrase* "with its sugary fruit" *to the dependent clause* "which was not known in the Middle Ages."

PARALLEL: The peach tree, which has a sugary fruit and which was not known in the Middle Ages, seems to have developed from the almond.
Now the and *joins two dependent clauses, each introduced by* which.

FAULTY: Thelonious Monk, with his deft fingers and who recorded for decades, was one of the great jazz pianists.
The and *tries to join the prepositional phrase* "with his deft fingers" *to the dependent clause* "who recorded for decades."

PARALLEL: Thelonious Monk, with his deft fingers and his decades of recording, was one of the great jazz pianists.
Here the and *successfully joins the two objects of the preposition* with — fingers *and* decades.

FAULTY: Walt Whitman, influenced by Emerson and whom multitudes loved, was the first great American poet to praise cities in his verse.

The and *tries to join the phrase* "influenced by Emerson" *to the clause* "whom multitudes loved."

PARALLEL: Walt Whitman, whom Emerson influenced and whom multitudes loved, was the first great American poet to praise cities in his verse.

The and *joins two clauses,* "whom Emerson influenced" *and* "whom multitudes loved."

PARALLEL: Walt Whitman, whom Emerson influenced and multitudes loved, was the first great American poet to praise cities in his verse.

Here the second whom *has been dropped, but the parallelism is maintained between* "Emerson influenced" *and* "multitudes loved."

Exercise 8.3   Revise the following structures as necessary to make good parallel constructions.

1. The movie *Gone with the Wind,* filmed in Technicolor and which cost millions of dollars to make, was the first talking movie about the Civil War to be a success at the box office.
2. Television, the great rival to the movies and which movie people hated at first, was not allowed to show the Academy Awards until 1952.
3. General Douglas MacArthur, American leader against Japan in World War II, maker of the Japanese Constitution afterward, and who was fired by President Harry Truman during the Korean war, wanted to become President.
4. She hoped to win her first marathon, the one she entered at Boston and which led over a hilly course.
5. He brought home a new car, large, fire-engine red, expensive, and which he could not afford.

CHAPTER NINE

Emphasis

When you arrange information carefully in a sentence, you can emphasize your most important ideas and can put less emphasis on less important ideas.

In most declarative sentences, the subject comes first, followed by a predicate that makes a statement about the subject. This form gives readers the feeling that the subject and the statement made about the subject are of equal importance. In very simple sentences, this balance between subject and predicate is easy to see and feel.

Mark *is swimming.*
The subject, Mark, *and the verb phrase,* is swimming, *are equally important to the sense of the sentence.*

More complicated sentences can also show balance.

The vast internal migration of the early 1940's *has continued, in a somewhat lower key, in the postwar period.*
—WILLIAM MANCHESTER
A subject is set down, and a statement is made about it; readers do not feel any special emphasis on either the subject or the predicate. They both seem equally important.

But sometimes the balance of a sentence may tip heavily to one side or another. In the following example, an enormous weight of emphasis is placed on the subject, but the predicate is so light that it is disappointing.

The battered trees, bending in the screaming winds of the storm, their branches ripped away by the gale, their leaves blowing like a green haze through the driving rain, *were diseased anyway.*
The subject is full of drama and movement, but the predicate is limp and disappointing.

If you are going to place dramatic elements at the beginning of a sentence, you must have a predicate strong enough to carry such a strong subject.

The sight of the bodies in the water, the strain of the long trip in from the transport ships, and now the ominous nearness of the flat sands and the dunes of Utah Beach *jerked men out of their lethargy.*
— CORNELIUS RYAN

9a
Learn to emphasize your main point by using a periodic sentence.

A periodic sentence is a sentence that has a strong word or phrase at the end, just before the period. The complete meaning is apparent only when you come to the last few words of the sentence. Study the following periodic sentences:

If asked to name the central quality in Faulkner's work, one is likely to give the quick answer "Imagination."
— MALCOLM COWLEY

It was always a great affair, the Misses Morkan's annual dance.
— JAMES JOYCE

It was the kind of party where everyone knew everyone else, except no one knew men.
— LINDA BIRD FRANCKE

Sometimes a periodic sentence ends with a striking thought rather than with a striking word.

The original Hopalong Cassidy was created by Clarence E. Mulford, a Brooklyn marriage-license clerk who at the time had never even seen the West.
— JAMES HORWITZ

The striking thought occurs at the end of the sentence, where we learn that the hero of so many books and movies about the West was created by a man who had never been there.

When you have several facts that you want to convey in a sentence, it is nearly always a good idea to put the more important ones toward the end to give a sense of building to a climax that will be memorable.

Loose: John Muir, the naturalist who was more responsible than any other single person for establishing Yosemite National Park, took long, solitary walks and let his beard grow long and tangled. *The most important fact in this sentence is not John Muir's long and tangled beard but his part in establishing Yosemite National Park— the detail that should come last, making a periodic sentence.*

Revised: John Muir, a naturalist who took long, solitary walks and let his beard grow long and tangled, was more responsible than any other person for establishing Yosemite National Park.

9b

emph

Often when you write your first draft, you may simply jot down a list of events or facts that you can combine to make periodic sentences in later drafts.

First Draft: At last, the hang glider settled softly and safely to earth. Its daring pilot had lunged into space from the cliff above. The cliff was three thousand feet above the valley floor. He knew that if he touched the face of the cliff, he would plunge to his death. He caught the morning winds and drifted down. *The most important fact in these sentences is that the hang-glider pilot landed safely after a daring flight. Here is a revision to make a periodic sentence.*

Revised: The daring pilot of the hang glider lunged into space from the cliff three thousand feet above the valley floor, caught the morning winds, and drifted down, knowing that to touch the face of the cliff was to plunge to his death, at last coming softly and safely to earth.

9b
Do not undermine your sentences by ending them with weak or parenthetical expressions.

Weak: Young people in 1946 and 1947 turned from the horrors of World War II to a love affair with the jukebox, however.

Better: Young people in 1946 and 1947, however, turned from the horrors of World War II to a love affair with the jukebox. *The reader learns of the contradiction early in the sentence when however is placed after the subject.*

WEAK: The huge demonstrations in Washington against the Vietnamese war in the 1960s may not have been supported by a majority of the American people, nevertheless.

BETTER: Nevertheless, the huge demonstrations in Washington against the Vietnamese war in the 1960s may not have been supported by a majority of the American people.

Nevertheless at the beginning of the sentence states a contradiction with something that has been said before and allows the sentence to end on a strong note.

Exercise 9.1 Rewrite the sentences below to make periodic sentences. If necessary, delete some words and phrases or invent others that capture the central idea.

1. Adlai Stevenson, laboring against the awesome power of Dwight Eisenhower's smile, lost the presidential elections of 1952 and 1956, as everyone knows.
2. Fiction writers do not often talk very well to interviewers about how they write, so Malcolm Cowley says.
3. The inspector found the body in the kitchen. When she had arrived on the scene, the house was locked and silent. She had the officers break down the door.
4. The gravity of the sun did bend lightwaves passing nearby from distant stars, as experiments during a solar eclipse proved.

9c

Write cumulative sentences by adding modifying elements to the predicates of independent or dependent clauses.

In a **cumulative sentence**, several free modifiers or absolutes are added to the end of the predicate, thus bringing new layers of meaning to the basic assertion of the clause.

Free modifiers follow the word they modify, and quite often they are participial phrases that follow a verb and modify the subject. The free modifiers in the following sentences are in italics.

The motorcycle spun out of control, *leaving the highway, plunging down the ravine, crashing through a fence, coming to rest at last on its side.*

The ocean beat against the shore in long swells, *roaring above the sound of the wind, threatening the tiny houses, slamming against the great rocks on the beach.*

Absolutes (see 5c, page 169) include both a noun and a participle. They may be placed at the end of a sentence to add texture and meaning to the whole. The absolutes in the following sentences are in italics.

> He crossed the finish line in record time, *his lungs nearly bursting with his effort.*
> The barn burned, *the flames rising two hundred feet into the night sky.*

Sometimes an absolute uses a noun with an unwritten or understood participle of the verb *to be.*

> She walked into the room, her face bright and cheerful.
> *The sentence may be understood in this way: "She walked into the room, her face* being *bright and cheerful."*

A cumulative sentence may use absolutes or free modifiers or both. In contrast, a noncumulative sentence completes its thought with a subject complement, a direct object, or an adverb or adverbial phrase. The sentence below concludes its thought with an adverbial phrase.

> The house stood silently *on the hill.*

But the sentence can be revised so that it completes its thought with absolutes and free modifiers:

> The house stood silently on the hill, baking in the hot sunshine, its broken windows gaping open to the ragged fields, its roof collapsing, its rotting doors hanging open, its glory departed.
> *The participial phrase* baking in the hot sunshine *is a free modifier modifying* house; *the phrases* its broken windows gaping open to the ragged fields, its roof collapsing, its rotting doors hanging open, *and* its glory departed *are all absolutes.*

Study the following cumulative sentences, and see how elements added to the end of the predicate help accumulate force.

> He emptied them thoroughly, *unhurried, his face completely cold, masklike almost.*
> —WILLIAM FAULKNER
> *The phrases in italics add an accumulating force to the sentence.*

Another characteristic was that once a Veragua had caught and gored a man or a horse he would not leave him but would attack again and again, *seeming to want to destroy his victim entirely.*

——ERNEST HEMINGWAY

The participial phrase seeming to want to destroy his victim entirely *is a free modifier, describing a breed of bull called a Veragua that is the subject of the sentence. The modifying phrase comes at the end of the sentence.*

Exercise 9.2   Combine the following sentences to make cumulative sentences.

Example

He sat at the typewriter. His teacup was at his left. The wind was blowing outside. The clock was ticking over the fireplace.

He sat at the typewriter, his teacup at his left, the clock ticking over the fireplace, the wind blowing outside.

1. She studied the map of the block. She was thinking of the fine old buildings that would have to be torn down. She was thinking of her own creation that would take their place. Her ideas were rushing in her head like a flood.
2. He got down from the train and looked around. He saw the courthouse. He saw the city square. It was vacant at this hour of the morning.
3. She saw him. He was sitting in a rocking chair. He was holding a large, black book. It was his family Bible.

Exercise 9.3   Look around the room where you are sitting, and write three cumulative sentences that describe some of the things you see.

9d

Give emphasis to the actor or agent in your sentences by using the active rather than the passive voice.

In the active voice, the subject of the sentence performs the action of the verb; in the passive voice, the subject of the sentence is acted upon (see 20e).

WEAK PASSIVE: His decision not to run for reelection to the presidency in 1968 was announced on television on March 31 of that year by Lyndon Johnson.

STRONGER ACTIVE: On March 31, 1968, President Lyndon Johnson announced on television that he would not run for reelection in the fall.

You can use the passive to build a dramatic periodic sentence in which the agent remains a surprise until the end. But such a sentence is valuable only if the surprise is worthwhile, as it may be in a humorous sentence:

9e

emph

The burglar alarms were set clanging, the police were brought running with drawn guns, and the customers in the bank were sent flying out the doors by a signal set off in the vault by a lost puppy.

You cannot use such a device often, and you must be sure that the surprise is real. Readers are likely to feel annoyed by writers who try to surprise them with the obvious:

Macbeth was written by the most brilliant of English playwrights, the Sweet Swan of Avon, the man whose work millions have known and loved, William Shakespeare.

As a rule, use the passive voice only when the actor or agent in the sentence is much less important to your statement than the recipient of the action.

Estes Kefauver *was elected* to the Senate in 1948.

She *was taken* to the hospital last night.

9e
Occasionally give emphasis by repeating key words or phrases in several consecutive clauses or sentences.

Let every nation know, whether it wishes us well or ill, that we shall pay *any* price, bear *any* burdens, meet *any* hardship, support *any* friend, oppose *any* foe to assure the survival and the success of liberty.

—JOHN F. KENNEDY

President Kennedy intended the word any *to pound home his message to the American people and the world.*

Such repetition is effective when used only occasionally to make an emphatic argument against important doubts. It can easily be overdone.

9f

Give special emphasis to ideas by writing a very short sentence to follow several long ones.

The real objection to capital punishment doesn't lie against the actual extermination of the condemned, but against our brutal American habit of putting it off so long. After all, every one of us must die soon or late, and a murderer, it must be assumed, is one who makes that sad fact the cornerstone of his metaphysic. But it is one thing to die, and quite another thing to lie for long months and even years under the shadow of death. *No sane man would choose such a finish.*

—H. L. Mencken

Exercise 9.4   Write a short paragraph in which you repeat a key word several times. You can write about anything you want, but it will probably help to assume that your paragraph is part of a controversial argument.

Example:
    Many protest nuclear energy, and they may be right. But they are wrong when they turn to coal as an alternative source of fuel. Coal is a destroyer. Coal kills the land where it is mined and the men who mine it. Coal dirties the air and blackens our cities. Coal smothers the delicate smells and strews a black dust over the green land. Coal eats at our skin and corrupts our lungs.

Exercise 9.5   Rewrite the following sentences to give emphasis to the elements you think are most important or most dramatic. You may change or delete words and phrases as long as you keep the central idea. Try to find several ways of dealing with each sentence.

1. The college library was locked up by the head librarian, G. W. Cranshaw, who said he got tired of seeing all those careless and sweaty students handling the books.
2. How strongly we believe in something, especially when it is something we think we ought to believe and maybe don't but won't admit it, and

222   Writing Clear and Effective Sentences

somebody comes and asks us if we believe it, is not measured well by statistics.

3. Now swimmers can buy little floats with bright colors on the top and clamps on the bottom under the water, and they can swim out to sea and take off their bathing suits and clamp them with the clamps and go skinny dipping if they want to.

4. An artificial climate has been made by central air-conditioning and central heating, and we are used to it now and cannot think of being without it, although we may have to get along without it someday.

5. Only a few fiction writers have also been good poets because the crafts are different, and not many people can manage both, although Edgar Allan Poe, Thomas Hardy, William Faulkner, and James Joyce have all done their best.

9f

emph

CHAPTER TEN

Variety

Sentence variety is the spice of lively writing, and you should strive to write sentences varied enough to hold your readers' attention throughout your paper.

10a

Vary the patterns and the lengths of your sentences to keep your readers alert and involved.

If you repeat any sentence pattern too often, you will bore your readers, so it is a good idea to learn and practice variations in the basic writing pattern. The basic pattern in modern English writing is *subject + predicate* (see 5c).

         Subject.   Predicate.

My father and my stepmother left on the noon plane to Atlanta.

The most common variation on this basic pattern is to begin with some kind of adverbial opener.

     ADVERBIAL PHRASE: *By the late afternoon,* they will be at home.

     ADVERBIAL CLAUSE: *Because they live so far away,* we see them only once or twice a year.

SIMPLE ADVERB: *Tomorrow* they will telephone.

Another variation is to begin a sentence with a participle or a participial phrase that serves as an adjective.

PARTICIPLE: *Smiling,* he walked confidently into the room.

PARTICIPIAL PHRASE: *Stunned by the stock market crash,* many brokers committed suicide.

10a

var

Sentences also can open with an infinitive phrase or a coordinating conjunction.

INFINITIVE PHRASE: *To protect my mother,* I'd made up stories of a secret marriage that for some strange reason never got known.
—SHERWOOD ANDERSON

COORDINATING CONJUNCTION: *But,* say you, it is a question of interest, and if you make it your interest, you have the right to enslave another. Very well. *And* if he can make it his interest, he has the right to enslave you.
—ABRAHAM LINCOLN

The repetition of the common pattern *subject + predicate* is less monotonous than the repetition of the other patterns, but it grows tiresome if it is combined with choppy, disconnected sentences. In the first passage below, the sentences all begin with the subject; they are all about the same length; and they are all short. They are clear and understandable, but notice the improvement in the second passage, where the combined and embedded elements create a pleasing variety in both length and sentence structure.

REPETITIOUS

He dived quickly into the sea. He peered through his mask. The watery world turned darker. A school of fish went by. The distant light glittered on their bodies. He stopped swimming. He waited. He thought the fish might be chased by a shark. He satisfied himself that there was no shark. He continued down. He heard only one sound. That was his breathing apparatus. It made a bubbling noise in operation.

10b

var

He dived quickly into the sea, peering through his mask at a watery world that turned darker as he went down. A school of fish went by, the distant light glittering on their bodies, and he stopped swimming and waited a moment to see if the fish might be chased by a shark. Satisfying himself that there was no shark, he continued down. The only sound he heard was the bubbling noise of his breathing apparatus.

The improved version combines thoughts and reduces the number of sentences in the passage. The repetition of the pronoun *he* is also reduced and the sentence patterns are more varied and interesting.

10b

Ask an occasional rhetorical question.

A rhetorical question heightens attention by suddenly requiring the reader to participate more actively in your prose. A rhetorical question allows you to give an answer as the writer does in the following example:

> The movie is called *Rock 'n Roll High School,* and for anyone not into punk, it has only one conceivable point of interest: Can Van Patten act as well as he hits a tennis ball? The answer is no, which is not to say that he isn't a promising young actor. It's just that as a tennis player he is a good deal more than fine.
>
> —*Sports Illustrated*

Sometimes writers ask a question or even a series of questions without giving an answer because to them the answer is obvious:

> Is not marriage an open question, when it is alleged, from the beginning of the world, that such as are in the institution wish to get out; and such as are out wish to get in?
>
> —RALPH WALDO EMERSON

You may ask questions that you know will be asked by your opponents in argument. You can then answer them in ways that support your side. You also can gain an advantage in the argument by raising the difficult questions in a way that helps your cause. Study the following passage with its questions posed, on behalf of his opponents, by Martin Luther King, Jr. It is from his "Letter from Birmingham Jail."

One may well ask: "How can you advocate breaking some laws and obeying others?" The answer lies in the fact that there are two types of laws: just and unjust. I would be the first to advocate obeying just laws. One has not only a legal but a moral responsibility to obey just laws. Conversely, one has a moral responsibility to disobey unjust laws. I would agree with St. Augustine that "an unjust law is no law at all."

Now, what is the difference between the two? How does one determine whether a law is just or unjust? A just law is a man-made code that squares with the moral law or the law of God. An unjust law is a code that is out of harmony with the moral law. To put it in the terms of St. Thomas Aquinas: An unjust law is a human law that is not rooted in eternal and natural law. Any law that uplifts human personality is just. Any law that degrades personality is unjust. All segregation statutes are unjust because segregation distorts the soul and damages the personality.

Avoid beginning an essay by asking broad rhetorical questions that might better be phrased as sharp thesis statements. Inexperienced writers use this device so often that it loses its effect quickly. "Why should we study *Huckleberry Finn*?" "How did TVA begin?" "Was Alger Hiss guilty as charged?" Readers may suspect that the writer of such broad questions will not take the trouble to think of a better opening. It is usually better to save your rhetorical questions for an occasional paragraph that comes in the body of a paper after the subject has been introduced in some other way.

10c

Use an exclamation on rare occasions for special effects.

Occasionally an exclamation helps you vary a series of declarative sentences:

Clearly, even if there were a limit on the length of sentences to twenty words, it would not be possible to characterize any individual's knowledge of English by claiming that he carried around a list of all its sentences in his head! But there is in fact no limit to the length of a sentence. A sentence twenty-one words in length can be made longer by adding another modifier or a subordinate of some kind—and so on.

—HELEN S. CAIRNS AND CHARLES E. CAIRNS

10d

Invert the subject and the verb occasionally.

For variety you can put the verb before the subject. This is another device that should be used only rarely:

> Beyond is another country.
>
> —ROBERT M. PIRSIG

> From high above in the swirl of raging wind and snow came a frightening, wonderful, mysterious sound.
>
> —MARK HELPRIN

Exercise 10.1 Revise the following sets of simple sentences to form two coherent paragraphs made up of sentences that are varied in style and in length. You may change or add words but not facts. Look for places where you can subordinate one idea to another, both to reduce the number of words and to create a pleasing style.

Experiment. Rearrange some sentences to make the verb come before the subject. Convert a sentence into a question, and either begin an answer or point your reader toward an answer. Compare your versions with the work of others in your class.

SET 1

1. Bluegrass music was popular in the rural south before World War II.
2. Radio and recordings have made it popular everywhere.
3. It features hand-held instruments.
4. These include the banjo, the guitar, the fiddle, the mandolin, and sometimes the dulcimer and the bass fiddle.
5. Bluegrass does not use drums.
6. Bluegrass songs are in the tradition of the mountain ballad and the Protestant hymn.
7. It began as the music of poor southern American mountaineers.
8. They had to make their own entertainment.
9. Bluegrass songs are about love affairs gone wrong.
10. Sometimes they speak about the fear of hell.
11. Sometimes they describe conversion experiences.
12. Sometimes they express the yearning of the soul for heaven.
13. Bluegrass bands never use electrified instruments.

1. D. W. Griffith was the first great American filmmaker.
2. He made the shot the most important element in filmmaking.
3. Others had made the scene the most important element.
4. He combined shots into scenes.
5. He understood the importance of cutting and composition.
6. He combined scenes into sequences.
7. He combined sequences into plots.
8. He began as an actor.
9. He made five dollars a day.
10. He became a director in 1908.
11. He made 150 films between 1908 and 1913.
12. He had the chance to experiment.
13. Others wanted to photograph the whole human figure.
14. These other film directors thought people wanted whole figures.
15. Griffith used the close-up shot.
16. The close-up shot provided emotions.
17. He made his actors stop making extreme gestures.
18. He tried to make actors seem like real people.

10e

Occasionally use free modifiers and absolutes at the end of a sentence to achieve variety (see 9c).

A free modifier, you have learned, is a participle or participial phrase occurring at the end of a clause and modifying the subject.

The plane climbed slowly, *fighting for altitude.*
The participial phrase fighting for altitude *is a free modifier describing the subject,* plane.

We walked home, *delighting in the autumn colors.*
The participial phrase delighting in the autumn colors *modifies the subject,* we.

An absolute, to review, consists of a noun combined with a participle and usually comes at the end of a clause. Absolutes modify the entire clause where they appear.

> The plane climbed slowly, *its engines shrieking.*
> *The phrase in italics is an absolute. The noun* engines *is joined to the participle* shrieking.

> We walked home, *our eyes delighting in the autumn colors and our hearts singing.*
> *Two absolutes come at the end of this sentence. The noun* eyes *combines with the participle* delighting *to make the first one, and the noun* hearts *combines with the participle* singing *to make the second one.*

Free modifiers and absolutes allow variety. Writers who use them can combine thoughts that might otherwise have to be expressed by simple sentences. We could say this:

> The cows grazed in the field. They made the day seem tranquil.

But by using a free modifier we can say this:

> The cows grazed in the field, making the day seem tranquil.

We could say this:

> She gathered up her portfolio. Her hands moved slowly and precisely.

But with an absolute we can say this:

> She gathered up her portfolio, her hands moving slowly and precisely.

You can combine absolutes and free modifiers to write fairly long sentences that do not become confusing:

> The car moved slowly up the dirt road, wheezing, banging, lurching along, the rust showing through its thin paint, its windshield cracked, its engine smoking.

Exercise 10.2   Combine the following sentence groups to make free modifiers and absolutes.

1. The bookshelf stood in the corner. It was overburdened with books. Its paint was worn off.
2. The computer hummed on my desk. Its green monitor was flashing at me in a friendly way.
3. He had stayed at home all his life. He had taken care of his family's farm.
4. The full moon rose over the graveyard. Its face looked ghostly. It frightened me.

10e

var

Part *3*

PART THREE

USING WORDS
EFFECTIVELY

	Chapter
Appropriate Diction	**11**
Imagery and Figurative Language	**12**
Including Needed Words	**13**
Avoiding Wordiness	**14**
Sexist Language	**15**
Using a Dictionary and Thesaurus	**16**

CHAPTER ELEVEN

Appropriate Diction

In writing, you always should use language that is appropriate to your subject by choosing words that state your meaning exactly and that convey a clear sense of it to your readers. You should avoid a writing style that is too informal or chatty, but you also must beware of stiffness and pomposity.

To get a sense of appropriate language, you should be as honest as you can be, and you should read as much as you can. Being honest means that you do not try to persuade readers by proclaiming passionate emotions that you do not feel or by assuming an authority that you do not have. An understated language that does not draw undue attention to itself is almost always the best voice for communicating ideas. A highly colored language often sends unwanted messages to readers, telling them that you believe you are superior to them or that you are cute or that you are interesting because of the feelings you have rather than because of the information you communicate. If you do feel highly emotional about an issue, it is much more effective to tell your readers the information that stirs your emotions than to tell them that you have the feelings. For example, if you object strongly to some practice like killing baby seals for their fur, you may win readers over by giving them a simple, factual narrative of how seal hunts are carried out. Understate your own feelings, but give all the details that create these feelings if you want to be persuasive. You will not win anybody if you use a shouting, insulting language that simply gives vent to your emotions. That is probably the least effective way of creating these emotions in your readers. For example, a student conducting interviews wrote this sentence in her paper:

As absurd as all the responses to my previous interviews were, none approached the repulsiveness of my last one.

She would have done much better to report what her interviewees had said so that her readers could judge whether the statements were "absurd" and whether they exhibited "repulsiveness."

The best way to gain a sense of appropriate language is to read as much as you can. Whether you are preparing to write about literature or natural science or history, take some time to read what writers who know the subject have written. Try to use their tone as a model for your own style. Strive to be serious and to be taken seriously, but do not get so serious that you become humorless and stiff. Take the attitude that you want your readers to learn something from you and to appreciate the way you convey information. Your readers should be able to enjoy your writing unless your topic itself is depressing or painful. But even then, your writing should be so clear that it creates sympathetic feelings in your readers to match the subject of your essay.

Some writers work hard to display themselves as vital, interesting people, truly excited about their subject and up to date in their use of language. Unfortunately, their strained efforts at informality often make them sound pretentious, self-conscious, and excessively emotional, as if they would rather be cute than correct:

> Now I want to tell you about this real, cool cat, David Farragut, see? At the time I'm getting ready to tell you about, he'd been out there on the deep blue sea for the U.S. Navy for more than fifty long years. When he was just a little kid, he was hauling powder up to the guns of a boat they called the *Essex* back there when we kicked the living daylights out of the Brits in the War of 1812. And you know what the old geezer did every time he had a birthday? He did a flip! That's right! He told one of his junior officers that he wouldn't think he was old until he couldn't do that any more. I wonder if he ever did get that old! Must have, since he's dead now! (Ha! Ha!) Well, when the big rip came in 1861, he was settled down there in ole Virginie, in Norfolk by the sea, and he told those Johnny Rebs in his hometown that they were going to catch the devil — that's exactly what he said — before it was all over. Then he split and got himself north to fight for Old Glory. So there he is when we get down to this part of his tale, getting ready to put the evil eye on ole New Orleans, piling all his boats into the river, and getting ready to ram his fleet right smack into the city.

Almost as bad as the slangy, overinformal prose above is this stiff, dead version:

> David Glasgow Farragut had served his country loyally in the United States Navy for over fifty years, more than half a century.

As an extremely young sailor, scarcely more than a boy, he had fulfilled the acutely dangerous task of carrying highly explosive gunpowder from the storage magazines below decks to the cannon stationed on the deck of a ship called the *Essex* of the frigate class, a ship well known in the heroic annals of the American navy. At the time of the outbreak of hostilities in the Civil War, Farragut possessed the strength and vitality of a much younger man, qualities which he exhibited each and every year by doing a handspring on his birthday, much to the astonishment of his younger subordinates, who, it may be assumed, expected actions of a more dignified nature from their commander! He told one of these subordinates one time that he would not suppose himself to be truly growing old until he found himself entirely unable to do such a handspring on his natal day. When the tragic conflict began its bloody pageant across the American stage he had been dwelling in the city of Norfolk in the state of Virginia, and he delivered himself of a stern verbal warning to those neighbors of his in this important port who believed in withdrawing their allegiance to the Union with its capital in Washington in the District of Columbia. "You fellows will catch the Devil before you get through with this business" was his somewhat brusque and perhaps ungallant but altogether sincere remark to these secessionists, as they were called at that time. He thereupon closed down his house, which we may suppose was a fine one, befitting his long service in the country's military, and departed for the northern climes, where he affirmed his undeviating and eternal loyalty to the government in Washington and resumed his proper position in that floating part of the military establishment destined to carry the war into the Atlantic frontier of the United States. Now he was the supreme commander of the naval fleet of fighting ships that had been sent down from the north to fight against and if possible capture the important port city of New Orleans, "Queen of the Mississippi," and he was undertaking the expedition of small, heavy ships and gunboats up into the river that led in the direction of the city.

Before readers get very far into either of these versions, they start having trouble. Here is Bruce Catton's version in his book *This Hallowed Ground:*

Farragut had been in the navy for more than half a century — had served as a very juvenile powder monkey on the famous frigate *Essex* when she cruised the Pacific in the War of 1812, and was still spry enough for a midshipman. He had a habit of turning a handspring on every birthday and told an amazed junior that he would not think he was growing old until he found himself unable to do it. He had been living in Norfolk, Virginia, when the war started; had warned his secessionist fellow townsmen, "You fellows will catch the Devil before you get through with this business," and then had closed his house and gone north to stick with the old flag. Now he was in command of the fleet that had been appointed to attack New Orleans, and he was getting heavy sloops and gunboats up into the river.

Catton's diction is informal without being stuffy or chatty. He does not use slang, although he does use the informal expression "powder monkey" because it was common in Farragut's time. He does not weigh his prose down with unnecessary explanations or dreary qualifications. He treats his material seriously, but he adds the humorous information that Farragut turned a handspring on his birthday every year. Catton does not intrude himself into his narrative; he does not tell us what he thinks about everything he says. He gives us information and lets us make up our own minds. We can see that he likes Farragut, that he even admires him. But we can perceive Catton's emotions only by what he chooses to tell us about his subject. He does not say, "David Farragut was an extremely admirable man because of what he did when the Civil War broke out." Catton tells us what we need to know, and he leaves us to make up our own minds about whether the people he describes are good or bad and whether their actions are admirable or not.

You should use a similar discretion. When you write, choose a tone that will not interfere with what you want your reader to know. Catton's style is an example of a common and attractive tone in American prose today. In general, it is a good tone to imitate because it is simple and straightforward and unemotional.

You should always choose the tone and the diction that fit your subject. You should not use a breezy, informal tone for a paper on cancer or for an essay on famine in Africa. And you should not use a sober, humorless tone in writing about the World Series or the Super Bowl.

11a

Use slang sparingly and only when it is appropriate to the subject and the tone you choose for your essay.

INAPPROPRIATE: In *Heart of Darkness,* we hear a lot about a dude named Kurtz, but we don't see the guy much.

REVISED: In *Heart of Darkness*, Marlow, the narrator, talks almost continually about Kurtz, but we see Kurtz himself only at the end.

INAPPROPRIATE: When Thomas More saw how Henry VIII was going, he might have run off to France to save his hide, but he stayed on and got his head chopped off for his trouble.

REVISED: When he saw the direction of Henry's mind, Thomas More might have fled to France to save himself, but he stayed on until he was imprisoned and put to death.

In both inappropriate examples above, the use of slang and informal diction contradicts the seriousness of each topic.

Some slang terms are always entering the mainstream of the language, and many American journalists assume a breezy, informal tone. But even these journalists do not fill their prose with slang. Instead, they use slang occasionally to fit a special mood that they are trying to convey.

But Boston is also a city that historically has pricked the social conscience of many well-heeled undergraduates.

—HOWARD HUSOCK, *The New York Times Magazine*

The writer of a more formal essay would probably not use the term well-heeled.

Minutes before the camera's ruby light flashed on, cable TV's garrulous impresario was already well into his inaugural address before a gathering of Atlanta VIPs.

—*Time*

TV as an abbreviation for "television" is so common now that it is not considered slang and can be used even in formal writing; VIP for "Very Important Person" would probably still be considered too slangy for formal writing.

Many wisecracky lines are assigned to the spinster, and Joan Pape, when given a chance, delivers them well.

—*The New Yorker*

The word wisecracky *is an arresting coinage that many would consider slang, unsuitable for a formal subject. But it is at home in a theater review.*

Harvey Shapiro is a plump, middle-aged Cherry Hill business man who's been married to the same woman for 26 years. They have two kids.

—*Philadelphia Magazine*

In informal writing, the word kids *is appropriate. But no historian would write this sentence in a scholarly article: "Henry VIII had only one kid by his first marriage who survived into adulthood."*

You must use slang if it is part of a direct quotation. There the prose is not yours but that of your source, and you must quote that source exactly if you are using quotation marks.

Postell said that there is very little illness among students right now, adding, "If you've got a lot of sickness, you've got a lot of people sicking out."

The term sicking out *is slang for pretending illness to evade some responsibility—like taking an exam on time.* Sicking out *is a catchy phrase, but it would be glaringly out of place in a term paper about religion:* "Bishop John Fisher did not wish to attend the Parliament; so he sicked out and refused to come."

11b

Avoid writing in dialect.

Some inexperienced writers try to use dialect to show the ethnic or regional origins of people, but dialect is difficult to express in writing. Inexperienced writers frequently get it wrong and may appear to be laughing at the people they are writing about.

DIALECT: "Ah'm a-goin' raght over thar," she said, "an if'n you'd go along, hit'ud be a big hep, and Ah'd be much obleeged."

REVISED: "I'm going right over there," she said with a strong Appalachian accent, "and if you'd go along, it'd be a big help, and I'd be much obliged."

11c

Avoid jargon that inflates language and that makes your thoughts seem more complicated than they really are.

Jargon is a language that uses ordinary English words in ways that are unfamiliar to most people. Sometimes jargon enables people with specialized interests to talk with each other. For example, people who use computers talk to each other in a language nearly incomprehensible to people who know nothing about computers. Computer users speak of "booting a disk" and of making "hard copies" and of "accessing the program." These words communicate very well to the vast number of computer users in our country, and they turn up in computer magazines. "Input is a snap, since the entire program is menu driven (see Figure 2), and Help messages will flash on the screen if you don't understand the significance of an assumption (see Figure 3)." That sentence, from *PC Magazine*, is nonsense to the rest of us because it uses a special jargon with words like "input" and "program" and "Help messages."

Such jargon has its place in both speaking and writing. All too often, though, writers use jargon to make simple thoughts seem complicated and to imply that they have special knowledge that is superior to that of outsiders. Experienced readers see jargon as a false front, and they rarely take it seriously. Consider this paragraph written by an academic author:

> Romantic love is characterized by a preoccupation with a deliberately restricted set of perceived characteristics in the love object which are viewed as a means to some ideal ends. In the process of selecting the set of perceived characteristics and the process of determining the ideal ends, there is also a systematic failure to assess the accuracy of the perceived characteristics and the feasibility of achieving the ideal ends given the selected set of means and other pre-existing ends.

The paragraph means something like the following:

11d

d

> People in love see only what they want to see in the beloved. They want to believe in an ideal, so they do not question the accuracy of what they see or ask themselves if the ideal they imagine can be attained.
>
> *Notice the wordiness of the original, especially in expressions like* perceived characteristics *and* love object *and in the repetition of words like* ends. *We read that "Romantic love is characterized by . . . characteristics." Throughout the passage, the writer uses the passive voice, which is often a signal of jargon.*

When you think you may be writing in unnecessary jargon, break your sentences down into simple core assertions, keeping subjects close to verbs, limiting modifiers, removing repetitions. Write the simplest sentences that will still keep the meaning you want to convey. See if you can make them so direct that any literate person can understand them.

11d

Do not use obsolete and foreign words and technical terms unless you are sure that they are appropriate to your audience.

1 Avoid obsolete or archaic words and expressions that confuse your reader or misstate your meaning.

OBSOLETE: In Anthony Trollope's novel *Barchester Towers*, Slope insists on making love to Eleanor Bold in a carriage, despite her efforts to resist his advances.

In Trollope's day, to make love *meant to announce one's love to someone and to propose marriage, and Trollope uses the phrase in that sense in all his novels — as did all nineteenth-century English novelists. A scholar of literature might inadvertently fall into using Trollope's phrases today, thus confusing readers to whom the phrase* make love *means something else.*

OBSOLETE: It was clear ere she left that the problems had not been resolved.
The word ere *is used frequently in early modern English to mean "before," but it seems archaic now and may confuse modern American readers.*

But if you know your readers have read a piece of literature containing obsolete language, you may use it, sometimes humorously, when you write about the piece:

Anyone who hits on an interpretation of Hamlet's character and ponders it for a while is likely to find his resolution sicklied o'er with the pale cast of thought. No single interpretation seems adequate.
The line resolution sicklied o'er with the pale cast of thought *comes from a famous speech by Hamlet. The writer assumes that readers know both the play and the line and therefore uses the line, although it involves archaic language. Note that you do not place a well-known literary allusion in quotation marks when you are not referring to the quotation itself and when you are clearly not claiming to have originated the line yourself.*

2   Use foreign words only when they are necessary.

It is pretentious to use foreign expressions when English will do.

PRETENTIOUS: He used foreign expressions to show how superior he was to the *hoi polloi* because he had discovered *par hasard* that some of the beautiful people were deeply impressed by words they could not understand.

BETTER: He used foreign expressions to show how superior he was to ordinary people because he had discovered by chance that some of the beautiful people were deeply impressed by words they could not understand.

PRETENTIOUS: Her collection of exotic clamshells was her only *raison d'être.*

BETTER: Her collection of exotic clamshells was her only reason for living.

PRETENTIOUS: Sarah's *Weltanschauung* extended no further than her daily whims.

BETTER: Sarah's view of the world extended no further than her daily whims.

3   Avoid using technical terms unless you are writing for an audience that understands what these terms mean.

The advice that applies to jargon (see 11c) applies here. Sometimes technical terms work well when they are used for a specialized audience that understands them. But technical terms thrown into a paper for a general audience often seem pompous, and they can only confuse the average reader.

11d

d

POMPOUS: Baxter felt a pang of existential anxiety when he contemplated his English exam.

BETTER: Baxter worried about his English exam when he thought about it.
The words existential *and* existentialist *have a philosophical meaning understood by students of modern intellectual thought. They should not be used indiscriminately as synonyms for* personal *or* thoughtful.

CORRECT: The potential audience for the existentialists consists of those who feel that, when they ask for bread, the most competent English-speaking philosophers offer them a stone.
—WALTER KAUFMANN
The philosopher Walter Kaufmann uses the term existentialists *to describe a group of thinkers. He does not use it as a casual term for any kind of anxiety.*

Exercise 11.1   Rewrite the following sentences to change language that might be inappropriate in a formal paper. Try to keep the meaning of each sentence. To do so, you will need to consider what we mean when we use some common slang words—words that are often emotional but inexact.

1. Told by the British that he must die, Nathan Hale made a laid-back reply: "I regret that I have but one life to give for my country."

2. When the ump called nine consecutive strikes on three batters, Manager Sparky Anderson got his back up.
3. When the Germans were presented with the Treaty of Versailles in 1919, they really got sore.
4. Maybe the concert of the Boston Symphony Orchestra will be so wicked that the audience will fork over megabucks to go with the flow.
5. John Foster Dulles, Eisenhower's first Secretary of State, was a shrewd old geezer who saw red whenever the Commies did some dirt.
6. Some people think that if Marie Antoinette had not been so stuck up, the French mobs might not have cut her head off in the revolution, but maybe the Frenchies were so riled up over everything in general that they would have beheaded her if she had been as pure as Julie Andrews.
7. In the history of fashion, men's clothing was much more spiffy than women's until the nineteenth century.
8. The President promised to go to Moscow anon.
9. Mr. Thomas B. Cartwright, official flack for the State Department, told a press conference that the United States and China were boogying along toward lasting peace between the two countries.
10. Leonard Bernstein was top dog for the New York Philharmonic Orchestra for many years, although now and then he was accused of showboating.

11d

d

Exercise 11.2 Discuss in class the kinds of papers where the following expressions or words might be appropriate. Compose sentences using them.

1. rip-off	**6.** hobo
2. freaky	**7.** team player
3. bull session	**8.** loner
4. on the lam	**9.** flying high
5. hang out	**10.** narc

Exercise 11.3 Rewrite the following sentences to eliminate foreign words or stilted expressions. You may need to look up the foreign words or stilted expressions in your desk dictionary. Don't try to translate the foreign words literally; try rather to put their meaning into fresh, idiomatic English.

1. The freshmen thought that the *summum bonum* of college life was to own a convertible.

2. Max said that if his roommate kept on smoking cigars in bed at night, it would be a *casus belli.*

3. The mail carrier made her quotidian march *lentemente* from domicile to domicile, wearing her official blue culottes and dropping off little missives in the postal receptacles while phoebus showered the sidewalks with his lethal darts and myriads of canines kept up their iterant ululations.

4. A common multidimensional learning problem for students of the typewriter and the violin is the dexterity factor, for in both cases erroneous application of the fingers has the end result of a negative production response.

5. A sophomore is a kind of *tertium quid* between freshmen and upper-class students.

6. The professor tried to find a *via media* between unceasing research and talking to students all day long in her office.

11e

Use idioms according to standard practice.

Idioms are habitual ways of saying things, and when we violate them, we cause readers to stumble. All languages have their own idioms. The French say, "How many years does he have?" while we say, "How old is he?" The Germans say of something they do not understand, "That comes to me like Spanish." We say, "That's Greek to me." Spanish speakers say, "What hour is it?" We say, "What time is it?" The French say, "What do you have?" We say, "What's wrong with you?" The French also say, "I have heat," and we say, "I'm hot." The modern Greeks say, "It's going to make heat today." We say, "It's going to be hot today." Americans in the rural, mountainous South say, "What do you say?" Other Americans say, "Hello," or "How are you?" or "Hi" or "Howdy."

Idioms cannot usually be translated from one language to another, and they sometimes cannot be transferred from one region to another within a country. If you say in French to a Frenchman, "I'm going to eat a hot dog with mustard," he will probably be appalled at your taste for puppies. If you ask a mountain southerner in the United States for a poke, he will hand you a paper bag; if you ask a New Yorker, he may hit you in the mouth.

Teachers often write *id* (for incorrect idiom) in the margin of a paper when the student has mangled some standard English word or phrase. If you write, "The South was angry against Lincoln," your teacher may write *id* at *against* because we commonly say that we are *angry with* someone or *angry at* someone, not angry *against* the person. The same is true of the phrase *different from.* We say, "Fred is *different from* his older brother," not, "Fred is *different than* his older brother." When you disagree with a friend, you say, "I *differed with* her about the interpretation of the news," meaning that you had discussed the news and argued about it. But if you say, "He *differed from* me because he wore tweed pajamas," you are only noting how you and someone else are different without saying whether you have ever discussed the matter. We do not say, "She *laughed on* the joke"; we say, "She *laughed at* the joke."

From these examples, you can see that idioms often involve prepositions and that getting an idiom right is often a matter of using a preposition correctly. You know that there is a big difference between these two sentences: "He made off with the money." "He made up with his friend." There is also a big difference between these two sentences: "He bet on the horses every week." "He bet at a window at the racetrack." Sometimes we use the improper idiom by using the wrong preposition. We should not say, "He stayed *to* Boston last Sunday afternoon." We should say rather, "He stayed *in* Boston last Sunday afternoon." Sometimes we use a preposition when none is necessary. We should not say, "We will meet *up with* him in Denver." We should say only, "We will meet him in Denver."

Sometimes idiom refers to diction — how we use some words. We do not say, "On July 1, 1863, the Union Army of the Potomac and the Confederate Army of Northern Virginia *affronted* each other at Gettysburg." We do not mean that these two armies merely offended each other; we mean something stronger, and the idiomatic usage would be this: "On July 1, 1863, the Union Army of the Potomac and the Confederate Army of Northern Virginia *confronted* each other at Gettysburg." It is not idiomatic to say, "*Previous to* the game, the band performed on the field." We say, "*Before* the game, the band performed on the field."

Idiom refers to custom, and no book can give you all the ways idioms may be misused. Neither can a book give you a set of rules that will enable you to get idioms right all the time. Inexperienced writers most often have trouble with idioms when they use unfamiliar words or expressions and do not know how to put them together the way experienced writers use them. We learn idioms one at a time, and we remember them as we grow in experience with language and as we use them in our writing and speaking.

Exercise 11.4 Rewrite the following sentences to correct mistakes in idiom. Don't be afraid to make a mistake. Remember that idiom is very difficult because it often has no logic. It is a reflection of customary speech patterns, and custom often refuses to obey logical rules. You may wish to consult a dictionary that includes examples of how words are used. The dictionary examples will help you understand the idioms in question.

Example: Jack was angry against Leo.

Correct idiom: Jack was angry with Leo.

1. We celebrate Labor Day at the first Monday after the first Sunday in September.
2. Lyndon Johnson became President on November 1963.
3. My mother introduced me with her friend.
4. Previous to the meeting, we agreed to talk only an hour before adjourning.
5. Newton's general principle states that all bodies have a force of gravity proportionate with their mass.
6. Jazz music has been traditionally centered around the experience of black musicians playing in small groups.
7. He deaned the faculty for ten years and then returned to teaching because he wanted to make something of himself.
8. The sun arose that morning at six o'clock.
9. They promised to meet up with our group on the trail.
10. Computers promise to us much more efficiency than typewriters could ever give.
11. She loved to stay to home and read in the evening.
12. A sailboat race is different than a car race in how the racers start.
13. She had a good relationship to him.
14. His date was still not ready, and he had to wait on her in the dorm.
15. Bernadette was quite impatient of his behavior as she wondered where he was at.

11f

d

11f

Choose words with connotations you wish to convey.

The definition of words is complicated because words have both primary and secondary meanings. These secondary meanings are the impressions or *connotations* the words convey, connotations that allow some words to work in some contexts and not in others. The connotations of words are like the clothing we wear for special occasions. As the occasions differ, so do our clothes. A man who steps out of his house in a tuxedo is probably not going to the barn to milk the cows. A woman who emerges wearing a business suit and carrying a briefcase is probably not on her way to a job as a welder. The man might sometimes milk and the woman weld, but they would do these jobs in different clothes.

Similarly, ideas may be expressed in words that wear slightly different clothes to do different jobs. You can say that your friend Murdock *evaded* the requirement that everyone learn how to swim before graduation, or you can say that he *flouted* it, or you can say that he *escaped* it. Either way we know that Murdock did not learn how to swim and that he did not obey the rule. But if he *evaded* the rule, he slipped away from it; he was sly; he got around the requirement by some quiet and perhaps devious or clever way. If he *flouted* the requirement, he may have announced publicly and arrogantly that he did not intend to observe the requirement and that for all he cared, the administration could withhold his diploma if it wanted to. If he *escaped* the requirement, something may have happened accidentally to make the college forget to enforce the rule for him.

You can say that your boss *requested* that you come to a meeting on Thursday morning or that she *demanded* to see you as soon as you came in. The word *request* is a polite, perhaps neutral term, but when your boss starts making *demands*, you may be in trouble.

If you say that the audience was *hypnotized* by a speech, you imply that the speaker was so good that the audience forgot everything else except what the speaker was saying and believed everything; but if you say that a speech *put the audience to sleep*, you mean that the speech was a bore.

You may say that your parents *ignored* your request for money, implying a deliberate act of will on their part; but if they *neglected* your request, they may simply have put it off or forgotten about it.

If you say that someone is *unsympathetic* toward your views, you mean that she may have considered them but that she is not inclined to accept them. But if she is *intolerant* of your opinions, she probably does not want to hear them or talk to you about them or perhaps even be friendly toward you when you express them.

If you say that a shortstop was *confused*, you may mean that when a hard ground ball was hit to him with a man on first, he thought there were two outs when there was only one and in his confusion did not throw to second fast enough to get the double play. But if you say that he was *dazed*, you may mean that he was hit on the head by a line drive and that he could not tell whether he was in the ballpark or a bathtub.

Studying the connotations of words can be enjoyable, but beginning writers often have trouble with connotations. The best remedies are to note how experienced writers use different words and to study the dictionary for the use of **synonyms** — words having similar meanings but different connotations.

Exercise 11.5 Write sentences that use the following words correctly. You may use several of the words in one sentence if you can do so gracefully.

1. ambitious, greedy
2. successful, enterprising
3. proud, arrogant, haughty
4. hit, smash, collide
5. drink, guzzle, sip
6. eat, gobble, pick at

CHAPTER TWELVE

Imagery and Figurative Language

You can enliven your writing with imagery, that is, by creating word pictures for the reader. Using concrete nouns and verbs that appeal to the senses, you can change an abstract idea into something vivid and specific. If you write, "The trees were affected by the bad weather," you do not give your readers much to picture in their minds. But if you write, "The small pines shook in the wind," the concrete nouns *pine* and *wind* and the concrete verb *shook* create an image.

Figurative language helps you build images. A figure states or implies a comparison between your subject and something else. If you write "The small pines shook in the wind," you are being literal. If you write "The small pines trembled with fear like children scolded by the wind," you are being figurative. The figure compares the trees to frightened young children and the wind to a person scolding them. Our language is rich in figures because they help us express ideas more clearly and succinctly than we otherwise could.

12a

Use nouns and verbs that convey clear, concrete images or that report action.

Avoid nouns and passive verbs that merely report the existence of something but do not report that something happens. Examine this paragraph:

Often the positions people take on energy are an index to how they stand on other issues. Conservatives, liberals, and radicals tend to group their causes, and if you tell me where you think we ought to get our energy, I can probably tell you what you think about what we ought to eat and how we ought to spend our time. But nearly everybody on every side of every current issue agrees that we should use solar energy.

This paragraph contains no errors in grammar, and it is fairly clear. But its prose style does not engage our attention, and when we finish reading it, we have a hard time remembering it. Words like conservative, liberal, *and* radical *are so vague that we don't know what they mean unless the writer explains them — something few writers do who use these terms. A concept that sounds concrete, like* solar energy, *conveys many meanings to different people, and we don't know which meaning the writer intends.*

12a

fig

Now study this version (italics added):

Every source of energy seems to have become a political issue. Tell me whether you think the path to a happy future lies with *solar heating* or with *nuclear furnaces*, tell me how you feel about *oil shale* and *coal* and *corn-fed gasohol*, and I'll tell you where you stand on *welfare reform, environmental policy, vegetarianism, busing, backpacking*, and *abortion*. But there is one kind of energy that attracts a diverse following: *photovoltaics*, the art of converting *sunlight* into *electricity*.

— Tracy Kidder

Look at all the nouns in italics that call up concrete images in this paragraph. At the end we know just what aspect of solar energy — photovoltaics — the writer is talking about. He uses a technical term and immediately defines it.

Now study this paragraph:

In the 1930s, color started being used for movies, first in cartoons. Walt Disney was a pioneer in this field and made several short cartoons before he expanded the technique to make the first feature-length animation, *Snow White and the Seven Dwarfs*, which was very popular.

This paragraph has some concrete details, including the name of the movie Snow White and the Seven Dwarfs. *But compared with the following one, it is still vague and general.*

Color was coming in, but only in cartoons was it really successful. The *Silly Symphonies*, animating *flowers, birds, bees*, and *animals*, mocking well-loved pieces of classical *music*, using the freedom of *design* and *line* and *color* to create funny, moving, dramatic, and sometimes terrifying *effects,* are probably *Walt Disney's master-pieces. Mickey Mouse,* the dog *Pluto,* the *three little pigs* were added to, and often borrowed from the world's *folk-lore. "Who's Afraid of the Big Bad Wolf?"* took on a special meaning from the threats in *Hitler's speeches.* As for *Snow White and the Seven Dwarfs,* a reputedly hard-boiled and widely syndicated *American columnist, Westbrook Pegler,* thought it "the happiest thing that has happened in this world since the *Armistice."*

—ALAN JENKINS

Notice all the concrete details set in italics, and notice the quotation at the end, which gives a special force to the whole.

Exercise 12.1   Read the following short paragraphs and discuss the number of concrete details with your class.

In the smallest of these huts lived old Berl, a man in his eighties, and his wife, who was called Berlcha (wife of Berl). Old Berl was one of the Jews who had been driven from their villages in Russia and had settled in Poland. In Lentshin, they mocked the mistakes he made while praying aloud. He spoke with a sharp "r." He was short, broad-shouldered, and he had a small white beard, and summer and winter he wore a sheepskin hat, a padded cotton jacket, and stout boots. He walked slowly, shuffling his feet. He had a half acre of field, a cow, a goat, and chickens.

—ISAAC BASHEVIS SINGER

The police broke down the front door and found the hall impassable, then they hoisted a ladder to a second-story window. Behind it Homer was lying on the floor in a bathrobe; he had starved to death. Langley had disappeared. After some delay, the police broke into the basement, chopped a hole in the roof, and began throwing junk out of the house, top and bottom.

—MALCOLM COWLEY

12b

Use metaphors and similes to make your prose more vivid, but be sure that these devices are appropriate to your subject, your tone, and your audience.

Similes and metaphors make comparisons to convey a vivid impression. **Similes** use the word *like* or *as.*

My love is *like* a red, red rose.

—ROBERT BURNS

Tom Birch is as brisk *as* a bee in conversation.

—SAMUEL JOHNSON

Mortality weighs heavily upon me *like* an unwilling sleep.

—JOHN KEATS

Sometimes in modern journalism, similes are especially striking because they are unexpected.

He sat in the Speaker's vast office, his huge 260-lb. torso looking like a giant plum pudding, his long white hair falling over his blue eyes.

—*Time* (on Tip O'Neill, former Speaker of the House of Representatives)

Metaphors, implied comparisons, speak of things or of actions as if they were something other than what they are. Because of its compression, a metaphor may have stronger force than a simile.

12b

fig

The dice are the gods of the backgammon wars.

—E. J. KAHN, JR.

Marcel Duchamp once referred to dealers as "lice on the backs of artists"—useful and necessary lice, he added, but lice all the same.

—*The New Yorker*

As their first-quarter earnings painfully show, the nation's airlines are in a sickening dive.

—*Business Week*

At least half of all writers, major or minor, have suffered from writing blocks—from inner resistance to dragging oneself, hour after hour, to the bar of self-judgment, and forcing oneself, before it, to confront that most intimidating of objects to any writer: the blank page waiting to be filled.

—WALTER JACKSON BATE

When similes and metaphors work, they enliven writing. But when they are bad, they are embarrassing and often confusing as well. The general rule is that you should not use a simile or metaphor if you have any doubt about it.

The following extended simile goes wrong because it repeats the same idea again and again like someone telling a bad joke and having to repeat the punch line. Remember that comparisons work only when they clarify an important point or teach us something we need to know. This simile does not teach us anything about William Faulkner's short story "A Rose for Emily," which the writer is trying to address.

Miss Emily Grierson's house was like hell itself. First of all, it was in Mississippi, where it gets hot in summer—just like hell.

Second, it was dark and gloomy — just like hell. And third, all sorts of horrible things happened there — just like hell. Miss Emily lived out her existence there and never could escape, and her only real companion was a dead man. Nobody wanted to visit her. People who get into hell have only the dead for companions, and they never can get out, and no one wants to go there for a visit.

Yet the writer could make a short simile, leaving an impression that is striking but not tediously prolonged. A good simile or metaphor — like a good joke — makes its point quickly and sharply:

The stunning, macabre end of Faulkner's story "A Rose for Emily" fills us with both horror and pity — *as if* we had unexpectedly opened a door into hell and found roasting there someone whom we had always thought a little foolish and inferior.

Some extended similes or metaphors may be effective if they are executed with a light touch. But extended comparisons can easily become thin and pointless. Some people, for example, might admire the following extended simile, while others might find it strained:

Getting through college is a lot like driving a car in heavy traffic. Just as the good driver must know her destination, the college student must know what she wants to get out of her education. And just as the good driver must be aware of all the other cars in the street, the college student must be aware of other students and be willing to give them a piece of the road. As in driving, a little competition may be essential, but too much competition can kill. The good driver must concentrate on what she is doing, and so must the college student. But at the same time, the driver and the student should be relaxed and confident. Too much tension in either case can provoke a serious accident.

In short, similes and metaphors are natural to human thinking, and they enliven prose. But you should use them with caution.

Exercise 12.2   Complete the simile that will describe each of the following actions or objects. Try to avoid any similes that you have heard before. Add as many words as you need. Discuss your similes with other students in your class.

Example

The snow was as white as_____ .
The snow was as white as <u>sugar</u> .

1. My mother was as angry as _____.
2. The biscuits were as light and fluffy as _____.
3. The coin gleamed in his hand like _____.
4. My flower garden was as wild as _____.
5. Our football team was as inept as a group of _____.
6. My summer job was as boring as _____.
7. The music sounded like _____.
8. The sky was as blue as _____.
9. Learning to operate the computer was as difficult as _____.
10. The rain pounded against the glass like _____.

Exercise 12.3 Take the current issue of a magazine such as *Time, Sports Illustrated, Rolling Stone, Popular Mechanics,* or anything else you enjoy reading, and find at least five metaphors and similes.

12b

fig

Exercise 12.4 Write a descriptive paragraph on each of the following subjects, using a simile and a metaphor in each.

Example

A violent thunderstorm

    The wind sprang up at four o'clock. We heard the first blast shake through the trees, and after it came the rain, blown against our windows like a clatter of stones. The thunder crashed overhead, and the lightning sent its sharp fingers ripping through the sky. Tova, our beagle pup, cowered under the table and whimpered softly, her brown eyes pleading with us to make it all stop so she could go back to sleep again and dream of beefsteaks and cats. But the storm went on, a great wild animal shrieking across our town, and we sat by the windows in silence and watched the rain roar down.

1. A sunny dawn in the spring
2. A child learning that her parents will be divorced
3. The announcement that your father has won a beauty contest
4. Deciding to buy a new car
5. Realizing suddenly that you have a friend who is an alcoholic
6. Something you are proud of having done

12c

Avoid using worn-out expressions and clichés.

A **cliché** is an overworked expression. The moment we read the first word or two of a cliché, we know how it will end. If someone says "She was as mad as a _____," we expect the sentence to be completed by the words *wet hen* or *hornet.* If someone says "My biscuits were as light as _____," we expect the sentence to be completed by *a feather.* If someone says "His prose is as heavy as _____," we expect the sentence to end with *lead.*

Some of these expressions once had power to evoke an image or strong feelings in the minds of people who heard them. For example, in the days of wagons and muddy roads, when people on the way to market got stuck in the mire, someone *put his shoulder to the wheel.* Unafraid of exerting himself or getting dirty, he got the wagon moving again. When someone then wrote that the way to succeed in business was *to put your shoulder to the wheel,* readers could visualize the scene and think, "Yes! That is how to succeed — by hard, patient effort." But nobody can put his shoulder to the wheel when a car gets stuck in the mud. We have heard this expression so often that our minds are dead to it even when we understand what it means, and it no longer creates a vivid picture in our imaginations.

Other expressions create a similar deadness. We hear that we must understand *the cold, hard facts,* and we don't think of the facts as icy or hard; they are simply unpleasant. We hear that something is *an integral part* of something else, and the moment we hear the word *integral,* we know that *part* is sure to follow. We don't stop to wonder why the writer or speaker does not use another expression. If he is describing the *integral part,* won't his description tell us how necessary the part is to the whole? Do we need the word *integral?* When journalists write about the weather, why do they always talk about *weather conditions?* Why don't they tell us about *weather?*

Look over the following clichés, and think of others not on the list. Avoid them when you speak or write.

abreast of the times	brave as a lion	deaf as a post
acid test	brown as a nut	deep, dark secret
add insult to injury	brutal murder	depths of despair
agony of suspense	bustling cities	diabolical skill
beat a hasty retreat	calm, cool, and	distaff side
better half	collected	doomed to
beyond the shadow	cold, hard facts	disappointment
of a doubt	come to grips with	drunk as a lord
blind as a bat	cool as a cucumber	every dog has his day
blue as the sky	crazy as a loon	face the music
bolt from the blue	dead as a doornail	fair sex

Imagery and Figurative Language **255**

few and far between
fire-engine red
flat as a pancake
gild the lily
green with envy
heave a sigh of relief
heavy as lead
hit the nail on the
 head
in this day and age
ladder of success
last but not least
little lady
live from hand to
 mouth
livid with rage
nose to the
 grindstone
one hundred and
 ten percent

the other side of the
 coin
paint the town red
pale as a ghost
pass the buck
poor but honest
poor but proud
pretty as a picture
primrose path
proud possessor of
quick as a flash
quiet as a church-
 mouse
reigns supreme
right as rain
rise and shine
rise to the occasion
sadder but wiser
sharp as a tack
shoulder to the
 wheel

sink or swim
smart as a whip
sneaking suspicion
sober as a judge
straight and narrow
tempest in a teapot
tired but happy
tried and true
ugly as sin
undercurrent of
 excitement
walk the line
wax eloquent
white as a ghost
white as a sheet
worth its weight in
 gold

12c

fig

You may sometimes achieve a new effect with a cliché by changing
the words:

Scott Hamilton is a good wind who blows us no ill.
— LEONARD FEATHER
The cliché is It's an ill wind that blows no good. *Here the author turns
it around to make a clever comment on a tenor saxophone player.*

You may try your hand at inverting clichés. But usually the best thing
to do with a cliché is to rephrase it as simply as you can in plain language.

CLICHÉ: When John turned his papers in three weeks late, he
had to *face the music.*

BETTER: When John turned his papers in three weeks late, he
had to take the consequences.

CLICHÉ: Harvey *kept his nose to the grindstone.*

BETTER: Harvey gave close and unceasing attention to his work.

Exercise 12.5 Rewrite the following sentences, eliminating the
clichés. You may want to substitute the simple, literal meaning of a cliché.
Or you may be able to create a fresh and lively expression to replace a
cliché. Be adventurous. Try to think up some similes or metaphors that
convey the meaning of a cliché without repeating its tiresome words.

1. Although he had worked like a dog all week long, the conductor seemed as cool as a cucumber and as fresh as a daisy when he mounted the podium and raised his baton to his orchestra.
2. The letter announcing the prize came to her like a bolt from the blue, making her friends green with envy, while she herself felt worth her weight in gold.
3. Bollinger believed that he had a right to be president of the university, since he had paid his dues as a lower functionary for years, sometimes feeling in the depths of despair over the way people treated him like a dog, believing often that he was doomed to disappointment in life, but determined to put his shoulder to the wheel.
4. The bustling cities of the Renaissance had their share of brutal murders, for men believed that they had to be as brave as lions whenever anyone got under their skin.

Exercise 12.6   Write a paragraph about any subject that you and your teacher agree on. Count the number of details that carry an image and make you see something in your mind. Use metaphors, similes, or simple narration, but include lots of concrete details.

12c

fig

CHAPTER THIRTEEN

Including Needed Words

Be sure to include all the words that are necessary to make your sentences clear and complete.

13a
Include all the necessary parts of verbs.

Many forms of the verb require more than one word to make clear English sense. Be sure you include all the words necessary to make a correct verb phrase.

1   Include necessary helpers.

In some dialects of English, past participles serve as **finite verbs,** that is, verbs that report the action of subjects and that control predicates. Correct written English requires helping verbs with these participial forms.

NONSTANDARD: He *writing* about the beehives.

STANDARD: He is *writing* about the beehives.

NONSTANDARD: I *seen* what he *done.*

STANDARD: I *have seen* what he *has done.*

NONSTANDARD: She *taken* a minute to rest.

STANDARD: She *has taken* a minute to rest.

If you have trouble with the principal parts of verbs, see 20a, and study your dictionary when you are in doubt about correct forms.

2 Do not leave out part of a compound verb when the tense of one part of the verb varies from the tense of the other part.

INCOMPLETE: Caldwell has long and always will be sympathetic to those who think jogging is boring.

COMPLETE: Caldwell has long *been* and always will be sympathetic to those who think jogging is boring.

13b

∧

13b

Include the subordinating conjunction *that* when you need it for clarity (see 8e).

UNCLEAR: He sent the message canoes were unable to navigate the Platte River.

CLEAR: He sent the message *that* canoes were unable to navigate the Platte River.

Sometimes *that* can be omitted, especially in short sentences with a simple subordinate clause:

Loretta Lynn sang songs women love.

You could say, "Loretta Lynn sang songs *that* women love," but in a sentence as short as this one, the *that* is unnecessary. But often — especially in longer sentences — the omission of *that* makes readers stumble.

Exercise 13.1   Check the following sentences for missing words. Add words where they are needed. Place a check mark by the numbers of the sentences that are clear and grammatical as they stand.

1. He told the staff men and women deserve equal pensions.
2. He taken the car to a junkyard and found many people in suits now go to junkyards to get parts for old cars they want to keep running a few more years.
3. I been here now for thirty years and never seen so little rain.
4. Air travel getting so expensive only the rich and people on business able to afford it now.
5. She told her daughter driving across the country and staying in motels were much more expensive than flying.
6. I have always and will continue to keep the promises I made when I was running for office.
7. Many outstanding athletes in college plead poverty and hardship so they can be eligible for the pro draft before their senior year.
8. He had and always will be taken for an easy mark.
9. They seen the wreck by the time they came to tell the police investigating it was a hit-and-run accident.
10. The little boy working hard getting the tricycle up the hill.

13c

Include necessary articles, prepositions, and pronouns.

1 Include the articles that are necessary for idiomatic expressions.

NOT IDIOMATIC: All people in the room had quit smoking.

IDIOMATIC: All *the* people in the room had quit smoking.

NOT IDIOMATIC: Dog that bites should be kept on leash.

IDIOMATIC: *A* dog that bites should be kept on *a* leash.

2 Include the article when the sentence clearly refers to the specific rather than to the general.

He gave me *the* books he liked best.
Omission of the article the *would make the sentence awkward. Because the subordinate clause* he liked best *tells us of specific books, we need the article* the *to balance the clause.*

3 Include prepositions as they are needed.

NOT IDIOMATIC: This type dog is noted for its affection.

IDIOMATIC: This type *of* dog is noted for its affection.

NOT IDIOMATIC: He did not like taking or giving to the fund.

IDIOMATIC: He did not like taking *from* or giving to the fund.
Each participle requires a different preposition here; taking *requires* from, *but* giving *requires* to.

NOT IDIOMATIC: He loved her for her intelligence, for her beauty, and her money.

IDIOMATIC: He loved her for her intelligence, for her beauty, and *for* her money.
In formal writing, the preposition for *is required to make all the parts of this parallel construction grammatically equal.*

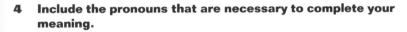

13c

∧

4 Include the pronouns that are necessary to complete your meaning.

NOT IDIOMATIC: The parachutist jumped with the red chute, fell into the lake.

IDIOMATIC: The parachutist *who* jumped with the red chute fell into the lake.
Perhaps the writer of the first sentence tried for a special effect, but the sentence is confusing. The addition of the pronoun who *after* parachutist *helps.*

5 Include all the words that are necessary to make comparisons clear.

Include a possessive form when you are comparing possessions.

UNCLEAR: Plato's philosophy is easier to read than Aristotle.
The possessive in the first term of the comparison requires a possessive in the second term.

CLEAR: Plato's philosophy is easier to read than *that of* Aristotle.

CLEAR: Plato's philosophy is easier to read than Aristotle's.

Use *other* and *else* to show that people or things belong to a group with which they are being compared.

UNCLEAR: Professor Koonig wrote more books than anyone in the department.
Was Professor Koonig not a member of the department, too? He did not write more books than he himself wrote.

BETTER: Professor Koonig wrote more books than anyone *else* in the department.

UNCLEAR: Professor Koonig's account of how he put a tribe of cannibals to sleep by reading to them from his collected works was longer than any book I have read.
Was Professor Koonig's account written as a book? If so, the writer of this sentence confuses things, since in effect, the sentence means that Professor Koonig's book is longer than Professor Koonig's book.

CLEAR: Professor Koonig's account of how he put a tribe of cannibals to sleep by reading to them from his collected works was longer than any *other* book I have read.

Use the word *as* twice when you use it to compare people or things.

INCOMPLETE: His temper was mild as milk.

COMPLETE: His temper was *as* mild as milk.

Avoid the vague comparison implied in the word *that* used as a weak synonym for *very*.

INCOMPLETE: Professor Koonig was not *that* dull.
How dull? People who use that *in this way never tell us. They assume that we have some idea of complete dullness, and they want to assure us that Professor Koonig was not as dull as that unstated standard.*

COMPLETE: Professor Koonig was not *very* dull.
Although very *is an extremely weak adverb, it is still stronger than a* that *which does not refer to anything.*

When you are tempted to use *that* as a vague comparative, think of something concrete and lively, and use the comparative form *as . . . as* instead of *that*. Or use *so . . . that* and a clause:

Professor Koonig was not *as* dull *as* some cows I have known.

Professor Koonig was *so* dull *that* he could make flowers droop from the first word of a lecture.

Be sure that your comparisons are always complete. If you have just said, "Professor Koonig is dull," you can say immediately afterward,

"Professor Donovan is more interesting." But you cannot say in isolation, "Professor Donovan is more interesting." You need to name who or what forms the rest of the comparison. You may say, "Professor Donovan is more interesting than Professor Koonig."

Exercise 13.2 Add words as they are needed in the following sentences. If a sentence is correct as it stands, put a check by the number.

1. She was happy as I have ever seen anyone when she graduated from West Point.
2. He took the car in to have the transmission replaced, the body painted, and seats covered.
3. This type grass seed does not do that well in shade.
4. The car I drove to the beach was worse than any car I have ever driven.
5. Pete Rose was not that fast, but he always played hard as a boy even when he was forty years old.
6. He had always and will continue to play well because of his hard work.
7. The night was more clear.

13c

$\wedge$

CHAPTER FOURTEEN

Avoiding Wordiness

If you can eliminate words that add only dead weight to your prose, you can make every word count. Tight, economical, meaning-laden sentences that flow easily and directly seldom appear in first drafts. Even famous authors must rewrite their sentences to make their thoughts more clear and less wordy.

Avoiding wordiness does not mean that you must write in short, choppy sentences or that you must reduce your prose to its bare bones. It does mean that every word should add something significant to your thought, because words that add nothing will obscure your meaning and will bore your readers.

14a
Edit carefully, eliminating unnecessary words.

The following paragraph, a response to an assignment requiring an explanation of *expository writing*, is a good first draft, but it is entirely too wordy. The writer, correctly, tried to put down thoughts as fast as they came to mind, without pausing to edit the piece. Then she edited the first draft to eliminate wordiness, without rewriting anything:

~~Briefly,~~ Expository writing ~~is the kind of writing~~ ~~that~~ develops an idea. It is not ~~quite the same as~~ narration, which tells a story, though ~~you and I~~ ~~both know that~~ narratives may contain ~~many~~ ideas. But that is not their main purpose. If I tell you that last night I ~~was eating~~ in a restaurant ~~and~~ found a pearl in my oysters, that is narration. ~~And~~ expository writing does not ~~is~~ ~~the kind of writing that~~ describes something, though descriptions may include ~~several of the most~~ important ideas. ~~that a writer~~ ~~considers significant.~~ If I describe ~~how~~ the campus ~~looks~~ under a deep, ~~thick, white~~ snow and ~~describe~~ the way people wade through the snow and leave tracks, ~~on its pure and immaculate surface,~~ ~~then~~ that is description. But if I ~~go to the theater and~~ see a play and ~~come home and~~ write ~~down~~ an interpretation of it, ~~then~~ I am doing expository writing even if part of the exposition is to describe the action of the play itself. And if I ~~go on and~~ talk about the ~~aforesaid~~ snow, ~~that I have talked~~ ~~about falling on the campus~~ and if I tell ~~the story~~ ~~about~~ how the history department ~~got out in it and~~

14a

wdy

started ~~aggressively and energetically~~ throwing

snowballs at the dean, and if I ~~then go on and~~ try

to explain why historians on this campus are ~~at this~~

~~point in time and always have been~~ bellicose, ~~then~~ I

am combining description, narration, and expository

writing. ~~But the main thing I want you to~~ be

conscious of ~~is~~ how you should classify the kinds of

writing that are likely to go on in a single piece,

~~of writing,~~ and ~~you've simply got to~~ remember that it

is not ~~an example of~~ expository writing unless it ~~is~~

~~writing about~~ expounding an idea.

Here are some questions the writer asked herself while editing the first draft:

1. Since snow is never anything but white when it first falls, do I have to say that it is white?

2. Are members of the history department throwing snowballs at the dean indoors?

3. As for "aggressively and energetically," do people throw snowballs any other way? Again, don't state the obvious.

The revised paragraph still needs more editing. Consider this puzzling sentence: "If I describe the campus under a deep snow and the way people wade through the snow and leave tracks, that is description." The sentence says that to describe is description — defining a word by itself. It is like saying, "To build something is to make a building." And do you have to see a play to write an interpretation of it, as the next sentence implies? The more you look, the more you see that even this draft is a little wordy, a little fuzzy. So the writer has to edit again, this time rewriting some of the sentences and changing some of the words. Remember that she is trying to preserve everything essential in the paragraph, and she is also trying to write concisely without sounding like a primer.

After making further changes, the writer produced this paragraph:

> Expository writing develops ideas; narrations tell stories; descriptions tell how things look. If I tell you that last night in a restaurant I found a pearl in my oysters, I am narrating. If I write of a deep snow on campus and how people wade through it and leave tracks, I am describing. But if I interpret a play, I am writing exposition, even if part of my essay describes the action of the play itself. And if I describe snow, and tell how the history department threw snowballs at the dean, and try to explain why historians at this university are bellicose, I am combining description, narration, and exposition. Remember that all three kinds of writing may appear in a single piece, but only expository writing interprets an idea.

The writer has recast the paragraph itself, as well as several sentences, and she has found more ways to shorten sentences too. She has presented her definitions in the beginning as quickly as possible, and by using three short, independent clauses connected with semicolons, she has saved many words. The paragraph now begins with expository writing and ends with it. No one will misunderstand the purpose of the piece — to define expository writing by comparing it with other kinds of prose. You may think of other revisions, but this third draft achieves a short, clear paragraph while saying everything important that was in the first version.

As you revise for wordiness you should look out for redundant words and phrases, the unnecessary repetitions that slip easily into first drafts. Conscious, deliberate repetition can help you emphasize ideas (see 9e); but meaningless repetition makes only flabby sentences. You should avoid redundant constructions like the following.

REDUNDANT: The candidate repeated the answer again.

IMPROVED: The candidate repeated the answer.
The verb repeated *means "to say again." The adverb adds nothing here.*

REDUNDANT: He expressed a number of clever expressions much to the audience's delight.

IMPROVED: He delighted the audience with his clever expressions.
Repeating the root express *is careless; the revision makes the point without distracting the reader with the repetition.*

REDUNDANT: The exam was very trying, and I kept trying to finish on time without making too many errors.

IMPROVED: The exam was very difficult, and I kept trying to finish on time without making too many errors.
The word trying *used twice, each with a different meaning, jars readers. The improved sentence eliminates the needless repetition.*

REDUNDANT: In the movie *Apocalypse Now* there were several dull parts that I found boring.

IMPROVED: I found several boring parts in the movie *Apocalypse Now.*
Both dull *and* boring *say the same thing. The writer of the improved sentence has removed the redundancy.*

Exercise 14.1 Edit the following paragraphs, and make them more concise:

14a

wdy

I am going to tell you how much fun and profit there is in it for you to build your own house. If you have the time and a little energy and common sense, then you can build your very own house, save a ton of money, and have lots and lots of fun as you build your house. When it's all done and your house is standing there, built by you and maybe some members of your family, you will be proud of it, really proud.

Most of us, including probably you and me, usually think there is some kind of strange, secret mystery to the occult art of carpentry, but building things with wood is not a mystery at all. It takes lots and lots of care and lots and lots of hard work, but just about anybody can do it.

Now what do we mean by *care?* Well friends, we mean attention to detail. Among those many details that ought to have a lot of attention are making sure the joints in the wood fit together tightly, driving nails carefully so you don't leave those ugly and unnecessary and thoroughly disgusting hammer marks around the heads of your nails, hanging your doors so they are straight and true, being absolutely and completely and carefully exact in your measurements, sawing your planks exactly and precisely and unwaveringly along the marks you make with a pencil or some other writing implement, perhaps even with a sharp nail and sometimes with your fingernail. All these things are a part of care.

Exercise 14.2 Explain the redundancies in the following examples.

1. at three A.M. in the morning
2. in modern times in the twentieth century today

3. return to the old neighborhood again
4. in my opinion, I think
5. the autobiography of her life
6. resultant effect of the report
7. quite tiny in size
8. the surrounding environment
9. unemployed workers now out of work
10. rectangular in shape

14b

Eliminate common phrases that take up space and burden your style without adding anything to your meaning.

When we speak, we often use phrases that serve as "waiting words"— they let us keep talking while we wait to think of something more to say. These waiting words often creep into our writing, where they take up valuable room without doing any work. Common waiting words include *like, you know, sort of, kind of, what I mean is, so to speak, in other words,* and *in the final analysis.*

Other common phrases are cumbersome, roundabout, habitual ways of saying something when we need only a word or two. And some of them are junk—words we can get rid of altogether without losing any of our real meaning.

Study the following examples and their recommended substitutions.

at the present time
in the present circumstances
at this point in time   } Use *now* or *today* or *nowadays.*
at this moment
in this day and age

at that point in time
in those days   } Use *then.*
in that period

in many cases   Use *often.*
in some cases   Use *sometimes.*
in exceptional cases   Use *rarely.*
in most cases   Use *usually.*

consider as, consider as being
  I consider study as being neces-   Use: I consider study necessary to
     sary to success.   success.

despite the fact that regardless of the fact that	Use *although*.
due to the fact that for the purpose of by virtue of the fact that the reason is because	Use *because*.
in a position to, in order to	Use *can*.
in the area of	Use *near* or *in*.
in the event that in the event of in case of	Use *if* with a verb.

In the event that fire breaks out, leave the files behind.
If fire breaks out, leave the files behind.

in terms of
[Should usually be revised out of your prose.]

The new curriculum was designed in terms of student needs and faculty
    ability.
The new curriculum considers both student needs and faculty ability.
The new curriculum was designed to match faculty ability with student
    needs.

in the final analysis	Use *finally*, or drop the phrase entirely.
in no uncertain terms	Drop the phrase, or use *firmly* or *clearly*.
in the nature of things of that nature	Use *like* or *things like that*.
refer back	Use only *refer*.
He is of a complex character. She is of a generous nature. The car was of a green color.	Use: He is complex. Use: She is generous. Use: The car was green.
The weather conditions are bad. Traffic conditions are congested.	Use: The weather is bad. Use: Traffic is congested.

Exercise 14.3 Edit the following paragraphs to eliminate unnecessary words and phrases. You may find some words and phrases that are not on the list above. Think hard about each sentence to see if you can eliminate padding and wordiness.

Due to the fact that at this point in time we have an energy crisis of a severe nature, we need to devote ourselves to a good rethinking of the academic calendar. At the present time, schools in the area of the United States begin in September and end in

May or June. The reason is because schools once upon a time used to begin right after the harvest in societies of an agricultural character. But by virtue of the fact that buildings must be heated in the wintertime, schools in the cold regions of the earth are now paying out millions of dollars for fuel bills — money that might do much more good if it were put into faculty salaries, student scholarships, the library fund, the athletic program, or things of these kinds and of that nature. A solution to the problem may be of a simple nature: make the academic calendar according to the weather conditions prevailing in the different areas where the schools happen to be located.

In the southern United States, where it is in the nature of winters to be mild, schools could continue in many cases to go on operating just as they always have. To cool buildings in the summer would cost more in such regions than heating them in the wintertime. But in the northern areas, the academic year could begin in March and end early in November, providing in many cases for the great fuel economies that could be thereby effected.

14c

Combine sentences to avoid wordiness.

Combining sentences, along with editing, will pull your thoughts together and make your writing clearer and more readable. Combining also gives variety to your prose (see Chapters 7 and 10).

Read these choppy declarative sentences:

> The flashlight illuminated the rest of the chamber. It was square. Carter christened it the Treasury. It contained chests. It contained caskets. It contained tall boxes. The boxes were black. They were thin. They were ominous. They were closed and sealed. They were standing against all sides of the room. Several dozen boats were on top of the boxes. The room looked as if somehow it was supposed to be the surface of the Nile itself. A flotilla was ready to sail. Some boats were simple little vessels. They were like sampans. Others were full-fledged sailboats. They had complex rigging. Their sails were furled. They looked as if one had only to give a command. Then a crew of a hundred or more would prepare them for their voyage.

Early in the composing process, when you first jot down your ideas, such sentences would play a valuable role in the formation of your essay. But combining some short sentences and subordinating some ideas to others will make this passage much more concise — and much more elegant (see 7a-2 and 7b-1).

The flashlight illuminated the rest of the square chamber, which Carter christened the Treasury. Chests, caskets, and tall, thin, ominous-looking black boxes, closed and sealed, were standing against all sides of the room. And on top of them were several dozen boats, as if the room were somehow the surface of the Nile itself, with a flotilla ready to set sail. Some were simple little vessels like sampans, others full-fledged sailboats with complex rigging and sails furled, looking as if one had only to give the command and a crew of a hundred or more would prepare them for their voyage.

—THOMAS HOVING

Exercise 14.4

14c

wdy

1. Combine the sentences in the following paragraph as economically as you can:

> Before the invention of the motorcar, this was a rural land. Geography dominated. Geography determined where and how we would live. Geography determined where and how we would travel. But then everything changed. The automobile spread communities. It merged them. It ended their distinctiveness. It brought the motel. It brought the fast-food chains. It brought the suburbs and the death of the inner city. It changed courting practices. It took young men and women from front-porch swings. It rolled them down lovers' lanes. It took them by lapping lakes in private and dark backseats. In some ways it added to American democracy. Gasoline was 20 cents a gallon. Factory workers packed their lemonade and their bologna sandwiches. They packed their hampers and their suitcases. They left hot factory neighborhoods in Detroit, Cleveland, Chicago, Milwaukee. They drove north to the woods, islands, and lakes of northern Michigan, Wisconsin, and Minnesota.

2. Now check what you have done by comparing your revision with the original:

> Before the invention of the motorcar, this was a rural land. Geography dominated, determining where and how we would live, where and how we would travel. But then everything changed. The automobile spread communities, merged them, ended their distinctiveness. It brought the motel, the fast-food chains, the suburbs and the death of the inner city. It changed courting practices, taking young men and women from front-porch swings and rolling them down lovers' lanes, by lapping lakes, in private and dark back seats. In some

ways it added to American democracy: with gasoline at 20 cents a gallon, factory workers packed their lemonade and bologna sandwiches, their hampers and suitcases and left hot factory neighborhoods in Detroit, Cleveland, Chicago, Milwaukee and drove north to the woods, islands, and lakes of northern Michigan, Wisconsin, and Minnesota.

—William Serrin

14d

Do not inflate simple thoughts with jargon-ridden, overblown language (see 11c).

14d

wdy

INFLATED: Owning a gun for protection could be a consequence of several other factors. It could be the logical extension of a general home defense orientation. One mode of behavior for individuals who are vulnerable to crime is to increase their personal security, which leads them to a general home defense orientation and the acquisition of a gun.

BETTER: Some people buy guns to defend their homes, especially when they feel threatened by crime.

INFLATED: Lucinda Childs' early development as a choreographer in the 1960s paralleled the rise of minimalist art. And while her work is extremely complex in its patterning and ordering, this complexity is grounded in the permutations of simplicity expressed in a few steps and their repetition.

BETTER: Lucinda Childs' early choreography in the 1960s developed alongside the work of the minimalist painters. Although she created complex patterns and sequences, she uses only a few simple steps repeated with slight changes.

Exercise 14.5 Edit the following sentences to make them more concise and clear. You may want to make two sentences where the writers have written one. Discuss your results with the class. Use the dictionary when you must.

1. A total site signage program is being studied, and if the study analysis dictates to relocate the stop sign, it will be done as a part of the total signage program and not as a result of your suggestion.

2. Dissatisfaction over the lack of responsiveness and accountability of decision makers is itself a primary source of the recent precipitous decline in confidence and trust that citizens hold for the national government.
3. Many theories of gaze interaction assume that a stare is physiologically arousing and that this arousal accounts in part for the efficacy of eye contact as a communication channel.
4. We were not micromanaging Grenada intelligencewise until about that time frame.

CHAPTER FIFTEEN

Sexist Language

In recent years, feminist writers have called attention to the ways language can imply that women are inferior to men or that women must behave in certain ways to be socially acceptable. Distinctions of this sort are called **sexist**. Thoughtful writers try to avoid sexist language because they know that such language is offensive to many readers.

15a

Avoid sexist labels and clichés that condescend to women or that imply that women are inferior to men or different from men in intelligence, morals, the careers they can choose, or the talents they possess.

Many cliché labels for women imply that there is one "right" way for women to behave and many "wrong" ways. Consider the implications of such cliché words as *lady* or *ladies, the distaff side, the weaker sex, the fair sex, the better half, girl* or *girls, gals, broads, dames, working wives, working mothers,* and *housewives.*

All such terms imply that women have a special, expected role in society. For example, to call a woman *ladylike* implies that she is polite and cooperative but unwilling to assert herself as men are expected to do in a competitive society.

While some people consider *ladylike* a compliment, others reject the implied suggestion that women must behave like ladies if they are to be acceptable people. Careful writers keep such distinctions in mind and avoid any clichés and labels that might turn women into stereotypes.

1   Do not refer to women as if they were appendages to men.

NOT: Lily Roundtree, wife of used-car dealer John T. Roundtree, has been cited by the *New England Journal of Medicine* for isolating a rare virus.

BUT: Dr. Lily Roundtree of Brookhaven Laboratories has been cited by the *New England Journal of Medicine* for isolating a rare virus.
Lily Roundtree is obviously a distinguished medical researcher. To identify her by reference to her husband is to imply that only her marriage makes her worthy of notice.

2   Avoid identifying a woman by referring to her children.

NOT: Molly Burdine, mother of six, will represent Sourmash State University at the national meeting of the American Association of University Professors to be held in Washington in June.

BUT: Molly Burdine, professor of government, will represent Sourmash State University at the national meeting of the American Association of University Professors to be held in Washington in June.
If Professor Burdine's children figure in your paper, you can mention them later—but would you mention the children if Professor Burdine were a man?

15b
Whenever possible, revise sentences to avoid using the pronouns *he*, *him*, *his*, and *himself* as indefinite personal pronouns.

A satisfactory way to avoid masculine singular pronouns is to use the plural forms:

SINGULAR: Every student who signed up for the class had to pay *his* fee in advance and to pledge *himself* to attend every session.

PLURAL: Students who signed up for the class had to pay *their* fees in advance and to pledge *themselves* to attend every session.

Often you can avoid the masculine pronouns by revising the sentence to eliminate the pronouns altogether.

Every student who signed up for the class had to pay the fee in advance and to pledge to attend every session.

15c

In general, avoid cumbersome constructions such as *his or her, his/her,* or *s/he.*

On occasion, it may be perfectly natural to use *he or she* or *his or her.*

> The student who spray-painted the insulting graffiti on the blackboard last night may have thought that he or she was being original and bold, but it was a cowardly act.
> *Nobody knows who committed the vandalism; the culprit could have been male or female.*

Such usage generally is cumbersome, though, and it becomes unbearable when it is repeated several times in a paragraph.

> Each student in the psychology class was to pick up a different book according to his or her interests, to read the book overnight and do without his or her normal sleep, to write a short summary of what he or she had read the next morning, and then to see if he or she dreamed about the book on the following night.

Some writers now alternate *he* and *she, him* and *her,* using one gender in one paragraph and the other gender the next time a singular pronoun is called for. This alternative can become distracting, too. Many speakers and some writers use a plural pronoun to refer to an impersonal singular antecedent: "The *person* who left *their* suitcase on the bus can call for it at the office." However, such usage is regarded as nonstandard by most writers and editors.

Some writers use the neuter impersonal pronoun *one* to avoid the masculine pronoun: "The American dream has always been that if one is willing to work, one can succeed in life."

Most professional writers and editors still use the masculine pronoun to refer to an impersonal, singular antecedent: "The American dream has always held that if anybody was willing to work, he could get ahead in life."

15d

Avoid artificial coinages that are cumbersome to read and to write.

Many English words ending in *-man* have traditionally applied to both men and women who occupy the positions the words describe: *freshman, chairman, councilman, fellow man, sportsman, workman, policeman, fireman, repairman, statesman,* and *salesman* are among these words.

The new awareness of sexist distinctions in language has led many writers and editors to substitute *-person* for *-man* in such words. Unfortunately, the result is often clumsy and hard to say. The best course seems to be to choose synonyms that use neither *-person* nor *-man*. The *newsman* can become a *reporter* or a *journalist* or a *writer*. The *chairman* can become the *chair*, the *weatherman* the *weather forecaster* or the *weather reporter* or the *meteorologist*, the *freshman* the *first-year student*, the *policeman* the *police officer*, and so forth.

Exercise 15.1   Rewrite the following sentences to eliminate sexist language.

15d

sxl

1. An ambassador must learn the customs of the country where he is stationed. He should also learn the language.
2. When machinery breaks down in the home, we must grit our teeth and call the repairman, knowing that he will charge too much money and that we may have to call him again soon.
3. Any country musician worth his guitar knows that true bluegrass music does not use drums. He would also not use an electric guitar.
4. Every organizational man knows the value of pleasing the boss. The boss may be a fool or a beast, but he is still the boss.
5. Anybody who goes to college knows that he has to work hard to earn good grades and that his grades do not always show how much he has learned.

Exercise 15.2   Write synonyms for these words that use masculine beginnings or endings. (Avoid using *-person* as a substitute.)

1. policeman
2. fireman
3. newspaperboy
4. mailman
5. mankind
6. sportsman
7. repairman
8. congressman

CHAPTER SIXTEEN

Using a Dictionary and Thesaurus

A good dictionary is an essential tool for every writer. You should consult your dictionary every time you have the slightest doubt about the spelling, meaning, proper use, pronunciation, or syllabication of a word.

16a
Learn about the most useful dictionaries for the college writer.

Desk Dictionaries

Buy at least one hardbound, abridged dictionary that you can keep comfortably on your desk and use frequently. Paperback dictionaries are handy because they can be carried easily, but they have fewer words than you will need as a college writer, and they fall apart quickly.

A standard desk dictionary contains 140,000 to 170,000 entries. It may include drawings as well. Illustrations are useful because they can show something that otherwise cannot be defined easily.

The following desk dictionaries are all useful for the college student:

***The American Heritage Dictionary of the English Language,* 2d College ed. (Boston: Houghton Mifflin, 1982).**

This dictionary has more than 200,000 entries, including biographical and geographic listings set alphabetically in the body of the work among the other words and expressions.

Most words in English have more than one meaning. The *American Heritage Dictionary* lists definitions in numeric order, beginning with the primary meaning suggested by the etymology or source of the word. The first listing is usually the most common definition of the word. The dictionary proceeds through other senses that are progressively more abstract or less common.

For example, the first meaning of the word *shuffle* is "to drag (the feet) along the floor or ground while walking or dancing; to scuffle." This meaning is closest to the Low German *schueffeln*, from which "shuffle" comes, a word meaning "to walk clumsily; to shuffle cards." The second meaning given by the dictionary is "to move (something) from one place to another." The third meaning is "to mix together in a disordered, haphazard fashion."

A valuable feature of this dictionary is the usage note appended to many definitions. The usage notes reflect the opinions of a panel of professional writers, editors, and speakers on what they consider good or bad usage of troublesome words. As the editors of the dictionary recognize, many writers and speakers disagree among themselves about how some words should be used. The usage notes help show these divisions of opinion and allow users of the dictionary to make up their minds in an informed way.

Webster's Ninth New Collegiate Dictionary (Springfield, Mass.: Merriam-Webster, 1983).

The word *Webster's* is not under copyright, and anybody can put out a "Webster's dictionary," supposedly based on Noah Webster's first dictionary of American English, published shortly after the American Revolution. But the Merriam-Webster dictionary is the most popular and authoritative dictionary bearing the Webster name. It is based on *Webster's Third New International Dictionary*, generally regarded as the standard one-volume unabridged dictionary in English.

Biographical and geographic entries are placed in appendixes, leaving the body of the dictionary for general words. The dictionary has about 160,000 entries and is by far the richest of all the dictionaries in vocabulary from the sciences. It lists the meanings of words in the historical order in which the words came into use. For example, the first meaning given for the word *prevent* is "to be in readiness for," a meaning labeled "archaic" to show that this meaning is rarely used now. Exemplary sentences from well-known writers illustrate usage, and an occasional usage note will offer guidance in the choice of a meaning for a word. In general, the editors view usage rules rather loosely. For example, they approve of the word *hopefully* as a synonym for "it is hoped," and they take a casual attitude toward the distinction most careful writers make between *imply* and *infer*.

The Random House College Dictionary of the English Language (New York: Random House, 1980).

This dictionary has 170,000 entries, a great number of them geographic and biographical. It is rich in scientific vocabulary and in entries that contain more than one word. The typeface is small, and there are few drawings. It does not contain nearly as many examples of usage as the Merriam-Webster and the American Heritage dictionaries, and the examples it does include are not from well-known writers.

Unabridged Dictionaries

In theory, an unabridged dictionary should include every word in the language. In practice, such inclusiveness is impossible. The English language is too rich, and it changes too often to be contained in any one work. A couple of unabridged dictionaries come close to the ideal, and college writers should learn about them and should continue to use them long after college.

Webster's Third New International Dictionary of the English Language (Springfield, Mass.: G. and C. Merriam, 1976).

This enormous volume is housed in the reference room of any respectable library, usually on a lectern in a prominent place. When it first appeared in 1961, purists greeted it with howls of outrage, and a few people burned it in protest. The dictionary included *ain't* and other words not regarded as standard English, and some people thought that it was not so much a dictionary as a symbol of the decay of the language. Critics objected to the editors' philosophy that a dictionary should include words used by a substantial part of the population, even if those words are not regarded as "literate" by more educated people. The dictionary also takes a casual attitude toward usages of certain standard words. For example, it accepts as a meaning for *disinterested* this definition: "not interested." But most literate people define *disinterested* as "impartial" or "unbiased" and believe that a judge can be *interested* in a case but *disinterested* in making a decision about it. The *Third New International Dictionary*, in the opinion of many authorities, can lead inexperienced writers astray because it does not warn them that certain usages are unacceptably casual or confusing.

The Oxford English Dictionary, 13 vols. (Oxford, England: Oxford Univ. Press, completed 1933).

There are four supplements. Volume 1, A–G, appeared in 1972; Volume 2, H–N, appeared in 1976; Volume 3, O–S, appeared in 1982; the last volume appeared in 1986. The original thirteen volumes have been available since 1971 in a photographically reduced two-volume edition printed on opaque paper, easily read with the strong magnifying glass furnished with the set.

Indisputably the greatest dictionary of the English language, this work traces each word from its first known appearance in writing to the present. Each variety of meaning is illustrated by sentences drawn from writers in the period when the word was so used. Variations appear in the citations from century to century. The thirteen original volumes include no words that might have offended proper Victorians, but the modern supplements include all such words.

Despite its great reputation, the *Oxford English Dictionary* is more valuable for the literary historian than for the general college writer.

Other Useful Dictionaries

16a

di/th

Many highly specialized dictionaries may be found in the reference room of any good library — medical dictionaries; dictionaries of legal terms; dictionaries of philosophy, sociology, engineering, and other disciplines; dictionaries of slang, of word origins, of famous quotations. These dictionaries may often help you write an essay, and you should always browse through them when you are pondering a topic. Your reference librarian can help you locate the dictionaries that will be most helpful.

Here are some dictionaries that might prove especially interesting or helpful in your general writing.

Dictionaries of Slang

Partridge, Eric. *Dictionary of Slang and Unconventional English.* 7th ed. New York: Macmillan, 1970.

Wentworth, Harold, and Stuart Berg Flexner. *Dictionary of American Slang.* 2d ed. New York: Thomas Y. Crowell, 1975.

Dictionaries of Usage

These dictionaries answer questions that all writers ask now and then about the appropriate use of words. As we noted earlier, many dictionaries will not tell you which of the various definitions is more acceptable than another. But a dictionary of usage will give advice. If you don't know whether to use *like* or *as* or whether to use *infer* or *imply* or whether you should split an infinitive or whether to use *slow* as an adverb, a dictionary of usage will give you helpful advice and will offer alternatives. The three leading dictionaries of usage are the following:

Follett, Wilson. *Modern American Usage.* Ed. Jacques Barzun. New York: Hill and Wang, 1966.

Fowler, H. W. *A Dictionary of Modern English Usage*, 2d ed., revised and edited by Sir Ernest Gowers. Oxford and New York: Oxford Univ. Press, 1965.

Morris, William, and Mary Morris. *Harper Dictionary of Contemporary Usage*. New York: Harper and Row, 1975.

16b

Learn how to read the entries in a standard desk dictionary.

All dictionaries contain guides that help readers use them. In these guides, usually located in the front, you will find the meanings of the abbreviations used in the entries, and you will also find a list of the special cautions dictionaries use for words that the editors consider *slang, vulgar, informal, nonstandard,* or something else worthy of notation. When you use a dictionary for the first time, study these instructions carefully. They usually contain sample entries that will help you get the most from the time you spend consulting the dictionary.

Here is part of a column of words as they are entered in the *American Heritage Dictionary*, 2d College edition. Study it and the following suggestions to see what you can learn from a good desk dictionary.

com·pare (kəm-pâr′) *v.* -**pared, -paring, -pares.** —*tr.* **1.** To represent as similar, equal, or analogous; liken. Used with *to.* See Usage note below. **2.** *Abbr.* **cf., cp.** To examine in order to note the similarities or differences of. Used with *with.* See Usage note below. **3.** *Grammar.* To form the positive, comparative, or superlative degrees of (an adjective or adverb). —*intr.* **1.** To be worthy of comparison; be considered as similar. Used with *with.* See Usage note below. **2.** To vie; compete. —**compare notes.** To exchange impressions. —*n.* Comparison. Usually used in the phrase *beyond* or *without compare.* [Middle English *comparen,* from Old French *comparer,* from Latin *comparāre,* to pair, match, from *compar,* like, equal : *com-,* mutually + *pār,* equal (see **pere-** in Appendix*).] —**com·par′er** *n.*

Usage: In formal usage, *compare to* is the only acceptable form when *compare* means representing as similar or likening, according to 71 per cent of the Usage Panel: *compare a voice to thunder.* In such comparisons the similarities are often metaphorical rather than real; the things compared are of fundamentally unlike orders, and a general likeness is intended rather than a detailed accounting. *Compare with* is the only acceptable form in the sense of examining in order to note similarities or differences, according to 70 per cent of the Panel: *compare Shelley's poetry with Wordsworth's.* Here the things compared are of like kinds, and specific resemblances and differences are examined in detail. Informally, *to* and *with* are often used interchangeably in the foregoing examples. In formal usage, only *compare with* is acceptable when *compare* intransitively means being worthy of comparison, according to 94 per cent of the Panel: *Promises do not compare with deeds.* In such constructions, *compare to* is infrequent, even in informal usage.

com·par·i·son (kəm-păr′ə-sən) *n.* **1.** A comparing or being compared; a statement or estimate of similarities and differences. **2.** The quality of being capable or worthy of being compared; similarity; likeness. **3.** *Grammar.* The modification or inflection of an adjective or adverb to denote the three degrees (positive, comparative, and superlative). [Middle English *comparisoun,* from Old French *comparaison,* from Latin *comparātiō,* from *comparāre,* COMPARE.]

Spelling, Syllabication, and Pronunciation

Entries in a dictionary are listed in alphabetic order according to standard spelling. In this dictionary, the verb *compare* is entered as **com · pare.** The dot divides the word into two syllables. To break a word at the end of a line, always divide it between the syllables (see 30g). Never break a syllable. Phonetic symbols in parentheses show the correct pronunciation; explanations of these symbols appear across the bottom of the pages in this dictionary. In the word *compare,* the second syllable receives the greater stress when you pronounce the word correctly. You say "comPARE." In this dictionary, the syllable that receives the primary stress is given an accent mark at the end like this: ´. Down the column in this section of the dictionary, you find the word *compartmentalize.* It is pronounced with the heaviest stress on the syllable *men,* and it has a secondary stress on the syllables *com* and *ize.* The syllable with the heaviest stress has the darkest accent mark; the syllables with the secondary stress receive lighter accent marks. Other dictionaries use a simple apostrophe to show accents. Study the accent marks in whatever dictionary you use.

16b

di/th

Parts of Speech and Various Forms

The symbol *v.* immediately after the pronunciation tells you that *compare* is most frequently used as a verb. The *-pared* shows the simple past and the past participle forms. If the past participle differed from the simple past, both forms would be included. (Look at the verb *drink* in your dictionary; you will see the forms *drank* and *drunk.*) The *-paring* gives you the present participle form and shows that you drop the final *e* in *compare* before you add the *-ing.* The *-pares* tells you the third-person singular form of the verb so that you know to write "She compares."

The symbol — *tr.* shows that the verb is used transitively. That is, the verb *compare* can be used to take a direct object. A little further down in the entry the symbol — *intr.* shows that *compare* is also used as an intransitive verb, one that does not take a direct object. The symbol — *n.* still further along in the entry shows that *compare* is occasionally used as a noun, and to illustrate this usage, the dictionary gives the phrases *beyond* or *without compare.* The form *comparer* in boldface at the end of the main entry shows that by adding the simple suffix *-er,* we can get the noun meaning "one who compares."

Definitions

The several meanings of the word are arranged according to the parts of speech that the word plays in different contexts. Meanings used in special contexts are often noted by editors. For example, for the verb *compare*, the editors of the dictionary note that in grammar the word has a special and technical meaning, which they indicate by putting *Grammar* in italics. The editors will also note in italics whether a word or a particular meaning of a word is *nonstandard, informal, slang, vulgar, archaic, rare, poetic, regional,* or *foreign.* For example, the *American Heritage Dictionary* gives the word *e'en* meaning "evening" but notes that it is *poetic* so that you would not use it in an essay unless you were quoting from a poem.

Word Origins

At the end of nearly every entry in this column is an etymology — a brief history of the word, usually beginning with its entry into English and tracing its forms from there to the present. We see that *compare* came from *comparen* in Middle English, the English in use during Chaucer's time, in the fourteenth century. *Comparen* came from the French word *comparer*, used by the Normans, who introduced a wealth of French words into Anglo-Saxon speech. *Comparer* came from the Latin verb *comparare;* Latin was the language of the Roman West, and French evolved from it.

A study of word origins often helps you understand what words mean. But always remember that in a living language like ours, words are in flux, and some words have changed drastically from their original meanings.

Usage

The usage note in the *American Heritage Dictionary* is appended to some main entries in the dictionary. The only usage note in this column explains some things about the verb *compare.* Here we see the dictionary's panel of experts divided over *compare with* and *compare to.* Since the majority of the usage panel holds that *compare with* is the more acceptable idiom for comparisons of similarities and differences, you would be well advised to follow the lead of those experts. If you were comparing geometry and trigonometry, for instance, you would note many ways in which they were alike and many ways in which they were different; so you would compare geometry *with* trigonometry.

But if your comparison were entirely with differences or entirely with similarities, you would use *compare to.* If you write "Compared to Paul, Margaret is kind and generous," you are talking only about a difference, not about both similarities and differences. You mean that Paul is not as kind and generous as Margaret. Again, the idiom is *compare to.*

Exercise 16.1   Which of the following words can be used as verbs? What cautions does your desk dictionary offer about using them? Indicate with a T or an I whether a verb is transitive or intransitive. Put a TI before verbs that can be used both transitively and intransitively.

1. total	6. victory	11. land	16. water
2. outside	7. hipster	12. paper	17. help
3. fritter	8. radio	13. grind	18. into
4. freeze	9. slop	14. language	19. cool
5. consider	10. postulate	15. rap	20. sullenly

Exercise 16.2   Write out your own short definition for each of the following words, noting the part or parts of speech that you think each word may serve. If you can, discuss the words with the class. Then check your definitions with those in a standard desk dictionary. If you don't know a word, try to guess what it means before you look it up in the dictionary.

1. effete	8. relationship	15. digital
2. jejune	9. mucus	16. agenda
3. jangle	10. buckboard	17. poignant
4. parameter	11. buttress	18. masterful
5. pestilent	12. sprocket	19. infer
6. nomenclature	13. habiliment	20. dark horse
7. manufacture	14. media	

Exercise 16.3   Look up the etymologies of the following words in your desk dictionary. Discuss with the class how the origins of a word help you understand its modern meaning.

1. gynecologist	6. dimension	11. harlequin
2. gymnasium	7. populist	12. courage
3. geology	8. democracy	13. shrewd
4. manufacture	9. helicopter	14. physics
5. center	10. muck	15. theology

Synonyms and Antonyms

Here is the entry from the *American Heritage Dictionary*, 2d College edition, for the word *include*. Study the *synonyms*. Note that the editors explain the slightly different sense that each of these synonyms conveys. If you study the synonyms in your dictionary, you will develop a greater understanding of what the words connote. That is, you will develop a sense for the extended meanings that words carry around with them.

> **in·clude** (ĭn-klo͞od′) *tr.v.* **-cluded, -cluding, -cludes. 1.** To have as a part or member; be made up of, at least in part; contain. **2.** To contain as a minor or secondary element; imply. **3.** To cause to be a part of something; consider with or put into a group, class, or total. [Middle English *includen,* from Latin *inclūdere,* to shut in : *in-,* in + *claudere,* to close (see **kleu-** in Appendix*).] **—in·clud′a·ble, in·clud′i·ble** *adj.*
>
> **Synonyms:** *include, comprise, comprehend, embrace, involve.* These verbs mean to take in or contain one or more things as part of something larger. *Include* and *comprise* both take as their objects things or persons that are constituent parts. *Comprise* usually implies that all of the components are stated: *The track meet comprises 15 events* (that is, consists of or is composed of). *Include* can be so used, but, like the remaining terms, more often implies an incomplete listing: *The meet includes among its high points a return match between leading sprinters. Comprehend* and *embrace* usually refer to the taking in of intangibles as part of a broader subject: *Law and order comprehend much more than exercise of police power. A person's tastes in reading need not embrace every subject fashionable at the moment. Involve* usually suggests the relationship of a thing that is a logical consequence or required condition of something more inclusive: *A heavy scholastic schedule involves extra effort.*

Antonyms have an opposite or nearly opposite meaning from the dictionary definition of any given word. The antonym of *large* would be *small.* The antonym of *young* would be *old.* Antonyms are generally less useful to writers than synonyms, and many dictionaries do not include them.

16c

di/th

Exercise 16.4   Look up both words in each pair of synonyms, and write sentences using each to show that you understand the connotation of the word.

Example

mournful/lugubrious

The funeral procession made its *mournful* way to the graveyard under the dripping trees and threatening skies.

He tired of the *lugubrious* outpourings of her insincere grief.

1. walk/ramble	5. rebut/refute	9. reporter/informer
2. ask/demand	6. decline/reject	10. ideal/visionary
3. urbane/suave	7. bright/gaudy	11. optimistic/utopian
4. mercenary/pecuniary	8. cheap/tawdry	12. plan/scheme

Geographic and Biographical Entries

The handy size of a standard desk dictionary limits the information that each entry can include. But you can find the correct spellings of important place names, the official names of countries with their areas and populations, and the names of capitals. Biographical entries give the birth and death years and enough information about the person to justify a listing in the dictionary.

16c

Use a thesaurus with caution.

16c

di/th

A **thesaurus** (the word means "treasury" or "collection" in Latin) is a dictionary of synonyms, usually without definitions. Three standard thesauruses are available:

Roget's International Thesaurus. 4th ed. New York: Thomas Y. Crowell, 1977.

The Synonym Finder. Ed. J. I. Rodale. Emmaus, Pa.: Rodale Press, 1978.

Webster's Collegiate Thesaurus. Springfield, Mass.: Merriam-Webster, 1976.

All three thesauruses give many synonyms for each listed word, and the words are indexed in the back of the book. Pocket thesauruses arranged in dictionary form are available but are limited in their number of entries and, hence, in their usefulness. The index entry for *walk* in *Roget's Thesaurus* shows that the noun synonyms may be located under entries for *sphere, slow motion, ramble, gait, circuit, sphere of work, path,* and *arena.* Verb synonyms can be found under entries for *go slow* and *travel. Walk* as a noun is listed with *leisurely gait, snail's* or *tortoise's pace, creep, crawl, saunter, stroll, slouch, shuffle, shamble,* and several more.

A thesaurus does not define words. Thus it is most useful for someone who already knows the definitions of the words and merely wants to be reminded of synonyms that may add color or more precision to a piece of prose. Thesauruses have misled many inexperienced writers by encouraging them to use a word without understanding its connotations (see 11f). The effects may be either laughable or seriously misleading.

For example, if you wanted to find just the right word for the colorless quality of a twilight just fading into complete darkness, you might look under "colorlessness" in *Roget's Thesaurus* and discover the adjective "ghastly." You might write, "Just before the darkness fell, the light under the trees in the forest turned ghastly." One of the meanings of *ghastly* is "with a ghostlike pallor," and "pallor" led Roget's editors to put "ghastly" among the adjectives of colorlessness. But the connotations of *ghastly* all relate to death, to horror, to dread, or to something equally terrible. So the sense of the word *ghastly* in the sentence above is that something about the light under the trees in the forest was horrible. If you were writing a murder mystery or a ghost story, the word might be the one you would want to use. But if you were describing the peaceful appearance of the woods on a pleasant spring evening, your meaning would go completely awry.

Again, use the thesaurus with extreme caution. If you do not fully understand a synonym that you are about to use in your own writing, look it up in a good dictionary to be sure it is just the word you want to use.

The thesaurus can also be dangerous to a writer tempted to use a fancy style. Most of the time the simple word is much more efficient and forceful than the complicated word in expressing meaning and in creating a good effect. If you use the thesaurus too often, even correctly, you risk creating stiff and pretentious prose.

Exercise 16.5 Find five synonyms for the word *excitement* in a thesaurus. Write a sentence for each of the synonyms, using the words correctly. Use a desk dictionary if you need to check on the connotations of a word.

16c

di/th

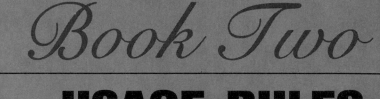

Book Two

USAGE RULES AND OPTIONS

PART FOUR
Understanding Grammar and Writing Correct Sentences

PART FIVE
Understanding Punctuation

PART SIX
Understanding Mechanics

PART FOUR 4

UNDERSTANDING GRAMMAR AND WRITING CORRECT SENTENCES

	Chapter
Correcting Run-ons and Comma Splices	17
Correcting Sentence Fragments	18
Agreement of Subject and Verb	19
Verb Forms	20
Pronouns	21
Adjective and Adverb Modifiers	22
Dangling Modifiers and Misplaced Parts	23
Confusing Shifts	24

CHAPTER SEVENTEEN

Correcting Run-ons and Comma Splices

Run-on errors occur when two independent clauses run together. **Comma splices** occur when two independent clauses are linked by a comma. Appropriate punctuation and conjunctions can correct these common sentence errors.

In the example below, you can see both of these errors.

> Fuel emissions at Yosemite National Park can disrupt the delicate ecological balance, [A] authorities have acted firmly against pollution [B] they have banned the automobile in Yosemite Valley. *(A)* Comma splice: *Only a comma marks the point of contact between two independent clauses here (see 5d). Commas alone are too weak to mark off independent clauses. (B)* Run-on sentence: *The end of one independent clause is not marked off by any punctuation.*

There are many ways to join or separate independent clauses.

17a _____
Use a period or some other suitable end mark to set off independent clauses from one another.

A period at the end of an independent clause, followed by a capital letter, will give you two distinct sentences.

> Fuel emissions at Yosemite National Park can disrupt the delicate ecological balance. Authorities have acted firmly against pollution. They have banned the automobile in Yosemite Valley.

You may sometimes use a question mark or an exclamation point to separate the clauses.

RUN-ON SENTENCE: Are liberal arts graduates desirable employees in business many corporations report their strong interest in women and men with humanities backgrounds.

CORRECTED: Are liberal arts graduates desirable employees in business? Many corporations report their strong interest in women and men with humanities backgrounds.

COMMA SPLICE: I made it, I passed the bar exam, I can be a lawyer!

CORRECTED: I made it! I passed the bar exam! I can be a lawyer!
A question mark corrects the run-on error after business *in the first example; the exclamation point replaces the commas and corrects the comma splices in the second example.*

Exercise 17.1   The items below contain one or more run-on errors or comma splices. Correct them by creating complete sentences separated by appropriate end punctuation and, where necessary, appropriate capitalization.

1. Many states outlaw the sale of fireworks, every year they cause many children to lose their hands and eyes.
2. Despite the rise in fares, short ocean voyages continue to draw vacationers from all over America now "cruises to nowhere" have grown in popularity.
3. The art of welding is necessary to modern industry welding is an art that requires much care and patience.
4. How can noise ordinances protect urban dwellers against loud portable radios cradled like babies in the arms of strolling adolescents the police seem reluctant to arrest young offenders, since a loud radio is not a violent crime.
5. When my mother first started working, I had to make some sudden adjustments, I had to deal with an unexpected feeling of abandonment the first time I came home from grade school to an empty house and realized that Mom was not there to greet me and that everything seemed still and dead.
6. I stepped out onto the road with care, expecting a joke, and kicked the abandoned purse gently, it jingled.

17b

Use a comma to join two independent clauses only when it comes before a coordinating conjunction—*and, but, or, nor, for, yet,* or *so*.

A comma alone is not strong enough to mark off one independent clause from another (see 5d). Notice how conjunctions serve correctly in the following examples.

Fuel emissions at Yosemite National Park can disrupt the delicate ecological balance, so authorities have acted firmly against pollution. *The comma and the conjunction* so *coordinate the independent clauses, giving us a compound sentence.*

COMMA SPLICE: Cortez first introduced chocolate to Europe, the Spaniards later added sugar for sweetening. *The comma after* Europe *incorrectly splices two independent clauses together.*

CORRECTED: Cortez first introduced chocolate to Europe, and the Spaniards later added sugar for sweetening. *The conjunction* and *added after the comma correctly joins two independent clauses in a compound sentence.*

COMMA SPLICE: Shakespeare's *Macbeth* is a morality play, it shows that some crimes are punished not only by society but also by the guilt criminals feel about their crimes.

CORRECTED: Shakespeare's *Macbeth* is a morality play, for it shows that some crimes are punished not only by society but also by the guilt criminals feel about their crimes. *The comma and the conjunction* for *correctly link the independent clauses.*

17c

Use a semicolon between two independent clauses when those clauses are closely related in meaning, form, or both. (See 27a.)

When the ideas in two independent clauses are closely related, semicolons help stress the connection in meaning. The first word after a semicolon begins with a lowercase letter unless the word is a proper noun. When a conjunctive adverb such as *also, however,* or *therefore* or a transitional expression such as *for example* or *on the contrary* (see 17e) appears between two independent clauses, you can separate them with a semicolon. Remember, however, that the period is a more usual mark of separation than a semicolon. When you use a period, you of course have two sentences; if you use the semicolon, you have one sentence.

> Federal authorities in Yosemite National Park have acted firmly against pollution; they have banned the automobile in Yosemite Valley.
> *By connecting the independent clauses, the semicolon stresses the point that the second clause is a consequence of the first.*

COMMA SPLICE: A good researcher may not know all the facts however, she should know where to find them.
The word however *is not a coordinating conjunction, and the comma before or after it cannot set off the independent clauses.*

CORRECTED: A good researcher may not know all the facts however, she should know where to find them.
The semicolon before however *corrects the comma splice.*

RUN-ON SENTENCE: Young children often watch television unsupervised – as a result, they can see violence, fear, and danger in their own living rooms.
The expression as a result *cannot join the clauses sufficiently.*

CORRECTED: Young children often watch television unsupervised; as a result, they can see violence, fear, and danger in their own living rooms.
The semicolon joins the two clauses and helps emphasize the close relation between them that as a result *suggests.*

In each example above, a period followed by a capitalized first letter would correct the run-on error or the comma splice by turning the two independent clauses into two distinct sentences.

Occasionally a writer will use both a semicolon and a conjunction to mark off independent clauses (see 27a).

> Nothing could be more racy, straightforward, and alive than the prose of Shakespeare; but it must be remembered that this was dialogue written to be spoken.
> —W. Somerset Maugham
> *Both the semicolon and the coordinating conjunction* but *join the independent clauses appropriately; but instead of using the semicolon, the author could have used a comma before* but.

When independent clauses are short and closely related in structure and meaning, some writers occasionally join them with a comma to achieve a special effect.

17c

ro/cs

The sense fails in two ways. Sometimes it gives no information, sometimes it gives false information.

—FRANCIS BACON

You fly in with the goods, you fly out with the lucky.

—JOHN LE CARRÉ

The writers use commas to stress the close joining of the thoughts in the two independent clauses. A semicolon after information *or after* goods *would have the same effect as the comma. A period, or a coordinating conjunction and a comma, would also connect the clauses correctly, but the writer would sacrifice the closeness of thought that the comma helps to establish.*

Exercise 17.2 Correct run-on errors and comma splices in the following sentences. Use either a coordinating conjunction and a comma or a semicolon, but be sure that your corrections yield logical sentences. Mark any correct sentences *C*.

1. The snow started falling at five o'clock then the wind began to blow hard from the north.
2. The best way to keep warm in icy weather is to wear layers of clothing moreover wool is much warmer than cotton.
3. She saw the cat spring through the air onto the bluebird she yelled.
4. Fewer jobs are open for teachers every year, yet many college students major in education to obtain teaching certificates.
5. The heavy black clouds meant rain, they came on swiftly with thunder and lightning.
6. Metro-Goldwyn-Mayer worked hard to make Tarzan's yell sound like that of a real animal, in the 1930s sound-effects specialists recorded and studied, among others, the cries of a hyena, the growls of a dog, and the wail of a mother camel whose young had been taken away.
7. The head on some old engines was nothing more than a cast-iron lid, cast iron was strong and heavy, just right to contain the explosions going on thousands of times a minute in the cylinders.
8. Cross-country skiing is cheaper than downhill skiing you can outfit two people with cross-country equipment for the price of outfitting one person with everything needed for downhill skiing.
9. Cramming for exams rarely helps, nevertheless many students stay up until dawn studying on the night before a big test.
10. Do not send cash or a check now simply phone in your order with a credit card number.

17d

Use subordination occasionally to correct a sentence with independent clauses that are incorrectly joined with a comma splice or that are run together.

COMMA SPLICE: Fuel emissions at Yosemite National Park can disrupt the delicate ecological balance of the region, authorities there have acted firmly against automobiles.

CORRECTED BY SUBORDINATION: Because fuel emissions at Yosemite National Park can disrupt the delicate ecological balance of the region, authorities there have acted firmly against automobiles.
The subordinator because *links the major thoughts in these clauses firmly by making the first clause dependent on the second.*

RUN-ON SENTENCE: Authorities have acted firmly against pollution – they have banned the automobile in Yosemite Valley.

CORRECTED BY SUBORDINATION: Authorities who have banned the automobile in Yosemite Valley have acted firmly against pollution.
Here the relative pronoun who *(see 5b-3) subordinates the clause following it, making that clause an adjective modifying the noun* authorities.

Acting firmly against pollution, authorities have banned the automobile in Yosemite Valley.
The writer has changed one of the clauses into a participial phrase, acting firmly against pollution. *The phrase serves as an adjective modifying* authorities.

Exercise 17.3   Use an appropriate method of subordination to correct run-on errors and comma splices below. Mark any correct sentences *C*.

1. Learning to read lips is not easy young children can adapt to this preferred method of teaching language to the deaf more easily than older people can.
2. At Bourda Market in Georgetown, Guyana, daybreak stirs a rush of activity, vendors set up their wares for the 6:30 A.M. opening.
3. Play, which allows a child's free expression, helps early childhood education. However, children must keep some real control over the situation if play is to encourage real learning.

ro/cs

4. Different careers and different ambitions often separate childhood friends, they share only memories after a while and do not share any common experiences in the present.
5. The Super Bowl in January has now become an unofficial national holiday, people who hardly follow professional football during the regular season gather at parties before huge color television sets, eating and drinking and enjoying each other and sometimes watching the game.

Exercise 17.4 Correct the run-on errors and comma splices in Exercise 17.1 (page 296), this time by joining complete thoughts either through coordination (see 17b and 17c) or through subordination (see 17d).

17e

Become alert to words, phrases, and punctuation that may cause run-on errors or comma splices.

17e

ro/cs

Certain conjunctive adverbs (see 5b-4), transitional expressions (see 4b-5), or subject pronouns (see 5b-3) at the beginning of a sentence can mislead you into producing a run-on error or a comma splice. If you look for such words in your writing, you can proofread more carefully for comma splices and run-ons.

Conjunctive adverbs in this category include words such as *accordingly, also, anyway, as a result, besides, consequently, finally, furthermore, hence, however, incidentally, indeed, instead, likewise, meanwhile, moreover, nevertheless, nonetheless, now, otherwise, still, suddenly, then, therefore,* and *thus.*

COMMA SPLICE: The price of gold varies greatly every year, nevertheless, speculators purchase precious metals in large quantities and hope always for a price rise.
A comma before nevertheless *incorrectly marks the boundary between the two independent clauses.*

CORRECTED: The price of gold varies greatly every year; nevertheless, speculators purchase precious metals in large quantities and hope always for a price rise.
A semicolon correctly joins the two clauses before the conjunctive adverb (see 27b). A period and a capital letter would also separate the two clauses appropriately by converting them into two sentences.

RUN-ON SENTENCE: Salt air corrodes metal easily – therefore, automobiles in coastal regions require frequent washing even in cold weather.

Therefore neither links nor separates the clauses adequately.

CORRECTED: Salt air corrodes metal easily. Therefore, automobiles in coastal regions require frequent washing even in cold weather.

The period before therefore and the capital letter correct the run-on error and create two complete sentences. A comma and the conjunction and, or a semicolon alone, would work just as well here.

Some of the transitional expressions that may lead to comma splice or run-on errors are the following: *after all, after a while, as a result, at any rate, at the same time, for example, for instance, in addition, in fact, in other words, in particular, in the first place, on the contrary,* and *on the other hand.*

COMMA SPLICE: Richard Rodgers's music continues to delight audiences everywhere, in fact, revivals of *Oklahoma, Carousel,* and *The King and I* pack theaters every year.

The transitional expression in fact *made this writer believe that the two independent clauses are correctly joined. But* in fact *is not a coordinating conjunction, and a comma is not strong enough to help the expression connect the two clauses.*

CORRECTED: Richard Rodgers's music continues to delight audiences everywhere. In fact, revivals of *Oklahoma, Carousel,* and *The King and I* pack theaters every year.

A period after everywhere *followed by a capital letter establishes the boundaries of the two sentences.*

RUN-ON SENTENCE: Americans continue their love affair with the automobile _ at the same time they are more successful than ever before in restricting its use.

The transitional phrase at the same time *does not serve to bind the two independent clauses together grammatically.*

CORRECTED: Americans continue their love affair with the automobile, but at the same time they are more successful than ever before in restricting its use.

The coordinator but *joins the two clauses correctly.*

The subject pronouns that may lead to comma splices and run-on sentences are the following: *I, you, he, she, it, we, they,* and *who.*

COMMA SPLICE: Disneyland is fun for everyone, I think I enjoyed it as much as my ten-year-old niece did.
The comma does not adequately set off the two independent clauses.

CORRECTED: Disneyland is fun for everyone; I think I enjoyed it as much as my ten-year-old niece did.
The semicolon coordinates the two independent clauses correctly. A period placed where the semicolon is would make two complete sentences.

RUN-ON SENTENCE: The weather disappointed Vermont vacationers—they wanted snow in January, not warm, sunny skies.
The subject pronoun they, *despite its close connection to the noun* vacationers, *its antecedent in the previous clause, cannot join the two clauses grammatically.*

CORRECTED: The weather disappointed Vermont vacationers because they wanted snow in January, not warm, sunny skies.
The addition of the word because *connects the two clauses by subordinating the second one.*

In divided quotations or in consecutive sentences within a quotation, be sure to punctuate complete sentences correctly.

In a dialogue, commas are not sufficient to set off independent clauses.

COMMA SPLICE: "Speak up, amigo," Juanita said, "I can't hear you."
Commas frequently precede quotations (see 26j), but in constructions like this one, we have two distinct sentences, and the punctuation should show that fact. One sentence ends after said; *another begins with the word* I.

CORRECTED: "Speak up, amigo," Juanita said. "I can't hear you."
The period separates the two sentences correctly.

RUN-ON SENTENCE: Finally he shrugged and said, "You don't love me—you never have loved me!"
Although only one person speaks the words within the quotation marks, the sentence boundaries must be properly marked.

CORRECTED: Finally he shrugged and said, "You don't love me! You never have loved me!"
An exclamation point keeps the independent clauses apart and stresses the emotion of the speaker. You could use a period or a semicolon instead of the exclamation point; the semicolon would not be followed by a capital letter.

Exercise 17.5   Use the word in brackets correctly in the sentence that follows. Correct the punctuation and capitalization where necessary.

1. [they] The use of copying machines has replaced note-taking for many students _____ simply photograph text pages instead of taking notes on their readings.
2. [however] His car skidded and struck the telephone pole _____, he was not hurt.
3. [however] He said _____ that the car would never run again.
4. [it] The dulcimer has a soft, sweet tone _____ was long ago replaced by the guitar in bluegrass music.
5. [I] "Not I," she replied with a scowl "_____ never liked him."
6. [on the contrary] He expected his lawyer to plead his case vigorously to the jury _____, she said only, "I think this man ought to be put away for life."

17f

Examine drafts of your papers carefully for run-on errors and comma splices.

If you have trouble with run-on errors and comma splices, spend extra time trying to locate and correct them in your papers. If you read over your drafts with an eye to avoiding these errors, you can locate them before you produce a final draft.

1   Read your papers aloud slowly.

When you read aloud slowly, your ear probably will pick out the independent clauses. They will sound like complete sentences, and you are likely to pause for breath at the end of each one. When your voice clearly stops and drops, look for a period or a semicolon at that point.

2   Before you write your final draft, count your sentences.

Number your sentences all the way through the draft of your paper. Then see if you have separated them properly with the right punctuation and capitalization. Too few sentences on several pages of a draft may signal run-on errors.

3 Read your papers backward from the last sentence to the first.

When you use this technique, you can consider each sentence as a separate unit of meaning apart from the surrounding sentences. Each sentence appears as a complete statement on its own, and implied connections, such as those made through transitional phrases, adverbs, and pronouns, cannot trap you into making errors. You must read very carefully, being sure that each group of words you read aloud forms a complete sentence or a complete independent clause.

4 Watch for the words and phrases that often cause run-on errors or comma splices at sentence junctures. (See 17e.)

Subject pronouns, transitional expressions, and conjunctive adverbs frequently appear at sentence junctures. Words and phrases in these groups can trap you into writing run-on errors and comma splices, and by looking especially for those words and phrases when you read over your drafts, you can often locate and correct your mistakes.

CHECKLIST: HOW TO CORRECT RUN-ON ERRORS AND COMMA SPLICES

1. Use a period, a question mark, or an exclamation point.
2. Use *and, but, or, nor, for, yet,* or *so,* preceded by a comma.
3. Use a semicolon to coordinate closely related ideas in consecutive independent clauses.
4. Use subordination to relate some ideas that might otherwise be expressed in independent clauses.

17f

ro/cs

Exercise 17.6   In each item below, underline the sentence element that gave rise to the run-on error or the comma splice. Correct the errors by using any of the methods explained in this chapter.

1. The deputy mayor enjoys speaking to civic groups, for example, she addressed the Kiwanis Club, the Young Republican Club, and the Daughters of the American Revolution all on one Sunday last month.
2. A hush fell over the crowd then a small man with an empty sleeve on his coat and a hideously scarred face got out of his seat and hobbled to the platform.

3. Public transportation is quick and safe on the other hand it does not offer the flexibility and privacy of travel by car.
4. Sidesaddles allowed women to ride horseback modestly in an age of long, thick skirts, however, such saddles were extremely dangerous because they did not allow women to grip the horse with their legs.
5. A two-cycle gasoline engine is excellent for lawn mowers and for boats using an outboard motor it is not good for larger machines because its lubrication is uneven at the higher temperatures larger machines generate.
6. "Many parents feel guilty about putting their young children in day-care centers," Mr. Carmichael said, "the children themselves usually seem to enjoy the experience."

Exercise 17.7 Correct the run-on errors and comma splices in the following passage. Do not change any correct sentences. Study the checklist on page 305.

(1) During my early childhood, there were two rules I hated in our house, mother enforced them too rigidly. (2) The first was the rule against talking in the bedroom after she turned the lights out, I can vividly remember whispering in the dark to my sister Lisa as we exchanged secrets before going to sleep in our bedroom. (3) I had always thought that nighttime was ideal for chatting and giggling, consequently, I went over everything I had done during the day, we planned things to do tomorrow. (4) "Do I hear talking in there?" my mother would shout, "I'd better not!" (5) We would laugh our pillows only partly muffled our giggling. (6) We stayed quiet for a while then, minutes later, the talking resumed. (7) Why mother insisted on enforcing this rule remains a mystery the second annoying rule I hated was that we were not supposed to eat in the living room. (8) I remember watching television one evening I was sprawled out on the sofa with my eyes glued to the tube after a while I heard mother's voice. (9) "Dinner's ready," she called, "everyone to the table." (10) While I hurriedly filled my plate, the telephone rang, and Mom turned to answer it, then I sneaked out of the kitchen and back to the living room and the television set, "Linda," I heard, "I've told you not to eat in the living room." (11) The next thing I knew Mom came walking into the living room with the pruning shears she used on her roses in the garden, unplugged the electric cord on the TV, and cut off the plug with her shears, consequently nobody watched television until we got a new cord for our set. (12) By that time everybody had color TV however I never did find out if Gilligan and all the others escaped from Gilligan's Island, somebody said they did.

CHAPTER EIGHTEEN

Correcting Sentence Fragments

End marks—periods, question marks, or exclamation points—separate grammatical units that are complete sentences. To be complete grammatically, a sentence needs both a subject and a predicate. A grammatically incomplete unit starting with a capital letter and closing with an end mark is called a **sentence fragment.**

In the following sentence fragments, the writer incorrectly makes an incomplete word group look like a sentence by using a capital letter for the first word and by placing a period after the last.

Through lively interviews and dramatic scenes.

And tried the hot tamales.

Watching ducks on the lake.

If they have empty home lives.

Who by that time had begun to get over their guilt feelings about Vietnam.

You can easily spot sentence fragments when they appear in isolation as these fragments do. But when a fragment is buried in surrounding sentences, you may have trouble seeing it and correcting it.

(A) Television brings current events to life. (B) *Through lively interviews and dramatic scenes.* (C) Newscasts flood our homes with interesting people and far-off places.
As a prepositional phrase (see 5d-1), the fragment—(B)—contains neither a subject nor a predicate. The writer assumed that the subject

and verb in (A), television brings, *or in (C),* newcasts flood, *could serve (B) as well. Standing alone as it does, however, (B) is a fragment.*

(A) We visited a new Mexican restaurant downtown. (B) *And tried the hot tamales.* (C) They burned my mouth for a week.
The fragment — (B) — is the second part of a compound predicate begun in (A). (See 5a-1 and 7a-1.) The writer is trying to say we visited *and* tried. *Without its own subject, though, (B) is a fragment.*

(A) On Sundays in May at Marjorie Post Park everyone relaxes. (B) *Watching ducks on the lake.* (C) Men and women sit everywhere beneath the flowering dogwoods and chat idly in the afternoon sun.
Although the participial phrase — *(B) — contains a word that looks like a verb, the present participle* watching *cannot serve as a complete verb without the aid of an auxiliary, or helping, verb (see 5b-1, and 20a). In addition, (B) has no subject, although the writer probably believed the subject in (A),* everyone, *or the subject in (C),* men and women, *would serve. But because it contains neither its own subject nor its own predicate, (B) is a fragment.*

(A) Unhappy teenagers can become runaways. (B) *If they have empty home lives.* (C) Escape at any cost may be attractive, even if it means being broke and alone.
Fragment (B) has a subject and a predicate, but the subordinator if *at the beginning makes the clause dependent on another clause, which is not present in the group of words here begun by a capital letter and ended by a period. Dependent clause (B) could be attached to the sentence before it — (A) — or to the sentence after it — (C). But as it stands, (B) is a fragment — perhaps because the writer had some trouble deciding whether to tack it on at the end of the previous sentence or to put it at the beginning of the next sentence.*

frag

(A) The capture of the American embassy in Iran by fanatical "students" angered Americans. (B) *Who by that time had begun to get over their guilt feelings about Vietnam.* (C) And the taking of American hostages created a new surge of patriotism across the United States.
Unit (B) is a relative clause, which must be embedded in a complete sentence. The writer intends the relative clause to modify the noun Americans *in (A). But to take part in a grammatically complete sentence, a relative clause must be attached to an independent clause that it modifies.*

Exercise 18.1 Identify the fragments and the complete sentences below. Explain your choices.

1. Without any funds from the federal government or from foundations.
2. Who found the lost keys.

3. Supported by heavy steel cables.
4. Driving through the California desert with the temperature at 114 degrees.
5. Johnny Cash sings many songs about prisons and prisoners, their loneliness and their hardships.
6. Since she spoke to the child's mother.
7. That woman holds two jobs.
8. Country music wailing with pain and loss.
9. A woman who holds two jobs.
10. Country music wails with pain and loss.
11. To learn a foreign language.
12. She wanted to learn a foreign language.
13. Because he cried and played the guitar woefully.
14. Fans at the Grand Ole Opry disliked him because he cried and played the guitar woefully and dressed in a tuxedo for his appearances.

Exercise 18.2   Identify the complete sentences and the fragment or fragments in each selection below, and explain your choices.

1. Alcohol can damage heart muscle tissue in a condition called *alcoholic cardiomyopathy.* Which can be fatal. Especially to people who cannot leave alcohol alone.
2. The United States Constitution gives three basic duties to Congress. Enacting laws, representing the people, and limiting the power of the executive branch.
3. Videodiscs and tapes have increased in popularity. As a result of this exciting new technology. Many more people can buy or rent their favorite movies. Seeing them without commercial interruptions on their own TV sets at home.
4. Human beings develop intellectually in leaps from one stage to another, say some important theorists in psychology. Such as Erik Erikson and Jean Piaget.
5. Working for the government sometimes requires great personal sacrifice, but the rewards of public service are great. By hard work and careful attention to detail, a government worker can do much good for the society at large.

18a

frag

18a
Correct sentence fragments by making them into complete sentences.

No handbook can give a complete set of rules for converting sentence fragments into sentences, but the following examples show some typical problems and some ways to remedy them.

1 **Join the fragment to the sentence that comes before it.**

FRAGMENT: Television brings current events to life. Through lively interviews and dramatic scenes.

CORRECTED: Television brings current events to life through lively interviews and dramatic scenes.
The prepositional phrase through lively interviews and dramatic scenes *completes the meaning of the independent clause; the independent clause and the prepositional phrase can be easily joined in a complete sentence.*

FRAGMENT: (A) Jean Rhys's *Good Morning, Midnight* is a novel about Sasha Jansen. (B) A lonely woman in Paris. (C) She searches desperately for escape from a dismal past.
As an appositive (see 5b-2), the fragment— (B) —depends for its meaning on sentence (A) or (C). However, lacking a subject, a verb, and a clear meaning on its own, (B) as it stands is incomplete.

CORRECTED: Jean Rhys's *Good Morning, Midnight* is a novel about Sasha Jansen, a lonely woman in Paris.
The appositive is joined to the previous independent clause by a comma.

FRAGMENT: We visited a Mexican restaurant downtown. And tried the hot tamales.

CORRECTED: We visited a Mexican restaurant downtown and tried the hot tamales.
The verbs visited *and* tried *make a compound predicate for the subject* We. *The fragment* and tried the hot tamales *is easily joined to the sentence before it.*

FRAGMENT: On Sundays in May at Marjorie Post Park everyone can relax. Watching ducks on the lake.

CORRECTED: On Sundays in May at Marjorie Post Park everyone can relax, watching ducks on the lake.
The participial phrase watching ducks on the lake *can be attached to the previous sentence; the phrase becomes a free modifier (see 5d-1 and 9c).*

FRAGMENT: Unhappy teenagers can become runaways. If they have empty home lives.

CORRECTED: Unhappy teenagers can become runaways if they have empty home lives.

The subordinate clause if they have empty home lives *cannot stand by itself, but it can be joined to the independent clause preceding it.*

FRAGMENT: The song "John Henry" tells the story of a man trying to save his job against a machine. An effort that killed him.

CORRECTED: The song "John Henry" tells the story of a man trying to save his job against a machine—an effort that killed him. *The dash joins the fragment to the previous sentence, and the fragment becomes an appositive. The dash adds emphasis to the appositive.*

2 **Correct a fragment by adding it to the beginning of the sentence that follows the fragment.**

FRAGMENT: Watching ducks glide across the lake. Men and women sit everywhere beneath the flowering dogwoods and talk softly under the afternoon sun.

CORRECTED: Watching ducks glide across the lake, men and women sit everywhere beneath the flowering dogwoods and talk softly under the afternoon sun.
The fragment watching ducks glide across the lake *is joined to the sentence after it and becomes a participial phrase modifying the subject* men and women.

FRAGMENT: If they have empty home lives. Escape at any cost may be attractive to some teenagers, even if it means being broke and alone.

CORRECTED: If they have empty home lives, escape at any cost may be attractive to some teenagers, even if it means being broke and alone.
The fragment if they have empty home lives *becomes, in the corrected version, an adverbial clause opening the sentence and modifying the verb phrase* may be.

FRAGMENT: (A) William L. Shirer wanted to travel the country beyond Iowa. (B) To see firsthand the people in the rest of Middle America. (C) He joined a tent crew for a road company of speakers, artists, and musicians.
Although the subject and predicate in (A), William L. Shirer wanted, *or in (C),* he joined, *may seem logically to serve in (B) to make it stand as a complete sentence, the fragment demands its own subject and predicate. The verbal unit in (B) is an* infinitive *phrase (see 5d-1).*

CORRECTED: William L. Shirer wanted to travel the country beyond Iowa. To see firsthand the people in the rest of Middle America, he joined a tent crew for a road company of speakers, artists, and musicians.
The infinitive phrase now opens the sentence that comes after it.

FRAGMENT: (A) My mother and I sound alike. (B) Whenever I answer the telephone. (C) Her friends mistake me for her.
As a subordinate clause, the fragment, (B), despite its close relation in meaning to neighboring sentences, cannot stand as a grammatically complete unit. The fragment does contain a subject and a verb, but the subordinator whenever *makes a connection to an independent clause necessary (see 5d-2).*

CORRECTED: My mother and I sound alike. Whenever I answer the telephone, her friends mistake me for her.
The subordinate clause now opens the second sentence.

Your intended meaning determines whether you connect a fragment to the sentence before or to the sentence after. Sometimes neither one of these options will produce a sentence that makes sense and pleases stylistically.

18a

frag

3 **Correct a fragment by adding or removing words to convert it into a complete sentence or by changing the wording of the fragment itself.**

FRAGMENT: On Sundays in May at Marjorie Post Park everyone can relax. Watching ducks on the lake.

CORRECTED: On Sundays in May at Marjorie Post Park everyone can relax. *Children enjoy* watching ducks on the lake.
Children, a subject, and enjoy, *a verb, have been added to the fragment to make a complete sentence and to change the emphasis somewhat.*

OR

On Sundays in May at Marjorie Post Park everyone can relax. *Children watch* ducks on the lake.
Now the participle watching *has been changed to a simple verb,* watch, *in the present tense, and a subject,* children, *has been added.*

FRAGMENT: Old Mr. Warren is outdoors this afternoon. *Working in his rose garden.*

CORRECTED BY ADDING WORDS: Old Mr. Warren is outdoors this afternoon. Unlike all the young people who have fled to the beach, he is working in his rose garden.

FRAGMENT: He wrote to his mother every day. *Which no one could understand.*

CORRECTED BY ADDING WORDS: He wrote to his mother every day. This was a devotion which no one could understand.

FRAGMENT: Although she worked at a tiresome job driving a cab all day long, she studied long hours at night. *Because she wanted with all her heart to become an architect.*

CORRECTED BY ELIMINATING A WORD: Although she worked at a tiresome job driving a cab all day long, she studied long hours at night. She wanted with all her heart to become an architect.

Exercise 18.3 Return to Exercise 18.1 on pages 308–309. Correct each fragment by using any one of the techniques explained in 18a. That is, create a complete sentence by adding a subject, a verb, or both; by changing participles or infinitives into verbs; or by removing subordinators and making whatever other changes sentence logic requires. Be sure that your new sentences make sense.

18a

frag

Exercise 18.4 Find the fourteen fragments in the following selection. Correct each one by adding it to an adjacent sentence, by adding words to it, or by removing words from it. Be sure that each sentence has a subject and a predicate.

We knew him as heavyweight boxing champion of the world. A joking, mocking, happy showman. He wrote poems about his foes. Bad poems. But they made people laugh. Paying attention. He bragged about himself in a sport. Where the athletes supposed to be humble. Not telling the world how good they are. But he was good. Maybe the best fighter in boxing history. Now he no longer heavyweight champion. He writes no more poems. On television speaks slowly. Hesitates. Looks puzzled and hurt. Fighting kills the brain of people who take too many blows to the head. He not now what he used to be. No one cheers for him anymore. His glory gone with the wind. People who made money off him gone too. They took all he gave them. And went away.

Exercise 18.5 Find the thirteen fragments in the following selection. Correct each one by adding it to an adjacent sentence, by adding words to it, or by removing words from it.

Looking weak and red above the housetops to the southwest. The sun seemed to sink wearily toward the horizon at the end of a January day. The red liquid in the thermometer just outside my window standing at zero degrees. Snow piled deep in the street. The world looking shut up and very still. There was not a cloud in the sky. As the sun sank out of sight. The color of the sky turned slowly dark. Looking like a dome of ice. The world was a giant igloo. Remembering summer. We thought we were remembering dreams. Because it seemed impossible that we had ever walked in these streets with our bare feet. Or in our shirtsleeves without layers and layers of warm clothing. That we had sat in Fenway Park in the open air at night, sipping cold drinks and watching the Red Sox play baseball. Summer a myth. A lost world. It seemed something that never was. Something that would never come again.

18b

Learn to recognize the words and phrases at sentence beginnings that can trap writers into producing fragments.

18b

frag

When you use present and past participles, infinitives, or certain adverbs, connectives, and subordinators as sentence openers, you may trap yourself into producing an incomplete sentence. If you check carefully when you proofread for words in these groups at the beginnings of your sentences, you may spot unwanted fragments.

Present participles are verb forms ending in *-ing*, such as *singing*, *running*, *speaking*, *trying*, *shouting*, *working*, and *flying* (see 5d-1, and 20a).

> **FRAGMENT:** *Running wildly in the hills.* The stallion looked untamed and beautiful and somehow ghostly.

> **CORRECTED:** Running wildly in the hills, the stallion looked untamed and beautiful and somehow ghostly.
> *The sentence opening, a participial phrase, is joined to a complete sentence and modifies the subject,* stallion.

Past participles are verb forms ending in *-ed, t, d,* or *-n,* such as *dressed, faded, hurt,* and *driven* (see 5d-1, and 20a).

> **FRAGMENT:** The toast popped up. *Burned black as coal.* It looked like a piece of volcanic rock.

CORRECTED: The toast popped up, burned black as coal.
The participial phrase burned black as coal *is a fragment that in the corrected version becomes a modifier describing the subject,* toast.

CORRECTED: The toast popped up. Burned black as coal, it looked like a piece of volcanic rock.
In this version, the fragment has been added on to the beginning of the next sentence so that it becomes a modifier describing the pronoun it.

CORRECTED: The toast popped up. It was burned black as coal.
In this version, the subject it *and the helping verb* was *have been added to the beginning of the fragment to convert it into a complete sentence.*

Infinitives are verb forms introduced by the word *to*, which is called the **infinitive marker** (see 5d-1). Infinitives include such forms as *to play, to scream, to study,* and *to eat.* Like participles and participial phrases, they express action vividly and sometimes seem so strong that writers may think them capable of standing alone as sentences.

FRAGMENT: The mayor spoke forcefully. *To convince her audience of the need for tax reform.*

CORRECTED: The mayor spoke forcefully to convince her audience of the need for tax reform.
The infinitive phrase contains the purpose of the mayor's speech. But it must be joined grammatically to the preceding sentence if it is to be a part of a complete statement.

CORRECTED: The mayor spoke forcefully. She worked hard to convince her audience of the need for tax reform.
Here words including a subject, she, *and a verb,* worked, *are added to the beginning of the fragment to convert it into a complete sentence.*

Adverbs, subordinators, and connecting words and phrases that often begin fragments include *also, as well as, especially, for example, for instance, just, like, mainly,* and *such as.* In speaking we often use fragments along with adverbs and connecting words, but when we write, we must be sure that adverbs and connecting words or phrases lead into complete sentences. Otherwise our readers will be confused.

FRAGMENT: An individual spectrum exists for each element. *For example, hydrogen.* It has a red, a blue-green, and a green line.

CORRECTED: An individual spectrum exists for each element. For example, hydrogen has a red, a blue-green, and a green line.

*In the corrected version, the fragment joins the independent clause
that follows it. The word* hydrogen *replaces the original subject,* It,
which is deleted.

FRAGMENT: Vegetarians should supplement their diets with
high-protein foods. *Like wheat germ and bean curd.*

CORRECTED: Vegetarians should supplement their diets with
high-protein foods like wheat germ and bean curd.
The fragment joins the complete sentence that precedes it.

Subordinators that may lead writers into making sentence fragments
include subordinating conjunctions, such as *as long as, after, although, as,
as if, as soon as, because, before, wherever, once, while, how, provided, if,
since, so that, though, unless, until, when, where,* and *whether,* and relative
pronouns, such as *what, which, who, whoever, whose, whom, whomever,
whatever,* and *that* (see 5b-3 and 5).

FRAGMENT: The University Government Association gives
students a voice in making policy. *Because they too should influence
the university administration in matters of academic, social, and
cultural welfare.*

CORRECTED: The University Government Association gives
students a voice in making policy because they too should
influence the university administration in matters of academic,
social, and cultural welfare.
*In the corrected version, the subordinate clause is added to the end of
the complete sentence in the first version.*

FRAGMENT: In Astoria in the late 1800s, an important community
figure was August Frederick Geipel. *Whose saloon on Newton
Road was a social center for German families in Queens.*

CORRECTED: In Astoria in the late 1800s, an important
community figure was August Frederick Geipel, whose saloon on
Newton Road was a social center for German families in Queens.
In the corrected version, the relative clause introduced by whose *is
joined to the independent clause to make a complex sentence (see
5d-3).*

FRAGMENT: Every winter morning he exercised by jogging
behind his two pet hounds. *That ran ahead of him, barking and
panting, and looking almost terrifying.*

CORRECTED: Every winter morning he exercised by jogging
behind his two pet hounds that ran ahead of him, barking and
panting, and looking almost terrifying.

18b

frag

The word that, *normally a demonstrative pronoun (see 5b-3), may serve as the subject of its own independent clause: "That was exactly what she wanted." In the fragment above, however,* that *is a relative pronoun. The clause it introduces is an adjective modifying* hounds. *As you see in the corrected version, the relative clause is now connected grammatically to an independent clause.*

Participles, infinitives, connectives, and *subordinators* make strong sentence openers, but you must give those words special attention at sentence beginnings to avoid fragments.

18c

Examine drafts carefully for sentence fragments.

Check papers for incomplete sentences by following these suggestions:

1 Read your sentences aloud, or get a friend to read them aloud to you.

Distinguish between the pause that a speaker may make for emphasis and the grammatical pause marked off by a period, a question mark, an exclamation point, or a semicolon.

2 Read your paper backward, from the last sentence to the first, or have a friend read the paper aloud in that way to you.

You may then judge the completeness of each sentence unit apart from the context. Stop after you read each sentence and ask, Is it complete? Does it make a complete statement or ask a complete question?

3 Check for subjects and predicates.

Every complete sentence must have at least one subject and one predicate (see 5a).

4 Look with particular care at sentences that begin with present and past participles, connective words and phrases, and subordinators. (See 18b.)

According to sentence logic and to your own stylistic tastes, take one of these steps:

1. Connect the fragment to the sentence *before* or *after*, making the choice that makes more sense.

2. Add a new subject, a new verb, or both, and add any other words that will help you make the fragment into a complete sentence.

3. Remove any words that keep the fragment from being a complete sentence.

4. Make a present or past participle into a verb by adding a helping verb such as *am, is, are, was,* or *were* before the participle or by changing the participle into a correct verb form.

5. When necessary, add a subject to the fragment to convert it into a complete sentence.

> **FRAGMENT:** Running away
> *present participle*
>
> **CORRECTED:** She is *running* away.
>
> OR
>
> She *runs* away.
>
> **FRAGMENT:** *Flown* above the city.
> *past participle*
>
> **CORRECTED:** The tiny aircraft *has flown* above the city.
>
> OR
>
> The tiny aircraft *flew* above the city.

6. Change an infinitive to a verb by removing *to* and by using the correct form of the verb. Or you can sometimes use *like, likes, want, wants, plan, plans, try, tries, am, is,* or *are* before the infinitive. Sometimes you will have to add a subject to fragments using an infinitive.

> **FRAGMENT:** To *watch* the sun rise over San Francisco Bay.
>
> **CORRECTED:** He *watches* the sun rise over San Francisco Bay.
>
> OR
>
> He *likes to watch* the sun rise over San Francisco Bay.
>
> OR
>
> We *are to watch* the sun rise over San Francisco Bay.

7. Make any necessary changes in the wording of the fragment to convert it into a complete sentence.

18c

frag

18d

Recognize acceptable uses of sentence fragments.

Although most formal writing requires complete sentences, sentence fragments occasionally can achieve some special effects. Writers of fiction regularly use fragments to record dialogue, since when we speak, we often use incomplete sentences. However, the context always makes the meaning of the fragment clear.

> Jean leaned back, her hands clasped round a knee, looking at the water below them. "I came to a decision last night, Dan." It was unexpected, and he glanced at her. "*Yes?*" She shrugged. "*Nothing momentous.* But I think I'll definitely try for a teacher training course when I get home. *If I can find a place.*"
>
> — JOHN FOWLES

> I had a sudden mad impulse to pack my bags and get away from both of them. Maybe it wasn't a question of choosing between them but just of escaping both entirely. *Released in my own custody. Stop this nonsense of running from one man to the next. Stand on my own two feet for once.*
>
> —ERICA JONG

Fragments may appear in nonfiction, especially when the writer is striving for an informal, conversational effect.

> But such was Autry's impact that even the action-all-the-way Cowboys had to have somebody in their films who could sing a few cowboy songs while the hero stood around listening and tapping his foot. Charles Starrett was good enough not to need any yodelers slowing up his action. But you couldn't buck the fashion. Anyway, Dick Weston did not exactly stop the show. *And never would if he went on calling himself Dick Weston.* The name was definitely not a bell ringer. *No matter how many times you said it.* It would never do for the Cowboy-Hero being groomed to challenge Gene Autry. It made him sound like a newsboy. It was too blah. They decided to call him Roy Rogers at Republic. *And gave him his own horse to sing to.*
>
> —JAMES HORWITZ

Questions and exclamations often have impact when written as fragments. To call attention to an idea, writers can use fragments effectively.

> *American culture?* Wealth is visible, and so, now, is poverty. Both have become intimidating clichés. *But the rest?*
>
> —PETER SCHRAG

The broadcaster is casually describing a routine landing of the giant gas bag. Suddenly he sees something. *A flash of flame!* An instant later the whole thing explodes.

— JOHN HOUSEMAN

Whatever economic sanctions can achieve will be duly tested. A semblance of Western resolve has been temporarily achieved. *At a considerable price.*

— *The New York Times*

Although they can be acceptable, as these examples show, fragments are still rare in the expository writing you will do in college. Use them carefully, and do not use them often. In writing for your courses, when you write a fragment, you may even want to mark it as such with an asterisk and a note at the bottom of the page. This will assure your teacher that you have made a deliberate choice and not a mistake.

Exercise 18.6 In each selection, correct each fragment by adding it to the sentence that comes before or after or by changing it into an independent sentence. Write *C* by the number of any selection that is correct as it stands.

1. In 1980, the Supreme Court ruled that scientists could patent bacteria made in laboratories. An important decision that has made profitable genetic engineering possible.
2. In and around Boston, the sixty-eight institutions of higher learning draw both full-time and part-time students, numbering more than 150,000. Of these over 60 percent come from states other than Massachusetts.
3. When I approached him after school for extra help with my algebra. He replied that he had already given me enough time. That I should try to find a tutor. Who could explain things slowly and carefully.
4. Although styles change quickly, the jeans phenomenon looks as if it is here to stay. Worn all over the world, jeans are especially popular with teenagers. But adults wear them, too, sometimes with jackets and neckties.
5. Abigail Adams championed women's rights. Writing about new legislation to her husband John early in the history of the United States. She said, "I desire you would remember the ladies and be more generous and favorable to them than your ancestors." A strong remark, considering the times.
6. Some garden pests may be controlled by means other than chemicals. To keep cutworms from destroying broccoli and cauliflower. A twelve-inch cardboard collar around each plant helps prevent damage.

Exercise 18.7 Return to Exercise 18.2 on page 309. Correct each fragment. Do not change correct sentences.

Exercise 18.8 Using these fragments, construct complete sentences. You may add anything you want to make the sentences complete.

1. Breaking away from the pack.
2. The coiled snake under my bed.
3. A woman of enormous strength and speed.
4. When I had discovered myself walking in my sleep.
5. If he should die before Saturday.
6. Ruined nevertheless.
7. For example, the personal computer and the typewriter.

Exercise 18.9 Identify the fragments in the following passages. Then explain why you think each writer used a fragment instead of a complete sentence. If you wanted to avoid the fragment, what would you do?

1. Mr. Fitzgerald and his wife, Kathy Fitzgerald, realized that if their hopes for filming the script were to be realized, they would need more help. Which they got in the form of Tom Shaw, a well known production manager and old friend of John Huston, who left a big-budget Barbra Streisand picture to take charge of *Wise Blood.*
   —LINDA CHARLTON
2. But how many women can name marriage itself as a source of our turbulence? More often than not, we were the ones who most wanted to get married. Besides, if not marriage, what *do* we want? Divorce? That is too fearsome.
   —NANCY FRIDAY
3. Milan is quite an attractive little city. A nice cathedral, *The Last Supper,* a very glamorous train station built by Mussolini, La Scala, and many other enjoyable sights.
   —FRAN LEBOWITZ
4. There have been three views about the purpose of art. First that it aims simply at imitation; second that it should influence human conduct; and third that it should produce a kind of exalted happiness.
   —KENNETH CLARK
5. Style is not the man, yet its presence or absence is part of the man. *Which part?* Not so easily pinned down, to take a trope from tailoring, yet the clothes a man chooses or disdains, are important facets of him.
   —JOSEPH EPSTEIN (ARISTIDES)

18d

frag

CHAPTER NINETEEN

Agreement of Subject and Verb

When a verb is singular, its subject must be singular; when a verb is plural, its subject must be plural. When a subject is in the first, second, or third person, the verb must match it (see 5b-1). This matching in number and person of subjects and verbs is called **agreement.**

In the present tense, the presence of the *-s* suffix at the end of a subject or verb usually indicates a plural subject or a singular verb.

> Our <u>dog</u> <u>sleeps</u> in the basement.
> *Third person singular subject,* dog; *third person singular verb,* sleeps
>
> Our <u>dogs</u> <u>sleep</u> in the basement.
> *Third person plural subject,* dogs; *third person plural verb,* sleep

The suffix *-s* (or *-es*) on a noun subject generally means that the subject is plural. The absence of the suffix *-s* (or *-es*) on a noun subject generally means that the subject is singular.

The suffix *-s* (or *-es*) on a present-tense verb usually tells you that the verb is singular. The absence of the suffix *-s* (or *-es*) on a verb usually tells you that the verb is plural.

Singular noun subjects, which usually *do not* end in *-s*, accompany singular verbs, which usually *do* end in *-s*.

Agreement: Singular Noun Subject; Singular Verb, Third Person, Present Tense

> Our <u>dog</u> <u>sleeps</u>.
>
> Singular subject;   Singular verb;
> no *-s* ending   *-s* ending

An *orchid* costs too much.

The *house* needs paint.

The *day* goes by quickly.

The absence of the suffix -s (or -es) after orchid, house, and day shows that all these noun subjects are singular. The suffix -s on costs and needs and the suffix -es on goes show that all these verbs in the third person are singular.

Plural noun subjects, which usually *do* end in *-s* (or *-es*), accompany plural verbs, which usually *do not* end in *-s*.

Agreement: Plural Noun Subject; Plural Verb, Third Person, Present Tense

<u>Dogs</u> <u>sleep</u>.

Plural subject; Plural verb;
-s ending no *-s* ending

Orchids *cost* too much.

The houses *need* paint.

The days *go* quickly.

The -s suffix on orchids, houses, and days shows that these subjects are all plural. The absence of the -s (or -es) suffix on the verbs shows that they are all plural.

19a

Use singular verbs with singular noun subjects that end in -*s*.

The letter -*s* at the end of a word is not always a suffix denoting the plural form. Some singular nouns end in -*s*, and they, too, must match singular verb forms.

<u>Glass</u>   <u>breaks</u>
Singular subject   *Singular verb*
ending in -s   *ending in -s*

<u>Moss</u> <u>grows</u>.

<u>Fungus</u> <u>spreads</u>.

19b

Use plural verbs with plural noun subjects that do not end in -s.

Some nouns do not use the suffix -s for the plural form (see 31c – 7). But no matter what the form is, a plural subject requires a plural verb.

<u>Children</u>	<u>giggle</u>.
Plural subject without an -s ending	*Plural verb*
<u>Men</u>	<u>guffaw</u>.
<u>Alumni</u>	<u>contribute</u>.

19c

Use singular verbs for the singular pronoun subjects *he*, *she*, and *it*.

The third person singular pronouns *he*, *she*, and *it*, like the nouns they replace, require singular verbs.

<u>She</u>	<u>raises</u>	tomatoes.
Singular pronoun in the third person	*Singular verb ending in -s*	

<u>He</u> <u>keeps</u> the cat away.

<u>It</u> <u>eats</u> all the seedlings.

19d

The pronouns *I* and *you* always take present tense forms that look plural, except for forms of *to be*.

Even though the pronoun *I* is singular, it always takes the present tense without a singular -s ending.

324 Understanding Grammar and Writing Correct Sentences

I *applaud.*

I *dream.*

I *write.*

I *cry.*

The pronoun *you* functions as both a singular and a plural. Only the verb form without the singular *-s* works correctly with *you*, whether *you* is singular or plural.

You *live.*

You *laugh.*

You *love.*
In each case, you may refer to just one person or to several people. However, the verb form remains the same for singular or plural, and this verb form is without the suffix -s.

I *am.*

You *are.*

She *is.*
The words in italics are all forms of the verb to be.

agr

19e
Use plural verbs for plural pronoun subjects.

<u>They</u>   <u>applaud</u>.
Plural pronoun   *Plural verb; no -s ending*

<u>They</u> <u>leap</u> to their feet.

<u>They</u> <u>shout</u>, "Bravo!"

<u>We</u> <u>sneer</u> at their bad taste.

Exercise 19.1   In the sentences below, subjects are underlined once, and verbs are underlined twice. If subjects and verbs are singular, make them plural; if they are plural, make them singular. You may need to change other words as well. Follow the example.

Example

A field <u>mouse</u> <u>takes</u> cover in the house when the <u>temperature</u> <u>drops</u>.
Field <u>mice</u> <u>take</u> cover in the house when <u>temperatures</u> <u>drop</u>.

Agreement of Subject and Verb   **325**

1. The <u>horses</u> <u>gallop</u> swiftly over the plains.
2. A <u>city</u> <u>provides</u> many interesting things for people to do.
3. Cigarette <u>smokers</u> <u>run</u> a high risk of getting certain diseases.
4. <u>I</u> <u>drive</u> her to class on Mondays, but on Thursdays <u>she</u> <u>insists</u> on taking the bus.
5. <u>Terror</u> <u>stalks</u> some neighborhoods; <u>people</u> <u>face</u> the possibility of violence every day.
6. Warm desert <u>winds</u> <u>carry</u> sand along the streets of Yuma and <u>sting</u> the eyes of people on the burning sidewalks.
7. <u>He</u> <u>urges</u> a balanced budget, although <u>they</u> <u>want</u> the government to pay for large social programs.
8. A direct-drive <u>turntable</u> <u>costs</u> more than a belt-drive, but my <u>friends</u> <u>swear</u> that <u>belt-drives</u> <u>are</u> just as good.

19f

Use a plural verb when *and* joins more than one subject.

<u>Pepper</u> and <u>garlic</u> <u>flavor</u> the soup.

The word *and* joins two   Plural verb;
singular subjects, giving   no *-s* ending
the sentence a plural
subject

Greed and arrogance *disgust* most people.

Queenie and Clarence *work* on cars.

When subjects joined by *and* suggest a single idea, they may take a singular verb, but such uses are rare.

The <u>tenor and star</u> of the show <u>is</u> out with the flu.

Two subjects are joined by *and*, but both   Singular verb
nouns refer to the same person, and so
the whole subject is grammatically singular.

Honest criticism and sensitive appreciation is directed not upon the poet but upon the poetry.

—T. S. Eliot

Eliot thought that "Honest criticism and sensitive appreciation" made one entity, that they were merely parts of the same approach to poetry, so he used the singular verb is in this sentence. But his usage here illustrates a danger, since to most people it is confusing. Most authorities would have been pleased if he had chosen to write "Honest criticism and sensitive appreciation are directed not upon the poet but upon the poetry."

The words *each* and *every* preceding singular subjects that are joined by *and* require a singular verb for the whole subject, even though the subject may sound plural.

In the Nittany Mountains, <u>each dawn and dusk</u> <u>fills</u> the sky with soft, pink light.

Compound subject, preceded by *each*   Singular verb

When every window and every door *shuts* out drafts, your furnace will burn less oil.

In the rare instances when *each* follows subjects joined by *and*, you may choose either a singular or a plural verb, whichever sounds better to you.

In the Nittany Mountains, dawn and dusk each *fill* (or *fills*) the sky with soft, pink light.

19g

For the verb *to be*, observe the rules of agreement in both the present and past tense. (See 20a-5.)

In the present tense, the various forms of *to be* are irregular and require selective use with subjects.

am: Use with the pronoun *I*.

When *I* **am** tired, I cannot think.

is: Use with all singular noun subjects and with singular pronoun subjects other than *I* and *you*.

The *door* **is rattling.**

Martha **is** late again.

He **is serving** tables.

It **is** dawn, and still *she* **is studying.**

are: Use with plural noun subjects, with plural pronoun subjects, and with the pronoun *you,* whether it is singular or plural.

The *waves* **are racing** to the shore.

They **are gardening;** *we* **are resting.**

When *you* **are finished,** you can go.

As you have seen, rules of agreement pertain to verbs in the present tense. In the simple past tense both singular and plural verbs use the same form for all subjects—except for the verb *to be,* which has two past tense forms, *was* and *were. Was* is singular, and *were* is plural.

was: Use with all singular noun subjects and with all singular pronoun subjects other than *you.*

The *ball* **was** high.

He **was** merely pink, but *I* **was** lobster-red.

were: Use with all plural noun subjects, with plural pronoun subjects, and with the pronoun *you,* whether it is singular or plural.

As *you* **were reading,** the *children* **were planning** their little surprise.

The *refugees* **were standing** patiently in line.

The rules of agreement also pertain to the present perfect tense (see 20a-2). In the present perfect tense, the helping verb *has* is singular, and the helping verb *have* may be either singular or plural.

I **have biked** across the country twice.
The single subject I *takes the helping verb* have *to form the present perfect tense of the verb* bike.

He **has** often **complained** about his back.
He, *a singular pronoun, takes the singular helping verb* has *in the present perfect tense.*

They **have been** out all night.
They *is a plural pronoun and takes the plural form* have *to form the present perfect tense of the verb* to be.

19h

Take care to make your verbs and subjects agree when misleading words or phrases come between them.

Large *amounts* of money *go* to national defense.
Although a singular noun, money, *stands close to the verb* go, *the true subject of the verb is the plural noun* amounts, *and that subject*

requires a plural verb. The verb go *is plural because its subject,* amounts, *is plural. The singular noun* money *is the object of the preposition* of *and is not the subject of the sentence.*

One *error* in a column of figures *throws* computations off by thousands.
Although it stands right before the verb throws, *the plural noun* figures *is the object of the preposition* of. *The subject,* error, *is singular; it requires a singular verb.*

Words such as *in addition to, as well as, along with, plus, including,* and *together with* do not affect the number of the subject. They usually serve as prepositions introducing the object of a preposition, which can never be the subject of a verb. (See 5d-1.)

A baseball *game* between the Philadelphia Athletics and the St. Louis Browns, along with my recollections of the bright colors of the grass and the uniforms and the excitement of the crowd, *makes* one of my happiest childhood memories.
The singular subject, game, *takes a singular verb,* makes, *and the combination of subject and verb is not affected by the extended prepositional phrase* along with my recollections of the bright colors of the grass and the uniforms and the excitement of the crowd.

Although such a sentence may be grammatically correct, it may still be awkward, and you should revise awkward sentences whether they are grammatically correct or not.

One of my happiest childhood memories is of a baseball game between the Philadelphia Athletics and the St. Louis Browns. I can still see the bright colors of the grass and the uniforms, and I can still feel the excitement of the crowd.

The *Marx Brothers,* including Groucho, still *make* audiences laugh in *A Night at the Opera,* filmed half a century ago.
The plural subject, Marx Brothers, *requires a plural verb,* make; *the phrase* including Groucho *does not influence the number of the verb.*

19i

When words such as *or, either . . . or,* and *neither . . . nor* connect singular subjects, use singular verbs.

A simple fungus *infection or a rash* between the toes is often extremely painful.

Either running or swimming **improves** the heart's performance significantly.

When a subject with *or* or *nor* contains both a singular and a plural part, the verb agrees with the nearest part of the subject.

> *Either fine art or old coins* **make** a good hedge against inflation.
> *The verb* make *is plural because its closest subject,* coins, *is plural.*

> Neither *Jack Miller* nor his friends *the Stanleys* **like** beer.
> *The verb* like *is plural because it follows the plural noun* Stanleys.

> *Either old coins or fine art* **makes** a good hedge against inflation.
> *In this example, the verb* makes *is singular because it follows the singular noun* art.

> Neither *the Stanleys* nor their friend *Jack Miller* **likes** beer.

Combined singular and plural subjects often sound awkward, and you should consider revising them to make compound subjects that may be expressed easily by a plural verb.

> **AWKWARD:** Either the lilacs or the magnolia tree is responsible for the sweet smell that now hangs on the night air.

> **IMPROVED:** Either the lilacs or the magnolia blossoms are responsible for the sweet smell that hangs on the night air.

> Old coins and fine art make a good hedge against inflation.

> Both the Stanleys and their friend Jack Miller dislike beer.

19j

With singular indefinite pronouns such as *anybody*, *anyone*, *anything*, *each*, *either*, *everybody*, *everyone*, *neither*, *nobody*, *none*, *no one*, and *one*, use singular verbs; the more ambiguous indefinite pronouns such as *all*, *any*, *more*, *most*, and *some* take singular or plural verbs, depending on their meaning in a particular sentence.

> *Everyone* **is** on strike.
> *Nobody* **likes** a losing team.

Use singular verbs with singular indefinite pronouns even when a prepositional phrase with a plural noun comes between the pronoun subject and the verb.

Everyone in all the departments **is** on strike.

Nobody among ardent fans **likes** a losing team.

In both examples, the presence of a plural noun as the object of a preposition between the subject and the verb has no influence on the choice of the verb; everyone *and* nobody *are singular pronoun subjects; they take singular verbs.*

Some speakers sometimes slip into using verbs that agree with nearby nouns instead of indefinite pronoun subjects. The error may not be noticed in speaking, but it may disrupt a reader's concentration if it turns up in writing.

HURRIED SPEECH: *One* of the shops *close* at five o'clock.

WRITTEN: *One* of the shops *closes* at five o'clock.

The more ambiguous indefinite pronouns such as *all, any, more, most,* and *some* take singular or plural verbs depending on whether their meaning is singular or plural in a particular sentence.

After the blizzard, workers made a huge pile of snow in the park. *Is* **any** of the snow left?

The pile of snow is singular; any, *in referring to it, takes a singular verb.*

Frank Sinatra once had thousands of young admirers who fainted when he sang. *Are* **any** of them still around?

The noun admirers *is plural;* any, *in referring to them, is also plural and takes a plural verb.*

She listens carefully to the children because *some* of them **have** mature ideas.

Children *is plural;* some, *a pronoun referring to the plural pronoun* them, *takes a plural verb,* have.

He made a cake last night; *some* of it **is** still on the table.

Cake *is singular;* some, *referring to it, is singular, too, and takes the singular verb* is.

The pronoun *none* has been a subject of much debate among writers. Strict grammarians point out that *none* means "no one" and should always take a singular verb:

None of my students **is** here yet.

But many writers make the same distinction with *none* that they make with *any.* When *none* refers to a plural noun, some writers use a plural verb. When *none* refers to a singular noun, these writers use a singular verb.

None of my students **are** here yet.
Since none *refers to the plural* students, *the verb* are *is plural.*

I read his *novel* and discovered that *none* of it **was** any good.
Since none *refers to the singular* novel, *it takes the singular verb* was.

19k

Make verbs agree with their subjects when you invert the normal sentence order.

Below the waves **lurks** a great white *shark.*
Shark is *the subject of the sentence, although it comes after the verb*
lurks. *As the object of the preposition* below *the noun* waves *does not influence the verb.*

Beside the brook **grow** *tulips* in a profusion of color.

19l

When verbs follow *there* or *here* at the beginning of a sentence, make sure that the subject that follows the verb agrees with it.

19m

agr

Here **lie** the *ruins* of a once-thriving civilization.
The subject, ruins, *is plural; its verb,* lie, *is also plural.*

There **are** five broken *pencils* on the desk.

There **is** a heavy glass *door* at the end of the corridor.

19m

When the relative pronouns *who, that,* and *which* appear as subjects, use a verb that agrees with the antecedent.

Readers learn about new products from advertisements *that*
sometimes **mislead** by making fantastic claims.
The antecedent of that *is* advertisements, *a plural noun; the verb*
mislead *must also be plural.*

Chow Leung is one of those physicians *who* **work** compulsively.
The antecedent for who *is the plural noun* physicians; *who is plural*

and takes a plural verb, work. *Even though the word* one *is singular, it does not influence agreement here.*

The word *only* placed before *one* can make a verb singular, even when the relative pronoun that later refers to it seems to have a plural antecedent.

The Glass Menagerie is the only one of Tennessee Williams's plays *that* **experiments** with slide photography.
The word only *establishes a singular context in the sentence, and because of that singular context, that refers to* one, *not to* plays. *No play by Tennessee Williams other than this one experiments with slide photography.*

19n

Use linking verbs that agree with their subjects, not with complements of the subjects.

Scholarship and study **are** her passion.
The plural subject, scholarship and study, *takes a plural verb,* are. *The complement,* her passion, *is singular, but it does not affect the verb.*

Her *passion* **is** scholarship and study.
The singular subject, passion, *takes a singular verb,* is. *The verb is unaffected by the plural complement,* scholarship and study.

If such sentences sound awkward, you can revise them to make them smoother.

Her passions are scholarship and study.

She loves scholarship and study.

19o

Use singular verbs with most collective nouns that stand for or suggest a unit.

Such nouns have singular forms, although they have plural meanings. Words such as *army, audience, class, committee, majority, minority, team,* and so on, take singular verbs because the words stand for a single body acting as a unit.

This *class* **meets** too early.

An *army* **needs** good leadership and a good cause.

The parking *committee* **issues** permits to students.

The football *team* **travels** to East Lansing tomorrow.

Sometimes writers may emphasize the individual actions of separate members over the unity of a group by using a plural verb.

A *number* of the members **were** opposed to the majority report.
The singular noun number *here takes a plural verb*, were.

However, many writers would revise such a sentence to make it sound less awkward.

Some of the members **were** opposed to the majority report.
The pronoun some *becomes plural because it refers to the plural noun* members *and takes the plural verb* were.

A *number* of the members **opposed** the majority report.
The singular number *now takes the verb* opposed *in the simple past tense. Using the simple past is a convenient way to avoid awkwardness in making subjects and verbs agree, since the simple past is the same for both singular and plural.*

Some plural nouns that specify quantities require singular verbs because the nouns suggest a single unit.

Ten minutes **is** not enough time to see the Acropolis.

A hundred *dollars* **is** not much to pay for a bike these days.
In these examples, a plural noun is taken as a single unit and takes a singular verb.

19p

Use singular verbs for those noun subjects that appear plural in form but are singular in meaning.

Gulliver's Travels **is** both a fantastic narrative and a serious satire on the human condition.
Although plural in form (shown by the −s ending on the word Travels*), the title takes a singular verb, since the subject is the title of a single book.*

Words like *mathematics, politics, athletics, ethics, kudos, pediatrics,* and many others are plural in form but nearly always take a singular verb.

Politics **is** both a science and an art.

Mathematics **is** difficult for many people.
In both examples, the noun subject may be plural in form, but the meaning of each is singular. Hence a singular verb is required.

Exercise 19.2   Change the infinitives shown in brackets into the correct forms of the *present tense* verb.

[to do]   1. The two books about health care for the senior citizen _____ not provide enough data.

[to like]   2. Neither she nor I _____ horror movies.

[to have]   3. Each of the children _____ to do some of the housework.

[to win]   4. The battery-powered car regularly _____ praise from environmentalists.

[to require]   5. Economics _____ careful study both for governments and for people planning to buy a new house or car.

[to give]   6. She is the only one of the trustees who _____ any consideration to what faculty members and students want.

[to be]   7. A pen and pencil _____ all you need.

[to recommend] 8. Our group unanimously _____ an end to parking fees.

[to need]   9. Each man and woman on the boat _____ a life jacket.

[to stand]   10. Beyond the elms _____ a small cabin.

19p

agr

Exercise 19.3   Circle the appropriate form of the verb in each sentence below.

1. There (is, are) the primaries and the convention to endure before a candidate in either party (claim, claims) victory.
2. C. P. Snow's book *The Two Cultures* (was, were) a controversial statement on how little scientists and humanists understand each other.
3. Ten dollars (is, are) too much to pay for lunch.
4. Either the physician or the nurse (was, were) checking the chart.
5. Although she (has, have) a set of antique dueling pistols that (earn, earns) praise for beauty, neither she nor her father (has, have) ever fired a shot.

6. Here (is, are) the pianist and the flautist surrounded by a cheering orchestra that (love, loves) their outrageous mistakes.
7. Black bean soup topped with chopped onions (makes, make) a nourishing lunch, but some people (hate, hates) it.
8. Along the river bank (was, were) a child and a dog playing in the grass and sometimes in the dangerous water.
9. One of the supervisors who (was, were) not promoted felt that there (were, was) too few opportunities for advancement in the office where all the bosses (was, were) men; therefore, she, as well as her best friend, (is, are) looking for another job.
10. None of the jurors (seem, seems) prejudiced against the defendant.

CHAPTER TWENTY

Verb Forms

Verbs can take a variety of forms, depending on the ways you use them. Learn how to make the various verb forms work for you.

20a

Learn the principal parts of verbs and their uses in showing verb tenses.

Tense means "time," and verb tenses show the time of the action described by the verb. To form tenses correctly, you must know the *principal parts* of the verb. The principal parts are the *present* form, the *past* form, and the *past participle*.

The *present* form (the *infinitive* form without the infinitive marker *to*) is listed alphabetically in the dictionary; it is often called the **dictionary form**.

DICTIONARY FORMS: sing, dance, delight, slice

INFINITIVE FORMS: to sing, to dance, to delight, to slice

The *past* form for most verbs is made by adding the suffix -*d* or -*ed* to the dictionary form of the verb.

I ask**ed**, you play**ed**, he danc**ed**, she slic**ed**, we calculat**ed**, they open**ed**

The *past participle* also is usually formed by adding *-d* or *-ed* to the dictionary form of the verb. But unlike the past form, the past participle always requires a helping verb to make the complete verb in a verb phrase. (The past participle form is sometimes used as a verbal; see 5d-1.) *Helping,* or *auxiliary, verbs* are made from the verbs *to be* and *to have.*

In the following sentences, the past participle is in italics:

I should have *predicted* that result.

We were *finished* by noon.

He had *planted* his garden before he left for work.

The present participle is an essential verb form, but since it is always formed by adding the suffix *-ing* to the dictionary form, it is not usually listed among the principal parts. (See 31b-6 for spelling changes in adding *-ing* to some verbs.) Remember that the *gerund* has the same form as the present participle, but gerunds are always used as nouns. Here are some present participles:

singing, dancing, delighting, slicing

A further note: The verb *do* in its various forms helps other verbs to make emphatic statements, to ask questions, or to make negations.

PRESENT EMPHATIC: I do work!

PRESENT QUESTION: Do I work?

PRESENT NEGATION: I do not work.

20a

vb

1   Learn the verb forms for the three simple tenses.

The *simple tenses* for any verb are the *present, past,* and *future.*

The *simple present* for most verbs is the *dictionary form,* which is also called the **present stem.** To form the third person singular from the simple present, you usually add *-s* or *-es* to the present stem.

I run	we run	she goes	they go
you run	you run	I join	we join
he runs	they run	you join	you join
I go	we go	it joins	they join
you go	you go		

The simple past is formed in regular verbs by adding *-d* or *-ed* to the present stem. The simple past does not change form.

I escaped	we escaped
you escaped	you escaped
he escaped	they escaped

Sometimes the simple past is irregular. Irregular verbs may not form the simple past tense with *-d* or *-ed.*

I ran	we ran
you ran	you ran
she ran	they ran

The simple future is made with the helping verbs *shall* and *will.*

I shall go	we shall go
you will go	you will go
she will go	they will go

Traditional grammar holds that *shall* should be used for the first person, *will* for the second and third person. In practice, this distinction is usually ignored; most people write "I will be twenty-five years old on my next birthday."

Helping verbs help form tenses. The common helping verbs are *have, has, had, am, is, are, was, were, be, being, been, do, does, did, shall, will, should, would, can, may, might, must,* and *could.* Helpers may also be groups of words like *have to, ought to, used to, is going to,* and *is about to.*

2 Learn the verb forms for the three perfect tenses.

In addition to the simple present, past, and future, verbs have three perfect tenses — the *present perfect,* the *past perfect,* and the *future perfect.* In grammar, the word *perfect* means that an act reported by one verb will be completed before an act reported by another verb. For that reason, a verb in the *perfect tense* should always be thought of as paired with another verb, either expressed or understood.

In the *present perfect* tense, the action of the verb started in the past. The present perfect is formed by using the helping verb *has* or *have* with the past participle.

I *have worked* hard for this diploma.
The sentence means that the work you began in the past has just ended. The writer implies this compound sentence: "I have worked hard for this diploma, but now my work is ended."

I *have worked* all my life.

The sentence means that the act of working began in the past and continues into the present. The writer implies this compound sentence: "I have worked all my life, and I am still working now."

She *has loved* architecture for many years, and now she *takes* architecture courses in night school.

The interest in architecture began in the past, and it continues into the present; as a result, she takes architecture courses in night school.

The *past perfect* tense reports an action completed before another action took place. The past perfect is also formed with the past participle, but it uses the helping verb *had*.

I *had worked* twenty years before I saved any money.

The act of working twenty years had been completed before the act of saving took place.

They thought they *had considered* all the dangers when they decided on the attack.

The act of considering all the dangers had been completed before the act of deciding took place.

Michelangelo *had painted* the ceiling of the Sistine Chapel and *had become* the most famous artist in Italy before he painted the great scene of the Last Judgment on the chapel's wall.

The acts of painting the ceiling and becoming a famous artist had been completed before the act of painting the great scene took place.

Often, as in the present perfect, use of the past perfect implies another act which is not stated in the sentence.

He *had told* me that he would quit if I yelled at him. I yelled at him, and he quit.

The past perfect had told *describes an action completed before the verbs* yelled *and* quit *in the next sentence.*

Abraham Lincoln *had dreamed* that he found the White House draped in black and that someone *had told* him that the President was dead.

The past perfect implies the obvious fact that Lincoln had dreamed *and that someone in his dream* had told *him of the President's death before he was assassinated and the dream came true.*

The *future perfect* tense reports an act that will be completed by some specific time in the future. It is formed by the helping verb *shall* or *will* added to *have* or *has* and the past participle.

20a

vb

I *shall have worked* fifty years when I retire.
The working for fifty years will be completed at retirement.

He *will have lived* with me ten years next March.
It is not yet March, but when March comes, his ten years of living with me will be past. He may go on living with me, but that particular period of ten years will be finished.

They *will have accepted* my invention by then.
They have not yet accepted my invention, but when that future time comes, they will have done so.

3 Learn the progressive form of the verb.

The progressive form of the verb is made with the present participle and a helping verb that is a form of *to be*. The progressive form is used with all tenses to show that an action continues during the time that the sentence describes, whether that time is past, present, or future.

PRESENT PROGRESSIVE: I am working.

PAST PROGRESSIVE: I was working.

FUTURE PROGRESSIVE: They will be working.

PRESENT PERFECT PROGRESSIVE: She has been working.

PAST PERFECT PROGRESSIVE: We had been working.

FUTURE PERFECT PROGRESSIVE: They will have been working.

Study the following progressive forms:

I *am working* on a new book.
The action of working is in progress throughout the time of the sentence.

I *was working* in the kitchen when the house caught fire.
The action of working was going on during the beginning of the fire.

They *will be working* in the garage tomorrow afternoon.
The action of working will be going on throughout the afternoon.

4 Learn how the various tenses of verbs show different divisions of time and different levels of force.

Present

Baseball *draws* millions of spectators every year.
The statement expresses a habitual act, something that happens every year.

Michael *is playing* outside.
The time of the sentence is the present, and all during the time that the sentence describes, the act of playing goes on.

John *does love* his friends.
The statement is emphatic. Someone may have asked, "Does John love his friends?" The reply states emphatically that he does.

Do you *remember* the St Louis Browns?
Use do *or* does *to ask a question in the present tense.*

Past

The Orioles *won* the 1983 World Series.
The sentence describes an action completed at a definite time in the past.

The cars *were pouring* out of the city on Labor Day weekend.
The past progressive shows that the action took place over the entire period of time described by the sentence.

He *has worked* for the university for twenty years.
The present perfect implies action begun in the past and continuing to the present.

Robert E. Lee *had served* honorably in the U.S. Army before Virginia left the Union.
The action took place before the definite time of the action described by the simple past tense left in the second clause.

Ted Williams *did play* brilliantly in Boston despite the hostility of sportswriters who continually insulted him.
The emphatic verb phrase "did play" contrasts with the negative, hostility. The emphatic use of the verb often is a reply to some negative statement: He did not play well. Yes, he did play *well!*

Did glaciers *contract* in the nineteenth century?
Did contract is the verb phrase. By beginning the sentence with did, *the writer asks a question.*

Future

The university *will build* a new library.
The verb phrase "will build" expresses a future time without reference to its duration.

I *shall have finished* by the time he arrives.
The future perfect reports an action that will be completed by a definite time in the future.

Next week I *fly* to Tucson.
The present form is used with an adverbial phrase that puts the action in the future.

He *is to be sentenced* Friday afternoon.
The present tense is used with an infinitive phrase and an adverbial phrase to indicate action in the future.

They *will be playing* all afternoon.
The future progressive form indicates action that will go on throughout the time of the sentence.

5 Learn the principal parts of the most common irregular verbs.

Although most verbs form their principal parts quite regularly, many of the most frequently used verbs are irregular. That is, their past tense and their past participle are not formed simply by adding *-ed*. The only way to master these irregular verbs is to memorize them.

The most important irregular verb is *to be,* often used as a helping verb. It is the only English verb that does not use the infinitive as the basic form for the present tense. Study the following forms:

20a

vb

TO BE		
	Singular	**Plural**
Present:	I am	we are
	you are	you are
	she is	they are
Past:	I was	we were
	you were	you were
	it was	they were
Past perfect:	I had been	we had been
	you had been	you had been
	he had been	they had been

If you are unsure of the principal parts of a verb, always look in a dictionary. If the verb is regular, a dictionary will list only the present form, and you will know that both the past and the past participle are formed by adding *-d* or *-ed*. If the verb is irregular, a dictionary will give the forms of the principal parts.

The following is a list of the principal parts of the most common irregular verbs. (Some verbs in this list are not irregular but are included because they confuse many people.) Read through it, and use it later on as a reference. Notice that some irregular verbs have more than one form for the past or the past participle.

Present stem	Past stem	Past participle
awake	awoke	awoke/awakened
become	became	become
begin	began	begun
blow	blew	blown
break	broke	broken
bring	brought	brought
burst	burst	burst
choose	chose	chosen
cling	clung	clung
come	came	come
dive	dove/dived	dived
do	did	done
draw	drew	drawn
drink	drank	drunk
drive	drove	driven
eat	ate	eaten
fall	fell	fallen
fly	flew	flown
forget	forgot	forgotten/forgot
forgive	forgave	forgiven
freeze	froze	frozen
get	got	gotten/got
give	gave	given
go	went	gone
grow	grew	grown
hang (things)	hung	hung
hang (people)	hanged	hanged
know	knew	known
lay (to put)	laid	laid
lie (to recline)	lay	lain
lose	lost	lost
pay	paid	paid
ride	rode	ridden
rise	rose	risen
say	said	said
see	saw	seen
set	set	set

20a

vb

shake	shook	shaken
shine	shone/shined	shone/shined
show	showed	shown
sing	sang	sung
sink	sank	sunk
sit	sat	sat
speak	spoke	spoken
spin	spun	spun
spit	spat/spit	spat/spit
steal	stole	stolen
strive	strove/strived	striven/strived
swear	swore	sworn
swim	swam	swum
swing	swung	swung
take	took	taken
tear	tore	torn
tread	trod	trod/trodden
wake	woke	waked/woke/wakened
wear	wore	worn
weave	wove	woven
wring	wrung	wrung
write	wrote	written

Exercise 20.1   In the following sentences, supply the correct form of the verb that appears in parentheses at the end of the sentence.

Example:

The book had <u>been published</u> before he knew anything about it. (publish)

1. The plane _____ before we can get to the airport. (go)
2. He will _____ the house by the time we get back from our vacation. (paint)
3. He _____ while we were singing in the living room. (cook)
4. They had often _____ together in the same place where the shark attacked. (swim)
5. On the western frontier, horse thieves were sometimes _____ without a trial. (hang)
6. Every day she comes down to the ocean and _____ out to sea. (look)
7. Macbeth was _____ from a great victory when he met the three witches. (return)
8. She _____ for you at this very moment. (search)
9. Johnson, whom you see over there at his desk, has _____ in this office for twenty years. (work)
10. He _____ to escape from his job whenever he can. (like)

20b

Review the various uses of the simple present tense.

The *simple present* has several uses:

It makes an unemphatic statement about something happening or a condition existing right now.

> The earth *revolves* around the sun.
>
> The car *passes* in the street.

It expresses habitual or continuous or characteristic action.

> Porters *carry* things.
>
> Dentists *fill* teeth and sometimes *pull* them.
>
> Rocky McKnuckle *fights* with everybody.
>
> The organization of his government always *seems* more important to an incoming president than the organization of his White House.
> —THEODORE H. WHITE

It expresses a command or a warning.

20b

vb

> *Watch* your step!
>
> Periodicals *are* not to be taken out of the room.

It reports the content of literature, documents, movies, musical compositions, objects of art, or anything else that supposedly comes alive in the present each time it is experienced by an audience.

> Macbeth *is driven* by ambition, and he *is haunted* by ghosts.
>
> E. B. White *advises* writers to prefer the standard to the offbeat.
>
> The Parthenon in Athens *embodies* grace, beauty, and calm.
>
> In *Casablanca* Humphrey Bogart *plays* the role of a nightclub owner who *has* the chance to save the husband of his former lover, Ingrid Bergman.

Occasionally some writers use the present tense to describe historical action on the theory that history happens to us again each time we read about it.

> Russia at the beginning of 1917 *is* bloody, famished, and weary.
> *Note that this historical present is awkward to sustain in English; in general, you should avoid it. A wise rule is to write about the past in the past tense.*

20c

Always observe the correct sequence of tenses.

If you have more than one verb in a sentence, you must be sure that the time of the verbs flows logically from one to the next. This means that past, present, and future actions must appear in sequences in a logical order.

While I *am writing*, I *like* to listen to the radio.
Two actions take place at the same time — the present. Both are reported in verbs using the present tense.

He *says* that Hamlet *felt* only self-pity.
The action of saying appears in the present; it is a comment on something that happened in the past.

Dickens *was* already famous when he *made* his first trip to America.
The two verbs both report past action; both are in the simple past.

The child *was crossing* the street when I *saw* the car bearing down on her.
The past progressive is used with the simple past, the action crossing *continuing to the definite point when I* saw.

He *had been* in Vietnam for a year when he *began* to write his book.
The past perfect "had been" *indicates an action in the past that continued before the action expressed in the simple past tense* began.

When I *get up*, he *will have been gone* for hours.
A future time is indicated by the adverb when *and the present* get up.
The future perfect "will have been gone" *indicates an action that will be completed before the action of getting up takes place.*

Ordinarily, a past tense in the first clause of a sentence cannot be followed by the simple present, the present perfect, or a future tense.

ILLOGICAL: Sir Walter Scott *wrote* many novels because he *is* always in debt and *needs* to make money.

ILLOGICAL: Sir Walter Scott *wrote* many novels because he *has been* in debt and *has needed* to make money.

ILLOGICAL: Sir Walter Scott *wrote* many novels because he *will be* in debt, and he *will need* to make money.

LOGICAL: Sir Walter Scott *wrote* many novels because he *was* always in debt and *needed* to make money.

However, you may use the present tense or the future tense in the second clause if it expresses a general truth always in force and follows a first clause containing a verb such as *say, tell, report, agree, promise,* and so on.

They *agreed* that relations between the sexes *are* difficult now.
The subjects in these sentences commented in the past that some statement is always valid.

He *says* that he *will pay* the bill next month.
The present tense in the first clause is followed by a future tense.

He *says* that he *has paid* the bill already.
The present is followed by the present perfect, indicating an action with effects that continue to the present.

He *says* that he *paid* the bill last month.
A simple present is followed by a simple past.

He *says* that he *had paid* the bill long before anyone *complained.*
A simple present is followed by a past perfect. The past perfect indicates action completed before the action of the verb complained *began.*

Exercise 20.2   Fill in the blanks with any verb that makes sense. Use the tense given in parentheses.

Example:

After John ___had been dancing___ for three hours, he realized that the band had stopped playing. (past perfect progressive)

1. He _____ to New York five times and plans to go again. (present perfect)
2. Tomorrow _____ the first day of the rest of my life. (future)
3. Ralph _____ in the bank when the robbery took place. (past perfect)
4. Hitchcock always _____ in his own movies. (present)
5. Canadian geese _____ continually while they fly. (present)
6. She _____ while she listened to the radio. (past progressive)

Exercise 20.3   Fill in the blanks with a logical tense of the verb given in parentheses.

1. They were going out the door when she _____. (call)
2. You will _____ home by the time you get this letter. (arrive)

348   Understanding Grammar and Writing Correct Sentences

3. They had been —————— for about an hour when the fire broke out in the boat. (sail)
4. Winter will have come and —————— by the time you come home from the army. (go)
5. They —————— supper right now. (eat)
6. The rain —————— since Sunday morning, but on Tuesday it stopped. (fall)

20d

Use the mood of the verb that accurately expresses your meaning.

The **mood** of a verb expresses the attitude of the writer by showing the way in which an association is made. Verbs have three moods — the *indicative*, the *subjunctive*, and the *imperative*.

1   The indicative is used for simple statements of fact or for asking questions about the fact.

It is by far the most common mood of verbs in English.

The tide *came* in at six o'clock and *swept* almost to the foundation of our house.
The indicative mood is used because this sentence makes a statement of fact not doubted by the writer.

Can he *be* serious?
The indicative is used because the question is asked with the expectation of a simple statement of fact as an answer. Questions are always in the indicative mood.

2   The subjunctive conveys a wish, a desire, or a demand in the third person, or else it makes a statement the writer thinks is contrary to fact.

He requested that his son *use* the money to go to college.
The verb use *is in the subjunctive because it reports an action that is desired but not certain to take place. We don't know if the son will honor the request or not. Notice that here, in the third person singular, the subjunctive form leaves off the customary final -s of the indicative. If the subject of the verb* use *were in the plural, the verb*

would be the same as if it were in the indicative; we would have to understand a subjunctive sense that is not shown by the grammatical form.

He requested that his sons and daughters *use* the money to go to college.

He asked that they never *forget* him.

For most verbs, the subjunctive form differs from the indicative only in the third person singular.

Although the subjunctive is not widely used in modern English, it is still alive in some common expressions:

She will finish her job, *come* hell or high water.
The form come *in the third person singular is subjunctive.*

All people should enjoy equal opportunity, *be* they rich or poor.
The form be *is subjunctive.*

Use the subjunctive in a clause beginning with *if* when the clause makes a statement contrary to fact:

If only I *were* in Paris tonight!
I am not in Paris, alas! So the were *in the* if *clause is in the subjunctive mood.*

With the verb *to be,* the present subjunctive is formed by using the form *were* for the first, second, and third persons, singular and plural.

If the moon *were* full on that night, he could have seen the murder as it happened.
The subjunctive were *tells us that the moon was not full on the fateful night; the indicative mood with* was *would tell us that the statement may be true.*

Were she my daughter, I would not permit her to date that member of the motorcycle gang.
She is not my daughter; therefore, the subjunctive were *is used as the verb.*

Use the subjunctive in clauses beginning with *that* after verbs that give orders or advice or express wishes or make requests.

He wishes that she *were* here.

She asked that he *draw* up a marriage contract before the wedding.

Sam suggested that Bill *get* a good night's sleep before the exam.

In all three of these examples, a request is embodied in a that *clause. Since no one can tell whether a request will be honored or not, the verb in each* that *clause is in the subjunctive, indicating uncertainty.*

Should and *had* may also express the subjunctive:

Should he step on a rattlesnake, his boots will protect him.
He has not stepped on a rattlesnake; it is uncertain that he will ever step on a rattlesnake. But if he should, his boots will protect him. Should *indicates a subjunctive mood.*

Had he taken my advice, he would not have bought stock in a dance hall.
Had, *the subjunctive, indicates a condition contrary to fact; he did not take my advice, and he did buy stock in a dance hall.*

I wish he *had* won the tournament.
The had *after the verb* wish *expresses a condition contrary to fact; he did not win the tournament.*

Be sure that when you use the word *had* as a past subjunctive, you do not confuse it with the conditional. Do not say "I wish we *would have* won the tournament." Say "I wish we *had* won the tournament."

Use the subjunctive in some commands or wishes expressed in the third person singular.

May the Good Lord *bless* and *keep* you.

Let there *be* light.

Grammar *be* hanged!

3 The imperative conveys a command or request in the second person.

The *imperative mood* is a particular kind of subjunctive. The imperative is used only to express commands in the second person, singular or plural, and the form of the verb is the same as the indicative. In the imperative sentence, the *subject* of the verb is always *you,* but the *you* is usually understood, not written out:

Pass the bread.

Drive me to the airport, please.

Leave the room!

He begged her, *"Become* an engineer!"

Sometimes the *you* is written for extra emphasis:

You give me my letter this instant!

Exercise 20.4   Identify the mood of the verbs in italics in the following sentences. Over each italicized verb, write *I* for indicative, *S* for subjunctive, or *IM* for imperative.

1. If she *was* awake, she must have heard the noise.
2. Prisoners in solitary confinement sometimes *dream* of enormous meals.
3. He said that Japan *has* one of the lowest crime rates in the world.
4. If Carlton Fisk *were* still *playing* for Boston, the Red Sox might not be so blue.
5. *Had* you *been* here, we might not have quarreled.
6. Please *send* me some postage stamps from the Vatican.
7. He asked that his father *stop* writing letters to the newspaper.
8. If he *used* a ballpoint pen, he could make six copies at once.
9. He asked that his friends neither *explain* him nor *excuse* him to others.
10 *Should* she *remember* me in her will, I would be astonished.

20e

Learn the difference between the active voice and the passive voice. Use verbs in the active voice in most sentences; use verbs in the passive voice sparingly and only for good reason.

The voice of a transitive verb tells us whether the subject is the actor in the sentence or is acted upon. (A transitive verb carries action from an agent to an object. A transitive verb can take a direct object; an intransitive verb does not take a direct object. See 5a-2.)

When transitive verbs are in the *active voice*, the subject does the acting. When transitive verbs are in the *passive voice*, the subject is acted upon by an agent that is implied, or an agent that is expressed in a prepositional phrase. (Intransitive verbs cannot be passive. You can say "My brother *brooded* too much," but you cannot say "My brother *was brooded*.") In the passive voice, the transitive verb phrase includes some form of the verb *to be*.

ACTIVE: She *mailed* the letter.

PASSIVE: The letter *was mailed* by her.

ACTIVE: John *washed* the dishes.

PASSIVE: The dishes *were washed* by John.

Readers usually want to know the agent of an action; that is, they want to know *who* or *what* does the acting.

ACTIVE: He made the bed.

PASSIVE: The bed was made **by him.**
The agent of the action here is identified by boldface.

Since the passive often fails to identify the agent of an action, it may be a means of evading responsibility.

PASSIVE: The Mustangs lost because a tackle *was missed* on the punt return.

ACTIVE: The Mustangs lost because Al Tennyson *missed* a tackle on the punt return.

Use the passive only when the recipient of the action in the sentence is much more important to your statement than the doer of the action.

My car *was stolen* last night.
Who stole your car is not important to this statement; you don't know who did it. The important thing in the sentence is that your car was stolen. So the verb phrase was stolen *can be in the passive voice.*

After her heart attack, she *was taken* to the hospital in an ambulance.
Who took her to the hospital is unimportant to this statement; the important fact is that she was taken.

In scientific and technical writing, researchers generally use the passive voice throughout a report on an experiment so that they can keep the focus on the experiment rather than on the experimenters.

PASSIVE: When the bacteria *were isolated*, they *were treated* carefully with nicotine and *were observed* to stop reproducing.

ACTIVE: When we *isolated* the bacteria, we *treated* them carefully with nicotine. They *stopped* reproducing.

A clear and direct writing style draws upon verbs in the active voice. Unless you have a special reason for using the passive, choose the active voice.

Exercise 20.5   Rewrite the following sentences to put the passive verbs in the active voice.

1. The paintings on the wall of my kitchen were done by my daughter.
2. The song "9 to 5" was written by Dolly Parton.
3. The movie *Citizen Kane* was made by Orson Welles, was the recipient of many awards, but was not viewed by Welles himself for years afterward.
4. In the 1950s, color was used by filmmakers to compete with television, where all the programs were still being shown in black and white.
5. The house was painted by Mr. Johnson last summer.
6. Poland was invaded by the Germans on September 1, 1939.
7. Our grass was cut by a neighborhood girl.
8. The home run was hit by Carlton Fisk in the bottom of the twelfth inning to win the game.
9. Disney's *Pinocchio* was being viewed by the fourth-grade children in the museum projection room.
10. The grass was watered despite the heavy rains last week.

Exercise 20.6   The following sentences were all written by professional writers. Analyze each verb to see whether it is in the active or the passive voice. Tell why the passive is used when you do find it.

20e

vb

1. Some birds can be identified by color alone.
   —Roger Tory Peterson
2. The radio was silenced, and all that could be heard was the echo of the Mayor's voice.
   —Mark Helprin
3. If you are bitten and the dog gets away, make every effort to find the dog and its owner.
   —Richard Ballantine
4. At this point, a doctor was summoned; a formal pronouncement of death was made; and Big Jim's carcass was dragged, feet first, and for the last time, through the front door of his saloon.
   —Joe McGinniss
5. Many statesmen feel that weapons are in themselves evil, and that they should be eliminated, as you would crush a snake.
   —E. B. White
6. There was much justification for these prophecies. By the time I was nine years old, I had been hit by a bus, thrown into the Harlem River (intentionally), hit by a car, severely beaten with a chain. And I had set the house on fire.
   —Claude Brown

7. The landscape too is dramatic, both in Israel and Jordan, which together make up the country of the Bible. Seeing it at first hand, one realizes that it was no accident that God was invented and two religions originated here.

—Barbara Tuchman

20f

Use the infinitive form of the verb to complete the sense of other verbs, to serve as a noun, and to form the basis of some phrases.

The word *to*, sometimes called the **infinitive marker,** is placed before the verb to identify the infinitive form.

The **present infinitive** describes action that takes place at the same time as the action in the verb the infinitive completes:

> He *wants* to go.
> *present*
> He *wanted* to go.
> *past*
> He *will want* to go.
> *future*

The *present infinitive* uses the infinitive marker *to* along with the simple present tense of the verb:

> to write, to dance, to play, to sing

The **present perfect infinitive** uses the infinitive marker *to*, the verb *have*, and a past participle:

> to have written, to have danced, to have sung, to have swum, to have run

The *present perfect infinitive* describes action prior to the action of the verb whose sense is completed by the infinitive. The present perfect infinitive often follows verb phrases that include *should* or *would*.

> I would like *to have seen* her face when she found the duck in her bathtub.
> *The* liking *takes place in the present and is expressed in the verb phrase* would like. *The phrase* would like *implies that the action*

expressed in the infinitive to have seen *did not take place. This wished-for seeing would have happened before the time of the verb phrase* would like.

Sometimes we say things like this:

> I wanted to have finished this paper before you arrived.
> *This usage is not incorrect, but it is unnecessarily wordy. We can say "I wanted to finish this paper before you arrived," and the present infinitive with the simple past tense would be enough to show that the finishing should have taken place before you arrived. If you wished to emphasize the* wanting *rather than the* finishing, *you would change the word order and say "Before you arrived, I wanted to finish this paper, but now that you are here, I don't want to finish it."*

An **infinitive phrase** includes the infinitive and the words that complete its meaning:

> Her attempt *to bicycle through a New York subway tunnel* was frustrated by an express train.
> *The infinitive* to bicycle *is modified by the prepositional phrase* through a New York subway tunnel. *In effect the prepositional phrase acts as an adverb modifying the infinitive, but the infinitive and its modifying prepositional phrase together make an* infinitive phrase.
> *To take such an immense journey* required courage and money.
> *The infinitive phrase in this sentence is the subject of the verb re-quired. The infinitive here has an object,* journey, *but the object is also part of the phrase and all the words in the phrase make up the subject of the sentence.*

Infinitives and infinitive phrases most often serve as nouns, but they can also be used as adjectives and adverbs.

> *To dance* was his whole reason for living.
> *Noun, subject of the sentence*
>
> Her only aim was *to dodge his flying feet*.
> *Noun, subject complement*
>
> He also wanted to *sing*.
> *Noun, direct object of the verb* wanted
>
> She was not a woman *to take chances*.
> *Adjective; the infinitive phrase modifies the noun* woman.

Infinitives and infinitive phrases may serve as adverbs when they answer the question *Why?* and modify the main verb.

He studied *to improve his voice.*
The infinitive phrase tells why he studied, modifying the verb stud-ied and thus acting as an adverb.

Sometimes the infinitive marker is omitted before the verb, especially after verbs like *hear, help, let, see,* and *watch.* Study the following examples.

She heard him *come* in.
The verbal come is an infinitive here, and the pronoun him serves as the subject of the infinitive. But by the conventions of English, we don't say "She heard him to come in." We omit the infinitive marker to.

They watched the ship *sail* out to sea.
The verbal sail is an infinitive here with the infinitive marker to omitted. Compare: "They expected the ship to sail out to sea."

She made him *treat* her with respect.
The verbal treat is an infinitive with the infinitive marker to omitted. Compare: "She asked him to treat her with respect."

In general, *avoid split infinitives.* A **split infinitive** has one or more words awkwardly placed between the infinitive marker *to* and the verb form.

Split Infinitive: He loved *to loudly sing.*
The adverb loudly *splits the infinitive* to sing

Better: He loved *to sing* loudly.

Some writers believe that split infinitives are acceptable:

The government was little altered as Mr. Bush touched down at Andrews Air Force Base at 6:30 p.m. *to gracefully assume* the duties but not the powers of the Presidency. [italics added]

— *Time*

The rule against split infinitives is not absolute: some writers split infinitives, and others do not. But the words used to split infinitives can usually go outside the infinitive, or they can be omitted altogether.

Split Infinitive: He told me to *really* try to do better.
The adverb really *is a weak intensifier that seldom adds anything to a sentence. It can be left out without harm.*

Better: He told me to try to do better.

Verb Forms   **357**

In general, related elements in a sentence should be kept as close together as possible to avoid confusion. When you split an infinitive with a long phrase, you violate this principle by moving the infinitive marker away from its related element, the verb form of the infinitive.

SPLIT: He intended *to carefully and completely revise* his paper.

BETTER: He intended *to revise* his paper carefully and completely. *Note that the revision places the adverbs after the noun that follows the infinitive. English idiom favors this positioning. We don't write, "She ran ten miles a day thoroughly to condition herself for the marathon"; we say, "She ran ten miles a day to condition herself thoroughly for the marathon."*

Exercise 20.7   Fill in the blank in each of the following sentences with the proper form of the infinitive of the verb in parentheses at the end of the sentence.

1. He asked her _____ his plane at 7:07 P.M. (meet)
2. I promise _____ your plane tomorrow. (meet)
3. He would have preferred _____ his education before he bought a car. (complete)
4. We often heard him _____ late at night in his shower. (sing)
5. She was not one _____ for opportunity to knock. (wait)

Exercise 20.8   Rewrite the following sentences to eliminate split infinitives.

1. She claimed to truly mean her promise to work hard.
2. They intended to speedily complete the job.
3. The pilot wanted to safely and happily complete the trip.
4. The United States Football League vowed to strictly refuse to sign college football players before they had played in their senior year.

20g
Beware of common errors in the use of verbs.

1   Avoid confusing the simple past and the past participle in irregular verbs. When it is part of a predicate, the past participle always needs a helping verb.

FAULTY: I *seen* her last night at the movie.
The past participle of the irregular verb see *is* seen; *the simple past tense is* saw.

CORRECT: I *saw* her last night at the movie.

FAULTY: We *taken* our books with us to camp.
The past participle taken *cannot serve as the simple past tense of the irregular verb* take.

CORRECT: We *took* our books with us to camp.
The principal parts of take *are* take, took, *and* taken. *The simple past* took *is used without a helping verb.*

CORRECT: We *had taken* our books with us to camp, and we were glad.
Here the helping verb had *combines with the past participle* taken *to make a correct verb phrase.*

FAULTY: I *done* the job myself.
The principal parts of the verb do *are* do, did, *and* done. *The past participle* done *must be used with a helping verb, or it must be changed to the simple past* did.

CORRECT: I *did* the job myself.
The simple past did *does not require a helping verb.*

CORRECT: I *have done* the job myself.
The helping verb have *with the past participle* done *makes the present perfect tense.*

2   **Recognize irregular verbs, and avoid the error of trying to make them regular.**

FAULTY: The artist *drawed* the portrait in an hour.
Ordinarily the suffix -ed *makes the simple past. But the irregular verb* draw *forms the simple past by becoming* drew.

CORRECT: The artist *drew* the portrait in an hour.

FAULTY: We *payed* for everything we got.
The simple past of the verb pay *is not* payed *but* paid.

CORRECT: We *paid* for everything we got.

20g

vb

3 Keep the distinction between *lay* and *lie*.

To lay means "to put down" or "to place." *To lie* means "to recline." *To lie* is an intransitive verb and cannot take a direct object.

I *lie* down to sleep every night at eleven o'clock.

To lay is a transitive verb and must always take a direct object.

I *lay* my books aside each evening to watch television.

The words *lay* and *lie* are often confused because they are both irregular verbs, and the past tense of *lie* is *lay*.

I *lie* down to sleep each night at eleven.
The verb lie *is in the present tense.*

Last night I *lay* down at eleven.
The past tense of lie *is* lay.

Yesterday I *laid* the keys on the table so he would find them when he came in.
The past tense of lay *is* laid.

We had *lain* there an hour when the clock struck midnight.
The past participle of lie *is* lain.

Although he could not find them, I had *laid* the keys on the table before I went to bed last night.
The past participle of lay *is* laid.

4 Keep the distinction between *sit* and *set*.

Sit is an intransitive verb and cannot take a direct object.

We all *sit* down.
No direct object

Set is a transitive verb and must always take a direct object when it means "to place."

We *set* the vase in the window when we want to signal our friends to come over.
The direct object is vase.

The principal parts of *sit* are *sit*, *sat*, and *sat*.

You sit to eat.
You sat all during yesterday's parade.
You have sat there an hour without speaking.

The principal parts of *set* are *set, set,* and *set.*

You set tables beautifully for your parties.

You set the clock last night before you went to bed.

You have set my teeth on edge with your horrifying tale.

5 Avoid illogical shifts in tense.

ILLOGICAL: The car *roared* down the street out of control, *hit* a tree, *bounced* over the sidewalk, and *comes* crashing into my living room.
The first three verbs — roared, hit, and bounced *— are in the simple past tense. The shift to* comes, *a present tense, is illogical and confusing.*

REVISED: The car *roared* down the street out of control, *hit* a tree, *bounced* over the sidewalk, and *came* crashing into my living room.

Exercise 20.9 Correct the errors in the following sentences. If a sentence is correct as it stands, place a check mark beside the number.

1. He come home last night and find the dog sick.
2. They taken the kickoff and get to work and have a touchdown in five minutes of the first quarter.
3. She worked hard and done a good job.
4. After a long day it's always good to lay down.
5. He lay his pants over the back of the chair last night and go right to sleep and don't wake up until this morning at ten o'clock.
6. Last year she lay the book on top of the chest, and she forget all about it until the library notice come yesterday.
7. I stood as long as I could, but finally I had to set down and taken a load off my poor feet.
8. Joey went down the slope first with a big whoosh, and then Helen go flying after him, and then here come Herman skiing like a windmill with his big feet sailing up in the air and his poles flying off, and he shouting like a fool, "Look at me!"

CHAPTER TWENTY-ONE

Pronouns

We use pronouns to avoid awkwardness, to simplify style, and to express certain ideas clearly. (See 5b-3 on identifying pronouns.)

Pronouns take the place of nouns in sentences. In the following sentence, if we had to repeat the noun *house* every time we wrote about the idea *house*, we would have awkward and unwieldy prose.

AWKWARD: The house stood on a shady street, and the house looked large and comfortable as if the house was perfectly suited for a large family and for two sets of grandparents who might visit the house for long periods.

The pronoun it *simplifies this sentence immediately.*

BETTER: The house stood on a shady street, and it looked large and comfortable as if it was perfectly suited for a large family and for two sets of grandparents who might visit it for long periods.

We could not express some ideas without pronouns. Many sentences require first-person pronouns (*I*, *we*, *our*, and *ours*) or second-person pronouns (*you*, *your*, and *yours*), and no other words can serve in their place.

By themselves, pronouns are indefinite words; therefore, most pronouns require an antecedent to give them content and meaning. The **antecedent** is the word that the pronoun substitutes for. The antecedent usually appears earlier in the same sentence or in the same passage.

The *snow* fell all day long, and by nightfall, *it* was three feet deep.

The noun snow *is an antecedent; the pronoun* it *looks back to* snow *so that in this sentence* snow *and* it *mean the same thing.*

Some pronouns are indefinite and take their meaning not from an antecedent but from the sentences where they are located.

Anybody who wants to see the Placido Domingo concert should get a ticket two months in advance.
Anybody standing by itself would have almost no meaning at all; it receives meaning from the sentence and especially from the clause who wants to see the Placido Domingo concert. *Nouns such as* John, house, garden, car, *and* dog *have a fairly clear meaning by themselves. An indefinite pronoun must have a sentence to give it meaning.*

Some pronouns are **reflexive.** They end in *-self,* and they add emphasis to the noun or pronoun they follow.

John *himself* admitted his error.
The legal battle about who owned the field went on for years while the field *itself* grew up like a jungle.
No matter how you may judge my actions, you *yourself* would have done the same thing in my situation.
I hurt *myself.*
All these reflexive pronouns stress their antecedents.

21a
Make certain that pronouns refer clearly to their antecedents. Keep pronouns as close to their antecedents as possible.

Pronouns that do not refer clearly to their antecedents or that are widely separated from them may confuse your readers. Often the only way to remedy a confusing reference of pronouns to their antecedents is to rewrite the sentence.

WEAK: Albert was with Beauregard when he got the news that his cigars had arrived.
Did Beauregard get the news, or did Albert? Did the cigars belong to Beauregard, or did they belong to Albert?

IMPROVED: Albert's cigars arrived, and while he was with Beauregard, Albert got the news that they had come.
Now the sentence is clear. The cigars belong to Albert, and he got the news of their arrival while he was with Beauregard. Readers would almost certainly understand another version: While he was with

Beauregard, Albert got the news that his cigars had arrived. Although the pronoun his could refer grammatically to either Beauregard or Albert, nearly all readers would assume that the two pronouns, he and his, had the same antecedent.

WEAK: The engine stopped, and McHale thought of the mechanic in the last small town on the highway amid the torrid, dusty summer of West Texas with its long and blinding stretches of treeless land burned brown by the sun, waterless and desolate, *who* had told him *it* was in excellent condition despite the strange noise *it* was making.
The relative clause beginning with who *is a long way from its antecedent,* mechanic, *and the two instances of the pronoun* it *are even farther from their antecedent,* engine. *Readers may be confused by the pronoun references.*

IMPROVED: The engine stopped, and McHale thought of the mechanic *who* had told him *it* was in excellent condition despite the strange noise *it* was making. That mechanic was now far behind him in the last small town on the highway amid the torrid, dusty summer of West Texas with its long and blinding stretches of treeless land burned brown by the sun, a land waterless and desolate.
A thorough revision yields two sentences instead of one and places the pronouns much closer to the antecedents to which they refer.

Avoid the use of *they* and *it* as indefinite pronouns in constructions such as *they say* or *it says*. Such constructions may be both awkward and unclear.

VAGUE: They say that the heat wave will break tomorrow.

BETTER: The weather forecast is that the heat wave will break tomorrow.

VAGUE: They say he dyes his hair.

BETTER: His former wife says he dyes his hair.
The improvement in both examples is to make the source of the information clear.

VAGUE: It says in the paper that we can expect a higher rate of inflation next year.

BETTER: A front-page article in today's paper says we can expect a higher rate of inflation next year.

The improved example is somewhat longer, and the source of the information is presented early in the sentence.

21b
Make pronouns agree in number with their antecedents.

Singular antecedents require singular pronouns.

The *house* was dark and gloomy, and *it* sat in a grove of tall cedars that made *it* seem darker still.

Plural antecedents require plural pronouns.

The *cars* swept by on the highway, all of *them* doing more than 55 miles per hour.
In the first sentence, house, *a singular noun, requires a singular pronoun,* it; *in the second, the plural* cars *requires a plural pronoun,* them.

Roosevelt and *Churchill* found radio a perfect medium for *their* speaking talents.
The antecedents are compound—that is, joined by a coordinating conjunction. A compound antecedent is plural and takes a plural pronoun—in this example, their.

Use a singular pronoun when all the parts of a compound antecedent are singular and the parts are joined by *or* or *nor*.

Either *Ted* or *John* will take *his* car.
Neither *Judy* nor *Linda* will lend you *her* horn.
But if Ted and John own one car in partnership, you should write, "Either Ted or John will take their *car." And if Judy and Linda own only one horn between them, you should write, "Neither Judy nor Linda will lend you* their *horn."*

Sometimes you must revise a sentence entirely because a single pronoun will not do.

Neither *Patricia* nor *John* would let me borrow *his* lawn mower.
Since we assume that Patricia is a woman and that John is a man, the

21b

pro

pronoun his *will not do unless Patricia has some control over John's lawn mower. The simplest way out of the problem would be to eliminate the pronoun: Neither Patricia nor John would let me borrow a lawn mower. Or you could write this sentence: John would not lend me his lawn mower, and Patricia would not lend me hers.*

When referring to collective nouns such as *team, family, audience, majority, minority, committee, group, government, flock, herd,* and many others, Americans usually use the singular pronoun.

The *team* won *its* victory gratefully.

In elections, the *majority* has *its* way.

The *committee* disbanded when *it* finished *its* business.

However, if the members of the group indicated by a collective noun are being considered as individuals, a plural pronoun is appropriate.

The hard-rock *band* broke up and began fighting among *themselves* when *their* leader was converted to Mozart.
Although band *is singular, the intent of the sentence is to stress the individuals in the group. Here* themselves *and* their — *both plural pronouns — are used to refer to the noun* band.

In British English, collective nouns usually take plural pronouns and plural verbs. In books first published in Great Britain or the Commonwealth, you often find sentences like these:

The cricket *team* quit playing when *they* discovered that *their* spectators had fallen into a profound sleep.

The government *refuse* to comment when *they* are asked about the prospects for peace in Poland.

Traditional writing textbooks direct you to use masculine singular pronouns to refer to nouns and pronouns of unknown gender.

Any *teacher* must sometimes despair at the indifference of *his* students.

Everybody can have what *he* wants to eat.

However, many people object that using the masculine pronoun when the gender of the noun is unknown or nonspecific creates sexist language. Chapter 15 explores the problem of sexist language and describes various remedies for it.

Exercise 21.1 Rewrite the following sentences to correct errors in pronoun reference. If you find no error in a sentence, put a check by it. You may rewrite a sentence to keep some pronouns, or you may eliminate the pronouns altogether.

1. The ship sailed under the Golden Gate Bridge as it put out to sea.
2. The painter complained to her model that she was too pale.
3. Blodgett met Whitney as he was returning from the swim meet.
4. It says in the menu that the special is fried eggplant.
5. The traveler bought a melon from the peasant as he stood in the shade on the road below Lamia, the city on the hill.
6. Anyone who loses their token will have to buy a new one if they want to ride the subway.
7. Neither Lewis nor Alfred brought their toothbrush.
8. If one wears polyester shirts, he will be much hotter in summer and much colder in winter than with cotton shirts, but he can enjoy them for years.
9. The gold team used the indoor tennis courts when they practiced in winter.
10. Neither Ellen nor Mike rode her bicycle to school that day, although they usually rode in together every morning.
11. They say that a penny saved is a penny earned, but they never considered how much you can spend when you try to save money at a half-price sale.
12. The control group was tested to see if they remembered the economics lecture as well as they remembered the soap opera.

21c

Avoid making broad references with the pronouns *this, that, they, it, which,* and *such.*

Some writers occasionally use one of these pronouns to refer not to a specific antecedent but to the general idea expressed by the whole clause or sentence.

> The members of Political Writers for a Democratic Society did not constitute a pack. They were too confident, competitive, proud, and self-sufficient for *that.*
>
> —TIMOTHY CROUSE
>
> *The pronoun* that *has as its antecedent the idea expressed in the first sentence, that the members of the organization called Political Writers for a Democratic Society did not constitute a pack.*

Babe Ruth, playing for the Boston Braves, hit three balls out of Forbes Field in Pittsburgh on May 25, 1935. *They* were his last home runs.

They, the subject of the second sentence, has as its antecedent the entire action of the first sentence rather than any one noun within that sentence.

But broad reference with pronouns is often awkward or misleading.

WEAK: Andy Warhol once made a movie of a man sleeping for a whole night, *which* was a tiresome experience.
Was the movie tiresome to watch? Or was making the movie the tiresome experience?

IMPROVED: Andy Warhol once made a tiresome movie of a man sleeping for a whole night.

IMPROVED: Andy Warhol once went through the tiresome experience of making a movie of a man sleeping for a whole night.

WEAK: That car gets good gas mileage and yet is so flimsy that it breaks up in the slightest accident. *This* ought to be a consideration to anyone thinking of buying it, but *this* is not likely when people live in a world like *this* where inflation is rampant.
Writers sometimes use the demonstrative pronoun this *far too frequently and far too broadly.*

IMPROVED: That car gets good gas mileage and yet is so flimsy that it breaks up in the slightest accident. Anyone thinking of buying it ought to consider its safety record, but safety may not come to mind in today's world where inflation is rampant.
Replacing the pronoun this *with specific nouns and revising these sentences help to clarify the meaning.*

21d
Learn the difference between the expletive *it* and the pronoun *it*.

The pronoun *it* always has an antecedent; the expletive *it* serves as a grammatical subject when the real subject is placed after the verb or is understood.

Pronoun *it*: When a barn burned in rural America, *it* often took with *it* a year's hard work for a farm family.
It, used twice in this sentence, has the noun barn *as an antecedent.*

Expletive *it*: When a barn burned, *it* was difficult for a farm family to recover from the loss.
The it *does not have an antecedent but serves as the grammatical subject for the independent clause that it begins. The sentence could read, "When a barn burned, to recover from the loss was difficult for a farm family." But such a sentence, although correct grammatically, does not conform to customary English usage, and it sounds awkward compared with the sentence with the expletive* it.

Expletive *it*: *It* will be a pretty day tomorrow.
The sentence could read, "Tomorrow will be a pretty day," but American usage often favors the expletive it.

Expletive *it*: *It* is hot now.
The subject is understood to be the temperature (the temperature *is hot now*) *or* the day (the day *is hot now*). *But the expletive* it, *without an antecedent, is favored in common usage.*

Try to avoid using the expletive *it* and the pronoun *it* one after the other.

Weak: What will happen to the kite? If *it* is windy, *it* will fly.

Improved: What will happen to the kite? It will fly if the wind blows.

21e
When you address your readers, use the pronoun *you* only when you are writing in an informal tone; use the pronoun *one* when you write more formally.

The book's no good to *you* now. Neither is scientific reason. *You* don't need any scientific experiments to find out what's wrong.
——Robert M. Pirsig
In his book Zen and the Art of Motorcycle Maintenance, *Pirsig announces that he will talk with the reader throughout as though in a discussion. So the tone is informal, and he frequently uses the pronoun* you.

One might have supposed that Abraham Lincoln's Gettysburg Address was disappointing because it was so short.
Here the tone is more formal, and the pronoun one *does the service that the pronoun* you *might perform in a less formal piece.*

21f

Let the tone and intention of your essay determine whether you will use the pronouns *I*, *my*, *me*, and *mine*.

Many writing teachers tell students to avoid using pronouns in the first person singular. The intention of these teachers is to prevent student writers from calling attention to themselves and getting in the way of the subject they should be writing about. Readers do not like to feel that the author is intruding unnecessarily into a piece of writing.

INTRUSIVE

> For the first few minutes I saw Carew whack screamers down the rightfield line, and I saw him frown at this unwanted consistency. I think Carew is a handsome man, but I don't mean that in the conventional sense. I think that the most arresting features on his face are a tiny turned-up nose and a mouth that in my opinion is a mile wide, and I believe it can exaggerate the mildest emotion. When he smiles, I believe the light can be seen as far away as Newport Beach. When he's downcast, I'd say there's an eclipse of the sun.

This kind of writing would quickly become tedious to all of us if it went on very long. Here is the way a writer for *Sports Illustrated* wrote about Rod Carew, first basemen for the California Angels baseball team:

NONINTRUSIVE

> For the first few minutes Carew whacked screamers down the right-field line, frowning at this unwanted consistency. Carew is a handsome man, but not in the conventional sense. The most arresting features on his face are a tiny turned-up nose and a mile-wide mouth that can exaggerate the mildest emotion. When he smiles, the light can be seen as far away as Newport Beach. When he's downcast, there's an eclipse of the sun.
>
> —RON FIMRITE

Fimrite is writing informally, but he is not writing about himself and his opinions; he is directing our attention to Rod Carew. We know that the opinions expressed here are Fimrite's because he wrote the article. He does not have to use the expression I think. *We know what he thinks without the personal pronoun.*

The first person singular pronouns are appropriate when you are writing about some experience of yours that is the center of your prose.

> From all available evidence no black man had ever set foot in this tiny Swiss village before I came. I was told before arriving that I would probably be a "sight" for the village; I took this to mean that people of my complexion were rarely seen in Switzerland, and also that city people are always something of a "sight" outside of the city. It did not occur to me — possibly because I am an American — that there could be people anywhere who had never seen a Negro.
>
> — James Baldwin

The first person singular pronouns are also acceptable when you are weighing two contradictory opinions and want to let readers know which side you are on.

> Many scientists believe that the universe will end in a general collapse in which all matter falls back to a central mass, which will eventually explode again in a "big bang" like that which has created the universe we know. Others believe that the stars will continue forever to fly apart from each other in space and that the universe will end in the solitary deaths of all those stars scattered at an infinite distance from one another. I am inclined to accept the second view.
>
> *The writer knows that much debate surrounds this issue; she expresses her own opinion at the last, and the effect of the use of the first person here is to admit of some doubt.*

The first person singular pronouns can be used in other kinds of writing, but you should always at least experiment with not using the first person. Avoiding the first person can help you avoid wordiness, but when you believe you must use it, you may do so with a good conscience. No rule of English holds that you should always avoid saying *I, me, my,* and *mine.*

21g
Avoid the unnecessary placing of a pronoun after a noun.

Some Americans tend to use a pronoun immediately after the noun to give the noun special emphasis. In this regional style of speech, these pronouns play the part of reflexive pronouns. In writing they should be avoided.

REDUNDANT: Harry Truman *he* played the piano.

IMPROVED: Harry Truman played the piano.
The noun Harry Truman *is sufficient; the pronoun* he *is unnecessary.*

IMPROVED: Harry Truman *himself* played the piano.
Here a true reflexive pronoun, himself, *adds emphasis to the noun* Harry Truman.

REDUNDANT: The newspapers *they* admitted that advertising sometimes influences their editorial policy.

IMPROVED: The newspapers admitted that advertising sometimes influences their editorial policy.
The pronoun they *is not needed in the sentence.*

IMPROVED: The newspapers *themselves* admitted that advertising sometimes influences their editorial policy.
The true reflexive pronoun themselves *may add emphasis to the noun* newspapers.

21g

pro

Exercise 21.2 Rewrite the following sentences to eliminate pronoun errors. If a sentence is correct, put a check beside it.

1. He liked to read in the bathtub in the summer and to regulate the water temperature with his toes and to keep the door shut and locked, which was inconvenient for others in the family, since the house had only one bathroom.
2. The movie *Apocalypse Now* was based partly on a novel by Joseph Conrad. It is likely that it suffered because Marlon Brando was so fat in it that it was hard to take him seriously. It looked as if he himself had not taken the movie seriously, and despite the money spent on promoting it, it is clear that it failed to meet expectations about it.
3. The movies *Godfather* and *Godfather II* made millions of dollars, which proves that crime does pay if it is possible to make it exciting on film.
4. The house it was small and cramped for a family of four, and my mother and father, they loved each other, and they made the house seem as big as all creation.
5. The readers of this page will forgive this writer perhaps if he indulges himself in a personal recollection of hearing Hank Williams sing at the Grand Ole Opry in Nashville.

6. I have read that World War I began in 1914. It seems to me that I remember that the Germans invaded Belgium to get to France, and I think that then the British came in to defend Belgium, which, as I recall, was neutral.

7. This time she promised to write the essay, and this was said to be acceptable by the teacher, who said that after this all her work had to be turned in on time and that this was completely reasonable in a class where late papers created a lot of work for the teacher.

8. You can see from the statistical evidence that smoking cigarettes is dangerous to your health.

9. Oil has become so expensive that it is natural that Americans should reduce their use of it, but it remains to be seen whether they can eliminate it as a major item in their budgets.

10. As for wood, it is a good fuel, but it is inconvenient for most people, and its smoke may be dangerous to health.

11. He had a bad temper, and that was one reason why he had so few friends.

12. It is to be expected that it will be cold in winter, and yet in this winter it was said of the temperature that it was much warmer than it had been before in all the history of the weather bureau.

21h
Use the proper cases for pronouns.

Pronouns often show *case* by their forms. **Case** refers to the grammatical relation of a pronoun to other words in the sentence. English has only three cases—the *subjective* (sometimes called the *nominative*), the *possessive* (sometimes called the *genitive*), and the *objective* (sometimes called the *accusative*).

Indefinite pronouns (*anybody, everybody:* See 5b-3), the pronoun *it*, and the pronoun *you* change their forms only for the *possessive* case. We speak of *anybody's* guess, *its* color, and *your* writing. The pronouns *I, we, he, she, they,* and *who* change forms in each of the three cases.

Subjective Case

Pronouns in the *subjective case* act as subjects or as subject complements.

He and *I* read books all summer long.

She was the candidate *who I* thought deserved the victory.

The pronouns in italics serve as the subjects of the clauses where they appear.

It could have been *anyone*.

Mark's best friends were *she* and *I*.
The pronouns in italics are subject complements.

Possessive Case

Pronouns in the *possessive case* show ownership or a special relation.

Their cat climbed up on *his* roof and ate *our* bird.

Her critics were louder than *her* admirers.

My uncle was *my* only relative *whose* tastes were like *mine*.

The decision was *theirs* to make after we had made *ours*.
The pronouns in italics are in the possessive case. See 5b-3 for a list of possessive pronouns.

Objective Case

Pronouns in the *objective case* are indirect objects, direct objects, objects of prepositions, or the subjects or objects of infinitives.

The company gave *her* a contract to design the building.
indirect object

Marlow told *them* his story.
indirect object

The team chose *me*.
direct object

The mouse ate *them*.
direct object

Just between *you* and *me*, I thought the play was terrible.
objects of a preposition

Who among *them* could possibly object?
object of a preposition

They believed *him* to be better qualified.
subject of an infinitive

They wanted *her* to be their friend.
subject of an infinitive

He expected *them* to wait for the late movie.
subject of an infinitive

She asked him to call *her* that evening.
object of an infinitive

1 **A pronoun that is the subject of a dependent clause is always in the subjective case, even when the dependent clause serves as the object for another clause.**

He promised the prize to *whoever* made the best grades.
Despite its position after the preposition to, *the pronoun* whoever *is in the subjective case because it is the subject of the verb* made *in its own clause. The entire clause* whoever made the best grades *serves as the object of the preposition* to.

She was the writer *who* I thought deserved to win the Pulitzer Prize.
Not whom *I thought: The pronoun* who *is the subject of the verb* deserved. *The words* I thought *form a separate, parenthetical clause.*

2 **Pronouns that serve as objects of prepositions, direct objects, and indirect objects must be in the objective case.**

It was a secret between you and *me*.
Me is correct because it is the object of the preposition between. *The subjective form* I *cannot be the object of a preposition. Thus,* between you and I *is incorrect.*

The old man pushed David and *her* aside and then hobbled down the stairs.
The pronoun her *is in the objective case because it is the object of the verb* pushed.

She gave the driver and *me* quite a lecture on road safety and courtesy.
As an indirect object of the verb gave, me *is in the objective case.*

Who's kicking *whom?*
Some people do write "Who's kicking who," *but this usage is sometimes considered illiterate, and writers should use it with caution.*

3 **In appositive constructions where a noun follows a pronoun, use the case for the pronoun that you would use if the noun were not present.**

He gave the test to *us* students.
You could say, "He gave the test to us." *The pronoun* us *is the object of the preposition* to *and must be in the objective case. Adding the noun* students *does not change the case of the pronoun.*

We students said that the test was too hard.
You could say, "We said that the test was too hard." *Adding the noun* students *does not change the pronoun* we.

4 **Use the correct case of the pronoun after *than* and *as*, which often serve as conjunctions introducing implied clauses.**

We do not need to write out some clauses because we understand the idea that follows a pronoun at the end of a sentence. The case of the pronoun depends on the way the pronoun is used in the *implied clause*, the clause we would make if we carried out the obvious thought suggested by the pronoun. (Sometimes implied clauses are called **elliptical clauses**. *Elliptical* comes from *ellipsis*, which means "something left out.")

I always thought that I was smarter than *he*.
If we filled in the implied clause at the end of this sentence, we would have an awkward but perfectly grammatical construction. "I always thought that I was smarter than he was smart." *The pronoun* he *must be in the subjective case because it is the subject of this implied clause.*

Odetta likes George more than *I*.

Odetta likes George more than *me*.
In the first sentence, Odetta likes George more than I *like George. In the second sentence, Odetta likes George more than* she likes me. *Notice how the difference in case changes the meaning of these two sentences.*

21h

pro

5 **Use the objective case for pronouns that are the subjects or the objects of infinitives.**

They thought *her* to be an excellent choice for department head.
The pronoun her *is the subject of the infinitive* to be *and must be in the objective case. The subject of the infinitive acts through the infinitive verb. You could change the sentence to read, "They thought that she would be an excellent choice for department head."*

Lincoln decided to consult Johnson and *him*.
The pronoun him *receives the action of the infinitive verb* consult *and is therefore the object of the infinitive and must be in the objective case.*

6 **Use the possessive case before gerunds. Use the subjective or objective case with present participles used as adjectives.**

A gerund is an *-ing* verb form used as a noun. (See 5d-1.)

His returning the punt ninety-six yards for a touchdown spoiled the bets made by the gamblers.
His, the possessive pronoun, puts the main emphasis on the act of returning the punt. Compare: "His ninety-six-yard punt return spoiled the bets made by the gamblers."

He, returning the punt ninety-six yards for a touchdown, spoiled the bets made by the gamblers.
In this example, the phrase returning the punt *includes the present participle* returning. *This form of the verb* return *is acting as an adjective. The emphasis of the sentence is on the person rather than on the act. This emphasis becomes clearer if we rewrite the sentence: "Returning the punt ninety-six yards for a touchdown, he spoiled the bets made by the gamblers."*

They remembered him laughing as he said goodbye.
The objective case him *is used with the present participle* laughing, *which is used as an adjective to modify* him.

7 **In compound and appositive constructions, use pronouns that agree in case with the nouns or pronouns with which they are paired.**

COMPOUND: *He* and Sebastian del Cano sailed around the world.
Not him *and Sebastian del Cano. The pronoun and the proper noun together form the subject of the sentence. So the pronoun must be in the subjective case.*

APPOSITIVE: The captain chose two crew members, *her* and *me*, to attempt the rescue.
Not she *and* I. *The appositive pronouns must correspond to the noun* members, *which in this sentence is the direct object. The pronouns must be in the objective case, too.*

APPOSITIVE: The last crew members on board, *she* and *I*, were given the first watch.
The pronouns she *and* I *are appositives to the noun* members, *which serves as the subject of the verb* were given. *The pronouns must be in the subjective case.*

Exercise 21.3   Circle the correct pronoun within the parentheses in the following sentences.

1. He wrote the book for Nini, for (she, her) of the quick quip.
2. Of all the English kings, Henry VIII was the one (who, whom) I think was most cruel.
3. Between her and (I, me) little difference could be seen.
4. I had no objection to (she, her) walking across the country.
5. The candidates seemed to most Americans, including (I, me), to represent a choice between foolishness and stupidity.
6. Just between you and (I, me), I have to say that Hawley was to blame.
7. Jackson is the sculptor (who, whom) I believe to be worthy of the Sting Memorial Award.
8. Clark Gable played the same role again and again for (whoever, whomever) directed him.
9. Unfortunately, he built (we, us) a solar house in the shade of Mt. Tom.
10. Eisenhower was the President for (who, whom) the college was named.
11. Smog hurts (we, us) biking commuters.
12. (We, Us) writers must work long and hard for a good style.
13. She asked (we, us) to tell (he, him) that (she, her) was flying to Las Vegas that night.
14. (His, He) greasing his hair made him look like an Elvis fan from the 1950s.
15. Two cooks, Geoffrey and (I, me), were chosen to explain the food poisoning to the health department.

CHAPTER TWENTY-TWO

Adjective and Adverb Modifiers

Adjectives and adverbs are describing words. Because they qualify in some way the meaning of other words, we say they *modify* other parts of speech.

Adjectives tell us what kind or how many. They include words such as *big, little, beautiful, red, sunny, crazy,* and *important.* We speak of the *big* house, or the *little* farm, or a *beautiful* day, or the *red* tulip, or the *sunny* weather, or the *crazy* joke, or the *important* plans.

Adverbs tell us where, when, why, and how. They include words such as *quickly, yesterday, beautifully, crazily,* and *rightly.* We say that the dog came *quickly,* or that she was sad *yesterday,* or that the dancing couples spun *crazily* around the room, or that he was *rightly* indignant about being ignored.

Some words can be both adverbs and adjectives and can have the same form in both instances. We speak of *fast* cars, and we say that someone can run *fast.* But most adverbs are formed by adding -*ly* to the end of the adjective form of the word. So we say "He weaves *beautiful* rugs" when we want to emphasize that the rugs are beautiful, but we say "He weaves *beautifully*" when we want to emphasize the techniques he uses as he weaves.

Adjectives modify nouns and pronouns; they do not modify anything else. Adverbs modify verbs (including verb phrases), adjectives, other adverbs, and sometimes whole sentences.

22a

Use adjectives to modify nouns or pronouns.

You can identify adjectives by locating words that answer one or more of these questions about nouns or pronouns: *Which one? How many? What color? What size? What kind?*

The adjectives in the following sentences are in italics.

> She was a *brilliant* architect and a *good* person.
> *The adjective* brilliant *tells us what kind of architect, and the adjective* good *tells what kind of person.*

> The road was *long, hard*, and *twisting*.
> *These adjectives, coming after the verb, serve as subject complements and tell what kind of road.*

> The *red* Buick belonged to my aunt.
> *The adjective* red *tells what color Buick and distinguishes it from other Buicks by telling us which one.*

> The *six large* men were brothers.
> *The adjective* six *tells how many; the adjective* large *tells what size the men were. The combination of adjectives tells us which ones.*

> Writing is always *difficult*.
> *The adjective* difficult *tells us what kind and modifies the subject* writing, *which is a gerund.*

> The *American hockey* team beat the Russians in the Olympics of 1980.
> *The adjectives* American *and* hockey *tell what kind of team.*

You may use adjectives before or after the noun or pronoun they modify.

> The building, *ugly* and *tall*, burned down last night.
> The *tall, ugly* building burned down last night.
> The *old* car, *battered* and *rusty*, finally died.

Present and past participles of verbs often serve as adjectives.

> *Running* hard, the bank robber fired back over his shoulder at the police.
> Running, *the present participle, modifies the subject*, robber.

> The trip was both *exhausting* and *rewarding*.
> *The present participles modify the subject*, trip.

The *gathering* night was *filled* with stars.
The present participle, gathering, *and the past participle,* filled, *both modify the subject,* night.

Buried alive for days, he survived to tell about the earthquake.
Buried, *the past participle, modifies the subject,* he.

Tired and *discouraged,* she dropped out of the marathon.
The past participles modify the subject, she.

A noun can be used as an adjective.

Cigarette smoking harms your lungs.

The *energy* crisis is not helped by people who drive six miles for a six-pack.

The *Marshall* Plan helped rebuild Europe after World War II.

Adjectives can serve as nouns.

The *unemployed* are not always the *lazy* and the *inept.*
All the italicized words are normally adjectives. But the sentence clearly means that the words modify an understood noun, people *or* persons, *which can be left out, turning the adjectives into nouns.*

22a

ad

1   Use adjectives after linking verbs to modify the subject of the sentence.

A linking verb always links a subject with an adjective or a noun that adds to the description of the subject.

Charles was *fast* and *reliable.*
Both adjectives modify the subject, Charles.

The road became *difficult.*
The adjective modifes the subject, road.

2   Avoid using nouns as adjectives if an adjectival form conveys the same meaning or if a revision of the sentence makes the meaning clearer.

Bureaucratic jargon often uses many nouns as adjectives when perfectly good adjectives are available.

JARGON: An *opposition education* theory holds that children learn Latin best under strict *discipline* conditions.

Adjective and Adverb Modifiers   **381**

BETTER: An opposing educational theory holds that children learn Latin best under strict disciplinary conditions.

Exercise 22.1   Draw a line under the adjectives in the following paragraphs.

The man in those pictures is the same man who was fascinated by Italian grand opera. I have never known just what my father saw in the spectacle, but he has told me that he would take my mother to the Opera House every Friday night — if he had enough money for orchestra seats. ("Why go to sit in the balcony?") On Sundays he'd don Italian silk scarves and a camel's hair coat to take his new wife to the polo matches in Golden Gate Park. But one weekend my father stopped going to the opera and polo matches. He would blame the change in his life on one job — a warehouse job, working for a large corporation which today advertises its products with the smiling faces of children. "They made me an old man before my time," he'd say to me many years later. Afterward, jobs got easier and cleaner. Eventually, in middle age, he got a job making false teeth. But his youth was spent at the warehouse. "Everything changed," his wife remembers. The dapper young man in the old photographs yielded to the man I saw after dinner: haggard, asleep on the sofa.

— RICHARD RODRIGUEZ

I fought him for three days. I beat him one day, and he beat me the next day. On the third day, we fought three fights. I had a black eye, and he had a bloody lip. He had a bloody nose, and I had a bloody nose. By the end of the day, we had become good friends. Somebody took us to the candy store and bought us ice-cream cones.

— CLAUDE BROWN

Exercise 22.2

1. Write a sentence in which the adjective *gigantic* appears before a noun subject and the adjectives *frightening* and *dreamy* appear as subject complements.
2. Write a sentence in which the adjective *happy* is used in a phrase immediately after the noun or pronoun that it modifies.
3. Write a sentence in which the adjective *young* is used as a noun.
4. Write a sentence in which the adjective *unwilling* is used to modify the subject.
5. Write a sentence in which the noun *baseball* is used as an adjective.

22a

ad

22b

Use adverbs to modify verbs, adjectives, and other adverbs.

The child ran *quickly* into the house.
The adverb quickly *modifies the verb* ran.

The game was *hotly* contested.
The adverb hotly *modifies the adjective* contested.

He spoke *more* slowly at the end than at the beginning.
The adverb more *modifies the adverb* slowly.

**1   Use adverbs to answer the questions *When? Where? How?
How often? How much? To what degree?* and *Why?***

Yesterday she was in Chicago.
Yesterday, *an adverb, modifies the verb* was *and answers the question* when?

The lamp is right **there.**
The adverb there *modifies the verb* is *and answers the question* where?

He came *painfully* to the door.
The adverb painfully *modifies the verb* came *and tells how* he came to the door.

She *seldom* comes to visit any more.
The adverb seldom *modifies the verb* comes *and answers the question* how often?

We were *greatly* relieved to receive your letter.
The adverb greatly *modifies the adjective* relieved *and tells* how much *we were relieved.*

She was *completely* surprised at the results.
The adverb completely *modifies the adjective* surprised *and tells* to what degree *she was surprised.*

Dickens mixed humor and pathos better than any other English writer after Shakespeare; *consequently* he is still read by millions.
The adverb consequently *tells why Dickens is read.*

22b

ad

Most adverbs are formed by adding *-ly* to the adjective form, but adverbs may also end in *-wise, -where,* or *-ward.* And many adverbs lack any special ending. Among these are *anew, soon, never, ever, almost, already, well, very, often, rather, yesterday,* and *tomorrow.*

The surest way to recognize adverbs is not by looking at their endings but by understanding how they work in a sentence.

Exercise 22.3 Fill in the blanks in the following sentences with adverbs that make sense.

1. She waited _____ at the airport for the team to make its way _____ home.
2. Lincoln was _____ witty, but he was also _____ sad.
3. _____ the sun was shining when I got up, and a great blue heron flew _____ over the waters of the lake.
4. Doctors have _____ accused boxing of being responsible for serious brain injuries among fighters.
5. She was _____ careful after the accident.
6. We believe that manual dexterity helps _____ in developing the brain.
7. The gasoline was _____ gone when we _____ came to the service station.

2　Use adverbs correctly as transitional expressions to carry readers smoothly from the ideas of one sentence or paragraph to the ideas of another.

Adverbs may help you tie your thoughts together from one part of your paper to another. Such transitional adverbs include *accordingly, also, anyway, besides, consequently, finally, furthermore, hence, however, incidentally, indeed, instead, likewise, meanwhile, moreover, nevertheless, next, nonetheless, otherwise, still, then, thereafter, therefore,* and *thus.*

These transitional adverbs can introduce sentences, but they cannot be used as conjunctions. Misuse of such transitional adverbs leads to the error called a comma splice (see 17e).

COMMA SPLICE: The Appalachian region is rugged and mountainous, moreover, it is covered with forests and rich in coal.

STANDARD: The Appalachian region is rugged and mountainous. Moreover, it is covered with forests and rich in coal.
In the standard version, the writer has made two sentences. The transitional adverb begins the second sentence.

STANDARD: The Appalachian region is rugged and mountainous, and, moreover, it is covered with forests and rich in coal.
In this version, the coordinating conjunction and *has been inserted after the first independent clause and before the transitional adverb* moreover.

STANDARD: The Appalachian region is rugged and mountainous; moreover, it is covered with forests and rich in coal.

A semicolon has been inserted before the transitional adverb moreover, *replacing the comma.*

22c

Be cautious when you use adverbs to modify whole sentences.

Sometimes adverbs may seem to modify whole sentences:

Unfortunately, the *Quiz Kids* lost its popularity as an afternoon game show.

Presumably, the climber was killed in an avalanche three years ago, although his body was never found.

Some authorities maintain that these adverbs modify the entire sentence, while others insist that these adverbs modify only the verbs in the clauses where they appear. In either case, the meaning of these sentences is clear. But other adverbs are much more ambiguous when they are used to modify full sentences. In common speech people often say things like this: "Hopefully, I will ride my bike to San Francisco." Grammatically, the sentence means that the speaker plans to pedal to San Francisco, feeling hopeful all along the way. Yet the speaker probably means that she hopes she will be able to bike to San Francisco.

This confusion leads many people to reject the use of *hopefully* to mean "I hope" or "they hope" or "she hopes."

Hopefully he will change his job before this one gives him an ulcer.
Who is doing the hoping? Is it the person who speaks the sentence or the person who is the subject of the sentence? The adverb hopefully *does not tell us clearly. But if we say, "My children and I hope that my husband will change his job before this one gives him an ulcer," the source of the hope is clear.*

Similar confusions occur when other adverbs are used to modify whole sentences:

Briefly, he was the source of the trouble.
Does this sentence mean that the writer wishes to say briefly that the subject he *was the source of the trouble? Or does it mean that* he *was briefly the source of the trouble and that he then changed and was no longer such a source?*

Happily, the mad dog fell dead before it could bite anybody.
Grammatically, this sentence means that the mad dog fell dead very happily before it could bite anybody. The writer probably means that people on the street were happy that the mad dog fell dead before it could bite one of them. Why not write that?

It is better to revise such sentences to avoid confusion and the air of loose construction that such use of adverbs conveys:

To put it briefly, I think he was the source of the trouble.

The mad dog fell dead before it could bite anybody.
Readers do not need to be told that this was a fortunate occurrence.

22d

Do not use adjectives when adverbs are clearly called for.

ad

In common speech we sometimes use adjectival forms in an adverbial way; in writing, this colloquial usage should be avoided.

NONSTANDARD: He hit that one *real good*, Howard.
Both real *and* good *are adjectives, but they are used here as adverbs,* real *modifying* good *and* good *modifying the verb* hit.

NONSTANDARD: She *sure* made me work hard for my grade.
The adjective sure *here tries to do the work of an adverb modifying the verb* made.

Both these nonstandard usages can be revised simply by changing the improperly used adjectives to adverbs. Thus, "He hit that one *really well,* Howard," and "She *surely* made me work hard for my grade" would substitute correctly for the nonstandard sentences above. But a better solution is to rethink the sentences to make them stronger. Improperly used adjectives are often a sign of a general vagueness of thought, and you can make better sentences by being more concrete:

He hit that one to the warning track, Howard.

She made me write a five-page paper every week.

22e

Use adverbs and adjectives correctly with verbs of sense and with certain other linking verbs.

Verbs of sense (*smell, taste, feel,* and so on) can be linking or nonlinking. You must decide whether the modifier after a verb of sense serves the verb or the subject. Study the following examples:

ADVERB: The dog smelled *badly.*
The adverb badly *modifies the verb* smelled *and tells us that the dog had lost its sense of smell and could not track anything.*

ADJECTIVE: The dog smelled *bad.*
The dog needed a bath. Mentally you can say, "The dog smelled as if he had been in something bad."

ADVERB: I felt *badly.*
My sense of touch was bad, perhaps because my fingers were numb.

ADJECTIVE: I felt *bad* because she heard me say that her baby looked like a baboon.
Mentally in this expression the person is saying, "I felt that I was bad because she heard me make such a terrible remark." A similar expression would be this: "I felt guilty *because she heard me make that remark." You would not say, "I felt* guiltily *because I hurt her feelings."*

ADVERB: He looked *calmly* to the crowd.
The adverb modifies looked *and describes the way that he swept his eyes over the crowd, perhaps waiting for some new response from them.*

ADJECTIVE: He looked *calm* to the crowd.
The adjective shows the opinion of the crowd; the people in it thought he was calm.

22f

Learn the words that have the same spelling in the adjectival and adverbial forms.

As you know, not every adverb is formed by tacking *-ly* onto the end of an adjective. In standard English, many adverbs do not require the *-ly*, and some words have the same form whether they are used as adjectives or adverbs. When you are in doubt, consult your dictionary (see 16b).

Adjective	Adverb
fast	fast
hard	hard
only	only
right	right or rightly
straight	straight

Exercise 22.4 In each of the following sentences, locate the words misused as adjectives and put the proper adverbs in their place or vice versa. You may simplify the sentence by eliminating the misused adjective or adverb.

1. I felt badly because he took my advice about the horse race and lost all his money.
2. He did terrific on the exam, and I sure was unhappy about his success.
3. John felt real good because he ran so fast in the race.
4. McDonald looked greedy at the fried chicken on his neighbor's plate and decided he would go to Kentucky real fast.
5. She sat still while the poisonous snake twined silent in the arbor just over her head, but her heart beat hard, and she was real scared.
6. She thought she had done good in the lacrosse game, and hopefully she would make the team.
7. Briefly, the speech went on for three hours, and I don't remember a word of it.
8. Interestingly, he turned out to be a bore, although he was supposed to be a fine writer.
9. Hopefully they would never see her again.

Exercise 22.5 Fill in the blanks in the sentences below with any adverb that makes sense. Avoid the easy choices of *very*, *well*, and *badly*.

1. As the rains grew heavier, the houses were _____ damaged by the flood.

22f

ad

2. The procession wound _____ through the narrow streets and across the square, where the police had _____ blocked off traffic.
3. One by one the graduates walked _____ across the stage, shook hands _____ with the college president, received their diplomas, and stood _____ for a moment while relatives snapped their pictures.
4. She ate _____, saying that diets might help some but that eating _____ did her much more good.
5. Jokes are _____ funny because we do not expect the punch line.

22g

Learn to use correctly the three degrees of adjectives and adverbs — the positive, the comparative, and the superlative.

Adjectives and adverbs are often used to compare. Usually an -er or an -est ending on the word or the use of more or most along with the word indicates degrees of amount or quality.

The simplest form of the adjective or the adverb is the *positive* degree, the form of an adjective or adverb used when no comparison is involved. This is the form you find in the dictionary.

POSITIVE: The dog ran *quickly* out of the house.
The running of the dog is not being compared with anything else, so the adverb quickly *is used in the positive degree.*

POSITIVE: The dog was *quick*.
A simple statement is being made about the dog; the dog is not being compared with anything else, so the adjective quick *is used in the positive degree.*

In the *comparative degree*, two things are being compared. For many adjectives the comparative degree is formed by adding the suffix -er, but the comparative degree can also be formed by using the secondary adverb *more* or *less*. For most adverbs the comparative is also formed by using the adverb *more* or *less*.

COMPARATIVE: The dog was *quicker* than the rabbit.
The adjective quicker *is used to make a comparison between the dog and the rabbit.*

COMPARATIVE: The dog was *more quick* than the rabbit.
Here again, two things are being compared, but the writer has chosen to use the adverb more *rather than the suffix -er to form the comparative of the adjective* quick.

COMPARATIVE: The dog ran *more quickly* than the rabbit.
Here the adverb more *modifies the adverb* quickly *to form the comparative of* quickly.

COMPARATIVE: The rabbit ran *less quickly* than the dog.
Here the adverb less *modifies the adverb* quickly *to form the comparative of* quickly.

Use the *superlative degree* for both adjectives and adverbs when you compare more than two things. The superlative degree of adjectives may be formed by adding the suffix *-est* to the positive form. It also may be formed by using the adverb *most* or *least* with the positive form. The superlative degree of adverbs is formed by using the adverb *most* or *least* with the positive form.

22g

ad

SUPERLATIVE: She was the *happiest* of the three women.
More than two women are being compared, so the superlative degree is used. The superlative degree, happiest, *is formed by adding -est to the end of the adjective* happy. *(For the change from y to i, see 31b-5.)*

SUPERLATIVE: George was the *most gloomy* person I ever knew.
The superlative of the adjective gloomy *is here formed by using the adverb* most *with the positive form of the adjective.*

SUPERLATIVE: They sang *most happily* when they had eaten well.
The superlative degree of the adverb happily *is formed by using the adverb* most.

1   Do not use the superlative for only two things or units.

NOT: Of the two brothers, John was *quickest.*

BUT: Of the two brothers, John was *quicker.*

2 Learn the forms of the adjectives and adverbs that are irregular in the comparative and the superlative.

Positive	Comparative	Superlative
bad	worse	worst
good	better	best
little	less	least
many/much	more	most
far	farther	farthest

3 Do not use the comparative and superlative degrees with absolute adjectives.

Absolutes are words that in themselves mean something complete or ideal, words like *unique, infinite, impossible, perfect, round, square, destroyed,* and *demolished.*

If something is *unique,* it is the only one of its kind. So we cannot say, "Her dresses were *more unique* than his neckties." Either something is unique or it is not. We should not say, "The answer to your question is *more impossible* than you think." Something is either possible or impossible; it cannot be *more* or *less* impossible.

22g

ad

4 Avoid using the superlative when you are not making a comparison with anything.

Dracula is the *scariest* movie!
The scariest movie ever filmed? The scariest movie you have ever seen? The scariest movie ever shown in town?

In common speech, we frequently use expressions like *scariest movie* or *silliest thing* when we are not in fact comparing the movie or the thing with anything else. In writing, such expressions lack the vocal emphasis we can give them when we speak. They become merely wordy and imprecise, taking up space without conveying any meaning.

5 Avoid adding an unnecessary adverb to the superlative degree of adjectives.

NOT: She was the *very* brightest person in the room.

BUT: She was the brightest person in the room.
The superlative degree of an adjective ending in -est does not take a supporting adverb.

NOT: The interstate was the *most* shortest way to Nashville.

BUT: The interstate was the shortest way to Nashville.

6 Avoid making illogical comparisons with adjectives and adverbs.

Illogical comparisons occur when writers leave out some necessary words.

ILLOGICAL: The story of the *Titanic* is more interesting than the story of any disaster at sea.
This comparison makes it seem that the story of the Titanic *is one thing and that the story of any disaster at sea is something different. In fact the story of the* Titanic *is about a disaster at sea. Is the story of the* Titanic *more interesting than itself? The sentence is illogical.*

LOGICAL: The story of the *Titanic* is the most interesting of all the stories of disasters at sea.
Here the superlative degree quickly identifies the story of the Titanic *as one about a disaster at sea and announces that in comparison with all the others, it is the most interesting.*

ILLOGICAL: Building houses with brick is harder than lumber.
What is being compared here? Is the act of building harder than the thing we call lumber? The comparison is illogical because acts are different from things and cannot be compared in a sentence like the one above.

LOGICAL: Building houses with brick is harder than *building* them with lumber.
Now it is clear that the comparison is between two acts of building, not between an act and a thing.

ILLOGICAL: Mr. Lincoln's speech was shorter than Mr. Everett.
In this sentence, one might suppose that Mr. Everett was six feet tall but that Mr. Lincoln's speech was only five feet.

22g

ad

LOGICAL: Mr. Lincoln's speech was shorter *than that* of Mr.
Everett.
*Now it is clear that Mr. Lincoln's speech is being compared with Mr.
Everett's speech and not with Mr. Everett himself.*

7   Avoid overusing adjectives.

Using too many adjectives in any one sentence will weaken the force
of a statement. Strong writers put an adjective before a noun or pronoun
only when the adjective is truly needed. They rarely put as many as three
adjectives before a noun unless they need to create some special effect or
unless one of the adjectives is a number.

Study the following paragraphs. The adjectives are in boldface.

I had imagined Siberia as having been filled up by waves of
settlers, much as the **American** West. But what impressed me most
on that **train** trip was the sparseness of humanity and the **enormous**
emptiness of the land. Cities would suddenly loom up without the
warning of suburbs and then, after we stopped briefly, would vanish
just as suddenly. The **petty** barter from ship-to-shore marked the
progress of our voyage across the continent. The **dining** car left Moscow well stocked with **fresh** apples, oranges, cucumbers, **chocolate**
candy and **other little** delicacies. At the **early** stops, townfolk would
rush to purchase these goodies from the **dining car** staff leaning out
doors and windows. But later, as supplies ran **low** and the menu
became more **restricted,** the trade shifted the **other** way.

— HEDRICK SMITH

The jet has radically altered the rate at which **Western** technology and culture have spread. When a **ten thousand foot** runway is
constructed in some hitherto **remote** spot, life in that area will begin
to change at once — probably faster than at **any** time since it was last
invaded in war. And because the **modern** traveler demands as far as
possible the comfort and lifestyle of his home, it becomes increasingly **difficult** to wake up in a hotel anywhere in the world and know,
instantly, where you are. **Local** customs and the **physical** shape of the
environment are changed to meet the requirements of visitors. The
rate at which this is happening has increased with the construction of
widebody jets, each capable of carrying nearly **four hundred** people.
As the standard of living in the West has risen steadily since the end
of the **last world** war, with a **consequent** increase in **disposable** income, the numbers of people **able** to afford holidays by air have risen
too. Because the **new** jets operate more efficiently than their prede-
cessors, costs have fallen and this has acted as a **further** stimulus to
travel.

— JAMES BURKE

Adjective and Adverb Modifiers   **393**

In the first paragraph, in 131 words we find only fifteen adjectives. In the second paragraph, we have 190 words and only eighteen adjectives (the numbers are counted as one adjective each, although each number in this selection has two words). Different writers will, of course, use adjectives at different rates. But it will help you limit your own use of adjectives if you study examples of writing you like to read and notice how economical good writers are in their use of adjectives.

Exercise 22.6   In the following sentences, use any adjectives you choose to fill in the blanks. But whatever adjective you write in must be in the proper degree — positive, comparative, or superlative. Be adventurous. Avoid common adjectives like *good* and *bad*.

1. President Franklin D. Roosevelt was a _____ man than many presidents who served before him.
2. Rhode Island is the _____ of all the states.
3. Lassie is a _____ actor than John Travolta.
4. Steam radiators are _____.
5. Percy owned the _____ leather vest in his motorcycle gang.
6. Rock records are generally the _____ of all records sold.
7. Rain is generally _____ than snow or ice.
8. The president of the university is _____ than the faculty.
9. The sea is _____ than the desert.
10. Dick Tracy was _____ than Batman.

Exercise 22.7   Choose a piece of nonfiction that you enjoy, such as an article in a popular magazine like *Sports Illustrated, Time, Newsweek, Popular Mechanics,* or *Rolling Stone.* Answer the following questions about the article you choose.

1. In three consecutive paragraphs chosen at random, what is the total number of nouns?
2. How many nouns have adjectives before them?
3. How many nouns have more than one adjective before them?
4. What is the total number of adjectives in these paragraphs?
5. How many times do you find two or more consecutive adjectives of more than one syllable in sentences taken from your randomly selected paragraphs?
6. What adjectives can be left out without injury to the clarity or to the tone of the piece?
7. What conclusions can you make about the use of adjectives by professional writers?

Exercise 22.8   Take any paper written by you or another student in the class, and ask the same questions you asked in Exercise 22.7.

Exercise 22.9   Eliminate as many adjectives as you can in the following paragraph:

> The old, bent, gray man stood still and thoughtful on the crowded edge of the crowded, busy, narrow street and looked down to the tall, lighted, brick building which loomed up in the thick, damp, gray mist of the early, chill, autumn, overcast, threatening night. He felt in the deep, warm, dark pocket of his new, wool, black, tweed overcoat for the hard, blue, loaded, automatic pistol and checked the tiny, metal safety catch on the lethal, heavy, criminal weapon. The important, threatening, dangerous gun was there, ready, waiting, eager to be fired.

CHAPTER TWENTY-THREE

Dangling Modifiers and Misplaced Parts

In English, clarity depends on the word order within sentences. We expect most adjectives and adjectival clauses and phrases to come either immediately before or immediately after the words they modify unless they are subject complements, joined to the words they modify by linking verbs (see 5a-1). For example, it is common to find sentences like this one:

> The **quick, brown** fox jumps over the **lazy** dog.
> *The adjectives, in boldface, come immediately before the nouns they modify.*

And it is common to find sentences like this one:

> The beggar, **sad** and **old,** held out his hand to me.
> *The adjectives* sad *and* old *come immediately after the noun they modify.*

But adverbs and adverbial phrases are often separated by other words from the words or phrases they modify. We say "They began their job **yesterday**," and we know without thinking much about it that the adverb *yesterday* modifies the verb *began*, although the words *their job* come between the verb and its modifier. It is not customary in English to say "They began yesterday their job." And we also write sentences like this one: "**When she was young,** she played softball every **Saturday.**" The adverbial clause *When she was young* modifies the verb *played*, and so does the adverb *Saturday*. But both the clause and the simple adverb are separated from the verb by other words.

So the trick in English is to know when you can separate modifiers from the words or phrases they modify and when you cannot. And in general you can separate adverbs and adverbials from the words they modify more easily than you can separate adjectives from the words they modify.

Yet even adverbs and adverbial phrases can be misplaced. In general, for example, an adverbial phrase modifies the nearest verb. It may be separated from that verb by other words, but English idiom makes us expect to join adverbs and adverbials to the nearest possible verb. When another verb gets in the way, our sentences get into trouble, as in the following sentences from one of the humorous squibs in *The New Yorker:*

> Wednesday morning, Lee's oldest son Mike signed a national letter of intent with Indiana University to play football for the Hoosiers in the family kitchen at 3838 Ashland Drive in West Lafayette.
> *The writer intended to make the adverbial prepositional phrase* in the family kitchen *modify the verb* signed. *But since it is nearer to the infinitive phrase* to play football, *it seems to modify that phrase, giving the impression that Mike is going to be running for touchdowns over the kitchen sink.*

> During the lecture, Johanson will describe the discovery of a band of the new species of hominids who appeared to have been killed simultaneously by some disaster with color slides.
> *The writer has intended to make the prepositional phrase* with color slides *modify the verb phrase* will describe. *But it is nearer to and appears to describe the noun* disaster *and seems to be an adjectival phrase.*

The lesson of errors like these should be to remind you to keep the related parts of a sentence as close to each other as you can. Otherwise you may create confusion for your readers.

23a
Avoid dangling or misplaced participles.

Introductory participles and participial phrases must modify the grammatical subject of the sentence. Participles that do not modify the grammatical subject are called **dangling** or **misplaced** participles. A *dangling* participle lacks a noun to modify.

DANGLING: After drying up the Turkish and Asian poppy supplies, Mexico became a prime supplier of Mexican Brown heroin.
— *Boston Globe, New England Magazine*

As written, the sentence means that Mexico somehow dried up the Turkish and Asian poppy supplies and took over these parts of the drug trade itself, as if the Mexican government intended such a course of event. But this was not the sense of the article at all. The participial phrase after drying up the Turkish and Asian poppy supplies *modifies nothing in the rest of the sentence. The writer has used a participle when we should have another form: "After Turkish and Asian poppy supplies dried up, Mexico became a prime supplier of a heroin called 'Mexican Brown.'"*

A *misplaced* participle occurs in a sentence containing a noun that the participle should modify. But since the participle is misplaced, it modifies the wrong noun instead.

MISPLACED: Born in 1812, the novel commonly called *The Pickwick Papers* made Charles Dickens famous by the age of 25.
Born in 1812, the past participle, should modify Charles Dickens. *Instead it seems to modify the noun* novel *so that the book appears to have been born in 1812.*

As noted above, the only way to correct dangling and misplaced modifiers is to make a complete revision of the sentence.

Born in 1812, Charles Dickens became famous at the age of 25 when he published the novel commonly called *The Pickwick Papers.*
The sentence has been rewritten to make Charles Dickens *the grammatical subject, modified by the introductory participial phrase* born in 1812.

dang

DANGLING: Having studied small-engine repair in night school, fixing the lawn mower was easy.
The subject of the sentence is the gerund fixing. *But the* fixing *cannot have studied small-engine repair in night school. The writer had a subject in mind when he started the sentence but forgot it when he wrote the rest, so there is nothing in the second part of the sentence for the introductory phrase to modify.*

REVISED: Having studied small-engine repair in night school, Jane found that fixing the lawn mower was easy.
The introductory phrase now modifies the subject, Jane.

REVISED: After Jane studied small-engine repair in night school, fixing the lawn mower was easy.
The opening has been changed to an adverbial clause.

DANGLING: Driving along Route 10, the sun shone in Carmela's face.
This sentence says that the sun was driving along Route 10.

REVISED: Driving along Route 10, Carmela found the sun shining in her face.
Now it is clearly Carmela who was driving along Route 10. The sentence has been revised to place a correct subject after the modifying participle at the beginning.

REVISED: When Carmela drove along Route 10, the sun shone in her face.
The introductory phrase has been rewritten so that the sentence now begins with a clause.

DANGLING: Using elaborate charts and graphs, the audience understood the plan.
The sentence says that the audience used the charts and graphs to understand the plan.

REVISED: Using elaborate charts and graphs, the mayor explained the plan to the audience.
The added noun mayor *becomes the subject of the rewritten sentence, and the introductory participial phrase now modifies the subject correctly.*

REVISED: Because the mayor used elaborate charts and graphs, the audience understood the plan.
Now the sentence begins with an introductory clause that serves as an adverb modifying the verb understood.

Although dangling participles usually come at the beginning of a sentence, they can come at the end.

DANGLING: The work was hard, sweating over hot machinery, bending in cramped spaces, sometimes mashing his fingers, skinning his knees, twisting heavy wrenches, and getting home late and exhausted every night.
The writer has attached a series of participial phrases to the end of the sentence. Such participial phrases at the end of the sentence, often called free *modifiers, should modify the subject of the sentence. But these modifiers cannot modify the subject,* work.

REVISED: He worked hard, sweating over hot machinery, bending in cramped spaces, sometimes mashing his fingers, skinning his knees, twisting heavy wrenches, and getting home late and exhausted every night.
Now all the participial phrases modify the subject, he.

Note: Avoid confusing absolute phrases with dangling participles. Absolute phrases contain both a noun and a present or past participle (see

dang

5d-1). They stand by themselves in sentences and do not modify single words, although they add to the meaning of the sentence as a whole.

ABSOLUTE PHRASES

> Intercollegiate athletic programs have become big business, their coaches paid more than presidents, their teams far better known than professors, their revenues contributing more to the general fund than tuition.
>
> *The absolute constructions are* their coaches paid more than presidents, their teams far better known than professors, *and* their revenues contributing more to the general fund than tuition. *Each of these absolutes names something, and each concludes with a participle that modifies what is named.*

> He remembered the old days in the now-abandoned railroad station, the steam locomotives puffing in and out, the newspaper boys shouting the headlines, passengers climbing down and looking around for taxis, a hum of activity filling the air.
>
> *This sentence includes a string of absolute phrases, each naming something with a noun, then modifying the noun with a present participial phrase. The absolute phrases do not dangle.*

USAGE NOTE

dang

Informal usage frequently accepts the following forms that combine an introductory participle with the expletive *it* (see 21-d), especially when the participle expresses a habitual or general action.

> Walking in the country at dawn, it is easy to see many different kinds of birds.
>
> *The statement is general, expressing something that would be done by anyone. Many writers and editors would prefer this revision: "Walking in the country at dawn is an easy way to see many different kinds of birds."*

> When beginning a new exercise program, it is good to have a complete physical examination by a doctor.
>
> *The statement is general, and to many writers it seems preferable to an informal statement like this one: "When you begin a new exercise program, you should have a complete physical examination by a doctor." Or a formal statement like this one: "When one begins a new exercise program, one should have a complete physical examination by a doctor." But many other writers — perhaps a majority — would revise the sentence to read like this: "Anyone who begins a new exercise program should have a complete physical examination by a doctor."*

Exercise 23.1   Rewrite any of the following sentences that have dangling or misplaced participles. If a sentence does not have a dangling or misplaced participle, put a check beside it. If a sentence contains an absolute, write an A beside it.

1. Daydreaming about his new job, the doorbell startled him.
2. Working hard through the night, the job was finished by daybreak.
3. Everything went off exactly as planned, the false Arab sheik sitting in costume on a sofa, the congressmen led in one by one, the bribes offered, the congressmen making excuses for themselves to have reasons for taking the money, the FBI moving at last to put them under arrest.
4. Riding hard through the night, Paul Revere spread the alarm through Middlesex County to the sleeping town of Lexington.
5. Backed into a corner and hurt, the bell barely saved him.
6. Walking along the street, the city seemed calm.
7. Using a word processor, he was able to revise his paper in a couple of hours and turn in the finished product the next day, every error corrected and some sentences rewritten in a much more effective style.
8. Having played hard, the loss was bitter.
9. Taking the ship from New York, the trip was now under way.
10. Having been aged in an oak barrel for twelve years, he discovered that the wine was exactly to his taste.
11. The marathon was difficult, running up hills, knowing his shoes were inferior, sweating hard, thirsting for water.
12. They enjoyed the meal, talking, laughing, telling old stories, and drinking too much.
13. Having cleaned up the house, the garage was next on the list.
14. Looking up, the long V-shaped flock of geese could be seen by everyone in the valley.
15. Turning the car down the valley road, he could see the long shadows cast by the stark white moon, the houses shut up against the night, and the road itself running like a stripe painted across the earth and disappearing into the dark in the distance.

23b

misp

23b
Avoid the misplaced prepositional phrase that modifies the wrong element in the sentence.

Prepositional phrases used as adjectives seldom give trouble. We use them commonly in speech, and these speech habits transfer readily to writing:

The book *on the table* belongs to me.
The prepositional phrase on the table *is used as an adjective modifying the noun* book.

We lived in a house *near the school.*
The prepositional phrase near the school *is used as an adjective modifying the noun* house.

Prepositional phrases used as adverbs are harder to place in sentences, and sometimes writers are led astray by their adverbial phrases.

MISPLACED: He saw the first dive-bombers approaching from the bridge of the battleship.
The misplaced prepositional phrase from the bridge *makes it seem that the dive-bombers were approaching from the bridge of the battleship.*

REVISED: From the bridge of the battleship, he saw the first dive-bombers approaching.
From the bridge now clearly modifies the verb saw.

MISPLACED: The German chancellor was introduced to Americans on television.
The position of the prepositional phrase on television *functions as an adjective modifying the noun* Americans.

REVISED: The German chancellor was introduced on television to Americans.
Now the position of the prepositional phrase makes it function as an adverb modifying the verb phrase was introduced.

MISPLACED: He ran the ten-kilometer race from the shopping mall through the center of town to the finish line by the monument in his bare feet.
The misplaced adverbial prepositional phrase in his bare feet *might make a rapid reader think that the monument was in his bare feet.*

REVISED: In his bare feet he ran the ten-kilometer race from the shopping mall through the center of town to the finish line by the monument.
In his bare feet is now close enough to the verb ran *to avoid confusion.*

REVISED: From the shopping mall, through the center of town to the finish line by the monument, he ran the ten-kilometer race in his bare feet.
This version preserves the sentence emphasis that the writer wanted in the first draft of the sentence, keeping the surprising phrase in his bare feet *until the end.*

23c

Avoid the misplaced clause that modifies the wrong sentence element.

MISPLACED: Professor Peebles taught the course on the English novel that most students dropped after three weeks.
Did they drop the course or the novel?

REVISED: Professor Peebles taught the course on the English novel, a course most students dropped after three weeks.
The repetition of the word course *before the adjectival clause makes the modification clear. Students dropped the course, not the novel.*

REVISED: After three weeks, most students dropped Professor Peebles' course on the English novel.
This version is a more thorough revision, and the need for a dependent clause has disappeared. The extent of such a revision will depend on the writer's view of what is most important in the sentence, a view that will be decided by the context of the sentence.

MISPLACED: For five years Dixon worked all day as an accountant to support her family and after supper went to night school to study law, which was hard, but finally she got her degree.
Was law hard, or was her schedule hard?

REVISED: For five years Dixon worked all day as an accountant to support her family and after supper went to night school to study law. It was a hard schedule, but she finally got her degree.

REVISED: For five years Dixon worked all day as an accountant to support her family and after supper went to night school to study law. Law was a hard field, but she finally got her degree.
In both revisions, a long original sentence has been broken into two shorter ones. When you have trouble with modification, you can often clarify your thought by using two sentences instead of one.

Exercise 23.2   Rewrite the following sentences to correct errors in modification.

1. Marco Polo traveled overland to China with his father and his uncle to visit the Mongol Empire, which was very dangerous.
2. He stood in the middle of the room and shouted at everyone in his pajamas.
3. He bought a digital watch at the jewelry shop which ran on tiny batteries.

4. She wrote the outline of her book on the wall in the kitchen with a black crayon.
5. When she was a little girl, she used to lie awake at night wishing that she had a horse in her bedroom.
6. The boat lost its sail in the hard wind which was made of canvas.

23d

Avoid the confusing adverb or adverbial phrase that seems to modify both the element that comes immediately before it and the element that comes immediately after it.

Place your adverbs so that they modify only one sentence element.

CONFUSING: To read a good book *completely* satisfies her.
Does reading a book satisfy her completely? Or must she read the book completely to be satisfied?

REVISED: She is completely satisfied when she reads a good book.

REVISED: She is satisfied when she reads a good book completely.

CONFUSING: Changing gears *continually* gives mental exercise to people who ride bicycles.
Does the writer mean that continually changing gears provides mental exercise or that changing gears gives mental exercise continually?

REVISED: Continually changing gears gives mental exercise to people who ride bicycles.

REVISED: Changing gears gives continual mental exercise to people who ride bicycles.
Notice that in the second revision, continual is an adjective. In the first revision, merely changing the position of continually clarifies the meaning of the sentence.

Exercise 23.3 Rewrite the following sentences to eliminate the confusion of adverbs that may modify two elements in a sentence.

1. The car starting easily made this the best day of my trip.
2. People who disliked long hair very much liked having ten-dollar bills with long-haired Alexander Hamilton's picture on the front.

3. A scholar who studies often goes to sleep over her books.
4. People who love to criticize books sometimes do not write books themselves.
5. She woke up suddenly pushing off the covers.

23e

As a rule, place one-word modifiers that define degree, extent, or limitation before the words or phrases that they modify.

These modifiers include words like *merely, completely, fully, perfectly, hardly, nearly, almost, even, just, simply, scarcely,* and *only.*

Note the differences in meaning in the following sentences:

The *almost* exhausted man finished the marathon.

The exhausted man *almost* finished the marathon.

The *completely* restored antique cars paraded proudly through the admiring town.

The restored antique cars paraded proudly through the *completely* admiring town.

In speaking, we sometimes put limiting modifiers in illogical places, but the sense of what we say is clear from the tone of our voice, our gestures, or the general context. In writing, lack of logic in misplaced modifiers can cause confusion.

misp

CONFUSING: He *only* had one bad habit, but it *just* was enough to keep him in trouble.
The only *in the sentence seems to modify the verb* had, *and the* just *modifies the adjective* enough.

REVISED: He had only one bad habit, but it was just enough to keep him in trouble.

CONFUSING: They were all *nearly* about to graduate, but they wouldn't *even* send one invitation because all of them decided *almost* that the commencement speaker would insult the intelligence of the audience.
The adverb nearly *seems to modify* about, *but the phrase* about to graduate *and* nearly *say something similar;* even *seems to modify* send, *and* almost *seems to modify the entire dependent clause that comes after it. The sentence is difficult to understand.*

Dangling Modifiers and Misplaced Parts **405**

REVISED: They were nearly all about to graduate, but they wouldn't send even one invitation because all of them decided that the commencement speaker would insult the intelligence of the audience.

Exercise 23.4   Use each of these modifiers in at least two sentences: *only, even, just, scarcely, almost, nearly.*

CHAPTER TWENTY-FOUR

Confusing Shifts

To keep your sentences clear and harmonious, you must be consistent in your use of verbs and nouns. You should avoid jarring shifts in point of view and sudden outbursts of emotion.

24a
Be consistent in your verb tenses.

INCONSISTENT: Every day the parking lot *fills* up by eight in the morning, and commuting students arriving after that *could* not find parking places.

The verb fills *is in the present indicative tense; the verb* could *is in the past tense.*

CONSISTENT: The parking lot *fills* up by eight in the morning, and commuting students arriving after that *can*not find parking places.

Both verbs are now in the present tense.

When you write about the content of any piece of literature, you usually use the present tense. Be careful not to shift out of the present tense when you have decided to use it for such a purpose. Take this care not only within sentences but from one sentence to another. Be especially careful when you quote a passage that is in the past tense. Do not shift

407

your description of the passage into the past tense if you have been using the present. Here is an example:

> David Copperfield *observes* other people with a fine and sympathetic eye. He *describes* villains such as Mr. Murdstone and improbable heroes such as Mr. Micawber with unforgettable sharpness of detail. But David Copperfield *was* not himself an especially interesting person.
>
> *The unexpected shift from present to past tense in the third sentence will jar readers.*

Avoid the temptation to fall into inconsistent tenses when you are telling an exciting story. Sometimes the events you are relating become vividly present to you as you speak or write, and you slip into the present tense. Such an inconsistency may be acceptable in conversation, but it confuses readers.

> **INCONSISTENT:** The wind *was howling* and *blowing* a hundred miles an hour when suddenly there *is* a big crash, and a tree *falls* into Rocky's living room.
>
> *The writer begins with the past progressive, or imperfect, tense (was howling . . . blowing) and in the excitement of describing a falling tree shifts the tense to the present (is and falls).*

> **CONSISTENT:** The wind *was howling* and *blowing* a hundred miles an hour when suddenly there *was* a big crash, and a tree *fell* into Rocky's living room.

shift

Inconsistency may creep into your writing when you combine present perfect and past perfect tenses with present and past tenses of verbs.

> **INCONSISTENT:** She *has admired* many strange buildings at the university, but she *thought* that the Science Center *looked* completely out of place.

> **CONSISTENT:** She *has admired* many strange buildings at the university, but she *thinks* that the Science Center *looks* completely out of place.
>
> *The present perfect tense* has admired *leads readers from a point in the past to the present and assumes that the activity described still goes on. So in making successive clauses you must be sure that you take into account the continuing action of the first clause. The thought expressed in the consistent sentence is like this: She has admired and still admires in the present many strange buildings at the university, but she thinks now in the present that the Science Center looks completely out of place.*

CONSISTENT: She *admired* many strange buildings at the university, but she *thought* that the Science Center *looked* completely out of place.
The simple past in the first clause names an action considered finished at some point in past time. The second clause can also use a simple past verb for an action which, like the action in the first verb, is considered past.

Verbs in successive clauses do not have to be in the same tense, but they should follow each other in tenses that make good grammatical sense and say what the writer wants them to say.

The present tense may be followed by another present tense:

Dogs *bark* to show that they *are* interested in something, or to show that they *are* afraid, or to announce that someone — perhaps another dog — *is invading* their territory.

The present tense may be followed by a past tense:

Michaelson *says* that transistors *made* stereo systems cheaper but *reduced* the fidelity of sound created by vacuum tubes.

The present can be used with the present perfect:

Quality control in the American automobile industry *is* a long-standing problem that *has made* millions of Americans think that Japanese cars are better.

The present can be used with the future tense:

We *predict* that word processors *will replace* electric typewriters in most offices by the end of this decade.

The present tense should not be used with the past perfect tense unless a suitable tense follows the past perfect.

INCONSISTENT: She *swears* that she *had registered* her car properly.

CONSISTENT: She *swears* that she *had registered* her car properly before she *received* a ticket for having an improper license plate.
In the consistent version, the past perfect comes before a clause that uses the simple past tense in its verb. The past perfect reports action that was finished in the past before some other past action occurred.

If you are not going to follow the past perfect with a clause using a verb in the past tense, change the past perfect tense to a more suitable form.

CONSISTENT: She *swears* that she *registered* her car properly.

The simple past can be followed by another simple past:

College football *was* so violent early in this century that President Theodore Roosevelt *threatened* to abolish it.

The simple past can be used with the imperfect:

Everyone *was* eager to know if she *was going* to enter the fifty-mile road race.

The simple past can be used with the future:

They *told* me that the tire shipment *will arrive* next week.

The simple past should not be used with the present perfect, although in informal speech we sometimes do use the two tenses together.

INFORMAL: She *reported* that she *has been running* nine miles every morning.

FORMAL: She *reports* that she *runs* nine miles every morning.

FORMAL: She *reported* that she *had been running* nine miles every morning.

24b

Be consistent in the mood of your verbs.

Mood is a change in a verb that shows the way in which an assertion is made in a sentence (see 20d). The indicative mood makes simple statements or asks simple questions. The conditional mood makes statements that would be true if something else were true. The subjunctive mood is now used rarely in English (see 20d-2), but when it is used, it often makes conditional statements known to be contrary to fact. (If I *were* in Rome on Easter morning, I would hear thousands of church bells. I am not in Rome on Easter morning, and I may not be there when Easter comes; so I use the subjunctive mood in the clause *if I were.*)

Inconsistent shifts from the indicative to the conditional or from the conditional to the indicative often cause trouble.

INCONSISTENT: He *will go* to night school and *would take* a course in hotel management.

The indicative will go *seems to be about to make a statement, a simple report that someone is going to night school. But the conditional* would take *makes us think that this is not a simple report at all but that some uncertainty is involved. Maybe he is not going to night school. The conditional makes us expect a clause beginning with if.*

CONSISTENT: If he *could go* to night school, he *would take* a course in hotel management.

Now the conditional verb could go *in the first clause makes us expect another conditional verb,* would take, *in the next clause. We have the uncertainty of his going to night school clearly stated.*

INCONSISTENT: If he *goes* to night school, he *would take* a course in hotel management.

Here the inconsistency arises because the indicative verb goes *seems to start the sentence by making a simple statement to answer the question "What will he do if he goes to night school?" But the change in mood with the conditional verb* would take *in the next clause brings in an unnecessary confusion. We know that it is not certain that he will go to night school. The* if *tells us that. But if he does go to night school, is there any uncertainty about what he will take? The conditional mood in the verb* would take *indicates that there is, but we are not told why.*

CONSISTENT: He *would go* to night school, and he *would take* a course in hotel management, if he *could get out* of jail.

Here the conditional mood used throughout in the verbs makes everything about this sentence seem uncertain. The use of the conditional implies that none of these acts is likely to happen. He is probably not going to get out of jail, and he is probably not going to go to night school and take a course in hotel management.

CONSISTENT: He *will go* to night school and *will take* a course in hotel management if he *gets out* of jail.

The mood throughout is indicative—and more optimistic. The sentence makes a simple statement of fact, telling what he will do if he gets out of jail. No uncertainty is involved in the verbs preceding the if *clause, although the conjunction* if *does imply that he may not get out of jail. Yet the indicative mood shows that he has a good chance of getting out of jail, since it implies much less uncertainty than the conditional mood.*

INCONSISTENT: If he *were* absent, he *will fail* the course.

The subjunctive were *indicates a statement contrary to fact. He is not absent, but if he were, something would happen. But then the indica-*

24b

shift

tive will fail *indicates a simple report of fact. The mood is inconsist-*
ent with the subjunctive that comes before it.

CONSISTENT: If he *is* absent, he *will fail* the course.
Now we have a simple statement. We do not know if he is absent or
not. But if he is absent, he will fail the course. The indicative is used
in both verbs.

CONSISTENT: If he *were* absent, he *would fail* the course.
The subjunctive were *indicates a conditional statement contrary to*
fact. He is not absent. It is followed by a conditional verb in the
following clause, would fail. *The conditional makes the sentence*
mean that if he were absent, he would fail the course, but he is not
absent, and he will not fail the course.

You can see here the value of the moods of verbs; without these
various moods, we would have a hard time saying some things.

24b

shift

Exercise 24.1   Correct the confusing shifts in the following sentences. If a sentence is correct as it stands, put a check by the number.

1. Hamlet has been in school in Wittenberg, and he came home to find
   his father dead and his mother married to his father's brother.
2. Mercutio has to die in *Romeo and Juliet,* or else he would have carried
   the play off from the two young lovers, who are not nearly as interesting as he was.
3. The band hit a sour note, and the drum major gets sore at the tuba
   section.
4. Parents who often get drunk embarrassed their children.
5. King James I, who died in 1625, had never taken a bath in his adult
   life, and those who prepared him for burial have to scour his underwear off his body.
6. If you travel abroad this summer, we would have enjoyed going with
   you.
7. She would design the building if she knows calculus.
8. If I were in Paris right now, I can hear the sounds of the streets.
9. If the queen will stop wearing those big, round hats, her people
   would think better of her taste.
10. She has been to automobile-mechanics school before she set up her
    business.

24c

Use the same voice for verbs in closely related clauses and sentences.

The voice of a transitive verb is either active or passive. In clauses with active verbs, the subject does the acting; in clauses with passive verbs, the subject is acted upon (see 20e). Inconsistency in voice sometimes arises from a writer's desire to use variety in sentence forms. But when the actor remains the same in successive clauses, you should not change voice.

INCONSISTENT: The Impressionist painters *hated* black. Violet, green, blue, pink, and red *were favored* by them.
The actor in the successive sentences is the same — the Impressionist painters. But the voices of the verbs are inconsistent because hated *is active and* were favored *is passive. The writer has bought variety at the expense of reader confusion.*

CONSISTENT: The Impressionist painters *hated* black. They *favored* violet, green, blue, pink, and red.
Now both verbs in the successive sentences are in the active voice.

Note that it is easy to go from a linking verb of simple description in the active voice to a verb in the passive voice in the next clause:

Today American Indians *are* often poor, uneducated, and unhealthy. They *have been isolated* from the rest of the country, *deprived* of the benefits of the land which was taken away from them by force, and *forgotten* by the people who robbed them.
The passive verbs have been isolated, deprived, *and* forgotten *follow naturally after the simple descriptive sentence* Today American Indians are often poor, uneducated, and unhealthy, *which has a simple linking verb,* is. *The shift in voice is unobtrusive.*

You should avoid a sudden shift in voice from clause to clause or sentence to sentence when you are writing about the same actor or agent. Your readers may expect a shift if you move from one agent to another. They will not expect a shift when you are telling of the actions of the same agent in successive clauses.

INCONSISTENT: The bulldozer clanked into the woods and bit into the ground. The trees and the earth were ripped up.

CONSISTENT: The bulldozer clanked into the woods, bit into the ground, and ripped up the trees and the earth.

shift

Consistent: McNabb *rode* his motorcycle through the plate-glass window and *was taken* to the hospital as soon as the ambulance could get there.

Here you could say, "McNabb rode *his motorcycle through the plate-glass window, and the ambulance driver* took *him to the hospital as soon as possible." But by changing to the passive voice with the verb* was taken, *the writer keeps attention on McNabb, the most interesting person in the action here reported.*

24d

Be consistent in the person and number of your nouns and pronouns and in the way you address your reader.

In speaking and writing in an informal tone, we often use the pronoun *you* instead of the more formal pronoun *one* (see 21e).

> If *you* smoke cigarettes, *you* run a high risk of getting lung cancer.

Problems arise when you mix the informal *you* with the formal *one:*

> If *one* smokes cigarettes, *you* run a high risk of getting lung cancer.

24d

shift

Here the pronoun *one* is inconsistent with the pronoun *you,* and the sentence must be revised. A more formal statement is this:

> If *one* smokes cigarettes, *one* runs a high risk of getting lung cancer.
> OR:
> *Anyone* who smokes cigarettes runs a high risk of getting lung cancer.
> OR:
> *People* who smoke cigarettes run a high risk of getting lung cancer.

If you address your reader directly as *you,* you may write in the third person from time to time. But you cannot shift from the third person to the second person or from the second person to the third person in the same sentence.

> **Consistent:** *You* will always find good writing to be hard work. *Good writers* never think that their craft is easy.
>
> *You, in the first sentence, addresses the reader directly. Good writers, the third-person subject in the second sentence, begins a statement consistent with the direct address in the first sentence. In effect, the reader is being addressed in both sentences and feels no discomfort with the shift from the second person to the third person.*

INCONSISTENT: *People* flying across the country nowadays discover that *you* can get many different fares to the same destination.
The shift in the same sentence from the third-person people *to the second-person* you *is confusing.*

Make your pronouns agree with their antecedents, but try to avoid sexist language (see Chapter 15 and 21b).

INCONSISTENT: *Anyone* who rides a bicycle every day will discover that *they* develop some muscles not developed in jogging.
Anyone *is an indefinite singular pronoun; the pronoun* they *is plural. Although in informal usage the pronoun* they *is used for the antecedent* anyone, *the usage is still not accepted by many editors, who hold that a pronoun must agree with its antecedent in number.*

CONSISTENT: *People* who ride bicycles every day will discover that *they* develop some muscles not developed in jogging.

CONSISTENT: *Anyone* who rides a bicycle every day will discover that *she* develops some muscles not developed in jogging.

CONSISTENT: *Anyone* who rides a bicycle every day will discover that *he* develops some muscles not developed in jogging.

CONSISTENT: *Anyone* who rides a bicycle every day will discover that *he* or *she* develops some muscles not developed in jogging.

You can make a much more sweeping revision:

Bike riders do not exercise some of the muscles used in jogging and usually discover that they get sore quickly when they try to run around the neighborhood at night.

24e
Avoid jarring shifts in point of view.

INCONSISTENT

He sat idly in his seat and looked down at the land pouring beneath the low-flying plane like some immense sea whose waters reached to the sky. The green of the forest enchanted him. Everything was primitive and nearly unspoiled. Here and there a house stood in a solitary clearing that, from above, looked like a raft afloat on the great ocean of green. He saw it for a moment, and then it was whisked away behind him. *In the houses, people were sitting down to supper, unfolding napkins, looking expectantly at the head of the table where the father gravely bowed his head to say grace.*

The point of view, quickly established, is of someone in an airplane looking down on the land passing underneath. But in the last sentence we shift to a scene that such a traveler cannot see. A reader must go back to look for what is missing because the shift is jarring. The last sentence can be easily fixed to match the point of view established in the rest of the passage.

He could imagine that in the houses people were sitting down to supper, unfolding napkins, looking expectantly at the head of the table where the father gravely bowed his head to say grace.

Exercise 24.2 Rewrite the following sentences to eliminate confusing shifts. If a sentence is correct as it stands, put a check beside it.

1. American landscape painters of the nineteenth century viewed the American wilderness as the handiwork of God; signs of God's work were seen by them in lakes, mountains, and prairies.
2. Government paperwork costs forty billion dollars a year, and government accountants are working to trim those costs—and making more paperwork as they do so; you can see the problem.
3. If anyone carries a pack on your back while they ride a bicycle up a mountain in the summer, be prepared to be hot and tired.
4. People who take a lot of pictures sometimes find that you get tired carrying a camera, and they often stop taking pictures all at once, the way some people stop smoking.
5. Anyone who writes a long letter of complaint is frustrated when they get a form letter in return.
6. Everybody who uses the library has to be responsible for the damage they may do to books.

7. Some of the new sun-screening lotions offer relief to people who sunburn easily—unless you happen to be allergic to the chemical agent in such lotions.
8. My Uncle Charley always brought his queen out on the third move when he played chess—something you'll have to admit was pretty stupid.
9. Ralph Waldo Emerson shocked people in the nineteenth century because he seemed so radical. You could be sure that a conservative school like Yale would not let him speak there.
10. Captain Ahab in *Moby Dick* was a figure for all those people so obsessed with the wrongs that they had suffered that they finally destroyed themselves in their quest for vengeance.

Exercise 24.3   Rewrite the following paragraph to correct the confusing shift.

> In Thomas More's book *Utopia,* which is the name for an island supposedly located off the coast of the new world, the people of his commonwealth wear unbleached wool, eat together in great halls, punish adultery with death when one is convicted twice of the offense, and allow husbands and wives to inspect each other naked before they are married so one will not be deceived by the other. The Utopians had no individuality. They tried as hard as they could to eliminate passion. More made no mention of any artists among them.

24f

shift

24f
Avoid sudden outbursts of emotion in your writing.

You may have strong feelings about a subject, and having discussed some of the issues in an essay, you may be tempted to conclude with a highly emotional ending so readers will know where you stand. Excessive emotionalism in writing is almost always a mistake. Most readers dismiss the opinions of a ranter, and if you rant in your writing, few people will take your thoughts seriously. You may embarrass even those people who agree with you because you present their opinions in such an irrational way. Sarcasm is one of the most objectionable devices in writing because it implies that the writer is a hateful person. Readers want to like the writer of the prose they read; otherwise they will not enjoy spending time in his or her company. Few readers like to spend time with an angry or overwrought or sarcastic person. They will almost inevitably dislike the prose that comes from such a person — or that seems to come from such a person.

Consider these two paragraphs on the military draft:

> The armed forces of the United States need brave men and women who stand ready to save this precious country from all the bloodthirsty rats ready to gnaw us to bloody pieces if we let our guard down for a minute. The President has brought back the military draft, and wouldn't you know it? All the long-haired, dirty, cowardly college punks are protesting their feeble brains out. They don't want to go to the army! Not those vermin! They're too good to go to the army and die for their country! All they're good for is sitting around smoking dope and shacking up with each other and putting fertilizer on their hair so it will grow longer. Once in a while they crack a book so they can seem intellectual and better than everybody else. They want to live in the country like worms in a pig, and they want somebody else to do their fighting and their dying for them. Well, let me tell you something: Red-blooded true Americans aren't going to resist the draft.

> *For the overwhelming majority of readers — even those who support the military draft — the frantic and ugly tone of this paragraph would be repulsive. It could please only those people already in support of the draft and unreasonably angry with those who do not believe in conscription. It could not convince anybody who does not already believe the writer's point of view.*

> The military draft has raised protests among America's young people, especially among college students. They do not remember the Vietnamese war, but they are convinced that the war was useless and that many Americans died uselessly in it. They think that the draft opens the way for similar wars, and they do not want to fight in them. But even among college students, few believe that the country could long survive without military force. Not many people like to be in the army, and although more Americans are killed on the highways every year than died in the entire war in Vietnam, most of us would rather be at home dodging cars than in the jungle dodging bullets. But it can be argued that the best way to avoid war is to be strong, and the draft is not the same as a declaration of war. It is rather a statement that we will defend our vital interests, and it does not push aside the fervent hope of

shift

Americans, both in and out of the army, that we never have to fight. The volunteer army has put the burden of military service on the poor and the ignorant. The American tradition of fair play makes many leaders think that military burdens should be borne by all who receive the benefits of safety that the military provides. And the desire for an able and efficient army makes these same leaders believe that sophisticated military technology cannot be left in the hands of the most poorly educated people in our society. The solution to these problems is the military draft.

By making his point rationally and calmly, the writer wins readers to his point of view and forces even opponents to think of arguments to counter the arguments here. They cannot merely dismiss his thoughts as the ravings of a lunatic. They must argue with him if they are to maintain their position.

Exercise 24.4 Write a short, argumentative paragraph on a controversial subject, one for which you have deep feelings. Convey your point of view without undue emotion and with full respect for those who may disagree with you.

Now do the best you can to make arguments for the opposite point of view. Write a paragraph that might convince you to reconsider your own opinions, one that would treat you—an opponent—with the respect that might win you over.

Exercise 24.5 The following passage is excessively overwrought. Rewrite it, using understatement, to convey the sense of the text:

Lord Crenshaw strode mightily into the room, his bushy eyebrows looking like forests waving in the mightiest of all God's storms, his cold blue eyes flashing like bolts of lightning as he looked around at the assembled guests. Philippa felt her heart go bang in her chest with a wild emotion, wilder than anything she had ever felt before, wild as the incandescent lava that bursts from a volcano and pours down the mountainside, burning up all the reserve and all the hesitation that she might have felt. This was the famous Lord Crenshaw, dauntless leader of Wellington's right at Waterloo, the bold, brave man who flung his great arms skyward and shouted at his troops to hold fast while all around his gallant head the bullets whizzed and whirled, the thunderhead of a hero whose voice sounded like ten thousand organs booming through ten thousand cathedrals. People nodded gravely to him, knowing his reputation for sudden anger, for the outburst that could lead to the duel at sunrise that had more than once snuffed out the tender flower of a young life before it could grow and flourish and become a mighty tree. As he entered the room, a silence like that of Judgment Day itself fell over everyone, and it seemed that the world held its breath while he walked to the buffet and thundered a command to the trembling waiter there. "Give me a ham sandwich," he said. "And hold the pickles."

PART FIVE
UNDERSTANDING PUNCTUATION

	Chapter
End Marks	25
Commas	26
Semicolons	27
Apostrophes	28
Quotation marks	29
Other Marks of Punctuation	30

CHAPTER TWENTY-FIVE

End Marks

In English as in most other languages, the system of end marks gives writers a means for separating sentences and for indicating other special operations.

25a

Use a period after a sentence that makes a statement, that gives a mild command or makes a mild request, or that asks a question indirectly.

Statements (Declarative sentences)

Soap melts in the bathtub.

Every year Americans buy more bicycles than cars.

The building burned down last night.

Mild Commands (Imperative sentences without strong emotion, often sentences that make a mild request)

Please go with me to the lecture.

Consider your opponent's views carefully when you are making an argument.

Lend me the car, and I'll do the shopping.
Commands showing strong emotion require exclamation points; see 25c.

Take the money and run!

Indirect Questions

People wonder why they have to pay such high taxes.

She asked me where I had gone to college.

They demanded to know who was responsible for the killings.

He wanted to know how I had come to that conclusion.

The words why, where, who, *and* how *in these sentences ask questions indirectly.*

Direct questions require question marks (see 25b).
For the use of the ellipsis marks, see 30f.

25b
Use a question mark after a direct question but not after an indirect question.

Who wrote *One of Ours?* *direct question*

She wanted to know who wrote *One of Ours.* *indirect question*

? If a question ends with a quoted question, one question mark serves for both the question in the main clause and the question that is quoted.

What did Juliet mean when she cried, "Oh Romeo, Romeo! Wherefore art thou Romeo?"

If a quoted question comes in a sentence that makes a statement, place a question mark before the last quotation mark for the quoted question, and put a period at the end of the sentence.

"What was Henry Ford's greatest contribution to the industrial revolution in America?" he said.

"What did the President know and when did he know it?" became the great question of the Watergate hearings.

Occasionally a question mark changes a statement into a question.

You expect me to believe a story like that?
He drove my car into your living room?

To give emphasis to parts of a series of questions, you can use question marks to separate them into fragments.

And what will we leave behind us when we are long dead? Temples? Amphora? Sunken treasure?

—MARYA MANNES

To express uncertainty about a word or a date, you may use a question mark. In such usage the question mark means that no one can be sure if the date or word is true. You should never use such question marks merely to show that you have not bothered to look up the information.

Napoleon Bonaparte's brother-in-law, Joachim Murat (1767?– 1815), was King of Naples for seven years.

25c
Use exclamation marks sparingly to emphasize strong emotion.

To convey surprise, outbursts, shock, or some other strong emotion, use exclamation marks.

The land of the free! This is the land of the free! Why, if I say anything that displeases them, the free mob will lynch me, and that's my freedom.

—D. H. LAWRENCE

Moon, rise! Wind, hit the trees, blow up the leaves! Up, now, run! Tricks! Treats! Gangway!

—RAY BRADBURY

Avoid using too many exclamation marks. If you use exclamation marks too frequently, you will dull the sensitivity of your readers to them, and they will not respond with the excitement that an exclamation mark is supposed to call up. For mild statements, use some other marks of punctuation.

"Ah, what a beautiful morning," she said, throwing the windows open onto the new day.
A comma rather than an exclamation mark is used after morning.

Socrates said, "Know thyself."
A period is used after thyself *rather than an exclamation mark.*

Exercise 25.1   Use periods, question marks, and exclamation marks where they are required in the sentences below.

1. He wanted to know if Mr. Kuhns worked for UNESCO or for the FBI
2. "Was it you," she asked, "who painted that wall purple"
3. What did he mean when he asked me, "Is your car an antique"
4. Stolen The money was stolen Right before our eyes, somebody snatched my purse and ran off with it
5. "Help me" he said "I want to learn how to dance"
6. "Isn't the true folk instrument the dulcimer" she asked
7. You expect me to believe that computers can think
8. Pick up the papers Don't you think it's fair for each of us to try to keep this room clean
9. She asked if the theft of credit cards has become a major crime in this country
10. "Where will it end" he asked

Exercise 25.2   Compare the effects of different punctuation marks on the sentences in each pair below. Discuss your responses in class. Imagine situations when you might have used each version of each sentence.

1. a. You don't have to tell me.
   b. You don't have to tell me!
   c. You don't have to tell me?
2. a. You mowed the lawn!
   b. You mowed the lawn?
   c. You mowed the lawn.
3. a. What will you contribute, your time, your talent, or your money?
   b. What will you contribute? Your time? Your talent? Your money?

25c

!

CHAPTER TWENTY-SIX

Commas

When you speak, you may pause to emphasize certain elements of a sentence or to catch your breath. Commas show these pauses within written sentences. Commas also set off sentence elements, clarify the relations of some sentence elements to others, and serve in standard ways for dates, addresses, and other conventions.

Notice how commas take the place of spoken emphasis in the following sentences. Without the commas, you might have to read each of these sentences a couple of times to perceive the correct meaning.

We are, counting the nonvoting delegates, fifty strong.

Although his first name was Abraham, Lincoln had little religious training and never joined a church.

26a

Use commas to set off independent clauses joined by the common coordinating conjunctions.

No one voted in the election, and the White House stood empty for four years.
A comma is used before the coordinating conjunction and, *which introduces an independent clause.*

He was an all-American quarterback, but no pro team drafted him.
A comma is used before the coordinating conjunction but, *which introduces an independent clause.*

The art majors could paint portraits, or they could paint houses.
The comma is used before the coordinating conjunction or, *which introduces the independent clause* they could paint houses.

Many Americans did not at first understand jazz, nor did they enjoy listening to it.

The rock singer did not like to stand with his back to the audience, for then he had to face the music.

The mechanic liked to be different, so he wore a tuxedo when he changed the oil.

Many people don't understand punctuation, yet they use it anyway.

Note that many writers and editors still prefer to use a semicolon rather than a comma before *so* and *yet*.

Printing has made language much less flexible than it once was; *so* the common rules of English grammar will probably not change soon again.

Nearly all of us think we write well; *yet* we all complain about the poor writing of others.

Note, too, that some writers do not separate short independent clauses with a comma.

He stayed at home and she went to work.

But it is always more clear to put the comma in such sentences.

He stayed at home, and she went to work.

26b

Use commas after long introductory phrases and clauses to keep these elements distinct from the core assertion of your sentences.

Although short introductory word groups do not require commas to set them off from the rest of the sentence, commas always make long introductory phrases and clauses easier to read and to understand.

After he had been in the hot tub for three hours, the fire department had to revive him.

When dieting to lose fifty pounds, people should take the advice of a doctor.

Because of many complicated and somewhat bizarre reasons, I could not hand my paper in on time.

These short opening phrases do not have to be set off by commas:

Leaving the game I drifted along with the happy crowd.

After her death he felt lonely and sad for years.

In the street he met his friend Dr. Johnson.

A few writers omit the comma even after long opening phrases in their sentences.

In a letter sent by courier to Richmond that same day he went more fully into this and other matters bearing on the issue.

—SHELBY FOOTE

Despite the occasional exception in the way writers use commas, you will make your sentences consistently more clear if you set off long introductory phrases with commas.

You should always put a comma after an introductory subordinate clause (see 7b-1).

When we came out, we were not on the busiest Chinatown street but on a side street across from the park.

—MAXINE HONG KINGSTON

Although the struggle and competition for national or international power may not be explained wholly and simply as analogous to the power drive in personal relations, the personal may provide significant insight into the political.

—KENNETH B. CLARK

Commas often set off introductory adverbs, especially transitional adverbs like *therefore, also, however, nevertheless,* and *thus.* Normally it is better to rewrite sentences with one-word adverbial openers so that the adverb comes later on.

However, Mr. Smith finally made justice triumph in Washington —at least in the movie.

Therefore, we should enjoy youth while we can and worry less about the future and its reponsibilities.

Nevertheless, we should do nothing in youth that might injure others and leave us with sad memories of our own wrongs.

Also, pitchers are subject to shoulder and elbow injuries.

These sentences may be revised so that they open in a different way.

But Mr. Smith finally made justice triumph in Washington—at least in the movie.

26b

/ ,

The however *that originally began this sentence has been changed to the shorter conjunction* but.

We should, therefore, enjoy youth while we can and worry less about the future and its responsibilities.
Therefore here *has been moved to a later position in the sentence.*

We should nevertheless do nothing in youth that might injure others and leave us with sad memories of our own wrongs.
The nevertheless *has been moved to a later position in the sentence.*

Pitchers are also subject to shoulder and elbow injuries.
The also *is moved to another position.*

The reason for not beginning a sentence with these transitional adverbs is that they are often weaker than another kind of beginning. The subject of a sentence, for example, is usually more vivid than a transitional adverb; if that is so, it is better to begin the sentence with the subject.

Other kinds of one-word adverbs regularly begin sentences, and they are frequently not set off by commas.

Yesterday I resolved to stop worrying about things I could not help.
Yesterday, the adverb that begins this sentence, is not set off by a comma.

26c
Use commas to set off absolutes.

Absolutes, you have learned, are phrases that combine a noun with a present or past participle and that serve to modify the entire sentence (see 5d-1). They usually appear at the beginning of the sentence or clause of which they are a part, but they may also come in the middle or at the end.

The bridge being built, the British set out to destroy it.
The absolute phrase, in italics, modifies the clause the British set out to destroy it.

The snake slithered through the tall grass, the sunlight shining now and then on its green skin, its forked tongue feeling its way, its body bending like a ribbon.
Three absolutes end this sentence. Each is set off by a comma.

26d

Use commas to set off participial modifiers at the end of a sentence.

Participial phrases modifying the subject may come at the end of a sentence. They are set off by commas.

> They toiled all night on the engine, grinding and adjusting the valves, polishing the cylinders, cleaning the pistons, replacing the rings, installing a new fuel pump, putting in new spark plugs and points.
> *This sentence ends with a succession of participial modifiers, each modifying the subject* they *and each set off by a comma.*

26e

Use commas whenever you need to separate elements of a sentence that may cause confusion if you do not separate them.

UNCLEAR: Every time John raced small boys could leave him behind.

CLEAR: Every time John raced, small boys could leave him behind.

UNCLEAR: No matter what he did to win her love was impossible.

CLEAR: No matter what he did, to win her love was impossible.

Exercise 26.1 Put commas wherever they are needed in the following sentences.

1. Many young people want to write fiction but they do not see that any kind of writing is an art.
2. The plane having left we had to take the bus to New York.
3. Although you need to know grammar exercises in grammar alone will not help you write well unless you also read.
4. Nevertheless Greek wine has become popular in America among non-Greeks and it is often sold in restaurants that do not specialize in Greek food.
5. You can read books or you can live forever in your own small world believing that your ignorance is bliss not knowing how ignorant you are supposing that people are all like you.

6. Strictly speaking there are no rules of grammar but there are conventions that most educated people use and you can violate these conventions only at the cost of making things hard on your readers and making your readers believe that you are ignorant.
7. Pay something if you can but if you cannot go in and enjoy the art anyway.
8. After he had watched television all night long his eyes turned to egg white and his brain became glue.
9. Economic circumstances being what they are a Ph.D. degree is not much help in getting a job.
10. Running hard now she began passing others in the race feeling her second wind feeling strength come back to muscles she had thought ready to die gaining confidence as she lunged forward hearing the cheers of the crowd seeing the finish line coming to meet her.
11. Turning their backs on the medieval scholars in the Renaissance tried to recapture the classical age of Greece and Rome.
12. Serving the rich and the famous cooks can become rich and famous themselves if they develop some new and popular dishes.

26f

Use commas to set off nonrestrictive clauses and phrases.

Nonrestrictive clauses and phrases can be lifted out of the sentences where they appear without changing the primary meaning of the sentences. The commas that set off a nonrestrictive clause or phrase announce that these words provide additional information for the main assertion of the sentence.

> My dog Lady, who treed a cat last week, treed the mail carrier this morning.
> *The nonrestrictive clause* who treed a cat last week *adds information, but the primary assertion of the sentence would be complete without it.*

> On this bright summer day, a day smelling of flowers and radiant with sunshine and cooled by soft winds, my wife and I celebrated our thirtieth wedding anniversary.
> *The appositive phrase* a day smelling of flowers and radiant with sunshine and cooled by soft winds *is set off by commas, since it is nonrestrictive. It adds information to the primary assertion of the sentence, but it could be removed without damaging the fundamental meaning.*

Setting off a phrase or a clause with commas can often change the meaning of a sentence.

The commencement speaker, who was a sleep therapist, spoke for three hours.

The commas make the clause nonrestrictive. There was only one commencement speaker, and that speaker happened to be a sleep therapist. The clause could be removed without damaging the primary assertion of the sentence.

The commencement speaker who was a sleep therapist spoke for three hours.

The absence of commas makes us think that there must have been several commencement speakers. The writer must, in some special way, single out the one who spoke for three hours. By calling the speaker a sleep therapist, the writer says that although there were several speakers, there was only one who was a sleep therapist, and that person was the one who spoke for three hours.

Exercise 26.2   Use commas to set off nonrestrictive clauses and phrases in the following sentences. In some you have a choice. You can make the clause or phrase restrictive by not setting it off with commas. In such cases, discuss the changes in meaning so that you may be clear as to what they are and why they occur. At times you must rely on simple common sense to tell you whether to make the clause restrictive or nonrestrictive.

1. The chain saw which had a two-cycle engine gave him a sense of immense power as he took it in his hand and walked into the woods filled with oaks and maples.
2. Fly-fishing a difficult and sometimes dangerous sport requires much more skill than fishing with worms from a boat on a still lake.
3. The McCormick reaper which was invented by Cyrus Hall McCormick vastly increased wheat production in the nineteenth century.
4. Farmers who are by profession often isolated and independent have never been drawn in large groups to communism, but they have been attracted by fraternal organizations that have helped them meet together to satisfy social and economic needs.
5. Bats flying mammals found all over the world probably seem odious to many people because they look like mice that fly.
6. Kit Carson who was illiterate became famous in the mid-nineteenth century as a guide and fighting man and made many friends among important people who ran the national government in Washington.
7. Edith Cavell an English nurse in Belgium was shot in 1915 by the Germans as a spy after she helped many British, French, and Belgian soldiers escape from German-occupied Belgium into neutral Holland.

26f

/,\

26g

Use commas to separate items in a series.

A series is a set of nouns, pronouns, adjectives, adverbs, phrases, or clauses that are joined to each other by commas and — usually — a coordinating conjunction.

A Series of Nouns

In 1940, when he became the prime minister, Winston Churchill told the English people that he had nothing to offer them but blood, toil, tears, and sweat.

A Series of Pronouns

He, she, and I all graduated from high school in the same class.

A Series of Adjectives

My teacher's notes were old, yellow, and worn.

A Series of Adverbs

The three outlaws walked slowly, silently, and cautiously into the Sunday school.

A Series of Phrases

The university raised fees, reduced maintenance, fired assistant professors, turned down the heat, and still went bankrupt.

A Series of Clauses

The traffic was heavy, the parking lot was full, and I was late.

26h

As a general rule, use commas to separate two or more adjectives before a noun or a pronoun.

The so-called "rednecks" of the South have been unforgettably evoked by Flannery O'Connor in her hard, tough, shrewd, unnerving stories.

—Robert Coles

But warfare for the Kiowas was preeminently a matter of disposition rather than of survival, and they never understood the grim, unrelenting advance of the U.S. Cavalry.

—N. Scott Momaday

Note that many writers do not use commas to mark off some adjectives that appear before nouns and pronouns, adjectives so closely related to what they modify that the whole phrase seems to stand as one unit.

A good test for whether or not you need a comma is to put a mental *and* between the adjectives. If the *and* fits easily between the adjectives, you may use a comma instead of the *and*. If it seems clumsy to use *and,* you should omit the comma. In the sentence above by Momaday, you could easily say, "They never understood the grim *and* unrelenting advance of the U.S. Cavalry." Because the *and* goes in so easily, you know to use a comma. But see how clumsy it would be to insert *and* between the adjectives in italics below:

Six thin green pines stood against the evening sky.

Adjectives that usually do not require the dividing comma when they appear in a series before nouns and pronouns are those that mention color, size, age, location, or number. But if you mention several different colors or sizes or numbers before your nouns, you should separate the adjectives with commas:

On the last day convertibles were made, the auto assembly line turned out a hundred green, gold, blue, black, silver, and red soft-topped cars.

The and *test works here too. You could write of the green* and *gold* and *blue* and *black* and *silver* and *red cars. Where you can say* and *you may use a comma.*

26i

Use commas to set off parenthetical words and phrases, including the sources of indirect quotations.

To be sure, Johnson was boring.

The class, however, should not have booed him.

It was, one student said, a moment of impolite truth.

The students, nevertheless, refused to apologize.

26j

Use a comma with quotation marks to set off a direct quotation from the clause that names the source of the quotation.

When the source comes before the quotation, the comma goes before the quotation marks, not within them.

She said, "I'm sorry, but all sections are full."

When the quotation comes before the source, the comma goes before the last quotation mark.

"But I have to have this course to graduate," he said.

Often a direct quotation will surround the clause that gives the source. When that happens, the same rules apply: the comma before the source goes before the final quotation mark, and the comma after the source goes before the opening quotation mark.

"A rule is a rule," she said sweetly, "and you will just have to postpone your graduation."

A comma is not used if some other punctuation mark is used within the quotation marks.

"Do you believe in grades?" he asked.

"Believe in them!" she cried. "I've had them."

A comma after the question mark or the exclamation point would be incorrect.

26k

Use the comma in direct address.

I'll say this to you, John, and I sincerely mean it.

Ethel, please bring me the soap.

The writer uses the names of the people addressed in these sentences.

Exercise 26.3   Place commas where they belong in the following sentences.

1. The old gray mare is not the superb creature she used to be says the old song.
2. Three happy young children came to the door shouting "Trick or Treat!"
3. The hospital smelled of wax linen and iodine.
4. She righted the boat ran up the sail grabbed the rudder and flew before the wind.
5. The storm broke suddenly and furiously the lightning crashed from a black sky and the cattle ran off into the dark.
6. "North Dakota is sky prairie wheat and hospitality" she said. "You must go there Charles. You will never see colors so pure land so vast or cities more manageable and clean."
7. The poor the speaker said commit far more violent crimes than do members of the middle class and the saddest thing he thought is that poor people are most likely to kill or maim members of their own families.
8. To be sure violent crime is not limited to the poor.
9. Nevertheless he said the frustrations of poverty often come to the boiling point in assault robbery and murder.
10. He spoke energetically sadly and eloquently.

26l

Use commas to substitute for words in a sentence.

Commas may frequently take the place of the conjunction *and*, and in some constructions, they can take the place of other words as well.

The comma can take the place of *and* in a compound verb.

Power staggers forward, then falls facedown into the dust.

—Philip Caputo

Instead of and *after* forward, *a comma connects* staggers *and* falls, *the compound verb.*

The comma can also take the place of *and* in a series.

The joke was stale, flat, vulgar.

In sentences that express a contrast, the comma can stand for several words.

Lincoln was impressive, not handsome.
Compare: Lincoln was impressive. He was not handsome. The writer of the sentence above leaves out He was *and substitutes a comma.*

She said that her automobile was big, bright, and powerful, not economical.
Compare: She said that her automobile was big, bright, and powerful. She did not say that it was economical.

26m

Use the comma occasionally to give special emphasis to words and phrases, even when the comma is not grammatically necessary.

It seems impossible to get a saint, or a philosopher, or a scientist, to stick to this simple truth.

—D. H. LAWRENCE

The commas after saint, *and* philosopher, *and* scientist *draw attention to the separate items in the series. The series would be correct without the commas.*

He found hamlets of three decaying houses with the corrugated iron of their roofs grinding and clanking in a hot wind, and not a tree for miles.

—WILLIAM GOLDING

The comma after wind *indicates a slight pause for emphasis before the final phrase* and not a tree for miles, *which gives a striking end to the sentence.*

26n

Use commas according to standard practice for places and addresses.

In Cleveland, Ohio, the river sometimes catches fire.
The comma is used to separate the city, Cleveland, *from its state,*

Ohio. *Another comma comes after* Ohio *to set off the state from the rest of the sentence.*

BUT:

He said he would come to Cleveland the next time he wanted a drink of fire water.

When Cleveland *is used by itself in the sentence without its state, it is not set off by commas.*

Commas set off parts of an address both in sentences and in addresses placed on letters and envelopes:

He lived at 1400 Crabgrass Lane, Suburbia, New York.

My address is:

63 Oceanside Drive, Apartment 3

Knoxville, TN 37916

Note that in the address as it would appear on an envelope, a comma does not go at the end of any line, and it does not go between the abbreviation of the state name and the zip code.

26o
Use commas in dates when the month, day, and year are included.

On June 6, 1944, a British and American force invaded France.

British writers and, increasingly, many Americans use a form of the date that does not require a comma.

She graduated from college on 5 June 1980.

26p
Put a comma before the coordinating conjunction in a series.

Human institutions such as marriage, law, and government do not just happen somehow.

—S. I. HAYAKAWA

The comma after law *helps set* law *apart from* government.

Some writers, especially British writers and writers for American newspapers and magazines, do not put a comma before the coordinating conjunction in a series.

Seldom can civil war have been accompanied by so little ill-feeling, so little deliberate cruelty and so much readiness to forgive and forget.

—MARY CLIVE

The comma is omitted after the word cruelty, *the second noun in a series.*

You should use a comma after each item in a series, including the item before the coordinating conjunction.

Exercise 26.4   Use commas correctly in the sentences below.

1. The speaker was rude pompous tiresome.
2. She purchased eggs rolls and butter from a small corner store in Cincinnati Ohio.
3. I shall be thirty on April 7 1987.
4. Dugan takes the motorbike Grady the sedan.
5. Water flows over the rocks then plunges fifty feet to a pond.

26q
Avoid faulty or needless commas.

A comma should not separate a subject from its verb or a verb from its object or complement unless the comma is needed to set off an intervening nonrestrictive clause or phrase.

> **FAULTY:**   John, sold his pet cat to the laboratory.
> *The comma improperly separates the subject,* John, *from the verb,* sold.
>
> John sold his pet, cat to the laboratory.
> *The comma improperly separates the direct object,* pet, *from the objective complement,* cat.
>
> **CORRECT:**   John, who never liked his cat anyway, sold him to the laboratory.
> *The intervening nonrestrictive clause modifies* John *and is set off by commas.*

Prepositional phrases that serve as adjectives are not set off by commas from the noun or pronoun that they modify.

FAULTY: The best part, of the meal, is coffee.
The prepositional phrase of the meal *serves as an adjective modifying the noun* part. *It should not be set off by commas.*

CORRECT: The best part of the meal is coffee.

Prepositional phrases that serve as adverbs are not set off from the rest of the sentence by commas.

FAULTY: He swam, with the current, rather than against it.
The prepositional phrase with the current *serves as an adverb modifying the verb* swam. *It should not be set off by commas.*

CORRECT: He swam with the current rather than against it.

The phrases in a series of prepositional phrases will be set off from each other by commas according to the normal rules for items in a series.

Lincoln expressed his hope that the suffering of the American Civil War would guarantee that government of the people, by the people, and for the people should not perish from the earth.
The prepositional phrases of the people, by the people, *and* for the people *are items in a series, and they are set off from each other by commas. Note, however, that the first phrase in the series — of the people — is not set off by a comma from the noun* government, *which is modified by that phrase and the other phrases.*

Do not divide a compound verb with a comma if the elements of the verb are joined by a coordinating conjunction unless the parts of the verb make a series.

FAULTY: He ran, and walked twenty miles.
In a compound verb of only two parts, ran *and* walked, *a comma should not divide the parts.*

CORRECT: He ran and walked twenty miles.

If the parts of a compound verb form a series, commas set off the parts of the verb.

He ran, walked, and crawled twenty miles.

Do not use a comma after the last item in a series unless the series concludes a clause or a phrase that is set off by commas.

26q

/,\

He loved books, flowers, and people and spent much of his time with all of them.

The series is not part of a clause or phrase set off by commas. Hence, a comma after people *would be incorrect.*

Three "scourges of modern life," as Roberts calls the automobile, the telephone, and the polyester shirt, were unknown little more than a century ago.

The series is part of a nonrestrictive clause, and nonrestrictive clauses are set off by commas. The last word in the series, shirt, *is the last word of the clause; so it is followed by a comma.*

Avoid commas with quotation marks when the effect of the commas would be to create a false parenthesis.

FAULTY: A song called, "Faded Love," made Bob Wills famous.

The commas make the title "Faded Love" seem like a parenthesis, but a parenthesis may be removed from a sentence without damage to the grammar of the sentence. If the title "Faded Love" were removed from this sentence, the grammar and the sense would be damaged. Hence the title should not be set off by commas.

CORRECT: A song called "Faded Love" made Bob Wills famous.

FAULTY: The so-called, Buckley Amendment, made some professors fear to write honest letters of recommendation.

Try to remove the title Buckley Amendment *from the sentence; the sentence will be nonsense.*

CORRECT: The so-called Buckley Amendment made some professors fear to write honest letters of recommendation.

Do not use commas to set off dependent adverbial clauses that come at the end of a sentence. In practice this rule means that you should not use commas before words such as *because, when, since, while, as, neither,* and *either.*

FAULTY: He looked forward every year to June, because he always made a long bike trip as soon as school was out.

The comma before because *incorrectly sets off an adverbial clause.*

CORRECT: He looked forward every year to June because he always made a long bike trip as soon as school was out.

BUT:

Because he always made a long bike trip as soon as school was out, he looked forward every year to June.

When the adverbial clause comes at the beginning of a sentence, it is set off by a comma. See 26b.

FAULTY: She searched for the familiar sights of home, while the plane dipped low toward the runway.

The comma after home *incorrectly sets off an adverbial clause at the end of the sentence.*

Exercise 26.5 Eliminate the unnecessary commas in the following sentences. Be careful! Some of the commas belong where they are. If a sentence is correct as it is written, put a check by it.

1. According to reports coming out of Russia, life there for the average man and woman, in the large cities, is one long round, of corruption, lines, and alcoholism.
2. Democracy, has often been called inefficient, and divisive, since it encourages political argument, and diversity of opinions about art, morals, education, religion, and many other important parts, of life.
3. Thousands of people crowded along the banks of the river, swarmed on the bridges, and cheered their favorites, as the boats in the race swept by.
4. The chill air of autumn, the falling leaves, the weak sunshine all told us that winter was not far away.
5. Mr. Giacometti, opened the doors of his establishment promptly at eight in the morning.
6. The apartment she rented in Omaha, was not far from the railroad museum.
7. It is sometimes not easy to tell, when you have drunk too much beer to drive safely.
8. Since divorce has become as common as it is in American society, more and more children are growing up without the company, of a mother or a father.
9. Many people, just starting careers in business and government, are afraid to express their true opinions, because they are afraid, they may damage their chances for promotion.
10. Central heating in private homes, was once considered a luxury, and with the rising cost of fuel, we may return to those days, since more and more people heat only one or two rooms, and leave the rest of the house cold.

CHAPTER TWENTY-SEVEN

Semicolons

The semicolon is a stronger mark of punctuation than the comma, and it can be used to join sentence elements that cannot be joined by a comma alone. Semicolons can join certain independent clauses and set off elements within a series when there are commas within the elements.

27a

Use a semicolon to join independent clauses, either with or without the help of a coordinating conjunction.

Silence is deep as eternity; speech is shallow as time.

—THOMAS CARLYLE

Before 8000 BC wheat was not the luxuriant plant it is today; it was merely one of many wild grasses that spread throughout the Middle East.

—JACOB BRONOWSKI

In each example, two clauses are closely related to each other—one of the reasons for using the semicolon. Each writer could have separated them with a period, but he chose the semicolon to stress the relation of ideas in the clauses.

In the first draft I had Bigger going smack to the electric chair; but I felt that two murders were enough for one novel.

—RICHARD WRIGHT

The writer could have placed a comma where he put the semicolon, but the semicolon adds emphasis to the second independent clause.

He stayed up all night to study for the exam; he opened the exam booklet to begin and fainted.

His staying up all night long is the implied cause for his fainting just as he began the exam. The semicolon emphasizes the cause-and-effect relation by closely joining the two clauses.

27b

Use a semicolon to join main clauses separated by a conjunctive adverb.

Conjunctive adverbs such as *nevertheless, moreover, then,* and *consequently* are not coordinating conjunctions and cannot join independent clauses (see 17e). Even a comma placed before them cannot give them the grammatical strength to link clauses.

INCORRECT: He had biked 112 miles in ten hours, nevertheless, he now had to do a marathon.

CORRECTED WITH A SEMICOLON: He had biked 112 miles in ten hours; nevertheless, he now had to do a marathon.
A semicolon is necessary before the conjunctive adverb nevertheless *to join the two clauses properly.*

Exercise 27.1 Review the following sentences for the proper use of semicolons. If a sentence is correct as it stands, place a check beside it. Supply semicolons where they are needed. Eliminate semicolons that are incorrectly used.

1. She was unable to keep the appointment; since she was delayed in traffic; because of the wreck.
2. The sun is our most potent source of energy, nevertheless, research in harnessing solar power has gone slowly.
3. The United States and Canada have relatively few varieties of poisonous snakes; but the climate is warm enough to allow many such snakes to flourish should they be accidentally introduced.
4. Western movies once showed hostile Indians attacking covered wagons drawn up in circles on the plains; although no such attack ever occurred in fact.
5. Videocassette recorders allow many people to rent movies on tape and to play them at home through their television sets moreover, the rental fee for the tape is much less than it would cost a family to see a movie in a theater.

27b

;/

6. Nuclear war is a horror that no one wants to imagine; yet imagining it may help us prevent it.
7. November is a month that is much abused and often unfairly so; true, the leaves fall, and cold weather begins; but November gives us three holidays—Election Day, Veterans Day, and Thanksgiving.

27c

Use a semicolon to separate elements in a series when some of those elements contain commas.

They are aware of sunrise, noon and sunset; of the full moon and the new; of equinox and solstice; of spring and summer, autumn and winter.

—ALDOUS HUXLEY

Two of the four elements in the series contain commas; separating the elements with semicolons prevents confusion.

CONFUSING SERIES: The committee included Dr. Curtis Youngblood, the county medical examiner, Robert Collingwood, the director of the bureau's criminal division, and Darcy Coolidge, the chief of police.
Readers of this passage would have trouble deciding how many people they were reading about.

SERIES WITH SEMICOLONS: The committee included Dr. Curtis Youngblood, the county medical examiner; Robert Collingwood, the director of the bureau's criminal division; and Darcy Coolidge, the chief of police.
Now the semicolons show clearly that the name of each man is followed by his title, which serves to identify him. We are clearly dealing with three men and not five or six.

27d

;/

27d

Use a semicolon to separate elements in elliptical constructions where words left out are clearly understood.

In America, traffic problems are caused by cars; in China, by bicycles.
We understand that the words left out would make the sentence read like this: "In America, traffic problems are caused by cars; in China,

traffic problems are caused by bicycles." The semicolon is used as if the missing words were present in the sentence.

27e

Use semicolons to separate elements in reference notes when those notes contain other punctuation marks.

The assignment will be to read Leviticus 21 : 1 – 20; Joshua 5 : 3 – 6; and Isaiah 55 : 1 – 10.

Exercise 27.2   For each set below, write a single sentence using semicolons correctly. Make reference to all the people and identify them by their jobs.

1. Dr. Mary A. Carter is a professor of history. Mr. Glenn G. Swenson is a football coach. Dean Sylvia Paoli was the moderator of the discussion. Dr. Carter and Mr. Swenson debated the place of intercollegiate athletics in education.
2. Ronald Martin is a designer of computers. Elizabeth Ingersol is an architect. Joseph Greenberg is a science teacher in Bradford High School. The three of them led a discussion on the future of home computers in business and in education.

Exercise 27.3   Punctuate the following sentences correctly.

1. Some were satisfied others disgruntled.
2. He needed seven hours of sleep a night she only five.
3. Cancer is more feared heart disease more fatal.
4. In her room there were three pictures in mine one in his none.

Exercise 27.4   Explain the use of the semicolon in each sentence below.

1. It was not in anger she had forsaken him; it was in simple submission to hard reality, to the stern logic of love.

—HENRY JAMES

27e

;/

2. Her presence brought memories of such things as Bourbon roses, rubies and tropical midnight; her moods recalled lotus-eaters and the march in "Athalie"; her motions, the ebb and flow of the sea; her voice, the viola.

—Thomas Hardy

3. The expansion that derives from city import replacing consists specifically of five forms of growth: abruptly enlarged city markets for new and different imports, consisting largely of goods from rural areas and of innovations being produced in other cities; abruptly increased numbers and kinds of jobs in the import-replacing city; new uses of technology, particularly to increase rural productivity; increased transplants of city work into non-urban locations as older, expanding enterprises are crowded out; and the growth of city capital.

—Jane Jacobs

27e

;/

CHAPTER TWENTY-EIGHT

Apostrophes

We use apostrophes to show possession, to indicate omitted letters in words written as contractions, and to form special plurals.

28a

Use an apostrophe to show possession of nouns and of indefinite pronouns. (See 5b-3.)

To indicate ownership — or, in special cases, to show that an entity has a particular attribute, quality, value, or feature — writers can often choose among different forms of the possessive case (see p. 148):

Children's toys could mean:
toys *of children*
toys *for children*
toys *belonging to children*
toys *owned by children*
toys *that children own*

Everybody's dreams could mean:
dreams *of everybody*
dreams *for everybody*
dreams *everybody has*
dreams *belonging to everybody*

Most writers would use the first form above without spelling out one of the full phrases. Without words such as *of, for, belonging to,* and *owned by,* only the apostrophe plus *s* ('s) conveys the intended sense of possession. Writers often use possessive forms even when the concept of possession seems uncertain. In the examples above, *everybody* does not possess *dreams* in the same way that *children* possess *toys*. Also, accepted usage requires apostrophes with concepts of duration and of monetary value:

An *hour's* wait   Two *minutes'* work

A *dime's* worth   Five *dollars'* worth

In these phrases, despite the required possessive forms, hours and dollars do not really possess anything.

Showing possession correctly with apostrophes usually requires two essential elements. Someone or something is the possessor, and someone or something is being possessed. The person or entity that possesses something takes an apostrophe, either along with an *-s* or alone if the word already ends in *-s*.

The person or entity being possessed usually appears just after the word with the apostrophe:

	Possessor	Thing, attribute, quality, value, or feature possessed
the woman's shovel	woman's	shovel
a child's bright smile	child's	bright smile
Juanita's son	Juanita's	son
the robbers' clever plan	robbers'	clever plan
five dollars' worth	dollars'	worth
everyone's plans	everyone's	plans
babies' books	babies'	books

In some instances, the thing possessed precedes the possessor:

The motorcycle is the student's.

Is the tractor Jan Stewart's?

The student possesses the motorcycle; Jan Stewart possesses the tractor; and the possessive forms (the nouns ending in -'s) come after the objects possessed.

In other cases, the sentence may not name the thing possessed, but its identity is clearly understood by the reader.

I saw your cousin at Nicki's.

The object possessed, Nicki's house or place, is implied.

Sometimes we indicate possession by using both the *of* form and an apostrophe plus *s* or a personal possessive pronoun.

a friend of Rocco's

Both Rocco's *and* of *carry the possessive here:* Rocco *is the possessor;* friend *is the entity possessed.*

this dress of Mother's

that child of his

1   Distinguish between plural forms and possessive forms.

Most nouns require -*s* endings to show the plural form: boy/boys; girl/girls; teacher/teachers; song/songs. Possessive forms require the apostrophe plus *s* ('s) ending: boy/boy's; girl/girl's; teacher/teacher's. The possessive form and the plural form are not interchangeable; yet errors involving a confusion of the two often occur.

INCORRECT: The teacher's asked the girl's and boy's for attention.

CORRECT: The teachers asked the girls and boys for attention.

An apostrophe plus *s* at the end of a word makes that word the possessor of something. In the incorrect sentence above, the teacher, the girl, and the boy possess nothing.

Apostrophes occasionally signal plurals, but only in very special cases (see 28c).

Exercise 28.1   Identify each word in the following list as plural or possessive; then use each word correctly in a sentence.

1. a. women   b. women's   c. woman's
2. a. man's   b. men's   c. men
3. a. child's   b. children   c. children's
4. a. cats   b. cat's   c. cats'
5. a. professor's b. professors   c. professors'

Exercise 28.2   In each of the following sentences, underline the word that shows possession and put an X above the word that names the entity possessed. (The entity possessed may be understood but not named.)

1. Plucking feathers on turkeys is not everyone's idea of a good job.
2. If the responsibility is the mayor's, then our citizens' group should push her to act.
3. At Mario's, the waiters serve with elegance; the diner's pleasure is the staff's only concern.
4. She brought me six dollars' worth of flour.
5. They went on a week's vacation together.
6. Gloria's smile welcomes students to the Writing Center.

2 To form a possessive, add an apostrophe plus *s* to a noun or pronoun not already ending in -*s*, whether it is singular or plural.

Noun/pronoun		As a possessive
baby	singular	a baby's smile
men	plural	the men's club
Wanda	singular	Wanda's sundae
hour	singular	an hour's time
anyone	singular	anyone's idea
children	plural	the children's papers

3 Add only an apostrophe (') to words already ending in -*s*, whether those words are singular or plural.

Word (-*s* ending)		Word used as a possessive
babies	plural	the babies' smiles
Luis	singular	Luis' ring
companies	plural	the companies' employees
Dickens	singular	Dickens' novels
hours	plural	three hours' time

Many writers add both an apostrophe and a final *s* to one-syllable singular nouns already ending in -*s*, especially if the word following the possessive begins with a vowel sound.

Keats's *a*rt, James's *a*dventure

452   Understanding Punctuation

However, the addition of the apostrophe alone is increasingly acceptable.

Note that proper names of geographic locations, associations, organizations, and so forth, sometimes exclude apostrophes:

Kings Point, Veterans Highway

4　**For hyphenated words and compound words and word groups, add an apostrophe plus *s* to the last word only.**

my father-in-law's job

the editor-in-chief's responsibilities

the union leader's supporters

5　**To express joint ownership by two or more people, use the possessive form for the last name only; to express individual ownership, use the possessive form for each name.**

Felicia and Elias' house
The two own the house together.

McGraw-Hill's book catalog

Felicia's and Elias' houses
Each one owns a house; notice that houses *is plural.*

the city's and the state's finances

Exercise 28.3　Change each word in parentheses into the correct possessive form by adding an apostrophe or an apostrophe plus *s*. A word may require a plural form before you change it to a possessive.

Example

The two (woman) <u>women's</u> cars blocked the driveway.

1. (Mr. Cass) _____ contribution to the primaries brought praise from the (governor) _____ reelection committee.
2. The (assistant editor) _____ idea was to run three (student) _____ biographies in each issue.
3. The (Lady) _____ Auxiliary League drew hundreds to its Fourth of July picnic; (everyone) _____ praise meant that the tradition would continue next year.
4. In (Dickens) _____ novel *Great Expectations*, (Pip) _____ adventures hold every (reader) _____ attention.

28a

'✓'

Exercise 28.4 Change the structures that show ownership to possessive forms that use apostrophes.

Example

The announcement of the Secretary of State

The Secretary of State's announcement

1. the car of Kim and Thai
2. a business belonging to my brother-in-law
3. the houses of Mr. Garcia and Mr. Youngblood
4. the smile of Doris
5. the value of three dollars
6. a term of six months

28b

Use an apostrophe to indicate letters or numbers left out of contractions, or letters omitted from words to show regional pronunciation.

In a contraction—a shortened word or group of words formed by omitting some letters or sounds—use an apostrophe in place of the omissions.

it's	(for *it is* or *it has*)
weren't	(for *were not*)
here's	(for *here is*)
comin'	(for *coming*)

Sometimes we abbreviate the numbers of years, using the apostrophe. For example, we say, "The '50s were a decade of relative calm; the '60s were much more turbulent." But it is usually better to spell these digits out when they refer to years. "Many claim that the fifties were much more turbulent than we remember and that the sixties only continued trends begun a decade earlier."

28c

Use an apostrophe plus *s* ('s) to show plurals of letters, numbers, and words stressed as words rather than for the meaning they convey.

Committee has two *m*'s, two *t*'s, and two *e*'s.
The letters are italicized, but not the final 's. See 34c.

There are twelve *no*'s in the first paragraph.

He makes his 2's look like 5's.

When no confusion results, it is equally acceptable to eliminate the apostrophe in these plurals.

1980's   **OR**   1980s

2s and 3s

Bs, Cs, and Ds
But to prevent confusion with the word as, *write the plural of* A *as* A's.

28d

To show possession for personal and relative pronouns and for the pronoun *it*, use the special possessive forms, which never require apostrophes (my/mine, your/yours, his, her/hers, our/ours, their/theirs, whose, and its).

His cooking won a prize.

Its fur was shedding.

They knew *our* secret.

Is he a friend of *yours?*

The rake is *hers.*

When an apostrophe appears with an *s* in a pronoun, the apostrophe probably marks omissions in a contraction.

It's too hot.
It's = It + is

Who's there?
Who's = Who + is

If you're awake, please call.
you're = you + are

Exercise 28.5 Correct any words in italics either by removing incorrectly used apostrophes or by adding apostrophes where they belong. Some words are correct and require no change.

1. *Iris* cat lost *its* way, but one *neighbors* boys helped her find it.
2. There *wasnt* enough attention placed on writing *skills'* in college English curricula in the *60s.*
3. In the word *occurrence,* the two *cs* and two *rs* confuse many grade school *students'.*
4. If the *ideas'* are *hers',* *it's* wise to give her credit for them.
5. Many *childrens parents'* bought these *dolls* before the *companies* recalled them at the *governments* request.

CHAPTER TWENTY-NINE

Quotation Marks

Quotation marks (" ") always work in pairs. They are used to enclose words, phrases, and sentences that are quoted directly. Titles of short works like poems, articles, songs, and short stories, when cited with other words, also require quotation marks, as do some words and phrases that you wish to use in a special sense.

29a
Use quotation marks to enclose direct quotations.

In a *direct quotation* you repeat the exact words of a speaker or of a text. Direct quotations from written material may be whole sentences or significant words or phrases taken from other sentences.

James Baldwin wrote of his experience of whites during his childhood, "The only white people who came to our house were welfare workers and bill collectors."

James Baldwin wrote that the only white visitors he saw in his home as a child were "welfare workers and bill collectors."

The "only" whites who visited Baldwin's childhood home, he wrote much later on, came to distribute welfare or to collect bills.

The following diagrams will help you see how direct quotations are used and punctuated in sentences.

Sentence: Quoted Words First

Quotation mark.—Capital letter.

"The first thing that strikes one about Plath's journals is what

End quotation mark.   End mark.

they leave out," writes Katha Pollitt in *The Atlantic*.

Comma inside quote.   Small letter.

Sentence: Quoted Words Last

Comma.

Small letter.   Capital letter.

In *The Atlantic* Katha Pollitt writes, "The first thing that

Quotation marks.

strikes one about Plath's journals is what they leave out."

End mark inside quote.

Sentence: Quoted Words Interrupted

Quotation mark.

Quotation mark.   Comma inside quote.

Capital letter.   Small letter.

"The first thing that strikes one about Plath's journals," writes

Quotation mark.   End mark inside quote.

Katha Pollitt in *The Atlantic*, "is what they leave out."

Comma.   Small letter.   Quotation mark.

In writing dialogue, use quotation marks to enclose everything a speaker says. When one person continues speaking, use quotation marks again if the person's quoted sentence is interrupted.

> "I don't know what you're talking about," he said. "I did listen to everything you told me."
> "You listened," she said, "but you did not try to understand."

In an *indirect quotation,* you paraphrase. That is, you express in your own words the meaning of someone else's words. Indirect quotations do not require quotation marks.

DIRECT QUOTATION

> Casey said, "What I like best about driving the locomotive is blowing the whistle."

INDIRECT QUOTATION

Casey confessed that he enjoyed blowing the whistle more than anything else he did as a locomotive engineer.

DIRECT QUOTATION

Odette asked me, "May I please borrow your chain saw?"

INDIRECT QUOTATION

Odette asked if she could borrow my chain saw.

When you quote more than five lines, type them double-spaced and set every line off by a five-space indentation from the left margin. Triple-space above and below the quotation. *Be sure that you indent every line in a block quotation.*

Block quotations are *not* set off by quotation marks. If the block includes a direct quotation, however, use quotation marks as they are found in the text. The example that follows shows you how to do this.

Some of the most interesting pages in Schorske's book describe how Sigmund Freud arrived at psychoanalysis and the interpretation of dreams and so made a revolution in our understanding of how the mind works. But as Schorske points out, the young Freud's first passion was not the working of the mind but classical archeology:

> He consumed with avidity Jakob Burckhardt's newly published *History of Greek Culture,* so rich in materials on primitive myth and religion. He read with envy the biography of Heinrich Schliemann, who fulfilled a childhood wish by his discovery of Troy. Freud began the famous collection of ancient artifacts which were soon to grace his office in the Berggasse. And he cultivated a new friendship in the Viennese professional elite—especially rare in those days of withdrawal—with Emanuel Loewy, a professor of archeology. "He keeps me up till three o'clock in the morning," Freud wrote appreciatively to Fliess. "He tells me about Rome."
>
> —CARL SCHORSKE

Note the quotation marks for material quoted within the block quotation.

Use block quotations sparingly. They cut down on the readability of your papers. When you are tempted to use long block quotations, try to paraphrase the material, and include it in your text, giving proper credit to your sources (see 37b, c, and d).

Short quotations from poetry may be run into your text, much like any other short quotation. Line breaks are usually shown with a slash.

> In the nineteenth century Wordsworth wrote of the weary acquisitiveness of our modern age: "The world is too much with us; late and soon,/Getting and spending, we lay waste our powers:/Little we see in nature that is ours."

Longer verse quotations are indented block-style like long quotations from prose. If you cannot get an entire line of poetry on a single line of your typescript, you may put the end of the line under your typed line near the right margin of your paper.

> Ah, what can ever be more stately and admirable to me
> than mast-hemmed Manhattan?
> River and sunset and scalop-edg'd waves of flood tide?
> The sea-gulls oscillating their bodies, the hay-boat in the twilight,
> and the belated lighter?
> What gods can exceed those that clasp me by the hand, and with
> voices
> I love call me promptly and loudly by my nighest name
> as I approach?
> —Walt Whitman

In American practice, a pair of single quotation marks (made with the apostrophe on the typewriter) is used to set off quotations within quotations.

> What happened when the faculty demanded an investigation of dishonest recruiting practices in the athletic department? The president of the university said, "I know you're saying to me, 'We want an honest football team.' But I'm telling you this: 'I want a winning football team.'"

British practice with quotation marks differs from American practice. Commonwealth countries usually enclose direct quotations within single quotation marks and use double marks to enclose quotations within quotations. Because many English books are now being reproduced photographically in America, you may see both systems. In your own writing, use the American system.

29b

Learn the conventional use of other punctuation with quotation marks.

A comma or period coming at the end of a quotation is always set before the last quotation mark. A question mark is set before the last quotation mark if the quotation itself asks a question. Punctuation marks that come before the quoted material are not included within quotation marks.

> "The worst movie I've ever seen is *Jaws*," he said.
>
> "How can you say that?" she asked. "I loved *Jaws*."
>
> "How can I say that?" he said. "I'll tell you how I can say that; I can say that because I saw it eight times!"
>
> She said, "I think *Jaws II* is even worse."
>
> "Yes," he replied, "I agree. I saw it only four times."

Standard American practice is to place the period or the exclamation point before the final quotation mark even when the quotation is only one or two words long. The question mark is placed after the last quotation mark if the quoted material is not itself in the form of a question.

> He had what he called his "special reasons."
>
> Why did he name his car "Buck"?
>
> "Because," she said, "people pass it all the time."

Standard American practice is to put colons and semicolons after the final quotation mark.

> "I think the jokes in this book are terrible"; she made the remark at the top of her voice, and since I wrote the book, I was hurt.
>
> Dean Wilcox cited the items he called his "daily delights": a free parking place for his scooter at the faculty club, a special table in the club itself, and friends to laugh with after a day's work.

Exercise 29.1 Punctuate correctly the following sentences. Some sentences require no additional punctuation.

1. I want you to write a book Ted told me one night.
2. He said Give me a manuscript, and I'll get it published
3. She told me that she would rather play tennis than eat
4. He said to his friend I bought the car on credit
5. The wind is rising she shouted Make the boats secure The hurricane is coming

6. They told me that the finance company would repossess my type-writer tomorrow, but I said It doesn't matter at all since I'm going to finish my novel tonight
7. These were what Mark called his showcase talents: friendliness, intelligence, good looks, and humility
8. We asked our secretary to account for the absence of the treasurer, and these were his exact words I'm afraid she's run off with all our money since she called me last night and said Jack, I don't think the club can ever forgive me But who knows Jack said Maybe she only meant that she had lost the account book

29c

Use quotation marks for titles of essays or chapters or other sections that occur within books or periodicals.

"How to Die: The Example of Samuel Johnson" is the title of a recent article in *The Sewanee Review.*

The chapter was called "Another Question of Location."

Note that the titles of songs and short poems are usually put in quotation marks. Titles of long poems are put in italics. In manuscripts, titles of long poems are underlined (see 34a).

Robert Herrick wrote the poem "Upon Julia's Clothes."

George Gordon Noel, Lord Byron, wrote *Childe Harold's Pilgrimage.*

29d

Use quotation marks to show that someone else has used a word or phrase in a special way, one that you or the general public may not use or agree with completely.

The "workers' paradise" of Stalinist Russia turned out to be a combination of slums, shortages, secret police, and slave-labor camps.

George had the "privilege" of working his way through school by cleaning bathrooms.

Quotation marks can let your readers know that a group or a person you are writing about uses words in a special sense.

For them, getting "saved" is clearly only the first step.
— Frances Fitzgerald

The "core curriculum" has now been in effect for several years.

29e

Avoid apologetic quotation marks.

Experienced writers rarely enclose slang or clichés in quotation marks, but inexperienced writers sometimes do so as if to show that such words or expressions do not belong in their writing. They believe that they are somehow excused if they show readers that they know better. In fact, such quotation marks only mark you as inexperienced and do not contribute to good prose.

People in California are "laid back."

You can accomplish great things only if you "keep your nose to the grindstone."

I thought he was "cute."

When you are tempted to use apologetic quotation marks, take time to think of a better way of expressing yourself.

People in California pride themselves in living for pleasure without taking anything too seriously.

You can accomplish great things only if you pay attention to what you are doing.

I thought he was attractive.

Exercise 29.2   In some of the following sentences, quotation marks are incorrectly used. Correct any incorrect usages, and put a check by those sentences where the quotation marks are used in the right way.

1. "Traditional Principles of Rhetoric" is the title of a chapter in Kenneth Burke's book *A Rhetoric of Motives.*
2. "Gee whiz," he said, "I could rap with you all night long."
3. When I waited to do my term paper until the night before it was due, I was really "up the creek without a paddle."
4. "Sweet Baby James" is the title of a song James Taylor sings.

5. I wanted to know if I could bring the "kids" to the party.
6. She was "put off" by my reaction to her paper.
7. "To His Coy Mistress" is a celebrated poem by Andrew Marvell.
8. Most "utopian" communities emphasize rigid conformity, hard work, and puritanical ethics.
9. "Lochinvar" is a rousing poem by Sir Walter Scott.
10. The word "trees" can be both a noun and a verb.
11. Most of the students here are "laid back" and "cool," but some of them are "nerds."

CHAPTER THIRTY

Other Marks of Punctuation

30a

Use the dash to set off words, phrases, and sometimes whole sentences so that they receive special emphasis.

Think of the dash as a very strong pause intended to give a special emphasis to what follows—and sometimes to what comes immediately before.

> A Wisconsin man traveling on horseback had the lower parts of his boots—brand-new ones, be it noted—eaten by wolves, but managed to save his toes.
>
> —Richard Erdoes

> I think this is the most extraordinary collection of human talent, of human knowledge, that has ever been gathered at the White House —with the possible exception of when Thomas Jefferson dined alone.
>
> —John F. Kennedy

On the typewriter the dash is made with *two* unspaced hyphens, and there is no space between the dash and the words on each side of it. Handwritten and typeset dashes are single, unbroken lines about as wide as a capital **M**.

```
Beer, cheese, and brevity--these are the marks of
a good study session in the dorm.
```

Often the dash is used to set off nouns placed for special emphasis at the beginning of a sentence and then summarized by a pronoun after the dash, as you see in the sentence above. The dash can sometimes set off an independent clause within a sentence. In such sentences, the content of the set-off independent clause is not essential to the main assertion of the sentence. It is added information.

> Grant had three divisions in line—reinforcements came up the Cumberland in transports, just behind Andrew Foote's gunboats—and he had them strung out in a long semicircle facing the Confederate trenches.
>
> —Bruce Catton
>
> *The pair of dashes sets off the independent clause starting with the word* reinforcements *and ending with the word* gunboats. *The main sentence can stand without this inserted clause, which adds interesting but nonessential information.*

Remember that overuse of the dash can distract your readers. You should use the dash only for special emphasis; if you try to emphasize everything, your readers will find the tactic tedious.

30b

Use the colon to link independent clauses, to introduce direct quotations and lists, and to set off words and phrases at the end of a sentence. Use the colon also as standard punctuation for Bible verses and for other specialized forms.

The colon links independent clauses when you want to emphasize the clause that follows the colon:

> Women in Switzerland have an overwhelming political disadvantage: they cannot vote.
>
> *Some writers might use a semicolon here instead of the colon. But the colon indicates that the second clause is an explanation of the first, a statement that makes the first clause more explicit and clear.*

You can use a colon to introduce a direct quotation:

> "Don't speak of it," she said in a reciting voice and choosing her words sadly and carefully: "It was a stroke."
>
> —V. S. Pritchett
>
> *The colon before* It was a stroke *emphasizes the close relation between the two quotations and the long clause between them.*

Later she recalled the hours Faulkner spent helping her to recover hope: "He kept me alive," she said.

—DAVID MINTER

A colon is more formal than a comma. The use of the colon before this direct quotation separates the independent clauses. The quotation amplifies the first clause.

To introduce block quotations, you should use a colon:

Dickens had a contempt for lazy people. His heroes and his heroines are always industrious, always active, always in motion. His worst characters are those who pretend to do honest labor and don't, or those who lie about, waiting for others to wait on them. Here is the way he introduces Mrs. Witterly in *Nicholas Nickleby:*

> The lady had an air of sweet insipidity, and a face of engaging paleness; there was a faded look about her, and about the furniture, and about the house altogether. She was reclining on the sofa in such a very unstudied attitude that she might have been taken for an actress all ready for the first scene in a ballet, and only waiting for the drop curtain to go up.

Colons also serve to introduce itemized lists:

During its first four years the Virginia venture had failed to meet three basic needs: political stability, economic prosperity, and peaceful Indian relations.

—ALDEN T. VAUGHAN

The words three basic needs *imply itemization, and the colon precedes the listing that follows.*

The colon *cannot* be used to introduce a simple series.

INCORRECT: During its first four years the Virginia venture had failed to meet: political stability, economic prosperity, and peaceful Indian relations.
The colon cannot interrupt an independent clause or a sentence. The colon used before a list must follow an independent clause. If you replace the colon with a period and eliminate the following list, the sentence should still make grammatical sense.

CORRECT: During its first four years the Virginia venture had failed to meet three basic needs.
The list, including the words political stability, economic prosperity, and peaceful Indian relations, *has been eliminated. The remaining sentence is grammatically complete.*

30b

:

Note that some writers still follow the old custom of capitalizing the first letter of the first word after a colon if a complete sentence follows the colon.

He is kind: Innumerable unknowns in dire need have received financial help from Sinatra.

—ISOBEL SILDEN

But most writers capitalize the first letter in the word following the colon only when they are writing titles. (A proper noun is, of course, capitalized wherever it appears. See 32b.)

Doing Without: Meeting the Energy Crisis in the 1980s

Colons intervene between Bible chapters and verses:

Young writers should take Proverbs 12:1 as a motto.

To indicate the time of day, use a colon between the hour and the minutes:

He woke up at 6:30 in the morning.

Colons follow salutations in business letters:

Dear Mr. Bush:

30c

Use parentheses to set off information that breaks the flow of your thought within a sentence or a paragraph.

[ ]

Parentheses enclose material that is not as important as material set off by commas or dashes.

The first money you get for a book will probably be your advance; as a rule, half of that is paid when you sign your contract (or as soon thereafter as the legal department and the accounting department fill out the appropriate forms), and the other half comes due when you deliver a satisfactory manuscript.

—JUDITH APPLEBAUM and NANCY EVANS

At another barrier a seaman held back Kathy Gilnagh, Kate Mullins, and Kate Murphy. (On the *Titanic* everyone seemed to be named Katherine.)

—WALTER LORD

Note that when parentheses enclose a whole sentence, a period comes after the sentence but before the final parenthesis, as in the example above. A sentence that appears within parentheses *within a sentence* is neither capitalized nor closed with a period.

> John Henry (he was the man with the forty-pound hammer) was a hero to miners fearing the loss of their jobs to machines.

But a question mark or an exclamation point may follow a parenthetical sentence within a sentence.

> John Henry (did he really swing a forty-pound hammer?) was a hero to miners fearing the loss of their jobs to machines.

> John Henry (he swung a forty-pound hammer!) was a hero to miners fearing the loss of their jobs to machines.

Parentheses are used to enclose many numbers within a text. In some forms of annotation (see 37e), parentheses enclose page numbers of a book referred to throughout the paper.

> Stevens writes that the demands of their offices turn the best university presidents into machines (43).

> Carmichael says that the argument Stevens makes is nonsense because (1) university presidents don't work as well as machines, (2) university presidents don't do any real work at all, and (3) universities would be better off if they were run by faculty committees.

Note that forcing readers to wade through many parenthetical numbers is usually distracting. In the example above, the numbers within parentheses could be left out, and the statements could be set off by commas, making the passage more readable.

30d

30d
Use brackets to set off material within quoted matter that is not part of the quotation.

Samuel Eliot Morison has written, "This passage has attracted a good deal of scorn to the Florentine mariner [Verrazzano], but without justice."

In this sentence, a writer is quoting Morison. But the sentence from Morison does not include the name of the "Florentine mariner." The writer adds the name — Verrazzano — but places it in brackets so readers will know the identity of the mariner Morison is talking about.

Sometimes material in brackets provides an explanation or a correction for something that is quoted.

Vasco da Gama's man wrote in 1487, "The body of the church [it was not a church but a Hindu shrine] is as large as a monastery."
The brackets in this example correct a mistake made by one of the early sailors who went to India with Vasco da Gama. The material within the brackets comes from the writer of the essay, who has quoted the report made by a member of da Gama's crew. If that material were in parentheses, readers might think that it was in the original source, and they would be confused.

Brackets are also used when you must change a quotation slightly to make it fit the style or grammar of your own sentence.

A Source to be Quoted

I went back to the country and farmed a crop of tobacco with my dad that next year. For all the work I put in I didn't make half as much as I'd been making at the factory, so, after market closed, I wandered back to town and started looking for another job.

— Ann Banks

The Source Quoted in a Paper

30d

[ ]

Jim Wells came off the farm to work in a cigarette factory in North Carolina during the depression. He was fired because he hit a foreman who mistreated him, and, he said, "I went back to the country and farmed a crop of tobacco with my dad that next year [but] I didn't make half as much as I'd been making at the factory." The only thing he could do was to go back to the city and look for another job.
The bracketed word but *eliminates the need for an ellipsis (three spaced periods), although several words,* For all the work I put in, *have been cut out of the quotation. The brackets show that the writer has changed the quotation to fit the style of the paper that uses the material.*

Brackets may enclose the word *sic* after a piece of correctly quoted information that a reader might believe had slipped into the text erroneously.

The dean said, "Those kids is [*sic*] going to get kicked out of school for saying I don't know no [*sic*] grammar."

The sic *in brackets shows that the dean did, in fact, make these errors in grammar.*

Brackets are frequently used, as they are in this book, to enclose editorial notes, page numbers, or other information inserted in a text. In formal essays they should be used sparingly.

30e

As a rule, use the slash only to divide lines of poetry written as a quotation within a sentence (see 29a).

Sophocles wrote of the uncertainty of human knowledge: "No man can judge that rough unknown or trust in second sight/For wisdom changes hands among the wise."

Occasionally the slash is used to show that something happened over a couple of calendar years.

The book sold well in 1976/77.

But it is usually better to write this:

The book sold well in 1976 and 1977.

The slash is sometimes used nowadays to substitute for the conjunction *or.*

The course was offered credit/noncredit.

The winner will be chosen by lot, and he/she will drive a new car home.

Most writers, however, consider such usage awkward. It is usually better to rephrase the sentence.

Students who took the course received no grades. If they satisfied the requirements, they got credit; if they did not, they received no penalty.

The winner, to be chosen by lot, will drive a new car home.

(For more on he/she, his/her, see Chapter 15, "Sexist Language.")

30f

Use three spaced periods, called an *ellipsis*, to show that words have been omitted from quotations.

To shorten a passage you are quoting, you may choose to leave out some words in the quotation. To show readers that you have left out some words, use ellipsis marks.

QUOTATION

"In the nineteenth century, railroads, lacing their way across continents, reaching into the heart of every major city in Europe and America, and bringing a new romance to travel, added to the unity of nations and fueled the nationalist fires already set burning by the French Revolution and the wars of Napoleon."

QUOTATION USED WITH ELLIPSIS MARKS

In his account of nineteenth-century society, Wilkins credited railroad building with increasing nationalism when he wrote that "railroads . . . added to the unity of nations and fueled the nationalist fires already set burning by the French Revolution and the wars of Napoleon."
The ellipsis shows that the second writer has left some words out of the original source.

Most writers do not use ellipsis marks to indicate that words have been left out at the beginning or the end of a quotation. Academic writers occasionally use ellipsis marks to show omissions at the beginning or at the end of quotations, but such usage is rare. The primary function of the ellipsis is to show that something has been left out of the middle of a quotation.

Ellipsis marks may be used at the end of a sentence if you mean to leave a thought hanging, either in your own prose or in something you are quoting. Such a usage suggests that you are not sure how the thought might be ended.

In the following passage, the writer — Dick Gregory — reports some thoughts he was having as a child.

Oh God, I'm scared. I wish I could die right now with the feeling I have because I know Momma's going to make me mad and I'm going to make her mad, and me and Presley's gonna fight. . . . "Richard, you get in here and put your coat on. Get in here or I'll whip you."

Gregory is saying that the consequences of all this are so unpredicta-
ble that he cannot even try to state them. Therefore, he ends his
sentence with ellipsis marks.

You should always use ellipsis marks honestly. That is, you should
never distort a writer's meaning by leaving out words in the material you
quote. The ellipsis should serve *only* as a means of shortening a quotation,
never as a device for changing its fundamental meaning or for creating
emphasis where none exists in the original.

Exercise 30.1

1. Write three sentences using the dash and three using parentheses.
   What difference, if any, do you find in the effects of using the two
   punctuation marks?
2. Go to the periodical reading room of your library, and look at *Time,*
   Newsweek, Sports Illustrated, Popular Mechanics, or *The New York*
   Times Magazine. Find sentences that use parentheses and sentences
   that use the dash. Copy as many of them down as you can find. What
   can you say about how these punctuation marks are used?
3. Write a paragraph in which you quote something and insert material
   within brackets in the quotation. Explain to your class what you have
   done.

Exercise 30.2   Explain the use of the punctuation marks in color in
each of the following examples. Is the punctuation appropriate to the
meaning? What other punctuation might serve as an alternative?

1. An air-cooled engine requires no antifreeze in winter (an advantage),
   but it must be fairly small for the cooling to work (a disadvantage).
2. Diesel engines are fuel-efficient and durable — but they are expensive
   to manufacture.
3. The Ford Motor Company paid workers five dollars a day (people said
   Henry Ford was undermining capitalism by paying so much) to build
   the Model T on assembly lines before World War I.
4. The rotary gasoline engine (the first popular model sold in the United
   States was the Japanese Mazda) was smooth, quiet, and durable, but it
   burned 15 percent more fuel than conventional engines — a reason
   for its swift demise.
5. Mechanical automobile brakes operated with springs, levers, and the
   physical strength of the driver — a strength that might not be sufficient to stop a car hurtling down the highway at forty miles per hour.
6. A high administration official said today, "All we can do now [to decrease the consumption of oil in the United States] is to let prices rise
   until it hurts to fill a gas tank."

7. Mr. Hatch told reporters, "When you see an antique car rolling down the interstate, it looks like a lot of fun [but] you are in fact looking at lethal danger."
8. Leslie Fiedler wrote, "The novel proper could not be launched until . . . the Seducer and the Pure Maiden were brought face to face in a ritual combat designed to end in marriage or death; the form and its mythology were born together, in the works of Samuel Richardson."

30g

Use the hyphen to divide a word at the end of a line only when such division is absolutely necessary. (See 31e for the use of hyphens to form compound words.)

Try to avoid breaking words at the ends of lines because such divisions slow your readers down. Never divide the last word on a page. Leave yourself wide margins and you will rarely have to divide a word.

When you must break a word, put a hyphen at the end of the first line only, and not at the start of the next line. Although the general rule is to divide words only between syllables, not every word can be divided according to this rule. If you are unsure about how to break a word into syllables, consult your dictionary (see 16b). The following pointers will help you to divide words correctly.

1. Never divide one-syllable words.

INCORRECT

None of us at the dean's luncheon thought that the dean would arrive in tattered jeans and a torn undershirt.

CORRECT

None of us at the dean's luncheon thought that the dean would arrive in tattered jeans and a torn undershirt.

None of us at the dean's luncheon thought that the dean would arrive in tattered jeans and a torn undershirt.

The one-syllable word would *has no natural break and cannot be divided. Fit the word in on the end of the first line, or write the entire word at the beginning of the second line.*

2. Never divide a word if the division leaves only one letter at the end of a line or only one or two letters at the beginning of a line. Avoid breaking words like *hap·py, could·n't, read·er, o·pen, light·ly, hat·ed,* and so on.

Naomi Lee Fong, who graduates today, never felt so happy in her life before.

Naomi Lee Fong, who graduates today, never felt so happy
in her life before.

Naomi Lee Fong, who graduates today, never felt so
happy in her life before.

3. Divide compound words into the words that make them up, or at the hyphen if the word contains a hyphen. Compound words like *hardworking, rattlesnake, bookcases,* and *paperwork* should be broken only between the words that form them: *hard-working, rattle-snake, book-cases, paper-work.* Compound words that already have hyphens, like *brother-in-law, self-denial, ex-convict,* and *anti-Semitic,* are broken after the hyphens only.

She loves being a detective, but she hates the paperwork.

30g

-

She loves being a detective, but she hates the paperwork.

I gave my old fishing rod to my brother-in-law, and he will sell it at his yard sale.

I gave my old fishing rod to my brother-
in-law, and he will sell it at his yard sale.

4. When two consonants come between vowels in a word you are
   dividing, make the split between the two consonants. Do not split
   the two consonants if the division does not reflect pronunciation.
   In the following words, for example, make the split where the dot
   appears:

> ter·ror   run·ning
> shel·ter   bril·liant

However in a word like *respire,* you would have to divide the
word after the prefix *re* and not between the *s* and the *p*, because
the word is pronounced *re·spire* and not *res·pire.*

5. Avoid confusing word divisions. Sometimes part of a divided
   word forms a shorter word that can mislead your reader. In such
   cases, write the complete word or break the word where it will
   not cause confusion. The following examples show some misleading divisions and some possible alternatives.

Divisions to avoid	Possible alternatives
a-toll	atoll
at-tire	attire
bar-row	barrow
fat-uous	fatuous
his-torian	histor-ian
im-pugn	impugn
mud-dled	muddled
pig-mentation	pigmen-tation, pigmenta-tion

30g

-

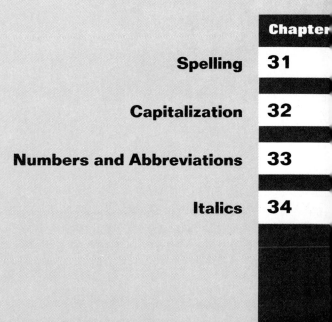

Part 6
PART SIX
UNDERSTANDING MECHANICS

	Chapter
Spelling	31
Capitalization	32
Numbers and Abbreviations	33
Italics	34

CHAPTER THIRTY-ONE

Spelling

Spelling is one of the chief signs of literacy. If you misspell words, your readers may understand you, but they will be less likely to take your thoughts seriously.

Teachers sometimes ignore misspellings, and even when they mark them, they may not count off for them. After all, your teacher has several months to get to know you and your work, and over a long period, misspelling may seem less important than the good things you do in a class and in your writing.

But in the public world of business and the professions, the people you write to are often in a hurry; they may not know you; and they have to read and judge your work quickly. If you misspell several words in a letter of application for a job, your reader may assume that you are a careless person or that you do not take your application seriously. There may be dozens of candidates for the same opening, and an application with misspellings gives the reader an excuse to reject it quickly. If you are writing a memo to your boss or to a committee, misspelled words in your memo may give the impression that your thoughts are as slapdash as your writing. In short, frequent or even occasional misspellings in your writing can make people believe that you are careless or ignorant, and if that happens, you will have to work twice as hard to make them take you and your thoughts seriously.

Here are some rules to help you toward better spelling. The rest of this chapter on spelling will expand on these rules and will give you some tips to make following them easier.

> Make yourself realize the importance of good spelling, and resolve to spell correctly.

2. Write down in a notebook all the words you misspell. Writing the word over and over again when you realize you have made a mistake will help fix the correct spelling in your mind and in your fingers. Good spelling is a habit of both mind and hand.

3. Try to group your errors. Misspellings often fall into patterns — errors with prefixes, with suffixes, with plurals, and so on.

4. Pronounce words carefully. Many people misspell words because they pronounce them incorrectly.

5. Learn the rules that generally hold for spelling, and learn the exceptions to those rules. Most of the rules have only a few exceptions, and by learning these words, you will make the rules themselves stick better in your mind.

6. Proofread your writing carefully. Misspellings creep into the prose of the best of writers when they are in a hurry, when they are thinking ahead to their next thought as they write something down, or when they do not wish to break their train of thought to look up a troublesome word.

7. Use your dictionary frequently when you proofread your work. Whenever you doubt the correctness of a word you have spelled, look it up. Writing continually and using a dictionary continually are two excellent ways to become a good speller.

31a
Read and pronounce words carefully.

Some common words are frequently misspelled because people misread them or mispronounce them. Of course, pronunciations vary from region to region, and no list can include all mispronunciations that lead to spelling trouble. But if you study the following list, you can train your eye and your ear to spot the parts of common words that often cause spelling errors.

accidentally	NOT	accidently
arithmetic	NOT	arithemetic
athletics	NOT	atheletics
candidate	NOT	cannidate
corporation	NOT	coperation
disastrous	NOT	disasterous
drowned	NOT	drowneded
everybody	NOT	everbody
everything	NOT	everthing
February	NOT	Febuary

generally	NOT	genrally or generly
government	NOT	goverment
height	NOT	heighth
hundreds	NOT	hundereds
irrelevant	NOT	irrevelant
laboratory	NOT	labratory or labertory
library	NOT	liberry
lightning	NOT	lightening
literature	NOT	litrature or literture
mathematics	NOT	mathmatics
mischievous	NOT	mischievious
optimist	NOT	optomist
peremptory	NOT	preemptory
performance	NOT	preformance
perspiration	NOT	presperation
prescription	NOT	perscription
production	NOT	perduction
program	NOT	progrum
publicly	NOT	publically
represent	NOT	repersent
strength	NOT	strenth
studious	NOT	studjous
temperature	NOT	temperture, temprature, or temperchoor
wondrous	NOT	wonderous

Be especially careful of those words that sound nearly alike but have different meanings and different spellings. (See also the Glossary of Usage.)

Affect/Effect

The new museum would *affect* our plans for acquiring new paintings.
"to influence," a verb

His speech did not have the *effect* he hoped for; the audience hated it.
"a result, a consequence," usually a noun, although it can also be a verb meaning "to cause"

Capital/Capitol

The *capital* of Kansas is Topeka.
The location of the seat of government

The legislature meets in the *capitol* building, which is located on a hill overlooking the city.

Waist/Waste

His *waist* was the same size as it was when he was in the army twenty years ago.

Some villages in the third world could live comfortably for a month on the *waste* thrown out after an average weekend in a college dining hall.

Some common plurals may be misspelled because they are mispronounced. This misspelling is especially common in the plurals of words ending in *ist* or *est*. The plural of *scientist* is *scientists*. The final combination *ts* sounds like the *tz* in *Ritz* or the *ts* in *fights*. Because this *ts* is difficult for some people to pronounce, they often leave it off, thinking almost unconsciously that the *s* sound in *ist* or *est* is sufficient to make the plural. But the plural of such words always requires a final *s*. So remember:

The plural of *humanist* is *humanists*.
The plural of *nest* is *nests*.
The plural of *socialist* is *socialists*.
The plural of *biologist* is *biologists*.
The plural of *racist* is *racists*.

Other words having a difficult *s* sound in the final syllable sometimes trouble writers forming the plural, but the rule is the same: the final *s* is necessary to make the noun plural.

disc/discs, rasp/rasps, desk/desks

Since words like these are much less common, they give much less trouble than words ending in *est* and *ist*.

31b

sp

31b
Learn as many principles of spelling as you can, and always use a dictionary when in doubt.

Some principles of English spelling are so generally true that learning them will help you be a better speller.

1   Consider the previous letter and the sound of the word when you are deciding between the combinations *ei* and *ie*.

When these letters sound like the *ee* in *see*, usually place the *i* before *e* — except after *c*.

believe, relieve, grief, chief, yield, wield, receive, deceive, ceiling, conceit

But there are exceptions:

species, seize, caffeine, codeine

When the sound is like *ay* in *bay* or *May*, the spelling is nearly always *ei*.

neigh, feign, neighbor

As for most other words with different sounds, memorize the spelling:

stein, weird, pietism, sierra, pierce, pier, pie, pied, fiery, sieve, foreign, height, forfeit

Exercise 31.1   Some of the following are misspelled. Spell them correctly. Put a check by each word in the list that is spelled correctly.

1. friendly	7. ceiling
2. weight	8. height
3. sieve	9. frieghten
4. beleif	10. wierd
5. beir	11. conceited
6. believing	12. concievable

Exercise 31.2   Fill in the blanks in the following words with *ei* or *ie* to make the words correct. Tell why you make your choices.

1. s ____ zure	7. d ____ gn	13. s ____ ge
2. rec ____ pt	8. hyg ____ ne	14. conc ____ t
3. perc ____ vable	9. th ____ f	15. dec ____ t
4. b ____ ge	10. fr ____ ze	16. perc ____ ve
5. r ____ n	11. l ____ n	17. conc ____ ve
6. v ____ n	12. p ____ ce	

2 **Before the suffix -*ing*, nearly always drop a final silent *e* from the root word.**

force/forcing, surprise/surprising, manage/managing, hope/hoping, scare/scaring, come/coming, pave/paving, become/becoming, fume/fuming

There are only a few exceptions to this rule:

dye/dyeing
To avoid confusion with dying.

age/ageing
But aging *is becoming common.*

shoe/shoeing
To avoid mispronunciation and confusion with showing.

hoe/hoeing
To avoid mispronunciation.

3 **A final, silent *e* on a root word is always dropped before the suffix -*ible*.**

force/forcible

4 **Though the silent *e* of the root is usually dropped before the ending -*able*, the *e* is retained often enough to make this principle uncertain. It is best to memorize the words.**

Drop *e* and add -*able:*

observe/observable, advise/advisable, move/movable (sometimes moveable), argue/arguable, debate/debatable

Do not drop the *e* when adding -*able:*

manage/manageable, peace/peaceable, notice/noticeable, change/changeable, embrace/embraceable

5 **Keep the final *y* on the root word or change it to *i* according to the nature of the root and the nature of the suffix.**

Keep a final *y* on the root word when adding -*ing:*

study/studying, rally/rallying, enjoy/enjoying, cry/crying, ready/readying, steady/steadying, lay/laying

When a final *y* follows a consonant in the root word, change the *y* to *i* before adding an ending other than -*ing*.

merry — merriment, merriest, merrier
happy — happier, happiness, happiest
rally — rallies, rallied, rallier
supply — supplier, supplies, supplied
pity — pitiless, pitiable, pitiful
mercy — merciful, merciless
kingly — kingliness
ugly — uglier, ugliest, ugliness

When a final *y* follows a vowel in the root word, keep the *y* when adding an *s* to make the plural of a noun or the third person singular of a verb.

valley/valleys, defray/defrays, delay/delays, dismay/dismays, enjoy/enjoys, toy/toys, ploy/ploys

The past tense of verbs ending in a final *y* preceded by a vowel is usually made by keeping the final *y* and by adding the suffix -*ed*.

play/played, dismay/dismayed, enjoy/enjoyed

But there are important exceptions:

pay/paid, say/said, lay/laid

Exercise 31.3 Add the suffix indicated for each of the following words. Be sure to change the spelling of the root word when such a change is appropriate.

31b

sp

1. advance + ing
2. highboy + s
3. learn + able
4. horrify + ing
5. quote + able
6. sally + s
7. sense + ible
8. pray + ed
9. quality + s
10. solicit + ing
11. fancy + ful
12. construct + ed
13. tally + ing
14. digress + ing

6 **Spell correctly words formed by adding a suffix that begins with a vowel to a root that ends with a consonant. These suffixes are *-ing*, *-er*, *-est*, *-ed*, *-ence*, *-ance*, *-ible*, *-able*, and *-ened*.**

With most words of one syllable ending in a consonant immediately preceded by a vowel, double the final consonant.

> grip/gripping, quip/quipped, stun/stunning, quit/quitting, plan/planned, sad/saddest, scar/scarring

If the root word ends with two consecutive consonants or with a consonant preceded by two consecutive vowels, do not double the final consonant before suffixes that begin with vowels.

> tight/tighter, stoop/stooping, straight/straightest, sing/singer, deep/deepened, creep/creeping, crawl/crawler

If the root word has more than one syllable, and if the accent of the root falls on the last syllable, usually double the final consonant.

> occur/occurrence, refer/referred, rebut/rebutting, concur/concurring

But if the final consonant of the root is preceded by a consonant or by two consecutive vowels, *or* if the accent shifts from the final syllable of the root when the suffix is added, don't double the final consonant.

> depart/departing
> *There are two final consonants in the root.*
>
> refer/reference
> *The accent shifts from the last syllable of the root when the suffix is added.*
>
> repair/repairing
> *The final consonant of the root is preceded by two consecutive vowels.*
>
> ferment/fermenting
> *The root ends with two consecutive consonants.*

This rule sounds so complicated that you may think it better to memorize the spelling of all these words rather than to memorize the rule. But give the rule a try; it does work!

31b

sp

7 **Add most standard prefixes without changing the spelling of the prefix or the root word. Before root words beginning with vowels, prefixes ending in vowels sometimes have a hyphen added, although the hyphen is tending to disappear in such forms (see 31e-4).**

appear/disappear

eminent/preeminent

operate/cooperate

usual/unusual

create/procreate

create/re-create
to create again

creation/recreation
recreation meaning to refresh oneself by doing something for the pleasure of it

satisfy/dissatisfy

Exercise 31.4   Use the rules you have learned to add the indicated suffixes to the root words below. Explain why you change some roots to add the suffix and why you leave other roots unchanged. The exercise will help you most if you discuss your choices with other members of the class.

1. attend + ance	10. map + ing	19. mad + est
2. din + ed	11. submit + ing	20. star + ing
3. strip + ing	12. reckon + ed	21. confer + ence
4. dine + ing	13. detest + able	22. hop + ed
5. mar + ed	14. soon + est	23. disdain + ed
6. despair + ed	15. omit + ed	24. drown + ing
7. bob + ing	16. silly + est	25. pretend + ed
8. accept + ance	17. depend + ence	
9. dip + er	18. prefer + ing	

31c

Learn the spelling of the regular and irregular forms of the plural.

1 **With most nouns, form the plural simply by adding s.**

grove/groves, boat/boats, cobra/cobras, bank/banks, scientist/scientists, moralist/moralists, gripe/gripes, gasp/gasps, disc/discs

The plurals of acronyms are formed by adding *s* to the acronym:

> It can be said that there have been two *FBIs*—the one before the death of J. Edgar Hoover and the one that came later on.
>
> Most nations believe that they cannot do without their *KGBs* and their *CIAs*.

The plurals of years are usually formed by adding *s*:

> The *1890s* were popularly called "The Gay Nineties" because of the extravagant pleasures of the rich during that decade.
> *Occasionally writers use an apostrophe plus s ('s) to make the plurals of acronyms, numbers, and dates. See 28c.*

2   When the singular of a noun ends in *s*, *x*, *ch*, or *sh*, add *es* to form the plural.

> kiss/kisses, Marx/the Marxes, Mr. Jones/the Joneses, church/churches, dish/dishes

A few words ending in a vowel and an *x* may change when the plural is formed.

> appendix/appendices, index/indices, vortex/vortices

But increasingly writers are making the plurals of these words simply by adding *es*:

> appendixes, indexes, vortexes

3   If a noun ends in a *y* preceded by a consonant, change the *y* to *i* and add *es* to form the plural; if the final *y* is preceded by a vowel, keep the *y* and add an *s* to make the plural.

> beauty/beauties, sally/sallies, glory/glories, city/cities, country/countries, destiny/destinies, crudity/crudities, ray/rays, boy/boys, joy/joys, valley/valleys

31c

sp

4   With nouns that end in *o* in the singular, form the plural by adding *s* or *es*.

Fortunately, nouns that end in *o* in the singular are so rare that you can memorize the plural forms of each without much trouble.

hero/heroes, solo/solos, tomato/tomatoes, tyro/tyros, potato/potatoes, hypo/hypos, flamingo/flamingos or flamingoes, piano/pianos

5   **With some nouns ending in *f*, change the final *f* to a *v* and add *es* to make the plural. With some nouns ending in an *f* and a silent *e*, also change the *f* to a *v*.**

leaf/leaves, hoof/hooves, beef/beeves, life/lives, wife/wives, self/selves

Here again modern practice favors the simpler form of making plurals, merely adding a final *s* to some of these words:

hoof/hoofs, beef/beefs

6   **With many hyphenated words that begin with a noun, form the plural by adding *s* or *es* to the first noun.**

mother-in-law/mothers-in-law, father-in-law/fathers-in-law, court-martial/courts-martial

7   **Memorize irregular plurals of nouns.**

Some nouns have irregular plurals that correspond to no rules and that must be memorized individually. Fortunately, most of these nouns are so familiar that the irregular plurals are not difficult.

child/children, man/men, woman/women, tooth/teeth

8   **Drop the singular ending *-um* or *-on* and add the plural *-a* to form the plural for many words that come from Greek or Latin.**

addendum/addenda, criterion/criteria, datum/data, medium/media, phenomenon/phenomena

Some editors and writers now use *data* as a singular, but the preferred practice is still to insist that *data* should take a plural verb: "The data *are* clear on this point; the pass/fail course has become outdated by events."
Like *data*, the word *media* should always be in the plural.

On the other hand, the word *agenda* is now fully accepted as a singular form.

A few English words with Latin roots ending in *-us* have plural forms made by changing the *-us* to *-i*.

alumnus/alumni, tumulus/tumuli, cumulus/cumuli, hippopotamus/hippopotami or hippopotamuses, calculus/calculi, cirrus/cirri

Even fewer words with Latin roots ending in *-a* have plural forms made by changing the *-a* to *-ae*:

alumna/alumnae

Exercise 31.5 Form the plural for each of the following words. Check yourself by the dictionary when you have finished. (See Chapter 16 for a discussion of how to use the dictionary.)

1. mess	12. harpy	23. harpist	34. soprano
2. harp	13. phlox	24. rabbi	35. locus
3. disco	14. rest	25. prophecy	
4. arch	15. flamingo	26. symposium	
5. potato	16. handful	27. rasp	
6. hello	17. day	28. fascist	
7. dodo	18. valley	29. scientist	
8. grief	19. father-in-law	30. musicologist	
9. fish	20. sheep	31. rest	
10. buffalo	21. cow	32. risk	
11. elegy	22. garnish	33. critic	

31d _____
Use spelling lists to help improve your spelling.

The following lists of words misspelled in student papers were compiled a few years ago by New York State. In the examination of over 31,000 misspelled words gathered by English teachers throughout the country, it was found that the following 407 words were misspelled more frequently than others. These words are arranged below in descending order of difficulty. Study the lists carefully. It will help if you have someone read the words aloud to you and if you try to spell them without looking at them.

believe
belief

benefit
benefited
beneficial

choose
chose
choice

definite
definitely
definition
define

description
describe

environment

exist
existence
existent

its
it's

lose
losing

necessary
unnecessary

occasion

occur
occurred
occurring
occurrence

perform
performance

personal
personnel

precede

principle
principal

privilege

professor
profession

receive
receiving

referring

separate
separation

similar

success
succeed
succession

than
then

their
they're
there

too
two
to

write
writing
writer

II. WORDS MISSPELLED **50** TO **99** TIMES.

accommodate

achieve
achievement

acquire

affect
affective

all right°

among

analyze
analysis

apparent

argument
arguing

began
begin
beginner
beginning

busy
business

category

comparative

conscience
conscientious

conscious

consistent
consistency

control
controlled
controlling

controversy
controversial

criticism
criticize

decision
decided

disastrous

31d

sp

° Although the spelling *alright* is also accepted by some dictionaries, it is listed as nonstandard usage by others. Many college teachers regard *alright* as a misspelling.

embarrass

equipped
equipment

excellent
excellence

experience

explanation

fascinate

forty
fourth

grammar
grammatically

height

imagine
imaginary
imagination

immediate
immediately

intelligence
intelligent

interest

interpretation
interpret

led

loneliness
lonely

marriage

Negro
Negroes

noticeable
noticing

origin
original

passed
past

possess
possession

prefer
preferred

prejudice

prevalent

probably

proceed
procedure

prominent

psychology
psychoanalysis
psychopathic
psychosomatic

pursue

realize
really

repetition

rhythm

sense

shining

studying

surprise

thorough

tries
tried

useful
useless
using

varies
various

weather
whether

---

accept
acceptance
acceptable
accepting

accident
accidentally

acquaint
acquaintance

across

aggressive

appear
appearance

article

athlete
athletic

attended
attendant
attendance

challenge

character
characteristic
characterized

coming

convenience
convenient

difference
different

disappoint

discipline
disciple

dominant
predominant

effect

exaggerate

sp 31d

foreign
foreigners

fundamental
fundamentally

government
governor

hero
heroine
heroic
heroes

humor
humorist
humorous

hypocrisy
hypocrite

incident
incidentally
independent
independence

liveliest
livelihood
liveliness
lives

mere

operate

opinion

opportunity

paid

particular

philosophy

planned

pleasant

possible

practical

prepare

quantity

quiet

recommend

ridicule
ridiculous

speech

sponsor

summary
summed

suppose

technique

transferred

unusual
usually

villain

woman

IV. WORDS MISSPELLED 30 TO 39 TIMES.

advice
advise

approach
approaches

author
authority
authoritative

basis
basically

before

careless
careful

carrying
carried
carries
carrier

conceive
conceivable

condemn

consider
considerably

continuous

curiosity
curious

dependent

desirability
desire

efficient
efficiency

entertain

extremely

familiar

finally

friendliness
friend

fulfill

further

happiness

hindrance

influential
influence

knowledge

laboratory

maintenance

ninety

oppose
opponent

optimism

31d

sp

parallel	relieve	therefore
permanent	religion	together
permit	response	undoubtedly
physical	satire	weird
piece	significance	where
propaganda	suppress	whose
propagate	temperament	you're

---

accompanying	attack	disease
accompanies	attitude	divide
accompanied		divine
accompaniment	boundary	
accomplish	Britain	especially
accustom	Britannica	excitable
actually	capital	exercise
actuality	capitalism	expense
actual	certain	experiment
adolescence	certainly	fallacy
adolescent	chief	fantasy
against	clothes	fantasies
amateur	completely	favorite
amount	counselor	fictitious
appreciate	counsel	field
appreciation	council	financier
approximate	curriculum	financially
arouse	dealt	forward
arousing	despair	

494 Understanding Mechanics

guarantee
guaranteed

guidance
guiding

hear
here

huge

hungry
hungrily
hunger

ignorance
ignorant

indispensable

intellect

interfere
interference

interrupt

involve

irrelevant

laborer
laboriously
labor

laid

later

leisure
leisurely

length
lengthening

license

likeness
likely
likelihood

luxury

magazine

magnificent
magnificence

maneuver

mathematics

meant

mechanics

medicine
medical

medieval

miniature

mischief

moral
morale
morally

narrative

naturally

noble

obstacle

omit

peace

perceive

persistent

persuade

pertain

phase

playwright

politician
political

primitive

regard

relative

remember

reminisce

represent

roommate

sacrifice

safety

satisfy
satisfied

scene

schedule

seize

sentence

sergeant

several

shepherd

simply
simple

sophomore

source

story
stories

straight

strength

strict

substantial

subtle

suspense

symbol

synonymous

tendency

themselves
them

theory
theories

those

thought

tragedy

tremendous

vacuum

view

whole

yield

31d

sp

31e

Use hyphens to form compound words and to avoid confusion.

1 Join two nouns with a hyphen to make one compound word.

Often in modern American English, two nouns are joined with a hyphen to make one compound word. Scientists speak of a *kilogram-meter* as a measure of force, while personnel managers speak of a *clerk-typist,* an employee who does general office work plus typing. The hyphen lets us know that the two nouns work together as one.

As new compound nouns come into general use, their hyphens often disappear. The nouns come to be written as one word, such as *housefly, firelight, firefight,* and *thundershower.*

2 Use a hyphen to link adjectives with nouns to make compound words.

Adjectives can be linked with nouns to make compound words. The compound word may be an adjective or a noun. To form the word *accident-prone,* an adjective, the noun *accident* is linked with the adjective *prone.* We say, "He was accident-prone," meaning that he seemed to have a knack for having accidents. To form the word *free-lancer,* a noun, the noun *lancer* is linked with the adjective *free.* We say, "She once worked for *The Daily Planet,* but she quit to become a *free-lancer* writing for various publications."

3 Use a hyphen to join modifiers when the absence of the hyphen might cause confusion.

Hyphens often help us sort out modifiers that come before the word they modify. If we say, "He was a hard running back," we might mean that he was hard and that he was also a running back. If we say, "He was a hard-running back," we mean that he ran hard. If we say, "She was a quick thinking person," we might mean that she was quick and that she was also thinking. If we say, "She was a quick-thinking person," we mean that she thought rapidly.

Notice that the hyphenated words in these examples employ adverbs *(hard, quick)* that do not end in *-ly.* When adverbs end in *-ly,* they do not require a hyphen if they modify an adjective that in turn modifies a noun.

They explored the *newly discovered* territories.

They endured his *clumsily arrogant* bragging.

Modifiers that are hyphenated when they are placed *before* the word they modify are usually not hyphenated when they are placed *after* the word they modify.

He was a crisis-and-confrontation politician.

His politics were a mix of crisis and confrontation.

It was a bad-mannered reply.

The reply was bad mannered.

4 Use hyphens to attach prefixes to certain words.

A hyphen often joins a prefix and a capitalized word.

un-American, pre-Columbian, anti-Semitic

In a few words the prefix is attached with a hyphen even though the main word is not capitalized.

ex-husband, all-conference

The prefix *self-* is usually joined to a word with a hyphen.

self-interest, self-control, self-centered

Some national names that are joined to make an adjective are hyphenated.

the Franco-Prussian war, the Sino-Japanese agreement, a Mexican-American heritage

Some numbers are hyphenated.

three-fourths of a gallon, twenty-five

Exercise 31.6 Rewrite the following sentences to correct misspellings. Hyphenate words when necessary.

1. He beleived that the badly damaged plane could land safly.
2. The love them today leave them tomorrow philosophy is probly on the decline becaus people now unnerstan it's hypocricy.
3. His nervous laff was a hinderence to his carreer.
4. She remained an optomist though her experence told her that optomists often have trouble acommodating themselves to a pityless city.
5. He had a tendancy to miss classes as a sophmore, and his teachers were bad mannered enough to take attendence.

31e

sp

CHAPTER THIRTY-TWO

Capitalization

Capital letters give readers signals about sentence patterns, names, titles, and pronouns. Most rules for capitalization have been fixed by custom, but some of those rules are more flexible than others. A standard dictionary is a good guide to those names that should be capitalized. Names that should always be capitalized are entered with capitals; all others are entered in lowercase, or small letters. (Remember that when we speak of capitalizing a word, we mean only that the first letter in the word is capitalized; all other letters in the word appear in lowercase.)

32a

Capitalize the first word of every sentence.

The capital letter at the beginning of a sentence is an essential signal to the reader that a new unit of thought is about to begin. The capital letter at the beginning of a sentence goes with the punctuation mark at the end of the previous sentence to make reading easier.

> The coming of the robot to the modern assembly line has raised both problems and possibilities. Because robots greatly reduce human error, the products they manufacture are of a much more uniform quality. But because they reduce human employment, robots risk eliminating part of the market for which their products are destined.

In sentence fragments used for special effects, capitalize the first word.

> But aside from good hair grooming, they are oblivious to everything but each other. Everybody gives them a once-over. Disgusting! Amusing! How touching!
>
> —Tom Wolfe

The three sentence fragments, used for special effect, begin with capitals.

> Why did she lie under oath on the witness stand to defend her husband? Because she knew he was innocent? No, because she knew he was guilty.

An immediate answer to a rhetorical question is often phrased as a fragment. Here, the two fragments represent answers to the question asked in the first sentence.

Some writers who ask a series of questions by using fragments do not capitalize the first word of each fragment.

> How many individuals can we count in society? how many actions? how many opinions?
>
> —Ralph Waldo Emerson

The first question is a complete sentence; the next two are fragments and are not capitalized.

The more common practice is to capitalize the first word in each fragment that answers a question.

> And what are the fundamentals? Reading? Writing? Of course not!
>
> —Sloan Wilson

Most writers do not capitalize the first word of an independent clause immediately following a colon:

> If a person suffer much from sea-sickness, let him weigh it heavily in the balance. I speak from experience: it is no trifling evil, cured in a week.
>
> —Charles Darwin

But sometimes writers do capitalize the first word after a colon:

> The answer is another question: How many days must go by before millions of people notice they are not eating?
>
> —*The New York Times*

32a

cap

The first word in an independent clause following a semicolon is never capitalized unless it is a proper noun (see 32b below).

All in all, however, outside support counted for little; the men of the village did the work themselves.

— Oscar Handlin

32b

Capitalize proper nouns and their abbreviations.

Proper nouns are the names of specific people, or things, names that set off the individual from the species. Proper nouns include names like *Jane* (instead of the common noun *person*), *France* (instead of the common noun *country*), and *Empire State Building* (instead of the common noun *building*).

The following are all proper nouns.

NAMES AND NICKNAMES OF PEOPLE

Wolfgang Amadeus Mozart, Ernest Hemingway, Jim Ed Rice, Ella Fitzgerald, John F. Kennedy, Sandra O'Connor, U. S. Grant, Gore Vidal, Joan Didion, the North Carolina Tarheels

NAMES OF PLACES

France, the U.S.A., the U.S.S.R., Tennessee, the Panama Canal, Back Bay, the Mississippi Delta, the North Shore, the Irunia Restaurant, the Sierra Nevada, the Great Lakes

OFFICIAL NAMES OF ORGANIZATIONS

Phi Beta Kappa, the U.S. Department of Defense, The Authors' Guild of America, the University of Notre Dame, Cumberland College, Ford Motor Company, the Roman Catholic Church, the American Red Cross, the Boy Scouts of America, the NCAA, the NAACP

DAYS OF THE WEEK, MONTHS, SPECIAL DAYS

Monday, July, Veterans Day, Christmas, Labor Day, Halloween, Yom Kippur, Earth Day, Pearl Harbor Day

32b

cap

ETHNIC GROUPS, NATIONALITIES, AND THEIR LANGUAGES

Greeks, Chinese, Americans, Arabs, Turks; Greek, Chinese, English, Arabic, Turkish

NOTE: *The words* blacks *and* whites *generally are not capitalized when they are used to refer to ethnic groups, but many writers use individual choice in this matter. The older and now less favored word* Negro *is capitalized.*

MEMBERS OF RELIGIOUS BODIES AND THEIR SACRED BOOKS AND NAMES

Jews, Christians, Baptists, Holy Bible, God, Allah, Hindus, Jesus Christ, Holy Spirit, the Koran, the Torah, Pentecostals, Christian Scientists

Note that many religious terms such as sacraments, altar, priests, rabbi, preacher, *and* holy water *are not capitalized. The word* Bible *is sometimes not capitalized in both English and American practice, and it is never capitalized when it is used as a metaphor for an essential book, as in this sentence: "His book* Winning at Stud Poker *was for many years the* bible *of gamblers."*

Sometimes words not ordinarily capitalized do take capitals when they are used as parts of proper names. We write, "My *aunt* is arriving this afternoon." But we write, "My *Aunt Lou* tells fantastic stories that I think she makes up." We write, "I have to go to the *bank* before we can leave." But we write, "The *Cambridge Bank* is on the corner." We write, "I graduated from *high school* in 1951," but we write, "I went to *Lenoir City High School.*"

Pronoun references to a deity worshipped by people in the present are sometimes capitalized, although some writers use capitals only to prevent confusion.

Allah, so Muslims believe, sent Mohammed to deliver *His* word to the world.

God helped Abraham carry out *His* law.

In each of the sentences above, the capitalization of the pronoun His *helps avoid confusion. If the pronoun were not capitalized, readers might not be able to tell if the* word *in the first sentence referred to Allah or Mohammed, or if the* law *in the second sentence was God's law or Abraham's law.*

God acts for *his* own purposes and according to *his* own wisdom.

In this sentence the pronoun his *is not capitalized, since no confusion would result. You may choose to capitalize the pronoun if you wish.*

32b

cap

Pronoun references to deities no longer worshiped are not capitalized.

Jupiter was the Roman god of thunder and lightning, and *he* led a tempestuous love life that often got *him* into deep trouble with *his* wife Juno.

Names like *Mother, Father, Cousin, Brother,* and *Sister* may replace proper names in some kinds of speech and writing. If you intend to refer to a specific individual, capitalize the word.

I still miss *Mother*, although she has been dead for over a decade.

He supposed that *Grandfather* would come to his aid again as he had so many times in the past.

But most of the time these words are not capitalized, since they do not replace a proper name. Whether you capitalize such words depends on your intention.

I asked my *mother* to wake me at 5:00 A.M.
The word mother *is not being used as a substitute for a proper name. It is being used in the more general way to denote a relation. It is not capitalized.*

Some titles that may be capitalized before a proper name are often not capitalized when they are used after the name.

Everyone knew that *Governor* Grover Cleveland of New York was the most likely candidate for the Democratic nomination.
The title Governor *before the name of Grover Cleveland is capitalized.*

The most likely candidate for the Democratic nomination was Grover Cleveland, *governor* of the state of New York.
The title written after the name is not capitalized.

Writers and editors do not agree on the capitalization of some titles. The title *President of the United States,* or the *President* (meaning the President of the United States), is almost always capitalized. But practice varies for other titles. Some writers say, "I will speak to the *Governor* about your wish to give him a new Cadillac for his personal use." Others say, "The *governor* of this state received a Cadillac last week from an old political friend and business associate." Most writers say, "The *president* of this university has seventeen honorary degrees." Others will say, "The *President* of this university would rather have a winning football team than seventeen honorary degrees."

In general, editors and writers are tending to capitalize less, but it is still important to be consistent. If you write "the *President* of the *University*," you should also write "the *Chair* of the *History Department*." If you write "the *president* of the *university*," you should also write "the *chair* of the *history department*." And, of course, if you say "the *President* of the *University*" in one place, you must capitalize in the same way whenever you write "the *President* of the *University*."

When proper names describe or identify common nouns, those nouns that follow are generally not capitalized.

Sanka brand, Russian history, French fries, Pennsylvania-Dutch shoofly pie, English literature

The words brand, history, fries, shoofly pie, *and* literature *are not capitalized because they are not considered part of the proper names they follow.*

Use capitals for abbreviations made from capitalized words or for words formed from the initial letters of words in a proper name. (These words are called acronyms. See 33e.)

WAC, FBI, NOW, UNESCO, U.S.A., ANZAC, NCAA, SWAT

Abbreviations used as parts of proper names usually take capitals.

T. S. Eliot; Sammy Davis, Jr.; George Sheehan, M.D.

Words derived from capitalized words generally keep the capitals of the original words.

Reaganomics, Miltonic, Hollywoodiana

32c

Capitalize the first and last words of the title of any piece of writing and of any work of art or architecture. Do not capitalize the articles (*a*, *an*, and *the*) or prepositions and conjunctions of fewer than five letters unless they begin the title. Capitalize the first word after a colon or semicolon in a title.

32c

cap

Pride and Prejudice
The Taming of the Shrew
the *Spirit of St. Louis*
the *Titanic*

the *Mona Lisa*

"Beating the Market: How to Get Rich on Stocks"

On Old Age

Two Years Before the Mast

Note that the preposition Before *in this last title is capitalized. The general rule is that a preposition or conjunction of five letters or more is capitalized.*

32d

Capitalize the first word of spoken dialogue included within quotation marks.

"You're going to kill us both!" she shouted.

"Calm down," he shouted back. "I spent just thirty minutes learning to drive this motorcycle, and we're already doing a hundred miles an hour."

"Help!" she said.

Indirect quotations and questions require no capitals for words attributed to a speaker or writer.

She said that jazz was one of the many contributions of blacks to world culture.

He asked me which I liked better, bluegrass music, without drums and electrically amplified instruments, or the more modern country music that is closely akin to soft rock.

Many authors in earlier centuries of the English language and some writers today — especially poets — have used capitals in eccentric ways. If you are quoting a text directly, reproduce the capitalization used in the source whether or not it is correct by today's standards.

Sun and moon run together in one of Pyramus's speeches, "Sweet Moon, I thank thee for thy sunny Beams."

— Elizabeth Sewell

32e

Use capitals consistently when you have a reason for doing so, but avoid unnecessary capitals.

Some inexperienced writers are tempted to use capitals for emphasis, and they capitalize too much. Unnecessary capitals may confuse readers or irritate them. In modern prose the tendency is to use lowercase whenever possible.

The Department of Agriculture and the Department of the Interior have often had conflicts because of overlapping jurisdictions. Both departments have responsibility for the American land. The secretary in charge of each department usually wants to increase his own power. The congress must sometimes step in and arbitrate the disputes between the two. But a strong Secretary of Agriculture or a greedy Secretary of the Interior can quickly undo any compromise made between the departments.

In this paragraph, the nouns department, departments, *and* secretary *are not capitalized when they appear as nouns that are not part of a complete title. Some writers today might have capitalized the word* congress. *But the tendency now is to capitalize as little as possible, and most writers and editors would prefer the version shown here.*

A REFERENCE CHART FOR CAPITALS

Consult this chart for ready reference about capitalization. Designed for quick reference, the chart highlights appropriate uses for capitals; the color numbers refer to the appropriate sections in the text.

Sentence conventions   32a, 32d

After periods, the pronoun I, quotations, after colons
They laughed. The child grinned.
When I finally spoke, I whispered.
She said, "Let me check your blood pressure."
This is clear: The (**or** the) lake is unfit for swimming.

BUT

They laughed; the child grinned.

Did she ask who arrived?

He said that fear can blind judgments.

People   32b

General George Patton

Justice Thurgood Marshall

D. K. Rivera, M.D.

Chancellor Joseph Murphy

The Governor (**OR** governor) waved to the crowd.

Uncle Kwok; hearing Uncle (**OR** uncle) speak

BUT

the general, the judge, a doctor, the chancellor, a governor, my uncle

32e

cap

Geographic locations   32b

Zimbabwe, Rhodesia

Pike's Peak

Tennessee

Main Street

Lake Placid

BUT

a new country, a historical mountain, this state, the street, a lake

Areas, regions, directions   32b

the Middle East

a Northerner

Northwest Territory

in the South

BUT

an eastern route, turn south, the territory

Historical events, names, movements, and writings   32b, 32c

World War II

the Louisiana Purchase

Modernism

the Bill of Rights

Moby Dick

"To Autumn"

BUT

a war, a bill, a philosophy, a document, amendments, laws, a novel, that event, the book

Institutions, groups, and organizations   32b

Democratic Party

Boston Red Sox

the High School of Music and Art

University of Maryland

the Knights of Columbus

Bank Leumi

McGraw-Hill Book Company

USN

32e

cap

BUT

political party, team, a high school, this university, the organization, our bank, the company, the navy

Academic subjects   32b

English, Chinese, Indian religions
Mathematics 13

BUT

language, theology, mathematics, psychology, history, senior class

Religion, race, nationality, sacred things   32b

Judaism, Catholics

Old Testament

Almighty God

Allah

Caucasian, Negro, black or Black

Pakistani

BUT

my religion, a race of people

Days, months, holidays   32b

Tuesday

June

Labor Day

BUT

tomorrow, this month, spring, summer, fall, winter

Plants, animals, games, illnesses   32b

African violet, Queen Anne's lace

Siamese cat

Monopoly

Addison's anemia

BUT

elm tree, rose, kiwi, baseball, measles, pneumonia

32e

cap

Exercise 32.1 Follow the directions in each item below, and write full-sentence responses. Observe the conventions of proper capitalization.

1. Name the professor in your school whose lectures you find most interesting.
2. Name the city and state (or city and country) where you were born.
3. Name a supermarket where you or your family members buy groceries.
4. What is your favorite season of the year?
5. In what direction must you walk or ride to get to campus?
6. In what region of the country did you grow up?
7. What two academic subjects do you enjoy most?
8. Name a book you enjoyed reading recently.
9. What is your favorite TV show?
10. Name your favorite holiday.
11. What is your favorite flower?
12. What was the name of your high school? (Use the words *high school* immediately after the name of the institution.)

Exercise 32.2 Fill in the correct capital or lowercase letters in the blanks below. Explain your choices.

1. _____hen _____overnor Blankenship stood on the steps of the state _____apitol _____uilding and said to the _____resident of the _____nited _____tates, "_____he states in the _____outh need more of the _____overnment's support," my neighbors on Main _____treet applauded wildly.
2. _____t the _____an _____iego _____oo last summer, I disliked the _____onkeys and the _____pes because they looked so much like little men and women in a cage, but I was fascinated by the reptile house, where I saw the _____frican _____ock _____ython as well as the _____ndian _____obras and the _____oa _____onstrictor.
3. _____ake _____ociology 320, a _____ourse in the _____ociology of _____eligion, where you learn to understand some of the strengths of _____rotestantism, _____udaism, and _____oman _____atholicism.

cap

Exercise 32.3 Rewrite the following sentences, using capital and lowercase letters correctly.

1. during Summer i like to visit the Ski Resorts in vermont, where few visitors disturb my meditations among the Fir Trees and the Maples that dot the Landscape.

2. when I was a child, thanksgiving day was one of the best holidays, not only because the family always got together for a huge dinner but also because thanksgiving came on thursday, and at Belmont high school, we were given both thursday and friday off.
3. in your sophomore course in english literature next fall, you may read at least one novel by daniel defoe, whose book *robinson crusoe* is sometimes called the first novel in the english language.
4. when we had our accident, we were taken to memorial hospital on greeley parkway, where a doctor named thomas babington examined us and told us there was nothing wrong with us. later, when i discovered that i had a fractured skull and that my brother had a broken leg, we sued the hospital, but the hospital claimed that dr. babington was only visiting the emergency room that day and was not an employee of memorial hospital at all.

32e

cap

CHAPTER THIRTY-THREE

Numbers and Abbreviations

Variations in the style of different authors and in the demands of different editors make it difficult to fix rules for figures and abbreviations. In some newspapers and some magazines the use of figures to express numbers may be common. In books, figures and abbreviations are less common, at least in the body of a text. In footnotes, bibliographies, scientific or technical reports, letters, charts, tables, and graphs, figures and abbreviations must be used no matter what the publication.

You should use figures sparingly for numbers in standard essays, and you should use abbreviations for words only when convention allows.

33a _____

In general, use words instead of figures for numbers that take only one or two words to spell out, and use figures instead of words for numbers that require three or more words to spell out.

When spelling numbers out takes a great deal of space, use figures, even in the body of an essay.

six cartons **BUT** 181 cartons
twenty-four dollars **BUT** $23.88
forty thousand children **BUT** 39,658 children

If you must begin a sentence with a number, you should usually spell the number out.

NOT: 450 motorcycles jammed the parking lot.

BUT: Four hundred and fifty motorcycles jammed the parking lot.
Here the number is spelled out because it begins the sentence.

Motorcycles — 450 of them — jammed the parking lot.
Motorcycles begins the sentence, and the number, written in figures, follows as an appositive.

33b

Use figures for numbers in prose that gives a great deal of statistical or quantitative information. Use figures for dates, times of day, and addresses.

In writing about some subjects, you may use numbers so frequently that to avoid confusion you should write the numbers as figures.

The original plan for the house called for a dining room that would be 18 × 25 and a living room that would be 30 × 34 with plate-glass windows at each end. The wall of the dining room was to include one enormous window measuring 16 × 5, to be set in the wall 1.5 feet above the floor.

Dates that include the year usually appear as figures, but some writers prefer to spell them out.

October 9, 1893	The ninth of October, 1893
9 October 1893	October ninth (NOT October 9th)
the 1960s	the nineteen-sixties
1929–1930	from 1929 to 1930

The time of day followed by the abbreviation A.M. or P.M. is always expressed in figures.

6:00 A.M., 6 A.M., 8:15 P.M.

six o'clock in the morning

a quarter past eight in the evening

Street and highway numbers almost always appear as figures except when a house number and the number of a street come together in an address. Then one of the numbers is written out.

1 Park Avenue   850 Fifteenth Street

Apartment 6J

Interstate 80

State Highway 2

33c

In formal essay writing, spell out most words rather than abbreviate them.

1   Common titles such as *Mister* and *Doctor* are abbreviated even in formal prose.

Other abbreviations may cut down readability, since a general audience may be unfamiliar with them or may not recognize them at all. But in some technical writing such as memos or reports intended for a limited audience, you may use abbreviations that are standard to that audience.

NOT: Dr. Ruth Smith and SOL Dean Th. Luciano discussed the std. rules about hab. corp. proceedings in the pol. cts. as they might apply to studs. arrested on DWI charges in the commercial dist. alg. Mass. Ave.

BUT: Dr. Ruth Smith and School of Law Dean Thomas Luciano discussed the standard rules about habeas corpus proceedings in the police courts as they might apply to students arrested on charges of driving while intoxicated in the commercial district along Massachusetts Avenue.
Readers may decipher the abbreviations of the first sentence, but the second sentence is much clearer and easier to read, even to those who know all the abbreviations in the first example.

President Jaworski said that the college should eliminate at least fifty full-time-equivalent positions. He said that for each FTE eliminated, an across-the-board raise of one hundred dollars would be possible for the remaining faculty.
Here the abbreviation FTE is acceptable, since the audience for whom this report is meant would be familiar with it. It is even more acceptable because it is explained in the first sentence.

If you use the name of an agency or an organization frequently in an essay or a report, you may abbreviate it to make the repetition less tedious. You are always safe if you write out the name of the agency or the organization the first time you use it and abbreviate it afterward. You may give the abbreviation in parentheses immediately after you mention the name the first time.

> The Student Nonviolent Coordinating Committee (SNCC) began earnest and often dangerous work in Mississippi and other parts of the South during the summer of 1964. SNCC was far to the left of other civil rights organizations, and its leaders often mocked the "conservatism" of Dr. Martin Luther King, Jr. SNCC quickly burned itself out and disappeared, but some scholars now give the organization much credit for some of the progress made in civil rights during those hard years.

2 **Spell out the names of countries, cities, boroughs, and states and the words _Avenue, Boulevard, Highway, Street, River_, and _Mountains_ and words like them used as parts of proper names when they appear in the body of your prose.**

> The Catskill Mountains (NOT _Mts._) of New York (NOT _N.Y._) flank the Hudson River (NOT _Riv._) to the west.
>
> Veterans Highway (NOT _Vets H'wy_) crosses Deer Park Avenue (NOT _Ave._)

3 **Spell out the names of months and days of the week; spell out people's names.**

> **NOT:** In Sept. and Oct. Chas. visits the botanical gardens every Sun.
>
> **BUT:** In September and October Charles visits the botanical gardens every Sunday.

4 **Avoid using the ampersand as a symbol for the conjunction _and_ unless the ampersand is part of an official name or title.**

> Loneliness and (NOT &) poverty often accompany old age.
>
> The A & P is one of the oldest supermarket chains in America.
>
> The stock index published by Standard & Poors is one of the most important economic documents in America.
>
> _In the last two examples, the ampersand is part of an official name._

5 **Spell out the words** *pages, chapter, volume,* **and** *edition,* **the names of courses of study, and words such as** *company, brothers,* **and** *incorporated* **except as they may appear in official titles.**

NOT: In Ch. 16 several pp. present new developments in open-heart surgery.

BUT: In Chapter 16, several pages present new developments in open-heart surgery.

Remember that you may use abbreviations for *page, chapter,* and *edition* in footnotes, endnotes, and bibliographical references (see 37c, d, and f).

Use the abbreviation *Inc., Corp., Co.,* or *Bros.* only when it is part of the official title of a company.

NOT: His bros. formed a toy co. called Kidstuff, Inc., and later changed the name to Goldstein Bros.

BUT: His brothers formed a toy company called Kidstuff, Inc., and later changed the name to Goldstein Bros.

6 **Avoid the use of** *etc.*

It is almost always better to name the items you intend to blanket under the abbreviation *etc.* than to use the abbreviation as a catchall. If you don't want to make a long list, use *and so on, and so forth, for example,* or *such as.*

NOT: This garden is good for planting lettuce, broccoli, spinach, etc.

BUT: This garden is good for planting lettuce, broccoli, spinach, radishes, onions, and other cool-weather vegetables.

OR

This garden is good for planting cool-weather vegetables— broccoli and spinach, for example.

OR

This garden is good for planting vegetables such as lettuce and broccoli.

When you do use *etc.,* do not put the conjunction *and* before it. The abbreviation *etc.* stands for the Latin *et cetera,* or *et caetera,* which means

n/ab

33c

"and the rest," so the *and* is included in the abbreviation itself. To add the English word is redundant. And note the spelling of the abbreviation: in *etc.* the *t* comes before the *c*, not after it.

33d

Use abbreviations for familiar titles that may stand before or after a person's name.

Some commonly abbreviated titles always go before the person's name. These include *Mr., Mrs., Ms., Dr., St., the Rev., the Hon., Sen., Rep.,* and *Fr.*

Fr. Louis joined our monastery twenty years ago.

Mrs. Jean Bascom designed the brick walkway in front of our building.

Dr. Epstein and Dr. Goodson consulted on the operation.

The Rev. Dr. Karl Barth visited Gettysburg, Pennsylvania, shortly before he died.

Note that the abbreviation Rev. *for* Reverend *should always be preceded by the article* the.

Many women now prefer to use the title *Ms.* instead of *Miss* or *Mrs.* (see Chapter 15). Strictly speaking, *Ms.* is not an abbreviation, since it does not stand for a word. But it is used in the same way *Mr.* and *Mrs.* are used—before a name. The title *Miss* is not an abbreviation, so it is not followed with a period. It, too, should precede the name.

Some abbreviations are always used after a proper name. Usually these indicate academic or professional degrees or honors. Note that a comma is placed between the name and the abbreviation and that a space follows the comma.

Kai-Y Hsu, Ph.D.

Maria Tiante, M.D.

Elaine Leff, C.P.A., LL.D.

Michael Bartlett, Esq.

Spell out most titles used without proper names:

NOT: Mr. Carew asked if she had seen the Dr.

BUT: Mr. Carew asked if she had seen the doctor.

33d

n/ab

Notice that when an abbreviation ends a sentence, the period at the end of the abbreviation itself will serve as the period of the sentence. If a question mark or an exclamation point ends the sentence, you must place such a punctuation mark *after* the period in the abbreviation:

When he was in the seventh grade, we called him "Stinky," but now he is William Percival Abernathy, Ph.D.!

Is it true that he now wants to be called Stanley Martin, Esq.?

33e

Abbreviate the names of agencies, groups, people, places, or objects commonly referred to by capitalized initials.

Some of these abbreviations use periods; others do not. Follow standard practice, and consult a dictionary if you have any doubts.

CIA OR C.I.A.

JFK OR J.F.K.

U.S. government OR US government

Washington, D.C. OR Washington, DC

Many government agencies known by their acronyms are regularly referred to with abbreviations, especially in publications where they are frequently mentioned. Often the abbreviations of these agencies are so well known that they do not require any explanation.

The FBI entered the case immediately, since under the Lindbergh Act kidnapping is a federal crime.

Both the Secretary of Defense and high officials in NASA worry about Russian military technology in space.

33f

n/ab

Abbreviate words typically used with times, dates, and figures.

6 P.M. OR 6:00 P.M.	A.D. 1066
9:45 AM OR 9:45 A.M.	6000 rpm
498 B.C.	

Note that in common practice, the abbreviation A.D. is written before the number indicating the year, and the abbreviation B.C. is written after the year number.

33g

Translate most Latin abbreviations into English in the body of your writing. Old systems of documentation do use Latin abbreviations in footnotes, endnotes, bibliographies, or parenthetical comments.

cf. should be "compare"

e.g. should be "for example"

et al. should be "and others"

etc. should be "and so on," "and so forth," or "and the rest"

ibid. should be "in the same place"

i.e. should be "that is"

vs. should be "versus"

Although new documentation systems for research papers use a minimum of abbreviations, you may come across these abbreviations in your own reading. A list of the most familiar of these appears on pages 600–601.

Exercise 33.1 Rewrite the following paragraphs, using numbers and abbreviations properly.

1936 was the year he moved to our town and set himself up as a doctor. He hung out the sign on his front porch saying, "Dr. Ezra Muscatel, M.D." His house was over on 2nd. Ave. next to the warehouse owned by the Ledbetter bros., & Doctor Muscatel used to sit out on the porch overlooking the ave. & stare at the mts. in the distance on the border between Tenn. and N.C.

Mister Ledbetter went to him first, with a stomachache in the early A.M., & Doctor Muscatel gave him 8 or 9 little pills that made him feel good right away, & after that people started going to Doctor Muscatel with stomachaches, headaches, rheumatism, etc. He was the only dr. in town who would make house calls. You could call him up at six PM, & he would come to your house & give you some pills, and etc., & you would feel better. He would come to your house to deliver a baby at three A.M. in the morning. He did not charge much money, & he was always serious about things. He listened to people and nodded his head when they told him their symptoms and never looked like one of those drs. that want to run off after 5 or 6 mins. with a patient. He sat there, looking sober and concerned, & afterward he would scribble something on his prescription pad & tell you to get it filled at the drugstore, & he would go shuffling off as if he was still thinking about you and what was wrong with you.

FDR was President of the U.S.A. back then, & we had a lot of people coming & going in our little town. One of them saw the old dr. one morning on Main St. and recognized him & began telling everybody that dr. Muscatel was an ex-con who had served thirty years in the Tenn. prison for manslaughter & that he had never finished high sch.

33g

n/ab

CHAPTER THIRTY-FOUR

Italics

To set off certain words and phrases from regular type, printers use *italics*, a typeface in which the characters slant to the right. Since most typewriters lack an italic face, and since it is impossible to make italics in handwriting, writers preparing manuscripts underline those words that a printer would place in italics.

HANDWRITTEN

Katharine Hepburn gives one of her best performances in <u>The African Queen</u>.

TYPED

```
Katharine Hepburn gives one of her best
performances in The African Queen.
```

PRINTED

Katharine Hepburn gives one of her best performances in *The African Queen*.

518

34a

To indicate italics underline in your manuscript the titles of books, magazines, journals, newspapers, plays, films, works of art, long poems, pamphlets, and musical works.

```
Joan Didion, a former editor of Vogue and The
National Review, received glowing reviews in The
New York Times for her novel A Book of Common Prayer.
```

In most titles, *a*, *an*, or *the* as a first word is capitalized and underlined. If titles of newspapers and magazines include the name of a city, you may decide whether to underline that name. You may write "the Los Angeles Times" or "The Los Angeles Times." Writers often do not underline or use italics for the initial *the* in the title of a periodical. But no hard-and-fast rule exists here. In most titles other than those of periodicals, *a*, *an*, or *the* as a first word is usually italicized and capitalized.

> Picasso's *Guernica* captures the anguish and despair of violence.
>
> Plays by Shakespeare provide details and story lines for Verdi's opera *Falstaff*, the musical comedy *Kiss Me Kate* by Cole Porter, and Franco Zeffirelli's film drama *Romeo and Juliet*.
>
> Edwin Newman's book *A Civil Tongue* is an amusing essay on modern language.
>
> This book is entitled *The McGraw-Hill College Handbook*.
>
> *If you were writing any of these italicized words in your own paper, you would underline them.*

Some publishers of newspapers, books, and magazines have special rules for the use of italics. They often use quotation marks either to save money in setting type or to conform to their preferred format. Usually such publishers give a style manual to their writers to ensure consistent styling. *The New Yorker,* for example, italicizes newspaper titles but places the titles of books, musical works, films, and plays in quotation marks. Most newspapers use quotation marks where formal writing requires italics.

> Nelson Gidding did the adaptation of the Shirley Jackson novel "The Haunting of Hill House."
>
> *— The New Yorker*
>
> On our way, dodging snowflakes, we picked up the Sunday *Times* to see what had happened to the world.
>
> *— The New Yorker*
>
> As readers of "Crazy in Berlin" and "Little Big Man" ought to know, you can never tell what to expect from a novel by Thomas Berger.
>
> — Christopher Lehmann-Haupt (in *The New York Times*)

Italics **519**

However, quotation marks usually mark off only the titles of short works—essays, newspaper and magazine articles and columns, short stories, television and radio programs, short poems, songs, chapters or other subdivisions in books, and unpublished dissertations and theses (see 29c).

> Elizabeth Cullinan's "Only Human" appears in a collection of her stories called *Yellow Roses.*
> *The title of the story requires quotation marks; the title of the book in which it appears, italics.*

Note that in referring to the Bible or other sacred books like the Koran, to court cases, or to government documents, you use neither italics nor quotation marks.

> The Book of Ecclesiastes provides some of the most haunting phrases in the Bible.

> In Brown vs. Topeka Board of Education, the United States Supreme Court handed down a far-reaching interpretation of the Constitution.

Do not underline the titles you give to your papers when you write them on the title page. When the titles of books appear on the jacket, the binding, or the title page, they are not italicized. The titles of articles are not italicized or placed in quotes when they appear in the title position in a journal or a book.

34b

Underline (to indicate italics for) foreign words and phrases not commonly regarded as part of English.

> They are wise to remember, however, one thing. He is Sinatra. The boss. *Il Padrone.*
> —GAY TALESE

> *Chota hasari*—the little breakfast—consists of a cup of tea at five-thirty or six in the morning, with possibly some fruit or toast served with it. At eleven or at midday a heavier meal is eaten, *chapatis*—thin unleavened wheat cakes—and curry, with *dal*—a kind of lentil soup—and curds and sweets of some sort.
> —SANTHA RAMA RAU

> Memphis, in fact, was definitely the mecca, yardstick and *summum bonum.*
> —TERRY SOUTHERN

34b

ital

Many originally foreign words have become so common in English that everyone accepts them as part of the English language, and they require no underlining or italics—words like rigor mortis (Latin), pasta (Italian), sombrero (Spanish), bête noire (French), and festschrift (German). In the sentence by Terry Southern above, a city in Saudi Arabia—Mecca—has given its name as a common noun meaning any place where large numbers of people go to have some exalting experience.

Some foreign words are still borderline, and some writers would underline them while others would not—words like *ex nihilo* (Latin for "from nothing"), *imprimatur* (Latin for "Let it be printed"), and *Weltanschauung* (German for "world view"). Often the preference of the writer or the need for a special effect dictates the decision to underline or not.

Dictionaries offer some help. By labeling as *French* a phrase like *mise-en-scène*, for example, a dictionary guides your decision to underline. Some dictionaries have special sections labeled "Foreign Words." Others italicize foreign words when they appear. But writers must use their own judgment about the borderline words. Here it is good to consider your audience and to try to imagine the expectations that readers may bring to your work.

34c

Use underlining (to indicate italics) to call attention to words or phrases you wish to stress as words rather than for the meaning they convey.

The use of the word *glide* at the end of the last stanza is effective and gives just the amount of emphasis required at the end of the poem.
— CLEANTH BROOKS and ROBERT PENN WARREN

And if the word *integration* means anything, this is what it means: that we, with love, shall force our brothers to see themselves as they are, to cease fleeing from reality and begin changing it.
— JAMES BALDWIN

Letters or numbers stressed as words also require underlining to show italics.

The word *bookkeeper* has three sets of double letters: double *o*, double *k*, and double *e*.

Some writers will use quotation marks to show that words are being spoken of as words.

When I was in graduate school in the late fifties, "criticism" was still a fighting word.

—Gerald Graff

34d

Underline (to indicate italics for) the names of ships, trains, and air or space vehicles.

I packed my valise, and took passage on an ancient tub called the *Paul Jones* for New Orleans.

—Mark Twain

Lindbergh had flown his tiny plane, *The Spirit of St. Louis*, from San Diego to New York, with one stop at St. Louis, in the elapsed time of twenty-one hours, clipping five hours from the transcontinental record.

—William L. Shirer

34e

Use underlining only occasionally for emphasis.

Reserve italics to show stress only occasionally. Too many words italicized to show emphasis in your writing will fatigue your readers; their eyes may leap over the underlined or italicized words—the very opposite effect from what you intended. Too much emphasis may mean no emphasis at all.

WEAK: You don't *mean* that your *teacher* told the whole *class* that *he* did not know the answer *himself?*

REVISED: It was your teacher, then, who astonished the class by not knowing the answer?
The new sentence through language and structure (and without italics) shows the surprise that the first sentence shows weakly with so many italicized words.

For special effects, an occasional word in italics helps you emphasize a point:

That advertisers exploit women's subordination rather than cause it can be clearly seen now that *male* fashions and toiletries have become big business.

—Ellen Willis

It now seems clear that we are not going to improve instruction by finding *the* method or methods that are good for all peoples.

—K. Patricia Cross

34e
ital

In written dialogue, writers may use italics to emphasize words to show the rhythms of speech used by characters.

> The lady, however, regarded it very placidly. "I shouldn't have gone if she *had* asked me."
>
> — HENRY JAMES

> As they turned to him, Blackburn said: "Can *you* give *me* a few minutes, Dr. Howe?" His eyes sparkled at the little audacity he had committed, the slightly impudent play with hierarchy.
>
> — LIONEL TRILLING

Exercise 34.1   Underline any words or phrases that require italics in the following sentences.

1. An advertisement in the San Diego Evening Tribune announced a cruise on the Queen Elizabeth II, but after I read Katherine Anne Porter's novel Ship of Fools, a vacation on the sea did not interest me.
2. Time reported that Da Vinci's painting The Last Supper had deteriorated seriously from pollution and neglect.
3. The word hopefully is common nowadays, but many people who take writing seriously object to it because they think the words I hope or we hope or it is hoped usually express the meaning more clearly.
4. By the time the police discovered the body, rigor mortis had set in, and Inspector Michaelson told reporters from the Times and the Globe that death had taken place about twelve hours before.
5. Russell Baker's column Observer appears in the New York Times several days a week.

Exercise 34.2   Rewrite the following sentences to eliminate excessive emphasis. You may change the wording—eliminating some words and adding others. You may also change the order of the sentences as you see fit.

1. Mr. Watt promised that this was *absolutely* the last time that he or *any other* member of his department would even *mention* digging a coal mine in Yellowstone National Park.
2. Who could *possibly* have known that the landing gear *was* defective and that the pilot was *drunk?*
3. The crew of the space shuttle *firmly* believed that the *engineering problems of the flight were less serious than the psychological problems of living so close together under such a demanding* routine.
4. *Anyone* desiring to change sections *must* file a form with the registrar *before* Friday afternoon.

34e

ital

Book Three

SPECIAL
WRITING TASKS

PART SEVEN
Writing a Research Paper

PART EIGHT
Other Writing Tasks

PART SEVEN

WRITING A RESEARCH PAPER

	Chapter
Starting a Research Project	35
Planning to Write from Sources	36
Citing and Documenting Sources	37
Developing, Writing, and Revising the Research Paper	38

CHAPTER THIRTY-FIVE

Starting a Research Project

Doing research is one of the fundamental activities for learning. From college and university classrooms to government agencies to corporate boardrooms, people trying to answer complex questions turn to research as a means for finding facts, for weighing varieties of evidence, and for reaching informed conclusions.

Research projects rely on careful investigation of many different sources in the library and elsewhere. These sources include not just the obvious books, periodicals, and reference items but also films, plays, concerts, television programs, videotapes, audiotapes, records, computer programs, microfilm, and microfiche. Anything that can uncover accurate information efficiently is a tool in the researcher's hands. Thus, research often involves interviews; a reporter, for example, digging into corruption among city officials, needs first-hand contact with municipal leaders and their aides. Often research involves telephone calls and casual conversations with your friends, teachers, or other experts who can help set you on the right path for finding information quickly.

As you prepare to do research and to write up your findings in a formal presentation, you should remember that a research paper must be more than just a summary of what you have read on a given topic. A research paper presents a thesis that you have developed by reading and thinking about your topic and your sources. Using careful documentation, you must cite evidence to make your thesis plausible to your readers.

The issue of documentation is critical in presenting your findings. Even during the early stages of your investigation, when you are simply checking sources for their usefulness, you should record publication data carefully. When you prepare a list of the works you cited to write your paper—a requirement for most written research projects—you should have available all the information you need.

To help you see how to develop a research paper from start to finish, the chapters in this part of the handbook focus on two papers. One is on a topic from literature, short stories by Willa Cather. The other paper is on a topic from science, the phenomenon of black holes. Good research and writing techniques apply to any subject, of course, but examining two different papers and seeing how they were developed will help you to expand your thinking about research papers. You can see how writers use research strategies for papers in different disciplines. You can also compare two documentation methods, one by the Modern Language Association of America and recommended for research in literature and the humanities; and the other by the American Psychological Association, recommended for research in the social sciences. You can see how diagrams and other visual techniques can help to clarify your final presentation. The conventions of writing about research vary from discipline to discipline; and the more you know about these conventions, the easier it will be for you to investigate sources and to present your findings for different courses of study.

Thinking through a research paper is much like thinking through any other written composition, even though research papers differ in content and format from other kinds of papers. Follow the planning guidelines set forth in these chapters to produce a successful research paper.

35a

Choose a subject that interests you, and develop a limited topic by doing prewriting exercises and using the library and by discussing the topic with friends or your instructor.

Select a general subject that fits your own interests to your instructor's assignment. Think about various specific topics within that general area of assignment; then discuss them with people you know. Try brainstorming, jotting ideas down in an informal list, asking yourself questions about your subject, writing nonstop, or developing a subject tree (see 1a).

Prewriting exercises will help you to explore what you already know about the subject and to identify areas that you would like to know more about. See, for example, how two different kinds of prewriting techniques have helped two writers narrow down a large subject to more limited topics. One writer used an informal list for her paper on Willa Cather. The other used nonstop writing as a way of getting into his paper on the search for black holes in space.

35a

res

<u>Willa Cather</u>

novel <u>My Antonia</u> my favorite in high school English

realistic picture of life on the frontier

hard existence for women

good descriptive detail

simple writing style, deep feelings though

hard to leave behind your families and move West

read one of Cather's short stories, ''Sculptor's
    Funeral''

good short story writer: picture of the hard life
    for the artist on the Western plains

maybe read some other stories by Cather?

women as central characters? difference of effects
    of hard life on men and women?

making a new life in a new territory you're not
    prepared for

dangers of famine, weather, Indians

Where and how was Cather educated?

What was her life like as a writer?

What did other writers think of her work? book reviews?

Cather's view of her art? What was she trying to
    achieve in her stories and novels?

NONSTOP WRITING

So, I have to do a research paper. About what? Wow! I

haven't done a research paper really ever except for

hurry-up jobs in high school. What interests me?

Astronomy. I have always loved astronomy. I remember when I used to look at the moon through dad's big binoculars. You could see the craters. Always gave me an eerie feeling. I remember the first time I saw a satellite. Thought it was a star, but it kept moving. Then I thought it was an airplane, but it was going too fast and didn't blink like airplane lights do. Funny that you don't hear much about satellites these days. How many out there now? What are they used for? Television. Telephones. Maybe I could write a paper on something about satellites. My teacher will probably say that is still too broad. Let's see. What else interests me in astronomy? Two ideas--black holes and the new things our space probes found out about Jupiter and Saturn. Black holes fascinate me. I saw a movie about them several years ago. What a great name--kind of like a cosmic Bermuda Triangle. Get too close to one in your space ship and you are swallowed up! I don't really know what a black hole is. Something about space being curved? I think that scientists say that nothing can escape from a black hole, not even light. If no light can escape, how do you see them or know they are there? That would be a good topic-- searching for black holes. Another topic is Jupiter or Saturn. From the news I guess those pictures from the space probe really baffle scientists. Those spokes on Saturn's rings. I think that a moon or something has a volcano or something. That would be another good paper-- what new problems we have discovered as a result of the space probes. The more I think about it, the more topics start pouring in. Comets, life on other worlds, all sorts of things. Well, time's up.

Once you have a preliminary idea for your research paper, you should browse through the library, checking the card catalog, general reference books, and periodical indexes to see what other people have written on your topic. Preliminary reading in books and magazines helps you to decide on the suitability of your topic and to limit and sharpen its focus. Also, this early exploring of books and magazines will help you to plan the development of your topic and to organize your later research successfully.

How narrow a topic must you choose? Answers to that question depend upon your interests, the nature of the assignment, the required length of the paper, the number and the quality of available library materials, and the time you have to do your assignment. But try to narrow your topic as much as possible, because narrow topics allow you to use enough specific examples and details to keep readers interested in your writing. Note in the following examples how prewriting exercises and preliminary library research have helped these students to narrow their topics through progressive stages until they have promising starting points for their papers.

Astronomy

Current questions about the universe ↓

Black holes ↓

How black holes might be located in space ↓

Various techniques used in the search for black holes

Literature

Short stories ↓

Willa Cather's short stories ↓

The theme of isolation in Cather's short stories ↓

The theme of isolation in two stories by Cather

As you pursue your research, you may discover that you need to limit your topic further. Carefully limiting your topic will help you exclude many fruitless areas before you investigate them. For instance, the writer of the paper on Cather's stories (see pages 613–643) would have wasted time researching Cather's later novels, her views on naturalism in fiction, or the ups and downs of her reputation among critics.

When you think that you have a workable limited topic, talk about it with your instructor or with friends before you begin your research in depth. At this point, discussions with people whose judgment you trust can help you test your ideas and can lead to important reshaping that may save time and hard work later on.

Exercise 35.1° Choose three of the general subjects below, and limit each subject to produce at least one topic suitable for a research paper. (You may wish to choose one of these narrowed-down topics for your own library paper. Exercises marked with an asterisk (°) in this chapter and in Chapters 36 through 38—that is Exercises 35.1, 35.2, 35.3, 35.4, 36.1, 36.2, 36.4, 38.2, 38.5, 38.6—are designed to help you with your own research project.)

1. Black entertainers
2. mental illness
3. Vincent Van Gogh
4. alcohol use in America
5. preschool education
6. urban novels
7. women corporate leaders
8. the history of the theater
9. cowboys
10. political essays
11. exercise
12. Carl Sandburg's poetry
13. jazz
14. existentialism
15. computers
16. mass transportation
17. dinosaurs
18. surrogate mothers
19. illegal aliens
20. one-act plays

35b

Learn about the various libraries available to you and the types of help they offer.

As you consider an appropriately narrow topic, check the library facilities on your campus and the surrounding community.

If your college has only one library, that may simplify your life, but it may also limit your resources. Most large universities have several specialized libraries scattered across the campus. Your school may have both an undergraduate library and a graduate or a main library, and it may have a science library and various other special collections. Many cities have large public libraries, and in some cities that have several colleges, students in one school often can use the libraries of all the others.

The concept of the library is changing rapidly because new technologies to preserve information are competing with books and periodicals for shelf space. Many libraries collect phonograph records, movie films, audio- and videotapes, photographs, and microfilm or microfiche. *Microfilm* is a film on which printed materials are photographed, greatly reduced in size. *Microfiche* is a sheet of microfilm that can accommodate and preserve many pages of printed text in reduced form.

Specialized off-campus libraries may offer a wide range of books and other materials closely related to your topic or rich in information not easily available elsewhere. A chapter of a local union, for example, may have a collection of documents related to the union's growth and development. Town, village, or city historical societies usually collect materials related to local history and make them available to students. Museums may house special book collections. Your local newspaper should have issues dating back to its origin and may provide valuable sources for your research. The college librarian can help you identify and visit special libraries.

Once you have chosen your topic and have put an initial limit on it, you should talk with a reference librarian, who can tell you what resources are available for your research. Librarians enjoy helping people, and you can save time if you let them help you. Most librarians know not only the resources available in their own libraries but also those you can consult elsewhere in the region. Ask for help at the very beginning. And as you write, ask for help whenever you need it.

35c

Find out what has been written about your subject and make a preliminary bibliography by using the library catalog, indexes to periodicals, reference books, and other sources.

1 Use the library catalog.

A library catalog names all the books owned by your library. Most libraries use *card catalogs.* Some libraries use bound volumes to catalog books. Modern automation makes catalogs available on microfilm, microfiche, computers, or a combination of these. Learn your library's catalog system as soon as you can; your librarian will help you use it efficiently.

Author Entry: Catalog from Automated Library System

Author's name → Cather, Willa, 1873-1947.
    Shadows on the rock. — New York: A. A. Knopf, 1931. 4 p., L.,
    3-280 p., 1 L.; 19½cm.—
      At head of title: By Willa Cather.
      "First edition."
      1. Canada – History – To 1763 (New France) – Fiction
      I. Title.   Other publication data:
      ■ PZ 3. C2858 Sh

Title of book and author's name → The troll garden / by Willa Cather; with an afterword by
    Katherine Anne Porter. New York: New American Library, 1971.   Name of special imprint of book
    151, [6] p.
      "A Plume book."
Call number →   Bibliography: p. [153]-[157] ←   Pages in bibliography
(Library of   I. Title.
Congress   → ■ PS 3505 A87 T7   (88497123)
System)

    Youth and the bright Medusa / by Willa Cather. — New York:
    Vintage Books, 1975, c1920. 279p.; 19 cm. ←   Size of book
      Contents: Coming, Aphrodite!—The diamond mine.—A gold
      slipper.—Scandal—Paul's case.— A Wagner matinée.—The
      sculptor's funeral.—"A death in the desert."
      I. Title
      ■ PZ 3 .C2858 Vo12

Title Entry: Catalog from Automated Library System

The Trojan woman. Adapted by Jean-Paul Sartre, English version by
Ronald Duncan.
Euripides. [1st American ed.] New York, Knopf, 1967. xv, 80 p.
20 cm.
Translation of Les Troyennes.
I. Sartre, Jean Paul, 1905– tr. II. Duncan, Ronald Frederick
Henry, 1914– tr. III. Title. IV. Title: Troades. English
■ PA 3976.7 .T8

The troll garden / by Willa Cather; with an afterword by Katherine
Anne Porter.
Cather, Willa, 1873-1947. New York: New American Library, 1971.
151, [6] p.
"A Plume book."
Bibliography: p. [153]-[157]
I. Title.
■ PS 3505 A87 T7

Title of book and author's name → The troll garden / by Willa Cather

Call number (Library of Congress System) → ■ PS 3505 A87 T7

Other publication data:

Author's birth and death dates

These cards are arranged alphabetically in the drawers, usually located near the circulation desk. In some large schools with several libraries, you will find a card catalog in each library. You may also find a union catalog in the main library listing all the holdings of the school's libraries, including the names of the libraries where the books can be found.

In the card catalog of your library, you will find that every book is listed on at least three cards: a *subject* card, a *title* card, and an *author* card. If it covers several subjects, the same book may be listed on several subject cards.

Libraries use a number system to organize books. To find a book in your library, you need the *call number*, which appears in the catalog entry and on the spine of the book. Many libraries use the Library of Congress classification system. Others use the older Dewey Decimal System or a combination of the two. Whatever catalog system a library uses will be displayed on charts near the catalog and the circulation desk.

As soon as you pick your topic, find the subject section of the catalog and list the books related to your topic. You will probably notice that some authors seem to be experts in the field you are exploring. They may have written other books and articles worth your time, even though these titles were not listed in the subject catalog that you inspected during your preliminary research. Look them up in the author cards.

Even at this early stage, you should list each promising source on a separate 3 × 5 bibliography card. Record full publishing data for all your sources. The data you will need include the author's full name, the title of the book, its date and city of publication, and the publisher's name. (See the sample bibliography card on page 538.) You should also copy down names of editors and translators as well as volume numbers, names and

Card Catalog Entries

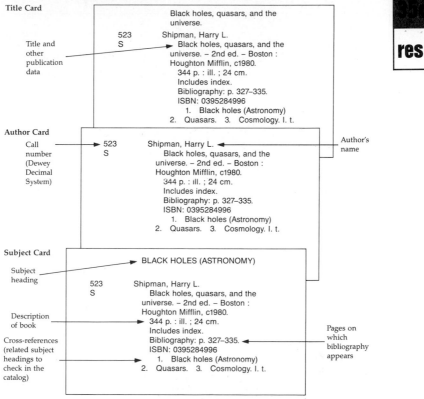

Title Card

Title and other publication data

Black holes, quasars, and the universe.

523
S
Shipman, Harry L.
Black holes, quasars, and the universe. – 2nd ed. – Boston : Houghton Mifflin, c1980.
344 p. : ill. ; 24 cm.
Includes index.
Bibliography: p. 327–335.
ISBN: 0395284996
1. Black holes (Astronomy)
2. Quasars. 3. Cosmology. l. t.

Author Card

Call number (Dewey Decimal System)

523
S
Shipman, Harry L.
Black holes, quasars, and the universe. – 2nd ed. – Boston : Houghton Mifflin, c1980.
344 p. : ill. ; 24 cm.
Includes index.
Bibliography: p. 327–335.
ISBN: 0395284996
1. Black holes (Astronomy)
2. Quasars. 3. Cosmology. l. t.

Author's name

Subject Card

Subject heading

Description of book

Cross-references (related subject headings to check in the catalog)

BLACK HOLES (ASTRONOMY)

523
S
Shipman, Harry L.
Black holes, quasars, and the universe. – 2nd ed. – Boston : Houghton Mifflin, c1980.
344 p. : ill. ; 24 cm.
Includes index.
Bibliography: p. 327–335.
ISBN: 0395284996
1. Black holes (Astronomy)
2. Quasars. 3. Cosmology. l. t.

Pages on which bibliography appears

numbers of series, and names of special imprints if any of this information appears in the catalog entry. When you get the book, you should check the data carefully against the information on the title page. Copying down full publishing data at this stage accomplishes two valuable goals. First, it assures you that all your notes are accurately and fully documented. Second, it saves you the trouble of going back to your reference materials to copy down data for your list of works cited (or reference list) after you have finished your research (see 37c-3 and 37d-2).

Always include the call number at the bottom of your card. You must have this number, whether you search for the book in the stacks or fill out a slip asking someone to find the book for you.

The call number identifies not only the book you want but also the general area in the library where you can find other books related to your topic. If you can go into the stacks in your library, check the shelves near the books you have found in the catalog. Look through them, and if they seem useful, jot down the titles on bibliography cards so that you can go back to them.

35c

res

> Shipman, Harry L.
> *Black Holes, Quasars and the Universe.*
> 2nd ed. Boston: Houghton Mifflin, 1980
>
> 523
> S

This student's bibliography card includes relevant bibliographic information. However, all information must be checked against the title page in the book.

Most of the sources you will use for a brief research paper will be *secondary,* although you should try to use *primary* sources whenever possible. **Primary** sources include works of literature, such as novels and poems; historical documents, such as diaries, letters, journals, speeches, and autobiographies; and interviews, private conversations, observations, and experiments. **Secondary** sources analyze and comment on other source material. The student writing about Willa Cather could use as a primary source one of Cather's short stories or novels or any of her other printed works; as secondary sources, the student could use books or articles written about Cather or her fiction. The student writing about black holes could use as a primary source any available reports of data from a satellite, the *Uhuru* for example. As a secondary source, the student could use books or articles commenting on the data.

2 Use indexes to periodicals.

Your reference librarian can show you several general indexes to periodical literature where you can look up journal articles pertaining to your topic. A good index usually lists articles by year of publication, under various subject headings; some indexes list by authors as well.

Make bibliography cards for any articles that you think might relate to your subject. The data you should record for periodicals include the name of the author, the title of the article, and the title of the journal. You also should copy down the volume number of the journal, the year of publication, and the page numbers on which the article appears. Look at the formats for periodical entries set down on pages 581–582 and pages 589–590 before you prepare bibliography cards for periodicals; these formats show some of the other data you might need when you set up your list of works cited or reference list.

Sample Bibliography Card: Periodical

> Daum, Bernard. "Willa Cather's Waste Land",
> South Atlantic Quarterly.
> Vol. 48
> 1949
> pages 589-601

The student will be able to use the information on this bibliography card to write an entry for her list of works cited. See page 581.

The periodical indexes have their own notation systems, and most of these do not match the formats for documentation required in your research papers. Unless you copy down data in the correct format on your bibliography cards, you may have trouble developing appropriate citations in your paper. You usually must check the article itself for information missing from the entry in the index—the author's first name, for example. Because index entries also include information not required in footnotes or endnotes, it is unwise to use an index entry as a model for your bibliography card.

The Readers' Guide is the best-known general guide to many popular periodicals. It is issued regularly (about every month) in paper covers throughout the year, and annual volumes appear in hard covers, fully indexed. Entries in *The Readers' Guide* are arranged by subject and by author. There is a helpful page of suggestions about how to use each volume, as well as a key to all abbreviations used in the index.

Sample subject and author entries appear below. Marginal notations explain the parts of the entries.

Subject Entry

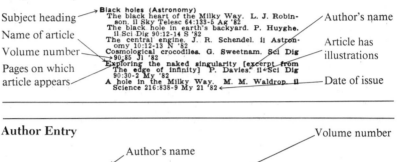

Subject heading → Black holes (Astronomy) → Author's name
Name of article → Article has illustrations
Volume number → Article appears
Pages on which article appears → Date of issue

Author Entry

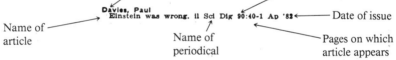

Volume number
Author's name
Name of article
Date of issue
Name of periodical
Pages on which article appears

Other Indexes

Access, 1975–.
This index bills itself as "the supplementary index to periodicals," meaning that it indexes periodicals not included in *The Readers' Guide* and other general indexes. Even so, *Access* limits itself to the kind of periodical that you might find in a large magazine store.

America: History and Life, 1964–.
An especially useful index for the research writer investigating any topic dealing with American (including Canadian) history and culture, *America* includes not only citations to the articles but also abstracts. **An abstract** summarizes the article, usually in a short paragraph, without criticizing it. Because this summary tells you much more than the title, it may save you lots of time.

The British Humanities Index, 1962–.
This British version of *The Readers' Guide* indexes periodicals published in Great Britain and has a much broader range than its American counterpart because it includes scholarly and professional journals. It succeeds the *Subject Index to Periodicals* published by the Library Association.

Essay and General Literature Index, 1900–.
This valuable index lists essays and articles in essay collections in the humanities and social sciences.

Humanities Index, 1974–.
Arranged by author and subject, the *Humanities Index* includes entries from more than 250 periodicals in archaeology, classics, language, literature, history, philosophy, religion, performing arts, and folklore. Book reviews appear in a separate section at the end.

MLA International Bibliography of Books and Articles on the Modern Languages and Literatures.
Anyone who does a research paper in literature should consult this annual five-volume bibliography from the Modern Language Association. Offering a classified list and index by subject of selections on modern languages, literatures, folklore, and linguistics, the *MLA International Bibliography* draws upon hundreds of books and periodicals as well as films, sound recordings, microfilms, and other machine-readable materials.

Here is a typical entry, with marginal notes explaining the parts of the entry.

Entry: MLA Index

Author of document   Title

Entry ⟶ [7689]   Gross, Barry. "Willa Cather and the American
number

Metaphysic." *Midamerica* ⟵————— Name or acronym
                                            of journal (check
                    1981;   8:   68–78.   master list at
Date of   front of volume)
publication   Volume   Page numbers

The New York Times Index, 1913–.
This is an indispensable index to researchers in history, government, the arts, sports, and other subjects of interest. Including all stories that have appeared in *The New York Times,* the *New York Times Index* gives the date of each story, the page and column number of the paper, and an abstract of the entry. Cross references are numerous.

Psychological Abstracts, 1927–.
Abstracts of thousands of articles in psychology published every year appear here, making this volume an excellent tool for any topic with a psychological dimension.

Public Affairs Information Service Bulletin (**P.A.I.S.**), 1915–.
Listing articles by subject, this volume is a rich resource for almost any topic dealing with politics, economics, international relations, city planning, or other aspects of social or political life.

Social Sciences Index, 1974–.
This index covers periodicals in the fields of anthropology, criminology, economics, law, political science, psychology, and sociology, among other areas of interest to social scientists. Here, too, a separate section of book reviews appears in each issue.

From 1965 to 1974, the *Humanities Index* and the *Social Sciences Index* were published as the *Social Sciences and Humanities Index.* From 1907 to 1965 the name of the combined index was the *International Index.*

Many other indexes to periodical literature deal with specialized fields and include citations from highly specialized journals. Some articles may help you in the later stages of your research, after you have summarized the information about your topic and have developed a general idea of what you want to say about it. Among the specialized indexes are the following:

Applied Science and Technology Index, 1913–
Art Index, 1929–
Arts and Humanities Citation Index, 1978–
Biography Index, 1947–
Biological and Agricultural Index, 1964–
Business Periodicals Index, 1953–
Current Index to Journals in Education, 1969–
Education Index, 1929–
Film Literature Index, 1973–
Index to U.S. Government Periodicals, 1974–
Music Index, 1949–
Social Sciences Citation Index, 1973–

Be sure to ask for help from your reference librarian, who will guide you to other indexes for topics dealing with other special fields.

Most periodicals publish an annual index of their own. When you work in a special field, consult the indexes of journals published in the field for articles that will be useful for your research.

3 Use standard reference books such as encyclopedias and dictionaries.

You must do much more than merely repeat information out of encyclopedias and dictionaries when you write a research paper. But it is always a good idea to use such reference works for background information and, perhaps, for inspiration in thinking of other ways to explore your topic. The reference room of your library has several encyclopedias. Here are a few standard works you may wish to consult.

Encyclopedias

Multivolume Encyclopedias
Collier's Encyclopedia
Encyclopaedia Britannica
Encyclopedia Americana
Because of the high costs to prepare each edition, encyclopedias are published every several years. However, these encyclopedias also publish yearbooks that try to keep up with general knowledge in various disciplines as it develops each year.

Single-Volume Encyclopedia
The New Columbia Desk Encyclopedia
The type is small, but the amount of information in this volume is staggering.

Many disciplines have encyclopedias of their own, and your reference librarian can help you find them. Here are a few that may prove especially useful for research papers.

American History
Dictionary of American History, 8 vols.

Art
Encyclopedia of World Art, 15 vols.
The McGraw-Hill Dictionary of Art

Canadian History and Culture
Encyclopedia Canadiana, 10 vols.

Classical Civilization
The Oxford Classical Dictionary, 2d ed.

Film

The International Encyclopedia of Film
The New York Times Film Reviews, 1913–

Music

Harvard Dictionary of Music
The New Grove Dictionary of Music and Musicians, 20 vols.

Religion

Encyclopaedia Judaica, 16 vols.
Encyclopaedia of Religion and Ethics, 13 vols.
The Golden Bough: A Study in Magic and Religion, edited by Sir James
G. Frazer, 13 vols.
New Catholic Encyclopedia, 15 vols.
The Oxford Dictionary of the Christian Church

Science and Technology

The McGraw-Hill Encyclopedia of Science and Technology, 15 vols.

Social Sciences

International Encyclopedia of the Social Sciences, 19 vols.

Literature

When you write research papers for literature courses, you have a large body of research materials to draw from, including several outstanding works.

The Oxford Companion to American Literature, 4th edition, edited by James D. Hart, offers biographies of American writers and summaries of literary works written in English by Americans. This volume pays little attention to literature not written by U.S. authors, and it ignores Latin American writers.

The Oxford Companion to English Literature, 4th edition, edited by Sir Paul Harvey, presents biographies of British writers and summaries of their important works; it also gives writers' biographies and plot summaries from European literature considered influential in Britain and America.

The Oxford History of English Literature comes in twelve volumes, each covering a period of literature and written by a distinguished specialist in that field.

The Year's Work in English Studies, published in London annually since 1920, contains graceful, well-written summaries of books and articles published each year in the entire field of English literature.

Contemporary Authors, 1962–, is a large, multivolume series giving short biographies and publication information for twentieth-century writers.

Contemporary Literary Criticism, 1976–, is another large, multivolume series. It presents excerpts from reviews written by prominent critics of contemporary literature. The series has recently expanded to include film criticism.

The Harvard Guide to Contemporary American Writing, edited by Daniel Hoffmann, 1979, surveys the most prominent recent American writers.

4 Do a computer search.

Automated libraries now can store extensive information on sources and make the information quickly available to researchers. Using electronic reference lists, or **data bases,** you can examine bibliographic information, as well as abstracts, cross-references, or summaries from hundreds of different sources. Good data bases currently exist in natural, applied, and social sciences, and you can save time by consulting one suited to your topic.

Your librarian will help you identify data bases relevant to your research and in all probability will carry out the search for you. But you may have to do the search yourself, and you probably will have to pay a fee. Find out about your library's computer search facilities. No doubt a set of guidelines is available, and you should study it carefully.

A successful electronic search starts with key words, or **descriptors,** that signal your area of interest and allow the computer to call up the articles that relate to your key words. You need to match the key words for your topic with the words that the data base uses to call up information. Lists of key words accompany most data bases to help you determine which to use. You should choose the most precise and specific descriptors that you can. A descriptor that is too general invariably produces an overly extensive list that will no doubt contain too many selections you will not be able to use. When your key word does not trigger enough information from the data base, your librarian can help you select more useful terms.

For most data bases you will be able to print out the titles that the computer produces for your key words. Before you do, examine the number of citations and the format in which they will appear. You may want to narrow your descriptors further or develop new combinations. You can command the computer to provide simple bibliographic data only, or you can request abstracts for articles as well as other relevant key words. Ask only for what you need.

The student researching black holes used the *Magazine Index*, a popular data-base index available at many libraries. Using *astronomy* as a descriptor, he learned that more than 2,500 entries were available, far too many to be useful. The descriptor *black holes and astronomy*, on the other hand, had 126 entries, focusing the list to more relevant titles. The student then chose to limit the list further by requesting all items published in 1986 or 1987. Narrowing the search in this way produced just three titles, which the student asked the computer to name. Narrowing the search by dates, however, is not the only method of creating a manageable list of sources from the data base. The student could have used one of these descriptors: *black holes and astronomy and evidence* or *black holes and astronomy and evidence or existence* among other possibilities.

Marginal notes explain the entries in the sample printout shown here.

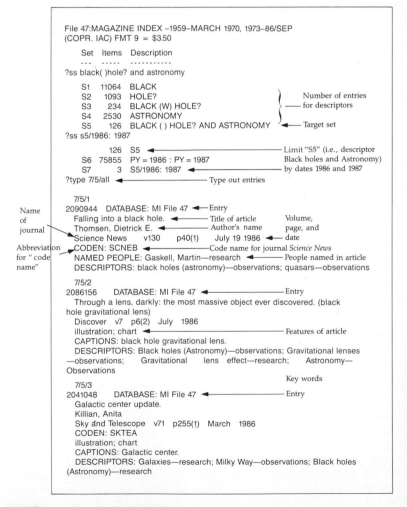

File 47:MAGAZINE INDEX –1959–MARCH 1970, 1973–86/SEP
(COPR. IAC) FMT 9 = $3.50

```
        Set   Items   Description
        ---   -----   -----------
?ss black( )hole? and astronomy

        S1   11064   BLACK
        S2    1093   HOLE?                                    Number of entries
        S3     234   BLACK (W) HOLE?                          for descriptors
        S4    2530   ASTRONOMY
        S5     126   BLACK ( ) HOLE? AND ASTRONOMY    Target set
?ss s5/1986: 1987

               126   S5                              Limit "S5" (i.e., descriptor
        S6   75855   PY = 1986 : PY = 1987            Black holes and Astronomy)
        S7       3   S5/1986: 1987                    by dates 1986 and 1987
?type 7/5/all                              Type out entries

        7/5/1
        2090944   DATABASE: MI File 47      Entry
```

Name of journal
```
        Falling into a black hole.        Title of article      Volume,
        Thomsen, Dietrick E.              Author's name         page, and
        Science News    v130    p40(1)    July 19 1986          date
```
Abbreviation for "code name"
```
        CODEN: SCNEB              Code name for journal Science News
        NAMED PEOPLE: Gaskell, Martin—research        People named in article
        DESCRIPTORS: black holes (astronomy)—observations; quasars—observations

        7/5/2
        2086156       DATABASE: MI File 47                 Entry
        Through a lens, darkly: the most massive object ever discovered. (black
        hole gravitational lens)
        Discover   v7   p6(2)   July   1986
        illustration; chart                           Features of article
        CAPTIONS: black hole gravitational lens.
        DESCRIPTORS: Black holes (Astronomy)—observations; Gravitational lenses
        —observations;    Gravitational    lens effect—research;    Astronomy—
        Observations
                                              Key words
        7/5/3
        2041048       DATABASE: MI File 47                 Entry
        Galactic center update.
        Killian, Anita
        Sky and Telescope   v71   p255(1)   March   1986
        CODEN: SKTEA
        illustration; chart
        CAPTIONS: Galactic center.
        DESCRIPTORS: Galaxies—research; Milky Way—observations; Black holes
        (Astronomy)—research
```

5 Use the bibliographies and notes in the works you consult to help you with your own research.

Look carefully at the scholarly books and articles you consult to find useful bibliographies and bibliographic notes. References to other books and articles often lead to new and useful sources of information.

In a 1984 collection, *Critical Essays on Willa Cather* by John J. Murphy, the student writing on Cather discovered a three-page list of sources after one of the essays. There she found a reference to a piece by Dayton Kohler in a 1947 issue of *College English*. Kohler's point about the effects of the barren landscape of the West on the human spirit helped the writer shape some of her ideas on Cather's stories.

*Exercise 35.2   For any topic you narrowed down in Exercise 35.1 (page 534), make a list of five indexes that you might use to help you locate articles in periodicals. Use the reference section of your library.

*Exercise 35.3   If your library can do a computer search, make a list of key words relevant to your topic and check the list against the data-base descriptions. Print out a limited, focused list of sources.

*Exercise 35.4   For any topic you narrowed down in Exercise 35.1, develop at least ten bibliography cards for books, periodicals, and other sources. Be sure to follow either the format suggested by your instructor or the format described in 35c-1 as you copy down the required data.

CHAPTER THIRTY-SIX

Planning to Write from Sources

Up to this point in your research project, you've concentrated on selecting and narrowing a topic suitable for research and on identifying appropriate libraries, reference tools, and other materials for investigation. Your main tasks now are to shape your thoughts about your topic by exploring some sources and taking notes. You should also develop a flexible plan for your paper. As you read and evaluate what you have read, your topic may change focus or emphasis, and your plan, too, will change. Reading, note taking, and planning will help you produce a well-written paper.

36a
Develop your thinking on your topic by exploring a few sources; then form a tentative thesis and develop a rough plan.

After prewriting and after limiting your topic, explore some of your resources for information about it. Your purpose in reading at this stage is to develop your ideas about the topic. You will find that you do have ideas, and you can develop them. Doing research is more than simply gathering information—it is developing something of your own to say about what you have read. Don't worry about the number of people who have written about your topic before you. Some careful thought about your resources at this stage and as you continue your research will stimulate your own original ideas on your topic. As your thoughts take shape, put together a hypothesis and a rough plan. Both of these will help you concentrate on the topic you expect to develop in your paper.

A **hypothesis** is an assumption, a debatable assumption that you have to prove. A hypothesis is an educated guess. After some early exploration of your topic you should state tentatively what conclusion you expect your research to support. Don't worry that your research is still developing. All researchers start with a hypothesis; it guides their investigations, helping them find appropriate sources and rule out others. Samples of early hypotheses and the topics from which they originated are shown below.

Topic	Hypothesis
Techniques used in the search for black holes	Black holes are almost impossible to find.
The theme of isolation in Cather's stories	In Cather's stories, characters isolated from familiar surroundings are severely affected physically and spiritually.

The student who chose the topic on black holes was struck early in his investigations by how uncertain researchers were in regard to the phenomenon. Physicists had defined black holes, predicted their presence, suggested their origins — but no one had reported having found black holes. Could they be found at all? The student formulated a hypothesis: His guess was that black holes were almost impossible to locate.

The student writing on Cather noted a remark one critic made about how the American West affected the lives of characters in Cather's novels, especially characters moving to the West from more "civilized" eastern societies. Was this true about characters in the short stories as well? As the student read Cather's stories and comments about them in secondary sources (see page 538), she could identify details that seemed to show the effects of separation upon the body and spirit of central characters. Her hypothesis reflects the connection she sees between isolation from familiar worlds and its effects upon people.

As you continue reading and exploring, your hypothesis — even your topic itself — may change markedly. Other investigators may have disproved your idea. You may find that what seemed like promising sources offer little or no help after all. You may discover a new area of thought that reshapes your thinking and pushes you into new territory. Remember, then, that your hypothesis at this stage is tentative, as is your plan for the research paper itself. As your reading continues and your hypothesis becomes more precise, you will refine your thoughts and language and will develop a carefully worded thesis for your paper. In the papers on Cather and on black holes you can see how the hypotheses above changed as the writers thought about their topics during the course of their research (see 38a).

Your tentative plan and your thesis will guide the rest of your research and will help you to eliminate from your reading list books and articles that you cannot use.

The tentative thesis statements and the rough plans that follow might well have guided the writers of the papers on pages 613–643 and pages 644–659.

Plan: Write about the search for black holes

Tentative thesis: The search for black holes presents complex problems for astronomers today.

1. Definition
2. History of the idea
3. Early search
4. Pulsars
5. Binary stars
6. Current search

Plan: Write about the effects of isolation in Willa Cather's short stories

Tentative thesis: Cather's stories " 'A Death in the Desert' " and "A Wagner Matinee" deal with the theme of isolation.

1. Effects on characters' spirits
2. Effects on their appearance
3. How music is important

These preparatory steps bring the topic into focus for note-taking and for real outlining. Of course, as you continue to read, you will make many changes, both in the thesis and in the rough plan.

*Exercise 36.1

Do some preliminary reading to shape your ideas about the topic that you chose in Exercise 35.1. Then, develop a tentative thesis and rough plan to guide your research.

36b

Read your sources with care, and take careful notes.

Whether you summarize, paraphrase, or copy quotations, always distinguish your own comments from the words and thoughts of your sources.

Write your notes on 3 × 5 cards, putting only one idea on each card.

Limiting your notes in this way will make it easier for you to organize your materials later (see 36c). Some students prefer larger index cards, but big cards make it tempting to copy down more information and more quotations than you need. Quote directly on your note cards only if you think you may use the quotation in your paper. It is wise to summarize or to paraphrase many of your sources. Summarizing and paraphrasing force you to absorb the thoughts of your source and to express them in your own words rather than merely repeat them.

A **summary** is a sharply condensed version of an original source, in your own words. A summary usually states the thesis briefly and gives the main idea of the original. Your purpose in a summary is to condense important information and to eliminate unessential points.

A **paraphrase** is a much fuller summary; it may cite some of the evidence and use some of the words in the original source. A good paraphrase follows the line of reasoning in the original source and the sequence of ideas as well. In both paraphrases and summaries, you must acknowledge your sources.

If you have a book lying on your desk, do not waste time copying down a long quotation or writing a paraphrase or a summary on a note card. Instead, make a signal card. On a **signal card,** you note the page numbers where the information appears and record your thoughts about how a quotation might be used in your paper. Of course, you can't keep library books forever; so when you write signal cards, you should be ready to write your paper.

If you think you may not have the book handy when you do write, copy down the material you need, either as a direct quotation or as a paraphrase. Because copying long direct quotations by hand leads to errors, you must proofread such copied passages with great care.

Copying machines are available in most libraries, and you can copy a page or two from a book or a periodical. (Such copying is strictly regulated by federal copyright laws, and your library may have regulations about the use of copying machines.) Remember that copying the source on a machine is no substitute for reading it. If you are going to use the source in your paper, you must read it carefully and make it part of your own thinking.

Often, when you are taking notes, ideas about what you are summarizing, paraphrasing, or copying will occur to you. Be sure your notes distinguish your words and ideas from those of your source. In your paper you will have to identify the sources of all the ideas you have borrowed. If you do not make clear in your notes just whose ideas are whose, you may find yourself committing plagiarism (see 37g). Use parentheses, asterisks, arrows, or some other means to identify your own thoughts in your notes. Also, be careful to note page breaks when a quotation continues to another page. Only a small piece of what you record on a note card may appear in the final draft of your paper, and you must be able to report the exact page reference for the quotation you use.

Below is an excerpt on black holes from page 37 of Preston Cloud's *Cosmos, Earth and Man: A Short History of the Universe* (New Haven: Yale UP, 1978). Various types of note cards prepared from the excerpt follow it. Note that the writer has identified the source at the top of each card in an abbreviated form. (Full bibliographic data will appear on the writer's bibliography cards; see 35c-1.)

SOURCE

As early as 1798 the French astronomer and mathematician Pierre Simon de Laplace suggested that, if a star were dense and massive enough, the velocity required for gravitational escape from its surface would be greater than the speed of light and that it would, therefore, be invisible. Even neutron stars cannot support a load greater than two or three solar masses. A more massive star must collapse until, consistent with relativity theory, light cannot escape and the condition visualized by Laplace is fulfilled. Such objects, assuming they exist, have been appropriately called *black holes.* A black hole may be thought of as a region in space of such fantastically high density that nothing ever leaves it. Volume at its center shrinks toward zero and density approaches infinity. Its ancestral star has essentially vanished from the visible universe — although, when quantum effects are taken into account, it appears that black holes actually do emit small amounts of radiation.

QUOTATION CARD

Cloud, *Cosmos* . . . , p. 37
"A black hole may be thought of as a region in space of such fantastically high density that nothing ever leaves it. Volume at its center shrinks toward zero and density approaches infinity."
→ Compare definition with definition in Thorne and elsewhere. Definitions are very similar. No dispute on terms?

The exact words of the source are in quotation marks; the quotation is not extensive and is one the researcher might want to use to define black holes. An arrow distinguishes the writer's thought from that of the source.

> *Cloud, Cosmos ..., p. 31*
>
> *Black holes confirm 1798 ideas advanced by French mathematician/astronomer Laplace. Very dense stars with high mass prevent escape of light and are invisible. Black holes: high-density places in space where nothing can escape.*

This summary highlights the major points in the passage that pertain to the writer's concerns and interests. Note all the details omitted from the source.

PARAPHRASE CARD

> *Cloud, Cosmos ..., p. 31*
>
> *French astronomer - mathematician Laplace in 1798 believed that if a star had a high enough mass and density, it would be invisible, because the velocity of light would be less than the velocity needed to break loose from the pull of gravity on the star. A massive star "must collapse until, consistent with relativity theory, light cannot escape." Black holes are in spots of space "of such fantastically high density" that escape is impossible.*
>
> *→ Gravity always increases as density decreases? Check.*

Here the notes closely follow the line of reasoning of the original, although the writer has used his own words to restate the point. The few words in quotation marks are exact words from the source, which may be useful to support an idea in the research paper. Again, the writer uses an arrow to set off his own thought from the ideas in the original.

Exercise 36.2   Take notes as you read and consult the various sources you have selected for your research. Use the note cards on pages 552 to 553 as models.

36c

Read and organize your notes carefully, and use them to help you focus your ideas and develop your plan.

Your early thesis statement and rough plan will guide your reading and note-taking and will shape your thoughts about the topic. Your thoughts, in turn, will suggest changes in your thesis and plan. Don't worry if your thesis and plan change many times as you develop your outline, rough drafts, and final draft for the paper. Following a preliminary plan too rigidly keeps you from making the major changes in emphasis and organization that later reading and thinking often suggest.

If you have done your research carefully, you will have many note cards on which you have collected quotations, paraphrases, statistical information, and other data from your sources. Only one idea should appear on each card. Now you have to read your notes over carefully and organize them so that you can develop your paper.

In reading through your note cards, you should find that your material falls naturally into subject groups. The headings in your rough plan were, of course, your guide for taking and organizing notes from the beginning. By now you have probably clustered related data from various sources around the general headings in this plan. Yet as you reread your note cards, you will think of new major headings that bear on your topic and discover some old main headings that do not. You will also think of subheadings that flesh out the main headings.

At this point, you are ready to expand your rough outline further, to prepare a formal outline, or to write a first draft. First, collect all your note cards, put them in order, and number them consecutively. Now you can prepare a summary guide that tells you, by number, where each note card fits into your plan. Excerpts from the summary guide developed for the paper on black holes are at the top of the next page.

This kind of guide to your note cards helps you arrange them according to tentative headings. And because the cards are numbered and each card includes the author's name and the title of the book or the article, you can keep track of your sources as you go along.

This system of organization allows you to experiment. You can group and regroup related data and ideas and shift the order of subject groups around before you make any final decisions about your plan. This experimentation also can help you to develop your plan by suggesting more effective headings and subheadings.

Headings	Note Cards
European investigation of black holes	3, 4, 6, 9, 22, 26
Definitions of black holes	1, 7, 12, 13, 14, 28
Finding black holes	2, 18, 32, 36, 37
Interpreting data	30, 31
Key researchers	5, 24, 25, 46, 53
Research methodology	5, 8, 17, 18, 55, 56, 57

You also may find it useful to think on paper about your topic in its current state. The following excerpt from several pages of notes shows how the writer of the paper on black holes began focusing his ideas and shaping the essay. These notes are experiments—attempts to build a design that will help the writer decide exactly what should be in the paper and what should not.

Writing notes like these will help you develop your information into a paper. Notice that there are questions, sentence fragments, thoughts that don't lead anywhere. All these are part of that initial shaping that eventually makes a paper.

NOTES ON BLACK HOLES

Topic: The search for black holes
Should of course define what black holes are. Definition will help explain why the search for them is worth a paper. Black holes are compressed objects, containing trillions and trillions of tons of matter in the volume of a pinhead or less. How can anybody imagine that! Jastrow says our intuitions tell us such objects cannot exist. But intuition told people the world was flat. Maybe they do exist.

Black holes are collapsed stars. Not just any star. Has to have a mass of at least three times the mass of the sun before gravity strong enough to make a black hole. Before a star collapses, energy from nuclear burning balances the gravity and holds the star in being. Like our sun. But as the star burns out its nuclear fuel, it begins to shrink. As star grows smaller, gravity grows greater, star shrinks more, until it disappears within itself.

Concept of black holes especially hard to grasp because we all grew up with Newton's idea of the universe as a great, silent machine, turning and turning. Newton's universe has no end; went on forever, at least mathematically. Had no beginning either. But the black hole idea means that it all ends in such compression that the elements themselves disappear. Atoms squeezed together in an undifferentiated mass. There goes Shakespeare! Nothing survives.

Religious people say this mathematical picture not necessarily true. God could intervene. God might have other plans. But can't treat that in a paper. Just say black holes are the end of the universe as we know it. Maybe don't even need to go into such things. Paper supposed to be nine or ten pages. Can't begin to cover everything!

Discuss discovery of pulsars. Pulsars only about ten miles across. They spin in space, throwing off radio waves from the friction of the atoms compressed in them. Jastrow says pulsars like the beam of light from a lighthouse. As the pulsar spins, it throws a pulse of radio waves toward earth. Can be picked up by radio telescopes. Should I explain radio telescopes? No, just say they are huge radio receivers that can be turned to different parts of the sky.

From the brief plan on page 550 and from the notes he developed in investigating the topic "black holes," the writer prepared this expanded plan.

Topic: The Search for Black Holes
Thesis: Astronomers are finding it almost impossible to discover and investigate black holes.

1. Definition of black holes
— Schwarzschild's theory
— Oppenheimer's move from theory to reality
— Problems of detection presented by the nature of black holes

2. The beginning of the search for black holes
— Why people did not search for them for a long time
— Discovery of a turbulent universe in the sixties
   a. The end of Newton's calm assumptions
   b. Possibility that people did not look for black holes because they did not want to prove such a bleak theory
— Discovery of pulsars, or neutron stars
— Relation of the compressed pulsar to the black hole

3. Russian work on black holes
— Idea that a black hole and a bright star might exist in a binary relationship
— Method of their search
   a. Examination of star catalogs for stars with unusual patterns
   b. X-ray emissions from stars

4. Continuation of the search among binaries
— *Uhuru* satellite and detection of x-rays
— V861 Sco

5. The search for black holes at the center of galaxies
— Qualities of galactic centers
— How phenomena may be explained by positing a black hole
— Galaxy M 87

6. Reinterpretation of existing data
— Cassiopeia A
— Qualities that need to be explained
— Iosef Shklovsky's theories

7. Conclusion

With an expanded plan like this, you can prepare a draft of the paper. You have a format, a fairly clear idea of what you want to say, and a collection of evidence to support your generalizations. But as you write, some things are bound to change. The plan may need to be simplified, or you may find it necessary to leave some things out. (It is always good to have more information than you can possibly use in your paper.) You may also realize that diagrams or charts would help to clarify some points that are hard to describe in words.

Exercise 36.3   Compare the rough plan on the topic "black holes" (page 550) with the later plan for the topic (pages 556–557). Discuss similarities and differences.

*Exercise 36.4   Continue reading about your topic and taking notes. Using the rough plan you formulated in Exercise 36.1, develop a more detailed plan.

CHAPTER THIRTY-SEVEN

Citing and Documenting Sources

By now you have a comprehensive set of note cards on your readings and an expanded plan for developing your paper. Before you prepare a draft, you need to consider ways to integrate source material into your own writing. A research paper requires a thoughtful balance between your own language and the words and sentences you borrow from other sources. Good, intelligent use of source material is the heart of research writing. Yet a perplexing issue is just how much to quote exactly and how much to restate in your own words (see 37a, pages 559–562). As a general rule of thumb, use quotations only when you feel that the original wording will add significantly to your point. Students are often tempted to quote lengthy passages verbatim, but it is not a good practice unless you have a clear, specific purpose for doing so. A lengthy passage can be tedious if the reader does not see why you didn't summarize it, perhaps quoting a line or two of the most important words. Select quotations carefully and always keep them as short as possible.

To write a paper that does more than simply restate the ideas of others, you must interpret and evaluate source materials, providing commentary to clarify points and to assert your own conclusions. And you must acknowledge every source you use; thus, you need to choose an appropriate and accepted method for citing and documenting materials you use in your paper.

37a

Integrate words and ideas from others with your own writing and provide commentary when needed.

1 Integrate source materials carefully with your own writing.

Integrating source material smoothly into your writing takes thought and care. The thesis of your paper will determine the points you make, but you will be supporting those points with ideas drawn from sources and written in a language and style that may be quite different from your own.

Following the different methods you used to record your data (see 36b), you could quote the source directly, you could summarize the source, or you could paraphrase it. Suppose you wanted to use part of this passage that appears at the end of the short story "A Wagner Matinee" by Willa Cather. The passage is about Aunt Georgiana, the main character.

SOURCE

The concert was over; the people filed out of the hall chattering and laughing, glad to relax and find the living level again, but my kinswoman made no effort to rise. The harpist slipped its green felt cover over his instrument; the flute players shook the water from their mouthpieces; the men of the orchestra went out one by one, leaving the stage to the chairs and music stands, empty as a winter cornfield.

I spoke to my aunt. She burst into tears and sobbed pleadingly. "I don't want to go, Clark, I don't want to go!"

I understood. For her, just outside the door of the concert hall, lay the black pond with the cattle-tracked bluffs; the tall, unpainted house, with weather-curled boards; naked as a tower, the crook-backed ash seedlings where the dishcloths hung to dry; the gaunt, molting turkeys picking up refuse about the kitchen door.
— Willa Cather

One option is to quote the source exactly. Depending on your purpose, you could quote a sentence or two to make your point, or you could present a longer quotation in block form, perhaps reproducing an entire paragraph. Either way, you must separate your ideas from those of your source. At the same time, you should blend your own words with the words of the writer you are quoting to produce a smooth and pleasing sentence. Later in this chapter you will learn the mechanics of documenting your sources in a variety of citation systems. Here we are concentrating on how to make smoother connections between your prose and the prose of your source.

In the last lines of ''A Wagner Matinee'' we can see the horrible tragedy of the transplanted artist, as Clark's aunt faces her life back home. Clark explains that ''just outside the door of the concert hall, lay . . . the tall, unpainted house, with weather-curled boards'' and ''the gaunt, molting turkeys picking up refuse about the kitchen door'' (115). It is the refuse of Aunt Georgiana's existence.

Notice how the writer uses her source to support the point she's making, the tragedy of the transplanted artist. Quotation marks are placed around each phrase copied from the source. The sentence that includes the quotation starting with "just outside the concert hall" follows smoothly from the sentence before it. The tag "Clark explains that" helps the writer integrate the quoted material with her own writing. The writer uses the conjunction "and" to connect two parts of Cather's sentence that are separated in the original. The spaced periods, called ellipses, shorten the quotation (see 30f). Note how the writer comments on the quotation with her own thoughtful observation: the turkeys' refuse is the refuse of Aunt Georgiana's existence. The parenthetical reference "(115)" is to the page number on which the quotation appears in Cather's story. Full documentation appears in the list of works cited (see 37c-3 and 37d-2).

QUOTATION FROM SOURCE

The final overwhelming images of the story show the utter horror of the transplanted artist:

> For her, just outside the door of the
> concert hall, lay the black pond with
> the cattle-tracked bluffs; the tall,
> unpainted house, with weather-curled
> boards; naked as a tower, the crook-

```
         backed ash seedlings where the
      dishcloths hung to dry; the gaunt,
      molting turkeys picking up refuse about
      the kitchen door.
```
The block form sets off a long quotation from the source. No quotation marks are used for block quotes of four typed lines or more. The quotation supports the point that the writer makes in the introductory sentence, which justifies the use of the long passage by calling attention to the "overwhelming images." Readers will read to see why the writer finds it overwhelming.

SUMMARY

```
         Cather leaves us with a grim picture of the
      life awaiting Aunt Georgiana after she leaves the
      concert hall and returns to her bleak homestead
      on the Nebraska frontier.
```

PARAPHRASE

```
         We see a stark, ugly world awaiting Aunt
      Georgiana. When she returns to her Nebraska
      homestead after the concert hall, she must face
      ''the black pond'' surrounded by cliffs, a
      weatherbeaten farmhouse, small ash trees, ''where
      the dishcloths hung to dry,'' and thin, bony
      turkeys pecking at garbage outside the kitchen (115).
```
In the paraphrase, which follows the original line of reasoning more closely than the summary, the writer uses quotation marks around the phrases from the original.

You must use your judgment about when to use quotation marks for individual words or for brief phrases borrowed from another source. Notice that the words *concert hall* appear in the original by Cather, but in the summary and the paraphrase, these words are not enclosed within quotation marks. A good general rule is that when you use three or more consecutive words from another source, you need quotation marks. Sometimes common sense will tell you that you need not use quotation marks, but the rule is a good one to keep in mind. It will make you think about what you are doing and will help you avoid the unconscious plagiarism that can get you into just as much trouble as the deliberate act (see 37g).

Exercise 37.1   Select a passage from a magazine article or a book, and write a paragraph in which you incorporate elements from the passage into your own writing by following the directions below. Use appropriate citations. Make a copy of the passage to show your instructor.

1. Write a brief summary of the passage as part of a paragraph that might appear in a draft of your paper.
2. Write a short paragraph in which you quote a few lines exactly from the passage.
3. Write a short paragraph in which you paraphrase the passage.

2   Comment on source material in order to clarify, interpret, or evaluate main points.

Although summaries of sources are important elements in most research papers, you should provide more than summaries alone. Readers expect you to guide them by explaining, interpreting, and evaluating source materials. You build paragraphs from summaries, paraphrases, or quotations by giving your own thoughts on your topic.

Extensive research will shape your thoughts and opinions, and as you continue examining different sources, you will formulate new ideas or modify existing ones. Some of your sources may provide conflicting data. Others may simply disagree in their interpretation of facts or even in their definitions of key terms. Still others may offer opinions that challenge what you have read elsewhere. Readers of your paper need your help in sorting out the contradictions, the important ideas from the routine, the facts from the speculations.

Commenting on source material is not easy, but it is important. There are no exact rules to follow. A sensitive researcher learns from experience just when to shed light on a complex point or when to interpret or challenge an important idea. You should respect your sources, of course, but should not be intimidated by them. In citing authorities it is right to question their conclusions, to lay them alongside conclusions drawn by others, or to use them as springboards for your own conclusions. The two examples on the next page demonstrate how a writer can integrate source material while providing useful commentary on it.

Cather's debut into fame was noted in volumes concerning American fiction, the first being Grant Overton's *The Women Who Make Our Novels*, issued late in 1918. A literary reporter rather than critic, Overton compiled information about all American female novelists of importance or popularity; but he did not prognosticate which of them, if any, might continue to be read fifty years hence. The order of his chapters was accidental and therefore meaningless; Willa Cather is sandwiched between one Grace S. Richmond, whose books were said to sell "faster than the books of any other American writer," and Clara Louise Burnham, author of "twenty-six books which have sold a half million copies." The thirteen pages Overton granted Cather are devoted largely to a biographical sketch (not always noted for accuracy) and to a summary of her achievement, drawn from reviews; these cover her work from *Alexander's Bridge*, which might have been written by Mrs. Wharton, through the indisputably personal triumph of *My Antonia*. Overton's judgments, reflecting a cross section of others' evaluations, emphasize the significance of Cather's early western experience, her controlled accessibility to it, her fidelity to character, and the esthetic delight furnished by her method.

—Philip Gerber

Much more than a summary appears here. Certainly we learn the essence of Overton's entry on Cather and two of her contemporaries. But Gerber's comments and evaluations guide our perceptions. Note how he judges Overton's credentials as a writer about Cather, how he calls the order of chapters in The Women Who Make Our Novels *meaningless, and how he questions the biographical accuracy in Overton's sketch of Cather. A reader unfamiliar with Overton has not only a summary of his work but also an assessment of it from Gerber's perspective.*

Two of the shorter pieces in *The Troll Garden,* "A Wagner Matinee" and "The Sculptor's Funeral," take firm grip on the fatality of deprivation which was an inherent part of Miss Cather's native Nebraska material. "A Wagner Matinee" is a bleakly effective *récit*, holding in concentration the terrible spiritual toll taken by frontier life, especially upon women. An old aunt of the narrator, grizzled and deformed, comes to visit her nephew in New York; she had been a music teacher at the Boston Conservatory, and marriage had taken her to a Nebraska homestead fifty miles from a railroad, to live at first in a dugout in a hillside. He takes her to a concert. At the *Tannhäuser* overture, she clutches his coat sleeve. "Then it was I first realized that for her this broke a silence of thirty years; the inconceivable silence of the plains. . . ."

—Dorothy Van Ghent

Van Ghent's purpose is to summarize the main action of "A Wagner Matinee," but she provides her own interpretations as well. She classifies the story as a récit—a term usually reserved for short novels with simple narrative lines.

Exercise 37.2   Read the following passage from the book *Sociology* by Horton and Hunt. Write a paragraph or two in which you integrate quoted or paraphrased material from the passage. Provide commentary on the quotes or paraphrases by offering your own clarifications, interpretations, or judgments.

Stereotypes.   A *stereotype* is *a group-shared image of another group or category of people.* Stereotypes can be positive (the kindly, dedicated family doctor), negative (the unprincipled, opportunistic politician), or mixed (the dedicated, fussy, sexless old-maid teacher). Stereotypes are applied indiscriminately to all members of the stereotyped group, without allowance for individual differences. Stereotypes are never entirely untrue, for they must bear *some* resemblance to the characteristics of the persons stereotyped or they would not be recognized. But stereotypes are always distorted, in that they exaggerate and universalize *some* of the characteristics of *some* of the members of the stereotyped group.

   Just how stereotypes begin is not known. Once the stereotype has become a part of the culture, it is maintained by *selective perception* (noting only the confirming incidents or cases and failing to note or remember the exceptions), *selective interpretation* (interpreting observations in terms of the stereotype: e.g., Jews are "pushy" while gentiles are "ambitious"), *selective identification* ("they look like school teachers . . ."), and *selective exception* ("he really doesn't act at all Jewish"). All these processes involve a reminder of the stereotype, so that even exceptions and incorrect identifications serve to feed and sustain the stereotype.

Stereotypes and humor.   Out-groups are often depicted in a stereotyped manner which emphasizes their alleged shortcomings. This prevents us from seeing them as individual human beings with the normal assortment of virtues and vices. Stereotypes thus enable us to apply a double standard under which we assume the best of our own group and the worst of others.

   Stereotypes form the basis of ethnic humor depicting alleged shortcomings of a particular group. Some years ago comedians used many ethnic stereotypes (thrifty Scots, money-grubbing Jews, quarrelsome Irish, dumb Swedes, etc.). Sometimes white Americans would be made up as blacks in minstrel shows in order to present the lazy, unreliable, yet somewhat cunning attitudes attributed to blacks. At other times dialect shows emphasized the inability of immigrants to speak proper English.

Today, dramatic presentations of these types are rare, but ethnic humor has not disappeared. Two changes have occurred. It is now permissible to portray stereotyped concepts of the majority group, while minority comedians may use negative stereotypes to illustrate attitudes which are now obsolete. On television, Archie Bunker exaggerated the stereotype of the conservative white blue-collar worker, while Maude on another TV show presented a stereotyped image of the white liberal determined to treat the maid as a companion whether she wished it or not. Several predominantly black programs utilized stereotypes as a put-down in confrontations between their characters. The present situation does indicate some degree of progress. At one time stereotypes in drama and story were accepted as true portraits. Today they are funny because they are regarded as burlesque rather than truth.

Stereotypes are important because people treat members of other groups in terms of the stereotyped views they hold of that group. They interact, at least initially, with the stereotype rather than with the true person. This results in many individual injustices, since only some persons in a group fully fit the stereotype. Most important, however, is the tendency for interaction in terms of stereotypes to encourage people to become more like the stereotype. In this sense the stereotype is an example of a self-fulfilling prophesy.

—Paul B. Horton and Chester L. Hunt

37b
Learn to use different formats for documenting sources.

You have already considered the importance of acknowledging information borrowed from others. Researchers often use other people's words and ideas but they always name the sources from whom they borrow.

The format for presenting information on the sources you use for research may vary, depending on the discipline in which you are doing research. Most up-to-date documentation systems require *internal* (or *parenthetical*) citation. With internal citation, sources are enclosed in parentheses and are named directly in the text of the paper instead of in footnotes. This system also requires a list of references or works cited.

Because academic disciplines vary in the precise forms they require for documentation, you must follow carefully the specific format that your instructor requests. Two of the most popular formats are those recommended by the Modern Language Association of America (MLA) in its 1984 *MLA Handbook for Writers of Research Papers* and in its counterpart for scholars, *The MLA Style Manual* (1985), and by the 1983 version of the *Publication Manual of the American Psychological Association* (APA). This chapter focuses on these formats. In addition, you will see how to use other parenthetical documentation systems as well as footnotes or endnotes. Your instructor may require the documentation format recommended in the University of Chicago Press's *The Chicago Manual of Style* or in Kate L. Turabian's *Manual for Writers of Term Papers, Theses, and Dissertations.* Many other manuals for researchers are also available.

37c

Use the MLA documentation format.

Most research papers in the humanities use the MLA format. The main features of this format include parenthetical citations directly in the text, a list of works cited, and, when necessary, explanatory endnotes.

1 Use parenthetical references to document your sources directly in the text of your paper.

The MLA system uses an abbreviated format for documentation within the text. (Full publishing data will appear in a list of works cited. See 37c-3.)

A citation in the text typically includes:

The author's last name.

The location of the material you borrowed. Usually the page numbers alone are enough; in a multivolume source, give the volume number as well. For literary works, you may want to give the act, scene, line, chapter, book, or stanza.

Remember: Complete bibliographic information must appear in your list of works cited at the end of the paper (see 37c-3). The following model will help you write your own sentences to indicate your sources.

The complete entry for Van Ghent's book appears in the list of works cited on page 641. (The full text from which the quotation in this model internal documentation is taken appears on page 563.)

The key to successful parenthetical documentation is your complete list of works cited at the end of the paper. Every reference you make in

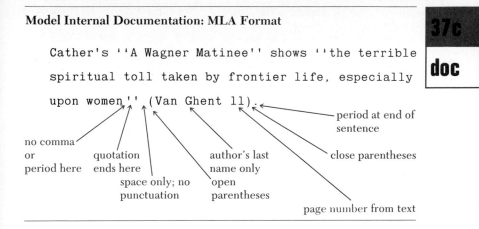

Cather's ''A Wagner Matinee'' shows ''the terrible
spiritual toll taken by frontier life, especially
upon women'' (Van Ghent 11).

period at end of sentence

no comma or period here

quotation ends here

space only; no punctuation

author's last name only

open parentheses

close parentheses

page number from text

your text must correspond to an entry on that list. Information you provide in the parenthetical documentation must match the information on your list of works cited.

Try to be concise and unobtrusive with your parenthetical references. Place them where pauses occur naturally in your sentences and as close as possible to the information you are identifying.

What you include in parentheses and what you include in the accompanying text will reflect your individual style as a writer. Feel free to experiment with different formats for references, remembering that what you include in your text determines what you include in the parenthetical documentation. If you use the author's name in a sentence, do not put that name in parentheses. If you do not name the author in your sentence, name him or her in parentheses.

No one can show all the stylistic possibilities for internal documentation, but the following examples illustrate the simplest options. Wherever possible, these examples correspond to examples presented in 37c-3 (preparing entries for the list of works cited) and 37f (preparing footnotes and endnotes).

Parts of Single-Volume Books or Articles

Van Ghent believes that ''A Wagner Matinee''
is a story about ''the terrible spiritual toll
taken by frontier life, especially upon women'' (11).

''A Wagner Matinee,'' as Van Ghent points out, ''is a bleakly effective <u>récit</u>, holding in concentration the terrible spiritual toll taken by frontier life, especially upon women'' (11).

In Cather's short story we see how life on the frontier imposes itself on a woman's spirit (Van Ghent 11).

The first two examples provide documentation that cites the author's name in the text. The third example is a paraphrase taken from Van Ghent; because the author's name does not appear in the sentence, the writer includes it in the parenthetical reference. Note in each case the page number from which the quotation or paraphrase is taken.

It may be true that some of Cather's writing shows ''the fatality of deprivation'' (Van Ghent 11), but certainly a story like ''A Wagner Matinee'' also is a tribute to the power of art in human life.

Van Ghent highlights the bleak, deprived life of Aunt Georgiana (11).

To cite an entire work rather than a part of it, name the author in your text and avoid a parenthetical reference.

Van Ghent comments on all of Cather's novels.

Morford and Lenardon have published an interesting collection of Greek and Roman myths.

Morgan, King, and Robinson have provided a basic text for beginning students of psychology.

Baugh et al. trace the growth and development of
English literature from the Middle Ages to the
twentieth century.

*The three citations directly above are all for books with more than
one author.*

Multivolume Works

Sir Thomas Browne's <u>Pseudodoxia Epidemica</u> was
''no hasty compilation, but was the product of
many years of patient thought, reading,
observation, and experiment'' (2: vii).

*The number before the colon in parentheses refers to the volume; the
number after the colon refers to the page number. (The vii tells you
that the quotation comes from the preface; pagination in the preface
or other front matter in a book is generally in lowercase roman numbers.)*

Modern readers may be mystified by the range of
classical allusions in the <u>Pseudodoxia Epidemica</u>
(Browne, vol. 2).

*This parenthetical reference is to an entire volume of a multivolume
work and not to any particular part of that volume. Here, you use a
comma to separate the author's name from the volume and you use
the abbreviation for volume.*

Works Cited by Title Only

Cather had already published <u>The Troll Garden</u> and
<u>Song of the Lark</u>, but it was <u>My Ántonia</u> that
widened her reputation in 1918 (''Cather'').

*For parenthetical references to a work that appears in the list of
works cited by title only, use a shortened version of the title. Omit the
page number if the article is brief; otherwise include the page number
after the title.*

Works by a Corporate Author

In 1980 the Commission on the Humanities
recommended that ''the humanities, sciences, and
technology need to be substantially connected''
(21), but we have made little progress in
achieving that goal.
The reference is to **The Humanities in American Life.**

Two or More Works by the Same Author

Bacon condemned Plato as ''an obstacle to
science'' (Farrington, Philosophy 35).

Farrington points out that Aristotle's father
Nicomachus, a physician, probably trained his son
in medicine (Aristotle 15).
*The title, or shortened form of it, is necessary in the parenthetical
reference to a work by an author who appears more than once on your
list of works cited. A comma follows the author's name if you use it in
the parenthetical reference. If you put the author's name in the text,
give only the title and the page reference, as in the second example
above. Two of Farrington's books,* **The Philosophy of Francis Bacon**
and **Aristotle: Founder of Scientific Philosophy,** *would appear on
the list of works cited in this case. See 37c-3 for how to list more than
one work by the same author on your list of works cited.*

Literary Works

In the opening sentence of Lord Jim, Conrad shows
us the physical power of his hero (3; ch. 1).

Marlowe says about Brown that what set him apart
from other scoundrels ''was the arrogant temper

of his misdeeds and a vehement scorn for mankind at large and for his victims in particular'' (Conrad 352-53; ch. 38).

For classical literary works in several editions, readers find it useful to have more than just page numbers in a reference. Chapter, book, or act and scene numbers make it easier to find materials in any copy of a novel or play. In the parenthetical reference, cite the page number first, then use a semicolon, and then give any other useful information, such as chapter, book, or act and scene numbers. Use accepted abbreviations.

More Than One Work in a Single Reference

Several critics refer to the place of music in Cather's art (Giannone; Brennan; Van Ghent 20-21).

Use semicolons to separate works when you cite more than one work in a single parenthetical reference. The first two entries ("Giannone" and "Brennan") are to complete articles; the last entry ("Van Ghent 20–21") is to specific pages in Van Ghent's article. Because a reference that is too long will distract your readers, you may want to use a footnote or endnote to cite multiple sources. See 37f.

Indirect Sources

Wolfe was upset at an anonymous criticism of his play <u>The Mountains</u>. He told his teacher at Harvard, George Pierce Baker, that ''if I knew who wrote that, I would no longer be responsible for my actions'' (qtd. in Turnball 54).

You should take material from original sources whenever you can. But when the original is unavailable and you have only an indirect source (for example, a published account of someone's spoken comments) use the abbreviation "qtd. in" in your parenthetical reference, right before your citation. Your list of works cited would include a reference like this:

Turnball, Andrew. <u>Thomas Wolfe</u>. New York:

    Scribner's, 1967.

You might choose to document your original source in a footnote or an endnote; see 37f.

37c

doc

Linda Lavin's performance in <u>Broadway Bound</u> by Neil Simon pleased most of the New York drama critics.

In <u>Heartbreak Ridge</u> Clint Eastwood continues to impress his audiences with his skills as an actor and a director.

Exercise 37.3 Write a sentence that summarizes, paraphrases, or quotes a portion of each selection below. Within your sentence, provide documentation for the source according to the MLA guidelines. Publishing data appears in parentheses; you will not have to use all the information, however.

1. "When Shakespeare came to London from Stratford-on-Avon, the new poetry, which was to crown the last decades of the sixteenth century and the beginning of the seventeenth, was already established. Its arrival had been announced in 1579 by the publication of Spenser's *The Shepherd's Calendar.*" (The selection is from *Shakespeare's Songs and Poems*, edited by Edward Hubler. The quotation is from pages xii–xiii. The book was published in 1959 by McGraw-Hill in New York.)
2. "Every summer, one of the nation's longest-running and most hotly contested photo competitions takes place at the offices of Sierra Club Books in San Francisco. Between 50,000 and 100,000 color transparencies are submitted for publication in the four Wilderness calendars, and the flood of entries keeps a small army of freelance photo editors and clerks busy from July to November." (The selection is from an article called "Wilderness Pin-Ups by Sierra Club" by Catherine Kouts in *Publishers Weekly*, volume 225, number 17, April 27, 1984, page 41.)
3. The Greeks' most important legacy is not, as we would like to think, democracy; it is their mythology. Even though in the second century A.D. a mysterious voice was heard exclaiming "great Pan is dead," the Greek gods and many obscure and irrational stories about them lived on in the imaginations of artists and writers, no matter how often or in how many different ways Christians and philosophers tried to dismiss the myths as frivolous or harmful. And even in the twentieth century, when man has acquired greater power than ever before to alter the natural world, the old myths continue to haunt us, not just in the form of nymphs and shepherds on vases or garden statuary, but in many

common assumptions about the shape of human experience. The notions — now presumably obsolete — that a man should be active and aggressive, a woman passive and subject to control by the men in her family, are expressed in virtually every Greek myth, even the ones in which the women seek to gain control of their own lives. That the most important phase of a woman's life is the period immediately preceding her marriage (or remarriage) is preserved in the plot of many novels, as is the notion that virginity, or at least celibacy, offers a woman a kind of freedom that she is no longer entitled to when she becomes involved with a man. (The selection is from page 207 of an article called "Women in Greek Myths" by Mary R. Lefkowitz. The article appears on pages 207-19 of the Spring 1985 *American Scholar*, volume 54, number 2. *The American Scholar* is a journal that numbers pages continuously throughout the annual volume and is published in Washington, D.C., by Phi Beta Kappa.)

2 Use explanatory notes to add information that you do not want in the text of your paper.

When you use parenthetical references in your research paper, you can provide additional information through footnotes or endnotes.

You can provide evaluative comments on your sources or other relevant information that does not fit neatly in your text paper. Or, you can use an explanatory note to list a number of citations. (See 37f for preparing footnotes and endnotes that cite sources.)

Indicate notes by a raised number in your text. Put your explanatory notes before your list of works cited (see 37c-3) on a separate page under the heading *Notes*.

Notes to Explain

Earlier, when Clark received the letter from Howard announcing Aunt Georgiana's arrival, Clark says that her name called up her figure ''at once pathetic and grotesque'' (107).[1]

[1] Cather's family and friends objected to her portrait of Nebraska life when this story first appeared in Everybody's Magazine. A good friend, Will Jones, complained that strangers would always

associate Nebraska with Aunt Georgiana's terrible

shape, her false teeth, and her yellow skin.

Cather denied that she wanted to disparage her

homeland but admitted that her family felt

insulted: ''They had already told her that it was

not nice to tell such things'' (Woodress 117).

In the above example the writer uses a parenthetical reference to cite the page, "(107)," from which she quotes the words "at once pathetic and grotesque." She uses the note to explain information that does not belong in the text itself. In addition, she cites a reference to a critical piece about Cather. See pages 567–568.

Note to Cite Multiple Sources

Music is a very important element in much of

Cather's fiction.²

² Giannone; Brennan, ''Willa Cather'';

Brennan, ''Music''; Gerber 71-73; Bloom and Bloom

123; Daiches 8; Van Ghent 20-21.

The note permits the writer to cite several sources. Including these many references in a parenthetical citation in the text itself would distract readers. See page 571.

3   Prepare a list of works cited.

You must provide a list of works cited for readers of your research paper. **A list of works cited** is an alphabetical list of books, articles, and other sources (like films, interviews, or dramatic productions) that you consulted in doing your research. All the citations in your paper will be keyed to this list of research materials. (If you use print materials only, your list will be called a **bibliography.**)

If you make bibliography cards carefully (see 36b), you can produce a list of works cited without much trouble. Each card will have the full data you need when you prepare your list for the final draft of your paper.

The following models show you how to document the usual kinds of sources for your research. If you cite some special sources (cartoons, computer programs, musical compositions, and works of art, for example), you should consult the *MLA Handbook* itself.

Model Entry (MLA) in a List of Works Cited: A Book with One Author

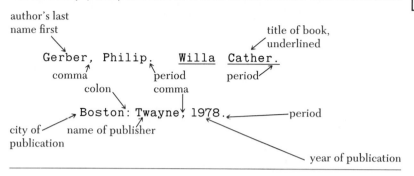

The periods set off three major divisions in the entry: the author's name, the title, and the publishing data. If the entry requires more than one line, indent the second line and all other lines five spaces.

Sometimes other facts than simply the author, title, and publishing information are required, as in the following sample:

McCray, Curtis L. ''Kaptain Kronkite: The Myth of

the Eternal Frame.'' <u>Television: The</u>

<u>Critical View.</u> Ed. Horace Newcomb. 2nd ed.

New York: Oxford UP, 1979. 319-33.

McCray is the author of an essay in the second edition of a book edited by Newcomb. Newcomb collected a number of essays and prepared them for printing, hence his designation as editor (Ed.) of the book. The book is in its second edition (2nd ed.), which means that one earlier version exists but that the researcher used the more recent book. Note the short form Oxford UP *for Oxford University Press. Short forms are acceptable.*

An Anthology

Wolfe, Don M., ed. <u>American Scene: New Voices</u>.

New York: Stuart, 1963.

The abbreviation ed. *says that Wolfe is the editor of this collection. If the author is a compiler (of a bibliography, for example) or a transla- tor, use* comp. *or* trans. *after the name.*

A Book by Two or More Authors

Morford, Mark P. O., and Robert J. Lenardon.

    <u>Classical Mythology</u>. New York: Longman, 1971.

Morgan, Clifford T., and Richard A. King.

    <u>Introduction to Psychology</u>, 2nd ed. New

    York: McGraw, 1961.

Note that only the first author's name is inverted.

Morgan, Clifford T., Richard A. King, and Nancy

    M. Robinson. <u>Introduction to Psychology</u>. 6th

    ed. New York: McGraw, 1979.

The abbreviation ed. *here stands for* edition. *An arabic number (with an appropriate suffix to show that the number is ordinal) indicates the edition number.*

Baugh, Albert C., et al. <u>A Literary History of</u>

    <u>England</u>. New York: Appleton, 1948.

The abbreviation et al. *is short for the Latin* et alii, *meaning "and others"; with more than three authors* et al. *replaces the names of all authors but the first, whose name is inverted as usual.*

Two or More Books by the Same Author

Brooks, Cleanth. <u>Fundamentals of Good Writing: A</u>

    <u>Handbook of Modern Rhetoric</u>. New York:

    Harcourt, 1950.

- - -. <u>The Hidden God: Studies in Hemingway,</u>

    <u>Faulkner, Yeats, Eliot, and Warren</u>. New

    Haven: Yale UP, 1963.

Brooks, Cleanth, and Robert Penn Warren, eds.

    <u>Understanding Poetry</u>. 3rd ed. New York:

    Holt, 1960.

Farrington, Benjamin. <u>Aristotle: Founder of</u>

    <u>Scientific Philosophy</u>. New York: Praeger, 1969.

- - -. <u>The Philosophy of Francis Bacon</u>. Chicago: U

    of Chicago P, 1964.

When you list more than one book by the same author, give the author's name in the first entry only. For each succeeding entry, instead of the author's name type three hyphens and a period, then skip a space and type the title. The hyphens always stand for the author's name exactly as it appears in the entry that comes directly before. (Brooks' name is repeated in the third entry because hyphens would have referred to his name only; in Understanding Poetry *he is one of two authors.) If the author is an editor, a compiler, or a translator, use a comma after the hyphens and write in the correct abbreviation — ed., comp., or trans. — before the title. Of course, all works listed for the same author appear alphabetically by title.*

A Book with Corporate Authorship

Commission on the Humanities. <u>The Humanities in</u>

    <u>American Life: Report of the Commission on</u>

    <u>the Humanities</u>. Berkeley: U of California P,

    1980.

A Book with No Author's Name on the Title Page

<u>Greece: 1974</u>. Athens: National Tourist

    Organization of Greece, 1973.

The entry begins with the title; on the list of works cited, alphabetize the entry by the first word other than an article.

A Selection from an Anthology

Sewell, Elizabeth. ''Bacon, Vico, Coleridge, and

    the Poetic Method.'' <u>Giambattista Vico: An</u>

    <u>International Symposium</u>. Ed. Giorgio

    Tagliacozzo and Hayden V. White. Baltimore:

    Johns Hopkins P, 1969. 125-36.

Page numbers indicate where the essay being cited appears in the longer work.

A Preface, an Introduction, a Foreword, or an Afterword

Blackmur, Richard P. Introduction. <u>The Art of the</u>

<u>Novel: Critical Prefaces</u>. By Henry James.

New York: Scribner's, 1962. vii-xxxix.

Fowles, John. Preface. <u>Islands</u>. By Fowles. Boston:

Little, 1978. 1-2.

The name of the writer of the preface, introduction, foreword, or afterword begins the entry, followed by the name of the part you are citing. Quotation marks or underlining is unnecessary. When the writer of the piece differs from the author of the book, use the word By after the title and cite the author's full name, first name first. If the writer of the piece is the same person who wrote the book, use only the last name after the word By. In the first entry, Blackmur wrote the introduction; James wrote the prefaces. In the second entry, the writer of the preface is also the author of the book.

A Work in More Than One Volume

Browne, Thomas. <u>The Works of Sir Thomas Browne</u>.

Ed. Geoffrey Keynes. 4 vols. London: Faber, 1928.

Browne, Thomas. <u>The Works of Sir Thomas Browne</u>.

Ed. Geoffrey Keynes. Vol. 2. London: Faber,

1928. 4 vols.

The first entry says that the work is in four volumes and that the researcher used them all. The second entry says that only the second volume was used.

An Edited Book

Buck, Pearl. <u>China as I See It</u>. Ed. Theodore F.

Harris. New York: Day, 1970.

Harris prepared this work of Buck's for publication. The entry indicates that citations in the text of the paper are to Buck's writing. If the citations are to the editor (his introductory comments, for example), his name would begin the entry. See the entry for Blackmur above.

A Translation

Maffei, Paolo. Beyond the Moon. Trans. D. J. K.

     O'Connell. Cambridge: MIT P, 1978.
Note that the MLA style of referencing does not include the abbreviation for the state after the city. If your citations are to the translator's comments, and not to the translation itself, use the translator's name to begin the entry. See the entry for Blackmur above.

A Publisher's Imprint

Farrington, Benjamin. The Philosophy of Francis

     Bacon. Chicago: Phoenix-U of Chicago P, 1964.
An imprint is the name a publisher sometimes gives to a special group of books to be published under that name. Doubleday, for example, uses the imprint Anchor; Avon uses Camelot; New American Library uses Mentor. When a publisher's imprint appears on the title page, give the imprint name before the publisher's name. Use a hyphen between them.

A Republished Book

Knowles, John. A Separate Peace. 1959. New York:

     Bantam, 1966.
The original edition appeared in 1959; the writer of the paper used the edition republished by Bantam in 1966.

Reference Books

''Kindergarten.'' Encyclopaedia Britannica:

     Macropaedia. 1974 ed.
Material from a well-known reference work like the Encyclopaedia Britannica *does not require full publication data, but you should note the year of publication. The title in quotation marks is the entry word for the topic in the encyclopedia. The title appears first in such an entry because the information under the subject is unsigned. That is, the author's name does not accompany the article.*

Moore, Norman. ''Hodgkin, Thomas, M.D.''

Dictionary of National Biography. 1908.

Naylor, John Henry. ''Peninsular War.''

Encyclopaedia Britannica: Macropaedia.

1974 ed.

For a signed article in an encyclopedia, include the author's name. Sometimes only initials appear after the article; in that case check the list of initials in the index or in some other volume of the encyclopedia to find out the author's full name.

Pamphlets, Bulletins, and Public Documents

United States. Congressional Budget Office.

Proposition 13: Its Impact on the Nation's

Economy, Federal Revenues, and Federal

Expenditures. Washington: GPO, 1978.

National Academy of Sciences. Committee on Water,

Division of Earth Sciences. Alternatives in

Water Management. National Research Council

Publication No. 1408. Washington: National

Academy of Sciences, 1969.

For a work by a government the name of the government comes first, then the name of the agency.

A Work in a Series

Swimming Medicine IV. International Series on

Sports Sciences 6. Baltimore: University Park

P, 1978.

Neither underlined nor in quotation marks, the name of the series appears after the title of the book.

Model Entry (MLA) in a List of Works Cited: An Article in a Journal with Pages Numbered Continuously Throughout the Annual Volume

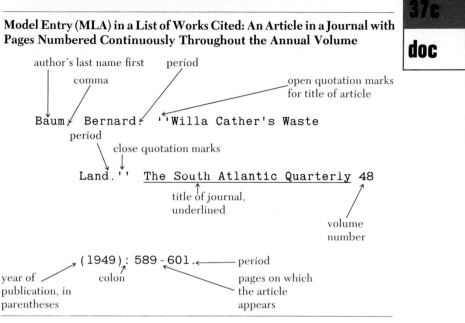

author's last name first   period

comma

open quotation marks
for title of article

Baum, Bernard. ''Willa Cather's Waste

period

close quotation marks

Land.'' The South Atlantic Quarterly 48

title of journal,
underlined

volume
number

(1949): 589-601.← period

year of
publication, in
parentheses

colon

pages on which
the article
appears

The author's name, the title, and the publishing data are the main divisions in the entry for a journal article, too. Note the titles both of the article and of the journal in which the work appears.

An Article in a Journal That Numbers Pages Separately in Each Issue of an Annual Volume

Jewell, Walter. ''The Contribution of

   Administrative Leadership to Academic

   Excellence.'' WPA: Writing Program

   Administration 3.3 (1980): 9-13.

If each issue in a volume is numbered, include the issue number in the citation. Write the volume number, then a period, then the issue number. If the journal uses only issue numbers, treat them like volume numbers.

An Article in a Monthly or Bimonthly Magazine

Arnold, Marilyn. ''Willa Cather's Nostalgia: A

   Study in Ambivalence.'' Research Studies

   Mar. 1981: 23-24.

An Article in a Weekly or Biweekly Magazine

Jones, Howard Mumford. ''The Novels of Willa

   Cather.'' <u>The Saturday Review of Literature</u>

   6 Aug. 1938: 3-4, 16.

The article is on pages 3 and 4, then jumps to page 16.

An Unsigned Article in a Magazine

''Return of the Sweatshops--They Flourish Anew.''

   <u>U.S. News and World Report</u> 14 Jan. 1980: 73-74.

An Article in a Daily Newspaper

Clark, F. Atherton. ''Metric Lengths Make

   Computation Easier.'' <u>San Antonio Express</u> 31

   July 1978: A13.

For the readers' convenience in locating the article, the section designation A appears along with the page reference, 13. If an edition is named on the masthead, specify the edition (natl. ed. or late ed., for example) after the date. Use a comma between the date and the edition.

Special Works

Unpublished Dissertations and Theses

Eisenberg, Nora. ''The Far Side of Language: The

   Search for Expression in the Novels of

   Virginia Woolf.'' Diss. Columbia U, 1977.

The abbreviation Diss. *stands for dissertation.*

Book Reviews

Fleming, Peter J. ''Nobel Lady.'' Rev. of <u>Pearl</u>

   <u>S. Buck: A Biography</u>, by T. F. Harris.

   <u>Catholic World</u> Dec. 1969: 138-39.

Recordings

Verdi, Giuseppe. <u>La Traviata</u>. With Joan

Sutherland, Luciano Pavarotti, and Matteo

Manuguerra. Cond. Richard Bonynge. National

Philharmonic Orch. and London Opera Chorus.

London, LDR-73002, 1981.

The entry starts with the composer, followed by the title of the work. The major performers appear after the word "with." Cond. is an abbreviation for Conductor and Orch. is an abbreviation for Orchestra. LDR-73002 is the catalog number.

Plays and Concerts

Brown, Arvin, dir. <u>American Buffalo</u>. By David

Mamet. With Al Pacino. Circle in the Square

Downtown Theatre, New York. 14 Aug. 1981.

Thomas, Michael Tilson, cond. American Symphony

Orch. Concert. Carnegie Hall, New York. 15

Feb. 1981.

In the first entry the abbreviation dir. is for director. In both examples the date of the performance is given.

Films and Television (or Radio) Programs

Redford, Robert, dir. <u>Ordinary People</u>. With Donald

Sutherland, Mary Tyler Moore, and Timothy

Hutton. Paramount, 1980.

<u>The Mother</u>. Writ. Paddy Chayevsky. Dir. Delbert

Mann. Philco Television Playhouse. NBC, 4

Apr. 1954.

Interviews

Sills, Beverly. Telephone interview. 6 Dec. 1981.

The interview by telephone took place on December 6, 1981.

FORMAT FOR FINAL LIST OF WORKS CITED

Your list of works cited, placed at the end of your paper, must include data for all the materials you used. A list that also includes data for materials consulted but not cited is entitled "Works Consulted." For a sample of a full "Works Cited" list, see pages 639–641.

━━━━━ **GUIDELINES FOR PREPARING A LIST OF WORKS CITED** ━━━━━

1. Set up your list on a separate page at the end of your paper.

2. Type the title ("Works Cited," or "Works Consulted," or "Bibliography") about one inch from the top of the page, and double-space before you type the first entry.

3. Arrange all your entries alphabetically according to the author's last name, but do not number them. The author's last name goes first, then the first and middle names.

4. See page 570 for listing two or more books by the same author.

5. List all entries without authors alphabetically according to the first important word in the title.

6. Do not separate books from periodicals. Strict alphabetical order guides the arrangement of entries. (For advanced research projects, writers sometimes separate primary from secondary sources.)

7. Start the first line of each entry at the left margin. Indent five spaces all the other lines within each entry. Double-space within entries and between them.

Model: MLA Style List of Works Cited (Excerpt)

```
                    Works Cited
   Bloom, Edward A., and Lillian D. Bloom. Willa
          Cather's Gift of Sympathy. Carbondale:
          Southern Illinois UP, 1962.
   Brennan, Joseph X. ''Music and Willa Cather.''
          University Review 31 (1965): 257-64.
   ---. ''Willa Cather and Music.'' University Review
          31 (1965): 175-83.
   ''Cather.'' World Scope Encyclopedia. 1955 ed.
   Cather, Willa. On Writing. New York: Knopf, 1949.
```

Exercise 37.4 Using the models in 37c-3, write correct entries for the following sources to be included in a list of works cited. (You may not need all the data that appear in each group.)

1. *Writing in the Arts and Sciences,* a 1981 textbook published by Winthrop Publishers, Inc., in Cambridge, Massachusetts. The authors, in the order that appears on the title page, are Elaine Maimon, Gerald L. Belcher, Gail W. Hearn, Barbara F. Nodine, and Finbarr W. O'Connor.

2. An article by Leo Seligsohn called "A Simple Service for Harry Chapin," in *Newsday,* a Garden City, New York, newspaper. The article appeared on Wednesday, July 22, 1981, on page 3.

3. A book by Stewart C. Easton called *Roger Bacon and his Search for a Universal Science,* published by Greenwood Press of Westport, Connecticut, in 1970.

4. In the quarterly journal *Sewanee Review,* an essay about Hart Crane, which was printed in the Spring of 1981 and called "Two Views of *The Bridge.*" Malcolm Cowley is the author. The article appears on pages 191–205.

5. Volume one of the two-volume edition of *Joseph Conrad: Life and Letters,* edited by G. Jean-Aubry and published in 1927 by Doubleday in Garden City, New York.

6. Bruno Bettelheim and Karen Zelan's "Why Children Don't Like to Read," which appeared on pages 25–31 in volume 248, number 5 (November 1981) of the *Atlantic,* an illustrated monthly magazine published in Boston by The Atlantic Monthly Company.

7. The Hemdale Film Corporation production of 1986, *Platoon,* directed by Oliver Stone and starring Tom Berenger, William DaFoe, and Charlie Sheen.

8. The fifth edition of the nine-volume *Grove's Dictionary of Music and Musicians,* published in 1954 by St. Martin's Press in New York City.

9. Rolfe Humphries' translation of Ovid's *Metamorphoses* published in London in 1957 by John Calder.

10. Henry Sambrooke Leigh's poem "The Twins" in *A Century of Humorous Verse: 1850–1950* edited by Roger Lancelyn Green and published in London by J. M. Dent and Sons. The poem appears on page 96.

Exercise 37.5 Return to Exercise 35.4 on page 547. For any five sources, write a complete entry for a list of works cited.

37d

37d

Use the APA documentation format.

doc

The *Publication Manual of the American Psychological Association* (APA) provides guidelines for writers of research papers in the social sciences and other academic areas. APA addresses its manual to writers aiming at publication in one of the many APA journals. It recommends that students writing papers in APA style follow supplementary guidelines established by their colleges. If you are told to use the APA *Publication Manual,* check with your teacher for further instructions. For example, APA manuscripts submitted for publication require an **abstract,** which is a short, comprehensive summary of the paper. Yet many undergraduate papers written in the APA format will use an outline instead of an abstract. The paper on black holes (pages 642–656) provides a topic outline instead of an abstract.

Like the MLA format, that of the APA recommends short references documented within the text and a complete list of sources, called **references,** at the end of the paper. The APA parenthetical citation includes the author's last name and the year of publication.

1 Use parenthetical references, including author's last name and year of publication, directly in the text.

Model Internal Documentation: APA Format

Scientists generally agree that a black hole is an

area in space with such a high density that

nothing can escape it (Cloud, 1978).

author's   comma   date of   period
name   publication

In the APA style a comma separates the author's name from the publication date.

Here are some other models that aim for a smooth integration of references and text:

```
This definition of black holes is one with which

Cloud (1978) would agree.

In 1978 Cloud pointed out that black holes are

definable, but many still find it difficult to

believe that they exist.
```
In the first example the author's name appears in the text; only the date is in parentheses. In the second example both name and date are woven directly into the text.

In the event that an author has more than one publication in a single year, after the date use an *a* for the first publication, a *b* for the second, and so on. These letters will also appear beside the date for the citations in your references list.

```
Bower (1977a) discusses the developing child's

perceptions.
```
The citation is to the first 1977 publication, to be marked a *on the list of references,* The Perceptual World of the Child. *Bower's second publication of 1977,* A Primer of Infant Development, *would be marked* b *in the references list.*

The three following examples show how to cite references with multiple authors. In the APA system, if a source has six authors or fewer, cite them all in the first reference. For two authors only, name them both each time you cite their material. For more than two but fewer than six authors, subsequent references use *et al.* after the first author's name. (As explained earlier, the abbreviation *et al.* is for the Latin phrase *et alii*, meaning "and others." Do not underline the abbreviation. Do not use a period after *et*; do use a period after *al.*) If your source has more than six authors, use *et al.* after the first name each time you cite the work. Use the date in each case.

Some psychologists see suicide attempts as a
gamble (Lester & Lester, 1971).
An ampersand replaces the word and.

An important study connects birth order and a
child's need to conform (Becker, Lerner, &
Carroll, 1966).
The names of all three authors are used.

Conformity also relates to group pressure (Becker
et al., 1966).
In this second reference to Becker, Lerner, & Carroll, the abbreviation et al. *replaces the names of the last two authors.*

If you want to cite a specific part of your source, put the page number you've taken your information from after the date.

A six-year-old child who could not speak, Isabelle
was ''apparently unaware of relationships of any
kind'' (Mason, 1942, p. 299).
Note the abbreviation for page. *To abbreviate the word* pages *use* pp.

Model Entry (APA) for a References Page: A Book with One Author

author's last name and initials

year of publication in parentheses

Cloud, P. (1978). Cosmos, earth and man.

periods here   title of book, underlined   period here

colon   period here

New Haven: Yale University Press.
city of   publisher's name
publication

---

2   Make a list of all the sources you cited.

At the end of your paper, on a separate page with a *References* heading, make a list of all the sources you cited.

A Book by Two or More Authors

Lester, G., & Lester, D. (1971). <u>Suicide: The</u>

    <u>gamble with death</u>. Englewood Cliffs, NJ:

    Prentice-Hall.
A comma and an ampersand separate the authors' names.

Lewis, M., & Rosenblum, L.A. (Eds.). (1974). <u>The</u>

    <u>effect of the infant on its caregiver</u>. New

    York: Wiley.
Lewis and Rosenblum are editors of this volume.

Model Entry (APA) for a References Page: An Article in a Journal with Pages Numbered Consecutively Throughout the Annual Volume

author's last
name and initials

periods

Schaefer, S. (1959)   A circumplex model for

year of publication,
in parentheses

title of article, no quotation marks: lowercase
initial letters for all words except first word

period

    maternal behavior. Journal of Abnormal
                   comma   period

    <u>and Social Psychology, 59</u>, 226-235.

volume number underlined

title of
journal is underlined,
no abbreviations.
Capitalize all major words.

pages on
which the
article appears

An Article in a Journal That Numbers Pages Separately in Each Issue of an Annual Volume

Labouvie-Vief, G. (1980). Beyond formal operations:

    Uses and limits of pure logic in life-span

    development. <u>Human Development, 23</u> (3), 141-161.
*The number 23 after the title is the volume number. The number 3 in
parentheses after the volume indicates the issue number.*

An Article in a Monthly or Bimonthly Magazine

Tresemer, D. (1983, October). Fear of success:

    Popular but unproven. <u>Psychology Today</u>, pp. 82-85.
A comma separates the year of publication from the month. Use pp. *to
abbreviate* pages *only for magazine and newspaper entries, not for
journals.*

An Article in a Daily Newspaper

Shepard, Nathaniel, Jr. (1981, October 11). Strong

    gun law sought in Chicago. <u>New York Times</u>, p. 38.

FORMAT FOR FINAL REFERENCES LIST

Like the list of works cited, the list of references names all sources cited in
the text. The list is alphabetical and appears on a separate page at the end
of the paper.

━━━━━ **GUIDELINES FOR PREPARING A REFERENCES LIST** ━━━━━

1. Type the word *References* at the center of a separate page placed at the
   end of your paper. Number the references page as you would other
   pages of your manuscript. Double-space between the word *References*
   and the first entry.

2. Arrange all entries in alphabetical order according to author's last name.
   Do not number entries. Do not separate books from periodicals.

3. Type the first line of each entry flush with the left margin. Indent two
   spaces all other lines within each entry. Double-space within entries and
   between them.

References

Cloud, P. (1978). Cosmos, earth, and man: <u>A short</u>

<u>history of the universe</u>. New Haven: Yale

University Press.

Dupress, A. K., & Hartman, L. (1979, October).

Hunting for black holes. <u>Natural History</u>, pp. 30-37.

Exercise 37.6   Return to Exercise 37.3. Revise your parenthetical documentation according to the APA format. Also, prepare a references page for the three sources.

Exercise 37.7   Return to Exercise 35.4. Select any five entries and prepare a references page according to the APA format.

37e

Use other systems of parenthetical references as your instructor requires.

Your instructor may recommend the number reference system or a full publication data system for citing sources in your paper.

The Number System

This definition of black holes is one with which

Cloud would agree (<u>2</u>, 37).

The number system requires arabic numbers for each entry in the list of works cited; these numbers appear in the parenthetical citation, too. A comma separates the number of the entry from the relevant page number, and the entry number is often underlined as you see above. With such a system, references included in the list of works cited may be arranged in any useful order, such as the order in which the writer cites the references in the text.

```
Cloud describes the shrinking of the volume in a

black hole to zero. (Cosmos, Earth and Man: A

Short History of the Universe [New Haven: Yale

UP, 1978] 37).
```
If you are required to give full parenthetical citation, use square brackets to replace the parentheses you would ordinarily use around city, publisher, and date. Full publication information in parenthetical references is rare; it distracts readers from the text and does not provide for a list of works cited that readers always find useful. Occasionally, however, you will see this system in a bibliographic study or in a work that cites only a few references.

37f
Use footnotes or endnotes to document your sources.

Many researchers use a system of notes to document their sources accurately. In such a system, notes provide full publishing information.

Footnotes appear at page bottoms, numbered consecutively throughout the paper. Endnotes are easier to set up because you number them consecutively and put them at the end of an essay. Footnotes and endnotes appear in both student papers and scholarly works.

Annotation must be clear and consistent. Your notes should make it easy for your reader to locate your sources, and they should be patterned consistently to avoid confusion. The following notes (based on the *MLA Handbook*) show you the most common style used in academic publications. Each note corresponds to an entry in 37c or 37d. For each source, therefore, you can compare the format for a footnote (or an endnote) with the format for an entry in the list of works cited or on the references page.

Books and Reference Works

A comma separates the author's name from the title. Parentheses set off the publishing data from the rest of the reference, and, as in bibliographic entries, you can always use the short form of the publisher's name. A period completes the entry. Raised a half space above the line, the number of each note comes after a five-space indentation.

Model Footnote Entry: A Book with One Author

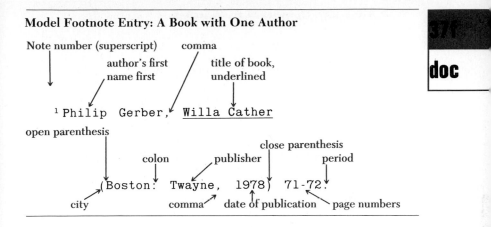

Note number (superscript) ↓

comma ↓

author's first name first ↓

title of book, underlined ↓

37f

doc

¹ Philip Gerber, Willa Cather

open parenthesis ↓

colon ↓

publisher ↓

close parenthesis ↓

period ↓

(Boston: Twayne, 1978) 71-72.

city · comma · date of publication · page numbers

An Anthology

² Don M. Wolfe, ed., American Scene: New Voices (New York: Stuart, 1963) xi-xii.

A Book by Two or More Authors

³ Mark P. O. Morford and Robert J. Lenardon, Classical Mythology (New York: Longman, 1971) 153-154.

⁴ Clifford T. Morgan and Richard A. King, Introduction to Psychology, 2nd ed. (New York: McGraw, 1961) 10.

⁵ Albert C. Baugh et al., A Literary History of England (New York: Appleton, 1948) 307.

⁶ Clifford T. Morgan, Richard A. King, and Nancy M. Robinson, Introduction to Psychology, 6th ed. (New York: McGraw, 1979) 296.

A Book with Corporate Authorship

[7] Commission on the Humanities, The Humanities in American Life: Report of the Commission on the Humanities (Berkeley: U of California P, 1980) 21.

A Book with No Author's Name on the Title Page

[8] Greece: 1974. (Athens: National Tourist Organization of Greece, 1973) 141.

A Selection from an Anthology

[9] Elizabeth Sewell, ''Bacon, Vico, Coleridge, and the Poetic Method,'' Giambattista Vico: An International Symposium, ed. Giorgio Tagliacozzo and Hayden V. White (Baltimore: Johns Hopkins P, 1969) 127-28.

A Preface, an Introduction, a Foreword, or an Afterword

[10] Richard P. Blackmur, introduction, The Art of the Novel: Critical Prefaces, by Henry James (New York: Scribner's, 1962) xvii.

A Work in More Than One Volume

[11] Thomas Browne, The Works of Sir Thomas Browne, ed. Geoffrey Keynes, 4 vols. (London: Faber, 1928) 2: 7.

The number 2 refers to the second volume. A colon and a space after it separate the volume number from the page number, here page 7. If you wanted to cite the entire volume, you would write vol. 2 right after the space following the final parenthesis. A period would complete the entry.

An Edited Book

[12] Pearl Buck, _China as I See It_, ed. Theodore
F. Harris (New York: John Day, 1970) 15.

A Translation

[13] Paolo Maffei, _Beyond the Moon_, trans.
D. J. K. O'Connell (Cambridge: MIT P, 1978) 19.

A Republished Book

[14] John Knowles, _A Separate Peace_ (1959; New
York: Bantam, 1966) 66.

A Work in a Series

[15]_Swimming Medicine IV_, International Series
on Sports Sciences 6 (Baltimore: University Park
P, 1978) 416.

Selections from Reference Books

[16] ''Kindergarten,'' _Encyclopaedia
Britannica: Macropaedia_, 1974 ed.

[17] Norman Moore, ''Hodgkin, Thomas, M.D.,''
Dictionary of National Biography (1908).

[18] John Henry Naylor, ''Peninsular War,''
Encyclopaedia Britannica: Macropaedia, 1974 ed.

Pamphlets, Bulletins, and Public Documents

[19] United States, Congressional Budget Office,
_Proposition 13: Its Impact on the Nation's
Economy, Federal Revenues, and Federal
Expenditures_ (Washington: GPO, 1978) 7-8.

[20] National Academy of Sciences, Committee on Water, Division of Earth Sciences, <u>Alternatives in Water Management</u>, National Research Council Publication No. 1408 (Washington: National Academy of Sciences, 1969) 3.

Journals, Magazines, and Newspapers

Model Footnote Entry: An Article in a Journal with Pages Numbered Continuously Throughout the Annual Volume

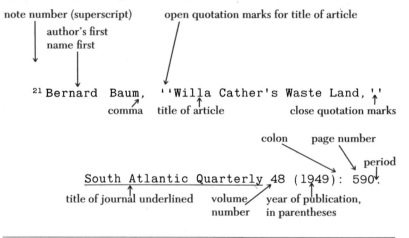

note number (superscript)

author's first name first

open quotation marks for title of article

[21] Bernard Baum, ''Willa Cather's Waste Land,''

comma   title of article   close quotation marks

colon   page number   period

<u>South Atlantic Quarterly</u> 48 (1949): 590.

title of journal underlined   volume number   year of publication, in parentheses

---

As in the reference to a book, commas separate the main elements here.

An Article in a Journal That Numbers Pages Separately in Each Issue of an Annual Volume

[22] Walter Jewell, ''The Contribution of Administrative Leadership to Academic Excellence,'' <u>WPA: Writing Program Administration</u> 3.3 (1980): 9-13.

An Article in a Monthly or Bimonthly Periodical

[23] Marilyn Arnold, ''Willa Cather's Nostalgia: A Study in Ambivalence,'' Research Studies Mar. 1981: 28.

An Article in a Weekly or Biweekly Magazine

[24] Howard Mumford Jones, ''The Novels of Willa Cather,'' The Saturday Review of Literature 6 Aug. 1938: 4.

An Unsigned Article in a Magazine

[25] ''Return of the Sweatshops—They Flourish Anew,'' U.S. News & World Report 14 Jan. 1980: 74.

An Article in a Daily Newspaper

[26] Atherton F. Clark, ''Metric Lengths Make Computation Easier,'' San Antonio Express 31 July 1978: A13.

Special Works

Unpublished Dissertations and Theses

[27] Nora Eisenberg, ''The Far Side of Language: The Search for Expression in the Novels of Virginia Woolf,'' diss., Columbia U, 1977, 29-30.

Book Reviews

[28] Peter J. Fleming, ''Nobel Lady,'' rev. of Pearl S. Buck: A Biography, by T. F. Harris, Catholic World Dec. 1969: 139.

Recordings

[29] Giuseppe Verdi, <u>La Traviata</u>, with Joan Sutherland, Luciano Pavarotti, and Matteo Manuguerra, cond. Richard Bonynge, National Philharmonic Orch. and London Opera Chorus, London, LDR-73002, 1981.

Plays and Concerts

[30] Arvin Brown, dir., <u>American Buffalo</u>, by David Mamet, with Al Pacino, Circle in the Square Downtown Theatre, New York, 14 Aug. 1981.

[31] Michael Tilson Thomas, cond., American Symphony Orch. Concert, Carnegie Hall, New York, 15 Feb. 1981.

Films and Television (or Radio) Programs

[32] Robert Redford, dir., <u>Ordinary People</u>, with Donald Sutherland, Mary Tyler Moore, and Timothy Hutton, Paramount, 1980.

[33] <u>The Mother</u>, writ. Paddy Chayevsky, dir. Delbert Mann, Philco Television Playhouse, NBC, 4 Apr. 1954.

Interviews

[34] Telephone interview with Beverly Sills, director of the New York City Opera, 6 Dec. 1981.

Later References to the Same Source

Once you provide full publishing data in a note, you can use a shortened form of citation in each later reference to your source. Generally, these references include only the author's last name and the page number. Although the *MLA Handbook* discourages the use of the Latin abbreviation *ibid.* for *ibidem,* meaning "in the same place," the form still persists in academic writing. The samples below of first and later citations show both styles.

¹ Bernard Baum, ''Willa Cather's Waste Land,'' <u>South Atlantic Quarterly</u> 48 (1949): 590.

² Philip Gerber, <u>Willa Cather</u> (Boston: Twayne, 1978) 71-72.

³ Baum 593.

⁴ Baum.

⁵ Gerber 72.

Notes 1 and 2 give all the data required as well for the sources in notes 3 and 5, respectively. Therefore, the shortened form appears in notes 3 and 5, with only the author's last name and the page number in each. Since the reference in note 4 is to the same page as the page in note 3, the author's last name alone is enough.

¹ Bernard Baum, ''Willa Cather's Waste Land,'' <u>South Atlantic Quarterly</u> 48 (1949): 590.

² Ibid. 592.

³ Philip Gerber, <u>Willa Cather</u> (Boston: Twayne, 1978) 72.

⁴ Ibid.

⁵ Baum 592.

Ibid. indicates that the citation appears in exactly the same source as in the preceding note. Capitalize ibid. as the first word of the sentence in the note, and always use a period after the abbreviation. In note 2, the reference is to the same book named in note 1, although the page number is different. Note 3 introduces a new citation. Ibid. in note 4, therefore, refers only to the source named in 3; because the page number is the same in both, no reference to pages is required in note 4.

When you use two or more sources by the same author, the author's name alone in later references would be unclear. Avoid confusion by using a shortened form of the title along with the author's name, but be sure that readers can recognize the source easily.

> [15] William Labov, ''The Study of Language in Its Social Context,'' <u>Studium Generale</u> 23 (1970): 68.

> [16] William Labov, <u>The Study of Nonstandard English</u> (Urbana: NCTE, 1970) 16.

> [17] Labov, ''The Study of Language'' 33.

> [18] Labov, <u>Nonstandard English</u> 18.

Notes 17 and 18 refer to different sources by the same author. A shortened form of the title identifies the source more specifically than the name alone.

Abbreviations

As noted before, the Modern Language Association recommends that writers avoid using some Latin abbreviations that at one time were standard in research papers. You will encounter abbreviations often in your reading, however, and you should know what they mean. The following list includes familiar abbreviations for bibliographic citations, along with some of the short forms of Latin terms that you may encounter.

anon.	anonymous
bk., bks.	book(s)
c., ca.	circa ("about"), used with approximate dates
cf.	*confer* ("compare")
ch., chs.	chapter(s)
col., cols.	column(s)
diss.	dissertation
ed., eds.	edition(s) or editor(s)
et al.	et alii ("and others")
ff.	and the following pages, as in *pp. 85ff.*
ibid.	ibidem ("in the same place")
illus.	illustrated by, illustrator, illustration(s)
l., ll.	line(s)
loc. cit.	loco citato ("in the place cited")
ms, mss	manuscript(s)

n., nn.	note(s), as in p. 24, n. 2
n.d.	no date (of publication)
no., nos.	number(s)
n. pag.	no pagination
n.p.	no place (of publication) or no publisher
op. cit.	opere citato ("in the work cited")
p., pp.	page(s)
pt., pts.	part, parts
passim	throughout
q.v.	quod vide ("which see")
rev.	revision, revised, revised by; or review, reviewed by
rpt.	reprint, reprinted
sec., secs.	section, sections
trans.	translator, translated by, translation
univ.	university
vol., vols.	volume(s)

Placement of Footnotes and Endnotes

Number your notes consecutively throughout the paper, starting with 1. Do not use asterisks or other symbols instead of numbers. In the text, type the arabic number of the note a half space above the line after all punctuation (except a dash). Note numbers always come in a logical place after a quotation or a paraphrase, and they should not distract the reader by breaking up a thought unit. Keep your notes as unobtrusive as possible.

The MLA recommends that you use endnotes (instead of footnotes) for research papers that require notes, unless you receive other instructions. Type endnotes on a separate page (or pages) after your last page of text. Use double spacing throughout the endnotes. Leave a one-inch space on top of the first page, then type the word *Notes*. Double-space beneath it before you type the first note of your paper. Here, too, place note numbers half a space above the line. Continue numbering the pages of endnotes as consecutive pages of your text. Thus, if your last page of text is page 10, the first page of endnotes will be page 11.

If you use footnotes, leave enough space to type them at the bottom of each page. Leave four blank lines between the last line of your text and the first footnote. Indent five spaces before typing the note number (again raised above the line), and leave one space after it. Only the first line of each note is indented; all other lines are flush with the left margin. Use single spacing between the lines in each note. Use double spacing between the notes themselves.

Exercise 37.8   Write footnotes or endnotes according to the following instructions.

1. In note 1 cite pages 28 to 29 in Sidney Verba and Norman H. Nie's 1972 book *Participation in America,* published in New York by Harper and Row.
2. In note 2 cite page 1 of an article called "Joint Project with University Aims at Revitalizing High School" by Beverly T. Watkins in *The Chronicle of Higher Education* dated May 16, 1984. *The Chronicle* is a weekly newspaper.
3. In note 3 cite page 8, column 2 of the same article.
4. In note 4 cite the Verba and Nie book again, page 40.
5. In note 5 cite the Verba and Nie book again, same page as in note 4.

37g
Credit all your sources to avoid plagiarism.

When you borrow something and use it in your own writing, you must leave no doubt in your reader's mind as to what you have borrowed. If you are conscious of your debts and try to show them, you will not commit plagiarism.

Plagiarism occurs whenever you present words or ideas taken from another person as if they were your own. The easiest way to avoid plagiarism is always to use quotation marks when you quote directly from a source, and always to acknowledge a source when you borrow or even allude to someone else's ideas and language, even though you may not have used that person's exact words. Sections 37c and 37d explain accepted methods of documentation and citation.

If you fail to follow these rules for borrowing from other writers, you may commit plagiarism. The most obvious plagiarism is simply **copying,** either word for word or with a few words added or shifted around. Anyone who compares the source and the copy can recognize plagiarism instantly.

Another form of plagiarism, called **mosaic plagiarism,** may result when a well-meaning, uninformed writer takes bad notes or when a dishonest one deliberately attempts to deceive readers. Here is an example in which the words are not copied entirely from the source. The writer may add words or sentences or even whole paragraphs. But anyone who reads the source and the plagiarism can tell that the latter entirely depends on the former:

A territory is an area of space, whether of water or earth or air, which an animal or group of animals defends as an exclusive preserve. The word is also used to describe the inward compulsion in animate beings to possess and defend such a space. A territorial species of animals, therefore, is one in which all males, and sometimes females too, bear an inherent drive to gain and defend an exclusive property.

In most but not all territorial species, defense is directed only against fellow members of the kind. A squirrel does not regard a mouse as a trespasser. In most but not all territorial species—not in chameleons, for example—the female is sexually unresponsive to an unpropertied male. As a general pattern of behavior, in territorial species the competition between males which we formerly believed was one for the possession of females is in truth for possession of property.

—ROBERT ARDREY

MOSAIC PLAGIARISM

Territory may be defined as an area of space, water, earth, or air, which animals defend as an exclusive preserve. The word *territory* also describes the inner compulsion in living beings to own and defend such a space. In a territorial species, males and some females are driven to gain and defend their exclusive property against fellow members of the species. The female of most territorial animals is not responsive sexually to a male without property, and the competition between males that we once believed was for the possession of females is really for possession of property.

Anyone can see that this paragraph depends entirely on the original. Some words have been changed or added, and many phrases have been altered, but the second passage is out-and-out plagiarism.

Plagiarism is a very serious offense. The prose we write ourselves is so individual that when we write something in a striking way or express a new idea, we have produced something that always belongs to us. To call someone else's writing your own is wrong and foolish. The student who plagiarizes can expect a failing grade on the paper, and in many schools for the whole course. Plagiarism is an honors-code violation and is often grounds for expulsion.

How can you avoid plagiarism? The following suggestions will help.

============ **AVOIDING PLAGIARISM: SOME POINTERS** ============

1. Study the subject you are writing on until you believe that you have something of your own to say about it. The more you think about your research, the more you will realize that you do have ideas of your own and that your opinions are worthy of being expressed. As you study, think, and write, you can come up with good ideas, and you won't have to copy the work of others.

2. Always keep your own notes and comments about a subject separate from the things you copy from other sources. Students sometimes commit accidental plagiarism because their note-taking fails to distinguish between what is their own and what they have copied.

   Read 36b on note-taking again. You may choose a different way of keeping your words separate from those of your sources. You could write your comments in a different color or keep them in a separate notebook or draw a circle around them or indicate them with an arrow. Whatever you do, do something! If you can see at a glance that some ideas came out of your own head and some from your sources, you'll avoid plagiarism.

3. Always acknowledge your sources. Here is how the writer of the mosaic plagiarism on page 603 could have avoided it by acknowledging the source of those thoughts, Robert Ardrey:

   > Ardrey defines territory as an area "whether of water or earth or air" that animals see as theirs exclusively and which they are driven by an "inward compulsion" to defend against members of their own species. A female in a territorial species is "sexually unresponsive to an unpropertied male." Ardrey believes that males do not compete for females. Instead, "the competition . . . is in truth for possession of property" (3).
   > *[This is a paraphrase that gives Ardrey credit for his points. Quotation marks enclose phrases and a clause taken directly from the original. The page number in parentheses shows exactly where in Ardrey's work these ideas appear. Full documentation would appear in the list of works cited. See 37c-3 and 37d-2.]*

4. Always use quotation marks when you are quoting directly, even if you choose to quote only a short phrase or clause.

5. Even when you are not quoting directly from a source, always be sure to attribute striking ideas to the person who first thought of them. Let your readers know the source of any novel ideas you use in your own paper, and you will be both honest and courteous.

6. You need not attribute information that is common knowledge. If you say that World War II ended in 1945, do not cite the source of your statement, since it is common knowledge. But if you do not know whether information is common knowledge or not, you should consult your teacher or an expert in the field.

CHAPTER THIRTY-EIGHT

Developing, Writing, and Revising the Research Paper

By this time you are ready to prepare a draft of your research paper. You have investigated many sources and have taken careful notes. You can see relations between ideas from one source to another. You note contradictions and differences of opinion. As a result your ideas form and re-form about your topic; your hypothesis changes; you read further to explore a point you missed or to check on a point you're not sure of.

You need to think carefully of your thesis now. Your reading and other research should focus your thoughts and allow you to state your point clearly and accurately. As you prepare to write, you may find that a formal outline helps you organize your paper. A formal outline provides an orderly visual scheme of the paragraphs with main and subordinated points clearly related. From your outline you can write first and subsequent drafts. You need to revise your research paper, paying attention to all the special details of documentation as well as to the general concerns of manuscript preparation. The students' research papers included in this chapter are useful models as your own writing progresses.

38a
Make any necessary revisions in your thesis.

After studying your rough plan, your tentative thesis, and your notes (which you now have in order), you should reevaluate your thesis in the light of what your reading has revealed about the topic.

The thesis of your research paper should be precise and should state clearly the problem you are addressing. The student developing the paper on black holes evolved a thesis, changing early versions until he produced a statement that satisfied him.

Tentative thesis	Revised thesis (1)	Revised thesis (2)
The search for black holes presents complex problems for astronomers today.	Astronomers are finding it very difficult to discover and investigate black holes.	Although the search for black holes goes on, they are by definition almost impossible to find.

The revised thesis (2) states the point of the paper clearly and appears in the student's outline. Yet as drafts of the paper developed, he changed his thesis again. The thesis that appears in the final draft of the research paper on pages 646–659 is:

> The trouble is that if black holes do exist, they are by definition almost impossible to find.

This thesis sentence is more precisely stated than any of the others. The writer is less interested in commenting on ongoing research than he is in raising a question about the existence of black holes. Note the elements of debate and paradox that win the reader's interest. Do black holes exist? If so, it would be almost impossible to find them. The research presented in the paper supports the major issues raised in the thesis.

Here are the various thesis sentences that the writer developed for the paper on Willa Cather:

Tentative thesis	Revised thesis (1)	Revised thesis (2)
Willa Cather's stories are about isolation.	Cather's " 'Death in the Desert' " and "A Wagner Matinee" show people who are isolated from familiar environments.	The central characters in Cather's stories " 'A Death in the Desert' " and "A Wagner Matinee" show the effects of an untamed country on people who go to live there from a stable, civilized world.

The thesis that appears in the final draft of the research paper on pages 617–639 is:

In two particular stories, "'A Death in the Desert'" and "A Wagner Matinee," the central characters bear the burden of escape and isolation from familiar, stable traditions to a "new country."

Exercise 38.1 Look at the hypothesis (see page 549) for the paper on Willa Cather. Then examine the thesis statements as they developed for the paper. Comment on the evolution of the thesis. What was the writer's original hypothesis? How did it change? How does the thesis reflect the concerns of the hypothesis?

*Exercise 38.2 Study your notes and make revisions in your thesis sentence as required.

38b

Write a formal outline if one is required or is useful at this stage, and revise your thesis if necessary.

Your instructor may require a formal outline, or you may find that one is useful in your efforts to refine your plan. A formal outline gives you an orderly visual scheme of your ideas, with supporting points subordinated to controlling ones. As you set down these ideas, use roman numerals for the most important points, capital letters for the next most important points, arabic numbers for supporting points under lettered points, and lowercase letters for the smallest items you include in the outline. Further subordination is possible, but you will rarely need to use all four degrees. For most papers, two or three degrees of subordination will do. The scheme is shown at the top of the following page.

Once you have grouped large related ideas in your notes, label them with accurate, mutually exclusive, logically arranged headings. Follow your rough plan in doing this. But at this stage it is more important to concentrate on making your headings sufficient in number and breadth to cover the topic properly.

As you look over these headings, some changes in organization may occur to you. Make whatever changes you need to shape your ideas, and then fill in supporting information under each major heading. Watch for and delete any overlap or repetition of ideas. The purpose of making a formal outline is to lay out your argument as clearly and as simply as possible.

All outlines follow the same format, but you can write them up as either topic outlines or sentence outlines. In a **topic outline,** you write out your points as brief capsules of meaning. Each item in a topic outline must

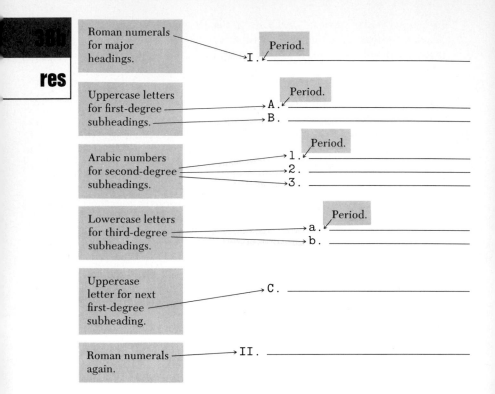

Roman numerals for major headings.

Period.

I.

Uppercase letters for first-degree subheadings.

Period.

A.

B.

Arabic numbers for second-degree subheadings.

Period.

1.

2.

3.

Lowercase letters for third-degree subheadings.

Period.

a.

b.

Uppercase letter for next first-degree subheading.

C.

Roman numerals again.

II.

communicate an idea, of course, but the items need not appear in full sentences. In a **sentence outline,** each point appears as a complete grammatical statement, with a subject and a predicate. The sentence outline requires more effort because it asks you not only to name what you are going to talk about but also to indicate what you are going to say about it. For this reason, a sentence outline may be more productive, but a topic outline can be just as helpful if you think it through just as carefully.

Two rules govern the construction of every formal outline, whether topic or sentence:

1. *Every entry requiring division must be divided into at least two parts.* Division must produce two or more parts. When you divide a topic, you must have two or more subheadings under it. If you can come up with only one subpart, incorporate it into the main heading; it belongs there. In short, a *I* requires a *II*; an *A* requires a *B*; a *1* requires a *2*; an *a* requires a *b*.

2. *Main headings must be parallel in form to each other, and subheadings under each main heading must be parallel in form to each other.*

These rules will help you to construct a clear and useful outline of your paper. But remember that you should never be bound to your outline as you write. Feel free to pull out of the air the thoughts that come to all writers, ideas they did not have in mind when they planned their work. In fact, you may very well prepare the formal outline *after* you write the paper. Every essay that works has a logic and structure that can be outlined; so you should be able to outline your essay once you have completed it. Then the outline will help you see that you have constructed a logical and clear piece of prose, that you have put everything in its proper place, and that you have developed a thesis in a thoughtful and attractive series of paragraphs leading to a conclusion.

The topic outline on pages 644–645 and the sentence outline on pages 614–615 show you the skeletons of the sample research papers on pages 646–659 and 617–639. Study them carefully, and use them as models for correct form and style.

Exercise 38.3 Discuss the strengths and weaknesses in the following outline for a paper. Look especially at the relation of the thesis to the points on the outline; at the appropriateness and parallelism of main headings and subordinate points; and at the form of the outline, including divisions and the use of numbers and letters.

```
                        Outline
Thesis: A study of liberal arts and sciences is
        valuable for students seeking careers in
        business.
   I. Exclusion of liberal arts and science courses
      from business curricula
      A. Need for specialized business courses for
         job training
  II. An understanding of people
      A. Value of psychology and sociology
         1. In a study of personality and group dynamics
      B. Value of natural sciences in seeing problems
         and in stating and in finding solutions to them
      C. Insights into human character from literature
         1. Complete personality studies from fiction
         2. Opportunities to share thoughts of
            pressured characters
 III. Recognition by businesses today of capabilities
      developing from employees' varied educational
      backgrounds
      A. Strong qualities of character
      B. Ability to deal with future technologies
  IV. Transmission of humanity's cherished values
```

Exercise 38.4   Compare and contrast the formal topic outline for the black holes paper (pages 644–645) with the earlier expanded plan (pages 556–557). What additions or deletions do you notice?

*Exercise 38.5   As your instructor directs, prepare a formal outline for your research paper. Use a *topic* or a *sentence* outline according to your instructor's wishes.

38c
Write the first draft of your paper.

Using your rough plan, your formal outline, and your note cards, write a rough draft of your research paper. This is not your final copy, and the point is not to say everything perfectly but simply to flesh out what you have to say. Once you have your paragraphs drafted, use them to adjust and refine your rough plan or your formal outline.

At this stage you will have a rough draft but a nearly final outline. Your outline should now be a trusted guide to your next draft, although as new ideas come to you in the process of creating that draft, you may need to refine the outline further. Throughout the writing process, the outline enables you to check the logic of your progress from one point to the next. Also, the outline helps you check the accuracy and the consistency of your argument.

As you write your draft, you will be drawing upon what you wrote on your note cards from your readings. Review 37a on integrating source material into your own writing. Be sure to acknowledge all sources, using the citation and documentation system your instructor requires.

The checklist below will guide you as you produce your drafts. (See also 3b.)

CHECKLIST: QUESTIONS TO ANSWER AS YOU REVISE YOUR RESEARCH PAPER

1. Is my thesis clear? Does it state accurately the intent of the paper?

2. Have I done more than simply summarize other sources? Have I made appropriate commentary on source materials?

3. Do my source materials—quotations, summaries, paraphrases— support my points throughout?

4. Do my ideas follow from each other logically? Are transitions clear?

5. Are all sources cited? Have I always indicated my source of ideas even when paraphrasing or summarizing? Are citations unobtrusive and correctly written?

6. Are my sources listed with full publication data on a separate page at the end of my paper?

res

You are bound to have other questions as you write your draft. At this stage, ask someone to read your draft before you go on. Perhaps your instructor will read it or will arrange for the class members to read each other's papers. If not, ask your roommate, some other trusted friend, or a family member. Nothing can help so much now as another pair of eyes.

Listen carefully to your reader's responses to the questions on the checklist and to any other questions you may have. Listen to any advice your reader offers. Before you prepare another draft, consider what your reader has said, and if necessary, address your reader's concerns as you revise.

38d

Once you have prepared an acceptable revised draft, edit it carefully for clarity of language and ideas and for conciseness.

Take the time to polish your expression and to check paragraph and sentence structure, grammar, spelling, and mechanics. Also, check the accuracy of quotations, paraphrases, and summaries. Avoid plagiarism by citing your sources clearly and consistently (see 37c and 37d).

38e

Prepare the final version of your research paper in acceptable form. Follow standard manuscript preparation requirements.

Most instructors ask that you type long papers, and you should follow the guidelines for manuscript preparation carefully (see 3d). Handwritten research papers are hard to produce neatly because of their length and are difficult to read. If, with your instructor's permission, you choose to handwrite your final copy, take special pains to produce a neat, clear manuscript.

Developing, Writing, and Revising the Research Paper **611**

Final copy for a research paper or a term paper usually includes, in this order:

1. A title page. The *MLA Handbook* suggests that the author's name, the class, the date, and so on, should appear on the first page of the paper, an inch down from the top and an inch from the right. The title is centered, four spaces above the text of the paper. But when formal outlines are required, many instructors prefer a title page. (See page 613 for a sample.) APA recommends a cover sheet.

2. A formal outline.

3. The body of the essay.

4. Endnotes. (If your instructor requires footnotes, place them at the bottoms of pages. If you use parenthetical documentation, endnotes or footnotes will be minimal.)

5. The list of works cited.

Number all your pages consecutively in the upper right hand corner, starting with page 1 of your text. Some writers type their last name before the page number in case pages are misplaced. Do not use a period, hyphen, or the word *page* (or the abbreviation *p.*) with the page number. Remember that endnotes and the list of works cited do count in the total pagination of your paper.

38f

Examine sample research papers.

The two research papers that follow illustrate many of the suggestions made in this chapter. The paper on Willa Cather employs the MLA system of citing sources in the text, while the paper on black holes demonstrates the APA citation system. Examine these sample research papers and the explanatory comments. Use the papers as models whenever you encounter problems in setting up research papers of your own.

*Exercise 38.6   After reading the sample papers and following the guidelines set forth in 38c, prepare the final copy of your research paper. Observe any requirements made by your instructor.

Note the punctuation of the story, " 'A Death in the Desert' "—single quotation marks enclosed by double quotation marks. Cather used double quotation marks around the title of the story to show her debt to Robert Browning. Browning's poem "A Death in the Desert" gave Cather her title. When we write the title of the story, then, we write it as a quote within a quote.

Place the title one-third down the page and double-space.

                    Isolation and Escape

                            in

        Cather's " 'A Death in the Desert' "

                           and

              "A Wagner Matinee"

Leave approximately two inches before typing the next line.

                            by

The writer's name appears here, and, on separate lines, double-spaced, the instructor's name, the course and section number, and the date the paper is submitted.

                    Shirley Hawkins

                     Mr. C. Prager

              English 101, Section 4

                   April 7, 1988

Thesis: The central characters in Willa Cather's
stories " 'A Death in the Desert' " and "A
Wagner Matinee" show the effects of an
untamed country on people who go to live
there from a stable, civilized world.

I. The main characters show the physical burden of
living in the barren West.

A. In " 'A Death in the Desert' " Katharine
Gaylord, self-isolated in the Cheyenne of
her youth, is dying from tuberculosis.

B. In "A Wagner Matinee" Aunt Georgiana is
misshapen and pathetic as a result of her
thirty years on the Nebraska frontier.

II. The characters are also burdened by the toll of
the untamed West on their spirits.

A. Wyoming is for Katharine a spiritual desert.

1. She misses her former life as a famous singer.

2. The emptiness of the desert intrudes on
the room she modeled after musical
studios in the East.

3. She will never realize her great longing
for a return to art.

4. Her death is no worse an isolation from
art than her life was.

B. Aunt Georgiana also suffers the spiritual

deprivation of a harsh frontier life.

    1. In a world of worries about survival she had little opportunity to enjoy the music she has loved so much.

    2. When she returns to Boston, the world of the prairie is always painfully close.

III. Cather uses music to identify the pains of separation from a traditional civilization to a primitive setting.

    A. For Katharine Gaylord music symbolizes the swiftly passing time of her own life.

        1. Both life and artistic achievement are too brief.

        2. In a new sonata she recognizes her own personal tragedy of isolation from the musical themes.

    B. The musical selections Aunt Georgiana hears at the matinee echo her particular condition.

        1. The overture to <u>Tannhauser</u> reflects her own struggle between art and the frontier existence.

        2. Other selections echo the battle of opposing forces in her life.

IV. Cather acknowledged that the theme of escape ran through her work.

(1-a) Title is centered two inches from the top of the page.

(1-b) *qtd. in Woodress* means that the source of the quote from Fisher is *Willa Cather* by James Woodress. (See the list of works cited on pages 641 and 643.) Fisher's original article was not available to the writer of the paper; hence she used a secondary source.

(1-c) *Gerber, preface* means that the quote appears in the preface, which is unpaginated in Gerber's book. (See the list of works cited on pages 641 and 643.)

(1-d) The thesis in its current form clearly states the topic. Notice how the introduction builds to the thesis. Notice, too, the changes the writer made from an earlier draft of the introductory paragraph:

Dorothy Canfield Fisher was a friend of Willa Cather's from college days at the University of Nebraska. She wrote an essay on Cather's works for the New York <u>Herald Tribune</u> in 1933. She said: ''the one real subject of all her books is the effect a new country--our new country--has on the people transplanted to it from the traditions of a stable, complex civilization'' (qtd. in Woodress 247). Fisher was answering complaints by critics about disconnectedness in Cather's novels. But even in Cather's short stories, you can see that Fisher is right. The central characters in the stories generally are hurt by their escape from familiar places to a new one.

Isolation and Escape in

(1-a) Cather's " 'A Death in the Desert' " and

"A Wagner Matinee"

In a 1933 essay for the New York <u>Herald Tribune</u>
Dorothy Canfield Fisher wrote about her friend from
college days at the University of Nebraska. "I offer
you a hypothesis about Willa Cather's work: the one
real subject of all her books is the effect a new
country--our new country--has on the people
transplanted to it from the traditions of a stable,

(1-b) complex civilization" (qtd. in Woodress 247). Fisher
was addressing complaints by contemporary critics
who saw disconnectedness in Cather's writing, and
Fisher wanted to show that novels like <u>A Lost Lady</u>

(1-c) and <u>Shadows on the Rock</u> had a common bond (Gerber,
preface). But even in Cather's first collection of
short stories, <u>The Troll Garden</u> published in 1905,
readers can see that Fisher's comment is valid. In

(1-d) two particular stories, " 'A Death in the Desert' "
and "A Wagner Matinee," the central characters bear

(2-a) The writer's last name and the page number of the paper appear about ¾ inch from the top of all pages after the first page of the paper itself. Margins of 1 to 1½ inches help create a readable, attractive manuscript.

(2-b) The words *character* and *story* and the repeated idea of separation connect the paragraphs smoothly. The first sentence of this paragraph corresponds to the major heading I. in the outline. The rest of this paragraph and the next develop the first-degree subheading I.A. in the outline.

(2-c) The summary gives only essential plot details to help readers who may not know the story.

(2-d) The quote from the story blends neatly with the writer's own prose. The parenthetical citation indicates that the quoted words appear on page 72 of the collection *The Troll Garden,* abbreviated here as *TG*. The title is required along with Cather's name in this citation because the list of works cited contains other works by Cather. Without the title, readers would not know which source by Cather was meant here (see the list of works cited on pages 641 and 643).

(2-e) The writer has paraphrased from the words Katharine Gaylord speaks in the story. Here is the original source:

Formerly, when it was not *if* I should ever sing Brunnhilde, but quite simply when I *should* sing Brunnhilde, I was always starving myself and thinking what I might drink and what I might not. But broken music boxes may drink whatsoever they list, and no one cares whether they lose their figure.

the burden of escape and isolation from familiar, stable traditions to a "new country."

(2-b)

   The physical appearance of the main character in each story shows the strain of the separations they lived through. When we first see her in " 'A Death in the Desert' " Katharine Gaylord, a former

(2-c) singer, is dying of lung disease in Cheyenne, Wyoming, the home of her youth. In the past she had lived in New York and Chicago and had travelled throughout Europe with the brilliant yet selfish composer Adriance Hilgarde, a man she loved deeply without his knowing it.

   Now Everett Hilgarde, Adriance's brother and an almost exact look-alike for the famous musician, observes Katharine, who is being destroyed by her long illness. Her loose-fitting gown could not hide

(2-d) "the sharp outlines of her emaciated body, but the stamp of her disease was there; simple and ugly and obtrusive, a pitiless fact that could not be disguised or evaded" (Cather, TG 72). She has stooped shoulders; she sways unevenly when she walks; and her face is "older, sadder, softer" (72) than when Everett saw her a long time ago. Self-exiled in the

(2-e) Gaylords' house, Katharine refers to herself as a

(3-a) The writer interprets the quotes she has presented.

(3-b) Corresponding to the first-degree subheading II.B. on the outline, this paragraph briefly summarizes important plot elements in "A Wagner Matinee." Note in the opening sentence the smooth integration of a quote from the story.

(3-c) The page number alone is enough in parentheses here. Readers know that the discussion is still about "A Wagner Matinee."

(3-d) The superscript 1 corresponds to the reference note 1 on page 639.

(3-a) broken music box (81). Her physical decay reflects her separation from the lively world of art she once knew.

(3-b) In "A Wagner Matinee" Aunt Georgiana, a former music teacher at the Boston Conservatory, returns to Boston--"the place longed for hungrily half a lifetime" (Cather, TG 110). For thirty years she had tended a ranch on the desolate Nebraska frontier. Her nephew Clark, who spent some of his boyhood years on the farm with her and his uncle Howard,

(3-c) notes her "misshapen figure" (108), her "soiled linen duster," and her stooped shoulders "now almost bent together over her sunken chest.... She wore ill-fitting false teeth, and her skin was as yellow as a Mongolian's from constant exposure to a pitiless wind and to the alkaline water which hardens the most transparent cuticle into a sort of flexible

(3-d) leather" (109).[1] Earlier, when Clark received the letter from Howard announcing Aunt Georgiana's arrival, Clark says that her name called up her figure "at once pathetic and grotesque" (107). Clark himself knows about the pains of that frontier life; when he thinks of corn husking days on the ranch he says "I felt the knuckles of my thumb ... as though they were raw again" (107).

(4-a) The opening sentence of this paragraph corresponds to the major heading II. on the outline. The first-degree subheading A. identifies the character to be discussed here. Second degree subheadings 1., 2., 3., and 4. correspond to details introduced and expanded upon in succeeding paragraphs.

(4-b) The quotation card for this source appears below. In the paper note how the writer quotes only the most relevant point from Kohler.

Kohler, "WC," 9.
"To a generation coming to maturity between wars Miss Cather already seemed a little old-fashioned. It was true that she did not always flatter the West, and her stories were filled with images of the waste that its barren loneliness imposed upon the human spirit."
* Good statement to support Fisher's point -- tough new world's effect on the spirit.

(4-c) The sentence identifies Porter as the source. Hence the parenthetical documentation gives only the page number. Readers can check the list of works cited for full publishing data.

(4-d) This paragraph develops the second-degree subheadings II.A.1. ("She misses her former life as a famous singer.") and II.A.2. ("The emptiness of the desert intrudes on the room she modeled after musical studios in the East.").

(4-e) The writer interprets and evaluates Cather's image.

(4-a)   But Cather's stories showed more than just the effects of the untamed West on a person's body. They also showed "the waste that its barren loneliness **(4-b)** imposed upon the human spirit" (Kohler 9). It is true that for Katharine Gaylord, life in the West did not cause her bodily pain. Still, her physical condition is a symbol for the barren life the former **(4-c)** artist must live now as she is dying of tuberculosis. As Katherine Anne Porter says in her 1952 Afterword to The Troll Garden about the singer, "Wyoming is for her not only an earthly desert but one of the heart, the mind, the spirit" (151). Forced to leave the life of musical fame that she once had, she is very unhappy, her brother says, dying "like a rat in a hole, out of her own world, and she can't fall back into ours" (Cather, TG 69).

(4-d)   We can see how much that former life meant to her and how deeply she misses it. It is easier to die in the West, she maintains: "to go East would be dying twice" (70). It is not that Wyoming is a new land for her--she grew up there as a child--but it **(4-e)** is a land now so alien to her spiritual needs. With a brilliant image Cather shows the conflicting forces of past and present in Katharine's life. In the

(5-a) Here is the signal card that the writer made and, below it, the quote from "A Wagner Matinee."

Cather, "Wagner Matinee," 74-75.
Quote about Everett talking with Katharine – as
desert suddenly glares through window -- good
to show contrast between two worlds tugging
at Katharine.

(5-b) Note the writer's interpretation.

Quotation from Source

"'I remember,' Everett said seriously, twirling the pencil between his fingers and looking, as he sat with his head thrown back, out under the red window blind which was raised just a little, and as it swung back and forth in the wind revealed the glaring panorama of the desert—a blinding stretch of yellow, flat as the sea in dead calm, splotched here and there with deep purple shadows; and, beyond, the ragged-blue outline of the mountains and the peaks of snow, white as the white clouds."

In the paper the ellipses help the writer shorten the quotation.
(5-c) This paragraph develops points II.A.3. and II.A.4. in the outline.

(5-d) The writer has paraphrased Bloom and Bloom. Here is the original source from which the paraphrase comes:

This avowed hostility between the artist and society gave her the subject for an undergraduate theme, which was published in the *State Journal,* on Thomas Carlyle's fierce withdrawal from social concerns. Later, in "'A Death in the Desert,'" she further alluded to the alienation as a "long warfare" so futile and enervating that it can only distract the artist's attention from his singular purpose.

(5-a) Wyoming house, the music room makes Everett feel
that he had stepped into a familiar New York studio
almost exactly like his brother's, "so individual
and poignantly reminiscent here in Wyoming" (71). As
he sits chatting with Katharine, a window blind
swinging in the wind reveals "the glaring panorama
of the desert--a blinding stretch of yellow, flat as
the sea in dead calm ..." (75). Blinding, yellow,

(5-b) flat, dead: so is Katharine's life away from the
East, even in the studio room she had tried so hard
to make like Adriance's.

(5-c)   Only Everett with his tales of city life and,
finally (at Everett's prompting), a letter from
Adriance with a copy of a new sonata he has just
written, cheer Katharine up somewhat. But it is very
clear from her regular conversations with Everett
that her desperate longing for the art she once knew
and her own fate not to achieve it are the great
ironies of the story. When the singer dies, Cather
writes, "the madness of art was over for Katharine"

(5-d) (86). As Bloom and Bloom have noted (151), Cather
was fascinated by the artist isolated from society.
In the portrait of Katharine Gaylord, we see that
the singer's death was no more terrible an isolation

(6-a) The opening sentence places the issues of frontier life and artistic fulfillment in a larger critical context and provides a thoughtful bridge to the discussion of "A Wagner Matinee." The parenthetical documentation identifies three critics who have called attention to the issue being emphasized here. This multiple reference does not distract the reader; any more than three consecutive citations would require a reference note. (See note 2, page 639.) The numbers after each name point to the pages in the respective sources. Full documentation is given in the list of works cited.

(6-b) The point here matches the first-degree subheading II.B. in the outline.

(6-c) Brief details of the plot explain Aunt Georgiana's separation from the music she loved.

(6-d) This paragraph develops the second-degree subheading II.B.2. in the outline.

from art than the final years of her life.

(6-a) Many critics note Cather's concern with the difficulties an artist has in leading a satisfying life on the harsh frontier (Gerber 44; Bloom and Bloom 8; Stouck 299). As with Katharine Gaylord, "the

(6-b) fatality of deprivation" (Van Ghent 11) has a serious effect on Clark's Aunt Georgiana in "A Wagner Matinee." Yet Georgiana's circumstances are somewhat different from Katharine's. Passionate love, not illness, removed her from the civilized world of

(6-c) Boston. Against her family's wishes, she eloped with a shiftless village boy who was nine years younger than she was. Howard led her to the Nebraska homestead, which she did not leave for many years. Their lives were always threatened by roving bands of Indians and insufficient supplies. A little parlor organ and church singing provided the only music she heard during all that time. Clark recalls that once, as he practiced at the organ, she told him in a quivering voice, "Don't love it so well, Clark, or it may be taken from you" (Cather, TG 110).

(6-d) Unlike Katharine's permanent exile, Aunt Georgiana returns to her former world of art. Clark takes her to a performance of the Symphony Orchestra.

(7-a) Compare the quotation in the paper with the complete paragraph by Cather from which it comes. The ellipsis in the paper indicates the omission of words that the writer felt were unnecessary for her point.

"The concert was over; the people filed out of the hall chattering and laughing, glad to relax and find the living level again, but my kinswoman made no effort to rise. The harpist slipped its green felt cover over his instrument; the flute players shook the water from their mouthpieces; the men of the orchestra went out one by one, leaving the stage to the chairs and music stands, empty as a winter cornfield."

(7-b) The writer's own evaluation here emphasizes the importance of the image and justifies the use of the long quotation.

(7-c) This quotation is more than four typed lines and, therefore, is set off from the text. Introduced by a colon, the quotation starts on a new line indented ten spaces from the left margin. Quotation marks are not used and all lines are double-spaced. The quotation is part of a single paragraph, making further paragraph indentation unnecessary. When a quotation is set off, the parenthetical reference comes after the punctuation mark. For a discussion of the various options to quote, paraphrase, or summarize from the original source, see 37a, pages 559 – 565.

Here, too, Cather's images weave together the civilized world and the grim prairie. Clark wonders how much of her ability to understand music "had been dissolved in soapsuds or worked into bread or milked in the bottom of the pail" (114). At the end

(7-a) of the concert, Aunt Georgiana sits weeping as the musicians file out, "leaving the stage ... empty as

(7-b) a winter cornfield" (115). The final overwhelming image of the story shows the utter horror of the transplanted artist:

(7-c)
> For her, just outside the door of the concert hall, lay the black pond with the cattle-tracked bluffs; the tall unpainted house, with weather-curled boards; naked as a tower, the crook-backed ash seedlings where the dishcloths hung to dry; the gaunt, molting turkeys picking up refuse about the kitchen door. (115)

It is the refuse of Aunt Georgiana's existence. Clark realizes that no matter how painful a human life, the soul always can be revived. Yet we must wonder if, in fact, he did a service for his aunt by reawakening her to the joys she had missed for so long. We understand, as Clark does at the end, when

(8-a) Note the pair of single quotation marks within the pair of double quotation marks. The quote from "A Wagner Matinee" begins with "burst into tears"; hence, double quotation marks precede it. Within that quote the writer of the paper indicates the beginning of Aunt Georgiana's spoken words with a single quotation mark before "I." Aunt Georgiana's spoken words and the quotation from the story end after the word "go"; therefore, both a single and double quotation mark follow the final punctuation.

(8-b) The opening sentence corresponds to major heading III. on the outline.

(8-c) The superscript "2" corresponds to the reference note on page 639.

(8-d) The citation indicates a paraphrase. Here is the original statement as it appears in Brennan's essay:

"It seems likely, too, that she subscribed to a prevalent nineteenth-century view (one prevalent even yet, for that matter) that music is the supreme act, that the musical experience—in its sensuous immediacy, its emotional intensity and profound spiritual appeal—is the most rapturous, most transcendent, the most certainly ineffable of all aesthetic experiences. In Willa Cather's fiction, at any rate, it is the musical moment which is generally employed to characterize a transcendent rhapsodic emotion that drenches the soul in its intensity but eludes all precise definition."

Although the writer's language is original, she nonetheless acknowledges the source of her ideas in the paper. Merely changing Brennan's words does not change the fact that the ideas are his.

(8-e) The opening sentence corresponds to outline point III.A. The rest of the paragraph develops outline points III.A.1. and III.A.2.

(8-a) she "burst into tears and sobbed pleadingly. 'I don't want to go, Clark, I don't want to go!' " (115). Yet, of course, go she must.

(8-b) It is obvious that Katharine and Georgiana were both very much involved in music, and in the two stories, music helps Cather show how dramatic the separation can be from civilized society for a person isolated in a primitive setting. Music is a very

(8-c) important element in much of Cather's fiction.[2] Of all the arts, Cather saw music as the most dynamic form in our culture--even more dynamic than literature. Through the power of music Cather characterizes an emotion so powerful that it goes beyond ordinary limits to saturate the human soul

(8-d) (Brennan, "Music" 175).

(8-e) Richard Giannone sees music for Katharine Gaylord in " 'A Death in the Desert' " as a symbol of how swiftly her time is passing. Though art is humanity's most supreme effort, it is futile, finally, because life and artistic achievement are so brief (41). Transplanted now from the life of art, she realizes her dilemma as she listens to Adriance's composition. As Everett plays the piece, Katharine recognizes its great tragic themes.

(9-a) The writer interprets the meaning of the image and relates it to the thesis of the paper.

(9-b) The opening sentence of this paragraph corresponds to III.B. in the outline (the echo of Aunt Georgiana's personal condition in the music she hears at the concert). The rest of the paragraph expands on III.B.1.

Adriance's achievement prods her own suffering. "This is my tragedy, as I lie here spent by the racecourse," she proclaims, "listening to the feet of the runners as they pass me. Ah, God! The swift feet of the runners!" (81). The feet of the runners

(9-a) are elements of that stable complex world, to use Fisher's terms again, from which Katharine was transplanted. Adriance's music tells her of the "tragedy of the soul" and "the tragedy of effort and failure, the thing Keats called hell" (Cather, <u>TG</u> 81). It is, of course, Katharine's own failure that she recognizes in the sonata.

(9-b) In "A Wagner Matinee" the musical selections at the concert echo the themes of the story. The first piece Aunt Georgiana hears is the overture to <u>Tannhauser</u>, one of Wagner's early operas. The overture starts with the Pilgrim's chorus, the solemn chanting of travelers on their way to Rome (Ewen 673). Giannone says that the motif in this chorus "represents the ecstasy of sacred yearnings" (43). Then the Venusberg motif begins, the music of the sensual, tempting, yet disturbing world of Venus and her followers. Giannone sees this as a contrasting world of profane longings. He points out that in the

(10-a) This paragraph develops point III.B.2. from the outline.

(10-b) The conclusion reminds readers of the introduction and the important point made by Dorothy Canfield Fisher. This paragraph is not simply a restatement of the introductory paragraph. The writer provides interesting background information as she explains Cather's own reaction to her friend's criticism. The conclusion builds further credibility for the thesis of the paper. The writer is implying that even Cather herself might acknowledge that the two stories treated the lives of women transplanted to a new country from stable civilizations.

overture to <u>Tannhauser</u>, Wagner presents the "struggle between the sacred and profane in man" (43). For Aunt Georgiana, the sacred is her higher yearnings for art and music; the profane is the dry prairie in an unfriendly world. The terrible tragedy here, Giannone suggests, is that "In the tug between 'the inconceivable silence of the plains' and 'the little parlor organ,' silence won" (43).

(10-a) Other selections that Aunt Georgiana hears at the matinee, including pieces from <u>The Flying Dutchman</u> and <u>Tristan and Isolde</u>, similarly reflect the battle between the opposing forces that she so fully embodies. The last piece, Siegfried's funeral march from the <u>Ring</u> cycle, signals the defeat of Wagner's hero, just as it predicts Aunt Georgiana's defeat, her return to Nebraska after the concert ends. Unlike many of Wagner's operas, "A Wagner Matinee" does not end in glory or victory with good overpowering evil. Art does not win here, nor do sacred yearnings. Nothing redeems Aunt Georgiana's fate (Giannone 45).

(10-b) By 1933, when Dorothy Canfield Fisher was writing her essay for the <u>Tribune</u>, Cather was highly sensitive to comments by critics. Honored for

(11-a) The citation "Cather" refers to an encyclopedia entry. See the list of works cited.

(11-b) Here the writer draws upon another primary source to make an important point. Note again the smooth integration of source material.

(11-c) The conclusion highlights major points made throughout the research paper.

literary accomplishments with the Prix Femina

(11-a) Americain ("Cather"), she nonetheless was attacked by many of her contemporaries (Murphy and Synnott 12–14). After she read a pre-publication copy of Fisher's essay, Cather sent her friend a telegram asking her to give up the project. About Fisher's idea that Cather's fiction deals with the effects of a new country on people removed to it from a civilized world, Cather unhappily "summarized this thesis in one word 'escape' " (Woodress 247). Yet she recognized that this theme ran through her work. Just a few years later she would write in a letter

(11-b) to The Commonweal, "What has art ever been but escape?" ("On Writing" 18). In " 'A Death in the Desert' " and "A Wagner Matinee" Cather explores the complex theme of escape by means of sympathetic

(11-c) women transplanted from civilized societies into hostile worlds.

(12-a) These notes correspond to the superscripts that appear on pages 3 and
        8 of the research paper. Notes generally go on a separate page at the
        end of the text with the word *Notes* centered one inch from the top.
        Notes are double-spaced and indented five spaces from the left margin.
        If more than one line is required, subsequent lines are flush with the left
        margin. Some instructors require the notes to be placed at the bottom
        of the page on which the matching numeral appears in the text. See 37f,
        page 592.

(12-b) Note the format of the multiple references here. The writer separates
        the references with semicolons. No page numbers follow the first three
        references. (Giannone; Brennan "Willa Cather"; Brennan "Music")
        because the writer of the paper is referring to the whole essay in each
        case.

(12-a)

Notes

[1]Cather's family and friends objected to her portrait of Nebraska life when this story first appeared in <u>Everybody's Magazine</u>. A good friend, Will Jones, complained that strangers would always associate Nebraska with Aunt Georgiana's terrible shape, her false teeth, and her yellow skin. Cather denied that she wanted to disparage her homeland but admitted that her family felt insulted: "They had already told her that it was not nice to tell such things" (Woodress 117).

(12-b)

[2]Giannone; Brennan, "Willa Cather"; Brennan, "Music"; Gerber 71–73; Bloom and Bloom 123; Daiches 8; Van Ghent 20–21.

Entries are listed alphabetically by author's last name or, as with unsigned works, by the first main word in the title. Books and articles are not separated.

(13-a) A book with two authors. The abbreviation UP stands for University Press.

(13-b) Three hyphens followed by a period indicate a piece by the author of the previous piece. Both selections here are journal articles with pages numbered consecutively throughout the annual volume. The articles are listed alphabetically by the first word in the title.

(13-c) An article in a reference encyclopedia.

(13-d) A republished book. The date of the original edition is 1905; the date of the current edition is 1971. Also, this NAL book has a special imprint, *Plume,* which precedes the publisher's name.

(13-e) Standard reference to a book with one author.

(13-f) An entry for an encyclopedia in only one edition. Ewen wrote the particular entry and the rest of the book as well. He is author of the article and author of the encyclopedia. Hence, his name appears in two places.

(13-g) Murphy's complete book is *not* cited in the text of the paper and hence might seem out of place here. However, since the writer of the paper used *two* articles from this anthology, she lists the collection itself and then cites the articles with *cross-references* to this main entry. See i. below.

(13-h) Murphy's name is spelled out here as well as in the previous entry. The first entry *(Critical Essays on Willa Cather)* is for a book published under his name alone. If other books appeared by Murphy as single author, three hyphens and a period would appear in place of his name for the second and subsequent entries. (See b. above.) The three hyphens, however, stand for only the name or names of authors in the preceding entry. Since the authors of "The Recognition of Willa Cather's Art" are Murphy *and* Synnott, both names are listed.

(13-i) A cross-reference. *Murphy 1–28* refers readers to *Critical Essays on Willa Cather,* the main entry for Murphy. The numbers *1–28* identify the pages on which the essay "The Recognition of Willa Cather's Art" are found.

Works Cited

(13-a) Bloom, Edward A., and Lillian D. Bloom. <u>Willa Cather's Gift of Sympathy</u>. Carbondale: Southern Illinois UP, 1962.

Brennan, Joseph X. "Music and Willa Cather," <u>University Review</u> 31 (1965): 257–264.

(13-b) ---. "Willa Cather and Music." <u>University Review</u> 31 (1965): 175–183.

(13-c) "Cather." <u>World Scope Encyclopedia</u>. 1955 ed.

Cather, Willa. <u>On Writing</u>. New York: Knopf, 1949.

(13-d) ---. <u>The Troll Garden</u>. 1905. New York. Plume-NAL, 1971.

(13-e) Daiches, David. <u>Willa Cather: A Critical Introduction</u>. Ithaca: Cornell UP, 1959.

(13-f) Ewen, David. "Tannhauser." <u>The New Encyclopedia of the Opera</u> By Ewen. New York: Hill, 1971.

Gerber, Philip L. <u>Willa Cather</u>. Boston: Twayne, 1975.

Giannone, Richard. <u>Music in Willa Cather's Fiction</u>. Lincoln: U of Nebraska P, 1968.

Kohler, Dayton. "Willa Cather: 1876–1947." <u>College English</u> 9 (1947): 8–18.

(13-g) Murphy, John J., ed. <u>Critical Essays on Willa Cather</u>. Boston: Hall, 1984.

(13-h)
(13-i) Murphy, John J., and Kevin A. Synnott. "The Recognition of Willa Cather's Art." Murphy 1–28.

(14-a) Porter's Afterword, published in 1952, appears in the volume of *The Troll Garden* already cited under Cather's name. The cross-reference "Cather, *Troll Garden*" is used instead of "Cather" because another book by Cather appears in the Works Cited list.

(14-b) Another cross-reference to *Critical Essays on Willa Cather.*

(14-c) A book in a series. When the title page of a book indicates that the book is part of a series, put the series name (without quotations or underlining) and number before the publishing data.

(14-a) Porter, Katherine Anne. Afterword. 1952. Cather,

Troll Garden, 134–151.

(14-b) Stouck, David. 1905. "Willa Cather's Last Four

Books." Murphy 290–304.

(14-c) Van Ghent, Dorothy. Willa Cather. U of Minnesota

Pamphlets on American Writers 36. Minneapolis:

U of Minnesota P, 1964.

Woodress, James. Willa Cather. 1970. Lincoln: Bison-U

of Nebraska P, 1975.

The Search for Black Holes

Richard Lanier

English 101, Section 6

November 7, 1988

Title of paper

Writer's name

Course and section

Date of submission

Thesis: Although the search for black holes goes on,
they are, by definition, almost impossible
to find.

 I. Black holes vs. ordinary stars

   A. Definition of black holes

   B. Contrary forces on ordinary stars

     1. Expansion from nuclear burning

     2. Compression from gravity

   C. Theory of black hole formation

     1. Crush of atoms

     2. Lack of light

 II. Beginnings in the search for black holes

   A. Problems in finding them

     1. Their invisibility

     2. Their infinitesimal size

     3. Their place in theories of the universe

   B. Discovery of pulsars, or neutron stars

Topic outline
(see 38b)

Letters and arabic numbers for subordinate points

III. Russian work on black holes

    A. Idea of binary relationship

    B. Method of search

       1. Examination of star catalogs

       2. Theory of stars' x-ray emission

IV. Continuation of search among binaries

    A. <u>Uhuru</u> satellite and x-ray detection

    B. X-ray star called V861 Sco

    C. Doubts from inadequate instruments

 V. The continuing hunt for black holes

The Search for Black Holes

Title

One of the most talked-about scientific concepts to emerge during the past two decades is the black hole. Astronomers are scanning the skies with all their amazing technology, accumulating evidence for the existence of black holes. The trouble is that if black holes do exist, they are by definition almost impossible to find.

Intro-
duction
builds to
thesis

Thesis:
compare
with early
versions
(see 38a)

What is a black hole? In theory it is a burned-out, enormous star that has collapsed. Its atoms have become so squeezed together that what is left of the star is almost infinitely dense. When density increases, so does gravity. In the black hole, the density is so great and the gravity of the object is so powerful that even light cannot escape from it.

Definition
and
explanation
of black
hole

In an ordinary "healthy" star like our sun, two contrary forces balance each other. As shown in Figure 1, one force is the expansion caused by nuclear burning pushing out toward the surface of the star. The other force is the star's own gravity, which tends to compress the star into a ball. It is much the same effect as the one we have observed

Reference to
diagram

Citations
unneces-
sary:
writer's
own words
and
ideas

with water floating in space when our astronauts have
journeyed into weightlessness. Water squeezes itself
into a ball, but the ball does not weigh enough to
crush the atoms that it contains.

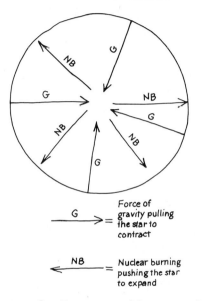

**Diagram marked
Figure 1**

Figure 1. Forces acting on stars.

All stars go through a complicated life cycle. **Outline
point I.C.**
The theory of black holes is based on the belief
that eventually the force of gravity within the star
becomes much stronger than the expanding force
generated by the nuclear reaction in the star. The
star literally burns itself out, and when its fuel is

exhausted, it begins to shrink. If the star is large
enough--at least three times larger than our sun--it
contains so much mass that its gravity begins to
crush its atoms. All atoms have a great deal of space
in them--much more space than substance. Gravity
squeezes the space out, making them more and more
dense and, of course, reducing the circumference of
the star (see Figure 2).

Outline
point
I.C.1.

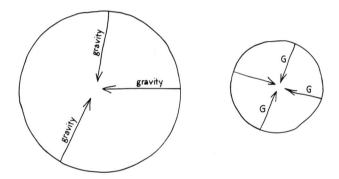

Figure 2. Gravity reducing star's circumference.

This crushing of atoms releases energy that
might take the form of light. But scientists who
believe in black holes think that the gravity of the
crushed star is so great that no light can escape
from it. Jastrow (1979) sums up the process in the
following passage, where he compares rays of light to
a ball thrown up from the earth and returning because

Author and
date

Citation
to *Red
Giants
and
White
Dwarfs*
(see
"Refer-
ences,"
page 659)

of the pull of gravity:

> But if the core of the collapsing star is
> squeezed into a very small volume, the force of
> gravity on its surface is very great. Suppose
> the core is squeezed down to a radius of a few
> miles. At that point, the mass is so compact
> that the force of gravity at the surface is
> billions of times stronger than the force of
> gravity at the surface of the sun. The tug of
> that enormous force prevents the rays of light
> from leaving the surface of the star; like the
> ball thrown upward from the earth, they are
> pulled back and cannot escape to space. All the
> light within the star is now trapped by
> gravity. From this moment on, the star is
> invisible. It is <u>a black hole in space</u>. (p. 65)

Long quotation double-spaced and set off without quotation marks

Page number on which quotation appears

This amazing theory has developed slowly. Karl
Schwarzschild, a German astronomer, first formulated
the idea of the black hole in 1916. He argued that
such an object <u>could</u> exist if we assume that light is
affected by the force of gravity ("Schwarzschild,"
1974).[1]

Commentary on source (see 37a-2)

Citation from encyclopedia article (see "References," page 659)

In 1939, J. Robert Oppenheimer--later to become
famous for his role in creating the atom bomb--and

his student Hartland Snyder suggested that a black
hole might result from the collapse of enormous,
massive stars several times larger than our own sun.
Their idea moved black holes from the realm of pure
theory into real possibility (Dupree & Hartman,
1979). But how could black holes be found?

The most obvious problem is that black holes
cannot be seen. No light can escape from them--an
almost total barrier to observing them directly.

Not only are black holes invisible; they also
may be tiny, even smaller than objects we can see
with a powerful microscope. Jastrow (1979) writes:

> The star's volume becomes smaller and smaller;
> from a globe with a two-mile radius it shrinks
> to the size of a pinhead, then to the size of a
> microbe, and still shrinking, passes into the
> realm of distances smaller than any ever probed
> by man. At all times the star's mass of a
> thousand trillion trillion tons remains packed
> into the shrinking volume. But intuition tells
> us that such an object cannot exist. At some
> point the collapse must be halted. Yet,
> according to all the laws of twentieth-century
> physics, no force, no matter how powerful, can

Reference to "Hunting for Black Holes" (see "References," page 659); Two authors' names separated by ampersand (&)

stop the collapse. (p. 65)

Abbreviate *page* with *p.*

Until the mid-1960s, few astronomers cared to undertake the detection of black holes. In fact, the idea of black holes challenged the concept of a calm, orderly universe, a concept inherited from Newton that guided the development of space theory for many years. As Thorne (1977) has observed, "Objects such as black holes . . . were too bizarre to fit naturally into our tranquil universe" (p. 67). But in the 1960s, scientists began to discover that the universe was much more turbulent than they had dreamed. In 1967 an astronomy student at Cambridge University in England discovered pulsars, which were soon recognized to be neutron stars. These were stars that had collapsed until the protons, the positively charged particles in atoms, and electrons, which are negatively charged particles, had been forced together to form neutrons, or electrically neutral particles (Thorne, 1977).

Page number of quotation

The inner space of the atoms in these neutron stars had been so reduced that the stars were only ten miles in diameter, far too small to be seen with optical telescopes. But they gave off powerful radio waves, the product of intense radiation created as

Outline point II.B.

the compressed atoms in the neutron stars collided
with each other. (Because they pulsate with radio
waves, these stars are called "pulsars.") Since a
neutron star is spinning rapidly, it flings radio
waves off into space as it whirls in orbit so that **Integrated quotation (see 37a-1)**
"the stream of radiation from its surface sweeps
through space like the light from a revolving
lighthouse beacon. If the earth happens to lie in
the path of the rotating beam, it will receive a
sharp burst of radiation once in every turn of the
pulsar" (Jastrow, 1979, p. 63). Neutron stars
exhibited the massive atomic collapse long theorized
for dying stars. Their discovery made many
astronomers think that black holes might also exist.

    If black holes do exist, it seems logical to **Outline point III.A.**
try to find them by studying their possible influence
on nearby objects. Even before pulsars were
discovered, two Russian astrophysicists had hit on
the idea of examining binary stars as a way to
discover black holes. Binary stars (double stars
that revolve around each other) are numerous in the
universe. Astronomers discovered long ago that in
many binaries a bright star is joined to a dark one,
one presumed dead; thus the bright star appears to

wink as the dark star comes between it and the earth in the extremely rapid rotation typical of such bodies.

Could a bright star be joined in a binary combination with a black hole? The black hole would be too small to make the bright star wink. But it might show its presence by the tremendous gravitational pull it should exert on the bright star, a pull that could be detected by the sophisticated means astronomers use to measure the movement of light in space. If they could find a bright star with a peculiarly vibrating light, they might have a binary pair that includes a black hole.

As early as 1964, two Russians, Y. B. Zel'dovich and O. K. Guseynov, began looking through lists of stars compiled by astronomers over the years together with a record of the kind of light the stars give off. They searched for any records that might show the fluctuating light that might be caused by the gravitational pull of a nearby black hole. In the end, reports Thorne (1977), the two Russians located five such stars.

Outline point III.B.1.

Astronomers made another assumption: if a black hole was near a visible star, the black hole must be pulling that star's gas into itself. This action is

Transition: "another assumption"

illustrated in Figure 3, with the black hole enlarged in scale compared with the visible star.

In theory, the stellar gas must be falling into the black hole at a speed approaching the speed of light, 186,000 miles per second (Dupree & Hartman, 1979). When the molecules of gas moving at such a terrific speed collide with each other and with the surface of the black hole itself, enormous quantities of x-rays should be generated. So a star with an apparent wobble in space, having no detectable companion such as a pulsar and yet giving off huge quantities of x-rays, might be a star paired with a black hole.

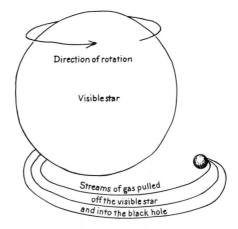

Figure 3. The pull of stellar gas.

But because the earth's atmosphere absorbs
x-rays, the search for such x-ray-emitting stars
could only be reliably conducted in space, and the
hypothesis could not be tested until a satellite
with an x-ray telescope had been launched into orbit.

In 1970, the United States and Italy jointly Outline point IV.A.
launched such a satellite, the Uhuru, and analysis
of the data from this satellite showed that the best
case for a black hole among the five stars the
Russians had found is one called Cygnus X-1. (Stars
are named for the constellations where they are
found and according to a system of grid marks set on
standard photographs of each segment of the sky.)
The mass of the unseen companion pulling on Cygnus
X-1 is estimated to be eight times that of the sun.
This mass is easily large enough to have the
gravitational pull that could produce a black hole.
Some astrophysicists have concluded that the unseen
companion is indeed a black hole (Thorne, 1977).

Another recently discovered x-ray star thought Outline point IV.B.
to be part of a binary pair is called V861 Sco. The
object appears to be connected to a dark companion,
and it is curious because it generates a large,
luminous ultraviolet flare. William Oegerle and

Ronald S. Polidan of Princeton University were struck by this flare. Thomson (1979) reported on their findings:

> From the optical properties of V861 Sco, they could determine an orbital period of seven days. They figure that the mass of the primary star is between 20 and 50 times that of the sun. The unseen companion is between 7.5 and 13 solar masses. That rules out a neutron star or a white dwarf. [White dwarfs are stars that have shrunk to a few thousand miles across, thus having enormous density but giving off an intense, white light.] Either ought to have much less mass. It is possible in theory to link the ultraviolet flare with an X-ray flare. X-ray flares are seen in these X-ray binaries, and they are explained by changes in the gas flow between the two objects. So it all looks good provided V861 Sco really is the X-ray source. (p. 25)

Thomson means that there is some slight chance that the x-rays detected by Oegerle and Polidan are coming from behind V861 Sco, from some more distant point in space.

Commentary on source (see 37a-2)

There always seems to be another possible

explanation for phenomena that might be caused by black holes. White dwarfs, those collapsing stars that still give off light although their mass is so great that a teaspoon of it would weigh ten tons (Jastrow, 1979), can draw gas from neighboring stars and produce x-rays. But so can neutron stars, and **Outline point IV.C.** some astronomers are doubtful that their instruments are yet sensitive enough to tell the difference between these bodies and black holes (Dupree & Hartman, 1979). Some astronomers like D. Hartman (personal communication, September 25, 1983) are still extremely doubtful that black holes even exist.

Personal communication cited in text but omitted from references list.

But still the search goes on, and hardly a **Conclusion** month goes by without the publication of an article in some scientific journal about yet another test for black holes. Human beings seem to have an unquenchable curiosity both about the way life begins and about the way the universe will end. If the universe does end in a black hole, the prospect is, appropriately enough, ultimately black. But no matter how bleak the prospect may be, the development of new technology, including much more sensitive instruments, is bound to mean that the quest for these strange objects will continue.

Commentary (see 37a-2)

Footnotes

Required
heading:
Foot-
notes

[1]In 1798 the French mathematician and astronomer
Pierre Simon de Laplace hinted at the possibility of
phenomena like black holes, but he never used the
term (Cloud, 1978).

References

Cloud, P. (1978). Cosmos, earth and man: A short history of the universe. New Haven: Yale University Press.

Dupree, A. K., & Hartman, L. (1979, October). Hunting for black holes. Natural History, pp. 30–37.

Jastrow, R. (1979). Red giants and white dwarfs. New York: Warner.

Schwarzschild, Karl. (1985). In Encylopaedia Britannica Micropaedia (Vol. 10, p. 548). New York: Encyclopaedia Britannica.

Thomson, D. (1979, July 14). V861 Sco's UV flare. Science News, p. 25.

Thorne, K. S. (1977). The search for black holes. In Cosmology + 1 (pp. 66–70). San Francisco: Freeman, 66–70.

References page for cited works (see 37d-2)

PART EIGHT

OTHER WRITING TASKS

	Chapter
Writing Logical Arguments	**39**
Writing About Literature	**40**
Writing an Essay Exam	**41**
Business Writing	**42**

CHAPTER THIRTY-NINE

Writing Logical Arguments

Use careful reasoning to write strong arguments.

We argue so we can persuade others to accept our point of view. In common speech, the word *argument* implies two or more opinions in conflict. In a sense, all papers may be seen as arguments in that writers always try to make readers believe something or do something.

But in general, we say that an argumentative paper strives courteously by reason and logic to address a disputed issue so convincingly that readers will accept the writer's point of view.

Some arguments are more disputable than others. If you write about your hiking trip in the Maine woods, no one is likely to tell you that you are wrong about your own experience. But if you write in favor of a candidate for mayor in an election in your town, many people will disagree with you, especially the other candidates. The word *argument* as we will use it in this chapter implies that there is another side, a point of view different from the one presented by the person making the argument. If there is no opposing point of view, we have no reason to argue.

39a
Use arguments to draw conclusions.

The word *argument* is unpleasant to some people. They associate it with quarreling and bickering. But argument should not imply bad feelings. A good argument is stated so carefully, so wisely, and in such confident good humor that it wins friends instead of making enemies.

To **argue** means to try to persuade someone to draw certain conclusions from evidence that is presented. We have been drawing conclusions all our lives. We must draw them to live. The first time most of us walk out into snow, we find that it is cold and wet; afterwards when we go out into the snow, we reach for boots and clothes to keep us warm. Most of us get a mild electrical shock sometime during our young lives, and afterwards we are wary of frayed electrical wires and broken outlets. People smile at us when we are children, and we learn that smiles usually mean goodwill. We draw conclusions from the evidence of our experience, and afterwards we act on those conclusions.

39a

arg

1   Consider books and other written sources as intellectual experience.

Part of our experience is what we learn from books or other sources. It is something we know because we have had the experience of reading. We may call information from texts *evidence.* We read the Surgeon General's statistics on cigarette smoking and disease, and we see that cigarette smokers have a much higher statistical probability of getting lung cancer and suffering heart attacks than do nonsmokers. So we can conclude—with the Surgeon General—that cigarette smoking helps cause these afflictions, though we do not know precisely how.

We read in the papers that a candidate for public office has been convicted in court for taking bribes, and we conclude that he is probably not worthy of our vote in the coming election. We read in a consumers' magazine that a certain brand of automobile has an excellent record for reliability, and we conclude that if reliability is our most important standard for a car, we would do well to buy that brand.

All these conclusions might be framed as arguments. They are based on experience, either something you know because it has happened to you or something you know because you have read it and have some reason to believe it. These conclusions make us believe or act in a certain way.

To write a good argument, you must be able to arrive at conclusions and to support them with evidence. Your raw opinions are not worth much unless you can support them with evidence that appears plausible to others. The truly educated person can reason about issues, arrive at conclusions, and present those conclusions to others in a convincing way.

2   Learn the difference between argument and persuasion.

Formal rhetoric, the science of spoken and written persuasion, sometimes distinguishes between *argument* and *persuasion.* **Persuasion** is the larger category that includes all the means—including argument—

by which we seek to influence others to accept our opinions. Persuasion may include such exhortations as "If you love me, you will do this" or "Don't ask me why I want you to do this; I'm your father; just do it."

Persuasion includes the commercials on television or advertising in periodicals where you may be told to buy a board game because it will make the whole family happy—and you see a picture of a happy family sitting around together playing the board game. Or overweight former professional athletes with loud voices will be shown guzzling a certain beer, telling you in one way or another that you ought to guzzle it, too. Never mind that overweight former athletes perhaps never touch the stuff off camera and that for being on camera, they are paid more for a thirty-second commercial than the average hard-working welder makes in a year. Advertisers do not care about such things. They realize that most people buy products on the basis of something called *name recognition.* That is, if consumers recognize a brand name, they will be more likely to buy the product, regardless of its quality. Any way to get consumers to remember the name favorably seems acceptable.

Much persuasive advertising is starkly illogical. One brand of cigarettes is advertised by a rugged-looking ranchhand riding or performing other work under open western skies; another sponsors women's tennis; still another shows sturdy-looking young men hiking or canoeing in the outdoors while pausing to light one of the cigarettes. The ads try to persuade us that cigarettes contribute to the healthy, active life. Since cigarette-related diseases kill about 300,000 people a year, it would be more logical to show cigarettes with tombstones, but that would not persuade people to buy cigarettes.

Persuasion often includes reasonable appeals. An automobile company may offer a five-year warranty (or fifty-thousand-mile warranty), giving evidence that it has enough confidence in its product to stand behind it, absorbing the costs for major repairs for the next five years. A jury may believe an eyewitness report if the witness has a reputation for honesty, though no one can prove or disprove that the witness saw what she claimed to see. A friend may persuade you to go to a movie by telling you that he saw it and liked it, and you go not because he has proved to you that the movie is good but because you trust his judgment.

39b
Use logic in your arguments.

Argument is a part of persuasion, but argument builds on logical connections. Argument may, of course, include emotional appeals, as we shall see in 39f-4. But the primary appeal of an argument is to reason, to judgment, to evaluating evidence, and to drawing conclusions that seem either inescapable or so plausible that they deserve serious considera-tion.

A **reasoned argument** is one that attempts to convince readers by the use of two common forms of reasoning—induction and deduction. An extended argument will usually include both types of reasoning, but one will usually predominate. The following long section treats induction; afterwards, we will discuss deduction.

39c

Inductive reasoning builds on specific instances to reach a conclusion.

Induction is the most common way we reason. We perceive that when people smile or laugh, they are usually in a good mood. After we have seen enough people smile and laugh, we conclude that laughing and smiling people are in a good mood. We get an electric shock, and we're careful about wires and sockets afterwards. We eat when we are hungry and feel the hunger pangs go away. We conclude that eating assuages hunger. We have known these things for so long that we may take them for granted and assume that we have always known them. But in fact they are the consequences of **induction**—working out meaning by consider-ing specific instances.

Sometimes you need a number of instances to draw a conclusion. Arguments about medical research often require careful study over years to determine if a substance is harmful or not. Few bike riders wore hel-mets until about ten years ago. But statistical studies done by medical researchers in hospitals showed that use of the helmet dramatically re-duced serious injury and fatalities among bike riders. Bike helmets are now common as bikers seek to increase their chances of survival should they fall or be hit by a car while they are riding. One could not draw a conclusion about the safety of a bike helmet from the study of only one rider, especially if that rider never had an accident and never put the helmet (or the lack of a helmet) to the test; studies had to be made of thousands of riders involved in accidents to arrive at a conclusion about the advantages of a helmet.

But some conclusions can be drawn from only one instance. If you accidentally burn yourself with a lighted match, you conclude that matches should be handled with care. You do not have to burn yourself again and again before you arrive at that conclusion. If you fall on the ice, you conclude that ice can be dangerous; you do not have to fall on the ice again and again to prove the danger to yourself. In these examples, only one instance is necessary to let us form a conclusion.

Scientists and mathematicians regularly draw sweeping conclusions from one experiment or proof. If the experiment or the proof can be duplicated by other scientists, broad general conclusions may be drawn. Louis Pasteur did not have to repeat dozens of times the experiment by which he killed the disease-causing bacteria in milk by heating the milk to 145 degrees Fahrenheit and then reducing the temperature quickly to less than fifty degrees. Once he arrived at his process and proved by means of the microscope that the bacteria were dead, he could form a general conclusion. Others could duplicate his experiments, and pasteurization has become a general practice. Pasteur could argue his case to the public according to the results; people who drank pasteurized milk did not get sick as often as did those who drank raw milk. But to other medical people, he did not have to repeat the experiment again and again.

But the inductive arguments we write usually require a gathering of many specific instances or facts. From these instances, we draw a conclusion that helps explain those instances and predict some things that may occur in the future. The medical evidence that has made the bike helmet popular is one example. Here, an argument based on induction is spelled out by Jane Brody, nutrition expert for *The New York Times*, in writing about cholesterol.

In a famous study of 12,000 middle-aged men in seven developed countries, Dr. Ancel Keys and his coworkers from the University of Minnesota found that the people of east Finland had the highest death rate from diseases of the coronary arteries—220 per 10,000 men in a five-year period—the highest percentage of saturated animal fats in their diet (22 percent of total calories were saturated fats, mostly from cheese, butter, and milk), and the highest blood cholesterol levels. The United States was not far behind in coronary deaths (185 per 10,000) and blood cholesterol levels.

But in Mediterranean countries like Greece and Italy, where the fat is mostly of vegetable origin and therefore unsaturated and lacking cholesterol, early death from coronary heart disease was far less common. And in Japan where only 10 percent of the diet is fat and most of that is polyunsaturated fat from vegetable sources (only 3 percent of total calories is saturated fat), the cholesterol levels were very low and the death rate from coronary artery disease was only 20 per 10,000. . . .

When people migrate from a country where saturated-fat consumption is low to one where it is high, their risk of developing heart disease early in life increases as they adopt the high-fat diet of their new country. Thus, Japanese migrants to Hawaii develop higher cholesterol levels and suffer more heart attacks than do the Japanese in Japan. And among Japanese migrants to California, the coronary death rates and cholesterol levels are higher still. About twenty experiments with humans have shown that an increase in cholesterol consumption usually raises blood levels of cholesterol as well.

There is some evidence that a reversal of atherosclerosis [a disease caused by clogging of the arteries with cholesterol] can occur in people who reduce their intake of saturated fats and cholesterol. A twelve-year study in two mental hospitals in Finland provides strong support for the health benefits of such a dietary change. In the first hospital, a cholesterol-lowering diet was instituted for six years, with soybean oil replacing the butterfat in milk and highly unsaturated margarines substituting for butter. At the end of six years, this experimental diet was begun in the second hospital for a second six-year period, and the first hospital went back to its regular diet. In each hospital, during the time the experimental diet was in effect, the death rate from coronary heart disease dropped significantly. When the first hospital returned to its original diet high in saturated fats, the death rate from heart disease more than doubled.

—JANE BRODY

Notice the progression of the argument here. Medical researchers gathered instances and converted those instances into statistics. Elsewhere in her book, Brody has pointed out that we do not understand the exact chemical relation between a diet high in animal fat and high levels of cholesterol in the blood, with the consequent clogging of the arteries and veins. But studies of various populations show that heart attacks are more common where diets are high in animal fat. The statistics allow us to conclude that cholesterol and heart disease are related. We do not see the relation; we infer that it exists. See 39c-2 and 3 below on inference.

We infer that cigarette smoking causes lung cancer because the disease is common among heavy cigarette smokers, relatively uncommon among those who do not smoke. But we do not precisely know what agent in cigarette smoke causes the cancer, and we cannot observe the cigarette smoke acting to make a cancer. Our conclusion is based on **statistics,** a number of instances that seem to have meaning when we construct a generalization that explains them.

1   Use inductive arguments to solve problems.

All arguments try to solve problems and answer questions. Being able to argue is partly based on the ability to ask the question "Why?" Inductive arguments are based on facts that help explain something and suggestions about conduct that derive from these explanations. Inductive arguments do not start with a random collection of facts. They begin as people study issues and raise questions that are not easily answered. Those questions then help sort out the kind of facts that may provide answers.

In the passage quoted above, Jane Brody considered the question "Why do people have heart attacks?" One part of that question was this: "Why do people have heart attacks because of clogged coronary arteries?"

She referred to research that involved the collection of facts from which some general principle might be derived. An important fact was the number of deaths from heart failure caused by clogged arteries per ten thousand middle-aged men in various cultures that used various diets. The higher the cholesterol in the diet, the larger the number of deaths from heart disease related to clogged arteries. The conclusion was that diets high in cholesterol were likely to cause clogged arteries and death.

This sort of conclusion from fact gathering always goes with inductive argument. Here are some simple examples:

arg

Fact	Conclusion
One thousand, one hundred thirty people were vaccinated against smallpox during a great epidemic that swept our state early in this century. Not one of those people got the disease. Not one of the people who got the disease had been vaccinated.	Vaccinations against smallpox prevented the disease.
My next-door neighbor got into a fight last week with the mail carrier because he said the mail carrier made too much noise walking up on the porch to deliver the mail. The same neighbor was arrested at our high school basketball game Tuesday night because he started a fight with an official over a foul call. He threatened to fight the trash haulers because they made so much noise with his garbage cans, and the paper boy refused to deliver papers any more after my neighbor yelled at him for being late.	My neighbor has a bad temper.

2   Use knowledge as a key to argument.

Before you can ask questions, you must know something. People do not argue well off the tops of their heads. Writers of good argument papers read books and articles, discuss things with their friends, take careful notes, and, above all, ask questions about what they know.

Charles Darwin, the nineteenth-century naturalist, always asked questions as he studied the facts. He wondered how certain plants growing in ponds and marshes were spread across the oceans so that the same varieties of such plants grew thousands of miles apart. This wonder came about because in his travels he had noticed that the same types of marsh grass grew in areas thousands of miles apart while the animals in these widely separated regions were considerably different from one another. It might be understandable, he says in the following passage, that aquatic plants (seaweed, and so on) would have a wide range. But how did terrestrial plants—plants with roots in earth—get spread around so over the earth? To solve the problem, he made an inference.

When we infer, we use some previous experience or knowledge to make sense of something we are observing. If someone smiles at us, we infer friendly feelings because in the past when people have smiled at us, they were showing friendly feelings. If we wake up in the night and hear a drumming of water on the roof, we infer that it is raining though we cannot see the rain fall; we have heard rain fall on our roof before, and we recognize the sound when we hear it. If we see fire trucks roaring down the street, their sirens wailing and all the firemen looking grim, we assume there is a fire somewhere.

Inference is not certain knowledge. A smile may mask an evil intent; some practical joker might have turned a hose on our roof; the firemen may be going out for coffee. But none of these possibilities is as likely as are the more normal expectations that we have from our experience. A smile is probably a sign of friendship; water drumming on the roof is probably rain; and the fire trucks screaming down the street are probably going to a fire.

Darwin considered the problem of the wide dispersion of certain plants. He made an argument to answer his question, How is it that the same varieties of plants grow so many thousands of miles apart?

With respect to plants, it has long been known what enormous ranges many fresh-water and even marsh species have, both over continents and to the most remote oceanic islands. This is strikingly illustrated, according to Alph. de Candolle [a French botanist], in those large groups of terrestrial plants, which have very few aquatic members; for the latter seem immediately to acquire, as if in consequence, a wide range. I think favourable means of dispersal explain this fact. I have before mentioned that earth occasionally adheres in some quantity to the feet and beaks of birds. Wading birds, which frequent the muddy edges of ponds, if suddenly flushed, would be the most likely to have muddy feet. Birds of this order wander more than those of any other; and they are occasionally found on the most remote and barren islands of the open ocean; they would not be likely to alight on the surface of the sea, so that any dirt on their feet would not be washed off; and when gaining the land, they would be sure to fly to their natural fresh-water haunts. I do not believe that botanists are aware how charged the mud of ponds is with seeds; I have tried several little experiments, but will here give only the most striking case: I took in February three tablespoonfuls of mud from three different points, beneath water, on the edge of a little pond: this mud when dried weighed only 6¾ ounces; I kept it covered up in my study for six months, pulling up and counting each plant as it grew; the plants were of many different kinds, and were altogether 537 in number; and yet the viscid mud was all contained in a breakfast cup! Considering these facts, I think it would be an inexplicable circumstance if water-birds did not transport the seeds of fresh-water plants to unstocked ponds and streams, situated at very distant points. The same agency may have come into play with the eggs of some of the smaller fresh-water animals.

—CHARLES DARWIN

Darwin is trying to make sense of his observations. He knows that the same plants grow thousands of miles apart. How are the seeds spread? He knows that the mud of ponds is charged with seeds. He proved that fact by taking small samples of mud from three different places under the water of a pond. Each of these samples contained abundant seeds, which sprouted when he observed them. If birds fly with such mud on their feet, he reasons, they must spread the seeds over thousands of miles. He did not see the birds spreading the seeds. But he knows that the birds have vast ranges, and he reasons that they are the likely carriers of the seeds—with their muddy feet.

39c

arg

3   Learn to form plausible conclusions.

To say that a conclusion is *plausible* is to say that we can believe it even if we cannot prove it by observation. Darwin's conclusion about the spread of seeds is plausible. He did not prove it. But most argumentation is based on plausible reasoning rather than on direct observation. When we can observe something directly, we do not have to argue about it.

Induction builds on a number of facts and arrives at an explanation that tries to account for everything we know. But we may lack the key observation that will prove our conclusion beyond all doubt. We can only **infer** a conclusion. That is, we can look at the evidence (the facts) and settle on the most plausible explanation of those facts that we can think of. Scientists often make observations of several facts (they usually call these facts *phenomena*) and try to explain them in a logical way. They arrive at a theory that explains the facts. **A theory** is an inference, a conclusion that seems to arise naturally from what we know.

Years ago, astronomers found the planet Neptune, eighth planet from the sun, and eventually measured its orbit precisely with their instruments. They discovered that Neptune's orbit around the sun varied slightly from what they thought it should be. Here was a fact—the planet Neptune, visible through telescopes, had an odd orbit. Here was a theory to account for the fact: there must be another planet beyond Neptune, and that planet's gravity was pulling on Neptune to make it seem to swing oddly in its orbit just as the moon pulls on the Earth to cause the tides. A few years later, astronomers found that other planet and named it Pluto. Pluto's existence was no longer a theory; it was a fact.

But the argument or theory that explained Neptune's oddly swinging orbit would have been a good one even if it had not been proved by the discovery of Pluto. An inductive argument may be good if it offers the most plausible explanation of the facts. A good inductive argument must take all the facts we know into account. Then the argument is **plausible.** That is, it can be believed because it seems to explain what we know or observe and it does not contradict the evidence.

An inductive argument proceeds from the gathering of facts and the explanation of how these facts are related to each other. That is, an inductive argument involves analyzing facts and deciding which of them are causes and which of them are effects. Sometimes that analysis leads to obvious conclusions: Cigarette smoking causes lung cancer. But sometimes the conclusions are not so obvious. When a fifty-five-mile-an-hour speed limit was imposed on American highways after the fuel crisis of 1973, traffic fatalities dropped dramatically. Did the lowered speed limit cause this drop? Or did the completion of the American interstate highway system that occurred about the same time cause the drop? One must study the issue a long time and gather a large quantity of data before one can make a compelling argument on either side.

Induction is used in all disciplines. An inductive argument may explain why the facts are as they are, or it may recommend some action to be taken as a result of that explanation, or it may both explain and recommend.

4   Remember that arguments often have two or more sides.

Inductive arguments may lead to a clearly preferable point of view. Once Neptune's wavering was observed, the most believable inference that could be drawn from that fact was that another planet must be out there at the edge of the solar system, its gravity strong enough to pull Neptune slightly out of its natural orbit. Once it was observed under the microscope that certain bacteria existed in the blood of everyone who had typhoid fever, the most plausible inference was that those bacteria caused the disease.

But often in the arguments you make in college papers, in position papers that set out arguments in business or professional life, and in writing about public issues, you discover that there are two or more plausible sides to an argument. Arguments that have only one side are rarely interesting. You must assemble the facts and decide what you want to argue from the facts. Your decision may depend on how you interpret those facts, or it may depend on what you value in those facts. In either case, you must gather as many facts as you can to be certain that you are being fair to the evidence and to let your readers know that you know what you are talking about.

Exercise 39.1 Construct brief arguments from the following groups of statements. Assume that each statement is true and, consequently, you can use each statement as evidence in your arguments. As you work your way through each group of statements, you will discover that you gather more and more information. As you gather more information, your arguments may change. The exercise will illustrate how much arguments depend on what you know.

When you have constructed each argument, share your work with the class. As you look at your arguments, pick out the facts from the collections of statements (your **evidence**) and distinguish between them and the assumptions that you brought to the argument. Discuss with your class how many of these assumptions you and the other students in your group share. What assumptions do you *not* share?

Example:

The library at Sourmash University will close from now on at five o'clock on Friday afternoons. The administration says that statistics show that the library is hardly used on Friday night and that it costs too much money to keep the library open. Administration accountants calculate that the library costs—in heat, lights, and personnel—an average of $984.62 a night to keep open. Closing the library will mean a saving of about ten thousand dollars every ten weeks, or approximately thirty thousand dollars a year. Those statistics also show that in a student population of seven thousand, an average of five readers and one professor will use the library on Friday night. An average of three books were checked out of the library on the last ten Fridays that the library was open. Some of the students who use the library on Friday nights drew up a petition, asking the administration to keep the library open. These students could gather only ten names for their petition, and three of those turned out to be the names of comic-strip characters. "We're trying to save money so student tuitions will not rise," President Prexy W. Bloot told the faculty in an open meeting. "The money ultimately has to come out of tuition fees paid by students. We want to keep tuition down so more students can come to Sourmash. This is one good way of doing it."

The administration of Sourmash University did the right thing to shut down the school library on Friday nights. Only about five students out of the seven thousand enrolled at Sourmash could be found in the library on any Friday night, and the cost of keeping it open for those five ran to almost a thousand dollars. Only one professor could be found regularly in the library on Friday nights. The university must cut costs, President Prexy W. Bloot said, or else some poorer students will be eliminated from Sourmash University. Students themselves seem uninterested in keeping the library open, adding validity to the argument that the library was not worth keeping open.

39c

arg

1. The administration of Sourmash University will shut the library on Friday nights from now on. An average of only five students use the library every Friday night. Seven thousand students attend Sourmash University. Only one professor uses the library on Friday nights. There are eight hundred professors at Sourmash University. It costs $984.62 in light, heat, and personnel for every night that the library stays open. If the university does not cut costs, tuitions must rise. Some poor students will then be excluded from Sourmash. One of the students who use the library every Friday night is senior Helen Walden. Her novel, *Late Hours*, last year won the Pulitzer Prize and has been translated into seventeen languages. Hardback sales in the United States have already passed the one million mark. Renowned critic Poser Eliot calls her the most promising American writer since William Faulkner. She has donated all the proceeds from her work to the Sourmash University medical school for cancer research. The one professor who uses the library on Friday nights is Judith Franklin. She has completed three volumes of a projected six-volume history of American woman writers. Her work has been widely praised. Critic and activist Helen Garfield Black says that Franklin's literary history of woman writers will change the way literature is taught in American universities for the next century. The football team at Sourmash lost eleven games this year and went into the red three million dollars. Coach Dixie Highball was fired at the end of the season. Newspaper reports say that the alumni athletic boosters have offered coach Pal Easter Blowhard of Enormous State University $250,000 a year to take the coaching job at Sourmash.

2. Professor Jimson Weed is the most popular professor at Sourmash University. Students crowd into his classes. His course is usually closed within an hour after registration begins. He makes everyone enjoy history. His lectures are filled with jokes and clever remarks. Laughter from Professor Weed's classes often disturbs other nearby classes. He outlines his lectures carefully for the class so that everyone

can follow him easily. He has never failed a student, and he gives nearly everyone an A or a B for the course. He spends much time with students, and he frequently has them as guests in his home. They notice that he has three pinball machines in his den along with several expensive computer games, but the only books in the house are the telephone company's Yellow Pages, the L. L. Bean catalog, and a book entitled *Stud Poker for Fun and Profit.* He has frequently spoken to alumni gatherings about Sourmash, and according to the university's development office, donations roll in after Professor Weed performs. The dean of Sourmash is his best friend and regularly invites him to dinner at the dean's residence and to play tennis on Saturday mornings. Professor Weed's book, *Why Russia Does Not Own California,* appeared last year and was condemned by every reviewer in every professional journal where it was reviewed. "Weed does not appear to realize that California is west of the Mississippi River," one reviewer wrote. "The only hope for this book," another wrote, "is that we might discover that Professor Weed meant it as a comedy." Professor Weed's students always do exceptionally poorly on the Graduate Record Exam. No student for whom he has written a recommendation has ever been admitted to graduate school. "Academics are not everything," Professor Weed says. "I work to develop the well-rounded student, able to go out into the world and have a good time." Professor Weed is being considered for tenure at Sourmash. According to general practice in the United States, tenure means the permanent employment of a professor. Once professors have received tenure, they have lifetime jobs at the institution that grants the tenure. If Professor Weed receives tenure, he will teach at Sourmash for as long as forty more years. Should he have tenure or not?

39d

Use deductive arguments to show the consequences of general truths.

Deductive argument is the application of a general truth to a specific case in order to draw a conclusion. A general truth is supposedly accepted by everyone likely to be interested in the argument. In **formal rhetoric** (which you will remember is the traditional science of spoken and written discourse), we say that deductive reasoning proceeds through a syllogism. The standard syllogism looks like this:

General truth: All men are mortal.

Specific case: Socrates is a man.

Conclusion: Socrates is mortal.

The general truth accepted by everyone is that all men are mortal. That is, all men will eventually die. No one reading the argument can doubt that assumption. The specific case here is a statement joining Socrates to the general truth by remarking that he is an individual member of that class of beings called men. The conclusion then follows.

You can visualize the syllogism like this:

39d

arg

All men are mortal;

since Socrates is a man,

he is mortal.

In a syllogism, the general truth includes the specific case and is the cause of the conclusion. You can always rephrase a syllogism to use the word "because" or "since" in the statements you make in conclusions derived from the general truth.

Inductive reasoning is the gathering of facts and the arrival at a general conclusion from them; in deductive reasoning, we begin with a general truth and use it to give some meaning or interpretation to a fact. As we have noted, in **formal logic,** the logic developed since Aristotle by professional philosophers, we call the general truth the *major premise.* The specific fact is called the *minor premise,* and the application of the major premise to the minor premise is called a **conclusion**—something that is true because the major premise is true and the minor premise is true. The major premise is always a broad generalization; the minor premise is always a statement that is somehow included within the general statement of the major premise. The conclusion then follows necessarily because of the relation of the major premise and the minor premise.

Like inductive reasoning, deductive reasoning applies to all sorts of ordinary situations in daily life. Here are some more syllogisms based on deductive reasoning:

Major premise: This textbook is revised every three years.

Minor premise: Three years have passed since the last edition of this textbook appeared.

Conclusion: A new edition of the textbook will appear this year.

Major premise: Rain nearly always falls soon after the barometer falls rapidly in climates where there is an abundance of warm, moist air.

Minor premise: The barometer is falling rapidly today, and the air is muggy and hot.

Conclusion: It will probably rain soon.

Major premise: Medical research has proved that excessive drinking of alcohol damages the heart, the digestive tract, and other organs of the body and that heavy drinking is often associated with cancer, insomnia, psychological depression, high blood pressure, and the breakdown of the immune system.

Minor premise: My Aunt Mabel drinks a quart of whiskey a day.

Conclusion: My Aunt Mabel is probably not going to live to a healthy old age.

Major premise: The ability to write well is a great advantage to business and professional people.

Minor premise: I write well.

Conclusion: I have an advantage if I decide to go into business or professional life.

These syllogisms are not quite as solid as the one about Socrates. Socrates has to be mortal because all men are mortal. But Aunt Mabel may live to be ninety-five years old, and the ability to write well does not guarantee success in business or professional life. In reasoning about most subjects to make an argument, the syllogisms we use may not fall together with the certainty of a good key turning a lock. If the major premise is not true, the syllogism will not be true. If the major premise is flawed or not accepted by others, the syllogism built on it will not be convincing.

Major premise: People who do not smoke cigarettes will never die.

Minor premise: My Cousin Horace does not smoke cigarettes.

Conclusion: Cousin Horace will never die.
We reject the syllogism immediately because we know that the major premise is not true. All people eventually die, whether they smoke cigarettes or not. And although Cousin Horace may live longer than someone who chain-smokes cigarettes, he will eventually die.

Major premise: First-rate rock composers have been much more creative than have classical-music composers.

Minor premise: John Lennon was a first-rate rock composer.

Conclusion: John Lennon was much more creative than Beethoven, a classical composer.
The syllogism might stand among those people who accept the major premise. But huge numbers of people would reject the major premise, saying it was untrue. Those lovers of classical music, especially lovers of Beethoven, would not accept the conclusion because they object to the supposed general truth from which the conclusion was derived. Lovers of the Beatles might accept the syllogism, but it would not convince anyone on the other side. If a syllogism is to persuade, it must begin with a general truth that all sides accept.

Writing Logical Arguments **677**

1 Syllogisms may be combined.

Syllogisms are often combined in arguments. That is, you may find several syllogisms in the same argument. We can find two syllogisms in the following paragraph.

In the Declaration of Independence, Thomas Jefferson wrote that government existed to preserve the rights of life, liberty, and the pursuit of happiness for all its citizens. The government of King George III of England had not protected those rights; it had, instead, violated them by taking the lives of Americans, by attempting to destroy their liberty, and by making it impossible for them to pursue happiness. Therefore, Jefferson argued, the English government was not a legal government; and since it was not a legal government, Americans were not obligated to obey it. Since they were not obligated to obey the English government, Americans had a right to revolt against it.

Here are the syllogisms:

Major premise: Governments exist to preserve the rights of life, liberty, and the pursuit of happiness.

Minor premise: The government of King George III violated these rights.

Conclusion: King George's government was not a legal government.

Major premise: People have a right to revolt against an illegal government.

Minor premise: King George's government was not a legal government.

Conclusion: Americans had the right to revolt against King George's government.

Exercise 39.2   Construct syllogisms from the arguments in the following paragraphs:

1. Universities exist to further the intellectual life of their students and faculty and society at large. The intellectual life is not cheap. It costs money for faculty, money for the buildings where classes are conducted, money for libraries, and money to keep those libraries open at night. Helen Garfield Black furthers the intellectual life every Friday night when she works in the library. The university should support her by keeping the library open so she can work. She is doing what Sourmash University exists to do.

2. Lightning can kill. Bike riders sometimes believe that they are protected from lightning because they are on rubber tires. They think that the rubber protects them by preventing the lightning that might hit them from running into the ground and killing them. But that belief is only a superstition. Lightning can strike bikers. It kills some cyclists every year. So when a thunderstorm blows up and you are on the road with your bike, take shelter at once. You won't dissolve in the rain. But you may die in the lightning.

3. Computers can do thousands of different things. With the right programs, they can work complicated math problems, construct graphic models for architecture, store and classify data, do word processing, and perform more tasks than any one person needs. The more elaborate your computer, the more you can do with it. But the more elaborate your computer, the more it will cost. Most students use their computers only for word processing, and cheap computers can do excellent word processing. Therefore, if you are going to use your computer only to write papers, you can save money by avoiding the expensive and elaborate machines.

Exercise 39.3   Take twenty-five minutes in class to construct a paragraph that contains a syllogism. Read your paragraph to other members of the class. See if your fellow students can pick out your syllogism.

2   Major premises of syllogisms may be unexpressed.

Many times in making a deductive argument, we do not spell out the entire syllogism. We assume that our readers know the major premise of the syllogism without our having to state it for them. We assume that they accept it. Sometimes we call an unexpressed major premise an *assumption*. Here is an example:

Professor Churl promised us that half our grade would depend on our research paper. We all worked night and day on those papers. I spent every night for three weeks in the library working on mine. But then he said that the term papers were all so good that he would have to give everyone in the class an A if he kept his promise. So he counted the term papers as only one-tenth of the grade and said the rest of the grade would come from the midterm and the final. All this was completely unfair.

This writer is arguing from a syllogism. But the major premise is implied; it is not stated.

Here is the syllogism with the major premise stated.

Major premise: Professors who break their promises to students are unfair.

Minor premise: Professor Churl broke his promise.

Conclusion: Professor Churl was unfair.

Many American students make a spelling mistake when they form the plural of words ending in -est and -ist—words such as *guest*, *nest*, *humanist*, *scientist*, and *colonist*. They do not add a final *s*. The plurals of these words should be *guests*, *nests*, *humanists*, *scientists*, and *colonists*. The error seems to come about because these students fail to pronounce the plural forms of these words correctly. It is difficult to make the *s* sound after -*ist*. And many Americans pronounce the singular and the plural the same way. So they spell them the same way. And so they misspell the plural form. The rule is simple. To make the plural of all words ending in -*est* or -*ist*, add the letter *s*.

A syllogism is embedded in this paragraph. The major premise is implied.

Major premise: Mispronunciation may cause misspellings.

Minor premise: Students often mispronounce words such as *guests*, *nests*, *humanists*, *scientists*, and *colonists*.

Conclusion: The mispronunciation causes these plurals to be spelled without the final *s* as if they were singular nouns.

Exercise 39.4 Find the implied major premise in each syllogism embedded in the following paragraphs.

1. Sylvester Pecks has been running for governor of the state telling us that he received the Congressional Medal of Honor in Vietnam. He has limped to the platform again and again to tell us how he was wounded in the leg trying to hold his position against overwhelming enemy attack. But now it turns out that he spent the entire Vietnam war in Switzerland acting as a security guard for a girls' school. The headmaster of that school has come forward to tell us that Mr. Pecks broke his leg when he fell through a kitchen window one night as he was making off with steaks from the school's refrigerator. The headmaster has produced medical records from a Swiss hospital that support his claim. Do not vote for Sylvester Pecks. He does not deserve to be the governor of our state.

2. Rattlesnakes abound in the Wyoming countryside around Independence Rock, one of the great landmarks along the old overland trail followed by the pioneers on their way to California and Oregon. Climbing up Independence Rock is a great adventure, and from the top you can see for miles across the rolling prairie. But be sure you wear tall boots as you walk through the high grass around the rock, and be careful where you put your hands.

3. A recent survey revealed that the average American watches seven hours of television a day. If the average American spent half that much time reading, we would have one of the most knowledgeable citizen bodies in the world. As it is, Americans, entertained by television and neglecting their books, are woefully ignorant of simple facts necessary to understand the world. Another recent survey disclosed that one-third of the students at a large American university could not locate the continent of Europe on a map of the world. Almost half of all Americans claim that they have never read a book through in their lives. Because they watch television and do not read, Americans run the risk of being unable to make policy decisions that may help them survive as a nation.

Exercise 39.5   Write a paragraph in which you imply a major premise to support an argument.

39e

You may frequently use two variations of argument from induction and argument from deduction: argument from authority and argument from testimony or personal experience.

1   To argue from authority means to quote someone or cite someone considered to be an authority on a certain subject.

Often that person is an authority because he or she has gathered facts, generalized about them, and gained a reputation for sound thinking. If you should write a paper arguing that the characters in Shakespeare's *A Midsummer Night's Dream* are not profound, you may quote Shakespearean scholar David Young, who has written on that subject and come to a similar conclusion. Young is an authority who adds to your case because he is known to have studied Shakespeare extensively and to have written a great deal about the plays, especially about the comedies.

Never be afraid to call up or drop by and see an expert to ask for help on a paper you are doing. People who have become authorities in their fields usually enjoy talking to students. Are you writing a paper on changes taking place in the Soviet Union? There is probably some professor on your campus who teaches Russian history, Russian politics, Russian government, or something else related to Russia and can give you some interpretation of events going on in the Soviet Union. Call on that person. He or she can become an authority for your paper. The opinions of such a person carry great weight because of the study that has gone into forming them.

39e

arg

Any time you quote facts from a book or an author's opinion to support your own in an argument paper, you are arguing from authority. (See 37c on the use of quotations and citations of sources.) When you are doing research, you know enough to be on the lookout for evidence that can give authority to the assertions you make in a paper. But even when you do random reading or when you listen to lectures in other disciplines or see things on TV or in the movies, keep your eyes open for materials you can use as authorities in your paper.

The following paragraphs represent an argument from authority. Historian David McCullough concerns himself with the recurring attacks of asthma that afflicted young Theodore Roosevelt, later President of the United States. What causes asthma? McCullough believes the disease is at least partly *psychosomatic*, that is, caused by the mental state of the victim rather than by germs, viruses, or some other physical entity. (The nickname "Teedie" in the selection was given young Theodore Roosevelt by his family, and McCullough uses it to indicate the child.)

In 1864, or two years after the infant Teedie's asthma had begun, a highly important work was published in Philadelphia, a book of 256 pages titled *On Asthma.* The author was an English physician, Henry Hyde Salter, a very keen observer who as the father of an asthmatic child has "experienced the horrors" of the disease. . . . Salter had found no abnormalities in the lungs of his asthmatic patients, no trace of the disease in either the respiratory or circulatory system, and hence concluded that the trouble lay in the nervous system. Asthma, a disease of "the direst suffering," a disease "about whose pathology more various and discrepant ideas prevail than any other," was "essentially a *nervous* disease."

Sudden "mental emotion," Salter said, could both bring on an attack and abruptly end one. He did not know why, only what he had observed. He reported on a patient whose attack ceased the moment he saw a fire outside the window and another who had his asthma stop when put on a fast horse. Still other patients found that as soon as they neared the doctor's office their asthma vanished, "suddenly and without any apparent cause except the mental perturbation at being within the precincts of the physician." The onset of an attack, he noted, was frequently preceded by a spell of depression or "heaviness" (what Teedie called feeling "doleful"), and twenty years in advance of what might be regarded as the first studies in the psycho-somatic side of asthma he reported on a small boy who "found his disease a convenient immunity from correction."

"Don't scold me," he would say, if he had incurred his father's displeasure, "or I shall have the asthma." And so he would; his fears were as correct as they were convenient.

— DAVID MCCULLOUGH

McCullough develops his argument that asthma was a symptom of young Teddy Roosevelt's extreme nervousness and that it contrib-uted to a miserable childhood. McCullough's method is to use the authority of a nineteenth-century doctor who had studied asthma at length. With that information, he can then explain many of the things Roosevelt's parents did to help their child but also many things they did without realizing that their actions often brought on the attacks.

2 In testimony, we say that something happened to us and that this happening proves a point that we wish to make in an argument or that it proves the entire argument.

Your personal experience may support an argument only if the expe-rience has given you enough information to make a generalization that will help the case you are trying to make. If you have not learned enough from your experience, your argument may be weakened by your inade-quate support.

PERSONAL EXPERIENCE

Disneyland has been criticized for giving a sanitized version of American history, for trivializing international relations and national differences, and for taking all the frightening moments out of fairy tales. But I visited Disneyland with my two children last summer and we loved it. Yes, it is a form of escapism. But why else do we go to an amusement park? Only a new form of puritanism requires us to be serious every moment about everything. Sometimes we have to relax. And I can't think of a time when I have been happier than I was sitting with my six-year-old and my four-year-old in Dumbo, the Flying Elephant, circling round and round, suspended over the crowds by the strong steel arms of a friendly Disneyland machine that rotated us in the friendly sunshine.

Here the writer has arrived at a concluding moment in his argument about the value of Disneyland, and he has tipped the balance by adding a personal experience. In an argument over whether Disney-land is good or bad, this experience would carry considerable weight.

Personal experience may damage your case if it is obviously too narrow or if it is unrelated to the argument at hand.

PERSONAL EXPERIENCE

I was in Paris last summer and discovered that the French were as rude as I had always heard they were. The woman in the little hotel where I stayed on the Left Bank ordered me not to wash any clothes in my room. I did a very small wash anyway, and when I hung my things up to dry, they dripped onto the floor and leaked through the ceiling of the room below mine. The people down there were rude enough to complain, and the hotel keeper came up and returned my money to me and ordered me out into the street that minute. All this proves to me that the French are rude and arrogant and that we should refuse to let them sell their cars in this country and that we should tell all Americans to stay away from France. If they insist on visiting France anyway, we ought to tax them a thousand dollars for every trip they make there.

The personal experience of being thrown out of a French hotel for violating the hotel's clearly announced rules is not sufficient to prove an argument about trade policy. To be useful, personal experience must have a clear relation to the argument.

39f

Observe the following checklist for making good arguments.

Now that we have classified the two main forms of arguments and considered a couple of variations on them, we have prepared you to think about some specific qualities of a good argument paper. Read over this section quickly. Then study the parts that give you the most trouble in writing your own arguments.

1 Choose a limited topic that you can argue well.

This requirement for a good argument is much like the requirement for writing any good paper. Avoid subjects that are so broad that you can do no more with them than to write a series of assertions. Any argument requires knowledge. You must gather enough information to know what you're talking about. Topics that are too broad require more knowledge than you can gather during the term. Fair-minded and informed readers will not believe your arguments if you display ignorance in setting forth your opinions.

You cannot argue in only a few pages that the American government is spending too much money for defense unless you are an expert on the federal budget, particularly on military spending. But you can argue in a brief paper that military spending involves a lot of waste—*if* you can gather evidence about that waste. You can get this information from newspaper and magazine articles and from budget hearings recorded in the *Congressional Record,* sources that are probably in your school library.

You cannot argue in a short paper that Herman Melville's *Moby Dick* was the greatest novel ever written. You would have to read all the novels ever written, arrive at some principles that define "greatness," and compare all those novels and *Moby Dick* to those principles—a task that you could not finish in a long lifetime. But you can read some articles written by literary scholars about Melville's work and argue that different readers have agreed on some of the qualities of greatness in *Moby Dick.*

You cannot argue that people who lived during the Renaissance had a completely different view of human ability than did people living in the Middle Ages. Can you read the works of all the people who lived during the Renaissance to see what they thought? And what about those millions and millions of people who did not write anything? How can you tell what *they* thought? But you can compare *The Prince* of Niccolò Machiavelli, written during the Italian Renaissance, and the pronouncements of two or three medieval popes about what kings should be, and you can argue that Machiavelli represents a radically different value system based on many of the same assumptions that popes made.

Exercise 39.6 Which of the following would make good arguments? Which cannot be argued in a college paper seven or eight pages long? Write a short paragraph explaining your response to each suggested argument.

1. William Faulkner used descriptions of light in his fiction to help emphasize the moods of his characters.
2. Mark Twain's novel *Huckleberry Finn* has much in it that can injure the feelings of modern American blacks.
3. The movie *Star Wars* was the most brilliant film ever produced by Hollywood.
4. The movie *Star Wars* uses a number of clichés developed in Hollywood westerns, but it makes them interesting by transforming them to outer space.
5. Everyone who drives to school would be much happier if the administration would provide more parking spaces.

2 Choose a topic that lends itself to debate.

A strong argument starts with a limited topic that lends itself to debate. If people can take sides on the issue, it's probably a good argumentative topic—provided it is limited enough to allow you to know it thoroughly and argue it convincingly. Using evidence and logic, others should be able to affirm or dispute your position. To test a topic for arguments, you might ask if it is debatable:

39f

arg

Topic	Debatable?
Shakespeare wrote some interesting plays.	No. Few people would disagree with this topic.
Radio stations should not be allowed by the federal government to play rock music with lyrics that glorify drugs or casual sex.	Yes. Many people think that something should be done to protect young children from such music; others think that a prohibition against such music would violate the First Amendment of the Constitution with its guarantee of free speech.
Private persons should not be allowed to own pistols.	Yes. Many people, citing the number of murders committed with pistols, think that private ownership of such weapons should be banned. Many others believe that such a ban would restrict the freedom of law-abiding gun owners.
We should find a cure for AIDS.	Almost no one would disagree with this topic. AIDS is one of the epidemic diseases of our age, and whether it should be cured or not is not a subject of serious debate.
AIDS victims should be quarantined.	Yes. Many people believe that AIDS victims should be kept away from society to protect those who do not have the disease. Others argue that the disease cannot be transferred by casual social contact and that quarantine is inhuman.

Controversy is not an essential condition for good argument. People do not have to be passionate about the subject. But the topic must be debatable. Often controversial topics (like abortion, welfare, funding the United Nations, or legalizing drugs) have been so extensively argued that fresh insights on them are hard to come by. Avoid topics that require you to state arguments that have been made again and again. Do not argue an issue unless you have something fresh to say about it.

Matters of taste are seldom debatable. It is difficult to argue that a movie or a novel or a short story or a play is good or bad. People disagree on such matters, and what seems like trash to one critic may seem like a masterpiece to another. Many people love the novel *Moby Dick;* others hate it. It is hard to argue that we should have a certain emotional response to something we read or see. Horror movies scare some people almost out of their wits; they strike others as silly.

You can argue that a movie or something you read contradicts itself or that it presents stereotypes or that it glorifies violence; you can argue that a movie is complicated, that it addresses this or that issue in society, that it strives for this or that effect. But the simple argument that the movie—or whatever—is "good" or "bad" will carry little weight.

Exercise 39.7 Discuss with your class the following suggested topics for argument papers. Which are debatable and which are not? Why?

1. A federal law should be passed banning smoking in all public places.
2. War is one of the great scourges of our time.
3. War is the great scourge of any time.
4. Women in the Army should take part in combat.
5. The President of the United States holds enormous responsibility.
6. *Casablanca* is a great movie.

3 A good argument considers contrary evidence.

As we saw in 39c-4, the facts rarely line up neatly on one side. Debatable topics are debatable *because* there are two sides. The same evidence may be interpreted in different ways. If you are to be fair-minded and reasonable, you must consider in your own argument the arguments others have made against your position.

Always be fair in dealing with opposing arguments and contrary evidence. It is unfair to misquote or misrepresent the opposition. You must think out the opposing point of view as carefully as you can, being sure you represent it correctly. (See 39f-5.)

In dealing with contrary evidence, you have three options.

1. You can argue that the contrary evidence is invalid because it has been misinterpreted by your opponents and that it therefore does not damage your position.

It is true that keeping the library open on Friday nights costs the university nearly a thousand dollars. Those who want to close the library argue that all that money would be saved if we take this step. But they have forgotten that we must still pay the salary of the guard who watches the building and the books at night when the library is closed. They have forgotten that even when the building is closed, the lights must remain on for security and the heat remains on to protect the books from damage from dampness. They have forgotten that library personnel on duty at night are students working their way through college and that to cut off their pay might be to exclude them from higher education here.

2. You can concede the contrary evidence but argue that your point of view is still superior to that of the opposition.

I do concede that only a handful of people use the library on Friday nights. Although those who want to close the library overestimate the money they would save, I concede that they would, indeed, save some money. But why does a university exist? It exists to promote the life of the mind, to expand the intellect and the imagination, to produce knowledge. By keeping the library open on Friday nights, the university confirms these purposes to the handful of people who work there. The books two of these people have written confirm the purposes of the university to the thousands of people who read these books. Through these writers, the university reaches out to readers who can never enter the campus.

The student union is also open on Friday nights. I have checked into the costs of operating the union on Friday nights. They amount to some six thousand dollars an evening. I am not opposed to keeping the union open on Friday nights. But I do say that a university that saves a little money by closing its library while it keeps open its poolrooms, its bowling alleys, its subsidized soda fountains, and its movie auditorium is selling its soul to the accountants, and it is losing its fundamental purpose.

3. A third option is to change your mind. You should never hold on to an argument once you see that the evidence is against you. Keep your mind open at all times, and when you feel that you do not have the evidence to support your position, be willing to admit it. Such an admission may not take the personal form of the following paragraph. In arguing for a position different from the one you started with, you do not always have to give your readers a history of your beliefs. But the following paragraph may illustrate one rhetorical effect of changing your mind.

I once believed in legalizing marijuana. Smoking the weed made people feel good. It seemed to have no harmful side effects, and it was not addictive like alcohol or nicotine. Users said that marijuana did not impair vision or judgment, so drivers high on marijuana could operate cars and trucks in perfect safety. But now a considerable body of research has been built up to prove that marijuana *does* have harmful side effects. Smoking marijuana is just as hard on the lungs as smoking tobacco. It does appear to be addictive. And marijuana has been implicated in several private-plane crashes, automobile wrecks, and, recently, train wrecks. It is not the harmless pleasure that it once appeared to be, and I think there are some powerful reasons *not* to legalize the drug.

4 A good argument is carried on in a courteous tone.

Too often, writers of argument papers believe that they can win their argument only by assaulting and insulting everyone who disagrees with them. Fair-minded readers quickly reject writers who argue as though they were at a shouting match. On rare occasions you can allow yourself to be emotional in an argument. But you should learn to argue by friendly persuasion, for that kind of argument nearly always carries the most weight with readers.

Avoid this sort of argument:

A lot of immoral, wicked people have argued that *The Prince* by Machiavelli is a good book! (Next thing you know, they'll be saying that Stalin had some good ideas!) To these so-called scholars, it's all right to lie, to cheat, to murder, and to keep people in fear. If we all lived the way Machiavelli taught, society would fall apart. Sure, he was writing in Renaissance Italy, where a lot of petty little tyrants were making people suffer. But you read Machiavelli, and he seems to think it was a good thing to make all those poor people grovel in the dirt and be afraid of the prince. Well, let me tell you something. I wouldn't trust my pocketbook to somebody who told me that he thought that disgusting, criminal Machiavelli was a great thinker.

This tone is much better:

It is the fashion today to argue that Machiavelli's *The Prince* is a work of genius and to condemn those who, for so many centuries, condemned Machiavelli. No doubt Machiavelli was a brilliant observer of the sixteenth century and understood the tactics of the petty princes who ruled the Italian city states. They were immoral men, and Machiavelli described their immorality in elaborate detail. Much of the criticism that has been made against Machiavelli through the years should, indeed, be directed against these princes. He considered himself a sort of reporter, describing in great detail how they grasped power and held on to it. One can even argue that like the Christian thinkers of the Middle Ages, Machiavelli believed that human beings were selfish and ignorant, slaves of a flawed human nature.

But despite the brilliance of his observations and the blame that can be placed on those he observed, Machiavelli himself can still be chilling. No particle of human sympathy for the victims of these princes penetrates the stately prose of his works. He seems to be above concern with the suffering of the innocent. He was passionately dedicated to building a strong Italian state able to stand off the French, German, and Spanish invaders of his homeland. But nothing shows him dedicated to human rights or even aware that human beings had rights. No matter how much good we say about his genius, something is lacking in his spirit.

The tone of the preceding two paragraphs, which might stand as the introduction to an argumentative essay about Machiavelli, does not insult those who have said that Machiavelli was a genius and that he has been judged too harshly by later writers. It makes an argument based on evidence and treats opponents gently, even though they have expressed different views.

Always be courteous and reasonable when you write an argument. Do not set out to destroy those who disagree with you. If you are courteous, there's a good chance you will begin to convince your opponents that your views are correct.

5 Avoid fallacious reasoning.

Fallacious reasoning may appear, at first, to be logical, but, on examination, the fallacies or errors in reasoning appear. Readers who catch you in fallacious reasoning will not be likely to take your work seriously. Here are some common fallacies:

Arguing from Cause to Effect

Do not argue from cause to effect merely because one thing happened after another thing happened.

In arguing from cause to effect, you must make a stronger connection than mere sequence.

FALLACIOUS REASONING

A black cat walked across my path last night, and when I got home, I discovered that my house had been robbed. The black cat brought me bad luck.

Many superstitions arise because people make connections between events that have no real relation to each other except that one happened before the other.

Thomas More wrote *The Dialogue of Comfort* over a century before John Milton wrote *Paradise Regained.* Therefore, Milton must have known More's work. And Milton must have been influenced by More.
You cannot assume that merely because one author wrote before another that the second author knew the work of the first. You must have stronger textual evidence from both works to prove that the later is influenced by the earlier.

Since radio, TV, and the movies began emphasizing stories about crime, crime has steadily increased; therefore, radio, TV, and the movies have been responsible for this increase in the crime rate.
In a complex society like ours, crime increases for many reasons. It is not a good argument to say that because crime increased after radio, TV, and the movies started emphasizing stories about crime, they caused that increase. We might make the argument if we could interview several convicted criminals and discover that they had been influenced by the broadcast media and the movies to commit crimes. Or if we could discover a rash of crimes identical to some crime that had been shown in a TV story or in a movie, we might have some proof that these media increased the crime rate. But the mere fact that the increase in the crime rate happened after these stories became popular in the media is not evidence that the media caused the crime. We might also discover that the crime rate had increased since TV started broadcasting more basketball games. Would anyone argue that the broadcasts of the basketball games had increased crime?

Generalizing from Too Little Information

In inductive reasoning, we gather facts and arrive at generalizations. If you don't gather enough facts, you may make a faulty generalization.

FAULTY GENERALIZATION

In many of his novels, William Faulkner wrote about some terrible happenings in the American South. Therefore, Faulkner must have hated the South.
Faulkner also wrote about many good things in the South. To learn whether Faulkner loved the South or hated it or both loved and hated it, we would have to gather much more information than that he wrote about some terrible happenings in the American South.

FAULTY GENERALIZATION

In his novel *The Turn of the Screw,* Henry James wrote about two ghosts who attempted to corrupt two little children. Therefore, James believed in ghosts.

You cannot generalize about a fiction writer's personal beliefs by seeing what one or two characters in a novel do or believe. Otherwise, the people who created Superman would have to believe in his incredible powers. The question of whether Henry James believed in ghosts is difficult, but we cannot resolve the problem from this one story.

When you make a generalization, always be sure that you have gathered enough information to support it.

Inappropriate and Unfair Either/Or Reasoning

This sort of fallacy resides in demands that we must accept one of two extreme positions.

EITHER/OR STATEMENT

Either we must stop our children from dancing to rock music or the moral foundations of civilization will crumble.

Rock music may damage the ears and even the imaginations of some children, but it seems extreme to say that if we do not stop children from dancing to it, the moral foundations of civilization will crumble.

EITHER/OR STATEMENT

Either you buy the new supercharged TurboLemon convertible by Friday when our sale ends, or you will never have such an opportunity again in your life.

The either/or statement implies that if you do not buy this car by Friday, you will lose something major in life; you probably won't lose anything since the TurboLemon will probably be on sale again somewhere next week.

Attacking Straw Men

The colloquial term "straw man" denotes an attack on an opponent for a position that opponent does not hold. The attack is designed to make readers (or hearers) think the opponent holds that position, one that is so terrible that no humane or sensible person could possibly hold it. Often the attack on the straw man is a variation of the either/or fallacy.

OPPONENT'S STATEMENT

In the United States, prayer in public schools offers many difficulties. It is extremely difficult for sincerely religious people to keep from trying to influence others to accept their point of view. Prayers may easily become sermons. Different people use different forms of prayer. Christians customarily pray with their eyes closed; Jews pray with their eyes open; some other religions held by Americans pray by means of chants. Children of various religious backgrounds are forced by law to go to school. But they should not be forced to worship God in a way that contradicts their own beliefs or the beliefs of their parents. The United States is the most religious of all the industrial countries, and we may suggest that religion has flourished here because it has not been forced on anyone. We would do well to ponder this question: Is religion helped by being prescribed by law, no matter how inoffensive the form may seem to those who prescribe it?

ATTACK ON A STRAW MAN

My opponent has questioned the value of prayer in the public schools. That proves that he is an atheist. He does not believe in God. He denies that we owe reverence to our Creator. He has blasphemed the Almighty by saying that little children should not pray to Him. It is his kind that will destroy this country, for if we forsake God, God will forsake us. I do not say that he is a Communist. But I say that he is playing into the hands of the Communists by denying God just as they deny God. If you vote for my opponent, my friends, you are voting against religion. *Nothing in the opponent's careful remarks about prayer in the public schools indicates that he does not believe in God. He has not said that children should not pray. And he has not spoken as a Communist but as someone attentive to traditional American values. But the attack on the straw man makes an either/or error. Either one must have prayer in the public schools or one is against God and religion. Such attacks are unfair, and Americans have traditionally rejected them.*

The attack on the straw man is closely related to another fallacy that you should avoid: the *argumentum ad hominem* or the "attack on the man." This is an attack that avoids meeting the central issue of the opponent's argument but, instead, attacks the character of the opponent's person.

39f

arg

My opponent spent an hour last night explaining his economic policies to the nation on television. He advanced columns of figures about jobs and about workers and employment and inflation. He gave us a six-point program that he said would reduce inflation, increase employment, strengthen the dollar, and control the federal deficit. These items were very interesting. But I could not think about them very much because as the cameras zoomed in on him, I realized that he dyes his hair. Now I ask you, what kind of man dyes his hair? Can you believe such a man? Would any of you women out there marry a man who dyes his hair? People who dye their hair are lying about themselves. And my friends, a man who lies about himself will lie about the budget of the United States. Look at me! I am totally bald. I have an honest, pure-bald head. Look at me, and see a man who believes in the truth. Look at my opponent and see a man who lies about his hair and his age and about anything else that will help him get elected President of the United States.

The argumentum ad hominem is often introduced into political arguments and even into arguments about literature and the arts. The black poet Langston Hughes dabbled in Communism in the 1930s; therefore, some people claim that none of his works have any value. North Carolina novelist Thomas Wolfe seemed absorbed in his own ego and, by most standards, was a terrible man; therefore, some people denounce his famous novel Look Homeward, Angel. *Actor Charlton Heston is conservative in his politics; so some people refuse to admit that he can act.*

Begging the Question

Begging the question occurs in deductive reasoning. The person who begs the question states the major premise in such a way that it is a conclusion, drawn without allowing an argument to decide the merits of the case.

BEGGED QUESTION

He could not be lying because he was president of the campus Society for Moral Uplift.

Here is how this statement would be set up in a syllogism.

Major premise: The president of the campus Society for Moral Uplift cannot tell a lie.

Minor premise: He is a president of the campus Society for Moral Uplift.

Conclusion: Therefore he cannot tell a lie.

If we accept the major premise, we have no argument. But if the president of the campus Society for Moral Uplift was charged with lying, the argument should turn on the evidence. Does the evidence show that he told the truth or not? The major premise is false.

Begging the question often goes hand in hand with another fallacy, that of the red herring. The original red herring was a smoked salt fish with a strong taste and smell. Sometimes during fox hunts, when poor farmers wanted to keep noble horsemen from galloping across their crops and ruining them, they would drag a red herring through the grass before the dogs came along. The smell of the herring would make the dogs lose the scent of the fox, who might have run through the crops, and the farmers' fields were saved because the dogs became confused and often ran in circles.

A **red herring** is any issue introduced into an argument that distracts attention from the main issue. People often introduce the red herring when they think they are about to lose an argument.

RED HERRING

That rugged, wonderful-looking cowboy smokes a famous cigarette in beautiful magazine ads that show stunning color photographs of the American West. You can almost smell the fresh air and feel the glory of space in those ads. You can look at that beautiful scene and that handsome face and know that cigarettes are not nearly as bad for your health as the Surgeon General claims they are.

The advertisers of cigarettes know that the medical evidence is solidly against smoking. So they present red herrings, beautiful ads that feature people doing athletic or robust things while they are smoking. The ads distract attention from the central issue, whether people should smoke or not.

Exercise 39.8   Read the following short argument paper and pick out the logical fallacies. Discuss the paper and the fallacies in your class.

The boring and worthless novel *Moby Dick* should never be required reading in a college English class because it has nothing worthwhile to teach. Herman Melville, its author, was a total failure in life. He was the son of a bankrupt father and had to go off to sea as a cabin boy when he was still a teenager—this at a time in the nineteenth century when sailors were often hardly better than vagabonds and criminals. Later, when he went as a sailor on a whaling ship, he deserted in the South Seas. Shipping out later on an Australian ship, he deserted once again and lived for a while as a common laborer and general vagabond in Tahiti where, as everyone knows, the morals were disgraceful.

He published a few short books that were fairly popular, but when he brought out *Moby Dick* in 1851, most readers justifiably lost interest in him. He eventually could not make a living from his writing—proving that what he wrote was no good—and he eventually became a customs inspector on the docks in New York City. When he died in 1891, hardly anyone noticed.

As if all this were not proof enough of how worthless he was as a writer, we have the long and boring novel *Moby Dick* itself. No one can read this book and enjoy it. The idea that people could go out and murder innocent whales is especially appalling. In my opinion, anybody who likes this book is in favor of destroying whales and making them extinct.

The main character in the book seems to be Captain Ahab, skipper of the *Pequod*, who is obsessed with finding and killing the white whale, Moby Dick, that earlier caused Ahab to lose his leg. Ahab is uninteresting because he is such a bad man. He is willing to sacrifice anything to get revenge on that whale, and, if you ask me, teachers who make us read stuff like this are teaching us the wrong values. We ought to read only books that are uplifting. This book is not uplifting because of its emphasis on Ahab's revenge. Therefore, we ought not to read it.

In the end, Ahab finds the whale and harpoons him, but the line on the harpoon gets tangled in Ahab's body, and when the great white whale dives into the sea, Ahab is carried along and drowned. A little while later, the whale rams the *Pequod* and sinks it, and the narrator, whose name is Ishmael, is the only person to be saved. This is unfortunate because he tells the story for hundreds and hundreds of boring pages, and we have to read it.

So the book is not only not uplifting, but it does not have a happy ending. I felt very depressed when I finished reading the book. And a literature course ought not to depress the students who are forced to take it.

The book had its good points. Ahab's death was one of them, and if he hadn't been the main character of the book, his being drowned would have been okay by me. I look at it from the whale's point of view. Years earlier, Ahab had tried to kill the whale and probably had sunk a harpoon into him. Ahab thought he was looking for the whale all during the book. But for all we know, the whale may have been looking for Ahab. In the end the whale got his revenge. And if you like animals, as I do, you have to be glad of that.

39f

arg

CHAPTER FORTY

Writing About Literature

Many of your English courses will require that you write about literature —novels, short stories, poems, or plays that you read on your own or that you study and discuss in class. An essay on a literary subject shows your understanding of the work you have read. Such an essay is always critical, meaning that it states your position on, attitude toward, or opinion of the work and provides details—usually quotations, summaries, and paraphrases—to support your point.

40a
Examine your assignment carefully.

Your teacher may have a specific goal in asking you to write about a piece of literature. For example, your assignment may be to write about sound images in *The Tempest,* to analyze the theme of Melville's story "Bartleby the Scrivener," to compare two love sonnets by Keats, or to trace the development of a character, Pip, for example, in Dickens' *Great Expectations,* or Mrs. Dalloway in Virginia Woolf's novel by that name. Or, your teacher may give a general assignment. She may identify a literary work and ask you to write about it, or she may tell you to choose a work on your own and write about it. In these last two cases you have to define the terms of the assignment yourself.

The student whose paper appears at the end of this chapter received this assignment: *Read "in Just-" by E. E. Cummings and write an essay of about two or three typed pages that explains the meaning of the poem.* The class was studying poetry and had read and discussed some of Cummings' other poems together. (The text of "in Just-" appears on pages 718–719.)

Both specific and open-ended writing assignments about literature almost always require **analysis.** When you analyze something, you scrutinize its parts in order to understand the whole. You look closely at the words and sentences, the motivations and the actions of the characters, the events of the narrative, and the writer's techniques, among other elements. Analysis often involves **interpretation,** an explanation of what you think the work means, and **evaluation,** your opinion and judgment about the literary work. Analysis and interpretation lead to evaluation, and you should base your judgments on thorough analysis and careful interpretation.

40b
Read the literary work with care and attention.

Don't plan on writing until you've read the work carefully several times. Poems and short stories can be reread easily, even under tight time pressures. You also should plan on reading and rereading longer works. You cannot write a good paper about literature that you have read only one time. When you read a text several times, you will begin to notice things that will deepen your appreciation and enlarge your understanding of it. The detailed knowledge will provide resources that enable you to write a good paper.

Read actively. If you own the book, underline words and phrases and make notes to yourself in the margin. Some students of literature make their own indexes on the blank pages in the back of a book, especially in longer works. They copy down a key phrase and the page number on which the phrase appears. Later, when they think and write about the work, they can find important passages easily.

Active reading of literature means raising questions. Stimulate your mind by posing questions about literary selections and seeking answers to them as you read. When you examine some of the approaches to writing about literature in 40e, you will find many questions that will help you understand a novel, short story, poem, or play that you are reading. Not all the questions will apply to every literary creation. But if you keep them in mind as you read, you will become a more attentive reader, and you will see things in the literature that will help you write about it.

See Appendix A, "Study Techniques," for other suggestions about how to read carefully.

40c

Use prewriting techniques and develop an appropriate thesis.

40c

lit

Follow the guidelines for prewriting in Chapter 1 as you prepare to write an essay about a piece of literature. Do brainstorming, make an informal list or a subject tree, or use a rough outline. Keep returning to the literary text as you shape your ideas.

Develop a tentative thesis for your paper. Before you begin writing your thesis statement, look at your assignment again. You may be able to use some of the language of the assignment in your thesis. For example, if your assignment is "Explain how Iago convinces Othello of Desdemona's guilt," your thesis might be "Iago convinces Othello of Desdemona's guilt by means of carefully developed circumstantial evidence." Note how the thesis draws upon the words and ideas in the assignment itself.

See the research paper on Willa Cather in Chapter 38. Willa Cather wrote about the harsh and grim life that people lived on the Great Plains and how that life deprived them of certain kinds of culture and beauty. You can see how the writer of this paper developed that theme in two of Cather's short stories. This development makes a good research paper that goes beyond a mere summary of the plot.

To develop such themes, you must study a text, think about it, read it again and again, and write down various ideas that you may try out as paper topics. These ideas may become an informal outline that is built around one central thesis. You may have to write a draft of a paper before your most important idea becomes clear; then you will have to write at least one more draft to develop it.

Use the guidelines in 2c as you formulate your thesis. Remember that your thesis should be flexible and probably will change as you write successive drafts. As with other kinds of writing, the thesis of a literary essay must be more than a statement of fact. Your thesis should state a concrete position that you can argue about. Both your topic and your opinion about it should be stated clearly.

The student who wrote about Cummings' poem developed his thesis in three stages:

Tentative thesis	Revised thesis 1	Revised thesis 2
Cummings' "in Just-" is about a group of children who respond to the whistle of the balloon man on a spring afternoon.	In the poem "in Just-" Cummings paints a child's world in the child's own terms.	In the poem "in Just-" E. E. Cummings presents a child's world filled with the delights and dangers of childhood.

The tentative thesis above is not a thesis at all. It is only a summary of the poem's action. It makes no arguable point. The first revised thesis does make an assertion, but it is too broad and not well focused. The second revised thesis makes an arguable assertion that is sufficiently limited for a brief literary paper. For the final draft the student revised the thesis again. See page 721.

When you get to a final draft, you must be sure to keep your paper focused on one leading idea. In the paper about Willa Cather in Chapter 38, the writer is not concerned about how Cather got from her birthplace in Virginia to Nebraska. Nor is the writer concerned about the many stories in nineteenth-century literature about artistic young women dying of tuberculosis. These are interesting subjects. They might make interesting topics for other papers. But this paper is about the effect of the vast spaces of the Great Plains and the hardships of life there on two people with a great love of music and the culture that music reflects. The writer would have spoiled the effect of the paper if she had been distracted into these other ideas and had neglected her central theme.

40d
Consider your audience and purpose.

Your audience for a paper on a literary subject is usually your instructor. In most cases your instructor is familiar with the work she has asked you to read and write about and does not need a detailed plot summary. Many students mistakenly provide long plot summaries when the assignment clearly calls for analysis.

Unless your assignment explicitly calls for it, you should avoid writing an extensive plot summary. Of course, you may have to refer to elements in the plot to make your point. But your instructor does not want to read a paper that tells her something she already knows quite well. In your essay, she wants to see your mind at work. She wants you to think about the piece and to develop some ideas that your reading has stimulated in your mind. Write your essay as if both of you know the work and you want to tell her some things you have learned about it by careful study and thought.

Your purpose in writing will influence the outcome of your paper on a literary subject. If you are writing an essay with limits defined by your teacher—about two pages (500–750 words), for example—make your point quickly and offer supporting detail and no more. Especially if the assignment is due within a few sessions after your teacher makes it, you should avoid an overly ambitious plan that draws upon extensive use of secondary sources and other library materials. For brief literary essays most teachers expect you to develop ideas from the primary text itself. On the other hand, if you have been given a substantial amount of time to carry out the assignment, library research is probably a requirement. Chapters 35 through 38 present a research paper on a literary topic and show you how the paper was developed.

40e

Consider a variety of approaches to literary analysis.

Literary study is varied, and you should be aware of the different approaches you might take when you write about literature and of the kinds of questions to raise as you think about your assignment.

1. Write about the *characters*. Who are the most important characters, *the protagonists,* in the work? How are the characters related to each other? How do the characters relate to each other? Does one character dominate the work, or do several characters share the action equally? What exactly do the characters do? Do they talk, or do they act? Do the actions of the characters match their talk? Or do they talk one way and act another? What do their actions and their talk reveal about the characters? What makes you sympathize with or like one or more of the characters? What makes you unsympathetic toward or dislike one or more of the characters? What moral values do the characters have? How do the characters judge their own situation?

2. Write about the plot and (or) the setting. The **plot** is the action of a work; the **setting** is the place and time of the action. But writing about the plot does not mean giving an extensive summary of the events. It means analyzing the relation of one event to another or the effects of the action on the characters or the effects of the characters on the action. Writing about the setting means trying to present your sense of why the author chose to create the scene as he or she did. The setting involves not only a specific location — a living room or a church — but also a broader environment of history and geography. You can raise many questions about plot and setting. How has the author arranged and connected the events? Are the events told in the order in which they occurred or in some other order? How does a single important event relate to other events? Where does the action of the work take place? Is there any significance to where the action takes place? What period or periods of time does the work embrace? Why do you suppose the writer set the work in that time? What surprises you in the work? Why are you surprised?

3. Write about the **structure** of the work. How has the author put the pieces together? How do the various chapters or stanzas or acts relate to each other? What particular chapter or stanza or act stands out for whatever reason? Why does it stand out? How is the work similar to or different from works in the same literary category, or **genre?** For example, the structure of a poem by E. E. Cummings is very different from the struc-

ture of a poem by John Keats or Thomas Hardy. And, despite similarities, one poem by Cummings is very different from other poems by Cummings. How does the author meet or challenge your expectations for the genre?

4. Write about the tone of the work. The **tone** is the author's attitude toward the subject. How does the author feel about the characters and their actions, and how does the author make you feel about them? Is the author impartial, serious, mocking, condemning, playful? What accounts for the author's attitude toward the subject? Why do you think the author wrote the work? Considering tone usually means considering the speaker, or **narrator,** the person through whose eyes and lips we learn about the events. All narrators have a **point of view,** or perspective. What is the narrator's point of view? Is the story told by a third-person narrator, someone who is not a character in the piece? Or is it told by a first-person narrator? Does the third-person narrator follow one character exclusively, or does the point of view shift from character to character? How much does the narrator know about the characters he or she describes? Are his or her perceptions reliable? How does the narrator's knowledge affect what we as readers know about the action in the work? You never should assume that the narrator in any work is the same as the author of the work. What is the relation, then, between those two, the narrator and the author?

5. Write about the author's language and style. The **language,** of course, comprises the words that the writer uses. **Style** includes the writer's language as well as sentence structure, usage, and diction. Imagery, figurative language, and symbolism (see Chapter 12 and 40h) contribute to the author's style. Some questions to ask about language and style are: Are the words informal, colloquial, formal? What kinds of words does the author seem to like? Which words does the author repeat frequently? Which of such words seem to have special meaning for him? Where and how has the author used sensory language? Are the images original? Can you identify a pattern in the uses of imagery? How do figurative expressions contribute to the style and meaning of the work? Does something in the work appear to stand for something else? That is, does some word, some action, some description or character make you think of something beyond it? How are the sentences structured—are they simple or complex, long or short? Which sentences do you like and why? What special qualities of style do you notice?

Keep in mind that fiction is fun to write about because it may embrace so much of the human experience.

Exercise 40.1   Read a short story, perhaps one assigned by your teacher, and see which of the questions in the preceding several pages can be asked about it. Answer ten of the questions. Do you have an idea of what you might write about?

40f

Pick a topic that you can develop into an essay.

Having asked yourself a number of questions about the short story you must write about, find those questions that help you pick a topic that you can develop adequately in a paper. Sometimes you may not be able to answer a question; or if you are able to answer it, you may not be able to extend your answer into a paper. There may not be enough material in the story. But you can often combine several questions from the above list around one major theme.

For example, as several questions above indicate, a consideration of the narrator in a story can often be developed into a good paper. The narrator is the person who tells the story. Narrators may be first person or third person. (You cannot easily have a narrator in the second person.) A first-person narrator, one who uses the word *I* or *we* in telling the story, is usually a character in the piece. In Herman Melville's huge novel *Moby Dick*, the character named Ishmael tells the story and takes part in the dramatic events, though he is not the book's major character. But you can tell a lot about Ishmael by the things he says about himself. In *Treasure Island* by Robert Louis Stevenson, the narrator Jim Hawkins is one of the principal participants in the action. Whenever you find a first-person narrator, study the work to see just how much that narrator takes part in the story. Is he or she merely a spectator? Does the narrator have any decisions to make that may change the action? Do the narrator's feelings have anything to do with the development of the story? What kind of personality does that narrator have, and does that personality make a difference? In John Updike's novel *Roger's Version*, the narrator is an extremely disagreeable professor in an unnamed divinity school whose view of reality may not be true. Deciding what that narrator knows and does not know can make an interesting paper.

You can usually tell more about the character of a first-person narrator than you can about a third-person narrator. Even so, some narrators are mysterious. Who is the narrator in William Faulkner's short story "A Rose for Emily," a story told in the first-person plural *we*?

> So the next day we all said, "She will kill herself"; and we said it would be the best thing. When she had first begun to be seen with Homer Barron, we had said, "She will marry him." Then we said, "She will persuade him yet," because Homer himself had remarked — he liked men, and it was known that he drank with the younger men in the Elks' Club — that he was not a marrying man. Later we said, "Poor Emily" behind the jalousies as they passed on Sunday afternoon in the glittering buggy, Miss Emily with her head high and Homer Barron with his hat cocked and a cigar in his teeth, reins and whip in a yellow glove.

Is the person telling the story a single individual? Or is the narrator the collective voice of the town where Miss Emily lived and died? The narrator seems to have lived a very long time — perhaps longer than Miss Emily lived, though she died as a very old woman. And what is the relation of the narrator to the story? The more we read the story, the more complicated the story seems. Trying to work out all the complexities of the narrator's role in the story will easily provide enough material for a substantial paper. The place of the narrator in this story can be the topic of an essay.

In many third-person narrations, the narrator may have little to do with the story, and the narrator's feelings may not matter or may not even be evident. In Shirley Jackson's chilling story "The Lottery," the narrator is detached and studiously factual. What does the narrator know? Does he or she know the thoughts of all the characters — or only the things the characters do and the words they speak?

At times narrators get very complicated. In Rudyard Kipling's story "The Man Who Would Be King," there are three main characters and two narrators. The first narrator is a reporter for an English newspaper in India during the time that Great Britain controlled India as part of the British Empire. Daniel Dravot and Peachey Carnehan are British vagabonds who embark on a wild scheme to make themselves kings of a tribe in the most remote regions of Afghanistan. The narrator tells us how he met both men, then how Dravot and Carnehan came to see the reporter to look at his books and maps before going off on their adventure, and then how they departed in a caravan, Dravot disguised as a mad priest and Carnehan pretending to be his servant.

Carnehan leaned down and shook hands. Then the camels passed away along the dusty road, and I was left alone to wonder. My eye could detect no failure in the disguises. The scene in the Serai [the central square in the town] attested that they were complete to the native mind. There was just the chance, therefore, that Carnehan and Dravot would be able to wander through Afghanistan without detection. But, beyond, they would find death, certain and awful death.

Carnehan returns, a dying man, and tells the reporter of the disaster that befell them because of Dravot's reckless pride. The first narrator, the reporter, repeats Carnehan's words.

"You went as far as Jagdallack with that caravan," I said at a venture, "after you had lit those fires. To Jagdallak, where you turned off to try to get into Kafiristan."

"No, we didn't neither. What are you talking about? We turned off before Jagdallak, because we heard the roads was good. But they wasn't good enough for our two camels — mine and Dravot's. When we left the caravan, Dravot took off all his clothes and mine too, and said we would be heathen, because the Kafirs didn't allow Mohammedans to talk to them. So we dressed betwixt and between, and such a sight as Daniel Dravot I never saw yet nor expect to see again. He burned half his beard, and slung a sheepskin over his shoulder, and shaved his head into patterns. He shaved mine, too, and made me wear outrageous things to look like a heathen. That was in a most mountaineous country, and our camels couldn't go along any more because of the mountains. They were tall and black, and coming home I saw them fight like wild goats—there are lots of goats in Kafiristan. And these mountains, they never keep still, no more than the goats. Always fighting they are, and don't let you sleep at night.

The reporter tells a story about being told a story. But Carnehan is clearly a different personality and speaks in a different style. By paying attention to these two narrative voices within the story, you can write an excellent paper about their differences and their similarities. You can join these ideas about the narrators by trying to answer the question "How are the characters related to each other?"

The point of view of the narrator is always a good place to begin thinking about a piece of fiction. The narrator may be straightforward, factual, never wrong. The narrator may know everything the characters do and think. Such narrators will probably not be as interesting to write papers about as narrators who are surprised, afraid, admiring, or disillusioned. Joseph Conrad's character Marlow, who narrates the story "Heart of Darkness," would be an interesting subject for a paper because Marlow comes to some conclusions about European imperialism in Africa. Those conclusions involve Marlow's encounter with the ivory trader Kurtz, supposedly an almost superhuman leader who Marlow discovers is evil and perverted. But who is more perverted, Kurtz or the white businessmen who have sent him into the jungle to exploit the native Africans for profit? So Marlow's consciousness can be a good subject for a paper.

You can find many other topics for papers about fiction beyond the narrators of the stories. Often the issue of why a story creates a certain mood will make an excellent topic for a paper. Stephen King's novels, for example, create feelings of horror and terror in most readers. Why are we so terrified by a Stephen King tale while Bram Stoker's late nineteenth-century novel *Dracula* about a vampire count in Transylvania is more likely to make us laugh at the wrong places when we read it today? If you pay close attention to your own reactions to a story and then try to see what in the story makes you have those reactions, you may produce a good paper on that subject.

Often people with special interests find illuminating subjects in fiction. People interested in various social issues may ask serious and important questions of fiction: How did Ernest Hemingway treat women in his books? What sort of women are characters in John Updike's works? What is the difference in the treatment of blacks in William Faulkner's work and in Alice Walker's *The Color Purple?* How are Jews portrayed in Saul Bellow's work and in that of Philip Roth?

If you observe and ask questions as you read, you can discover dozens of topics in a single short story. Some of these topics will overlap; so when you choose to write about one, you do not necessarily decide that you will not touch upon any of the ideas that you would have treated if you had decided on another topic.

Here are several topics that one might write about after a study of William Faulkner's short story "A Rose for Emily." If you are using an anthology of literature in your writing course, you probably have a copy of the story. If you study the story carefully, you will see that several of these suggested topics overlap.

40g

lit

1. The Sense of Time in William Faulkner's Story "A Rose for Emily"
2. Why Miss Emily Grierson Got Away with Murder
3. The Narrator in "A Rose for Emily"
4. The Place of Light Images in "A Rose for Emily"
5. What Miss Emily's Father Did to Ruin Her Life
6. Why "A Rose for Emily" Is a Horror Tale

Exercise 40.2   Read a story, a poem, or a play, asking the questions in 40e. Then write a short paragraph suggesting a paper topic in answer to one or more of the questions. Discuss your topic with the class and with your teacher with a view to seeing if the piece of literature gives you enough information to develop the topic into a good essay.

40g
Study poetry carefully to write about it.

Modern poetry is difficult; and if you write about it, you may have to study it a long time to make sense of it. It's always best to read the poem again and again and to see the relation of the various parts of the poem to one another. You may not be able to understand the precise meaning of every line. But you can often arrive at a general sense of the poem that will make most of it come clear. You sometimes have to think hard to decide how to fit the various parts of the poem to each other. But wrestling with that problem can enlighten you not only about reading that poem but about reading poetry in general. Modern poetry often requires much knowledge, for the poets write with many allusions to people and events and to ideas that they assume to be the common knowledge of their readers. Here is the first verse of a poem by Anne Sexton (1928–1974) called "Her Kind."

I have gone out, a possessed witch,
haunting the black air, braver at night;
dreaming evil, I have done my hitch
over the plain houses, light by light:
lonely thing, twelve-fingered, out of mind.
A woman like that is not a woman, quite.
I have been her kind.

You may look at this verse at first and be bewildered by it. What is the key word? It seems to be the word *witch;* and should you look up the word in an encyclopedia, you may discover that a witch is supposed to fly around at night on a broom, imagining the evil that she could do to people below. But what Anne Sexton seems to show here is not so much the evil of the witch but the isolation. She is not writing about the fear the witch inspires but the loneliness the witch feels. This feeling of difference, of separation, of alienation comes through every line in the poem. We see the line "lonely thing, twelve-fingered, out of mind." The poet seems to be saying, "I am isolated, too; I am like the witch cut off from all human society that I see only as lights below me." Witches were often supposed to have twelve fingers. That deformity set them off from other women. "A woman like that is not a woman, quite." Not a woman to whom? The witch is perhaps not regarded as a woman by others but as a creature possessed, having only the appearance of a woman. But who decides what a woman will be or not be? The poet says, "I have been her kind," acknowledging that the witch *was* a woman, no matter what the rest of society thinks. The poet identifies with the witch in her loneliness and in the misunderstanding that society brings to her condition. Sexton perhaps expects us to know that many people think that the persecution of witches in the late Middle Ages was one example of the hostility to women engineered by men in power in the society. However that may be, the poet is expressing a sense of unity with the persecuted and alienated women called witches in that bygone age.

We cannot tell that this explanation of this verse is what the poet intended. If we have only the poem, we cannot tell what the poet intended except from what we see in the lines of the poem itself. But we can make a plausible argument. We can look at this poem and start picking it apart and thinking of what it might mean, and we can write the meaning down, depending on the text of the poem for our evidence. But remember the encyclopedia, too. What we discover that people thought about witches in the late Middle Ages may help us understand what Sexton means by this poem.

708   Other Writing Tasks

Older poems may seem to be simpler, but that simplicity may be deceptive. That is, you may think that a poem is simpler than it is. Nearly everyone knows Alfred Lord Tennyson's poem, "Crossing the Bar," a work often recited at funerals. Tennyson himself requested that it always be placed at the end of any collection of his poetry that was published, and editors of anthologies still honor his wishes.

Sunset and evening star,
 And one clear call for me!
And may there be no moaning of the bar,
 When I put out to sea,

But such a tide as moving seems asleep,
 Too full for sound and foam,
When that which drew from out the boundless deep
 Turns again home.

Twilight and evening bell,
 And after that the dark!
And may there be no sadness of farewell,
 When I embark;

For though from out our bourne of Time and Place
 The flood may bear me far,
I hope to see my Pilot face to face
 When I have crost the bar.

At first reading, this poem looks like a supreme profession of faith. But one may ask many questions about it. What is the "moaning of the bar"? And what is the relation of crossing the bar to the moaning of the bar? Instead of the moaning of the bar, the poet wants "such a tide as moving seems asleep, too full for sound and foam." What does that mean? And consider these lines, "And may there be no sadness of farewell, / When I embark." Who should not have this sadness, the people who see the voyager / poet off to the great sea, or the voyager / poet himself? Is it possible that the poet is expressing a desire for himself, that he not be sad at departing this life when he dies?

And so one may go on, asking questions of this apparently simple poem. As in reading novels and short stories, we must be sure to put the poetry we read together in our minds. We must try to see it as a whole and to see the relations of the parts to one another. Sometimes the best papers about poetry merely explain, like the paper at the end of this chapter, what the poem may mean, what it says, what experiences it evokes.

40h

Become familiar with some key literary devices and terms.

Writers have often used certain literary devices to help them tell their stories with more effect. When you come on such a device in a piece of literature, you are likely to enjoy a mild sort of surprise and to see in a sudden flash of recognition what the writer is getting at. Often these devices help integrate the whole piece for the reader, perhaps revealing an unexpected meaning that makes the text more vivid and more memorable.

The great hope of any good writer is to produce a text that readers will read and read again because they find in it the delights that only literature can bring. So through the centuries writers in many languages have developed devices that intensify the novelty and enjoyment of literature.

When you recognize such devices and know their names, you can write about them more effectively and make your papers about literature more interesting. Often you can understand the meaning of a story by recognizing how a writer has used one device or another. In using the device of irony, for example, a writer says some things that he or she obviously does not mean. But then what is the meaning? In Jonathan Swift's "A Modest Proposal," the eighteenth-century writer suggests that Irish children be raised for food like farm animals. Swift obviously does not mean that we should eat children. But what *does* he mean? Searching for that meaning can make an excellent paper.

Climax

The climax of a literary work is that point toward which the entire piece seems to be directed. Usually literary works end shortly after the climax. The problems are resolved or made clear; some point of understanding is reached; the major action of the story takes place.

The climax of Faulkner's "A Rose for Emily" is the point at which the astonished citizens of Miss Emily's little town break into a long shut room of her house after her funeral and discover the corpse of Homer Barron lying in the bed and a strand of Miss Emily's "iron-gray" hair lying on the pillow beside the corpse.

The climax of Robert Browning's "My Last Duchess" occurs at the line where the narrator, a cruel Duke of Ferrara, having shown a visitor the portrait of the late Duchess on the wall and having described her sweet and gentle character, says this:

. . . Oh sir, she smiled, no doubt
Whene'er I passed her; but who passed without
Much the same smile? This grew; I gave commands;
Then all smiles stopped together. There she stands
As if alive.

The Duchess smiled at everyone; the Duke was jealous; he apparently had her put to death because she was too friendly for his taste. Shortly afterward, the poem ends — with the Duke negotiating for another bride.

The climax of Shakespeare's tragedy *Macbeth* comes at the moment when Macbeth, having committed a string of murders to take the throne of Scotland, realizes that he cannot evade the fate prophesied by the three witches, that he must fight his rival Macduff, and that he will certainly die in the battle.

Being able to identify the climax will help you see more clearly all the devices the author is using to keep you reading to see how everything turns out, and to see the relation of the various parts of the work to the whole. Once you perceive the climax, everything else in the work may then fall into place. In a good story or narrative poem, you read toward the climax not knowing why the author is giving you this or that piece of information. But once you reach the climax, the purpose of everything you have read should become more clear. If you read the story again, you see the author leading you along.

Irony

A writer or speaker using irony means something different from the literal meaning of the words. Sometimes the writer means something entirely opposite from the words in the text. The most famous bit of irony in English is Jonathan Swift's "A Modest Proposal." Swift, enraged by the exploitation of Ireland by England in the eighteenth century, was especially concerned with the neglect of poor Irish children while members of the English upper classes lived in luxury. He wrote:

I have been assured by a very knowing American of my acquaintance in London, that a young healthy child well nursed is at a year old a most delicious, nourishing and wholesome food, whether stewed, roasted, baked, or boiled, and I make no doubt that it will equally serve in a fricassee, or a ragout.

I do therefore humbly offer it to public consideration, that of the hundred and twenty thousand children already computed, twenty thousand may be reserved for breed, whereof only one fourth part to be males, which is more than we allow to sheep, black-cattle or swine, and my reason is that these children are seldom the fruits of marriage, a circumstance not much regarded by our savages, therefore one male will be sufficient to serve four females. That the remaining hundred thousand may at a year old be offered in sale to the persons of quality, and fortune, through the kingdom, always advising the mother to let them suck plentifully in the last month, so as to render them plump, and fat for a good table. A child will make two dishes at an entertainment for friends, and when the family dines alone, the fore or hind quarter will make a reasonable dish, and seasoned with a little pepper or salt will be very good boiled on the fourth day, especially in winter.

Swift is not serious about serving little Irish children up for food. But he is serious in his belief that the rich, especially the rich English lords of Ireland, were treating the poor like animals. Irony often makes a serious point while seeming to say something ridiculous. Most of the time irony is easy to recognize in fiction, and the purposes of an author's irony can make a good topic for a paper. As mentioned above, the question to ask when you see that an author is using irony is this: What does the author want me to understand? Writing about the positive thing the author wants to say will create good papers about irony.

Dramatic Irony

Simple irony may appear in essays where the author says something in his or her own voice that is not meant to be taken literally. Dramatic irony comes from characters in plays, poems, or stories who present or encounter a reality that is the opposite of appearances. The poem "Richard Cory" by Edwin Arlington Robinson illustrates dramatic irony:

Whenever Richard Cory went down town,
We people on the pavement looked at him:
He was a gentleman from sole to crown,
Clean favored and imperially slim.

And he was always quietly arrayed,
And he was always human when he talked;
But still he fluttered pulses when he said,
"Good-morning," and he glittered when he walked.

And he was rich—yes, richer than a king—
And admirably schooled in every grace:
In fine, we thought that he was everything
To make us wish that we were in his place.

So on we worked, and waited for the light,
And went without the meat, and cursed the bread:
And Richard Cory, one calm summer night,
Went home and put a bullet through his head.

The dramatic irony is that Richard Cory seemed to have everything to live for, and yet he killed himself. We do not know why he killed himself; we do not have to know that. We do know that what his life seemed to other people did not seem so to himself. Dramatic irony conveys the common human experience that things are not what they seem. One use of dramatic irony has always been to make us realize that there is much more to human life than the superficial appearances.

Shakespeare often uses dramatic irony in his plays. Macbeth is told that he will not die until Birnham Wood comes to Dunsinane Castle. He thinks he is secure because he does not believe a forest like Birnham Wood can move; but then Macduff's soldiers cut branches from the trees of Birnham Wood and use them as camouflage to disguise their movements, and so Birnham Wood comes to Dunsinane — and Macbeth is defeated and killed. Dramatic irony is a common form in all literature. It adds mystery and surprise. It conveys the common human perception that we are sometimes overwhelmed by events, that no matter what we intend, something else results. Dramatic irony was often used in the classical literature of Greece and Rome to show that the fate of human beings lay with the gods and not with human will. When you discover dramatic irony in a work of literature, you often have an indication of a moral code that the writer wishes you to accept, a code that involves the necessity for humility and sometimes the necessity for resignation. When you discover dramatic irony, you may have a key to writing a paper about the value system that the author wants us to accept.

In all irony, the audience must know that it is irony. Therefore in well-done ironic pieces, we know throughout that we are reading something not meant to be taken literally. Inexperienced writers often fail in their own use of irony because they know they are writing ironically but they do not give any clues to their readers of the irony. Therefore the readers take them literally.

Hyperbole

Hyperbole is akin to irony in that the writer does not intend for the text to be taken literally. Hyperbole is exaggeration beyond what anyone might expect to be taken for the truth.

The father of this pleasant grandfather, of the neighbourhood of Mount Pleasant, was a horny-skinned, two-legged, money-getting species of spider, who spun webs to catch unwary flies, and retired into holes until they were entrapped. The name of this old pagan's God was Compound Interest. He lived for it, married it, died of it. Meeting with a heavy loss in an honest little enterprise in which all the loss was intended to have been on the other side, he broke something — something necessary to his existence; therefore it couldn't have been his heart — and made an end of his career.

—Charles Dickens, *Bleak House*

Dickens here amuses himself by going back into the genealogy of the Smallweed family, people he does not like in his novel Bleak House. *He wants to show us that the entire family of Smallweeds was greedy, heartless, and cruel. He makes these points by hyperbole or exaggeration.*

When you encounter hyperbole, you should ask yourself what the author means by it. Often you will discover that hyperbole, like irony, is related to a set of moral values that the author wants you to embody. Dickens here is assaulting greed by means of hyperbole. You can write a paper on Dickens' view of the correct way to use money, a paper triggered by your recognition that in this hyperbole Dickens is making a moral statement as well as a literary one.

Understatement

Like exaggeration, understatement often pops up in ordinary speech, especially in humorous statements intended to defuse a tense situation. Your roommate comes home and starts throwing his books against the wall one by one and screaming at the top of his voice because he has received a grade of C— on a paper that he was certain would get an A. And you say, "I believe you're upset."

Here is Mark Twain, in *The Innocents Abroad*, describing a celebration of the Fourth of July on an American ship in the Mediterranean during one of his trips to Europe:

The speeches were bad — execrable, almost without exception. In fact, without *any* exception, but one. Capt. Duncan made a good speech; he made the only good speech of the evening. He said:

"LADIES AND GENTLEMEN: — May we all live to a green old age, and be prosperous and happy. Steward, bring up another basket of champagne."

It was regarded as a very able effort.

The understatement is in the sentence, "It was regarded as a very able effort," a sentence that expresses the enormous relief of the passengers that they were not going to have to listen to a long speech and that they were more interested in the champagne than they were in the talk. Twain often used understatement.

Understatement is particularly valuable when you are dealing with strong emotions that cannot be adequately set down in words. We often experience feelings all in a great rush, and the feelings themselves are complex. If we intellectualize those feelings by trying to put them into words, we may kill the emotion by describing it at too great length. Understatement works best when the writer describes in some detail without much emotion those things that cause the emotion but uses understatement to indicate the emotion itself. Twain describes the speech that he considered the best one of the evening. Then with understatement he describes the emotional response this speech created.

Allusion

In allusions writers refer to something without precisely identifying it. They refer to something indirectly. That may be a literary work, a historical event, a work of art, a person, or something else. In writing papers about literature, you should be especially interested in the allusions writers make to other written works:

> Methought I saw my late espoused saint
>   Brought to me like Alcestis from the grave
> Whom Jove's great son to her glad husband gave,
> Rescued from death by force, though pale and faint.
>   —John Milton, "On His Dead Wife"

In the beginning of this famous sonnet, Milton alludes to the classical myth of Alcestis, the wife of King Admetus of Thessaly. She sacrificed her life to save her husband, and later Zeus (or Jove as the Romans called him) permitted Hercules to go down into the realm of the dead and bring her back to her husband. Milton also alluded frequently to the Bible.

Occasionally titles are allusions. *Absalom, Absalom,* the title of one of William Faulkner's most famous novels, alludes to King David of Israel's lament when his son Absalom was killed rebelling against him. "And the king was much moved, and went up to the chamber over the gate, and wept: and as he went, thus he said, O my son Absalom, my son, my son Absalom! would God I had died for thee, O Absalom, my son, my son!" The allusion instructs us to prepare for the rebellion of a son against a father in Faulkner's novel and for the father's subsequent grief at the son's death.

Allusions can often be used as the topic of papers about literature since the allusion may provide a key to understanding the work of literature. In poetry, particularly, an allusion may give the key to the entire work, as we saw above in the mention of the witch in Anne Sexton's poem.

Symbols and Images

Fiction writers, dramatists, and poets sometimes use language that makes us think both of the literal truth they are describing and of something beyond that truth. Knowledge of the symbol may intensify the meaning of the literary work where it appears.

In Faulkner's story "A Rose for Emily," the title is probably symbolic. The family of the dead person at a southern funeral traditionally puts a rose or a bouquet of roses on the coffin as a final tribute. The story, told as we have seen earlier by a first-person plural narrator, is itself probably the rose, the tribute of a town telling of the life of Miss Emily Grierson. We do not have to know that a rose has that significance in the funeral customs of the South. But knowing of that symbolic use of the rose may increase our pleasure at the story.

Matthew Arnold (1822–1888) wrote his poem "Dover Beach" of a narrator standing by the English Channel at Dover, listening to the waves pound on the beach as the tide withdrew in the dark. He wrote these lines as the third stanza of his poem:

> The Sea of Faith
> Was once, too, at the full, and round earth's shore
> Lay like the folds of a bright girdle furled.
> But now I only hear
> Its melancholy, long, withdrawing roar,
> Retreating, to the breath
> Of the night-wind, down the vast edges drear
> And naked shingles of the world.

The retreating tide becomes for Arnold a symbol of the seeming retreat of religious faith in the nineteenth century under the attacks of Darwinism and other isms. The narrator in "Dover Beach" yearns to believe but feels belief passing away from him in a great dark of the soul. The more one looks in the poem, the more one finds symbols of the religious situation in the period when Arnold wrote.

Some things have such powerful associations that they become symbolic images whenever they appear. The cross, for example, appears often in poetry and sometimes in prose as a symbol of sacrifice, especially by the innocent.

> Still falls the Rain—
> Dark as the world of man, black as our loss—
> Blind as the nineteen hundred and forty nails
> Upon the Cross.
> —Edith Sitwell, "Still Falls the Rain"

The English poet Edith Sitwell wrote these lines about the German air raids over London in 1940 early in World War II. We may see in the image of the cross the suffering of innocent humankind from war throughout the 1,940 years since Christ.

To find images and symbols in literature, you must read the text carefully and look closely at individual words to see what special meanings the writer may have poured into them. Look especially at words that are frequently repeated. In James Joyce's short story "The Dead," often reprinted in anthologies, the word *snow* is repeated again and again, and the story ends with an account of the chief character in the story watching the snow fall. Is the snow an image of some larger thought that Joyce wants to convey to us? An exploration of such an image would make a good paper. Any time you see the repetition of an important word or phrase throughout a story or a poem, ask if it may have some larger meaning, something that goes beyond the events in the story to stand for a general truth.

40i

lit

Exercise 40.3   Choose a poem or a short story to use as the basis of an essay. Read the work carefully, rereading as many times as necessary until you understand the work fully. Consider the various approaches to writing about literature and decide on a strategy for your paper. Study the literary terms and devices in 40h to see how they apply to the poem or story you have selected.

Exercise 40.4   Plan your paper. Do prewriting. Develop a thesis.

40i
Write the first and subsequent drafts of your paper.

Use your prewriting to guide you as you develop the first and later drafts of your essay on a literary topic. Be prepared to revise your thesis as your ideas take shape. Return often to the work you are writing about.

Write your essay as you would an essay on any topic. Write an introduction followed by body paragraphs that support your points with specific details. Make your conclusion a natural ending for your paper.

One further point: Write about your literary topic in present tense verbs: "Cummings *uses* words and images that a child would use"; "But beneath this simple world *is* a much more complex one"; "the poet only *raises* the questions but *provides* no definite answers."

The following checklist will help you to write and revise your drafts.

1. Did I examine the assignment carefully?
2. Did I read and reread the literary work actively so that I understand it well?
3. Did I do prewriting to develop my ideas on the work?
4. Did I state my thesis as a hypothesis that I can argue intelligently?
5. Did I offer specific details to support my thesis?
6. Did I quote accurately? Did I enclose in quotation marks any exact words that I used from the literary work?
7. Did I avoid extensive plot summaries?
8. Did I demonstrate my understanding of the work by analyzing it carefully? Did I address literary terms and devices, where appropriate?
9. Did I consider my audience and purpose?
10. Did I revise my essay carefully?

40i

lit

The following essay about a literary subject was written in response to the assignment asking for an analysis of E. E. Cummings' poem "in Just-." The full text of the poem appears below.

in Just-
spring   when the world is mud-
luscious the little
lame balloonman

whistles   far   and wee

and eddieandbill come
running from marbles and
piracies and it's
spring

when the world is puddle-wonderful

the queer
old balloonman whistles
far   and   wee
and bettyandisbel come dancing

from hop-scotch and jump-rope and

it's
spring
and
   the

      goat-footed

balloonMan   whistles
far
and
wee

(1-a) This brief paper opens with a short introduction that states the thesis succinctly. Compare this final thesis with the tentative and revised theses on page 700.

(1-b) The writer analyzes the language and draws specific details from the poem. All quotations are enclosed in quotation marks. Note the use of the slash to divide the poetic line that ends with "and" from the line that begins with "piracies." See 30e.

(1-c) Note how the writer avoids plot summary. A plot summary is not necessary for readers to understand this essay. Note too how the writer shows his own thinking on the poem.

Delights and Dangers of Childhood

(1-a)   E. E. Cummings' poems show an inventive, playful use of words and sentence structure to force readers to consider common ideas and feelings in a new context. The poem "in Just-" presents an entirely familiar world of children at play in the spring. Yet the poet's unusual use of language shows us the subtle dangers lurking about the delights and pleasures we all associate with childhood.

(1-b)   Cummings uses words and images that a child would use. He calls the world "mud-luscious" and "puddle-wonderful." With those phrases we can feel a child's delight at springtime. The games abandoned at the balloonman's call--"marbles and / piracies" and "hop-scotch and jump-rope"--accurately show us children at play. Cummings runs the names of the children together on the page so that we hear them just as children would say them, "eddieandbill" and "bettyandisbel." In addition the balloonman

(1-c)   "whistles far and wee," a child's excited expression certainly. The words "it's spring" are repeated twice, again to show the innocent excitement of youngsters outdoors after the spring rain.

(2-a) The conjunction "But" and the phrase "this simple world" connect the point of this paragraph with the preceding paragraph.

(2-b) The literary technique of *allusion* is pertinent for the discussion here. By explaining the allusion to the satyrs, the writer enriches our understanding of the poem.

(2-c) The writer comments on the structure of the poem. A repeated phrase in a short poem should be considered. Here the writer addresses the phrase "far and wee" and uses it to make an interesting point.

(2-d) Again, an explanation of an allusion helps the reader understand the poem in a broader context.

(2-e) Here the writer is discussing his view of the theme of the poem. Readers can tell that he arrived at the theme after considering many important issues in the poem, such as language, plot, style, character, and setting.

(2-a)   But beneath this simple world is a much more complex one. The balloonman has a peculiar, ominous power over the children. They stop everything, running and dancing to see him. On one level, of course, it is not surprising for children to greet a neighborhood visitor who sells balloons. Yet

(2-b) Cummings calls him "lame," "queer," and "goat-footed." In Greek mythology, the satyrs, creatures who enjoyed wild merrymaking, were humanlike gods with goats' features. By alluding to the satyrs, the poet implies something sinister.

       The phrase for the sound of the balloonman's

(2-c) whistle,"far and wee," which is used three times in this poem of twenty-four very short lines, also suggests something unusual, even dangerous. Why "far" we must ask? Will the sound transport the children far away? Can children far away hear it? Although Cummings' piper is more contemporary--he uses a whistle instead of a flute--the poet certainly

(2-d) is alluding here to the Pied Piper of Hamelin, who enchanted all the children with his magic flute and took them away from their town.

       In a sense, then, the poem may be viewed as a

(2-e) story of the loss of innocence awaiting children as they grow up. In a secure world of play there are no

(3-a) Analyzing a key phrase, and relating it to the structure of the poem, is a good strategy here.

(3-b) The questions are interesting, especially in light of the writer's conclusion: "the poet only raises the questions but provides no definite answers."

Exercise 40.5 Write a draft of your essay on a poem or short story, using the checklist and the sample essay above as guides. Revise your paper so that you are ready to submit it by the deadline your teacher has given.

troubles. But evil and danger are imminent, maybe even necessary for passage into adulthood. These

(3-a) ideas help call attention to the phrase "in Just- / spring." (Cummings probably used an uppercase letter for the j in <u>Just</u> for emphasis. The only other capital letter in the poem is for the word <u>Man</u> in <u>BalloonMan</u>, when the word appears for the third time. Even the children's names are set in all lowercase letters.)

(3-b) Does the word <u>Just</u> mean "only," suggesting that spring alone, the season of growth and renewal, is the time of joy in a child's life? Or is the message darker, perhaps even ironic? If spring is "just," meaning fair or honorable, where is the justice in children (or their childhoods) being stolen away? Perhaps Cummings is saying that spring is not just at all, that its delights are merely seductions. What makes the poem so compelling and provocative is that the poet only raises the questions but provides no definite answers.

CHAPTER FORTY-ONE

Writing an Essay Exam

Most college courses require students to write a midterm and a final examination and perhaps other exams as well. The pressure of time during an examination makes this kind of writing especially challenging, but essay examinations call for the same skills demanded by other kinds of writing. Therefore, you should use writing to help you prepare to take an examination. Writing can be one of your most effective tools for learning both from what is said in class and from what you read outside of class, and if you practice your writing as you learn, you may find that the exam itself is almost easy.

41a
Review all your notes.

If you have taken useful notes on lectures and assigned readings, preparing for your exam should not be overwhelming (see Appendix A). Read what you have written in the margins of your text and in your notebooks. Underline key words and phrases. Develop outlines. Your goal should be to highlight the major concepts and details that the exam is likely to cover.

41b

Write out in advance any questions that you think your teacher might ask in the examination.

Imagine that you are the teacher giving an examination on material covered in class and in assigned readings. Write out the questions that you would give in your teacher's place. Merely writing those questions down helps you organize your mind to answer them, and you will often be surprised at how close you can come to the questions that appear on the examination. If you have paid attention to what your teacher has said in class, and if you have read the material outside of class carefully, and if you have made good notes on the lectures and the readings, you will have a clear idea of what the teacher thinks is important.

41c

Read each examination question carefully, and briefly outline your response before you start to write.

Once the fateful hour comes and you have the exam before you, you should take several steps. First, read the entire examination carefully and spend a minute or two thinking about it. You may find that a later question will remind you of information that will be useful in an earlier question. Be sure you understand exactly what each question is asking you to write. A great many students go wrong on exams because they read the questions hastily and misunderstand them.

Next, take a moment to review the first question several times, until you are sure you have it right. Then jot down a few words to help guide your answer. You can write short phrases or short sentences. They will provide a brief outline for you to use in developing your answer, and they will nearly always stimulate your mind to think more clearly about the question. The two or three minutes you spend reading the question clearly and writing down words to help you answer it will save you much time in the actual writing of the exam. Suppose you have a question like this:

What were the major causes of the First World War? Which of these causes do you think was most important in the conflict that broke out in the summer of 1914? Justify your opinion.

As you read the question carefully, you see that it is really two questions. The first one requires you to name several causes of the First World War. The second part of the question requires you to make a choice among the various causes that you have named — and then to give reasons for your answer.

Once you understand the question, you are ready to start jotting down a few words and phrases to help guide your answer. You begin by asking yourself who took part in the war as it developed in the summer of 1914 — information you should remember readily if you have taken careful notes from your lectures and your reading. You remember that Germany and Austria-Hungary stood on one side and that against those two powers stood Serbia, Russia, Belgium, France, and Great Britain. You might write those countries down. Then you write phrases like these:

Russia vs. Austria-Hungary in the Balkans/Sarajevo

Germany vs. France and England; Alsace-Lorraine/naval race

Germany vs. Russia; Germans fear Russians; Schlieffen Plan

Neutral Belgium in the way of German army

Most important cause: German fear of Russia

From these quickly jotted notes, you are then able to start writing.

41d

When you write your answer give concrete details that justify the opinions you express.

Many responses to essay questions are so vague and general that teachers wonder whether the students who wrote them know anything or not. A good examination answer mentions names, dates, facts, specific details, and other concrete data. A good examination answer also carries an argument and makes a point — just as any other good piece of writing does.

A good beginning for the essay question about World War I might read something like this:

In the summer of 1914, Europe was an arena of peoples who hated each other. The Germans hated the English because the English had a great empire, making the Germans feel cheated out of an empire of their own. The English hated the Germans because, since 1896, the Germans had been building a huge navy under the goading of the German Kaiser, Wilhelm II. The British believed that this German navy was to be used against them, and when the Kaiser sided with Britain's enemies in the Boer War, the British people saw their darkest suspicions confirmed.

The French hated the Germans because the Germans had annexed the French territories of Alsace and Lorraine after the

Franco-Prussian War of 1870–1871; the French wanted their land back and spoke continually of "revenge." The Germans heard that talk about revenge and hated the French for not adjusting to the new reality of Europe, which in the German view meant German domination of the Continent.

The writer establishes the theory that national hatreds were a major cause of World War I by giving specific reasons for each country's hatred of another country, including appropriate names and dates.

41e

Read over your response, and make any necessary changes and additions.

Once you have written your response, take a moment to read it over. Though you cannot rewrite it, you can often improve your response by making minor corrections and additions. Look for ways to strengthen general statements by making them more specific. Simply adding a name, a date, or a factual detail may transform a vague claim into a specific reference that will demonstrate your knowledge of the subject.

VAGUE: Though others flew before them, the Wright brothers are credited as the first to fly.

SPECIFIC: Because their powered flights of December 17, 1903, were recorded by witnesses and photographs, the Wright brothers are credited as the first to fly.

CHAPTER FORTY-TWO

Business Writing

Whenever you send out a business letter, a job application, a memo, or a résumé, you can expect to be judged on the form of what you have written as well as on the content. If you misspell words, type over errors without erasing them, or leave smudges and stains on what you send out, you can expect your readers to conclude that you are sloppy and careless in your work. If you do not use the standard forms of business writing, your readers will assume that you do not know how to use them. If you do not communicate information in a clear and structured way, your readers will think you are disorganized. But if your business correspondence is written clearly, directly, and neatly, your business audience will be inclined to pay serious attention to you.

42a
Write letters according to accepted business standards.

1 Formats for business letters vary, but you are always safe using the block or modified-block style, single-spaced.

Block Style

In the block style, the major parts of the letter are set flush with the left margin. Do not indent for paragraphs. Indicate paragraphs by leaving a line of space between the last line of one paragraph and the first line of the next.

Letterhead Stationery

If you are writing for a business firm or a professional organization, you will probably use stationery with a printed letterhead at the top. The letterhead will give the name of the firm, its address, and often some sort of advertising slogan. You begin such letters with the date, written a couple of spaces under the letterhead. You may center the date, or you may move it to the right hand of the page.

Space down three or four lines, and write the name and address of the person to whom you are sending the letter. The address of the recipient of your letter is called the *inside address.* Space down another couple of lines and write the salutation. Skip a line, and begin your first paragraph. Do not indent the paragraph. At the end of the paragraph, skip another line and begin the next paragraph.

When you have finished the letter, skip a couple of lines and write the complimentary close, again starting flush with the left margin. Space down four lines, and type your name. If you have a title, write it just under your typed name. Sign your name with a pen in the space between the complimentary close and your typed name.

If you enclose anything with the letter, space down another two lines and write "Enclosure" or "Enclosures" flush with the left margin.

Here is an example of a business letter on letterhead stationery, typed in block form:

carry pistons, rods, and crankshafts for that engine. We can supply them within one week after receipt of your order.

I am enclosing a price list for the various parts of the 1948 Chevrolet Fleetmaster engine. Note that shipping charges are included in the prices. We ship by United Parcel Service on the same day that orders are received. We can arrange overnight delivery at an additional charge.

We accept payment by Visa, MasterCard, or American Express credit cards, and of course we accept money orders and certified checks.

Thank you for thinking of International Automobile. I look forward to receiving your order for the Chevrolet Fleetmaster parts and to supplying you with other automotive parts for your future needs.

Yours sincerely,

Roderick Usher

Roderick Usher
President and General Manager

Enclosure

Stationery Without a Letterhead

If you write to a business or to an institution, you should type your letter on unlined, sturdy bond paper, 8½ × 11 inches. Type your own address at the top right side of the page. Put the date under your address. Make the other parts of the letter the same as you would if you were using letterhead stationery.

28 Horseshoe Lane
Fair Hills, New York 10020
March 15, 1989

Mr. Basil Carmine
Ajax Industrial Chemicals
3939 Gentilly Boulevard
New Orleans, Louisiana 70126

Dear Mr. Carmine:

Last week I bought a fifty-gallon drum of your industrial-strength floor cleanser for my automotive repair business. According to your full-page advertisement in last week's Mechanic's Companion, your cleanser, sold under the brand name Wipe Out, is guaranteed to remove every trace of oil and grease from the floor of a garage.

I carefully followed your directions in applying the cleanser. I put on rubber gloves and spread the powder over all the grease and oil stains on the floor of my establishment. I then hosed down the powder with water. You can imagine my astonishment when your cleanser began to boil violently and to give off thick red fumes that forced us to evacuate the building.

When we were finally able to reenter the building the next day, we discovered that Wipe Out had not only removed the oil and grease stains but had also eaten large holes in the concrete floor underneath the stains.

I have discussed the situation with my lawyer, Rosalyn Eastwick, of Eastwick, Burns, and Tavern, and she has advised me to ask you to pay for repairs on my building. To that end, I am having several reputable contractors give me estimates on these costs. I shall forward these estimates to you.

If you are unwilling to pay for these repairs, we shall have no recourse but to sue you and your firm under state and federal laws regulating interstate commerce and false and misleading advertising.

I hope that a lawsuit will not be necessary. And I look forward to your reply.

Yours sincerely,

Glenda Ruby

Glenda Ruby
President, Southside Garage Inc.

Modified-Block Style

In the block format, every line of the letter except the heading begins flush with the left margin. Such a format is common in business writing because it is efficient. Word processing programs on computers can be easily set up to produce the block format automatically, and the writer can move swiftly through the letter.

Some businesses prefer the modified-block format. The only difference here is that the complimentary close is centered and the first letter of the typed name of the letter writer is placed four lines directly under the first letter of the typed complimentary close.

42a

bus

2 Remember to give the title of the person to whom you write.

The title may be given immediately after the name. Or it can be given in the second line of the name and address of the person who is to receive the letter.

> Ms. Glenda Ruby
> President, Southside Garage Inc.
> 28 Horseshoe Lane
> Fair Hills, New York 10020

> Ms. Glenda Ruby, President
> Southside Garage Inc.
> *Notice that when the title is on the second line, the name is not followed by a comma; when the title is on the same line as the name, the name is followed by a comma.*

Never abbreviate titles of people. Do not write this:

> Ms. Glenda Ruby, Pres.
> Southside Garage Inc.

or this:

> Mr. Sylvan Glade, Asst. Mgr.
> Micawber Loan Company

Instead, write:

> Ms. Glenda Ruby, President

and

> Mr. Sylvan Glade, Assistant Manager

Some titles can be placed before the name of the recipient of your letter in the inside address. Note that some of these titles can be abbreviated:

Dr. Ishmael Romer
Dean Ivy Wallace
Bishop Bernard Law
The Rev. Jerry Falwell
Captain Jennifer Jones
Sister Mary Annunciata

3   Use an appropriate salutation.

The salutation, always followed by a colon in a business letter, greets the person who receives the letter. It is placed flush with the left margin, below the inside address, and separated from the inside address by a double space.

Use the addressee's last name in the salutation. Do not address the person by his or her first name unless you are very good friends. Never address a person by his or her first name if you have not met the person or if you know the person only slightly.

Always say "Dear _____." Do not say "Hi," "Hi there," "Greetings," or anything else that attempts to be cute. The conventions of business writing require the traditional salutation.

Here are several examples of salutations acceptable to most people.

Dear Ms. Ruby:
Dear Dr. Fang:
Dear Messrs. Doolittle and Kreisburg
Messrs. *is the abbreviated plural for* Mister *and also for the French* Monsieur.

Dear Mmes. Cohen and Grey:
Mmes. *is the abbreviated plural for* Madame *and is used when* Mrs. *requires a plural.*

Dear Miss Williams:

To avoid unnecessary reference to marital status, many writers favor *Ms.* as a title for women. (See 33d.) This usage has won wide acceptance, and many women prefer it for its neutrality. However, *Miss* and *Mrs.* still do appear, and you should use one of these forms of address if you know that the person you are addressing prefers it. (One way to learn this preference is to see how that person has signed any letters written to you or to see how the name is listed in the posting for a job.) Use the first name alone only if you know the addressee well as a friend.

In writing to business organizations or to someone whose name you do not know, use one of the following salutations:

Dear Registrar:
title of the person

Dear American Express:
name of the organization

Dear Sir or Madam:

Dear Sir:
if you know that the recipient is a man

Dear Madam:
if you know that the recipient is a woman

Gentlemen:
if you know that everyone is male in the group you are addressing

Mesdames:
if you know that everyone is female in the group you are addressing

Dear Colleagues:

To whom it may concern:

A good dictionary will provide correct forms for addresses and salutations in the special cases of elected government officials, religious leaders, military personnel, and so on.

4   Get to the point quickly in the body of your letter, and give enough information to let your reader know what you want him or her to do.

Business letters are like college papers in that they should have a thesis. You write a letter to get the recipient to do something or to believe something. You do not write a business letter to ramble on about all sorts of things that may be on your mind. You may write a business letter to apply for a job, to report on something that you have done, to request information, to complain, to apologize, to ask advice, to give information, to develop a plan, or for many other reasons. You should make your purpose clear within the first two sentences of your letter.

LOOSE AND RAMBLING

Dear Mr. Armstrong:

As you may know, I have been concerned for a very long time about the emissions from your factory located on the Hiwassee River. I have written you several times about this problem. It has seemed to me that your factory has been polluting the river, and I have often thought that you were violating many federal standards. The enormous number of fish that have died and floated to the surface of the river near your pipes discharging various chemicals into the river seems to prove that you are polluting the river that belongs not just to you but to all of us. Consequently I have decided to bring suit against you in federal court. I am being joined in this suit by a number of like-minded citizens. We call ourselves "The Environmental Coalition."

CLEAR AND DIRECT

Dear Mr. Armstrong:

As president of the Environmental Coalition, I am sending you this letter by certified mail to inform you that we are suing you in federal court to shut down your factory on the Hiwassee River. I have written you several times on this matter, but you have not responded. In the meantime, the pollutants from your factory have gone on killing fish by the thousands. So we have no recourse but to sue, and we have taken the first steps to get our suit before the court. You will be hearing from the court and from our lawyers shortly.

LOOSE AND RAMBLING

Dear Dr. Fang:

I have often passed your building and seen the sign bearing your distinguished name at the front door of your establishment. I have heard of you from many friends, and, even more important, many of my friends have had their dental work done by your competent hands. I feel awed by the thought of meeting a dentist as renowned as you are. I think that perhaps I might be speechless if we were to meet. But nevertheless, I feel it incumbent upon me to ask you if there might possibly be a chance that you would consider me for the position of dental hygienist in your office.

Dear Dr. Fang:

I would like to apply for the job of dental hygienist that you have advertised in this morning's edition of the *Morning Bugle.* I worked as a hygienist for ten years in Dallas, Texas, before my wife was transferred here by her business. I am enclosing my résumé, and I look forward to being able to talk with you about the position.

42a

bus

Business people do not have time to study a letter in search of the writer's meaning. They want to know right away what the writer wants of them. You should express that purpose as quickly and as directly as possible. Practice getting to the point as quickly as you can.

5 Use a simple and direct style in business letters.

Many people suppose that a good business letter must be bland and impersonal. Often they think that a business letter must use complicated language so that the recipient will be impressed. Less frequently, they think they must use slang or other informal language to attract attention. In fact, a business letter should be simple and direct, without jargon and without flourishes of informality.

UNNATURAL VOICE: I want to take this opportunity to inform you of the important fact that I am most seriously interested in the announcement of the accounting job that you advertised last week.

TOO INFORMAL: The accounting job you guys are offering in the latest *Daily Snort* sounds like a real grabber. Count me in. I look forward to pressing the flesh and to throwing all the facts on the table.

NATURAL: I want to apply for the accounting job you announced in today's *Times-Standard.*
Don't repeat yourself unnecessarily in a business letter, and don't use complicated language when simple language will do.

UNNECESSARILY COMPLEX: In your recent communication dated March 16, you asked us to enumerate, categorize, and prioritize the need-based scholarship applicants eligible for financial aid under Title 6 of the Federal Grants Act of 1987. We are able to report that we have now enumerated, categorized, and prioritized the need-based scholarship applicants eligible for financial aid under Title 6 of the Federal Grants Act of 1987.

SIMPLE AND DIRECT: In your letter of March 16, you asked us to count the students who need financial aid, to classify them according to the sort of help they need, and to decide which of them should have preference. We have done what you asked. Here are our findings.

6 Be brief.

Whenever possible, you should keep a business letter to one page. Longer letters burden the hurried people who must read them. They often obscure your meaning. Since business letters almost always ask for some action on the part of the recipient, you may feel that you have to argue your case at length. Sometimes you do indeed have to write a longer letter. But it is usually much better to make your request clearly, briefly give reasons for your request, and close the letter as quickly as possible. Readers of business letters appreciate brevity and clarity.

7 Let the recipient of the letter know clearly what you want.

Close the body of your letter by saying clearly what you want the recipient to do next. You may be ordering merchandise; you may be asking for information; you may be requesting agreement; you may be asking for a proposal; you may be asking how a complaint will be met; you may be asking for a response to a report. These and many other reasons make people write business letters. Now and then you may not want a response to the letter. You may, for example, acknowledge receipt of a report and thank the writer for her hard work in putting together information you have requested. You do not expect the recipient to write you in response to a thank-you note. But much of the time you will expect a response to your letter, and you should spell out clearly what that response should be. Do you want the person to telephone you? Do you want to meet with the person? Do you want a report? Do you want someone to replace faulty merchandise? Decide what you want the recipient to do next, and state your wishes clearly.

Here is a model outline for a typical business letter:

1. In the first sentence, give the purpose of the letter.
2. Tell the recipient what you want.
3. Give brief reasons for what you want.
4. Tell the recipient what he or she can do next.
5. Close the letter.

Dunham Engineering
31 Pine Crest Industrial Park
Atlanta, Georgia 30375

November 21, 1988

Mr. Michael Elia, President
Rocky Mountain Scenic Railroad, Inc.
1313 Grand View Street
Boulder, Colorado 80832

Dear Mr. Elia:

I want to arrange a day-long scenic excursion on
your railroad for approximately a thousand people on
Saturday, May 6, 1989. At that time, the National
Association of Subdivision Engineers will be having
its annual convention in Denver. We are sure to have
at least a thousand who would enjoy such a trip. We
would like to leave around 9:00 A.M. and to return
to Boulder around three-thirty or three o'clock in
the afternoon. We would like to charter our own
train, and we would like to stop for a picnic lunch
in the middle of the day.

Please let me know if your line is available for
such a trip, and, if it is, quote me your group
rates. Please tell me also if you are able to provide
the lunch or if we should arrange to have it catered
by another firm.

Many people have spoken to me of the beauty of your
rail route and the courtesy of your service. I look
forward to an enjoyable day on your line.

Yours sincerely,

David Dunham

David Dunham
President

8 Avoid clichés in your closing.

You should always maintain a courteous and businesslike tone in your letters, but you can avoid some of the clichés of letter writing. Don't end your letters with worn-out expressions of gratitude such as "Thank you for your time," "Thank you for your consideration of this request," or "I await the courtesy of a reply." If you write in a friendly tone, you can close the letter immediately after you have stated your business and no one will accuse you of discourtesy. If you want to thank your recipient for something specific, you can do that. The writer of the preceding letter closed with a friendly expression of expectation. You can often close with a pleasant word about future relations. But avoid formulaic closings.

9 At the end of your letter, include the complimentary close, your handwritten signature, and your typed name (and title, if appropriate).

Letters usually close with one of the endings below. A capital letter always starts the first word of the complimentary close; a comma always follows the complimentary close.

Yours truly,	Sincerely,
Very truly yours,	Sincerely yours,
Yours very truly,	Yours sincerely,
Cordially,	Cordially yours,
Respectfully,	Respectfully yours,
Regards,	Best regards,

The signature appears in a four-line space between the complimentary close and the typed name of the writer. Most writers avoid adding a professional title (such as attorney-at-law) or a degree (such as Ph.D.) after their typed name. However, to indicate their official capacity, writers who have a business title sometimes use it.

Sincerely yours,   Very truly yours,

Carolyn Garfield   W. Prescott Blast
Marketing Manager   Dean of the Faculty

Address envelopes clearly and completely, following postal guidelines.

Address envelopes to include all essential information required for postal delivery. The address centered on the envelope is the same as the inside address; the return address in the upper left of the envelope includes the sender's name and address. Write out all words according to standard practice (see 33c-1 and 2) except for official post office abbreviations for names of states.

bus

```
Julie Holden
3200 Lake View Drive
State College, PA 16801


            Ms. Delores Smith
            Personnel Manager
            Farm Journal, Inc.
            230 West Washington Square
            Philadelphia, PA 19105
```

Fold 8½ × 11 stationery in thirds so that it fits a standard 4 × 9½ envelope. Fold the bottom third up, then the top third down, leaving about a quarter inch between the top edge of the paper and the bottom fold so that your recipient can open the letter easily. For smaller business envelopes, fold standard paper in half from the bottom up; then fold the paper in thirds, left side first, right side over left.

42c

Write clear and direct memos.

Modern business runs on **memos,** short communications exchanged within an office or between offices in the same firm. As the name indicates, a *memo* refers usually to something that should be remembered by people on the staff. Most conferences in a well-run business result in a memo that records what was decided. Supervisors in such businesses use memos to make announcements. Memos are usually kept on file. They are often used to trace the development of policy.

A good memo has many of the qualities of the business letter. But since the memo usually goes out to several people — perhaps hundreds of people — at once, it usually lacks some of the more personal conventions of letters.

1 Use the correct heading for a memo.

42c

bus

Memos begin with a date in the upper right hand corner of the page. But instead of the salutation "Dear Ms. Adams," the memo begins with a general address, usually preceded by the word *to* followed by a colon.

The recipients are assumed to be within the organization; so the memo does not include an inside address other than the classification of the people who are to receive the memo.

The memo does not have a complimentary close, and it usually does not have a signature. Instead, the writer of the memo gives his or her name after "From" followed by a colon. The writer then puts his or her handwritten initials next to the name. The writer of the memo may or may not give his or her title.

Good memos announce the subject on a third line after the word *subject* followed by a colon. Here are some standard headings for memos:

```
To: All the staff
From: RCM    RCM
Subject: Midterm grades

To: All coaches
From: Jack Booster, president of the university JB
Subject: The upcoming NCAA investigation of our
athletic program

To: Department supervisors
From: Michele Johnson, Affirmative Action Officer MJ
Subject: Affirmative Action guidelines
```

2 Limit your memo to one page, and treat only one subject in each memo.

Like a good business letter, a good memo should be brief and to the point. It should treat only one subject. It should be clear. If some response is required, that response should be spelled out. The memo does not have a complimentary close and a signature at the bottom. Here is a sample memo:

July 29, 1989

To: All members of the staff
From: LB
Subject: Dental care

We have recently made arrangements with the North
Slope Community Health Group for complete dental
care for employees of the company and their families.
Your cost will be a $2.00 monthly fee that will be
added to the medical insurance deduction in your
paycheck. The company will defray all other costs
for each employee enrolled in the dental plan.

The enclosed brochure from the North Slope Community
Health Group will answer many of your questions
about the plan. If you have further questions, please
call Dr. Jerry Pullem at North Slope at 524-7529.

You must enroll in the plan by September 30. If you
wish to enroll, please sign the enclosed form and
return it to me. Your payroll deduction will begin
with your October paycheck.

If you do not wish to enroll, you need not do anything.

42d

When you apply for a job, send a letter along with a full résumé.

1 Write a letter that catches attention by its careful statement of your qualifications.

Among the scores of responses a personnel director receives after a
job is advertised, your letter must stand out if you are to receive the
consideration you want. Yet your letter must not be vulgar. It must not
violate the conventions of courtesy and restraint that have developed in
business correspondence over the centuries. You are best served if you
present your strongest qualifications clearly, briefly, and carefully.

A job-application letter usually accompanies a full résumé, which
gives the applicant's educational background, work experience, and
other interests. Your letter should show that you bring special talents to
the position. Make your letters specific. Don't be satisfied with saying "I
have had much valuable experience that will help me do this job." Tell
what that experience has been.

The letter from Julie Holden reproduced below is an example of a forceful and concise application letter. Note that each paragraph serves a specific function. The first states the writer's purpose in sending the letter. The second describes how the writer's background would help her do the job well. The third paragraph explains how the writer's education has prepared her for this job. The last paragraph asks for an interview. Everything is to the point.

```
                              Route 2, Box 9
                              Manheim, PA 17545
                              February 22, 1982



Ms. Delores Smith
Personnel Manager
Farm Journal, Inc.
230 West Washington Square
Philadelphia, PA 19105


Dear Ms. Smith:

I would like very much to become an editorial
assistant at Farm Journal. My four years of education
at the Pennsylvania State University and my twenty
years' experience as the daughter of a farming couple
have given me the knowledge and background necessary
to do this job.

Like many of your readers, I was born and raised on
a farm. I have planted corn, mowed hay with a
tractor, delivered calves, and built fences. I share
with your readers an appreciation of farm life and
an understanding of many of the problems of the
independent farmer.

As you will see on my résumé, I am graduating from
the university in June with a bachelor of arts degree
and a double major in English and sociology. I have
studied the problems of writing, editing, and
producing a magazine. In my classes, I have practiced
and refined my knowledge of writing and editing. Now
I would like to apply what I have learned.

I will be in Philadelphia for a week starting March
25. If we could arrange for an interview on the
```

morning of March 27, I would be most grateful.
I will call you before that day to see if it is
convenient or to see if we can make an appointment
at another time.

I look forward very much to meeting you.

Sincerely,

Julie Holden

Julie Holden

Encl.

2 Prepare a standard résumé that accurately presents your education, your work experience, your interests, and other pertinent personal data.

Formats for résumés differ. Some are in the form of paragraphs, giving full information about past experience relevant to the job application. Others are brief summaries. All good résumés include the information potential employers need to know about their workers. As the sample shows, you should type your résumé and lay it out attractively. Because a brief résumé helps a prospective employer evaluate your record quickly, you should try to keep your presentation to a single page unless you have extensive qualifications that you feel you must describe. Do not inflate your résumé with unnecessary details in an effort to make it seem more impressive than it really is. If you are just starting a career, no one will expect you to be rich in experience and skills.

Personal Data

Give your name, current address, home address (if it is different from your current address), zip codes, and telephone number with the area code. Mention any special abilities such as fluency with languages other than English or experience in using business machines or computers. Mention any travels that might be relevant to your job.

Career Objective

Express your interest in a specific kind of position by stating your immediate and perhaps also your long-range objectives realistically.

Education

List the schools you attended, beginning with high school. Start with your most recent school and work backward. Give your dates of attendance and the degrees you received, and include any honors or awards you won, your major, and any courses you think qualify you especially for the job you are seeking.

Experience

List the jobs you have held, the dates of your employment, the names of your supervisors, and a brief description of your duties. Again, start with the most recent job and work backward.

Special Interests

To reveal details about yourself as an individual, you may wish to include information about hobbies, about membership in clubs and organizations, about volunteer work, or about any special talents you have. Be sure to mention any interests that might be useful in the job you are applying for.

References

Give the names, addresses, and telephone numbers of people who will attest to your character and skill as a student and a worker. (Be sure to ask permission from anyone you list as a reference, and be sure to select people who know you well and will write or speak strongly in your behalf.) People you use as references should write directly to the prospective employer. You may send letters that you have received in the past, commending you for your work, and sometimes you may send letters of recommendation that you have solicited from various people. But some employers tend to disregard such letters, preferring instead those written directly to the employer on your behalf.

Résumé

JULIE HOLDEN

Campus Address   Home Address
8200 Beaver Avenue   R.D. 2, Box 9
State College, PA 16801   Manheim, PA 17545
Phone: (814) 998-0004   Phone: (717) 777-7888

Career Objective
A position of responsibility on the editorial staff
of a magazine or publishing firm.

Education
1978–1982   The Pennsylvania State University,
                     bachelor of arts in English (June
                     1982).
                     Grade point average: 3.25 of 4.0.
                     Honors: Dean's List.
                     Major courses: Article Writing,
                     News Writing and Reporting,
                     Techniques of Fiction, Technical
                     Writing, Advanced Technical
                     Writing and Editing, Magazine
                     Journalism, Problems of Style,
                     Nonfiction Writing; also, in my
                     area of knowledge--Sociology,
                     Rural Social Psychology,
                     Intergroup Relations, and Rural
                     Community Services.

1975–1978   Central High School, Manheim,
                     Pennsylvania
                     Academic diploma (1978)

Experience
Summers of 1980   Employed as a clerical assistant
and 1981   at Central High School under the
                     supervision of Mr. Horace K.

Williams, Manheim, Pennsylvania.
Duties included microfilming
confidential permanent records,
typing, and filing.

Summers of 1978
and 1979

Worked as a farmhand on the
Schwarzmuller Dairy Farm under the
supervision of Mr. Robert Wilkes,
Manheim, Pennsylvania. Duties
included field work (operating
tractors and implements) and barn
work (feeding and cleaning).

Special
Interests

Painting, photography, gardening,
macramé.

References
Professor Bernard Krimm
Department of English
The Pennsylvania State University
University Park, PA 16802
Phone: (814) 987-4994

Professor Carolyn Eckhardt
Department of English
The Pennsylvania State University
University Park, PA 16802
Phone: (814) 987-2268

Mr. Horace K. Williams
Guidance Counselor
Central High School
Manheim, PA 17545
Phone: (717) 998-8768

APPENDIX A

Study Techniques

Develop your study skills by applying techniques for improving your comprehension and retention of what you read. Learn to take useful notes when you read and when you listen to lectures. Studying is an active, continual process that requires planning, repetition, and *writing* to help you remember and use newly acquired information.

First, plan a reasonable study schedule.

Examine your week's activities, and develop a realistic plan for studying. Consider all the demands on your time—eating, sleeping, attending classes, doing homework, exercising, socializing, commuting, watching TV—and set aside time for regular studying. Some students make a weekly chart of their activities so that it's easier to keep track of their hours. If you do block in regular activities and study time on a calendar, leave a number of free periods so that you have time for relaxing and for making adjustments. When exams or special projects come up, for example, you'll need blocks of time over several days, even weeks, to complete your work on time. Try to avoid cramming for tests, because the stress it produces prevents deep learning and memory. If you must cram, try to outline the major points you need to cover and concentrate on learning the central ideas and facts.

Learn and retain information by reading actively.

You can improve your ability to learn and retain material by approaching your reading with a clear plan and by taking various kinds of notes.

1 Survey your text before you read it carefully.

Surveying—looking at the text for information without reading every word—gives you an outline of the material so that you can focus on what you are about to read. When you survey a book, look for chapter titles and subtitles, headings and subheadings, charts, graphs, illustrations, and words in boldface or italics. Skim the opening and closing paragraphs of a chapter or of chapter sections. Surveying like this can give you the sense of a book very quickly.

study

2 Write out questions in advance so that you can read with a purpose.

Once you have looked quickly through the reading material, jot down some questions about it. Writing will help make things stick in your mind, and your written questions will provide a good short review. It is always better to write your own questions about a text you are reading, but if questions do appear at the end of a chapter, consider them carefully before you read. Then let them guide your reading.

Keeping specific questions in mind as you read will get you actively involved in the material at hand. Your reading then has a purpose: you are trying to find answers to your questions.

3 Take notes on your reading.

Take notes on what you read. Learn how to make summaries. When you read, try to summarize every paragraph by composing a simple, short sentence. Be ruthless in cutting out the nonessential, and put the author's thoughts into your own words. Don't try to duplicate the style of the book or article you are reading. Putting somebody else's ideas into your own words is a good way of making sure that you truly know those ideas.

Many students underline as they read. Underlining has several disadvantages. Obviously, you cannot underline in a library book; so if you underline material, you will have to own the book. Underlining is also a passive way of learning; it is merely a signpost to tell you that something here is worth remembering. But often, when students come back to passages they have underlined, they cannot remember why they put those lines down in the first place. Often, too, they underline too much, and too much emphasis becomes boring and confusing. Underlining is never as effective as writing down a short summary sentence for each paragraph. Writing a summary sentence ensures that you will reconsider the thoughts in the book, translate them into your own words, and put them on paper.

4 Look up your reading topic in some reference books.

You can also aid your memory by looking for the same information or closely related information in another source. Your teacher may require you to buy one or more books for the course, and you should read these books and make notes about them. But it is also an excellent idea to check information mentioned in your reading by looking things up in some of the many reference books available in the library. Try an encyclopedia, various dictionaries, and other reference books your librarian may help you find. (Many of these reference books are listed in 35c-3 of this handbook.) When you read the same information several times, presented in slightly different ways, you will find that each source has some details that the others do not have. This seeking of variety in your learning will provide wonderful help to the mind in remembering. If you have taken careful summary notes on the various things you have read, your memory will be all the more strengthened.

5 Learn to analyze what you read by asking questions about it.

Another skill required in study is the ability to analyze, to tell what things mean, to discover how they fit with other things you know. Here again, writing will help you to study. Many writing teachers advise students to keep a notebook in which they can jot down their notes from sources on one page and then jot down their thoughts about those notes on a facing page. If you ask yourself questions about the things you put down, you will develop your analytical powers. Pay attention to your own feelings. Do you like a book? Make yourself set down reasons why you like it. Do you dislike a book? Again, write down the reasons for your preference. Whether you feel interested, bored, repelled, or excited, ask yourself what there is in the book (or movie or whatever else you may be studying) that rouses such feelings. Then write your reasons down. Don't think that you have to like a work of literature or art or a study in history merely because someone else does. But you should be able to justify your opinions, not merely to others but to yourself. And as you get into the habit of writing out these justifications, you will find your analytical ability improving steadily.

6   Look up unfamiliar words, practice using them, and build them into your vocabulary.

With the aid of a dictionary (see 16b-1 through 3), keep a record of new words; write them on index cards or in a notebook. Include correct spelling, pronunciation clues, clear definitions that you write yourself, and a phrase or a sentence using the word properly. Arrange the words in related groups to help yourself study (business words, economics words, psychology words, literature words, and so on). Incorporate new words in your speaking and your writing vocabulary. Here is an example of a word written down for further study.

```
                    puerile (PYOO ar il)
        juvenile in a bad sense. People who are puerile
        are not just children; they are childish. He was
        puerile when he refused to let her name appear
        before his on the program for the play.
```

7   Review your notes and your reading assignments.

Immediately after you finish reading, and at convenient intervals thereafter, look over whatever questions, notes, summaries, or outlines you have created from your reading. Don't try to read every word of the original material in the book or article every time you review. Skim over it. You will learn better from many rapid readings than from one or two slow readings. Skimming will help you get the shape of the material in your mind, and as you study your own notes, you will recall many of the supporting details.

Use your written work to help you complete your assignments. It often helps if you close your book, put away your notes, and try to jot down from memory a rough outline of what you are studying. The more different ways you can write about material you are learning, the more effectively you will learn it.

Learn to write useful notes on your lectures, and compare notes with your classmates.

Taking good notes during a lecture is a skill that requires practice. Some students tape-record lectures so they can listen again to what the teacher has said. But even if you have a tape recorder and the teacher is willing to be recorded, writing can still help you understand and remember the lecture.

Never try to write down everything you hear in the lecture as it is going on. Unless you know shorthand, you cannot write as fast as a person speaks, and while you are struggling to get a sentence down, the lecturer will have gone on to another point. In your haste, you may garble both what has been said and what is being said.

Your best bet is to write down words, phrases, and short sentences. Use these jottings to stimulate your memory later on. As soon as possible after the lecture is over, take your notes to a quiet place and try to write down as much of the lecture as you can remember. If you do this regularly, you probably will find yourself remembering more and more of each successive lecture.

Once you have written up your notes, compare what you have with the notes taken by another member of the class. If four or five of you get together to share your notes, you will each acquire an amazingly complete set, and in your discussions of gaps and confusions, you will further your learning.

Take breaks.

Don't try to sit for hours without a break, writing notes about your reading or your lectures. Get up every forty-five minutes or so and walk around the room and stretch. Then sit back down quickly and go to work again. Taking a break will relax your body and perhaps stimulate your mind to some new thought that you can use when you start studying again.

APPENDIX B

Writing with a Word Processor

Many users of this book will be writing papers with the aid of computers and word processing programs. Computers eliminate much of the painful physical labor of writing. You still have to work hard and think deeply to write well. No computer can think for you or tell you what you ought to say. But the computer, a good word processing program, and a printer will make some of your choices easier. Computers can make revision much easier, and as we have said frequently in this book, revision is the heart of writing. Here are some suggestions for the use of computers in your writing:

1   Use computers to take notes.

You can make many of your notes with a computer and a word processor. Book stands that will hold books open and upright beside your keyboard are available in all office-supply shops and in many campus bookstores. If you can use a keyboard at all, you can type much more quickly and with much less fatigue than you can write in longhand. You are also likely to take notes more accurately with a keyboard than in longhand, especially if you learn how to touch-type.

Taking your notes on a computer gives you several advantages. You can find them quickly by using the search command on your word processing program. For example, suppose you are reading stories by the writer Peter Taylor for a literature paper on his work and you notice how often he mentions mirrors. You think you might mention that detail, perhaps even making a paper out of it. But you don't yet know. So you make this note:

756

The person in the mirror now eyed him curiously, even incredulously, and momentarily he resented the intrusion of this third, unfamiliar person on the scene, a person who, so to speak, ought still to have been asleep beside his wife back there in the family's guest room.

—"At the Drug Store," *The Collected Stories of Peter Taylor*, New York, Penguin Books, 1986, p. 117.

You might want to add something to this direct quotation, some thought of your own about the use of the mirror in this passage. (In making notes, you may make a file in which you put the full bibliographic information down for every source you consult. If in that file you have the full bibliographic information for *The Collected Stories of Peter Taylor*, you need only write "Taylor" and a page number with your note on mirrors.)

When you have made several dozen notes in preparation for writing your paper, you may want to recover all those places where Taylor mentions a mirror. All you have to do is to command your word processor to search for the word *mirror* and you can find those mentions almost instantly. It is a much faster process than keeping notes on 3 x 5 cards and having to shuffle through them when you sit down to work on your paper.

All good word processing programs have another feature that you can use in your writing. By using only a few keystrokes, you can copy any of your notes from your note file into the body of the paper you are writing. If you wanted to quote the passage above from Peter Taylor, you would not have to type it again. You could move it quickly from your note file to the essay you are writing on your computer. Not only is the process much easier than typing the note all over again; it will also cut down your chances of making a copying error.

In taking notes with a computer, you should avoid the temptation to take too many notes or to copy too much **verbatim** (word for word) from the source. You should summarize most information, perhaps using only sentence fragments or abbreviated sentences. So, for the quotation above, you might write:

Taylor, mirrors, p. 117, *Collected Stories*

Then your computer file serves as an annotated index of your sources. Seeing the word *mirrors* on your computer, you can pick up the book of short stories and turn quickly to it. It is always good to take notes and to make comments on the notes you take. Your thoughts as you write the note down should also go into your computer file, marked in some clear way that allows you to distinguish between what you are thinking and what you are seeing in the source. But avoid taking so many notes that doing the research becomes a substitute for writing the paper. Many writers, both experienced and inexperienced, take so many notes and do so much resarch that they never get around to the hard job of writing the paper.

2 Use your word processing program to outline your paper.

The same features that make a word processing program a good note file can also help you in outlining a paper.

You can construct your outline on your word processor — and then move the various parts around easily to achieve a more effective organization.

As you work, you can gradually fill in your outline, using sample sentences and paragraphs that you can later fit into your paper. You can try out introductions and conclusions to see which of them best express your purposes.

If you have consulted several sources, you can often put your paper together by transferring notes from your note file to the place where you think they ought to fit in your outline. You can try different arrangements for your notes and experiment with different organizations of your paper.

You can save the various versions of your expanded outlines, print them out, and compare them to see which one of them seems to suit your purposes best.

Some word processing programs now have special outlining functions built in, and some outlining programs with special functions are on the market in computer stores and catalogs. These outliners can be extremely helpful, and they allow you to put your final paper together easily from an extended outline merely by pressing a few function keys. But by using the search and copy functions of any program, you can use it as an outliner.

If you use the computer to outline and to arrange your notes in organized blocks, you will see more clearly that writing is seldom a linear process in which one sits down and starts writing a paper from the beginning and goes straight through to the end. Writing is nearly always a process by which we bring chunks of material to an essay and then blend them into a whole.

3 Use the dictionaries that come with many word processing programs.

Many word processing programs come with dictionaries that allow you to check the spelling of words in your text. These dictionaries are usually small compared to standard desk dictionaries. A collegiate desk dictionary will usually list about 150,000 words; a dictionary on a word processing program usually has around 50,000 words. Geographic, biographical, and specialized names are not usually included in a computer dictionary. But you can usually add words to the dictionary. Computer dictionaries do not define words; they only list words with their correct spelling. So you must be sure that you are using the word in the right sense; the computer program will not usually tell you what the word means.

The computer dictionary, often called a *spell checker*, is usually activated by pressing one or more function keys while the cursor is on the word whose spelling you wish to examine. The computer will usually give you a message telling you whether the word is in the computer's dictionary. If it *is* in the dictionary, you may assume that you have spelled it correctly. If it is *not* in the dictionary as you have spelled it, either you have misspelled it or the computer dictionary does not include it. You might get a message, for example, that the word *dilettante* is not in your computer's dictionary. But on consulting your desk dictionary, you discover that you have spelled the word correctly! So you should never depend on the computer dictionary alone; you should use it in conjunction with a good desk dictionary.

Computer dictionaries can be a great help in ensuring the accuracy of spelling. But you have to use them. If you have any doubts about your spelling of a word, check it with the computer dictionary. And if your spelling is not listed in the computer dictionary, look it up in a desk dictionary.

Some dictionary programs can be set to work as you are typing. A quiet buzzer sounds each time you type a word not in the computer's dictionary. Such a function not only helps you with your spelling but also warns you against typographical errors. The computer will buzz if you misspell the word *believe* by writing "beleive." It will also buzz if you reverse letters in the word *the* so that you get "teh." So the computer dictionary becomes a valuable aid in proofreading.

wp

4   Back up all your work, and print out copies whenever you can.

Computer data are stored by means of electric impulses that are translated onto discs by much the same sort of process that allows us to make tape recordings. Small discs, measuring either 3½ inches or 5¼ inches across, are called *floppies* and can be carried around and used in various compatible computers. Hard discs with vast storage capacities are sealed and fixed in the computer and are not intended to be moved from computer to computer.

All these discs are extremely fragile. Floppies can be ruined by being placed too close to the speakers in a stereo or even too close to the video monitor on the computer itself. Floppies are also extremely sensitive to dust, to cracker crumbs, to fingerprints, to spilled coffee, or to anything else that touches the magnetic surface. Hard discs are sealed against dust and may give good service for several thousand hours. But all hard discs fail eventually. The failure comes suddenly, without warning. The hard disc simply fails to record data or to give data back to the computer screen.

Once a disc is ruined, the data you have put on it — a copy of your research paper, for example — may be gone forever. And even if you can retrieve the data by some of the technology now available, the process is time consuming and sometimes expensive.

So you should always make backup copies of your work. That means that you should copy the work on one disc to another and keep the two discs in separate places so that if something happens to one, you will not lose your data. If you are using a hard disc, back your work up on floppies. If your computer fails, you can take your floppies to another compatible computer and go back to work with a minimum of lost time and with no lost data. It's a good idea whenever you can to print your work out at the end of a session with the computer. Printing the work out takes more time than making a backup disc. If you have a printed copy of your work, you may suffer the inconvenience of having to type it over again. But at least you have your work.

wp

5 Revise your work carefully.

When you have used a computer for a while, you will learn to revise on the screen, inserting here, deleting there. But you should always print your work out and read it on paper, at least for your final run-through. Read with a pen in hand to mark those places where you want to revise.

Be sure to give special attention to two errors common in word processing. One is deleting too much; the other is not deleting enough.

Often a writer on a word processor will produce a sentence like this:

> Mr. Harrington, who has been convicted of car theft, said that his criminal record had nothing to do with his present effort to become city fire inspector since cars had nothing to do with city buildings.

The writer, looking at this long sentence, naturally thought of ways of shortening it. And so he deleted some words. But as people often do in using computers, he deleted too much.

Mr. Harrington, of car theft, said that his criminal record had nothing to do with his present effort to become city fire inspector since cars had nothing to do with city buildings.

He had to insert a word he had accidentally deleted:

Mr. Harrington, convicted of car theft, said that his criminal record had nothing to do with his present effort to become city fire inspector since cars had nothing to do with city buildings.

Another type of error comes from not deleting enough. A writer wrote this:

Custer seemed to think that a dramatic victory over the Sioux Indians in 1876 would make him a national hero and might make him President in the election later that year.

In looking at his sentence, he decided to revise and came up with this:

Custer seemed to think that a slaughtering the Sioux Indians would make him a national hero and might make him President in the election later that year.

The writer has decided to make Custer's intentions more vivid by changing "a dramatic victory over" to "slaughtering." So he has deleted and inserted. But he has not deleted the article *a*, thus leaving the sentence confused. It should be this:

Custer seemed to think that slaughtering the Sioux Indians would make him a national hero and might make him President in the election later that year.

Computers allow you to move groups of words or, indeed, whole pages from one part of your essay to another by using a few function keys. You can try out a great many forms for the information you present. But be sure that you make the parts you move fit into their new spot. Read your work over again to be sure that you have not moved something without proper regard for the new context or that you have not left a noticeable hole in the place where the moved text was originally located. Working a computer grants marvelous efficiency to the writing process. But it does not take away the requirement of any writer to read the text again and again and again to see that everything hangs together as it should.

Keep your successive drafts, either on backup discs or in printouts or both. You may decide that you want to return to an earlier version of a sentence or a paragraph.

6 Use the computer to check on stylistic mannerisms or tedious repetitions.

All writers have certain words or expressions they like and therefore tend to use too often. If you think you have used some stylistic mannerism too frequently, use the search function on the word processing program to see how many times you have used it during your paper. For example, you may like the word *doggedly*. Search your paper to see how many times you have used it. If you have used it more than once, you should probably find a synonym.

Sometimes, especially in a long paper, you are likely to repeat information unnecessarily. If you write a paper about southern literature, you might mention Peter Taylor as someone whose writing has little to do with the agrarian tradition of much southern writing. Suppose you are writing and think you may have said that earlier. It's easy to search for "Taylor" in your preceding text to see if you have given the information before.

wp

You can use parts of this handbook more effectively by searching in your writing for some words that you were warned against in these pages. Are you afraid that you have used needless intensifiers such as *absolutely, definitely,* and *incredibly?* Search for them on the computer and decide if you want to eliminate them. Do you think you may have overused modifiers such as *very, rather,* and *really?* Search for them on the computer, and see if you can eliminate them where they turn up.

7 Be courteous to readers of text produced on a computer.

The technology of computers makes life easier for writers but sometimes harder for readers. Be sure you do not let that technology burden your readers. You can be courteous in the kind of printer you use for your final drafts and by how you manage computer paper.

Computer printers come in three main sorts. Laser printers are expensive. They are fast, and they have the clearest typeface. Letter-quality printers are heavy and slow, but they also have an excellent typeface, comparable to that of a good electric typewriter. Dot-matrix printers are perhaps the most common and reliable printers generally available. They make characters out of combinations of tiny dots; the dots are pressed onto the paper by tiny wires pushed through an inked ribbon, and the effect is like the appearance of lights in a scoreboard that create different letters and numbers within a square.

Dot-matrix type has improved dramatically over the years, but some models still make characters that are difficult to read. If you use a dot-matrix printer, be sure that it makes letters with true descenders. That is, the *g, p, q,* and *y* should have tails that come below the baseline of the rest of the type. The dots should also be close enough together to make legible letters. Before you use or buy a dot-matrix printer, look at a document that printer has produced. Can you read the document without being distracted by the type? If you have any doubts, find another printer.

Other sorts of printers are on the market. You should beware especially of printers that work with a special thermal-sensitive paper. These printers are often advertised as needing no ribbon; they make an impression by applying the great heat of a dot-matrix printer to specially treated paper. Such printers are fast and quiet. But often the type fades quickly as chemical changes take place in the paper. You can write something on thermal-sensitive paper and discover in a few months that you have nothing but blank sheets in your file! (Always be careful around any kind of dot-matrix printer; in operation, the printing head is extremely hot and can cause severe burns.)

Be sure the ribbon on your printer is dark enough to provide legible print. The ribbons on dot-matrix printers wear out rapidly. A faint, scarcely legible type in dot matrix can make life even more difficult for a hard-pressed teacher.

Paper for a computer is usually fed into the printer on a continuous roll. A perforated strip on each side allows a tractor feed to roll the paper line by line into the printer so that there is no wrinkling up or twisting on the roller. When you hand in your paper, be sure to tear off the perforated strip that has been used by the tractor feed. Be sure, too, to separate the pages. Don't hand in a continuous roll of printed pages! You don't want to have people suspect that you think of your work as akin to toilet paper, which also comes on a continuous roll. Teachers become justifiably annoyed if they have to separate your individual sheets and put your work together.

Computer paper is notoriously poor in quality. But nearly all computer printers will accept ordinary white bond paper. You must feed bond paper into the printer one sheet at a time. This is a slower process than continuous-feed printing. But the greatly improved appearance will justify the extra effort.

8 When you format a document, be sure to consider the convenience of your readers.

When we format a document, we lay out a page by adjusting the margins, setting material (including page numbers) at the head and the foot of each page, determining the position of the subheads, deciding whether the page will be single- or double-spaced, and setting the number of lines of type that will appear on a page.

In word processing, as in typing, take care to provide ample margins —usually an inch and half on the left side and at least an inch at the top,

wp

the right side, and the bottom. A little practice with your computer and your word processing program should make it easy for you to set these margins.

Always number your pages. Word processing programs can set numbers at the top or the bottom of each page, and they can either center the number or set it on the right or left side. It's usually a good idea to number your pages at the top.

You can also set headers and footers. A **header** is a line of type that goes across the top of every page; a **footer** is a line of type that goes across the bottom of every page. Headers and footers should be separated from the body of the text by one line of space if the text is single-spaced and by two lines of space if the text is double-spaced.

Page numbers are usually set as headers or footers. You can add other information as well — the title of your paper, your last name, the date, or whatever. It's generally good to keep headers and footers simple so they will not distract from the body of the text.

Be sure that you do not end with a subhead at the bottom of the page. When you prepare the computer to paginate, you must tell it how many lines to put on a page. If you double-space on 8½ x 11 paper, you will usually have a header with a page number and about 27 lines of text. Sometimes the page will end with a subhead, and the material that the subhead introduces will not begin until the next page. This arrangement can be confusing to readers, and it makes your work look sloppy. With a little practice, you can learn to insert blank lines to make the computer move your heading to the top of the next page, where it belongs. Every time you repaginate after inserting into or deleting from your text, you should check through your work to be sure that you have not pulled or pushed a subhead to the bottom of a page.

Don't overuse the variety of types your computer may offer you. With some printers, the temptation is great to use as many of the available typefaces as possible. But in general, you should avoid eccentric typefaces. Boldface and italic are the only special typefaces you need for most work. Never turn in papers written in a script or gothic typeface.

With most word processing programs, you can justify the right margin. That is, you can make the right margin as straight as the left margin. This is standard practice in book and magazine publishing. Most printers, however, will justify the right margin by leaving extra spaces between words. In book and magazine publishing, printers use proportional spacing so that a printed *i* will take up much less space than a printed *m*. Spacing can be set so that there is apparently little difference in the length of spaces between words. When you justify the right margin *without* proportional spacing — leaving widely diverse lengths of space between words — you make things more difficult for a reader. Unless your word processing program and your printer will do proportional spacing, it's always better to leave your right margin unjustified.

By all means learn to use computers and word processing programs before you leave college. The computer is rapidly becoming a standard medium of communication. Word processing programs enable you to make sweeping revisions or small changes with relative ease. They are fun to use, and they often give writers a sense of control over their work that they lacked when they were doing everything with a pencil, or even with a typewriter.

Choose a word processing program that you can learn easily. Always choose a program that is being used successfully by someone you know. Manuals are notorious for the poor writing that goes into them. If you cannot understand the manual, you can always call for advice from a friend who knows the program.

Learn to compose at a keyboard. It is a much faster and more convenient way of writing than longhand. If you are going to use a computer, you must be able to use a keyboard. A little practice will show you that composing at a keyboard will make you much more productive. You can do it!

wp

APPENDIX C

A Sampler of Prose for Imitation

Inexperienced writers often fail to use enough variety in their sentences. They often write the same sentence form again and again and again. The English sentence is enormously flexible. You can make your writing style more flexible by studying and by trying to imitate the work of various authors who do things well. The following examples illustrate many devices that make for strong writing, and the notes that follow each example describe the techniques that make the examples effective.

To exercise your own talents, practice imitating these examples. Follow each model as closely as you can. When you read a sentence that begins with an adverbial clause or with a prepositional phrase, begin your own sentence in the same way. If the model sentence contains a simile or a series of verbs or an absolute phrase, your sentence should include these elements, too. Don't worry if you find the process awkward at first; imitation is difficult. But it will quickly become easier and more rewarding with practice, and you will discover that your writing style will grow more flexible as you gain confidence in doing different things.

It is best to do these imitations in small groups. You and your friends can each try your hand at an imitation. Then you can read your efforts to one another.

1. They had their orchestras and theater groups, their picnics and outings, their lectures and entertainments.

— FRANCIS RUSSELL

English has a great fondness for groups of three. Here is a sentence with three couples of direct objects — six direct objects in all. The direct objects are all acted upon by the single verb had. *Russell could have written "They had orchestras, theater groups, picnics, outings, lectures, and entertainments." But that would have been much more monotonous and difficult than the sentence he wrote. An imitation of the sentence would be this: "They gathered their husbands and their children, their books and their papers, their dogs and their cats."*

2. In his fiction, Kipling presents a number of heroes—the common soldier, the freebooter, and the imperial officer.
— JOHN A. MCCLURE

Here is another group of three, presented this time as an appositive to the noun heroes, object of the preposition of. The triple enlarges on the word heroes, telling you of what sorts these various heroes were. The triple enumeration after the dash enlarges or complements the meaning of the noun.

3. The Greeks knew what it was to have a country, a native religion, a beautiful noble way of living, to be defended to the death.
— GEORGE SANTAYANA

Yet another triple appears here, this time three objectives of the infinitive "to have." The sentence is complicated by a final infinitive phrase, "to be defended to the death."

4. By now the troopers who followed him were groggy with fatigue, the column was strung out, and he could not locate his mare Fanchon. He therefore detailed a sergeant with six men to poke up the stragglers, shoot exhausted horses so the Indians could not use them, and bring the mare forward.
— EVAN S. CONNELL

Here are triples in consecutive sentences. In the first, we have three clauses, one after the other. In the second sentence, we have three infinitives. Connell could have written, "He . . . detailed a sergeant with six men to poke up the stragglers, to shoot exhausted horses so the Indians could not use them, and to bring the mare forward." But because of the close connection of the triple, he uses the infinitive marker to only once to form the infinitive of all three verbs. Try to imitate the passage as it stands—with two sentences that flow together—using triples. But if you have trouble, imitate each sentence separately, without having them develop one subject.

5. He climbed trees, went for picnics in the woods, swam in the local lake, and larked about with the other village children.
— COLIN SIMPSON

Here is a sentence with four verbs expressing action by one subject. The verbs climbed, went, swam, and larked about all refer to action of the subject he. Multiple verbs give a sense of vitality to a sentence. The subject does several things, one after the other. The verbs give a sense of pace to the sentence. The triple-compound verb in American sentences is more common than the quadruple-compound verb that we have here. But the principle is the same whether there are three verbs or four in the sentence; action is compressed and made more vivid.

6. Behind Wilson's speeches were thought and profound belief and ideas which pierced through to men's hearts, aroused minds, and awakened hopes.

— Barbara Tuchman

Notice the triple-compound verb in the clause "which pierced through to men's hearts, aroused minds, and awakened hopes." The triple-compound verb gives the subject three related actions and helps speed up the pace of the sentence.

7. One who breaks an unjust law must do so openly, lovingly, and with a willingness to accept the penalty.

— Martin Luther King Jr.

Another triple, this one as an adverb modifying the verb phrase "must do so." How must one do so? "Openly, lovingly, and with a willingness to accept the penalty." Notice that the last adverbial form is made as a prepositional phrase and an infinitive phrase. A suitable imitation would be this: "A student of literature must work slowly, carefully, and with a capacity to endure frustration."

style

8. Never in the field of human conflict was so much owed by so many to so few.

— Winston Churchill

This famous short sentence has three rhetorical features. It is an inverted sentence; that is, the verb was comes before the subject much. The sentence also has a repeated word, so, which carries the thought along vigorously. And it also uses antithesis: "so much" and "so many" are in dramatic antithesis to "so few." Notice that like most inverted sentences, this one begins with an adverb. Churchill was writing of the debt that all the British people owed to a few hundred Royal Air Force pilots, who defeated the German Air Force during the Battle of Britain early in World War II.

9. There is another very interesting sailors' superstition—that a ring of gold is an amulet against drowning.

— John Fowles

This sentence puts a noun clause as a subject complement after the subject in an inverted sentence. Fowles could have written the sentence like this: Another very interesting sailors' superstition is that a ring of gold is an amulet against drowning. But as he has written it, the sentence builds from a low-key "There is" to a final surprise, that a ring of gold (usually worn in the ear) was a good-luck charm (or amulet) against drowning. The sentence has a periodic tone. (See 9a, p. 216.)

10. He was always coming back—back from Korea, back from a broken collarbone, a shattered elbow, a bruised heel, back from drastic bouts of flu and ptomaine poisoning.

— John Updike

Updike is writing about Ted Williams, the great outfielder for the Boston Red Sox. The pattern of repetition in the sentence, emphasized by the repeated use of the word back *and supported by specific details, echoes and enhances Updike's statement about Williams' persistence. You do not have to use the word* back *in imitating the sentence. The pattern is the main thing. Here is an example: "She was always running—running to work, running to an appointment, a meal, a meeting, running to departing trains and early planes."*

11. Even though the bikes were fresh out of the government-run factory, they looked old and shabby, the olive-drab paint flaking off, the handlebars rusting.

—Lewis M. Simons

In this sentence, about bicycles on sale in present-day Vietnam, the author uses two absolute phrases, "the olive-drab paint flaking off" and "the handlebars rusting." An absolute phrase comprises a noun followed by a participle. The participles in these absolutes are both present participles; that is, they end in -ing. Without the absolutes, the sentence might be broken down like this: "Even though the bikes were fresh out of the government-run factory, they looked old and shabby. The olive-drab paint was flaking off. The handlebars were rusting." Use of the absolutes allows for compression and a swifter pace in a sentence. Absolutes are common now in good writing. In imitating this sentence, you may work only with the independent clause that includes the absolute phrases. Then you might get a sentence like this about a house: "It looked poor and miserable, the roof falling in, the walls decaying."

12. A rough rectangle of carved stone, it stood about 200 yards long and 150 wide, its basilica walls covered by murals by Luca Giordana, its library filled with 100,000 volumes.

—Otto Friedrich

The description is of the Italian monastery of Monte Cassino destroyed by American bombing in 1943. In the sentence are absolute phrases using past participles instead of present participles. So we have "its . . . walls covered . . . its library filled. . . ." An absolute phrase can combine a noun with a past participle. The sentence is also interesting because it begins with an absolute in which the participle is implied but not written. The opening phrase implies the participle being, *so that if it were written out, it would be like this: "Being a rough rectangle of carved stone, it stood about 200 yards long and 150 wide. . . ." In imitating these absolute phrases, we might have a sentence like this one, describing an automobile: "A black vision of polished steel, the limousine stood twenty-five feet long and five-passengers wide, its seats covered with leather from Italy, its dashboard equipped with twelve instruments."*

13. The first thing he did was to put in electricity, wiring the place with his own hands.

—Dorothy Day

This sentence uses a free modifier, *a participle set off by a comma at the end of a sentence (or a clause), introducing a phrase that modifies the subject. Dorothy Day could have written this sentence like this: "Wiring the place with his own hands, the first thing he did was to put in electricity." Strings of free modifiers can be run together at the end of a sentence, all of them modifying the subject: "He worked with his hands, painting the walls, repairing the roof, polishing the floors, oiling the hinges, replacing broken windows." All of these free modifiers describe something about the subject,* he. *Though it would be awkward to do so, we could put them at the beginning of the sentence. Free modifiers allow a sentence to contain a lot of action, but because they all modify the subject, they do not become confusing. They are extremely common now in American English.*

style

14. Besides ordinary blubber oil, the sperm whale yielded finer and more valuable "case oil" from the reservoir in its head—the precious spermaceti from which were made the clearest and longest-burning candles.

—J. H. Perry

Set off by a dash, the final clause of this sentence defines something mentioned in the main clause. Case oil *is what nineteenth-century whaling men called the oil in the sperm-whale's head. It could be boiled down to* spermaceti, *a substance used to make candles. In imitating this sentence, use a term that has to be defined in a final clause set off from the first part of the sentence with a dash. Here is a possibility: "Besides selfish arrogance, King Lear was possessed by a more deadly quality—a lack of judgment from which was to come madness and death."*

15. Some ministers, remembering their early years, said in all seriousness that they had spent half of their active life in the saddle.

—Richard Erdoes

A participial modifier is found here after the subject. The sentence could be written like this: "Remembering their early years, some ministers said in all seriousness that they had spent half their active life in the saddle." But variety is obtained by putting the participial modifier in apposition to, or after, the noun that it modifies.

16. According to Dinsmore, Dante's chief legacy was his stress on "the accountability of man, the supremacy of moral law, the certainty of its rewards and punishments."

—Jackson Lears

What is to be imitated here is the use of a partial quotation. In quoting from a source, avoid quoting too much. Sometimes you will quote whole sentences. But often you can take some significant phrases out of a sentence and quote those phrases in a sentence of your own. Here author Jackson Lears quotes the nineteenth-century critic Charles Dinsmore on the late medieval Italian poet Dante. It would have slowed the pace of Lears' narrative to quote at length from Dinsmore; instead, he has quoted these three phrases. (Note that the triple was used as frequently in the nineteenth century as it is today.) Notice, too, that the quotation marks are sufficient to set off the quoted material. You do not need ellipsis marks. Lears did not write, "According to Dinsmore, Dante's chief legacy was his stress on ". . . the accountability of man, the supremacy of moral law, the certainty of its rewards and punishments." You do not need ellipsis marks at the beginning of a quotation. (See 30f.)

17. Born in 1895, the son of a grocer who owned his own small business, Schimpf had as a child watched his father lose his store and take a job as a machinist in a nearby steel company.

— ALAN BRINKLEY

This is a complicated sentence, but not too complicated to be imitated. A participial phrase and a noun modified by an adjective clause both modify the subject. Much information is therefore compressed. A possible imitation would be this: "Published in 1885, a novel that had been serialized in a magazine, Huckleberry Finn did not make an immediate impression."

18. Matilda listened, emotionally drained from her own weeping and praying since her Chicken George had been gone.

— ALEX HALEY

In this sentence, we have a short independent clause followed by a free modifier that acts as an adjective for the subject, Matilda. Alex Haley describes the separation of a slave from her husband in the American South before the Civil War. The long concluding modifier has the effect of a periodic sentence, putting great weight toward the end. A suitable imitation, in, say, a paper about Faulkner's "A Rose for Emily," would be this: "Miss Emily withdrew, isolated from the town by her loneliness and her solitude since her lover had departed."

19. Because the speed you attain and the amount of time you spend on the treadmill or bicycle provide a good indication of what kind of shape your heart, lungs, and blood vessels are in, stress test results are increasingly being used to make exercise prescriptions and to measure progress in fitness programs.

— JANIS GRAHAM

The adverbial clause beginning with the word because opens the sentence, giving variety. A more common way of using this clause would have been to put it at the end of the sentence. But by putting it first, the author was able to put the more interesting information early in the sentence.

style

20. Does housework, then, have any redeeming psychological value? Nervousness, insomnia, heart palpitations, headaches, dizziness, fainting, nightmares, trembling and perspiring hands, and above all, inertia. Housewives suffered more from every one of these symptoms of psychological distress than did working women, according to data collected by the Department of Health, Education, and Welfare in 1970.

—GAIL SHEEHY

The quality to be imitated here is the question followed by an answer. Notice that the answer here is a sentence fragment, a list of the symptoms of distress referred to in the third sentence. In some more informal kinds of writing, you can use this fast-paced style to give vigor to an argument. This would be an acceptable imitation: "Does memorizing poetry have any redeeming educational value? Discipline, confidence, mental alertness, true familiarity with a text, simple pleasure, and a sense of the rhythms of language. All these benefits come to the person who commits a large quantity of poetry to memory."

21. In eighteenth-century England, the concept of literature was not confined as it sometimes is today to "creative" or "imaginative" writing. It meant the whole body of valued writing in society: philosophy, history, essays, and letters as well as poems.

—TERRY EAGLETON

Here is a negative statement followed by a positive statement. The first sentence tells us what literature was not in eighteenth-century England; the second sentence tells us what it was. Such contrasting statements help us define important words. The second sentence has an additional quality: it gives specific examples of the term "valued writing in society" after a colon that announces a list. In the list are philosophy, history, essays, letters, and poems. You can imitate the sentence with a sentence like this: "In the Renaissance, the idea we call humanism *was not related, as it sometimes is today, to absence of a belief in God. Renaissance humanism embodied the entire classical tradition of Greece and Rome: history, languages, philosophy, and art."*

22. His words leap across rivers and mountains, but his thoughts are still only six inches long.

—E. B. WHITE

The sentence expresses antithesis—*two thoughts that seem, at first glance, to be opposite in meaning. White speaks of someone with great oratorical skill, someone who speaks with great power. But the thoughts behind the words are weak. So White gives us two metaphors—words leaping over rivers and mountains like a giant and thoughts that are only six inches long, like some kind of worm.*

APPENDIX D

Glossary of Usage

It is almost always best to use words and expressions in their traditional meanings. Although the meanings of words often change through the years, clear communication is enhanced when these changes take place slowly and the meanings of words are kept as constant as possible. The following words and expressions are often misused or used in nontraditional ways. Studying this list will help you to improve your vocabulary and to develop a sense of precision about the use of words.

ACCEPT/EXCEPT *Accept* is a verb meaning "to receive willingly."
Please *accept* my apologies.
Except is a preposition meaning "but."
Everyone *except* Carlos saw the film.

ADVICE/ADVISE *Advice* is a noun; *advise* is a verb. The c in *advice* is pronounced like the c in *certain;* the s in *advise* is pronounced like the last s in *surprise.*

AFFECT/EFFECT The verb *affect* means "to impress, to move, to change."
The noun *effect* means "result."
The verb *effect* means "to make, to accomplish."
The noun *affect*, meaning a feeling or an emotion, is used in psychology.
Inflation *affects* our sense of security.
Inflation is one of the many *effects* of war.
Inflation has *effected* many changes in how we spend money.
To study *affect*, psychologists probe the unconscious.

AIN'T This is an eighteenth-century contraction that has become a sign of illiteracy and ignorance; it should not be used in formal writing or speech.

ALL/ALL OF; MORE/MORE OF; SOME/SOME OF Except before some pronouns, the *of* in these constructions can usually be eliminated.

> *All of* us wish you well. [The pronoun *us* requires the *of* before it here.]
> *All* France rejoiced.
> *Some* students cut class.

ALL RIGHT/ALRIGHT The spelling *alright* is becoming more common, but most educated readers still think it is incorrect.

> I told him it was *all right* to miss class tomorrow.

ALL TOGETHER/ALTOGETHER *All together* expresses unity or common location; *altogether* means "completely," often in a tone of ironic understatement.

> At the Imitators-of-Elvis national competition, it was *altogether* startling to see a swarm of untalented, loud young men with their rhinestones, their dyed and greased hair, and their pretensions, gathered *all together* on a single stage.

ALLUSION/ILLUSION *Allusion* means an indirect reference to something; *illusion* means a fantasy that may be confused with reality.

> He wrote to her of an "empty house," an *allusion* to their abandoned love affair.
> They nourished the *illusion* that they could learn to write well without working hard.

ALMOST/MOST *Almost,* an adverb, means "nearly"; *most,* an adjective, means "the greater part of." Do not use *most* when you mean almost.

> He wrote her about *almost* [NOT most] everything he did.
> He told her about *most* things he did.

AMONG/BETWEEN *Between* is usually said to express a relation of two nouns; *among* is supposed to express a relation involving more than two:

> The distance *between* Boston and Knoxville is a thousand miles.
> The desire to quit smoking is common *among* people who have smoked for a long time.

But throughout the history of English, *between* has sometimes been used for more than two nouns. It often has the sense of "within":

> He covered the space *between* the four corners of his yard with concrete.

Between is sometimes used for more than two when each noun is considered individually:

> The treaty that was signed was *between* the United States, Israel, and Egypt. [Each country signed the treaty individually.]

Between usually expresses a more precise relation, and *among* is more general, but no rule completely satisfies everyone.

774 Appendix D

us/gl

AMOUNT/NUMBER Things measured in *amounts* usually cannot be thought of as having any individual identity; things measured in *numbers* can be sorted out and counted separately.

> The *amount* of oil left underground in America is a matter of dispute.
> But the *number* of oil companies losing money is tiny.

The word *number* often makes for wordiness in a sentence and may be eliminated by a little revision.

CLUMSY: A large number of people booed the band.
BETTER: Many people booed the band.

ANXIOUS/EAGER Careful writers distinguish between these two words when they are used to describe one's feelings about something that is going to happen. *Anxious* means fearful; *eager* signals strong interest or desire.

> I am *anxious* when I visit the doctor.
> I am *eager* to get out of the hospital.

ANY MORE/ANYMORE *Anymore* is an adverb. *Any more* may be an adjective and a pronoun as in the sentence "I can't stand any more." Or it can be an adverb and an adjective as in the sentence "I don't want any more peanut butter."
Anymore is always used after a negation: "I don't enjoy dancing *anymore*."
Anymore should not be used *before* the negation in a sentence.

ANYONE/ANY ONE; ANYBODY/ANY BODY; EVERYONE/EVERY ONE; EVERYBODY/ EVERY BODY Observe the difference between the indefinite pronouns *anyone, anybody, everyone,* and *everybody* and the noun *body* modified by the adjectives *any* and *every*.

> *Anybody* can make a mistake.
> A good murder mystery accounts for *every body* that turns up in the story.
> The Scots always thought that *any one* of them was worth three of the enemy.
> *Anyone* can see that this book is complicated.

APT/LIABLE/LIKELY Careful writers will distinguish between these three words.
Apt means that someone has a special talent for doing something: "The President is always *apt* to explain away his failures."
Liable means having legal responsibility: "If my singing breaks your chandelier, I am *liable* for damages."
Likely conveys a general expectation or consequence: "People who picnic in the woods are *likely* to get poison ivy."

As Careful writers do not use *as* as a synonym for *since, when, while,* or *because.*

> UNCLEAR: I told him that he should visit Alcatraz *as* he was going to San Francisco.
>
> BETTER: I told him that he should visit Alcatraz *since* he was going to San Francisco.

> UNCLEAR: *As* I complained about the meal, the cook said he didn't like to eat there himself.
>
> BETTER: *When* I complained about the meal, the cook said he didn't like to eat there himself.

> UNCLEAR: *As* American Indians fought as individuals and not in organized groups, no wagon train in the history of the West ever had to circle up and fight off a mass attack by an Indian tribe.
>
> BETTER: *Because* American Indians fought as individuals and not in organized groups, no wagon train in the history of the West ever had to circle up and fight off a mass attack by an Indian tribe.

As/Like In formal writing, avoid the use of *like* as a conjunction. Although this usage is becoming more common even among the educated, it still irritates so many people that you would be wise to avoid it.

> NOT: He sneezed *like* he had a cold.
>
> BUT: He sneezed *as if* he had a cold.

Like is perfectly acceptable as a comparative preposition.

> He rode his horse *like* a cavalry soldier.
>
> The peas were *like* bullets.
>
> At the closing bell, the children scattered from the school *like* leaves before the wind.

It is unnecessary to substitute *as* for *like* any time *like* is followed by a noun unless the noun is the subject of a dependent clause.

> She enjoyed tropical fruits *like* pineapples, bananas, oranges, and mangoes.
>
> They did the assignments uncomplainingly, *as* they would have done nothing, uncomplainingly, if I had assigned them nothing.

Some authorities on writing claim that you should use *like* when you are making comparisons between one thing and one or more other things and that you should use *such as* when you name a class of things and then name several things belonging to that class.

> He had a voice *like* thunder.
>
> She enjoyed tropical fruits *such as* pineapples, bananas, oranges, and mangoes.

There is nothing wrong with making such a distinction, but many writers ignore it.

At Avoid the use of *at* as a false particle to complete the notion of *where.*

> Where is Carmichael?
>
> NOT: Where is Carmichael *at*?

AWFUL/AWFULLY   Careful writers use *awful* and *awfully* only when they mean to convey emotions of terror or wonder.

The vampire flew out the window with an *awful* shriek.

Careful writers avoid the use of *awful* and *awfully* when they mean *very* or *extremely*.

NOT: It was an *awfully* good meal.

NOT: It's *awful* that you have a cold.

A WHILE/AWHILE   *A while* is an article and a noun:

Many authors are unable to write anything else for *a while* after they publish their first novel.

Awhile is an adverb:

Stay *awhile* with me.

BECAUSE   Avoid expressions like this one: "*The reason is because* I don't have the time."

Write: "The reason is that I don't have the time."

BEING AS/BEING THAT   These terms should not be used as synonyms for *since* or *because*.

NOT: *Being as* the mountain was there, we had to climb it.

BUT: *Because* the mountain was there, we had to climb it.

BESIDE/BESIDES   *Beside* means "next to" or "apart from."

The ski slope was *beside* the lodge.

She was *beside* herself with joy.

Besides means "in addition to" or "except for."

Besides a bicycle, he needed a tent and a pack.

BETTER   Avoid using *better* in expressions of quantity.

Crossing the continent by train took more than [NOT better than] four days.

BUT THAT/BUT WHAT   Avoid writing these phrases when you mean *that* in expressions of doubt.

NOT: I have no doubt *but that* you can learn to write well.

BUT: I have no doubt *that* you can learn to write well.

NOT: I doubt *but what* any country music singer and writer has ever had the genius of Hank Williams.

BUT: I doubt *that* any country music singer and writer has ever had the genius of Hank Williams.

CAN'T HARDLY   This is a double negative that is ungrammatical and self-contradictory.

NOT: I can't hardly understand algebra.

BUT: I can hardly understand algebra.

OR: I can't understand algebra.

CASE/INSTANCE/LINE   These words are often used in expressions that can be revised, made more clear, or shortened.

us/gl

NOT: In Murdock's case, I had to decide if he was telling the truth.
BUT: I had to decide if Murdock was telling the truth.

NOT: In that instance, Murdock lied.
BUT: Murdock lied.
OR: Murdock lied then, but he told the truth the rest of the time.

NOT: Along that line, Murdock lied.
BUT: Murdock lied when he said he was allergic to cats.
In many sentences, the use of "in that instance" or "along that line" or some other similar phrase keeps writers from being specific and keeps their prose from being lively.

CENSOR/CENSURE   To *censor* is to keep a part or all of a piece of writing, a film, or some other form of communication from getting to the public. To *censure* is to scold or condemn someone for doing something wrong. Sometimes the censure is a formal act; sometimes it is a personal expression.

The Argentine government *censors* newspapers.

The House of Representatives *censured* Congressman Larsonee for stealing from the Post Office.

COMPARE WITH/COMPARE TO   When you wish to stress either the similarities or the dissimilarities between two things, use *compare to;* when you wish to stress both similarities and differences, use *compare with.*

She compared his singing to the croaking of a wounded frog.
She thought that nearly everything about his singing was like the croaking of a wounded frog.

Compared to cigarette smoking, smoking a pipe is much safer.
No effort is made to sort out the similarities and the dissimilarities between smoking a pipe and smoking cigarettes. The dissimilarity is stressed.

He compared Omaha with San Francisco.
The use of "compared with" means that he found some things alike in Omaha and San Francisco and some things that were not alike and that he mentioned both the similarities and the dissimilarities.

COMPLEMENT/COMPLIMENT   A *complement* is something added to something else to complete it.

He insists that sauerkraut is a perfect *complement* to hot dogs.
A *compliment* is an approving remark.

She received many *compliments* because she made a memorable speech.
Complimentary is an adjective referring to something freely given, as approval or a favor.

All veterans received *complimentary* tickets.

His remarks were *complimentary*.

us/gl

CONTACT Many writers and editors frown on the use of *contact* as a verb because it is weak, imprecise, and overused in common speech. You should not *contact* all the members of your club who have not paid their dues; you should call, *write, threaten,* or *speak to* them.

CONVINCE/PERSUADE *Convince* usually means to win someone over by means of argument; *convince* should always take *that* with a clause.

The experiment *convinced* him *that* light was subject to gravity.
Persuade means to move to some form of action or change by argument or by some other means. *Persuade* is often followed by *to.*

I *persuaded* him *to* buy stock in the company.
Careful writers usually do not write, "I persuaded him that it was so."
They say rather, "I convinced him that it was so."

COULD OF/SHOULD OF/WOULD OF These are ungrammatical forms of *could have, should have,* and *would have.* Avoid them and use the proper forms.

DIFFER FROM/DIFFER WITH *Differ from* expresses a lack of similarity; *differ with* expresses disagreement.

The ancient Greeks *differed* less *from* the Persians than we often think.
Aristotle *differed with* Plato on some important issues in philosophy.

DIFFERENT FROM/DIFFERENT THAN The idiom is *different from.* Careful writers avoid *different than.*

The east coast of Florida is *different from* the west coast.

DISINTERESTED/UNINTERESTED To be *disinterested* means to be *impartial.* A disinterested party in a dispute has no selfish reason to favor one side over another.

We expect members of a jury to be *disinterested.*
To be *uninterested* means to have no concern about something, to pay no attention, to be bored.

Most people nowadays are *uninterested* in philosophy.

DON'T/DOESN'T *Don't* can only be a contraction for *do not. Doesn't* is the contraction for *does not.*

You *don't* know what you're talking about.
He *doesn't* either.
Some American speakers say *he don't* and *she don't.* But such usage is nonstandard and should be avoided.

DUE TO/BECAUSE *Due to* is an overworked, wordy, and often confusing expression when it is used to show cause.

WORDY: Due to the fact that I was hungry, I ate too much.
BETTER: Because I was hungry, I ate too much.
Most writers accept the causative use of *due to* in short phrases.
His failure was *due to* laziness.

us/gl

Such constructions can be vague and confusing. Whose laziness? His or someone else's? The sentence does not tell us. We may assume that it is his laziness. But what about a sentence like this one: Their divorce was due to infidelity. Whose infidelity, his or hers? Or were both partners unfaithful? Such sentences that are changed to include an agent are almost always clearer and more vigorous.

He failed because he was lazy.

His unfaithfulness to her caused their divorce.

A good rule of thumb is to use *due to* only in expressions of time in infinitive constructions.

The plane is *due to* arrive at five o'clock.

EACH AND EVERY   Use one or the other but not both:

Every cow came in at feeding time.

Each bale has to be put in the barn loft.

EAGER/ANXIOUS   *See* Anxious/Eager.

EITHER . . . OR/NEITHER . . . NOR   Always singular when followed by a singular noun or pronoun.

Neither Kant *nor* Hegel enjoys much popularity today.

When things get calm, *either* he *or* she starts a fight.

Either has an intensive use that *neither* does not, and when it is used as an intensive, *either* is always negative.

She told him she wouldn't go *either.*

EMINENT/IMMINENT/IMMANENT   *Eminent* means "exalted," "celebrated," "well known."

The *eminent* Victorians were often melancholy and disturbed.

Imminent means "about to happen" or "about to come."

In August 1939, war was *imminent.*

Immanent refers to something invisible spread everywhere through the visible world.

Medieval Christians believed that God's power was *immanent* through the universe.

ENTHUSED/ENTHUSIASTIC   Most writers and editors prefer the word *enthusiastic.*

The Secretary of the Interior was *enthusiastic* [NOT enthused] about the plans to build a high-rise condominium in Yosemite National Park.

ETC.   This is a Latin abbreviation for *et cetera*, meaning "and others" or "and other things." Since the *and* is included in the abbreviation, you should not write "and etc." In a series, a comma comes before *etc.* just as it would come before the coordinating conjunction that closes the series. CAUTION: Inexperienced writers often overuse *etc.* It should seldom be used because it is vague and often implies more knowledge than the writer may have.

EVERYONE/EVERY ONE *See* Anyone/Any one.

EXCEPT/ACCEPT *See* Accept/Except.

EXPECT Avoid the use of *expect* as a synonym for *suppose* or *presume.*
I *suppose* [NOT expect] that he lost money on the horses.

FARTHER/FURTHER *Farther* is used for geographic distances.
Ten miles *farther* on is a hotel.
Further means "in addition" when geography is not involved.
He said *further* that he was annoyed with the play, the actors, and the stage.
The Department of State hired a new public relations expert so that *further* disasters could be more carefully explained to the press.

FEWER/LESS *See* Amount/Number.
Fewer is the adjective for groups or collections whose parts can be counted individually; *less* is used for things in bulk not commonly considered collections of individual entities.
There were *fewer* people at commencement this year.
There is *less* substance to your argument than you think.

FLAUNT/FLOUT *Flaunt* means to wave, to show publicly. It connotes a delight tinged with pride and even arrogance.
He *flaunted* his wealth by wearing overalls lined with mink.
Flout means to scorn or to defy, especially in a public way without seeming to care for the consequences.
He *flouted* the traffic laws by speeding, driving on the wrong side of the road, and running through a red light.
The suffragettes often *flouted* all the conventions accepted by women in their day, cutting their hair, wearing shorter dresses, and smoking cigarettes in public.

FORMER/LATTER These words can only refer to one of two persons or things—in sequence, named first, named last.
John saw *Star Wars* and *The Empire Strikes Back.* He liked the former better than the latter.
If you are speaking of three or more things, use *first* and *last.*
Guy's closest friends were Paul, Curtis, and Ricco. The first was Greek, the second was English, and the third was Italian.
CAUTION: All these terms can be confusing, and it is usually better not to use them.
John saw *Star Wars* and *The Empire Strikes Back.* He liked *Star Wars* better.

GET *Get* is one of the most flexible verbs in English. But in formal writing, you should avoid some of its more colloquial uses, as in *get with it, get it all together, get-up-and-go, get it, get me,* and *that gets me.*

GOOD/WELL *Good* is an adjective; *well* is an adverb except when it refers to good health in which case it is an adjective. Avoid confusing them.

I felt *good* after the doctor told me that I looked *well.*
Both good *and* well *are adjectives in this sentence.*

She did *well* on the exam.
Well is an adverb.

He hit that ball real *good.*
Here, good *tries to masquerade incorrectly as an adverb.*

HALF/HALF A/A HALF OF Write *half, a half,* or *half a,* but not *a half a* or *a half of* or *half of.*

Half the baseball players went out on strike.

Half a loaf is better than none unless you are on a diet.

I want *a half* dozen eggs to throw at the candidate.

HANGED/HUNG People are *hanged* by the neck until dead. Pictures and all other things that can be suspended are *hung.*

HOPEFULLY Since the 1960s, *hopefully* has come into common use as an adverb modifying an entire sentence. Usually, adverbs modify only verbs, adjectives, or other adverbs, although there are exceptions to this practice. Many careful writers and speakers object to *hopefully* as a modifier of an entire sentence because it does not tell who has the hope; it is usually uneconomical, and it may be confusing.

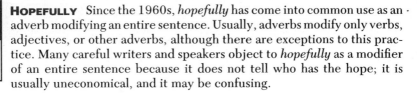

Hopefully Franklin will play poker tonight.
Does this sentence mean that Franklin will play poker with hope in his heart? Who has the hope, Franklin or the other players who hope to win his money? Or perhaps the hope is held by someone who yearns for Franklin to be out of the house this evening.

I *hope* Franklin is going to play poker tonight.

Franklin *hopes* to play poker tonight.

All his gambling friends *hope* that Franklin will play poker with them tonight.
In these sentences, the source of the hope is identified, confusion is eliminated, and economy is preserved.

IF . . . THEN Avoid the common redundancy that results when you use these words in tandem.

REDUNDANT: *If* I get my license, *then* I can drive a cab.

BETTER: If I get my license, I can drive a cab.

BETTER: Once I get my license, I can drive a cab.

IMPLY/INFER To *imply* means to suggest something without stating it directly; to *infer* means to draw a conclusion from evidence.

By pouring hot coffee on his head, she *implied* that he should stop singing.

When she dozed off in the middle of his declaration of love for her, he *inferred* that she was not going to marry him.

IN/IN TO/INTO   *In* refers to a location inside something.
>   Charles kept a snake *in* his room.

In to refers to motion with a purpose.
>   The dorm supervisor came *in to* kill it.

Into refers to movement from outside to inside or from separation to contact.
>   The snake escaped by crawling *into* the drain.
>   The supervisor ran *into* the wall, and Charles got *into* trouble.

INCREDIBLE/INCREDULOUS   The *incredible* cannot be believed; the *incredulous* do not believe. Stories are *incredible;* people are *incredulous.* Avoid using *incredible* and *incredibly* so loosely that your reader can tell that you were too lazy to think of a more precise and more vivid word. The writers of the following senseless sentences did not heed this advice:
>   I had an *incredible* time at the sociology department party.
>   She is just an *incredible* teacher, but I still got *incredibly* bad grades.

INDIVIDUAL/PERSON   Avoid the use of *individual* as a pompous synonym for *person,* and avoid using *individuals* when *people* will do. *Individual* as either a noun or an adjective should be used only to show a contrast between a person or a single entity and the group. Even then, *person* or one of its cognates may often be used.
>   The Bill of Rights guarantees *individual* liberties.
>   OR: The Bill of Rights guarantees *personal* liberties.

>   The speech was directed to every *person* in the square.
>   BUT: One of the oldest political questions is the relation between the *individual* and society.

It is a good idea for writers to discipline themselves not to use *individual* as a noun.

INSIDE OF/OUTSIDE OF   The *of* is unnecessary.
>   He was *inside* the house watching the pro football game on television.
>   She was *outside* the house mowing the lawn.

IRREGARDLESS   This is a nonstandard form of *regardless.* The construction *irregardless* is a double negative, since both the prefix *ir-* and the suffix *-less* are negatives.

IT'S/ITS   *It's* is commonly the contraction for *it is;* sometimes it is a contraction for *it has. Its* is a possessive pronoun.
>   *It's* clear that *its* paint is peeling.
>   *It's* often been said that English grammar is difficult.

KIND/KINDS   *Kind* is a singular form and must take singular verbs and modifiers.
>   *This kind* of house *is* easy to build.
>   *These kinds are* better than those kinds.

US/gl

Kind, sort, and *type* are often overused in writing. Always try to do without them unless the classification they imply is necessary.

AWKWARD: She was a happy kind of person.

BETTER: She was a happy person.

LIE/LAY *Lie* means to recline; *lay* means to place.

I am going to *lie* down to sleep.

He said he would *lay* the clothes carefully on the bed.

Part of the confusion in the way we use *lie* and *lay* comes because the principal parts of the verbs are confusing. Study the following sentences:

I often *lie* awake at night. [present]

He *lay* on his stomach for a long time and listened intently. [past]

He had *lain* there for an hour before he heard the horses. [past participle]

He will *lay* the bricks in a straight line. [present]

She *laid* her book on the steps and left it there. [past]

He had *laid* away money for years to prepare for his retirement. [past participle]

LITERALLY *Literally* shows that an expression often used in a figurative way is to be taken as true in the sentence where *literally* appears.

Literally thousands of people gathered for the funeral.

The writer knows that thousands *is sometimes used to mean merely "a great crowd." He wants people to know that if they counted the crowd at the funeral, they would number thousands.*

Literally is often incorrectly used as an intensive adverb. Avoid this usage, which can make you sound misleading or even ridiculous.

He *literally* scared Grandpa to death.

He did something so frightening that Grandpa fell over and died.

His blood *literally* boiled.

The use of literally *means that his blood rose to 212 degrees Fahrenheit and bubbled.*

Her eyes *literally* flashed fire.

This is an extremely dubious statement.

MAYBE/MAY BE *Maybe* is an adverb; *may be* is a verb.

Maybe he can get a summer job selling dictionaries.

That *may be* a problem because he doesn't know how to use one.

MORAL/MORALE The noun *moral* means "lesson," especially a lesson about morals or one that is supposed to grant a general wisdom about life. It is most commonly used in the idiom *the moral of the story.*

The noun *morale* means "attitude" or "mental condition."

Morale dropped sharply among the students in the class when they discovered that they would be penalized for misspelling words.

us/gl

MORE IMPORTANT/MORE IMPORTANTLY The correct idiom is *more important*, not *more importantly*.

> *More important,* if Jackson had not won the battle of New Orleans, the city might have remained in British hands.
> *The phrase is elliptical: What is "more important" is that Jackson did win the battle, and the Mississippi River became a highway from the center of the United States to the Gulf.*

MYSELF (HIMSELF, HERSELF, ETC.) All the pronouns ending with *-self* are best used as reflexives that intensify the stress on the noun or pronoun that serves as the antecedent.

> "I cleaned the stables *myself*," Hercules said.
> *He wanted to stress that he did the job without delegating it and without having help from anyone.*
> Standing in the doorway was Count Dracula *himself* with a silver goblet in his hand.
> We *ourselves* have often been guilty of the same fault.

Although in casual speech some people use the *-self* pronouns instead of ordinary pronouns, you should always avoid nonstandard usages like the following:

NONSTANDARD: The quarrel was between him and *myself.*
STANDARD: The quarrel was between him and me.

NONSTANDARD: John and *myself* shoed the horses.
STANDARD: John and I shoed the horses.

Sometimes when you are unsure of whether to use *I, me, she, her, he,* or *him* after a verb, you may be tempted to substitute one of the reflexive pronouns, which sounds safer: "The guest list included Roxie Jones and myself." But such usage is wrong, and you should avoid it.

NOHOW/NOWHERES These are nonstandard for *anyway, in no way, in any way, in any place,* and *in no place.*
Don't use these words in writing.

OF/HAVE *See* Could of/Should of/Would of.

OFF OF Omit the *of.*
NOT: He knocked the hide *off of* the ball.
BUT: He knocked the hide *off* the ball.

PARAMETER *Parameter* is most properly a mathematical term, especially one used in computer science. It is often misused as a synonym for *perimeter,* or *limit,* especially in the plural.
NONSTANDARD: The *parameters* of his biography of Theodore Roosevelt were set by Roosevelt's birth and death.

us/gl

STANDARD: The limits of his biography of Theodore Roosevelt were set by Roosevelt's birth and death.

Parameter can be used correctly in speaking of computers:

The *parameters* were set to give the standard deviation from many different distributions.

Parameter can sometimes be used correctly outside of mathematics to mean some constant whose value varies, allowing us to measure other variables by it:

Religion has been one of the *parameters* of life for as long as human beings have been on this planet, allowing us to observe how it affects the relation between family and society.

The word is so technical, however, that you can easily avoid it in general writing.

PLUS In formal writing, avoid using *plus* as a substitute for *and.*

NONSTANDARD: He had to walk the dog, wash the dishes, and take out the garbage, *plus* he had to write a book.

STANDARD: He had to walk the dog, wash the dishes, take out the garbage, and write his book.

PRACTICABLE/PRACTICAL *Practicable* is an adjective applied to things that can be done.

A tunnel under the English Channel is *practicable*, given today's machinery and engineering skills.

Practical means "sensible."

The English don't think such a tunnel is *practical* because they think of the English Channel as their first line of defense.

PREVIOUS TO/PRIOR TO Avoid using these wordy and somewhat pompous substitutes for *before.*

PRINCIPAL/PRINCIPLE *Principal* is an adjective meaning first in importance or a noun referring to the highest office in an organization. *Principle* is a noun referring to a standard for life, thought, or morals, or else the underlying unity that joins distinct phenomena.

The *principal* objection to our school's *principal* is that he had no *principles.*

REAL/REALLY Avoid the use of *real* when you mean *very.*

The cake was *very* [NOT real] good.

It is grammatically correct to use *really* for the adverb *very,* but *really* is overworked nowadays and should be given a rest, especially because it rarely adds anything worthwhile to a sentence. The overuse of *really* makes you sound insincere, as if you were trying to convince somebody of something without having any evidence at your command. Any time you see a *really,* you are likely to think, "Really?"

REASON IS BECAUSE Don't use this redundant expression.

The reason he fell on the ice is that [NOT because] he cannot skate.

us/gl

RELATION/RELATIONSHIP A short while ago *relationship* was most commonly used for *blood kin*. Now it has almost replaced *relation*. *Relationship* is called a *long variant* of *relation* by H. W. Fowler, a great authority on the English language. It says nothing that *relation* does not say, but often writers use it because it lets them imagine that they are saying much more than they are.

RESPECTIVE The word is almost always unnecessary in constructions like the following, and you can usually leave it out.

> Charles and Robert brought in their *respective* assignments.
> *Unless we are told otherwise, we would not expect Charles to bring in Robert's assignment or Robert to bring in Charles's assignment.*

SET/SIT *Set* is usually a transitive verb, taking a direct object. Its principal parts are *set*, *set*, and *set*.

> DiMaggio *set* the standard of excellence in fielding.

It is occasionally intransitive.

> The concrete took a while to *set*.

Sit is always intransitive; it never takes a direct object except in the idiom *he sits his horse*, meaning that he sits *on* his horse — so some would argue that *horse* is not a true direct object. The principal parts of *sit* are *sit*, *sat*, and *sat*.

> The dog *sat* on command.

SHALL/WILL Not long ago, *shall* was the standard first-person future of the verb *to be* when a simple statement of fact was intended; *will* was the future for the second and third person. But to say *I will, you shall, she shall*, or *they shall* implied a special determination to accomplish something.

> I *shall* be forty-eight on my next birthday.
> I *will* eat these cursed beets because they are good for me.

Now the distinction is blurred in the United States, although it is still observed in Britain. Most writers use *will* as the ordinary future tense for the first person.

> We *will* come to New York next week.

Shall is still used in a few emphatic constructions in the second and third person.

> They *shall* not pass.
> You may take my life, but you *shall* not rob me of my dignity.

SOME Avoid the use of the adjective *some* in place of the adverb *somewhat*.

> He felt *somewhat* [NOT some] better after a good night's sleep.

SOMEWHERES Don't use this nonstandard form for *somewhere*.

SURE Avoid confusing the adjective *sure* with the adverb *surely*.

> The hat she wore on the streetcar was *surely* [NOT sure] bizarre.

SURE AND/SURE TO *Sure and* is often used colloquially:
>Be *sure and* get to the wedding on time.

In formal writing, *sure to* is preferred:
>Be *sure to* get to the wedding on time.

THAT/WHICH A few writers use *that* as a restrictive pronoun to introduce restrictive clauses and *which* to introduce nonrestrictive clauses.
>The bull *that* escaped ran through my china shop, *which* was located on the square.

Though such a distinction might be useful if generally adopted, it has never been so widely observed or respected that it can be considered a rule of grammar. The distinction offers no help for restrictive and nonrestrictive phrases or for *who* and *whom* clauses, which can be restrictive or nonrestrictive. The best rule is to set off the nonrestrictive elements with commas and to avoid setting off restrictive elements with commas.

THEIR/THERE/THEY'RE *Their* is a possessive pronoun:
>They gave *their* lives.

There is an adverb of place:
>She was standing *there.*

They're is a contraction for *they are:*
>*They're* reading more poetry than they once did.

THIS HERE/THESE HERE/THAT THERE/THEM THERE Avoid these nonstandard forms.

TRY AND/TRY TO Use *try to.*
>*Try to* understand.

USE/UTILIZE *Utilize* seldom says more than *use,* and simpler is almost always better. We must learn how to *use* [NOT utilize] computers.

WAIT FOR/WAIT ON People *wait on* tables or customers; they *wait for* those who are late. Don't say, "Wait on me at the bus stop"; say, "Wait for me."

WHICH/WHO/WHOSE *Which* is used for things, *who* and *whose* for people.
>The plane, *which* was late, brought the team home from California.
>My lost fountain pen was found by a man *who* had never seen one before, *whose* whole life had been spent with ballpoints.

But *whose* is increasingly being used for things in constructions where *of which* would be awkward.
>The cathedral, *whose* towers could be seen from miles away, seemed to shelter its city.

Some writers, however, would insist on this form:
>The cathedral, the towers of which could be seen from miles away, seemed to shelter its city.

us/gl

APPENDIX E

Glossary of Grammatical Terms

ABSOLUTE PHRASE A phrase made up of a noun and a participle, extending the statement made by the sentence but not modifying any particular element in the sentence.

> The sun rose at six o'clock, *its red light throwing long shadows in the forest.*

When the participle is some form of the verb *to be*, it is often omitted.

> He flung the ball from center field, *his throw* [being] *like a bullet.*

Absolutes are common in modern English style; they allow compression of action and provide variety in sentences.

ABSTRACT NOUN A noun that does not call up a concrete memory involving sensual experience. Examples of abstract nouns are *relation, idea, thought, strength, matter, friendship, experience,* and *enmity.* An abstract noun refers to some quality *abstracted,* or drawn, from many different experiences, and it may be used to name many different kinds of experiences. In writing you should always be sure that abstract nouns do not dominate your prose. Abstract nouns require the help of concrete nouns if they are to make sense.

ACRONYM A noun made of the initials of an organization and sometimes pronounceable as if it were a word. Common acronyms in recent history include **FBI** (Federal Bureau of Investigation), **CREEP** (Committee to Re-elect the President), **SNCC** (Student Non-Violent Co-ordinating Committee), and **HEW** (Department of Health, Education, and Welfare). The forms of acronyms usually do not change, but the possessive case and the plural are formed in the same way as for other nouns.

> SNCC's first leader was Bob Moses.

ACTIVE VOICE The voice of a verb used to report that the subject does something.

>The guitar player *sang* tenor.

The active voice always makes a stronger sentence than the passive voice. (See *passive voice*.)

ADJECTIVAL Refers to any word or group of words (a phrase or a clause) that can be used as an adjective to modify a noun or pronoun. In the following examples, the adjectival words are in italics:

>*my* book, *your* picture, *his* anger, *her* success
>She painted the house *next door*.
>The table *in the corner* belonged to me.
>Writers *who write truly* always have readers.

ADJECTIVE Any word that modifies a noun or pronoun by describing some quality.

>The *red* coat; the *blue* book

Adjectives can come before or after a noun:

>The roof of the *old red* barn collapsed.
>The barn—*old, weather-beaten,* and *abandoned*—finally collapsed in the last snow.

Adjectives can also come after a verb when they modify the subject. In this position they are *predicate adjectives*.

>The barn was *red*.

Adjectives often have special forms in comparisons:

>Her car is *big*.
>Jack's car is *bigger*.
>My car is the *biggest* of all, and I can't afford to drive it.
>She bought an *expensive* meal at the Ritz.
>She bought a *more expensive* meal at the Algonquin.
>But she bought her *most expensive* meal at Tommy's Lunch, since it gave her food poisoning, putting her in the hospital for a week.

ADJECTIVE CLAUSE A clause used to modify a noun or pronoun.

>The car *that I drove then* appears in these old snapshots.

ADJECTIVE PHRASE A phrase such as a prepositional phrase that modifies a noun or pronoun.

>He came to the end *of the road*.

ADVERB A word used commonly to modify a verb, an adjective, or another adverb. Increasingly in modern English, adverbs are being used to modify whole sentences, though here the effect may be confusing.

>They left *yesterday*.
>The sun was *insufferably* hot.
>The *more frequently* used room deteriorated *more seriously*.
>*Happily*, the car hit the wall before it could hit me.

Adverbs tell us *when, where, why,* or *how*.

gt/gl

ADVERB CLAUSE   A clause that acts as an adverb, usually modifying a verb in another clause but sometimes modifying an adjective or another adverb. Adverb clauses often begin with subordinators like *when, because, although, since, if, whether, after,* and *before.*

> *After he lost at Gettysburg,* Lee knew he could not invade the North again.
>
> We often think that women's fashions in the nineteenth century were dull *because we see them only in black-and-white photographs.*

ADVERBIAL   A word sometimes used to describe phrases and clauses that act as adverbs. Sometimes nouns are pressed into service as adverbials.

> Many Americans go to church *Sundays.*
>
> We plan to go *home* for Thanksgiving.

ADVERB PHRASE   Any phrase used as an adverb. The most common adverb phrase is the prepositional phrase.

> You may find me *at home* this evening.
>
> We groped around *in the dark.*

AGREEMENT BETWEEN PRONOUNS AND ANTECEDENTS   A matching in number and gender between pronouns and the nouns to which they refer.

> Most *Americans* pay too little attention to *their* bodies.
>
> *Emma Bovary* hated *her* dull life in *her* little town.
>
> *Flaubert* created in her *his* greatest character.

AGREEMENT BETWEEN SUBJECTS AND VERBS   A matching in number between subjects and verbs. A singular subject must take a singular verb; a plural subject must take a plural verb.

> The *general* over all the armies *was* Eisenhower.
>
> The *horses run* nearly every day at Suffolk Downs.

The greatest trouble in agreement between subjects and verbs usually comes in the third person singular, made by adding *s* or *es* to the dictionary form of the verb.

> *She dances* with grace and strength.
>
> *He yearns* to return to the South.

The common contractions *don't* and *doesn't* give particular difficulty. Remember that *doesn't* is used in the third person singular in the present tense; *don't* is used in all other forms of the present tense:

> It *doesn't* matter now.
>
> They *don't* believe us.
>
> She *doesn't* live here any more.

APPOSITIVE   A noun or noun phrase that identifies another noun or pronoun, usually by naming it again in different words. Appositives usually come after the nouns they identify.

> This is my brother *John.*
>
> They loved Chinese food — *tofu, rice, and sweet-and-sour sauces.*
>
> Clarence Penn, *the children's leader at the YMCA,* loved to lead hikes.

gt/gl

Notice that the appositives have the same relation to the rest of the sentence as the nouns they identify. You can leave out either the appositive or the noun identified by the appositive and have a grammatically complete sentence:

The children's leader at the YMCA loved to lead hikes.

ARTICLE The *indefinite articles* are *a* and *an*; the *definite* article is *the*. Articles (sometimes called *determiners*) set off a noun or noun substitute in a sentence or phrase.

AUXILIARY VERB A verb used to help form the proper tense of another verb in a clause. Common auxiliary verbs are *am, is, are, was, be, been, were, have, has, had, shall, will, may, might, can, would, should, must*, and *ought*.

He *had been* sleeping before the earthquake hit.

Rock music *must* have some strange power over children.

They *have* invited Norman to the party, but he *has* not yet accepted.

CASE An inflected form of a noun or pronoun that shows a grammatical relation to some other part of the sentence. English has only three cases: the nominative (or the subjective), the possessive, and the objective. Only pronouns change their form from the nominative in both the possessive and the objective case. Nouns commonly change their form only in the possessive.

To form the possessive of a singular noun, add *'s*. For nouns ending in *s*, add only an apostrophe.

Erasmus/Erasmus', Dick/Dick's, Germany/Germany's

Some pronouns have different forms of all three cases.

Nominative	Possessive	Objective
I	my/mine	me
who	whose	whom
we	our/ours	them
they	their/theirs	them
he	his	him

Some pronouns have only two forms.

Nominative	Possessive	Objective
you	your	you
it	its	it
she	her/hers	her

CLAUSE A group of words that includes a subject and a predicate. An independent clause may stand alone as a sentence; a dependent clause acts as a noun, an adjective, or an adverb for some element of another clause. Independent clauses are sometimes called *main clauses;* dependent clauses are sometimes called *subordinate clauses.*

He thought his book was a failure *because it lost money.*

The independent clause (beginning with "He thought") can stand alone as a sentence; the dependent clause (in italics) acts as an adverb modifying the verb *was* in the independent clause.

COLLECTIVE NOUN   A noun naming a group of people or things. In American English it is usually considered a grammatical singular.

The *team* was upset because of the penalty.

The *government* is the plaintiff in the case.

The *majority* is opposed to the measure.

COMMA SPLICE/COMMA FAULT   The misuse of a comma to join two independent clauses without the help of a coordinating conjunction. The comma splice can be mended either by using a coordinating conjunction or by replacing the comma with a semicolon.

COMMA SPLICE: They gathered the wood, she built the fire.

REVISED: They gathered the wood; she built the fire.

REVISED: They gathered the wood, and she built the fire.

COMMON NOUN   A noun that is not specific enough to be capitalized within a sentence. Common nouns are words like *desk, typewriter, chair, aircraft, automobile, glue, cow,* and *football.*

COMPARATIVE DEGREE (See *comparison.*)

COMPARISON   Adjectives and adverbs can make comparisons. They indicate degrees with different inflected forms.

The positive degree is the form that makes no comparison: *swift, quickly.* The comparative degree compares no more than two things: a *swifter* boat, runs *more quickly.* The comparative degree is formed by adding *-er* to the modifier or by using the word *more* before the uninflected form of the modifier.

The superlative degree compares three or more things: the *swiftest* boat, runs *most quickly.* The superlative degree is formed by adding *-est* to the modifier or by using the word *most* before the uninflected form of the modifier.

COMPLEMENT   A word or group of words that extends the meaning of some other element in a clause.

A subjective complement usually follows the verb but adds something to the meaning of the subject. Subjective complements can be predicate nominatives or predicate adjectives·

PREDICATE NOMINATIVE: Her work was her *life.* [The noun *life* defines the subject, *work.*]

PREDICATE ADJECTIVE: Her work was *difficult.* [The adjective *difficult* modifies the subject, *work.*]

Both the predicate nominative and the predicate adjective are subjective complements.

gt/gl

An objective complement follows immediately after the direct object of a verb or another object in the sentence and extends or provides the meaning of the object.

I wrote a letter to my sister *Nancy*. [*Nancy* is the complement of the object of the preposition, *sister*.]

The university named her *president* last week. [*President* is the complement of the direct object, *her*.]

COMPLETE PREDICATE   (See *predicate*.)

COMPLETE SUBJECT   (See *subject*.)

COMPLEX SENTENCE   A sentence with an independent clause and at least one dependent clause.

If you want to write well, you must work hard.

COMPOUND SENTENCE   A sentence with at least two independent clauses joined by a comma and a coordinating conjunction or by a semicolon or a colon.

We faced strong opposition, but we won.

She washed the clothes; he did the dishes.

Their point was this: men and women should receive equal pay for equal work.

COMPOUND-COMPLEX SENTENCE   A sentence that has at least two independent clauses and at least one dependent clause.

The Russians declared war on Germany, and the Germans invaded Belgium, because a Serbian nationalist killed an Austrian prince far down in the Balkans.

CONJUGATION   A listing of the various forms of a verb to show tense, person, number, voice, and mood.

CONJUNCTIONS   Words that join elements of sentences to one another. The coordinating conjunctions are *and, but, or, nor, for,* and sometimes *so* and *yet*. The coordinating conjunctions can join independent clauses. *And* is the most frequently used coordinating conjunction, and it can be used to join many different elements in a sentence, but all the elements joined by *and* must be grammatically equal. That is, you should not write a sentence like this one: "The house was large, old, and it had not been painted in years." You should make the elements joined by *and* equal as in this revision: "The house was large, old, and weather-beaten."

Some conjunctions are called *subordinators* because they mark a dependent clause to come. Examples of subordinators are *although, after, because, when,* and *before*. Some relative pronouns such as *that* and *which* act as conjunctions and introduce dependent clauses.

Some adverbs have a conjunctive sense, linking two clauses or sentences. These adverbs are words such as *however, nevertheless, moreover, indeed, in fact,* and *as a result*. These conjunctive adverbs are not strong enough

gt/gl

to join two clauses without the help of a strong punctuation mark such as the semicolon as in this sentence: "The sea voyage was long and difficult; however, Darwin seemed to enjoy it." Conjunctive adverbs may be used to begin a sentence, indicating a strong relation between that sentence and the one immediately before it.

> Another way is not inevitable. Indeed, nothing in human life is inevitable except death.

CONNOTATION AND DENOTATION The *connotation* of a word is the traditional collection of associations that surround its use. If I say, "I *demand* an answer," the connotation is much less friendly than if I say, "I *request* an answer." If I say, "The orchestra *slogged through* Beethoven's Sixth Symphony," the impression is much less flattering to the orchestra than if I say, "The orchestra *marched* through Beethoven's Sixth." The *denotation* of a word is the strict, dictionary definition. It is often difficult to separate connotation and denotation.

CONTRACTION A combination of two words with the help of an apostrophe. Contractions include forms such as *doesn't* for *does not, can't* for *cannot,* and *won't* for *will not.* Contractions are common in informal speech and writing; they are generally not used in formal writing. You may find contractions in a magazine article; you will probably not find them in a history book.

COORDINATING CONJUNCTION (See *conjunction.*)

COORDINATION A grammatical structure that joins sentence elements so that they are of equal importance.

> They flew, but we drove.
> The bird tumbled from its perch and did a flip.

CORRELATIVES Pairs of words that connect sentence elements. Common correlatives are *either . . . or, neither . . . nor, not only . . . but also, both . . . and,* and *whether . . . or.*

DANGLING MODIFIER An adjectival element, usually but not always at the beginning of a sentence, which does not correctly modify the grammatical subject.

> DANGLING MODIFIER: *Crushed by the debt on her credit cards,* it was difficult for her to understand that she was making $40,000 a year and was still broke.
> REVISED: Crushed by the debt on her credit cards, she could hardly understand that she was making $40,000 a year and that she was still broke.

DECLARATIVE SENTENCE A sentence that makes a statement rather than gives a command or asks a question. Some writers define a *declarative sentence* as a sentence that begins with the subject followed by a verb without any intervening phrases or clauses.

DECLENSION A table of all the forms of a noun or pronoun, showing the various cases. In English, a declension would include the forms of the nominative, the possessive, and the objective in the singular and the plural.

DEGREE (See *comparison.*)

DEMONSTRATIVE ADJECTIVE An adjective like *these, those, this,* or *that* which points out a noun or noun substitute.

DEMONSTRATIVE PRONOUN (See *pronoun.*)

DENOTATION (See *connotation.*)

DEPENDENT CLAUSE (See *clause.*)

DETERMINER (See *article.*)

DIAGRAMMING A pictorial method of showing relationships among various grammatical parts of a sentence.

DIRECT AND INDIRECT QUOTATION In a *direct quotation,* the exact words of a source are given within quotation marks.

> DIRECT QUOTATION: The chair of the board said today, "I will not permit that no-good turkey of a president to dictate to this corporation."

In an *indirect quotation,* the sense of what has been said is given in a paraphrase; the exact words of the source are not used.

> INDIRECT QUOTATION: The chair of the board declared that he would not allow the president to tell the corporation what to do.

An indirect quotation is not enclosed within quotation marks.

DIRECT OBJECT (See *object.*)

DOUBLE NEGATIVE A substandard construction that makes a negative statement by using two negative forms. A double negative can be a single word such as the nonstandard *irregardless,* a word that has a negative form, *ir-,* at the beginning and another negative form, *-less,* at the end. A double negative is more commonly two negative words, as in this non-standard sentence: "I *don't* have *no* reason to go there." To correct the sentence, remove one of the negatives, as in this version: "I *don't* have a reason to go there," or in this one: "I have *no* reason to go there." A common double negative is the phrase *can't hardly,* as in the sentence "I *can't hardly* do that assignment." The phrase should read, "I *can hardly* do that assignment."

ELLIPSIS An omission from within a direct quotation, marked off by three dots made with the period on the typewriter. You should mark an ellipsis by making a space after the last word you quote; setting a period after the space; making another space, another period, another space, a third period, and another space; and then typing the first word of the quotation beyond the omitted material.

A sentence from David McCullough's *Mornings on Horseback:*

He must bide his time, maintain perfect decorum and silence, and so passive a role did not sit at all well with him.

The sentence quoted with an ellipsis:

"He must bide his time, . . . and so passive a role did not sit at all well with him," McCullough said.

Notice that the comma after *time* is included before the ellipsis marks.

ELLIPTICAL ELEMENTS   Phrases or clauses that we understand although some words have been left out.

[what is] *More important,* we learned to write well.

They are older *than she* [is old].

We enjoyed France more than [we enjoyed] *Switzerland.*

EXPLETIVE   The use of *there, here,* or *it* followed by a form of *to be.*

We saw that *there were* feathers beneath the fence.

"*Here are* footsteps in the mud!" she exclaimed.

It was only Lucinda the cat who had torn a pillow to shreds.

When *it* is used as an expletive, this pronoun is the grammatical subject of a clause, the *it* having no antecedent.

It is said that his grandfather did time in prison.

It was all a mystery, and we were baffled.

FINITE VERB   A verb with a tense that reports action done in the past, present, or future. A subject must control a finite verb to make a clause. Nonfinite verbs are verbal forms without time in themselves, forms like *infinitives, participles,* and *gerunds.*

FRAGMENT   (See *sentence fragment.*)

FREE MODIFIER   A modifier, usually in the form of the present or past participle, serving as an adjective modifying the subject but appearing after the verb. Free modifiers may be multiplied almost infinitely without confusing the sentence:

Hank Williams began his country music career as a young boy in Alabama, *playing* nightclubs called blood buckets, *writing* songs in cars between engagements, *drinking* too much whiskey, *making* his way painfully to the Grand Ole Opry and national fame.

FUSED SENTENCE   (See *run-on sentence.*)

FUTURE PERFECT TENSE   (See *tense.*)

FUTURE TENSE   (See *tense.*)

GENDER   Nouns and pronouns can have a masculine, feminine, or neuter *gender,* the name given to sexual reference in grammar. Many writers now make a special effort to use nouns that do not specify gender when both males and females may be included in the name: *police officer* rather than *policeman, chair* or *chairperson* rather than *chairman, flight attendant* rather than *stewardess.*

gt/gl

GENITIVE CASE   Another name for possessive case. (See *case.*)

GERUND   A verbal (a nonfinite verb) in the form of the present participle (with the ending *-ing*). It is used as a noun.

   Bicycling is my favorite exercise.

HELPING VERB   (See *auxiliary verb.*)

IDIOM   A word or expression that conveys a meaning established by custom and usage rather than by the literal definition. According to American English idiom, *making out* with someone is different from *making up* with that same person. If you say you are *burned out* at your job, you are saying something different from what you mean if you say you are *burned up* with your boss.

IMPERATIVE MOOD   (See *mood.*)

INDEFINITE PRONOUN   A pronoun (like *anybody* or *everyone*) that does not require an antecedent noun or pronoun, although it may refer to a noun or pronoun that comes after it in a sentence or a paragraph. (See *pronoun.*)

INDEPENDENT CLAUSE   (See *clause.*)

INDICATIVE MOOD   (See *mood.*)

INDIRECT OBJECT   (See *object.*)

INDIRECT QUOTATION   (See *direct quotation.*)

INFINITIVE   A verbal (nonfinite verb) in the form of the simple present and usually marked by the infinitive marker *to*. Infinitives can be used as nouns or adjectives or adverbs.

   NOUN: *To die* may not be the worst thing one can do.

   ADJECTIVE: She believed she had many books *to write.*

   ADVERB: Most Americans are willing *to work.*

Sometimes the infinitive appears in a sentence without the infinitive marker *to*.

   She can *do* anything. [You can write, "She is able *to do* anything."]

INFLECTIONS   The changes in nouns, pronouns, verbs, adjectives, and adverbs to make these words serve various functions in sentences. The inflections of nouns and pronouns are called *declensions,* the inflections of verbs are called *conjugations,* and the inflections of adverbs and adjectives are called *comparisons.* (See *declension, conjugation,* and *comparison.*)

INTENSIFIERS   Adjectives and adverbs that supposedly add emphasis to the words they modify. They are often unnecessary. Some common intensifiers are *very, really, absolutely, definitely,* and *too.* When you are tempted to use an intensifier, you should always ask yourself if you need it. Too many intensifiers will make readers think that you shout all the time.

gt/gl

INTENSIVE PRONOUN   (See *pronoun.*)

INTERJECTION   A part of speech usually somewhat disconnected from the sentence where it appears and used to express sudden or strong feeling.
> *Ouch!* That hurts!
> *Hey!* You can't do that to me!

INTERROGATIVE PRONOUN   (See *pronoun.*)

INTRANSITIVE VERB   A verb that reports an act or a state of the subject without taking a direct object.
> Jack *ran* all the way home.

Intransitive verbs that join a subject with a subject complement are called *linking verbs.*
> He *was* sick all that week.
> She *had been* an architect in Missouri.

INVERTED OBJECT   A direct object that comes before the subject in a sentence:
> Whiskey he drank by the barrel.

INVERTED SENTENCE   A sentence where the subject comes after the verb. The most common inverted sentences begin with the adverb *there:*
> There is something in what you say.

But other inverted sentences sometimes occur in English:
> Ding, ding, ding went the bell.
> Far, far away sounded the trumpets against the hills.

IRREGULAR VERB   Sometimes called a *strong verb,* a verb whose simple past and past participle are not formed with the addition of the suffix *-ed.* Irregular verbs are verbs such as come/came/come; think/thought/thought; and sit/sat/sat.

LINKING VERB   A verb that joins a subject to its complement. The most common linking verbs are forms of the verb *to be,* but all the verbs of sense are also linking verbs, so you should follow them with an adjective form:
> I felt bad because he disliked my play.
> The spring rain smelled good.

MAIN CLAUSE   (See *clause.*)

MISPLACED MODIFIER   A modifier that is misplaced in the sentence so that it modifies the wrong thing.
> Mrs. Hotchkiss, who loved Indian customs, served the Thanksgiving turkey in a sari and sandals.

MODIFIER   Any word or group of words used as an adjective or adverb to qualify another word or group of words. Modifiers help set off elements from other elements in a class. The *red* truck is set off from trucks that are not red, and the horse *in the field* is set off from horses not in the field.

gt/gl

MOOD The form of a verb that shows whether the writer or speaker thinks the action reported is true, false, or desirable.

The *indicative mood* reports actions that the writer assumes to be true:
> Cat books now *crowd* the best-seller list.

The *subjunctive mood* reports actions that the writer assumes are untrue or at least uncertain:
> If I *were* rich, I would do nothing but farm.

The subjunctive mood can report actions or states that may not be true but that the writer thinks are desirable:
> Let justice roll down like waters and righteousness as a mighty stream.

The *imperative mood* expresses a command or a request for an action that the writer or speaker thinks is desirable.
> *Get* out of here!
> *Bring* the books with you when you come.

NOMINATIVE CASE (See *case.*)

NONRESTRICTIVE MODIFIER A clause or phrase that adds to the description of the word it modifies without being essential to the core assertion of the sentence. Nonrestrictive modifiers are usually set off by commas from the word they modify.
> Faulkner, *who never finished college,* became one of America's greatest writers.
> He ran toward the sound of the train, *stumbling in the tall grass, laughing, longing to see the locomotive and the engineer.*
> The DC-3, *one of the most durable aircraft ever built,* still flies the skies in some parts of the world.

NOUN Nouns are names of persons, places, things, ideas, actions, etc. Any word can be a noun if in a given context it can be a name. A sure test for a noun is whether it can have one of the articles—*a, an,* or *the*—placed before it. The plurals of nouns are usually formed with the addition of *s* or *es,* but there are exceptions: sheep/*sheep,* child/*children,* and man/*men,* for example. *Common nouns* name things according to a general class: *desk, street, tractor, welder,* and so on. *Proper nouns* name specific people, places, or things and are spelled with initial capital letters: *Italy, the Department of Agriculture,* and *Abraham Lincoln,* for example. *Abstract nouns* name entities that lack any specific associations with sense experience: *friendship, ambition, relationship, haste, details. Concrete nouns* name entities that we may recall from our own sense experience—*wood, house, computer, cigar, highway, truck stop, bulldozer. Collective nouns* name groups—*team, crew, church, synagogue, audience, department.* The categories of nouns may overlap. The collective noun *community* is also an abstract noun, since the idea of community is abstracted from how we see people acting together. *George Washington* is a proper noun, since the name refers to a specific person and is capitalized; but it is also a concrete noun, since the man George Washington was a person whom we can identify by his picture and by works that have been written about him.

NOUN CLAUSE A dependent clause used as a noun.

> They told me *where we would meet in Athens.*
> *The clause in italics is a noun, acting as the direct object of the verb* told.

NUMBER The form of a noun, verb, pronoun, or demonstrative adjective that indicates singular or plural.

OBJECT A noun or noun substitute that receives the action reported by a verb, a preposition, or a verbal. (Verbals are infinitives, participles, and gerunds.) Objects usually but not always come after the element that conveys action to them. A direct object receives the action of a verb (or a verbal) and generally follows the verb in a sentence.

> Politicians must raise *money* to be elected. [direct object]

An indirect object is a noun or pronoun placed before a direct object and used to show for whom or to whom the action is conveyed by the verb.

> He promised *me* a hot cup of coffee. [indirect object]

Infinitives and verbals may take objects too.

> We hoped to give her the *victory.* [object of an infinitive]
> Pushing *the couch*, she injured her back. [object of a verbal]

Prepositions always take objects.

> They swam across the *river* together. [object of a preposition]

OBJECT COMPLEMENT A word or group of words appearing after an object in a sentence and further defining that object.

> He named his son *John.*
> They called the storm a *hurricane.*

OBJECTIVE CASE Properly speaking, we say that any noun or noun substitute is in the objective case when it is a direct object, an indirect object, or the object of a preposition or verbal. (See *case.*)

ORDINAL NUMBERS Numbers such as *first, second,* and *third,* distinguished from the cardinal numbers — *one, two, three,* etc.

PARENTHETICAL ELEMENT An element not essential to the main assertion of the sentence. If a parenthetical element represents a large interruption of the flow of a sentence, that element is usually placed within parentheses or dashes.

> Herbert Hoover detested Franklin Roosevelt (Hoover would scarcely speak to him during Roosevelt's inaugural in 1932) and went on denouncing the New Deal for years.
> He disliked the country — its loneliness appalled him — and he refused to visit it, even to ski or picnic or hike.

Nonrestrictive modifiers are sometimes called parenthetical, since they can be removed without making the main assertion of the sentence unintelligible. Some words and expressions such as *incidentally* and *to be sure* are also considered parenthetical.

PARTICIPIAL PHRASE (See *phrase*.)

PARTICIPLE (See *past participle* and *present participle*.)

PARTS OF SPEECH The names given to words to describe the role they play in communication. The eight parts of speech are noun, pronoun, verb, adjective, adverb, preposition, conjunction, and interjection.

PASSIVE VOICE The form of a verb phrase that causes the subject of a clause to be acted upon. The passive is always made with some form of the verb *to be* and a past participle.

> Lincoln *was elected* President in 1860.
> The houses on the hill *were* all *built* alike.

(See *active voice* and *voice*.)

PAST PARTICIPLE The third principal part of verbs, the form of a verb used with the auxiliaries *have* and *had*. It usually ends in *ed*, but irregular verbs have different endings. The past participle finds common use as an adjective:

> The hymn, *sung* by the mighty choir, rolled out into the night.
> Their *worn* faces showed the futility of their effort.

The past participle, used with some form of the verb *to be*, is necessary to the passive voice:

> Jefferson Davis *was captured* while trying to escape to South America.

PERSON The form of a pronoun that tells whether someone or something speaks (I, me, we, our), is spoken to (you, your), or is spoken about (he, she, it, their, them).
Verbs also change to show person in some tenses, especially in the third person singular.

> First person: *I cry* (or *we cry*) at sad movies.
> Second person: *You cry* at sad movies.
> Third person: *He cries* (or *they cry*) at sad movies.

PERSONAL PRONOUN A pronoun that refers to a person, such as *I, you, he, she, who, whom,* or *they.* (See *pronoun*.)

PHRASE A group of related words. It has neither subject nor predicate, and it serves as a part of speech in a sentence.

> Verb phrase: We *are toiling* in the vineyard. [verb]
> Prepositional phrase: We must work *until sunset*. [adverb]
> Participial phrase: *Leaping the fence,* the horse carried me swiftly to safety in the woods. [adjective]
> Infinitive phrase: Lyndon Johnson yearned *to be somebody important*.

Gerund phrase: *Walking the dog* was his own exercise. [noun]
Absolute phrase: The car crashed through the house, *the front wheels coming to rest on the living room sofa.*

POSITIVE DEGREE   (See *comparison.*)

POSSESSIVE CASE   The form of a noun or pronoun that indicates possession or a special relation. Some pronouns can only indicate possession — *my, mine, our, ours, your, yours, their.* Their possessive of nouns (singular or plural) and some pronouns is formed by adding an apostrophe (') and an *s* at the end — *anybody's, everyone's, Gertrude's, Hubert's, women's* bank, *children's* toys. The possessive of nouns ending in *s* (singular or plural) is generally formed by adding only an apostrophe — *James', Erasmus',* the *class'* responsibility, the *states'* governors. Some writers prefer to add *'s* even to those nouns that end in *s* in the singular — James*'s*, Erasmus*'s*. (See *case.*)

PREDICATE   Everything in a clause or sentence besides the subject and its immediate adjectives. The predicate declares something about the subject. The *complete predicate* comprises everything in the sentence but the subject cluster; the *simple predicate* comprises only the verb or verb phrase.

> The art of the late twentieth century [subject cluster]
> *has departed* [verb phrase; simple predicate]
> *from all the rules that supposedly guided both painting and sculpture for centuries.*
> *The complete predicate, including the simple predicate, is in italics.*

PREDICATE ADJECTIVE   An adjective, coming after a verb and modifying the subject.
> She was *dignified.*

(See *complement.*)

PREDICATE NOUN   A noun coming after the verb and helping to identify the subject of the sentence.
> Ms. Smythe was an *architect.*

(See *complement.*)

PREFIX   A letter or a group of letters, often derived from Latin or Greek, added to the beginning of a word to form another word. Common prefixes are *dis, ir-, un-,* and *a-,* implying some kind of negation, as in the words *disbelief, irreplaceable, unreliable,* and *asymmetrical; ad-* means something added or joined to something else, as in *admixture.*

PREPOSITION   A word, usually short, that does not change its form and that, by joining with a noun object, helps bring the strength of the noun into the sentence to act as an adjective or adverb. Common prepositions are *about, above, across, after, against, outside, toward,* and *within.* A preposition and its object, the noun (or noun substitute), make a prepositional phrase, and the prepositional phrase almost always serves as an adjective or an adverb in the sentence where it is found.

PREPOSITIONAL PHRASE (See *phrase.*)

PRESENT PARTICIPLE The form of a verb that ends with *ing.* With the aid of auxiliary verbs, the present participle forms the progressive of the various verb tenses. Standing by itself, the present participle can be an adjective or an adverb.

> ADJECTIVES: *Staggering* and *shouting,* he protested his innocence.
> ADVERB: They went *singing* through the streets at Christmas.

PRESENT PERFECT TENSE (See *tense.*)

PRESENT STEM For all English verbs except *to be,* the present stem is the form used with the personal pronoun *I* in the present tense (I go, I stop). It is also the form of the infinitive (to go, to stop). For regular verbs, the simple past is formed by adding *ed* or *d* to the present stem, and the present participle is formed by adding *ing* to the present stem. If the present stem ends in *e,* that letter is almost always dropped before *ing* is added. Dictionaries list words in alphabetical order according to the spelling of the present stem; so the present stem is sometimes called the *dictionary form* of the verb.

PRESENT TENSE (See *tense.*)

PRINCIPAL PARTS OF A VERB The present stem, the simple past, and the past participle of a verb. The various tenses of verbs are formed from their principal parts.

> Present stem: smile, do
> Simple past: smiled, did
> Past participle: smiled, done

(See *tense.*)

PROGRESSIVE TENSE (See *tense.*)

PRONOUN A word used in place of a noun. Many pronouns have an antecedent that comes before them either in the sentence where they are found or in an earlier sentence. But some pronouns such as *I, you, we, anybody,* and *everyone* may lack a formal antecedent, and sometimes the noun to which a pronoun refers may follow the pronoun in the text. Pronouns are generally classified in the following ways:

Personal: I, you, we, they, he, she, our
Relative: who, whom, which, that
Interrogative: who? which? what?
Demonstrative: this, that, these, those
Indefinite: anybody, anyone, everyone, everybody
Reciprocal: each other, one another
Reflexive: myself, yourself, oneself
Intensive: myself, yourself, oneself

gt/gl

The difference between reflexive and intensive pronouns depends on how they are used in a sentence. Their forms are the same. If the subject is in the same person as the pronoun and acts on it, the pronoun is reflexive, as in the sentence *I did all the damage to myself.* But if the pronoun serves to make a statement much more emphatic than it would be without the pronoun, we say that it is intensive, as in this sentence: *I said it myself.*

PROPER NOUN (See *noun.*)

RECIPROCAL PRONOUN (See *pronoun.*)

REFLEXIVE PRONOUN (See *pronoun.*)

REGULAR VERB A verb whose simple past and past participle are both formed with the addition of *ed* to the present stem: play/played/played. (See *irregular verb.*)

RELATIVE PRONOUN (See *pronoun.*)

RESTRICTIVE ELEMENT A modifying element that cannot be removed from a sentence without confusing the sense of the main assertion.

> The bicycle *that I rode to the coast* had eighteen speeds.
> *You are not talking about just any bicycle; you are talking about the one* "that I rode to the coast." *So the clause is restrictive.*
>
> The man *in the gray suit and white hat* held the gun.
> *The phrase* "in the gray suit and white hat" *provides an essential bit of information about the subject,* "man"; *so the phrase is a restrictive element: not just any man, but the man in the gray suit and the white hat.*

RHETORICAL QUESTION A question asked so that the writer or speaker may provide an answer or may demonstrate to the audience that the answer is obvious.

> How long are we going to let a government of the people be the chief destroyer of the people's land?
> How can we explain the seeming shift between Thomas More's early humanism and his later fury toward the Protestants?

The rhetorical question is often a convenient device for getting into a subject or for shifting emphasis within an essay, but you should not overuse it.

RUN-ON SENTENCE Two independent clauses run together with no punctuation to separate them.

> FUSED SENTENCE: Scientists, grammarians, and artists are all alike in one respect they depend on the work of others like themselves.
> REVISED: Scientists, grammarians, and artists are all alike in one respect: they depend on the work of others like themselves.

gt/gl

SENTENCE A statement, question, or command made by creating a grammatical union between a subject and a predicate. The subject must be a noun or noun substitute, and the predicate must include a finite verb. The subject controls the verb, and the subject and the verb must agree with each other in number. In sentences that are not commands, the predicate makes a statement about the subject. In questions, the statement is made in the form of an inquiry that asks to know if the statement is true.

The personal computer *will soon become as common in the American home as the sofa in the living room.*
The predicate, in italics, makes a statement about the subject, "The personal computer."

Will the personal computer soon become as common in the American home as the sofa in the living room?
The question asks whether the statement made by the predicate is true.

gt/gl

SENTENCE FRAGMENT A group of words that begins with a capital letter and ends with a closing mark of punctuation, so that at first glance it looks like a sentence, but does not include a subject in grammatical union with a predicate.

Correct a sentence fragment by giving it a subject or predicate (or both, when necessary) or by adding it to the sentence that comes directly before or after, if the revision is logical.

SENTENCE FRAGMENTS (in italics)

The telephone dropped. *Onto the floor.*
Working at her desk. She suffered terribly.
Dr. Leyton introduced the visiting surgeon. *Who spoke formally without looking up from her notes.*

CORRECTED SENTENCES

The telephone dropped. It fell to the floor.
Working at her desk, she suffered terribly.
Dr. Leyton introduced the visiting surgeon, who spoke formally without looking up from her notes.

SIMPLE PREDICATE (See *predicate.*)

SIMPLE SENTENCE A sentence with only one clause. Some simple sentences are not very simple.

Catherine arrived in England in 1501 and immediately encountered the English hatred of foreigners, a hatred shown in the scorn heaped on her retainers, in the bitter stinginess of her royal father-in-law Henry VII, and in the indifference of those around her to her comfort and even to her dignity.

SIMPLE SUBJECT (See *subject.*)

SQUINTING MODIFIER A modifier so confusingly located that readers are not sure whether it modifies the element before it or the one after it.

The speech he was giving *slowly* put the audience to sleep.
Was he giving the speech slowly, or was the audience slowly going to sleep?

SUBJECT The noun or noun substitute about which the predicate of a clause or sentence makes its statement. The *simple subject* is the noun or noun substitute; the *complete subject,* or the *subject cluster,* includes all the immediate modifiers of the subject.

The absurd and angry group that assembled in a beer hall in Munich that night in 1923 were to create, a decade later, the most bloody revolution in German history.
The simple subject in the sentence above is the noun group. *The complete subject, or subject cluster, includes all the modifying elements gathered immediately around the simple subject, including the adjective clause* "that assembled in a beer hall in Munich that night in 1923."

SUBJECT COMPLEMENT (See *complement.*)

SUBJECTIVE CASE (See *case.*)

SUBJUNCTIVE MOOD The mood of the verb that indicates the writer's doubts about the truth of the statement made in the sentence.

If we *were* in Athens now, we could see the sun shining on the Acropolis.
We are not in Greece; the verb were *is in the present subjunctive.*
I fear lest we *be* too optimistic about the outcome.
We may not be too optimistic, but the writer fears that we may be so.

SUBORDINATE CLAUSE (See *clause.*)

SUBORDINATING CONJUNCTION (See *conjunction.*)

SUBORDINATION The act of placing some elements in sentences in a dependent relation with others so that readers can follow the flow of discourse, knowing what is more important and what is less important.

So-called choppy sentences are usually sentences without adequate subordination.

> The hunters walked for miles.
> They did not know where they were going.
> They had never been in the woods before.
> Although the hunters walked for miles, they did not know where they were going, since they had never been in these woods before.

SUFFIX An ending that changes the meaning of the word to which it is attached. The suffixes in the following words are in italics:

> care/care*less*, delight/delight*ful*, boy/boy*ish*, visual/visual*ize*

SUPERLATIVE DEGREE (See *comparison*.)

SYNTAX The part of grammar that considers the relations between sentences and between parts of sentences. In English syntax, the subject usually comes before the verb; prepositional phrases include a preposition and a noun or noun substitute that acts as the object of the preposition; and clauses serve as nouns, adjectives, or adverbs.

TENSE The form of a verb that indicates time, whether present, past, or future. The *simple tenses* include the present, the past, and the future.

> Present: I *speak*, she *laughs*
> Past: I *spoke*, she *laughed*
> Future: I *shall* (or *will*) *speak*, she *will laugh*

The *perfect tenses* indicate time previous to the simple tenses. Perfected tenses are formed with the past participle and an auxiliary verb, *have* or *had*.

> Present perfect: I *have spoken*, she *has spoken*
> Past perfect: I *had spoken*, she *had spoken*
> Future perfect: I *shall have spoken*, she *will have spoken*

The *progressive tense* indicates continuing action. It is formed with the present participle and a form of the verb *to be* as auxiliary.

> I *am speaking*.
> She *was speaking*.
> They *had been speaking*.

TRANSITIVE VERB A verb that conveys action from a subject to a direct object. (See *verb*.)

VERB A word that reports an action or a condition; a word that makes an assertion. *Main verbs* combine with *auxiliary verbs* to form the various tenses. *Intransitive verbs* report that the subject acts or exists in a certain condition; these verbs do not take a direct object. *Transitive verbs* carry action from the subject to an object. Sometimes the same verb can be either transitive or intransitive, depending on its use in the sentence.

> Jackson *smoked*. [intransitive]
> Jackson *smoked* a pipe. [transitive, since *pipe* is a direct object]
> *Linking verbs* join a subject with a complement, either a noun or an adjective. (See *linking verb*.)

VERBAL A nonfinite form of a verb, that is, a form that does not express tense. Verbals are gerunds, participles, and infinitives. A verbal cannot make an assertion about a subject by itself, though it can do so with a helping verb or with another verb phrase. (See *gerund, infinitive,* and *past participle.*)

VERB COMPLEMENT A direct or indirect object. (See *object.*)

VERB PHRASE A main verb and its helpers, or auxiliary verbs. A verb phrase gives a complete statement of tense.

> I *am helping* with the project.
> He *had been seen* in the vicinity.

VOICE The active or passive form of a verb. In the active voice, the subject acts through the verb; in the passive, the verb asserts that some action is done to the subject.

> ACTIVE VOICE: Cecil Cooper *hit* the ball out of the park.
> PASSIVE VOICE: A ball *was hit* out of the park by Cecil Cooper.

WORD ORDER The order of words in an English sentence. Most English sentences begin with the subject, but many English sentences begin with an adverb or an adverbial. Relatively few English sentences begin with participles or conjunctions. The subject usually comes before the verb. The direct object usually comes after the verb. An indirect object always comes between the verb and the direct object. Most adjectives come immediately before or after the noun or noun substitute they modify. Predicate adjectives modify the subject of a clause but come after the verb. Adverbs may be separated by several words from the word or phrase they modify.

gt/gl

Acknowledgments

Note: Text quotations have been excerpted from the following works.

Adler, Mortimer J., and Van Doren, Charles. *How to Read a Book.* Copyright © 1940, 1967 by Mortimer J. Adler. Copyright © 1972 by Mortimer J. Adler and Charles Van Doren. Reprinted by permission of Simon & Schuster, Inc.

American Heritage Dictionary of the English Language, 2nd College Edition. Copyright © 1982 by Houghton Mifflin Company. Reprinted by permission.

Ardrey, Robert. *The Territorial Imperative.* Copyright © 1966 by Robert Ardrey. Reprinted by permission of Atheneum Publishers, a division of Macmillan, Inc.

Baldwin, James. *Notes of a Native Son.* Reprinted by permission of the publisher, Beacon Press.

Bartoshuk, Linda. "Separate Worlds of Taste." Copyright © 1980, American Psychological Association. Reprinted with permission from *Psychology Today Magazine.*

Bate, Walter Jackson. *Biography of Samuel Johnson.* Copyright © 1975, 1977 by Walter Jackson Bate. Reprinted by permission of Harcourt Brace Jovanovich, Inc.

Bereiter, Carl. "Genetics and Educability: Education Implications of the Jensen Debate," in *Disadvantaged Child. Compensatory Education: A National Debate,* vol. 3, edited by Jerome Hellmuth. Brunner, Mazel, publisher. Reprinted by permission.

Bird, Caroline. *The Crowding Syndrome: Learning to Live with Too Much and Too Many.* David McKay, publisher. Copyright © 1972. Used by permission of the author.

Bloom, Edward A., and Bloom, Lillian D. *Willa Cather's Gift of Sympathy.* Copyright © 1962 by Southern Illinois University Press. Reprinted by permission of the publisher.

Brennan, Joseph X. "Willa Cather and Music," *The University Review 31* 1965, pp. 175–183. Reprinted with permission of the Curators of the University of Missouri-Kansas City.

Brody, Jane E. "The Evidence Builds against Marijuana," *New York Times,* 5/21/80. Copyright © 1980 by The New York Times Company. Reprinted by permission.

Brody, Jane E. *Jane Brody's Nutrition Book.* Copyright © by Jane E. Brody. Reprinted by permission of W. W. Norton & Company, Inc.

Brown, Claude. *Manchild in the Promised Land.* Copyright © 1965 by Claude Brown. Reprinted by permission of Macmillan Publishing Company.

Burke, James. *Connections.* Text copyright © 1978 by James Burke. By permission of Little, Brown and Company.

Cairns, Helen S., and Cairns, Charles E. *Psycholinguistics: A Cognitive View of Language.* Copyright © 1976. Used by permission of Holt, Rinehart and Winston, Inc.

Carson, Rachel. "A Fable for Tomorrow," from *Silent Spring.* Copyright © 1962 by Rachel L.

Carson. Reprinted by permission of Houghton Mifflin Company.

Cather, Willa. "A Death in the Desert" and "A Wagner Matinee" in *Troll Garden*. Reprinted by permission of NAL Penguin, Inc.

Catton, Bruce. *This Hallowed Ground*. Reprinted by permission of Doubleday & Company, Inc.

Charlton, Linda. Interview with Michael Fitzgerald, *The New York Times*, 2/17/80. Copyright © 1980 by The New York Times Company. Reprinted by permission.

Chute, Marchette. *Shakespeare of London*. Copyright © 1949 by E. P. Dutton, renewed 1977 by Marchette Chute. Reprinted by permission of the publisher, E. P. Dutton, a division of NAL Penguin, Inc.

Colson, Bill. "Act Two for Bionic Boy." Reprinted courtesy of *Sports Illustrated* from the February 18, 1980 issue. Copyright © 1980, Time, Inc. All rights reserved.

Connell, Evan S. *Son of the Morning Star*. Copyright © 1984 by Evan S. Connell. Published by North Point Press and reprinted by permission.

Cowley, Malcolm. *The View from 80*. Copyright © 1976, 1978, 1980 by Malcolm Cowley. Reprinted by permission of Viking Penguin, Inc.

Cummings, E. E. "in Just-" from *Tulips & Chimneys*. Copyright 1923, 1925 and renewed 1951, 1953 by E. E. Cummings. Copyright © 1973, 1976 by The Trustees for the E. E. Cummings Trust. Copyright © 1973, 1976 by George James Firmage. Reprinted by permission of Liveright Publishing Corporation.

Cuthbertson, Tom. *Anybody's Bike Book*. Copyright © 1979. Used with permission of Ten Speed Press, Box 7123, Berkeley, CA 94707.

Dary, David. *Cowboy Culture*. Used by permission of Alfred A. Knopf, Inc.

Didion, Joan. "Some Dreamers of the Golden Dream," from *Slouching towards Bethlehem*. Copyright © 1966, 1968 by Joan Didion. Reprinted by permission of Farrar, Straus, and Giroux, Inc.

Donald, David Herbert. *Look Homeward: A Life of Thomas Wolfe*. Copyright © 1987 by Magnus Ltd. Unpublished material by Thomas Wolfe copyright © by Paul Gitlin, administrator CTA of the Estate of Thomas Wolfe.

Epstein, Joseph. "Dandies Askew," *The American Scholar*, vol. 48, Winter 1978–79. Copyright © 1979 by the author. By permission of the publisher.

Faulkner, William. "A Rose for Emily" from *Collected Stories of William Faulkner*. Copyright © 1931. Used by permission of Random House, Inc.

Fiedler, Leslie. *Love and Death in the American Novel*. Copyright © 1966 by Leslie Fiedler. Reprinted with the permission of Stein and Day Publishers.

Fimrite, Ron. "Portrait of the Artist as a Hitter." Reprinted courtesy of *Sports Illustrated* from the June 13, 1983 issue. Copyright © 1983, Time, Inc. All right reserved.

Fitzgerald, Frances. *Cities on a Hill*. Copyright © 1986 by Frances Fitzgerald. Reprinted by permission of Simon & Schuster, Inc.

Fowles, John. *Daniel Martin*. Copyright © 1977 by J. R. Fowles Limited. By permission of Little, Brown and Company.

Frye, Northrop. *The Educated Imagination*, pages 63–64. Reprinted by permission of Indiana University Press.

Gallo, Robert C. "The AIDS Virus," *Scientific American*, 1/87. Reprinted by permission of Dr. Robert C. Gallo, National Cancer Institute, Department of Health and Human Services.

Gerber, Philip. *Willa Cather*. Copyright © 1975. Reprinted by permission of G. K. Hall & Company, Boston.

Graham, Janis. "A Guide to Stress Tests," *New York Times Magazine*, 3/29/87. Copyright © 1987 by The New York Times Company. Reprinted by permission.

Gregory, Dick. From *Nigger: An Autobiography* by Dick Gregrory with Robert Lipsyte. Copyright © 1964 by Dick Gregory Enterprises, Inc. Reprinted by permission of the publisher, E. P. Dutton, a division of NAL Penguin, Inc.

Haley, Alex. *Roots*. Reprinted by permission of Doubleday & Company, Inc.

Heilbroner, Robert, and Thurow, Lester. *Five Economic Challenges*. Copyright © 1981. Reprinted by permission of the publisher, Prentice-Hall, Inc. Englewood Cliffs, NJ.

Horney, Karen, M.D. *The Neurotic Personality of Our Time*. Copyright 1937 by W. W. Norton & Company, Inc. Copyright renewed 1964 by Renate Mintz, Brigitte Swarzenski, and Marianne von Eckart. Reprinted by permission of W. W. Norton & Company, Inc.

Horton, Paul B., and Chester, C. Hunt. *Sociology*. Used by permission of McGraw-Hill Book Company.

Horwitz, James. *They Went Thataway*. Copyright © 1976 by James Horwitz. All rights reserved. Reprinted by permission of the publisher, E. P. Dutton, a division of NAL Penguin, Inc.

Hughes, Langston. "Salvation" from *The Big Sea*. Copyright © 1940 by Langston Hughes. Copyright renewed by Arna Bontemps and George Houston Bass. Reprinted by permission of Hill and Wang, a division of Farrar, Straus, and Giroux, Inc.

Jackson, Dale, and the Editors of Time-Life Books. *Twenty Million Yankees*. Used by permission of Time-Life Books.

Jacobs, Jane. *Cities and the Wealth of Nations*. Used by permission of Random House, Inc.

Jastrow, Robert. *Red Giants and White Dwarfs*. Reader's Library, Inc. By permission of the author.

Jenkins, Alan. *The Thirties*. Copyright © 1976 by Alan Jenkins. Reprinted with permission of Stein and Day Publishers.

Jolly, Alison. "Madagascar: A World Apart," *National Geographic*, 2/87. Copyright © National Geographic Magazine, 1987.

Jones, LeRoi. "Home" from *Home: The Social Essays of LeRoi Jones*. Copyright © 1962, 1966 by LeRoi Jones. Reprinted by permission of William Morrow and Company.

Jong, Erica. *Fear of Flying*. Copyright © 1973 by Erica Jong. Reprinted by permission of Henry Holt and Company, Inc.

Kidder, Tracy. *The Soul of a New Machine*. Copyright © 1981 by John Tracy Kidder. By permission of Little, Brown and Company in association with Atlantic Monthly Press.

King, Martin Luther, Jr. "Letter from Birmingham Jail," from *Why We Can't Wait*. Copyright © 1963, 1964 by Martin Luther King, Jr. Reprinted by permission of Joan Daves.

Kingston, Maxine Hong. *The Woman Warrior: Memoirs of a Girlhood among Ghosts*. Used by permission of Alfred A. Knopf, Inc.

Kohler, Dayton. "Willa Cather: 1876–1947" *College English 9*. Copyright © 1947 by the National Council of Teachers of English. Reprinted by permission of the publisher.

Kouts, Catherine. "Wilderness Pinups by Sierra Club." Reprinted from the 4/27/84 issue of *Publishers Weekly*, published by R. R. Bowker Company, a Xerox company. Copyright © 1984 by Xerox Corporation.

Kowinski, William Severini. "Endless Summer at the World's Biggest Shopping Wonderland," *Smithsonian* 12/86. Used by permission.

Kuh, Katherine. *Breakup: The Core of Modern Art*. Used by permission of Little, Brown and Company.

Lefkowitz, Mary. "Women in Greek Myths," *American Scholar 54*. Copyright © 1985 by the author. By permission of the publisher.

Leo, John. "What's in a Nickname," *Time*, 1/19/87. Copyright © 1987 Time, Inc. All rights reserved. Reprinted by permission from *Time*.

Lorenz, Konrad Z. *King Solomon's Ring*. (Thomas Y. Crowell Company). Copyright © 1952 by Harper & Row, Publishers. Reprinted by permission of Harper & Row, Publishers, Inc.

McCullough, David. *Mornings on Horseback*. Copyright © 1981 by David McCullough. Reprinted by permission of Simon & Schuster, Inc.

Mariani, Paul. *William Carlos Williams: A New World Naked*. Copyright © 1981. Used by permission of McGraw-Hill Book Company.

Moses, Sam. "Gallant Victory for an Odd Bird." Reprinted courtesy of Sports Illustrated from the January 5, 1987 issue. Copyright © 1983, Time, Inc. All rights reserved.

National Geographic Society, The. *We Americans*. Copyright © 1975, 1981 National Geographic Society.

Orwell, George. *Homage to Catalonia*. Copyright 1952, 1980 by Sonia Brownell Orwell. Reprinted by permission of Harcourt Brace Jovanovich, Inc.; the estate of the late Sonia Brownell Orwell; and Secker and Warburg, Ltd.

Parkinson, C. Northcote. *Parkinson's Law*. Copyright © 1957 by C. Northcote Parkinson. Copyright © renewed 1985 by C. Northcote Parkinson. Reprinted by permission of Houghton Mifflin Company.

Raymo, Chet. "Science Musings," *Boston Globe*, 1/19/87. By permission of the author.

Rodriguez, Richard. *Hunger of Memory: The Education of Richard Rodriguez*. Copyright © 1983 by Richard Rodriguez. Reprinted by permission of David R. Godine, Publisher, Boston.

Roueché, Berton. *What's Left*. Used by permission of Little, Brown and Company.

Russell, Francis. *Sacco and Vanzetti: The Case Resolved*. Copyright © 1986 by Francis Russell. Reprinted by permission of Harper & Row, Publishers, Inc.

Schorske, Carl. *Fin-de-Siècle Vienna: Politics and Culture*. Used by permission of Alfred A. Knopf, Inc.

Serrin, William. "Detroit Strikes Back," *New York Times Magazine*, 9/14/80. Copyright © 1980 by The New York Times Company. Reprinted by permission.

INDEX

Index

Numbers in **boldface** refer to sections of the handbook; other numbers refer to pages; page numbers in *italic* indicate glossary entries.

A, an, the, 155–156, **5b**
  inclusion of, necessary, 260, **13c**
A half of, 782, **D**
A while, awhile, 777, **D**
Abbreviations, 512–517, **33c–33g**
  acronyms, 516, **33e**; *789*, **E**
  capitalizing, 503, **32b**
  avoiding, 512–514, **33c**
  capitalizing, 503, **32b**,
  in citation of sources, 599–601, **37f**
  Latin, 517, **33g**; 599–601, **37f**
  etc., 514–515, **33c**; *780*, **D**
  with numbers, 516, **33f**
  for titles with personal names,
    515–516, **31b**
-able suffix, spelling of words with,
    484, **31b**
Absolute adjectives, 391, **22g**
Absolute phrases, 169, **5d**; 399–400,
    23a; 767, **C**; *789*, **E**
  commas for setting off, 430, **26c**
  for emphasis, 219, **9c**
  for variety, 230–231, **10e**
Abstract nouns, *789*, **E**
Accept, except, 773, **D**
Access (periodical index), 540, **35c**
Accusative (objective) case, *801*, **E**
  of pronouns, 374–377, **21h**; *792*, **E**
Acronyms, 516, **33e**; *789*, **E**
  capitalizing, 503, **32b**
Active vs. passive voice, 352–355, **20e**;
    790, 802, 809, **E**
  consistency in use of, 413–414, **24c**
  for emphasis, 220–221, **9d**
Active reading, 752–754, **A**
  of literature, *699*, **40b**
Ad hominem attacks, 693–694, **39f**
Addresses:
  for business letters: on envelope,
    742, **42b**
  inside, 731, 734–735, **42a**
  commas in, 439, **26n**
Adjectival, defined, *790*, **E**
Adjective clauses, 172, **5d**; *790*, **E**
  parallelism of, 213–214, **8e**

Adjective phrases, 165–167, **5d**; *790*, **E**
Adjectives, 153–156, **5b**; 379–382, **22a**;
    790, **E**
  absolute, 391, **22g**
  articles, 155–156, **5b**; 260, **13c**; *792*,
    E
  commas between, 435, **26h**
  in comparisons, degrees of, 153, **5b**;
    389–393, **22g**; *793*, **E**
  in hyphenated compounds, 496, **31e**
  misuse of, for adverbs, 386, **22d**
  overuse of, avoiding, 393–394, **22g**
  with same spelling as adverbial
    forms, 387–388, **22f**
  with verbs of sense, adverbs vs.,
    387, **22e**
Adverb clauses, 172–173, **5d**; *791*, **E**
  faulty comma use with, 442–443, **26q**
Adverb phrases, 166, **5d**; *791*, **E**
  misplaced, 397, **23**; 402, **23b**
Adverbials, *791*, **E**
  as sentence openers, 224–225, **10a**;
    429–430, **26b**
Adverbs, 156–158, **5b**; 379, **22**;
    383–385, **22b**; *789*, **E**
  adjectives misused as, 386, **22d**
  in comparisons, degrees of, 153, **5b**;
    389–392, **22g**; *793*, **E**
  in compound modifiers, 496, **31e**
  conjunctive, 157–158, **5b**; *794–795*,
    E
  run-ons and comma splices caused
    by, 301–302, **17e**
  semicolon use with, 445, **27b**
  misplaced: limiting, 405–406, **23e**
  squinting, 404–405, **23d**; *807*, **E**
  position of, in sentence, 429–430,
    26b
  with same spelling as adjectival
    forms, 387–388, **22f**
  sentences modified by, 385–386, **22c**
  with superlative degree of adjectives,
    avoiding, 392, **22g**
  with verbs of sense, adjectives vs.,
    387, **22e**

Advertising, persuasive, 661, **39a**
Advice, advise, 773, **D**
Affect, effect, 481, **31a**, 773, **D**
Agreement, pronoun-antecedent, 365–366, **21b**; 415, **24d**; *791*, **E**
Agreement, subject-verb, 322–336, **19**; *791*, **E**
  for collective nouns, 333–334, **19o**
  for compound subjects: with *and*, 326–327, **19f**
  with correlatives, 329–330, **19i**
  with intervening words, 328–329, **19h**; 330–331, **19j**
  inverted order and, 332, **19k–19l**
  with linking verbs, 333, **19n**
  for plural forms with singular meanings, 334–335, **19p**
  in present perfect tense, 328, **19g**
  for pronouns, 324–325, **19c–19e**; 330–332, **19j**; 332–333, **19m**
  -s suffix, presence or absence of, 322–324, **19a–19b**
  with *to be,* 327–328, **19g**
Ain't, 773, **D**
All, all of, 774, **D**
All right, alright, 774, **D**
All together, altogether, 774, **D**
Allusion, illusion, 774, **D**
Allusions, 715, **40h**
Almost, most, 774, **D**
America: History and Life (periodical index), 540, **35c**
American Heritage Dictionary of the English Language, The, 279–280, **16a**
  parts of entries in, 283–287, **16b**
American Psychological Association (APA) documentation format, 586–591, **37d**
Among, between, 774, **D**
Amount, number 775, **D**
Ampersand, 513, **33c**
An, a, the, 155–156, **5b**
  inclusion of, necessary, 260, **13c**
Analysis:
  defined, 699, **40a**
  literary (*see* Literary essays)
  in paragraphs: causal, 113, **4c**
    process, 111, **4c**
  as study skill, 753, **A**
And, 196, **7a**
  ampersand for, 513, **33c**
  comma as substitute for, 196–197, **7a**; 437–438, **26l**
  and subject-verb agreement, 326–327, **19f**

Antecedents of pronouns, 150, **5b**; 362, **21**
  agreement with, 365–366, **21b**; 415, **24d**; *791*, **E**
  clear reference to, 363–365, **21a**
Antonyms, 287, **16b**
Anxious, eager, 775, **D**
Anybody, any body; anymore, any more; anyone, any one, 775, **D**
APA (American Psychological Association) documentation format, 586–591, **37d**
  for internal documentation, 586–588, **37d**
  for list of references, 588–591, **37d**
Apologetic quotation marks, avoiding, 463, **29e**
Apostrophes, 449–456, **28**
  for contractions, 454, **28b**
  for plurals, special, 455, **28c**
  for possessive case, 449–454, **28a**
    exceptions to, 455, **28d**
Application for job:
  letter, 744–746, **42d**
  résumé, 746–749, **42d**
Appositives, 149, **5b**; *791–792*, **E**
  pronoun cases for, 375, 377, **21h**
Apt, liable, likely, 775, **D**
Archaic and obsolete words, avoiding, 241–242, **11d**
Arguments, 663–697, **39**
  from authority, 681–683, **39e**
  defined, 22, **1c**; 663, **39**
  evidence in: conclusions from, 664, **39a**
    contrary, considering, 687–689, **39f**
  fallacies in, avoiding, 690–697, **39f**
    ad hominem attacks, 693–694, **39f**
    begging the question, 694–695, **39f**
    cause-and-effect arguments, faulty, 690–691, **39f**
    either/or statements, extreme, 692, **39f**
    generalizations, faulty, 691–692, **39f**
    red herrings, 695, **39f**
    straw men, attacking, 692–693, **39f**
  from personal experience (testimony), 683–684, **39e**
  vs. persuasion, 664–665, **39a**
  plausible, 671–672, **39c**
  reasoning in, 665–666, **39b**
    deductive, 675–676, **39d**; 694–695, **39f**

Arguments, reasoning in (*Cont.*):
  fallacious (*see* fallacies in, avoiding, *above*)
  inductive, 666–675, **39c**
  rhetorical questions in, 226–227, **10b**
  tone of, courteous, 689–690, **39f**
  topic of, requirements for:
    debatability, 686–687, **39f**
    limitation, 684–685, **39f**
  with two or more sides, 672–673, **39c**
Argumentum ad hominem, 693–694, **39f**
Articles, 155–156, **5b**; *790*, **E**
  necessary, including, 260, **13c**
  as test for nouns, 147, **5b**
As, 776, **D**
Assumptions (unexpressed major premises), 679–681, **39d**
At, 774, **D**
Audience, consideration of, 8, *1a*; 24–28, **2a**
  community of discourse, 25–26, **2a**
  journalistic questions for, 28, **2a**
  for literary essay, 701, **40d**
  and tone, 26–27, **2a**
Authority, argument from, 681–683, **39e**
Auxiliary (helping) verbs, 134, 135, **5a**; 144–145, **5b**; 339, **20a**; *792*, **E**
  necessary, including, 258–259, **13a**
  perfect tenses formed with, 328, **19g**; 339–341, **20a**; *808*, **E**
Awful, awfully, 777, **D**
Awhile, a while, 777, **D**

Backup discs, computer, 760, **B**
Be, forms of, 343, **20a**
  agreement with subject, 327–328, **19g**
  subjunctive mood, 350, **20d**
Because:
  vs. *due to*, 779–780, **D**
  with *reason is*, 777, 786, **D**
Begging the question, 694–695, **39f**
Being as, being that, 777, **D**
Beside, besides, 777, **D**
Better, 777, **D**
Between, among, 774, **D**
Bibliographic information:
  in list of references, 588–591, **37d**
  in list of works cited, 574–585, **37c**
    example, 638–641, **38f**
  in works consulted, 547, **35c**

Bibliography cards for research papers, 536–539, **35c**
Block and modified-block style for business letters, 730–734, **42a**
Block quotations, 459–460, **29a**; 560–561, **37a**
  colons for introducing, 467, **30b**
Blueprint beginnings, 120, **4d**
Books:
  catalog of, in library, 535–537, **35c**
  citing (*see* Citation of sources)
  footnote or endnote entries for, 592–595, **37f**
  in lists of sources, 575–580, **37c**; 588–589, **37d**
  parenthetical citations of, 566–571, **37c**; 586–588, **37d**
  reference (*see* Reference books)
  studying from, 752–754, **A**
Brackets, 469–471, **30d**
British Humanities Index, The, 541, **35c**
Business writing, 730–749, **42**
  job applications: letter, 744–746, **42d**
    résumé, 746–749, **42d**
  letters, 730–741, **42a**
    body of, 736–740, **42a**
    closing, 741, **42a**
    envelopes for, addressing, 742, **42b**
    job-application, 744–746, **42d**
    salutations, 735–736, **42a**
    style for, block and modified-block, 730–734, **42a**
    titles, personal, in, 734–735, **42a**
  memos, 742–744, **42c**
But that, but what, 777, **D**

Call numbers of library books, 536, 537, **35c**
Can't hardly, 777, **D**
Capital, capitol, 482, **31a**
Capitalization, 498–509, **32**
  after colons, 468, **30b**; 499, **32a**
  of proper nouns and abbreviations, 500–503, **32b**; 505–507, **32**
  of quoted dialogue, 504, **32d**
  reference chart for, 505–507, **32**
  at sentence beginnings, 498–500, **32a**
  of titles of works, 503–504, **32c**
  unnecessary, avoiding, 504–505, **32e**
Capitol, capital, 482, **31a**
Card catalog, library, 535–537, **35c**
Case, instance, line, **D**

Cases, *792,* **E**
  objective, 374, **21h**; *801,* **E**
    proper use of, 375–377, **21h**
  possessive (*see* Possessive case)
  of pronouns, 151–152, **5b**; 373–374,
    21h; *792,* **E**
    proper use of, 375–377, **21h**
Cases and statistics, use of, 107–108,
  4c
Catalog system, library, 535–537, **35c**
Cause and effect:
  in argument: fallacious, 690–691, **39f**
    inductive, 672, **39c**
  paragraph organization around, 113,
    4c
  in sentences, establishing, 184–188,
    6c
Censor, censure, 778, **D**
Characters, literary, writing about,
  702, **40e**
Chronological arrangement of
  information, 34, **2d**
  in paragraphs, 91, **4b**
Citation of sources, 565–602, **37b–37f**
  APA format for, 586–591, **37d**
    internal documentation, 586–588,
      37d
    list of references, 588–591, **37d**
  full publication data system for, 592,
    37e
  MLA format for, 566–585, **37c**
    internal documentation, 566–573,
      37c
    list of works cited, 574–585, **37c**
    notes, 573–574, **37c**; 592–602, **37f**
    number system for, 591, **37e**
    sample list of works cited, **38f**
Classification, use of, in paragraphs,
  112–113, **4c**
Clauses, 164–165, 170–173, **5d**;
  792–793, **E**
  dependent (subordinate) (*see*
    Dependent clauses)
  independent (main) (*see* Independent
    clauses)
  as misplaced modifiers, 403, **23c**
  nonrestrictive, *800,* **E**
    commas with, 432–433, **26f**
  sentence types from, 173–175, **5d**
Clichés, avoiding, 255–257, **12c**
  in closing of business letter, 741, **42a**
  mixed, 190–191, **6e**
  sexist, 275, **15a**
Climax of literary works, 710–711, **40h**
Closing of business letter, 741, **42a**
Closing paragraphs, 120–121, **4d**

Cognates, repetitious definitions using,
  192, **6f**
Coherence and unity, 36–37, **2d**
Coherent paragraphs, methods for
  building, 87–105, **4b**
  arrangement, logical plan of, 90–94,
    4b
  between-paragraph links, 101–103,
    4b
  chronological arrangement, 91, **4b**
  deductive arrangement, 93, **4b**
  importance, arrangement by, 91–92,
    4b
  inductive arrangement, 92, **4b**
  parallelism, 95–97, **4b**
  pronoun use, 94, **4b**
  repetition, 95, **4b**
  spatial arrangement, 90, **4b**
  transitional expressions, 97–101, **4b**
Collective nouns, *793,* **E**
  pronoun agreement with, 366,
    21b
  verb agreement with, 333–334, **19o**
Colons, 466–468, **30b**
  capitalization after, 468, **30b**; 499,
    32a
Comma splices and run-ons,
  correcting, 295–306, **17**; *793,*
  805, **E**
  with coordinating conjunctions, 297,
    17b
  with end marks, 295–296, **17a**
  by examining drafts, 304–305, **17f**
  misleading words, alertness to,
    301–304, **17e**; 384, **22b**
  with semicolons, 297–298, **17c**
  with subordination, 300–301, **17d**
Commas, 427–443, **26**
  absolutes set off by, 430, **26c**
  in addresses, 439, **26n**
  adjectives separated by, 435, **26h**
  confusion avoided by, 431, **26e**
  in dates, 439, **20o**
  in direct address, 437, **26k**
  for emphasis, 438, **26m**
  faulty or needless, avoiding,
    440–443, **26q**
  independent clauses joined by, with
    coordinating conjunctions,
    297, **17b**; 427–428, **26a**
  after introductory word groups,
    428–430, **26b**
  with nonrestrictive elements,
    432–433, **26f**
  parenthetical elements set off by,
    436, **26i**

Commas (*Cont.*):
  participial modifiers set off by, 431,
    26d
  with place names, 438–439, **26n**
  with quotation marks, 436, **26j**
  with series, 434, **26g**; 439–440, **26p**;
    441–442, **26q**
  as substitute for words, 196–197, **7a**;
    437–438, **26l**
Commentary on research sources,
    562–565, **37a**
Commercials, persuasive, 665, **39a**
Common nouns, 147, **5b**; 793, **E**
Community of discourse, 25–26, **2a**
Comparative degree, 153, **5b**; 389–393,
    22g; 793, **E**
Compare with, compare to, 778, **D**
  dictionary usage note on, 285,
    16b
Comparisons, 9, **1a**
  degrees of adjectives and adverbs
    for, 153, **5b**; 389–393, **22g**;
    793, **E**
  necessary words in, including,
    261–263, **13c**; 392–393, **22g**
  for paragraph organization, 111–112,
    4c
  parallelism for, 209, **8a**
  similes and metaphors for, 251–254,
    12b
Complement, compliment, 778, **D**
Complements, 139–140, **5a**; 793–794,
    E
  object, 139, **5a**; *794, 801*, **E**
  subject (predicate nouns; predicate
    adjectives), 139, **5a**; *793, 803*,
    E
Complete vs. simple predicates, 133,
    5a
Complete vs. simple subjects, 132–133,
    5a
Complex sentences, 175, **5d**; *794*, **E**
Compliment, complement, 778, **D**
Complimentary close of business letter,
    741, **42a**
Compound antecedents, pronoun
    agreement with, 365–366,
    21b
Compound-complex sentences, 175,
    5d; *794*, **E**
Compound constructions, pronoun
    cases in, 377, **21h**
Compound nouns, 147, **5b**
Compound predicates, 133–134, **5a**
Compound sentences, 174–175, **5d**;
    297, **17b**; *794*, **E**

Compound subjects, 133, **5a**
  verb agreement with, 326–327, **19f**;
    329–330, **19i**
Compound verbs, necessary parts of,
    including, 259, **13a**
Compound words:
  dividing, 475–476, **30g**
  with hyphens, 496., **31e**
Computer search in library, 545–546,
    35c
Computers, writing with, 756–765, **B**
  dictionaries (spell checkers), using,
    758–759, **B**
  manuscript requirements for, 62, **3d**;
    763–764, **B**
  notes, taking, 756–757, **B**
  outlining, 758, **B**
  paper for, 763, **B**
  printers for, 762–763, **B**
  protecting work, 759–760, **B**
  repetition and overuse, checking for,
    762, **B**
  revising, care in, 760–761, **B**
Concluding paragraphs, 120–121, **4d**
Conclusions:
  from evidence, 664, **39a**
  from instances (induction), 666–675,
    39c
  plausible, forming, 671–672, **39c**
  from premises of syllogisms
    (deduction), 676–680, **39d**
  begged questions, 694–695, **39f**
Concrete details:
  in examination answers, 728–729,
    41d–41e
  images from, 249–251, **12a**
Conditional mood, 410–412, **24b**
Conjugation, *794*, **E**
Conjunctions, 159, **5b**; 794–795, **E**
  in compound subjects and
    predicates, 133–134, **5a**
  coordinating, 159, **5b**; 196–198, **7a**;
    794, **E**
  commas as substitute for, 196–197,
    7a; 437–438, **26l**
  commas before, 297, **17b**;
    427–428, **26a**; 439–440, **26p**
  vs. conjunctive adverbs, 157–158, **5b**
  and subject-verb agreement,
    326–327, **19f**
  correlative, 159, **5b**; *795*, **E**
  parallelism with, 210, **8b**
  and subject-verb agreement,
    329–330, **19i**
  subordinating, 159, **5b**; 171, **5d**;
    200–201, **7b**; *794*, **E**

Conjunctions, subordinating
   (*Cont.*):
   inclusion of, for clarity, 259, **13b**
Conjunctive adverbs, 157–158, **5b**;
   794–795, **E**
   run-ons and comma splices caused
      by, 301–302, **17e**
   semicolon use with, 445, **27b**
Connotations of words, 247–248, **11f**;
   793, **E**
Contact, 779, **D**
*Contemporary Authors; Contemporary
   Literary Criticism*, 545, **35c**
Contractions, 795, **E**
   apostrophes in, 454, **28b**
Contrary evidence, considering, in
   argument, 687–689, **39f**
Contrasts, parallelism for, 209, **8a**
Controlling idea of paragraph, 75–84,
   4a
   supporting: with details, 105–110, **4c**
      with sentences, 84–87, **4a**
Convince, persuade, 779, **D**
Coordinating conjunctions
      (coordinators), 159, **5b**; 196–198,
      7a; 794, **E**
   commas as substitute for, 196–197,
      7a; 437–438, **26l**
   commas before: independent clauses
      joined by, 297, **17b**; 427–428,
      26a
      in series, 439–440, **26p**
   vs. conjunctive adverbs, 157–158, **5b**
   and subject-verb agreement,
      326–327, **19f**
Coordination, 195–198, **7a**; 795, **E**
   conjunctions for (*see* Coordinating
      conjunctions)
   in correction of run-ons and comma
      splices, 297–298, **17b–17c**
   improper, revising, 194–195, **7**
Correction of evaluated paper, 64–65,
   3e
Correlative conjunctions, 159, **5b**; 795,
   E
   parallelism with, 210, **8b**
   and subject-verb agreement,
      329–330, **19i**
Correspondence, business (*see*
   Business writing)
Could of, 779, **D**
Cover page, manuscript requirements
   for, 61, **3d**
   example, 63, **3d**
Cumulative sentences, 218–220, **9c**

Dangling or misplaced participles,
   397–401, **23a**; 795, **E**
Dashes, 465–466, **30a**
Data bases, use of, 545–546, **35c**
Dates, writing:
   commas in, 439, **26o**
   numbers in, 511, **33b**
Debatability as requirement for
   argument topic, 686–687, **39f**
Declarative sentences, 795, **E**
Declension, 796, **E**
Deductive arguments, 675–681, **39d**
   begging the question in, 694–695,
      39f
Deductive arrangement of paragraph,
   93, **4b**
Definitions:
   dictionary, 280, **16a**; 284–285, **16b**
   secondary (connotations), 247–248,
      11f, 795, **E**
   writing, 191–193, **6f**
   paragraphs for, 113–115, **4c**
Degrees of adjectives and adverbs,
   153, **5b**; 389–393, **22g**, 793, **E**
Deletion on computer, errors in,
   760–761, **B**
Demonstrative adjective, 796, **E**
Demonstrative pronouns, 151, **5b**
Denotations of words, 795, **E**
Dependent clauses, 164–165, 170–173,
   5d; 200–201, **7b**
   adjective, 172, **5d**; 213–214, **8e**; 790,
      E
   commas with: in nonrestrictive
      constructions, 432–433, **26f**
      at sentence beginnings, 428–429,
      26b
      at sentence ends, avoiding,
      422–443, **26q**
   pronoun cases in, 375, **21h**
      implied clauses, 376, **21h**
   and sentence types, 175, **5d**
Description, defined, 21, **1c**
Descriptors in computer search,
   545–546, **35c**
Desk dictionaries, 279–281, **16a**
   using, 283–288, **16b**
Details:
   concrete: in examination answers,
      728–730, **41d–41e**
   images from, 249–251, **12a**
   controlling idea of paragraph
      supported with, 105–110, **4c**
   as evidence, choosing, 28–31, **2b**
   irrelevant, eliminating, 180–183, **6a**

Development of paper, 24–39, **2**
  audience, consideration of, 24–28, **2a**
  community of discourse, 25–26, **2a**
  journalistic questions for, 28, **2a**
  for literary essay, 701, **40d**
  and tone, 26–27, **2a**
  evidence and details, choosing,
    28–31, **2b**
  ideas, handling, 33–39, **2d**
  expansion, 33, **2d**
  methods of arranging, 34–35, **2d**
  rough outline, creating and
    checking, 35–39, **2d**
  thesis, formulating and stating,
    31–33, **2c**
  for literary essay, 700–701, **40c**
  for research paper, 549–550, **36a**;
    605–607, **38a**
Diagramming, 796, **E**
Dialect, avoiding, 240, **11b**
Dialogue, quoted (*see* Quotations,
  direct)
Diction, appropriate, 235–248, **11**
  in business letters, 738–739, **42a**
  connotations, choosing words for,
    247–248, **11f**
  dialect, avoiding, 240, **11b**
  foreign words, unnecessary,
    avoiding, 242–243, **11d**
  idioms, use of, 245–247, **11e**
  necessary words, including,
    260–261, **13c**
  jargon, limiting, 240–241, **11c**; 273,
    14d
  obsolete words, avoiding, 241–242,
    11d
  slang, use of, 239–240, **11a**
    vs. inappropriate use, 236, **11**;
      238, **11a**
  technical terms, avoiding, 243,
    11d
Dictionaries, 279–288, **16a–16b**
  computer (spell checkers), use of,
    758–759, **B**
  desk, 279–281, **16a**
    using, 283–288, **16b**
  parts of entries in, 283–288, **16b**
  specialized, 282, **16a**
  of synonyms (thesauruses), 288–289,
    16c
  unabridged, 281–282, **16a**
  of usage, 282–283, **16a**
Dictionary form (present stem) of
    verbs, 337, 338, **20a**; *804*, **E**
  irregular verbs, 344–345, **20a**

Dictionary form of verbs (*Cont.*):
  past and future formed from,
    145–146, **5b**; 339, **20a**
Differ from, differ with, 779, **D**
Different from, different than, 779, **D**
Direct address, commas in, 437, **26K**
Direct objects, 137–138, **5a**
Direct quotations (*see* Quotations,
  direct)
Discs, computer, 759–760, **B**
Disinterested, uninterested, 779, **D**
Do, 338, **20a**
Documentation of sources, 565–602,
    37b–37f
  APA format for, 586–591, **37d**
    internal documentation, 586–588,
      37d
    list of references, 588–591, **37d**
  full publication data system for, 592,
    37e
  MLA format for, 566–585, **37c**
    internal documentation, 566–573,
      37c
    list of works cited, 574–585, **37c**
    notes, 573–574, **37c**; 592–602, **37f**
  number system for, 591, **37e**
  sample list of works cited, 638–641,
    38f
Don't, doesn't, 779, **D**
Dot-matrix printers, 762–763, **B**
Double negative, 796, **E**
Drafts of paper:
  examining: for run-ons and comma
      splices, 304–305, **17f**
    for sentence fragments, 317, **18c**
  final, 60–64, **3d**
    example, 65–73, **3e**
    research papers, 611–612, **38e**
  first: preparing, 40–49, **3a**; 610, **38c**
    revising, 49–60, **3b**; 264–266, **14a**;
      610–611, **38c–38d**
  literary essays, 717–718, **40i**
  research papers, 610–612, **38c–38e**
Dramatic irony, 712–713, **40h**
Due to, because, 779–780, **D**

e ending, silent, and suffixes, 484, **31b**
Each, subject-verb agreement with,
    327, **19f**
Each and every, 780, **D**
Eager, anxious, 775, **D**
Editing (*see* Revision)
Effect, affect, 481, **31a**; 773, **D**
ei vs. *ie*, spellings with, 483, **31b**

Either . . . or, 780, **D**
  in fallacious reasoning, 692, **39f**
Ellipsis and ellipsis marks, 472–473,
  30f; 796–797, **E**
Elliptical (implied) clauses, pronoun
  cases in, 376, **21h**
Elliptical elements, 797, **E**
  semicolons with, 446–447, **27d**
Embedding techniques, use of,
  202–204, **7b**
Eminent, imminent, immanent, 780, **D**
Emotion:
  excessive, avoiding, 235–236, 238,
    11; 417–420, **24f**
  in arguments, 689–690, **39f**
  exclamation marks for emphasizing,
    425, **25c**
  understatement for indicating, 715,
    40h
Emphasis in sentences, 183–184, **6b**;
  215–223, **9**
  active vs. passive voice for, 220–221,
    9d
  commas for, 438, **26m**
  cumulative sentences for, 218–220,
    9c
  dashes for, 465–466, **30a**
  periodic sentences for, 216–217, **9a**
  repetition for, 211–212, **8d**; 221–222,
    9e
  from short sentence after long ones,
    222, **9f**
  underlining (italics) for, 522–523, **34e**
  weak endings, avoiding, 217–218, **9b**
Encyclopedias, 543–544, **35c**
End marks, 423–426, **25**
  after abbreviations, 516, **33d**
  for correcting run-ons and comma
    splices, 295–296, **17a**
  exclamation marks, 425, **25c**
  parentheses and, 469, **30c**
  periods, 423–424, **25a**
  question marks, 424–425, **25b**
  with quotation marks, 461, **29b**
Endnotes and footnotes, 573–574, **37c**;
  592–602, **37f**
Enthused, enthusiastic, 780, **D**
Envelopes, addressing, 742, **42b**
Essay and General Literature Index,
  541, **35c**
Essay examinations, writing, 726–729,
  41
Etc. 514–515, **33c**; *780,* **D**
Etymologies in dictionary entries, 285,
  16b

Evaluated papers, correction of, 64–65,
  3e
Every, subject-verb agreement with,
  327, **19f**
Everyone, every one: everybody, every
  body, 775, **D**
Evidence:
  conclusions from, 660, **39a**
  contrary, considering, 687–689, **39f**
  and details, choosing, 28–31, **2b**
Exaggeration (hyperbole), 713–714,
  40h
Examinations, essay, writing, 726–729,
  41
Except, accept, 773, **D**
Exclamation marks, 425, **25c**
Exclamations, use of, 227, **10c**
Expect, 781, **D**
Explanatory notes in research papers,
  573–574, **37c**
Expletives, 797, **E**
  it as, 797, **E**
    introductory participle and, 400,
      23a
    vs. pronoun, 368–369, **21d**
Exposition, defined, 21, **1c**

Fallacious reasoning, 690–697, **39f**
  ad hominem attacks, 693–694, **39f**
  begging the question, 694–695, **39f**
  from cause to effect, 690–691, **39f**
  either/or statements, extreme, 692,
    39f
  generalizations, faulty, 691–692, **39f**
  red herrings, 695, **39f**
  straw men, attacking, 692–693, **39f**
Farther, further, 781, **D**
Fewer, less, 781, **D**
Figurative language and imagery,
  249–257, **12**
  clichés, avoiding, 190–191, **6e**;
    255–257, **12c**
  concrete details, use of, 249–251,
    12a
  literary symbolism, 716–717, **40h**
  metaphors and similes, use of,
    251–254, **12b**
  mixed, avoiding, 190–191, **6e**
Figures vs. words for numbers,
  510–512, **33a–33b**
Final drafts of papers, 60–64, **3d**
  example, 65–73, **3e**
  research paper, 611–612, **38e**
Finite verb, 797, **E**

First drafts of papers:
preparing, 40–49, **3a**
research paper, 610, **38c**
revising, 49–60, **3b**; 264–266, **14a**
checklist for, 50–51, **3b**
example, 52–59, **3b**
research paper, 610–611, **38c–38d**
First person of verbs, 142, **5b**;
324–325, **19d**
First person singular pronouns, use of,
370–371, **21f**
Flaunt, flout, 781, **D**
Floppies and hard discs, 759–760, **B**
Footers and headers in formatted
documents, 764, **B**
Footnotes and endnotes, 573–574, **37c**;
592–602, **37f**
Foreign expressions:
abbreviations for, 517, **33g**; 599–601,
37f
etc., 514–515, **33c**: *780,* **D**
underlining (italicizing), 520–521,
34b
unnecessary, avoiding, 242–243,
11d
Formal outlines for research papers,
607–610, **38b**
examples, 613–615, 644–645, **38f**
Format of paper, manuscript
requirements for, 61–62, **3d**
Formatting of documents, 763–764, **B**
Former, latter, 781, **D**
Fragments, sentence, 130, **5**; 307–321,
18; *806,* **E**
acceptable uses of, recognizing,
319–320, **18d**
beginnings of, recognizing, 314–317,
18b
capitalization of, 499, **32a**
checklist for correcting, 318, **18**
complete sentences from: by
addition to adjacent
sentences, 310–312, **18a**
by change of words in, 312–313,
18a
examining drafts for, 317, **18c**
Free modifiers, 797, **E**
commas for setting off, 431, **26d**
dangling, 399, **23a**
for emphasis, 218–220, **9c**
examples for imitation, 770, 771, **C**
for variety, 229–231, **10e**
Full publication data reference system,
592, **37e**
Further, farther, 781, **D**

Future tenses, 146, **5b**; 339, **20a**
different uses of, 343, **20a**
perfect, 340–341, **20a**

Gender, 797, **E**
General and specific points, arranging,
34–35, **2d**
Generalizations, faulty, 691–692, **39f**
limiting, 188–190, **6d**
Genitive case (*see* Possessive case)
Gerunds and gerund phrases, 168, **5d**;
798, **E**
possessive pronouns with, 377, **21h**
Get, 781, **D**
Glossaries:
of grammar, 789–809, **E**
of usage, 773–788, **D**
Good, well, 781–782, **D**
Grammar, sentence, 127–177, **5**
defined, 127, **5**
errors: in verb use, avoiding, 347,
20c; 358–361, **20g**; 407–414,
24a–24c
(*See also* Comma splices and run-
ons, correcting, Misplaced
modifiers, Sentence
fragments; Shifts, confusing)
glossary of terms in, 789–809, **E**
parts of speech, 140–162, **5b**; *802,* **E**
dictionary information about, 284,
16b
different, same word as, 162, **5b**
interjections, 161–162, **5b**; 799, **E**
prepositions, 160–161, **5b**; 246,
11e; 261, **13c**; *803–804,* **E**
(*See also* Adjectives; Adverbs;
Conjunctions; Nouns;
Pronouns; Verbs)
patterns, sentence, 127–131, **5**
recognizing, 163–164, **5c**
varying, 224–226, **10a**
subject, 131–134, **5a**; *807,* **E**
inversion of verb and, 228, **10d**;
332, **19k–19l**; 799, **E**
simple, 132–133, 136–137, **5a**
verb agreement with (*see*
Agreement, subject-verb)
types of sentences, 173–177, **5d**
complex, 175, **5d**; *794,* **E**
compound, 174–175, **5d**; 297, **17b**;
794, **E**
compound-complex, 175, **5d**; *794,*
E
simple, 173–174, **5d**; *806–807,* **E**

Grammar, sentence (*Cont.*):
  (*See also* Clauses; Phrases;
    Predicates)

Had as past subjunctive, 351, **20d**
Half, half a, 782, **D**
Handwritten papers, manuscript
    requirements for, 62–63, **3d**
Hanged, hung, 782, **D**
*Harvard Guide to Contemporary
    American Writing, The*, 545,
    35c
Headers and footers in formatted
    documents, 764, **B**
Headings for memos, 743, **42c**
Helping (auxiliary) verbs, 134, 135, **5a**;
    144–145, **5b**; 339, **20a**; 792, **E**
  necessary, including, 258–259, **13a**
  perfect tenses formed with, 328, **19g**;
    339–341, **20a**; 808, **E**
Honesty in paper, 8, **1a**; 235, **11**; 473,
    30f
Hopefully, 385, **22c**; 782, **D**
Humanities Index, 541, **35c**
Hung, hanged, 782, **D**
Hyperbole, 711–712, **40h**
Hyphens:
  spellings with, 496–497, **31e**
  for word division, 474–476, **30g**
Hypothesis for research paper, 549,
    36a

I, verb agreement with, 142, **5b**;
    324–325, **19d**
Ibid., 599, **37f**
Idioms, use of, 245–247, **11e**; 798, **E**
  necessary words, including, 260–261,
    13c
ie vs. *ei*, spellings with, 483, **31b**
If . . . then, 782, **D**
Illusion, allusion, 774, **D**
Imagery and figurative language,
    249–257, **12**
  clichés, avoiding, 190–191, **6e**;
    255–257, **12c**
  concrete details, use of, 249–251,
    12a
  literary symbolism, 716–717, **40h**
  metaphors and similes, use of,
    251–254, **12b**
  mixed, avoiding, 190–191, **6e**
Imitation of prose examples, 766–772,
    C

Imminent, immanent, eminent, 780,
    D
Imperative mood, 351, **20d**
Implied clauses, pronoun cases in, 376,
    21h
Imply, infer, 782, **D**
Importance, arranging information by,
    35, **2d**
  in paragraph, 91–92, **4b**
In, in to, into, 783, **D**
Incredible, incredulous, 783, **D**
Indefinite pronouns, 150, **5b**; 363, **21**;
    798, **E**
  possessive case of, 449, **28a**
  verb agreement with, 330–332,
    19j
Independent clauses, 164–165, **5d**
  coordination of, 197–198, **7a**;
    297–298, **17b–17c**; 427–428,
    26a
  dashes and colons with, 466, **30a,
    30b**
  incorrect joining of, correcting,
    295–306, **17**
    with coordinating conjunctions,
    297, **17b**
    with end marks, 295–296, **17a**
    by examining drafts, 304–305, **17f**
    misleading words, alertness to,
    301–304, **17e**
    with semicolons, 297–298, **17c**
    with subordination, 200–301,
    17d
  semicolon for joining, 198, **7a**;
    297–298, **17c**; 444–446,
    27a–27b
  and sentence types, 173–175, **5d**
Indexes to periodicals, 538–542,
    35c
Indicative mood, 349, **20d**
  shifts in use of, avoiding, 410–412,
    24b
Indirect objects, 138–139, **5a**
Indirect questions, punctuating, 424,
    25a
Indirect quotations, 458–459, **29a**; 796,
    E
  capitals not required in, 504, **32d**
Individual, person, 783, **D**
Inductive arrangement of paragraph,
    92, **4b**
Inductive reasoning, 666–678, **39c**
Infer, imply, 782, **D**
Inferences, 30, **2b**; 670, **39c**
  theories, 671–672, **39c**
Infinitive marker *to*, 355, **20f**
  omitting, 357, **20f**

Infinitives and infinitive phrases, 167,
5d; 355–358, 20f; 798, E
objective pronouns with, 376, 21h
sentence fragments beginning with,
315, 18b
Inflections, 798, E
Informal diction, use of, 239–240, 11a
inappropriate, 236, 11; 238, 11a
-ing words:
gerunds, 168, 5d; 377, 21h; 798, E
present participles, 314, 18b; 338,
20a; 377, 21h; 380–381, 22a,
804, E
spelling, 484, 31b
Inside address in business letters, 731,
734–735, 42a
Inside of, 783, D
Instance, line, case, 777–778, D
Intensifiers, 798, E
Intensive (-self) pronouns, 151, 5b;
363, 21; 785, D; 805, E
Interjections, 161–162, 5b; 799, E
Internal citations:
APA format for, 586–588, 37d
defined, 565, 37b
full publication data system for, 592,
37e
MLA format for, 566–573, 37c
number system for, 591, 37e
Interrogative pronouns, 152, 5b
Into, in, in to, 783, D
Intransitive verbs, 138, 5a; 797, E
Inversion of subject and verb, 228,
10d; 799, E
and agreement, 332, 19k–19l
Inverted object, 799, E
Irony, 711–712, 40h
dramatic, 712–713, 40h
Irregardless, 783, D
Irregular adjectives and adverbs, 391,
22g
Irregular verbs, 799, E
errors in use of, 348–351, 20g
principal parts of, 343–345, 20a
in simple past tense, 146, 5b; 339,
20a
to be, 343, 20a
agreement with subject, 327–328,
19a
subjunctive mood, 350, 20d
Irrelevant details, eliminating,
180–183, 6a
It:
as expletive, 797, E
introductory participle and, 400,
23a
vs. pronoun, 368–369, 21d

It (Cont.):
indefinite use of, avoiding, 364, 21a
Italics, 518–523, 34
for emphasis, 522–523, 34e
for foreign expressions, 520–521, 34b
for names of vehicles, 522, 34d
for titles of works, 519–520, 34a
for words as words, 521, 34c
It's, its, 783, D

Jargon, limiting, 240–241, 11c; 273,
14d
Job applications:
letter, 744–746, 42d
résumé, 746–749, 42d
Journalistic questions, asking:
in consideration of audience, 28, 2a
as prewriting technique, 14–15, 1a
and sentence logic, 178–180, 6
Journals:
footnote or endnote entries for, 596,
37f
indexes to articles in, 538–542, 35c
in lists of sources, 581, 37c; 589–590,
37d

Key words in computer search,
545–546, 35c
Kind, kinds, 783–784, D

Language:
appropriate (see Diction,
appropriate)
of literary works, writing about, 703,
40e
sexist, avoiding, 275–278, 15
(See also Imagery and figurative
language)
Latin abbreviations, 517, 33g; 599–601,
37f
etc., 514–515, 33c; 780, D
Latter, former, 781, D
Lay, lie, 360, 20g; 784, D
Lecture notes, taking, 754–755, A
Length:
of paragraph, 117, 4c
of sentences, varying of patterns
and, 224–226, 10a
Less, fewer, 781, D
Letterhead stationery, writing on,
731–732, 42a

Letters, business, 730–741, **42a**
  body of, 736–741, **42a**
  closing, 741, **42a**
  envelopes for, addressing, 742, **42b**
  job-application, 744–746, **42d**
  salutations, 735–736, **42a**
  style for, block and modified-block, 730–734, **42a**
  titles, personal, in, 734–735, **42a**
Liable, likely, apt, 775, **D**
Library facilities, use of, 18, **1a**; 533, **35a**; 534–547, **35b–35c**
  bibliographic information in works consulted, 547, **35c**
  card catalog, 535–537, **35c**
  computer search, doing, 545–546, **35c**
  encyclopedias, 543–544, **35c**
  indexes to periodicals, 538–542, **35c**
  literature, reference works on, 544–545, **35c**
Lie, lay, 360, **20g**; 784, **D**
Like, as, 776, **D**
Likely, apt, liable, 775, **D**
Limitation:
  of generalizations, 188–190, **6d**
  of subject for paper, 6–7, 19–21, **1b**
    argument paper, 684–685, **39f**
    research paper, 533, **35a**
Line, case, instance, 777–778, **D**
Linking verbs, 139, **5a**; 381, **22a**; 799, **E**
  agreement with subject, 333, **19n**
  of sense, 387, **22e**
  shift to passive voice after, 413, **24c**
Lists:
  colons for introducing, 467, **30b**
  of ideas for paper, making, 10–13, **1a**
    for research paper, 531, **35a**
  parallelism in, 211, **8c**
  of references, APA format for, 588–591, **37d**
  of spelling words, 490–495, **31d**
  of works cited: example, 640–643, **38f**
    as key to parenthetical documentation, 566–567, **37c**
    MLA format for, 574–585, **37c**
Literally, 784, **D**
Literary essays, 698–725, **40**
  approaches to, 702–703, **40e**
  assignment, examining, 698–699, **40a**
  audience for, considering, 699, **40d**
  drafts of, developing, 717–718, **40i**

Literary essays (*Cont.*):
  literary devices, recognizing, 710–717, **40h**
    allusion, 715, **40h**
    climax, 710–711, **40h**
    hyperbole, 713–714, **40h**
    irony, 711–712, **40h**
    irony, dramatic, 712–713, **40h**
    symbolic images, 716–717, **40h**
    understatement, 714–715, **40h**
  about poetry, 707–709, **40g**
    example, 718–725, **40i**
  present tense in, 407–408, **24a**
  purpose of, considering, 701–702, **40d**
  reading of literary work for, 699, **40b**
  reference works for, 544–545, **35c**
  research, use of (*see* Research papers)
  thesis, developing, 700–701, **40c**
  topic, picking, 704–707, **40f**
Logic (*see* Reasoning in arguments)
Logic, sentence, 178–193, **6**
  cause and effect, establishing, 184–188, **6c**
  in definitions, 191–193, **6f**
  emphasis, organizing for, 183–184, **6b**; 216–220, **9a–9c**
  generalizations, limiting, 188–190, **6d**
  irrelevant details, eliminating, 180–183, **6a**
  mixed images, avoiding, 190–191, **6e**
Loose paragraphs, revising, 122–124, **4e**
-ly, words ending in, 157, **5b**; 379, **22**

Magazines:
  footnote or endnote entries for, 597, **37f**
  in lists of sources, 581–582, **37c**; 590, **37d**
Main clauses (*see* Independent clauses)
Main verbs, 144, **5b**
Major premises, 676–678, **39d**
  and begging the question, 694–695, **39f**
  implied, 679–681, **39d**
-man, words ending in, 277–278, **15d**
Manuscript preparation, 60–63, **3d**
  formatting of document, 763–764, **B**
Margins, manuscript requirements for, 61, **3d**
  on formatted documents, 763–764, **B**

Maybe, may be, 784, **D**
Meanings of words (*see* Definitions)
Memos, 742–744, **42c**
Metaphors and similes, use of, 251–254, **12b**
Minor premises, 676–678, **39d**
Misplaced modifiers, 396–406, **23**; 799, **E**
    adverbs: limiting, 405–406, **23e**
        squinting, 404–405, **23d**; *807,* **E**
    clauses, 403, **23c**
    dangling or misplaced participles, 397–401, **23a**; 795, **E**
    prepositional phrases, 397, **23**; 401–402, **23b**
Mixed images, avoiding, 190–191, **6e**
MLA (Modern Language Association of America) documentation format, 566–585, **37c**
    for internal documentation, 566–573, **37c**
    for list of works cited, 574–585, **37c**
    for notes, 573–574, **37c**; 592–602, **37f**
MLA (Modern Language Association) *International Bibliography of Books and Articles on the Modern Languages and Literatures,* 541, **35c**
Modes of writing, 21–23, **1c**
Modified-block style for business letters, 734, **42a**
Modifiers, 799, **E**
    free (*see* Free modifiers)
    hyphenated, 496–497, **31e**
    misplaced (*see* Misplaced modifiers)
    (*See also* Adjectives; Adverbs)
Moods of verbs, 349–352, **20d**; *800,* **E**
    consistency in, 410–412, **24b**
    imperative, 351, **20d**
    indicative, 349, **20d**; 410–412, **24b**
    subjunctive, 349–351, **20d**; 411–412, **24b**; *800, 807,* **E**
Moral, morale, 784, **D**
More, more of, 774, **D**
More important, more importantly, 785, **D**
Mosaic plagiarism, 602–603, **37g**
    avoiding, 604, **37g**
Most, almost, 774, **D**
Myself, etc. (*-self* pronouns), 151, **5b**; 363, **21**; *785,* **D**; *805,* **E**

Narration, defined, 21, **1c**

Narrative paragraphs, 110–111, **4c**
Narrators of literary works, writing about, 703, **40e**; 704–706, **40f**
Negative relations in sentences, 186–187, **6c**
Neither . . . nor, 780, **D**
New York Times Index, The, 541, **35c**
Nohow, 785, **D**
Nominative (subjective) case of pronouns, 373–374, **21h**
    proper use of, 375–377, **21h**
None, verb agreement with, 331–332, **19j**
Nonrestrictive elements, *800,* **E**
    commas with, 432–433, **26f**
Nonstop writing, 15–17, **1a**
    for research paper, 531–533, **35a**
Nor, or:
    and pronoun-antecedent agreement, 365, **21b**
    and subject-verb agreement, 330, **19i**
Notes:
    computer use for taking, 756–757, **B**
    reference, semicolons in, 447, **27e**
    for research papers: organizing, 554–557, **36c**
        taking, 550–553, **36b**
    in research papers, 573–574, **37c**; 592–602, **37f**
    reviewing, for essay exams, 726, **41a**
    as study aids, 752–755, **A**
Noun clauses, 172, **5d**; *801,* **E**
Nouns, 147–149, **5b**; *800–801,* **E**
    as adjectives, 381, **22a**
    collective, *793,* **E**
        pronoun agreement with, 366, **21b**
        verb agreement with, 333–334, **19o**
    in hyphenated compounds, 496, **31e**
    plural forms of, 147–148, **5b**
        vs. possessive forms, 451, **28a**
    possessives of, 452, **28a**
        spelling, 482, **31a**; 487–490, **31c**
    possessive case of, 148, **5b**; 449–454, **28a**; *792,* **E**
    pronouns after, avoiding unnecessary use of, 371–372, **21g**
    proper, 147, **5b**
        capitalizing, 500–503, **32b**; 505–507, **32**
    verb agreement with (*see* Agreement, subject-verb)
Nowheres, 785, **D**

Number, *801*, **E**
    agreement in: of pronouns with
        antecedents, 365–366, **21b**;
        415, **24d**; *791*, **E**
    of subjects and verbs (*see*
        Agreement, subject-verb)
Number, amount, 775, **D**
Number reference system, 591, **37e**
Numbers, 510–512, **33a–33b**
    abbreviations with, 516, **33f**
    in parentheses, 469, **30c**

Object complements, 139, **5a**; *794,
    801*, **E**
Objective case, *801*, **E**
    of pronouns, 374, **21h**; *792*, **E**
    proper use of, 375–377, **21h**
Objects, *801*, **E**
    direct, 137–138, **5a**
    indirect, 138–139, **5a**
    pronoun case for, 375, **21h**
Obsolete words, avoiding, 241–242,
    11d
Off of, 785, **D**
One vs. *you*, 369, **21e**; 414, **24d**
Opening paragraphs, 117–120, **4d**
Or, 197, **7a**
    and pronoun-antecedent agreement,
        365, **21b**
    and subject-verb agreement, 330, **19i**
Ordinal numbers, *801*, **E**
Outlines:
    computer use in making, 758, **B**
    parallelism in, 211, **8c**
    for research paper: formal, 607–610,
        38b; 613–615, 644–645, **38f**
    plan, expanded, 556–557, **36c**
    plan, rough, 550, **36a**
    rough, creating and checking, 35–39,
        2d
Outside of, 783, **D**
*Oxford Companion to American
    Literature, The; Oxford
    Companion to English
    Literature, The*, 544, **35c**
Oxford English Dictionary, The,
    281–282, **16a**
*Oxford History of English Literature,
    The*, 544, **35c**

Paper, computer, 763, **B**
Paragraphs, 74–124, **4**
    coherence in, methods of achieving,
        87–105, **4b**

Paragraphs, coherence in (*Cont.*):
    arrangement, logical plan of,
        90–94, **4b**
    between-paragraph links, 101–103,
        4b
    chronological arrangement, 91, **4b**
    deductive arrangement, 93, **4b**
    importance, arrangement by,
        91–92, **4b**
    inductive arrangement, 92, **4b**
    parallelism, 95–97, **4b**
    pronoun use, 94, **4b**
    repetition, 95, **4b**
    spatial arrangement, 90, **4b**
    transitional expressions, 97–101,
        4b
    concluding paragraphs, 120–121, **4d**
    controlling idea of, 75–84, **4a**
        supporting details for, 105–110, **4c**
        supporting sentences for, 84–87,
            4a
    forms for, 110–117, **4c**
        causal analysis, 113, **4c**
        classification, 112–113, **4c**
        comparison, 111–112, **4c**
        definition, 113–115, **4c**
        narration, 110–111, **4c**
        process analysis, 111, **4c**
    length of, 117, **4c**
    opening paragraphs, 117–120, **4d**
    revising, 122–124, **4e**
Parallelism, 208–214, **8**
    for comparison and contrast, 209, **8a**
    with correlatives, 210, **8b**
    faulty, 196, 197, **7a**
    in lists and outlines, 211, **8c**
    for paragraph coherence, 95–97, **4b**
    with relative pronouns, 213–214, **8e**
    repetition for emphasizing, 211–212,
        8d
    series for, 208–209, **8**
Parameter, 785–786, **D**
Paraphrases:
    in direct quotations, 458–459, **29a**
    of research sources, 561, **37a**
        in note-taking, 551, 553, **36b**
Parentheses, 468–469, **30c**
Parenthetical citations:
    APA format for, 586–588, **37d**
    defined, 565, **37b**
    full publication data system for, 592,
        37e
    MLA format for, 566–573, **37c**
    number system for, 591, **37e**
Parenthetical elements, *801–802*, **E**
    commas with, 436, **26i**

Participles and participial phrases,
167–168, **5d**; 338, **20a**
as adjectives, 380–381, **22a**
dangling or misplaced, 397–401, **23a**;
795, **E**
free modifiers, 797, **E**
commas for setting off, 431, **26d**
dangling, 399, **23a**
for emphasis, 218–220, **9c**
examples for imitation, 770, 771,
C
for variety, 229–231, **10e**
imitating examples of, 769–771, **C**
past, 167–168, **5d**; 338, **20a**; 802, **E**
as adjectives, 381, **22a**
of irregular verbs, 344–345, **20a**
sentence fragments beginning
with, 314–315, **18b**
simple past confused with,
358–359, **20g**
present, 338, **20a**; 804, **E**
as adjectives, 380–381, **22a**
pronoun cases with, 377, **21h**
sentence fragments beginning
with, 314, **18b**
as sentence openers, 225, **10a**
fragments with, 314–315, **18b**
Particles added to verbs, 145, **5b**
Parts of speech, 140–162, **5b**; 802, **E**
dictionary information about, 284,
16b
different, same word as, 162, **5b**
interjections, 161–162, **5b**; 799, **E**
prepositions, 160–161, **5b**; 803–804,
E
in idioms, 246, **11e**; 261, **13c**
(*See also* Adjectives; Adverbs;
Conjunctions; Nouns;
Pronouns; Verbs)
Passive vs. active voice, 220–221, **9d**;
352–355, **20e**; 790, 802, 809,
E
consistency in use of, 413–414, **24c**
Past form of verbs, 337, **20a**
irregular, 344–345, **20a**
Past participles, 167–168, **5d**; 338, **20a**;
802, **E**
as adjectives, 381, **22a**
of irregular verbs, 344–345, **20a**
sentence fragments beginning with,
314–315, **18b**
simple past confused with, 358–359,
20g
Past tenses, 145–146, **5b**; 339, **20a**
different uses of, 342, **20a**
perfect, 340, **20a**

Past tenses (*Cont.*):
sequence of tenses, correct, with,
347, **20c**; 410, **24a**
simple past and past participle
confused, 358–359, **20g**
of *to be*, 328, **19g**
Patterns, sentence, 127–131, **5**
recognizing, 163–164, **5c**
varying, 224–226, **10a**
Perfect infinitive, present, 355–356,
20f
Perfect tenses of verbs, 328, **19g**;
339–341, **20a**; 808, **E**
inconsistencies with, 408–409, **24a**
Periodic sentences, 216–217, **9a**
passive voice for, 221, **9d**
Periodicals:
footnote or endnote entries for,
596–597, **37f**
indexes to, 538–542, **35c**
in lists of sources, 581–582, **37c**;
589–590, **37d**
Periods, 423–424, **25a**
Person, individual, 781, **D**
Personal experience, argument from,
683–684, **39e**
Personal pronouns, 150, **5b**; 802, **E**
errors, run-on and comma splice,
caused by, 303, **17e**
possessive, 455, **28d**
and sexism, problem of, 276–277,
15b–15c
verb agreement with, 324–325,
19c–19e
Persons of pronouns, 802, **E**
tone and, 369–371, **21e–21f**; 414,
24d
Persons of verbs, 142–144, **5b**; 802, **E**
and moods, 349–351, **20d**
(*See also* Agreement, subject-verb)
Persuade, convince, 779, **D**
Persuasion vs. argument, 664–665, **39a**
Phrases, 164–169, **5d**; 802–803, **E**
absolute, 169, **5d**; 399–400, **23a**; 769,
C; 789, **E**
commas for setting off, 430, **26c**
for emphasis, 219, **9c**
for variety, 230–231, **10e**
comma use after, at sentence
beginnings, 428–429, **26b**
nonrestrictive, 800, **E**
commas with, 432–433, **26f**
prepositional, 160, **5b**; 165–167, **5d**
agreement, subject-verb,
unaffected by, 329, **19h**;
330–331, **19j**

Phrases, prepositional (*Cont.*):
  commas with, avoiding faulty use
    of, 441, **26q**
  misplaced, 397, **23**; 401–402, **23b**
  verb, 134, **5a**; 144–145, **5b**; *809*, **E**
  necessary words in, including,
    258–259, **13a**
  verbal, 167–168, **5d**
  infinitive, 167, **5d**; 315, **18b**;
    356–357, **20f**; 376, **21h**
  (*See also* Participles and participial
    phrases)
  wordy, eliminating, 269–271, **14b**
Place names, commas with, 438–439,
  26n
Plagiarism, avoiding, 602–604, **37g**
Plan for research paper:
  expanded, 556–557, **36c**
  rough, 550, **36a**
Planning of paper, 5–23, **1**
  limiting subject, 6–7, 19–21, **1b**
  for argument paper, 684–685,
    39f
  for research paper, 533, **35a**
  modes of writing, choosing, 21–23,
    1c
  prewriting techniques, use of, 7–19,
    1a
  learning about topic, 8–9, **1a**
  listing ideas, 10–13, **1a**; 531, **35a**
  nonstop writing, 15–17, **1a**;
    531–533, **35a**
  questions about subject, asking,
    13–15, **1a**
  research, 18, **1a**
  for research paper, 530–533, **35a**
  subject tree, 17–18, **1a**
  thinking about subject, 8, **1a**
Plot, literary, writing about, 702,
  40e
  summary, avoiding, 701, **40d**
Plural forms:
  apostrophe in, 455, **28c**
  of nouns, 147–148, **5b**
  vs. possessive forms, 451, **28a**
  possessives of, 452, **28a**
  spelling, 482, **31a**; 487–490, **31c**
  of pronouns, singular pronouns vs.:
    agreement with antecedents,
    365–366, **21b**; 415, **24d**; *791*,
    E
  verb agreement with, 324–325,
    19c–19e; 330–332, **19j**;
    332–333, **19m**
  of verbs, 142, 143, **5b**
Plus, 786, **D**

Poetry:
  quotations from, 460, **29a**
  slashes for, 460, **29a**; 471, **30e**
  writing about, 707–709, **40g**
  example, 718–725, **40i**
Point of view:
  of literary narrator, 703, **40e**; 706,
    40f
  shifts in, avoiding, 415–416, **24e**
Positive degree, 153, **5b**; 389, **22g**
Possessive case, *803*, **E**
  apostrophes for, 449–454, **28a**
  exceptions to, 455, **28d**
  in comparisons, necessary inclusion
    of, 261, **13c**
  of nouns, 148, **5b**; 449–454, **28a**;
    792, **E**
  of pronouns, 151–152, **5b**; 374, **21h**;
    455, **28d**; *792*, **E**
  before gerunds, 377, **21h**
  indefinite, 449, **28a**
Practicable, practical, 786, **D**
Predicate adjectives; predicate nouns
  (subject complements), 139, **5a**;
    793, 803, **E**
Predicates, 131, 133–134, **5a**; *803*, **E**
  complements, 139–140, **5a**; *793–794*,
    E
  object, 139, **5a**; *794, 801*, **E**
  subject (predicate adjectives;
    predicate nouns), 139, **5a**;
    793, 803, **E**
  direct objects, 137–138, **5a**
  indirect objects, 138–139, **5a**
  (*See also* Verbs)
Prefixes, *803*, **E**
  spellings with, 487, **31b**; 497, **31e**
Premises of syllogisms, 676–678, **39d**
  begging the question with, 694–695,
    39f
  implied, 679–681, **39d**
Prepositional phrases, 160, **5b**;
    165–167, **5d**
  agreement, subject-verb, unaffected
    by, 329, **19h**; 330–331, **19j**
  commas with, avoiding faulty use of,
    441, **26q**
  misplaced, 397, **23**; 401–402, **23b**
Prepositions, 160–161, **5b**; *803–804*, **E**
  in idioms, 246, **11e**
  necessary, including, 261, **13c**
Present (dictionary) form of verbs, 337,
    338, **20a**; *804*, **E**
  irregular verbs, 344–345, **20a**
  past and future formed from,
    145–146, **5b**; 339, **20a**

Present infinitive, 355, **20f**
Present participles, 338, **20a**; *804*, **E**
  as adjectives, 380–381, **22a**
  pronoun cases with, 377, **21h**
  sentence fragments beginning with,
    314, **18b**
Present perfect infinitive, 355–356, **20f**
Present perfect tense, 328, **19g**;
    339–340, **20a**
Present tenses, 338, **20a**
  different uses of, 342, **20a**; 346, **20b**
  literature discussed in, 407–408, **24a**
  perfect, 328, **19g**; 339–340, **20a**
  sequence of tenses, correct, with,
    409–410, **24a**
  subject-verb agreement in, 322–325,
    19d; 327–328, **19g**
Previous to, 786, **D**
Prewriting techniques, use of, 7–19, **1a**
  learning about topic, 8–9, **1a**
  listing ideas, 10–13, **1a**; 531, **35a**
  nonstop writing, 15–17, **1a**; 531–533,
    35a
  questions about subject, asking,
    13–15, **1a**
  research, 18, **1a**
  for research paper, 530–533, **35a**
  subject tree, 17–18, **1a**
  thinking about subject, 8, **1a**
Primary vs. secondary sources, 538,
    35c
Principal, principle, 786, **D**
Principal parts of verbs, 337–338, **20a**;
    804, **E**
  irregular, 343–345, **20a**
Printers, computer, 762–763, **B**
Prior to, 786, **D**
Process analysis in paragraphs, 111, **4c**
Progressive forms of verbs, 341, **20a**;
    808, **E**
Pronouns, 149–153, **5b**; 362–378, **21**;
    804–805, **E**
  antecedents of, 150, **5b**; 362, **21**
  agreement with, 365–366, **21b**;
    415, **24d**; *791*, **E**
  clear reference to, 363–365, **21a**
  broad references with, avoiding,
    367–368, **21c**
  cases of, 373–374, **21h**; *792*, **E**
  possessive, 151–152, **5b**; 374, 377,
    21h; *792*, **E**
  proper use of, 375–377, **21h**
  for deities, 501–502, **32b**
  errors, run-on and comma splice,
    caused by, 303, **17e**
  vs. expletive, *it* as, 368–369, **21d**

Pronouns (*Cont.*):
  first person singular, use of,
    370–371, **21f**
  necessary, including, 261, **13c**
  after nouns, avoiding unnecessary
    use of, 371–372, **21g**
  one vs. *you*, 369, **21e**; 414, **24d**
  for paragraph coherence, 94, **4b**
  relative, 151, **5b**; 172, **5d**
    parallelism in use of, 213–214, **8e**
    verb agreement with, 332–333,
      19m
  with -*self*, 151, **5b**; 363, **21**; *785*, **D**;
    805, **E**
  and sexism, problem of, 276–277,
    15b–15c
  verb agreement with, 324–325,
    19c–19e; 330–332, **19j**;
    332–333, **19m**
Pronunciation:
  dictionary information about, 284,
    16b
  and spelling, 480–482, **31a**
Proofreading, 60, **3c**
Proper nouns, 147, **5b**
  capitalizing, 500–503, **32b**; 505–507,
    32
Psychological Abstracts, 542, **35c**
*Public Affairs Information Service
  Bulletin* (P.A.I.S.), 542, **35c**
*Publication Manual of the American
  Psychological Association* (APA)
  documentation format, 586–591,
    37d
Punctuation, 423–476, **25–30**
  apostrophes, 449–456, **28**
  brackets, 469–471, **30d**
  colons, 466–468, **30b**
    capitalization after, 468, **30b**; 499,
      32a
  correction of run-ons and comma
    splices with, 295–296, **17a**;
    297–299, **17c**
  dashes, 465–466, **30a**
  of ellipsis, 472–473, **30f**; *796–797*, **E**
  hyphens: spellings with, 496–497,
    31e
    for word division, 474–476, **30g**
  parentheses, 468–469, **30c**
  semicolons, 444–448, **27**
    independent clauses joined by,
      198, **7a**; 297–298, **17c**;
      444–446, **27a–27b**
  slashes, 471, **30e**
    with quoted poetry, 460, **29a**; 471,
      30e

Punctuation (*Cont.*):
as transitional device, 99, **4b**
(*See also* Commas; End marks;
Quotation marks)
Purpose of paper:
literary essay, 701–702, **40d**
and modes of writing, 22–23, **1c**

Question marks, 424–425, **25b**
Questions, 132, **5a**
exam, 727–728, **41b–41c**
journalistic, asking: in consideration
of audience, 28, **2a**
as prewriting technique, 14–15, **1a**
and sentence logic, 178–180, **6**
about literature, 699, **40b**; 702–703,
40e
paragraphs introduced with, 81, **4a**
punctuating, 424–425, **25a–25b**
on reading material, 752, 753, **A**
rhetorical, 226–227, **10b**; 805, **E**
about subject of paper, 13–15, **1a**
Quotation marks, 457–464, **29**
apologetic, avoiding, 463, **29e**
commas with, 436, **26j**
faulty, avoiding, 442, **26q**
for direct quotations, 457–460, **29a**
other punctuation with, 436, **26j**;
461, **29b**
single, 460, **29a**
with source use, 560–562, **37a**
for special uses of words, 462–463,
29d
for titles of works, 462, **29c**
italics vs., 519–520, **34a**
Quotations, direct, 770–771, **C**; 796, **E**
block, 459–460, **29a**; 560–561, **37a**
colons for introducing, 467, **30b**
capitalization in, 504, **32d**
italics for emphasis in, 523, **34e**
paragraphs introduced with, 80–81,
4a
punctuating, 303, **17e**; 424, **25b**; 436,
26j; 457–462, **29a–29b**
brackets within, 469–471, **30d**
colons for introducing, 466–467,
30b
ellipsis marks for omissions from,
472–473, **30f**; 796–797, **E**
within quotations, 460, **29a**
slashes for poetry, 460, **29a**; 471,
30e
from research sources, 558, 560–561,
37a
in note-taking, 551, 552, **36b**

Quotations, indirect, 458–459, **29a**;
796, **E**
capitals not required in, 504, **32d**

*Random House College Dictionary of
the English Language, The,* 281,
16a
Readers (*see* Audience, consideration
of)
*Readers' Guide to Periodical
Literature, The,* 540, **35c**
Reading:
of drafts for papers, 304, 305, **17f**;
317, **18c**
evidence from, 664, **39a**
of literary work, 699, **40b**
as study skill, 752–754, **A**
Real, really, 784, **D**
Reason is because, 777, 786, **D**
Reasoning in arguments, 665–666, **39b**
deductive, 675–681, **39d**
begging the question in, 694–695,
39f
fallacious, 690–697, **39f**
ad hominem attacks, 693–694, **39f**
begging the question, 694–695,
39f
from cause to effect, 690–691, **39f**
either/or statements, extreme,
692, **39f**
generalizations, faulty, 691–692,
39f
red herrings, 695, **39f**
straw men, attacking, 692–693, **39f**
inductive, 666–675, **39c**
Red herrings, 695, **39f**
Redundancies, avoiding, 267–269, **14a**
Reference books:
dictionaries, 279–289, **16**
desk, 279–281, **16a**; 283–288, **16b**
parts of entries in, 283–288, **16b**
specialized, 282, **16a**
of synonyms (thesauruses),
288–289, **16c**
unabridged, 281–282, **16a**
of usage, 282–283, **16a**
encyclopedias, 543–544, **35c**
on literature, 544–545, **35c**
as study aid, 753, **A**
Reference notes, semicolons in, 447,
27e
References, documenting (*see*
Documentation of sources)
References page, APA format for,
588–591, **37d**

Reflexive (-*self*) pronouns, 151, **5b**; 363, **21**; 785, **D**; 805, **E**
Regular verb, 805, **E**
Relation, relationship, 787, **D**
Relative pronouns, 151, **5b**; 172, **5d**
  parallelism in use of, 213–214, **8e**
  verb agreement with, 332–333, **19m**
Religious references, capitalized vs.
    lowercase, 501–502, **32b**
Repetition:
  computer check on, 762, **B**
  in definitions, avoiding, 191–192, **6f**
  for emphasis, 211–212, **8d**; 221–222,
    9e
  for paragraph coherence, 95, **4b**
  redundancies, avoiding, 267–269,
    14a
  of sentence patterns, avoiding,
    224–226, **10a**
Research on subject, 18, **1a**
Research papers, 529–656, **35–38**
  drafts of, 610–612, **38c–38e**
  library resources for (*see* Library
    facilities, use of)
  outlines for: formal, 607–610, **38b**;
    613–615, 644–645, **38f**
  plan, expanded, 556–557, **36c**
  plan, rough, 550, **36a**
  revisions in, 610–611, **38c**
  of thesis, 605–607, **38a**
  sample, 612–658, **38f**
  sources, use of (*see* Sources for
    research papers)
  subject for, choosing and limiting,
    530–534, **35a**
  thesis of, 550, **36a**
    hypothesis, 549, **36a**
    revising, 605–607, **38a**
Respective, 787, **D**
Restrictive elements, 805, **E**
  vs. nonrestrictive elements, 433,
    26f
Résumés, 746–749, **42d**
Revision:
  on computer, care in, 760–761, **B**
  of first drafts, 49–60, **3b**; 264–266,
    14a
    checklist for, 50–51, **3b**
    example, 52–59, **3b**
  of research paper, 610–611,
    38c–38d
  of paragraphs, 122–124, **4e**
  of thesis for research paper,
    605–607, **38a**
  for wordiness, 264–269, **14a**
Rhetorical modes, 21–23, **1c**

Rhetorical questions, 226–227, **10b**;
    805, **E**
Rough drafts (*see* First drafts of papers)
Rough outline, creating and checking,
    35–39, **2d**
Run-ons and comma splices,
    correcting, 295–306, **17**; 793,
    805, **E**
  with coordinating conjunctions, 297,
    17b
  with end marks, 295–296, **17a**
  by examining drafts, 304–305, **17f**
  misleading words, alertness to,
    301–304, **17e**; 384, **22b**
  with semicolons, 297–298, **17c**
  with subordination, 300–301, **17d**

-*s*, final:
  in plural spellings, 482, **31a**;
    487–488, **31c**
    vs. possessive forms, 451, **28a**
  presence or absence of: in
    possessives, 452–453, **28a**
    and subject-verb agreement,
    322–324, **19a–19b**
Salutations in business letters,
    735–736, **42a**
Scene-setting paragraphs, 79, **4a**
Search command on word processing
    program, use of, 756–757, 762,
    B
Second person of verbs, 142, **5b**; 325,
    19d; 328, **19g**
  in imperative mood, 351, **20d**
Secondary vs. primary sources, 538,
    35c
-*self* pronouns, 151, **5b**; 363, **21**; 785,
    D; 805, **E**
Semicolons, 444–448, **27**
  in elliptical constructions, 446–447,
    27d
  independent clauses joined by, 198,
    7a; 297–298, **17c**; 444–446,
    27a–27b
  with other punctuation marks, 446,
    27c; 447, **27e**
Sense, verbs of, 387, **22e**
Sensory details, use of, 106–107, **4c**
Sentence fragments, 130, **5**; 307–321,
    18; 806, **E**
  acceptable uses of, recognizing,
    319–320, **18d**
  beginnings of, recognizing, 314–317,
    18b
  capitalization of, 499, **32a**

Sentence fragments (*Cont.*):
  checklist for correcting, 318, **18**
  complete sentences from: by
      addition to adjacent
      sentences, 310–312, **18a**
    by change of words in, 312–313,
        18a
    examining drafts for, 317, **18c**
Sentence outlines for research papers,
    608, **38b**
  example, 613–615, **38f**
Sentence patterns, 127–131, **5**
  recognizing, 163–164, **5c**
  varying, 224–226, **10a**
Sentence types, 173–177, **5d**
  complex, 175, **5d**; *794*, **E**
  compound, 174–175, **5d**; 297, **17b**;
      794, **E**
  compound-complex, 175, **5d**; *794*, **E**
  simple, 173–174, **5d**; *806–807*, **E**
Sentences, *806*, **E**
  adverbs modifying, 385–386, **22c**
  capitalized beginnings of, 498–500,
      32a
  coordination in, 195–198, **7a**; *795*, **E**
    conjunctions for (*see* Coordinating
        conjunctions)
    in correction of run-ons and
        comma splices, 297–298,
        17b–17c
    improper, revising, 194–195, **7**
  cumulative, 218–220, **9c**
  emphasis in (*see* Emphasis in
      sentences)
  ending: with prepositions, 161, **5b**
    punctuation for (*see* End marks)
  first in paragraph, 76–82, **4a**
    and coherence between
        paragraphs, 101–102, **4b**
  fragment conversion into, methods
      for, 310–313, **18a**
  grammar of (*see* Grammar, sentence)
  logic of (*see* Logic, sentence)
  parallelism in (*see* Parallelism)
  periodic, 216–217, **9a**
  passive voice for, 221, **9d**
  subordination in, 199–207, **7b**;
      807–808, **E**
    conjunctions for (*see*
        Subordinators)
    for correction of run-ons and
        comma splices, 300–301,
        17d
    embedded elements, use of,
        202–204, **7b**
    excessive, avoiding, 206, **7b**

Sentences (*Cont.*):
  support of controlling idea with,
      84–87, **4a**
  topic sentence, 76–81, **4a**
  types of (*see* Sentence types)
  variety in (*see* Variety, sentence,
      techniques for)
  wordiness eliminated by combining,
      271–273, **14c**
Series, 208–209, **8**
  colon misuse with, 467, **30b**
  comma use with, 434, **26g**; 439–440,
      26p; 441–442, **26q**
  semicolon use with, 446, **27c**
Set, sit, 360–361, **20g**; *787*, **D**
Setting, literary, writing about, 702,
    40e
Sexist language, avoiding, 275–278, **15**
  -man, words ending in, 277–278, **15d**
  pronoun problems, 276–277,
      15b–15c
  stereotypical references, 275–276,
      15a
Shall, will, 787, **D**
Shifts, confusing, 407–420, **24**
  into emotional outbursts, 417–420,
      24f
  in mood of verbs, 410–412, **24b**
  in point of view, 415–416, **24e**
  in pronoun use, 414–415, **24d**
  in tenses of verbs, 347, **20c**; 361,
      20g; 407–410, **24a**
  in voice of verbs, 413–414, **24c**
Should of, 779, **D**
Sic in brackets, 470–471, **30d**
Signal cards for research papers, 551,
    36b
Similes and metaphors, use of,
    251–254, **12b**
Simple predicates:
  vs. complete predicates, 133, **5a**
  (*See also* Verbs)
Simple sentences, 173–174, **5d**;
    806–807, **E**
Simple subjects, 136–137, **5a**
  vs. complete subjects, 132–133, **5a**
Simple tenses of verbs, 145–146, **5b**;
    338–339, **20a**, *808*, **E**
  consistency in use of, 409–410, **24a**
  past participle confused with past,
      358–359, **20g**
  uses of present, 346, **20b**
Single quotation marks, 460, **29a**
Singular and plural nouns, 147–148, **5b**
  possessives of, 452, **28a**
  (*See also* Agreement, subject-verb)

Singular and plural pronouns:
  agreement with antecedents,
      365–366, **21b**; 415, **24d**; *791,*
      E
  verb agreement with, 324–325,
      19c–19e; 330–332, **19j**;
      332–333, **19m**
Singular and plural verbs, 142–143, **5b**
  (*See also* Agreement, subject-verb)
Sit, set, 360–361, **20g**; *787,* **D**
Slang:
  dictionaries of, 282, **16a**
  use of, 239–240, **11a**
    inappropriate, 236, **11**; 238, **11a**
Slashes, 471, **30e**
  with quoted poetry, 460, **29a**; 471,
      30e
Social Sciences Index, 542, **35c**
Some, 787, **D**
  vs. *some of,* 774, **D**
Somewheres, 787, **D**
Sources for research papers, 548–604,
      36–37
  bibliography cards for, 536–539, **35c**
  commenting on, 562–565, **37a**
  documentation of, methods for,
      565–602, **37b–37f**
    APA format, 586–591, **37d**
    full publication data system, 592,
      37e
    lists, 574–585, **37c**; 588–591, **37d**;
      640–643, **38f**
    MLA format, 566–585, **37c**;
      592–602, **37f**
    notes, 573–574, **37c**; 592–602, **37f**
    number system, 591, **37e**
    parenthetical references, 566–573,
      37c; 586–588, **37d**;
      591–592, **37e**
  exploring, 548, **36a**
  integrating into writing, 558–562,
      37a
  locating (*see* Library facilities, use of)
  notes from: organizing, 554–557, **36c**
    taking, 550–553, **36b**
  plagiarism of, avoiding, 602–604, **37g**
  primary vs. secondary, 538, **35c**
Spatial arrangement of information, 34,
      2d
  in paragraphs, 90, **4b**
Specific and general points, arranging,
      34–35, **2d**
Spell checkers, use of, 758–759, **B**
Spelling, 479–497, **31**
  ei vs. *ie,* 483, **31b**
  with hyphens, 496–497, **31e**

Spelling (*Cont.*):
  lists for, 490–495, **31d**
  of plurals, 482, **31a**; 487–490, **31c**
  with prefixes, 487, **31b**; 497, **31e**
  pronunciation and, 480–482, **31a**
  with suffixes, 484–486, **31b**
Split infinitives, 357–358, **20f**
Squinting modifiers, 404–405, **23d**;
      807, **E**
Stationery for business letters, writing
      on:
    letterhead, 731–732, **42a**
    without letterhead, 732–733, **42a**
Statistics, use of, 107–108, **4c**
Straw men, attacking, 692–693, **39f**
Structure of literary works, writing
      about, 702–703, **40e**
Study techniques, 751–755, **A**
  breaks, taking, 755, **A**
  for examinations, 726–727, **41a–41b**
  lecture notes, taking, 754–755, **A**
  reading, active, 752–754, **A**
  schedule, planning, 750, **A**
Style:
  for business letters, 738–739, **42a**
    block and modified-block,
      730–734, **42a**
  imitating examples of, 766–772, **C**
  literary, writing about, 703, **40e**
  mannerisms, computer check on,
      762, **B**
  (*See also* Tone)
Subheads in formatted documents,
      764, **B**
Subject of paper (*see* Topic of paper)
Subject of sentence, 131–134, **5a**; *807,*
      E
  inversion of verb and, 228, **10d**; 332,
      19k–19l; *799,* **E**
  simple, 132–133, 136–137, **5a**
  verb agreement with (*see*
      Agreement, subject-verb)
Subject complements (predicate
      adjectives; predicate nouns),
      139, **5a**; *793, 803,* **E**
Subject pronouns:
  in dependent clauses, 375, **21h**
  errors, run-on and comma splice,
      caused by, 303, **17e**
  verb agreement with, 324–325,
      19c–19e; 330–332, **19j**;
      332–333, **19m**
Subject tree, 17–18, **1a**
Subjective case of pronouns, 373–374,
      21h
  proper use of, 375–377, **21h**

Subjunctive mood, 349–351, **20d**; *800,
     807,* **E**
   shifts in use of, avoiding, 411–412,
     24b
Subordinate clauses (*see* Dependent
     clauses)
Subordination, 199–207, **7b**; *807–808,*
     E
   conjunctions for (*see* Subordinators)
   for correction of run-ons and comma
     splices, 300–301, **17d**
   embedded elements, use of,
     202–204, **7b**
   excessive, avoiding, 206, **7b**
Subordinators, 159, **5b**; 171, **5d**;
     200–202, **7b**; *794,* **E**
   including, for clarity, 259, **13b**
   omitting, 171–172, **5d**
   sentence fragments beginning with,
     316–317, **18b**
Suffixes, *808,* **E**
   spellings with, 484–486, **31b**
Summary of literary plot, avoiding,
     701, **40d**
Summary of research sources, 561, **37a**
   in note-taking, 551, 553, **36b**
Summary guide for research paper,
     554, 555, **36c**
Summary notes, taking, vs. underlining
     in books, 752–753, **A**
Superlative and comparative degrees,
     153, **5b**; 389–393, **22g**; *793,* **E**
Sure, 787, **D**
Sure and, sure to, 788, **D**
Surveying reading material, 752, **A**
Syllabication in dictionary entries, 284,
     16b
Syllogisms, 675–681, **39d**
   begging the question in, 694–695,
     39f
Symbols in literature, 716–717, **40h**
Synonyms:
   in dictionary entries, 286–287, **16b**
   dictionary of (thesaurus), 288–289,
     16c
Syntax, *808,* **E**

Technical terms, avoiding, 243, **11d**
Tenses of verbs, *808,* **E**
   and agreement with subject,
     322–325, **19d**; 327–328, **19g**
   different uses of, 342–343, **20a**; 346,
     20b
   perfect, 328, **19g**; 339–341, **20a**; *808,* **E**
   inconsistencies with, 408–409, **24a**

Tenses of verbs (*Cont.*):
   sequence of, correct, observing,
     347–348, **20c**; 409–410, **24a**
   shifts in, illogical, avoiding, 347, **20c**;
     361, **20g**; 407–410, **24a**
   simple, 145–146, **5b**; 338–339, **20a**;
     808, **E**
   consistency in use of, 409–410,
     24a
   past participle confused with past,
     358–359, **20g**
   uses of present, 346, **20b**
Testimony, argument from, 683–684,
     39e
Tests, essay, writing, 726–729, **41**
That:
   including, for clarity, 259, **13b**
   omitting, 171–172, **5d**
   subjunctive with, 350–351, **20d**
   as vague comparative, avoiding, 262,
     13c
   vs. *which,* 788, **D**
That there, 788, **D**
The, 156, **5b**
   inclusion of, necessary, 260, **13c**
Their, there, they're, 788, **D**
Them there, 788, **D**
Theories, formation of, 671–672, **39c**
There, they're, their, 788, **D**
Thesauruses, 288–289, **16c**
These here, 788, **D**
Thesis, formulating and stating, 31–33,
     2c
   for literary essay, 700–701, **40c**
   for research paper, 550, **36a**
   hypothesis, 549, **36a**
   revision, 605–607, **38a**
They, avoiding indefinite use of, 364,
     21a
They're, their, there, 788, **D**
Thinking about subject, 8, **1a**
Third person of verbs, 143, **5b**
   agreement with subject (*see*
     Agreement, subject-verb)
   in subjunction mood, 349–351, **20d**
This here, 788, **D**
Time of day, writing, 511, **33b**; 516,
     33f
Time of verbs (*see* Tenses of verbs)
Title of paper, manuscript
     requirements for, 61, **3d**
Titles of persons:
   abbreviated, 515–516, **33d**
   in business letters, 734–735, **42a**
   capitalized vs. lowercase, 502–503,
     32b

Titles of works:
  capitalizing, 503–504, **32c**
  quotation marks for, 462, **29c**;
    519–520, **34a**
  underlining (italicizing), 519–520,
    34a
To as infinitive marker, 355, **20f**
  omitting, 357, **20f**
To be, forms of, 343, **20a**
  agreement with subject, 327–328,
    19g
  subjunctive mood, 350, **20d**
Tone:
  of arguments, 689–690, **39f**
  audience and, 26–27, **2a**
  of literary works, writing about, 703,
    40e
  and pronoun use: first person
    singular, 370–371, **21f**
    one vs. *you,* 369, **21e**; 414, **24d**
Topic of paper:
  argument, requirements for:
    debatability, 686–687, **39f**
    limitation, 684–685, **39f**
  exploring, prewriting techniques for,
    7–19, **1a**
    for research paper, 530–533, **35a**
  learning about, 8–9, **1a**
  limiting, 6–7, 19–21, **1b**
    for argument paper, 684–685, **39f**
    for research paper, 533, **35a**
  literary essay, 704–707, **40f**
  modes of writing suited to, 21–23, **1c**
  questions about, asking, 13–15, **1a**
  research on, 18, **1a**
  thesis from, 31–33, **2c**
    for literary essay, 700–701, **40c**
    for research paper, 549–550, **36a**;
      605–607, **38a**
  thinking about, 8, **1a**
Topic of paragraph, 75–84, **4a**
  supporting: with details, 105–110, **4c**
    with sentences, 84–87, **4a**
Topic outlines for research papers,
  607–608, **38b**
  example, 644–645, **38f**
Topic sentence, 76–81, **4a**
Transitional expressions, 384–385, **22b**;
  429–430, **26b**
  errors, run-on and comma splice,
    caused by, 302, **17e**; 384, **22b**
  for paragraph coherence, 97–101, **4b**
Transitive verbs:
  defined, 137, **5a**; 808, **E**
  voice of, active vs. passive, 352–355,
    20e; 800, 802, 809, **E**

Transitive verbs, voice of, active vs.
    passive *(Cont.)*:
  consistency in use of, 413–414,
    24c
  for emphasis, 220–221, **9d**
Triple enumerations, examples of,
  766–768, **C**
Try and, try to, 788, **D**
Typed papers, manuscript
  requirements for, 62, **3d**

Unabridged dictionaries, 281–282, **16a**
Underlining in books, disadvantages of,
  752–753, **A**
Underlining to indicate italics,
  518–523, **34**
  for emphasis, 522–523, **34e**
  for foreign expressions, 520–521, **34b**
  for names of vehicles, 522, **34d**
  for titles of works, 519–520, **34a**
  for words as words, 521, **34c**
Understatement, 714–715, **40h**
Unified paragraphs, controlling idea
  for, 75–84, **4a**
  supporting: with details, 105–110, **4c**
    with sentences, 84–87, **4a**
Uninterested, disinterested, 779, **D**
Unity and coherence, 36–37, **2d**
Usage:
  dictionaries of, 282–283, **16a**
  glossary of, 773–778, **D**
  notes on, in dictionaries, 280, **16a**;
    285, **16b**
Use, utilize, 786, **D**

Variety, sentence, techniques for,
  224–231, **10**
  absolutes at end, 230–231, **10e**
  exclamations, 227, **10c**
  free modifiers, 229–231, **10e**
  imitating examples of, 766–772, **C**
  inversion of subject and verb, 228,
    10d
  pattern and length, varying,
    224–226, **10a**
  rhetorical questions, 226–227, **10b**
Verb complement, 809, **E**
Verb phrases, 134, **5a**; 144–145, **5b**;
  809, **E**
  necessary words in, including,
    258–259, **13a**
Verbals and verbal phrases, 167–168,
  5d; 809, **E**
  gerund, 168, **5d**; 377, **21h**; 798, **E**

Verbals and verbal phrases (*Cont.*):
 infinitive, 167, **5d**; 315, **18b**;
  355–358, **20f**; 376, **21h**; 798,
  E
 (*See also* Participles and participial
  phrases)
Verbs, 133, 135–136, **5a**; 142–145, **5b**;
  337–361, **20**; *808*, **E**
 agreement of, with subject (*see*
  Agreement, subject-verb)
 errors in use of, 358–361, **20g**
  shifts, confusing, 347, **20c**; 361,
   20g; 407–414, **24a–24c**
 helping (auxiliary), 134, 135, **5a**;
  144–145, **5b**; 339, **20a**; 792, **E**
 necessary, including, 258–259, **13a**
 perfect tenses formed with, 328,
  19g; 339–341, **20a**; *808*, **E**
 infinitive form of, 167, **5d**; 315, **18b**;
  355–358, **20f**; 376, **21h**; 798,
  E
 intransitive, 138, **5a**; 799, **E**
 inversion of subject and, 228, **10d**;
  332, **19k–19l**; 799, **E**
 linking, 139, **5a**; 381, **22a**; 799, **E**
  agreement with subject, 333, **19n**
  of sense, 387, **22e**
  shift to passive voice after, 413,
   24c
 moods of, 349–352, **20d**; *800*, **E**
  consistency in, 410–412, **24b**
  imperative, 351, **20d**
  indicative, 349, **20d**; 410–412, **24b**
  subjunctive, 349–351, **20d**;
   411–412, **24b**; *800, 807*, **E**
 necessary parts of, including,
  258–259, **13a**
 particles added to, 145, **5b**
 principal parts of, 337–338, **20a**; *804*,
  E
  irregular, 343–345, **20a**
 progressive forms of, 341, **20a**; *808*,
  E
 of sense, 387, **22e**
 tenses of (*see* Tenses of verbs)
 transitive: defined, 137, **5a**; *808*, **E**
  voice of, active vs. passive,
   220–221, **9d**; 352–355, **20e**;
   413–414, **24c**; *800, 802,
   809*, **E**
Verse quotations, 460, **29a**
 slashes in, 460, **29a**; 471, **30e**
Viewpoint:
 of literary narrator, 703, **40e**; 706,
  40f
 shifts in, avoiding, 415–416, **24e**

Vocabulary, adding to, 754, **A**
Voice of verbs, active vs. passive,
  352–355, **20e**; *800, 802, 809*, **E**
 consistency in use of, 413–414, **24c**
 for emphasis, 220–221, **9d**

Waist, waste, 482, **31a**
Wait for, wait on, 788, **D**
Waiting words, 269, **14b**
*Webster's Ninth New Collegiate
  Dictionary*, 280, **16a**
*Webster's Third New International
  Dictionary of the English
  Language*, 281, **16a**
Well, good, 781–782, **D**
Which, 788, **D**
 omitting, 171, **5d**
Who, whose, 788, **D**
Will, shall, 787, **D**
Word order, 396–397, **23**; *809*, **E**
Word origins in dictionary entries, 285,
  16b
Word processors, writing with,
  756–765, **B**
 dictionaries (spell checkers), using,
  758–759, **B**
 manuscript requirements for, 62, **3d**;
  763–764, **B**
 notes, taking, 756–757, **B**
 outlining, 758, **B**
 paper for, 763, **B**
 printers for, 762–763, **B**
 protecting work, 759–760, **B**
 repetition and overuse, checking for,
  762, **B**
 revising, care in, 760–761, **B**
Wordiness, avoiding, 264–274, **14**
 by combining sentences, 271–273,
  14c
 by editing, 264–269, **14a**
 jargon, eliminating, 240–241, **11c**;
  273, **14d**
 phrases, common, eliminating,
  269–271, **14b**
Words:
 dictionaries of (*see* Dictionaries)
 division of, with hyphens, 474–476,
  30g
 mechanics of (*see* Capitalization;
  Spelling)
 needed, including, 258–263, **13**
  articles, 260, **13c**
  in comparisons, 261–263, **13c**;
   392–393, **22g**
  prepositions, 261, **13c**

Words, needed, including (*Cont.*):
    pronouns, 261, **13c**
    subordinating conjunction *that*,
        259, **13b**
    verb parts, 258–259, **13a**
    for numbers, figures vs., 510–512,
        33a–33b
    unfamiliar, studying, 754, **A**
    unnecessary, eliminating (*see*
        Wordiness, avoiding)
    usage glossary of, 773–788, **D**
    as words, treatment of, 521–522, **34c**
    (*See also* Language; Parts of speech)
Would of, 779, **D**
Writing process, 5–7, **1**
    components in (*see* Paragraphs;
        Sentences; Words)
    with computers (*see* Word
        processors, writing with)
    correction of evaluated paper, 64–65,
        3e
    imitating prose examples, 766–772,
        C

Writing process (*Cont.*):
    proofreading, 60, **3c**
    stages in (*see* Development of paper;
        Drafts of paper; Planning of
        paper)
    in studying, 752–755, **A**
    types of writing: essay examinations,
        726–729, **41**
        (*See also* Arguments; Business
            writing; Literary essays;
            Research papers)

y, final, spelling rules concerning,
        484–485, **31b**; 498, **31c**
Year's Work in English Studies, The,
        544, **35c**
You:
    as implied subject, 132, **5a**; 351, **20d**
    vs. *one*, 369, **21e**; 414, **24d**
    verb agreement with, 325, **19d**; 328,
        19g

BOOK ONE   THE WRITING PROCESS

I Writing Essays and Paragraphs

1 *plan*
Planning a Paper 5
a Prewriting
b Limiting subjects
c Purpose and approach
2 *dev*
Developing a Paper 24
a Audience
b Evidence and details
c Writing a thesis
d Expanding and organizing ideas
3 *wri/rev*
Writing and Revising a Paper 40
a First draft
b Revision
c Proofreading
d Final draft
e Changes and corrections
4 ¶
Writing Strong Paragraphs 74
a Unity
b Coherence
c Supporting details
d Opening and closing paragraphs
e Revising

II Writing Clear and Effective Setences

5 *gr*
Basic Sentence Grammar 127
a Structure
b Parts of speech
c Sentence patterns
d Phrases and clauses
6 *log*
Sentence Logic 178
a Irrelevant details
b Emphasis
c Cause and effect
d Generalizations
e Mixed images
f Definitions
7 *co/sub*
Coordination and Subordination 194
a Coordination
b Subordination
8 *//*
Parallelism 208
a Comparisons
b Correlatives
c Lists and outlines
d Repetition
e Relative pronouns
9 *emph*
Emphasis 215
a Periodic sentences
b Parenthetical elements
c Cumulative sentences
d Active voice
e Repetition
10 *var*
Variety 224
a Sentence patterns
b Rhetorical questions
c Exclamations
d Inversions
e Free modifiers and absolutes

III Using Words Effectively

11 *d*
Appropriate Diction 235
a Slang
b Dialect
c Jargon
d Obsolete, foreign, and technical words
e Idioms
f Connotations
12 *fig*
Imagery and Figurative Language 249
a Concreteness
b Metaphors and similes
c Clichés
13 ∧
Including Needed Words 258
a Parts of verbs
b Use of *that*
c Articles, prepositions, and pronouns
14 *wdy*
Avoiding Wordiness 264
a Unnecessary words
b Common phrases
c Combining sentences
d Jargon
15 *sxl*
Sexist Language 275
a Labels and clichés
b Masculine pronouns
c Cumbersome uses
d Artificial coinages
16 *di/th*
Dictionary and Thesaurus 279
a Types of dictionaries
b Dictionary entry
c Thesaurus

BOOK TWO   RULES

IV Understanding Grammar and Writing Correct Sentences

17 *ro/cs*
Correcting Run-ons and Comma Splices 295
a End marks
b Commas and coordinating conjunctions
c Semicolons
d Subordination
e Causes of run-ons and comma splices
f Examining drafts
18 *frag*
Correcting Sentence Fragments 307
a Fragments into sentences
b Fragment signals
c Examining drafts
d Acceptable fragments
19 *agr*
Agreement of Subject and Verb 322
a Singular verbs and subjects
b Plural verbs and subjects
c Singular pronoun subjects
d *I* and *you*
e Plural pronoun subjects
f Subjects with *and*
g *To be*
h Intervening phrases
i *Or, either . . . or, neither . . . nor*
j Indefinite subjects
k Inverted sentences
l *There* or *here*
m Relative pronouns
n Linking verbs
o Collective nouns
p Plural subjects, singular meanings
20 *vb*
Verb Forms 337
a Principal parts
b Present tense
c Sequence of tenses
d Mood
e Active and passive voice
f Infinitives
g Common errors
21 *pro*
Pronouns 382
a Antecedents
b Agreement
c Broad reference
d *It*
e *One* and *you*
f *I, my, me,* and *mine*
g Placement after nouns
h Case